Weatherby

FOUNDATION 4 UNIT MATHEMATICS

Second Edition

By
S.K.Patel

PASCAL PRESS

Copyright © S.K.Patel and Pascal Press

ISBN 1 8753 1226 9

First Edition published by Pascal Press April 1989
Revised Edition published October 1989
Second Edition published January 1991

Pascal Press
P.O. Box 250
Glebe NSW 2037

Material can only be reproduced from this book as allowed under the **Copyright Act**. Otherwise, written permission from the publisher must be obtained.

Printed in Australia by Australian Print Group

PREFACE

In this second edition of **Foundations of 4 Unit Mathematics** some important changes have been made to reflect the recently published 4 Unit Mathematics Syllabus Notes. The chapters on Curve Sketching and Conic Sections have been thoroughly re-written and expanded in line with these notes. A whole new chapter on Harder Three Unit Topics has been added to provide students with the extra work they need in these areas. A few changes have also been made to the chapter on Polynomials. Other chapters are more or less intact with minor changes such as improved diagrams or better explanations. Obsolete material has been removed(the Energy and Work section in Chapter 7).

In carrying out these changes the size of the book has increased by about 80 pages. As in the previous editions, I have tried to retain all the qualities and features that users of these editions have found most useful. All the known errors have been corrected.

As always, my aim has been to impart the knowledge of mathematics to students who will need it in their later academic and professional work.

I would like to thank and acknowledge the help and contribution of the following individuals:
- Roger Myers of the Bankstown Technical College for his many thoughtful suggestions
- Judy Faulkner who typed the manuscript in the required time
- all my colleagues in the Technical Colleges and many other school teachers for their useful suggestions.

I sincerely hope that this new edition will be found to be even more useful than the previous one.

Suresh Patel
Bankstown Technical College
Sydney

CONTENTS

Page

CHAPTER 1　CURVE SKETCHING

1.1	Basic Curves	1
1.2	Method for Sketching the Curves	2
1.3	Graphs of Basic Functions	3
1.4	Curves with Vertical and Horizontal Asymptotes	8
1.5	Trigonometric Graphs	11
1.6	Exponential Curves	14
1.7	Drawing Graphs by Composition of Ordinates	15
1.8	Implicit Differentiation and Sketching Curves	24
1.9	Applications	26
1.10	Miscellaneous Curves Sketching	30
	Exercise: 1:A	40
	Exercise: 1:B	43

CHAPTER 2　INTEGRATION

2.1	Standard Integrals	49
2.2	Change of Variable: Substitution	51
	Exercise 2A	53
2.3	Integration by Part	54
	Exercise 2B	57
2.4	Trigonometric Integrals	58
2.5	Use of $t = \tan(x/2)$	61
	Exercise 2C	63
2.6	Reduction Formulas	64
	Exercise 2D	66
2.7	Trigonometric Substitution	67
	Exercise 2E	68
2.8	Integration of Rational Functions	68
	Exercise 2F	72
2.9	Method of Partial Fractions	73
	Exercise 2G	77
2.10	Completing the Square (Integration)	78
	Exercise 2H	80
2.11	Integration: Special Properties	81
	Exercise 2I	85
	Exercise 2J	86

CHAPTER 3 VOLUMES

3.1	Formulas for Volumes	88
	Exercise 3A	97
3.2	Volumes: Shell Method	99
3.3	Volumes: Washer Method	103
	Exercise 3B	104
3.4	Worked Examples (Miscellaneous)	105
	Exercise 3C	109

CHAPTER 4 COMPLEX NUMBERS

4.1	Introduction	112
4.2	Operations with Complex Numbers	113
	Exercise 4A	116
4.3	Complex Plane (Argand Diagram)	118
	Exercise 4B	121
4.4	Multiplication and Division of Complex Numbers Using Trigonometry	122
	Exercise 4C	124
4.5	Powers of Complex Numbers: De Moivre's Theorem	125
	Exercise 4D	126
4.6	Roots of Complex Numbers	127
	Exercise 4E	130
4.7	De Moivre's Theorem and its Applications	131
	Exercise 4F	134
4.8	Square Roots of a Complex Number	135
	Exercise 4G	136
4.9	Properties of Conjugate Complex Numbers	137
	Exercise 4H	138
4.10	The Complex Roots of Unity	139
	Exercise 4I	141
4.11	Miscellaneous: Factorisation over the Complex Field	143
	Exercise 4J	145
4.12	Geometric Representation of Complex Numbers	146
	Exercise 4K	149
4.13	Product and Quotient: Rotation	150
	Exercise 4L	152
4.14	Locus Problems with the Complex Variable z	153
	Exercise 4M	154
4.15	Miscellaneous Locus Problems (Including Inequations)	155
	Exercise 4N	159
	Exercise 4O	160

CHAPTER 5 POLYNOMIALS

5.1	Introduction	164
	Exercise 5A	167
5.2	Zeros of a Polynomial/Multiple Roots	168
	Exercise 5B	172
5.3	Polynomial over the Complex Field	173
	Exercise 5C	177
5.4	Relation between Roots and Coefficients of $P(x) = 0$	178
	Exercise 5D	183
5.5	Miscellaneous (Worked Examples)	185
	Exercise 5E	187

CHAPTER 6 CONIC SECTIONS

6.1	Introduction	191
6.2	Ellipse ($e < 1$): (Focus and Directrix Definition)	192
	Exercise 6A	195
6.3	The Hyperbola	196
	Exercise 6B	198
6.4	Shape of the Conics	199
6.5	Parametric Equations of the Circle and the Ellipse	201
6.6	Equations of chord, Tangent and Normal to the Ellipse	203
6.7	Parametric Equations of the Hyperbola	205
6.8	A Special (Rectangular) Hyperbola $xy = c^2$	206
	Exercise 6C	208
6.9	Miscellaneous Problems on Conics	209
	Exercise 6D	214
6.10	Tangents and the Chord of Contact	222
6.11	Geometric properties of the Ellipse	224
6.12	Geometric Properties of the Hyperbola	227
6.13	Properties of the Rectangular Hyperbola	228
6.14	Geometric Properties of Rectangular Hyperbola $xy = c^2$	229
	Exercise 6E	232

CHAPTER 7 ELEMENTARY PARTICLE DYNAMICS

7.1	Introduction	234
7.2	Laws of Motion – Force	234
	Exercise 7A	239

CHAPTER 8 MOTION PROBLEMS IN TWO DIMENSIONS

8.1	Introduction	240
8.2	Simple Harmonic Motion (Revision)	241
	Exercise 8A	244
8.3	Motion of a Projectile (Revision)	246
	Exercise 8B	249
8.4	Resisted Motion: Other Laws of Motion	252
	Exercise 8C	259

CHAPTER 9 CIRCULAR MOTION

9.1	Introduction	265
9.2	Angular Velocity: Period	266
9.3	Circular Motion: Tangential Velocity	267
	Exercise 9A	269
9.4	Acceleration of a Particle Rotating in a Circle	270
9.5	Uniform Circular Motion	271
	Exercise 9B	272
9.6	Conical Pendulum	273
	Exercise 9C	275
9.7	Banked Tracks	276
	Exercise 9D	278
9.8	Components of Acceleration (Variable Angular Velocity	279
	Exercise 9E	281
9.9	Miscellaneous (Worked Examples on Circular Motion)	282
	Exercise 9F	285

CHAPTER 10 HARDER 3 UNIT TOPICS

10.1	Harder Trigonometry	288
	Exercise 10A	291
10.2	3 Unit Co-ordinate Geometry: Circles (Harder Problems)	292
	Exercise 10B	296
10.3	Plane Geometry: Circles (Harder Problems)	297
	Exercise 10C	300
10.4	Inequalities	305
	Exercise 10D	307
10.5	Method of Mathematical Induction	308
	Exercise 10E	310
10.6	Properties of the Integrals	312
	Exercise 10F	315
	Appendix 1	316
	Appendix 2	317

Answers 318

Chapter 1: Curve Sketching

INTRODUCTION

A structure, no matter how complicated, is composed of basic building materials. In mathematics, the study of complicated functions such as $f(x) = \frac{1}{2}(e^x + e^{-x})$, $\log_e \frac{x-1}{x}$, $\sin^{-1} e^x$, etc. can be facilitated by sketching the graphs of these functions. But how can we best accomplish this? Firstly, by identifying them by the basic curves (listed below) and then using a number of systematic steps to produce reasonably good graphs. The objective is to draw a quick and neat sketch of the curve showing all the essential features (see section 1.2). Any thought of drawing the graph by brute force i.e. plotting scores of points must be abandoned, as it would most probably miss the essential features, such as asymptotes and the critical points.

1.1 Basic Curves

The following basic curves are well known to students. (See Chapter 1 for the graphs of the basic functions.)

	Function	Graph
1.	Linear: $ax + by + c = 0$; $y = mx + b$	A straight line
2.	Quadratic: $y = ax^2 + bx + c$	A parabola
3.	Cubic: $y = ax^3 + bx^2 + cx + d$	A cubic curve
4.	Quartic: $y = ax^4 + bx^3 + cx^2 + dx + e$	A quartic curve
5.	$y = \frac{k}{x}$, $x \neq 0$	A rectangular hyperbola
6.	$x^2 + y^2 + 2gx + 2fy + c = 0$ or $(x-a)^2 + (y-b)^2 = r^2$	A circle
7.	Exponential: $y = a^x$, e^x	An exponential curve
8.	Logarithmic: $y = \log_a x$, $\log_e x$	A logarithmic curve
9.	Trigonometric: $y = \sin x, \cos x, \tan x$	A sine curve, cosine curve, tangent curve
10.	Inverse Trig: $y = \sin^{-1} x, \cos^{-1} x, \tan^{-1} x$	An inverse sine curve etc.
11.	Type: $y = x^{1/n}$, $n = 2, 3$	

1.2 Method for Sketching the Curves

A sketch of the curve should convey the general shape of the curve, showing the following information.

1. **Intercepts on the axes**

   $x = 0$ gives the y-intercept, $y = 0$ gives the x-intercept.

2. **Symmetry**

   The curve is symmetric about the
   (a) y-axis if $f(x) = f(-x)$ (b) origin O if $f(-x) = -f(x)$

3. **Asymptotes**

   If $y = f(x)$ is a rational function of the form $f(x) = \frac{g(x)}{h(x)}$, where $g(x)$ and $h(x)$ are polynomials, then the:
   (a) vertical asymptotes are given by $h(x) = 0$
   (b) horizontal asymptotes are given by $\lim_{x \to |\infty|} f(x)$ if it exists, say $y = c$.

   Example: The vertical asymptotes of the curve $y = \frac{2x^2 + 1}{x^2 - 1}$ are given by $x^2 - 1 = 0$, i.e. $x = \pm 1$ and the horizontal asymptotes are given by
   $y = \lim_{x \to \infty} \frac{2x^2 + 1}{x^2 - 1} = 2$ and $y = \lim_{x \to -\infty} \frac{2x^2 + 1}{x^2 - 1} = 2$, i.e. $y = 2$.

4. **Critical points**
   (a) Relative maxima: $f'(x) = 0$, $f''(x) < 0$
   (b) Relative minima: $f'(x) = 0$, $f''(x) > 0$
   (c) Vertical tangent at $x = a$ if $f'(a)$ is undefined
   (d) Point of inflection at $x = a$, if $f''(a) = 0$ and $f''(x)$ changes sign as x increases through $x = a$.

5. **Rising and falling curves**
   (a) $f'(x) > 0$ for the increasing function (rising curve)
   (b) $f'(x) < 0$ for the decreasing function (falling curve)

6. **Concavity**
   (a) $f''(x) < 0$ indicates where the graph is concave down
   (b) $f''(x) > 0$ indicates where the graph is concave up

7. **Zones (regions) of exclusion:**

   The domain in which the graph of $y = f(x)$ does not exist (i.e. y is undefined) is an important consideration, because we don't have to worry about the graph in this interval.
   Example: $y = f(x) = \sqrt{9 - x^2}$
   The graph of this function is real if $-3 \leq x \leq 3$. It does not exist for $|x| > 3$. The curve is the upper half of the circle $x^2 + y^2 = 9$.

1.3 Graphs of Basic Functions

1. The graph of a linear function $y = mx + b$ is a straight line, with gradient m and y-intercept b.

   $x = b$ represents a vertical line.

   $y = c$ represents a horizontal line.

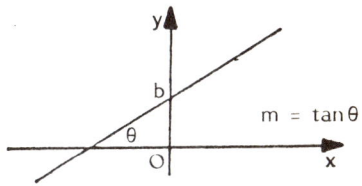

2. The graph of a quadratic function $y = ax^2 + bx + c$ is a parabola.
   Its vertex lies on the axis of symmetry $x = -\frac{b}{2a}$.
   If $a > 0$, y has a minimum at $x = -\frac{b}{2a}$.

   If $a < 0$, y has a maximum at $x = -\frac{b}{2a}$.

   Discriminant $\Delta = b^2 - 4ac$.

   If $\Delta < 0$, the curve does not intersect the x-axis.

   If $\Delta = 0$, the curve touches the x-axis.

   If $\Delta > 0$, the curve intersects the x-axis at $x = -\frac{b}{2a} \pm \frac{\Delta}{2a}$

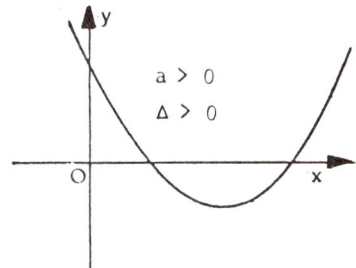

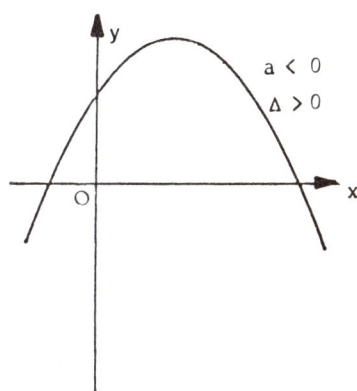

Examples: Sketch the curves:

(a) $y = x^2 - 4x + 3$ (b) $y = -x^2 + 2x$

(c) $y = x^2 + x + 1$

Solution:

(a) $y = x^2 - 4x + 3$

$a > 0$, $\Delta = 16 - 12 > 0$

The intersection with x-axis is given by $y = 0$

$\therefore (x - 3)(x - 1) = 0$

$A(1, 0)$, $B(3, 0)$

When $x = 0$, $y = 3$

Vertex at $x = 2$, $y = -1$

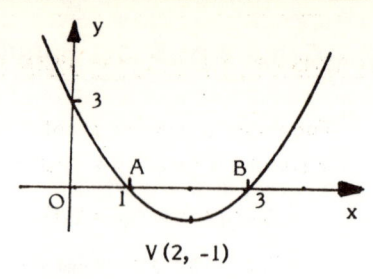

(b) $y = -x^2 + 2x$

$a < 0$

$y = 0$ gives $x(x - 2) = 0$

$O(0, 0)$ and $A(2, 0)$

Vertex $(1, 1)$

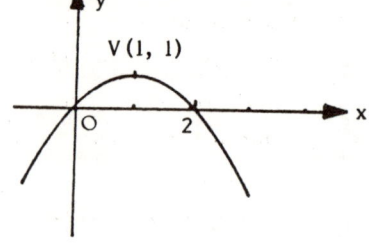

(c) $y = x^2 + x + 1$

$a > 0$, $\Delta = 1 - 4 < 0$

No intersection with x-axis

Vertex $(-\frac{1}{2}, \frac{3}{4})$

Some points on the graph

$A(1, 3)$, $B(0, 1)$, $C(-1, 1)$

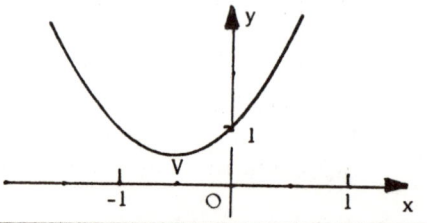

The equation of the form $x = ay^2 + by + c$ represents a parabola with its axis horizontal.

Vertex on axis of symmetry at $y = -\frac{b}{2a}$.

For $a > 0$ and $a < 0$, the shapes are as shown.

If $\Delta < 0$, the graph does not intersect y-axis.

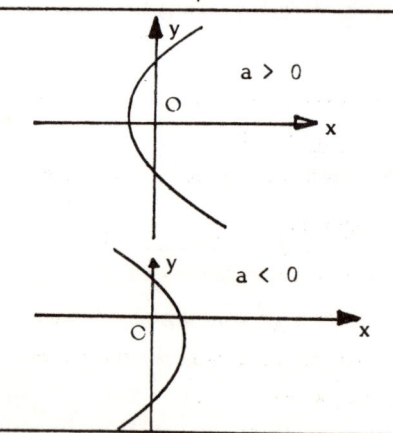

Example:
Sketch the curve $x = y^2 + 2y$

Solution:
$a = 1 > 0$.

Vertex: $y = -\frac{b}{2a} = -\frac{2}{2} = -1$, $V(-1, -1)$

$x = 0$ gives $y(y + 2) = 0$ i.e.

$(0, 0)$ and $(0, -2)$

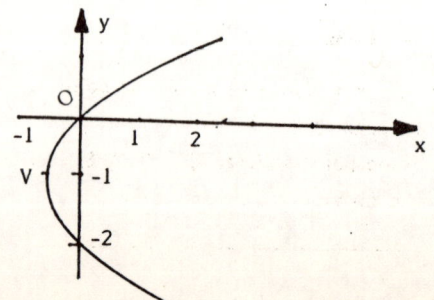

GRAPHS OF POLYNOMIAL FUNCTIONS

3. For sketching the graph of the polynomial function we need reasonably sufficient information, such as:

    a. The function $y = f(x)$ is an even function if $f(x) = f(-x)$.

    The graph of an even function is symmetric about y-axis.

    b. The function $y = f(x)$ is odd if $f(-x) = -f(-x)$ and the graph is symmetric about the origin.

    c. The intersection of the curve $y = f(x)$ with
    - the x-axis is given by $y = 0$. This is not always simple, but worth trying.
    - the y-axis is given by $x = 0$.

    d. The behaviour of the curve as $x \to \pm \infty$

    e. The nature of the turning points, i.e. a maximum or a minimum

    f. Concavity and points of inflexion   i.e. $f''(x) = 0$.

Example: (1)
Sketch the curves $y = x^3$ and $y = -x^3$

Solution:
$f(x) = x^3$ and $f(-x) = -x^3$
∴ The graph of $y = x^3$ is symmetric about the origin
$O(0, 0)$ is a point on the curve
As $x \to \infty$, $y \to +\infty$
$x \to -\infty$, $y \to -\infty$
$\frac{dy}{dx} = 3x^2$
But $x = 0$ is not a turning point, since $\frac{dy}{dx}$ does not change its sign in passing through O
Some points: $A(1, 1)$, $B(2, 8)$. This is reasonably sufficient information to sketch the curve.

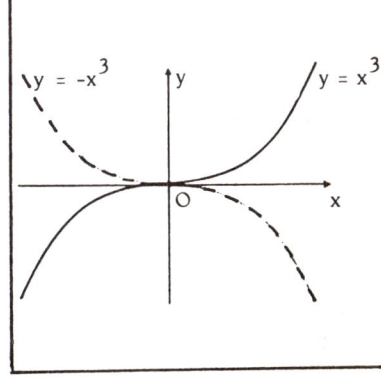

Example: (2)   Sketch the curve:
$y = (x + 2)(x - 1)(x - 3)$

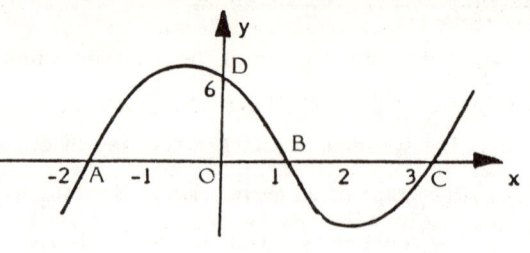

$y = 0$ gives $A(-2, 0)$, $B(1, 0)$, $C(3, 0)$
$x = 0$ gives $D(0, 6)$
$y \to \infty$ as $x \to \infty$
$y \to -\infty$ as $x \to -\infty$
Other points $x = 2, y = -4$
                        $x = -1, y = 8$

Example: (3)   Sketch the curve:

$y = (x + 2)(x - 2)^2$
$y = 0$ gives $A(-2, 0)$, $B(2, 0)$
The double zero $x = 2$ indicates that the x-axis touches the curve at $x = 2$
$y \to \pm\infty$ as $x \to \pm\infty$
$x = 0$ gives $y = 8$
Other points:
$C(-1, 9)$, $D(1, 3)$, $E(3, 5)$

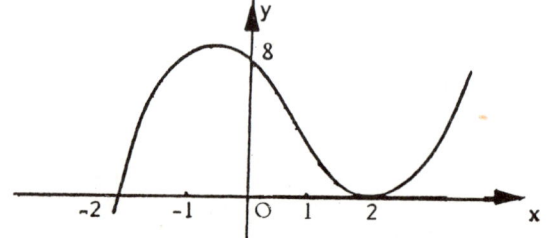

Example: (4)   Sketch the curve:
$y = (x + 2)(x + 1)(x - 2)(x - 3)$
The sketching is similar to that of Example 2, noting that $y \to \infty$ as $x \to -\infty$
$x = 0, y = 12$
$(1, 12)$ is another point

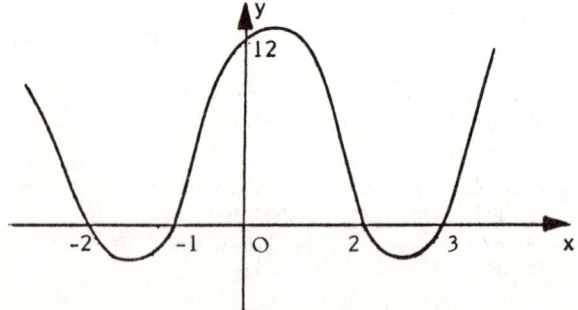

4. **Graphs of $y = x^{1/2}$ and $y = x^{1/3}$**

EXAMPLE: (1) Draw a sketch of $y = \sqrt{x}$ by analysing the behaviour of the function near $x = 0$.

SOLUTION:

The function $f(x) = \sqrt{x}$ exists and is continuous for $x \geq 0$.

Also $f(x) \geq 0$ for $x \geq 0$ and $f'(x) = \dfrac{1}{2\sqrt{x}}$ for $x > 0$.

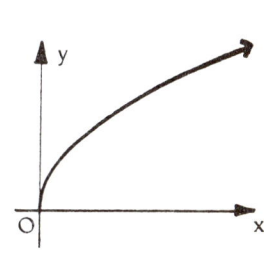

Graph of $y = \sqrt{x}$

The point $x = 0$ is a critical point as $f'(0)$ does not exist. The curve $y = \sqrt{x}$ has a vertical tangent at $x = 0$.

Since $f'(x) > 0$ for $x > 0$, $f(x)$ is an increasing function and $f(0) = 0$ is the absolute minimum, but $f(x)$ has no absolute maximum.

It may be noted that since $f''(x) = -\dfrac{1}{4} x^{-3/2} < 0$ for $x > 0$, the curve is concave down.

This is sufficient information for drawing a reasonable graph of $y = \sqrt{x}$.

Note: $y = \sqrt{x}$ is the upper half of the parabola $y^2 = x$.

EXAMPLE: (2)

Draw a sketch of $y = x^{1/3}$.

SOLUTION:

$y = x^{1/3}$, $\dfrac{dy}{dx} = \dfrac{1}{3} x^{-2/3}$, $\dfrac{d^2 y}{dx^2} = -\dfrac{2}{9} x^{-5/3}$.

$f(x) = x^{1/3}$ exists for all real x

$f(-x) = (-x)^{1/3} = -x^{1/3} = -f(x)$, so the curve has point symmetry about the origin.

$f'(x)$ does not exist for $x = 0$, so the curve has a vertical tangent, at $x = 0$.

Also $f'(x) > 0$ for all x, $x \neq 0$, so it is an increasing curve. $x = 0$ is a critical point.

$f(x) \to \infty$ as $x \to \infty$

$f(x) \to -\infty$ as $x \to -\infty$

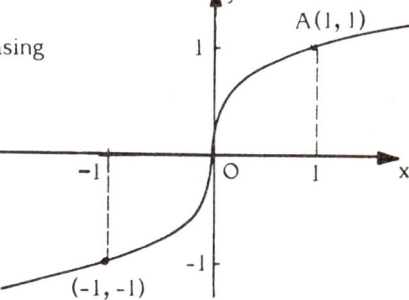

$f''(x) > 0$ for $x > 0$ and $f''(x) < 0$ for $x < 0$, so the origin is an inflection point.

Also $f''(x) > 0$ for $x > 0$ tells us that the curve is concave down, while $f''(x) < 0$ tells us that the curve is concave up for $x < 0$. A few simple points are O, A(1,1), B(-1,-1).

1.4 Curves with Vertical and Horizontal Asymptotes

Example: (1)

Sketch the curve $y = \dfrac{2}{x}$

y has same sign as x, hence curve in first and third quadrant

As $x \to \infty$, $y \to 0^+$ (from above)

As $x \to -\infty$, $y \to 0^-$ (from below)

The x-axis and y-axis are the asymptotes of the curve.

The asymptotes are very useful in sketching the curves. This curve is a rectangular hyperbola - rectangular because the asymptotes are perpendicular.

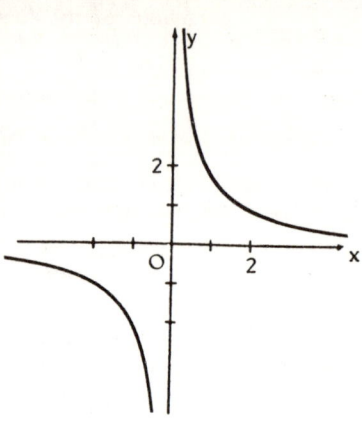

Example: (2)

Sketch the curve $y = x + \dfrac{1}{x}$

$y = x + \dfrac{1}{x}$, $x \neq 0$

Near $x = 0$, the term $\dfrac{1}{x}$ dominates, i.e. x is negligible compared to $\dfrac{1}{x}$

∴ The curve $y = x + \dfrac{1}{x}$ behaves like hyperbola $y = \dfrac{1}{x}$ near $x = 0$

As $x \to \infty$, $y \to x$ i.e. the curve approaches the line $y = x$

The graph is symmetric about the origin as $f(-x) = -f(x)$

The turning points are:

$\dfrac{dy}{dx} = 1 - \dfrac{1}{x^2} = 0 \Rightarrow P(1, 2)$
$\phantom{\dfrac{dy}{dx} = 1 - \dfrac{1}{x^2} = 0 \Rightarrow}Q(-1, -2)$

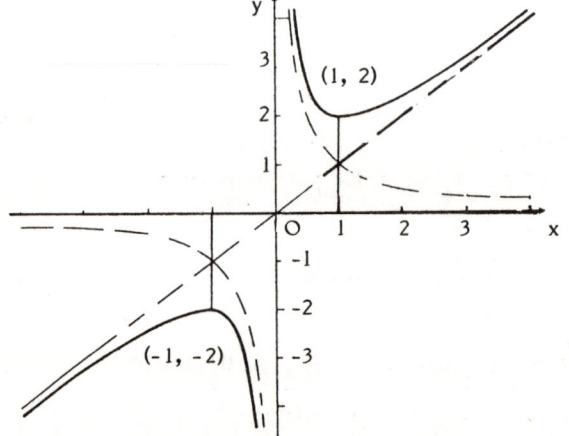

The curve does not intersect either axis

Other points: (2, 2.5), (-2, -2.5)

This is reasonable enough information to sketch this curve

Example: (3)

Sketch the curve $y = \dfrac{x-2}{x^2}$

Solution:

$y = \dfrac{x-2}{x^2}$

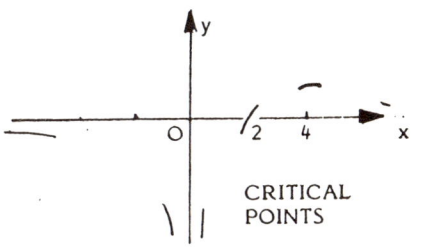
CRITICAL POINTS

The function is undefined at $x = 0$, i.e. y-axis is the asymptote

$x = 2$, $y = 0$. $A(2, 0)$

When $x > 2, y > 0$, $x < 2, y < 0$

Near $x = 0$, the graph behaves more like $-\dfrac{2}{x^2}$

As $x \to \infty$, $y \to 0^+$ from above

$\quad x \to -\infty$, $y \to 0^-$ from below

$\dfrac{dy}{dx} = \dfrac{-1}{x^2} + \dfrac{4}{x^3} = 0$ gives $x = 4$

$\therefore P(4, \tfrac{1}{2})$ is a maximum turning point.

The first sketch shows the important features, the second shows a complete graph

Other points: $(-1, -3), (-2, -1), (-3, -\tfrac{5}{9}), (1, -1)$

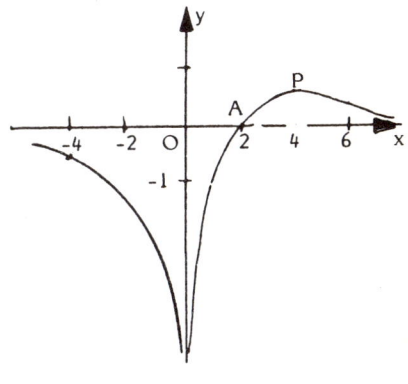

Example: (4)

$y = \dfrac{x^2}{(x-2)(x+2)}$

Solution:

The curve is undefined at $x = \pm 2$

$x = 0, y = 0$, $O(0, 0)$ is a point on the curve.

The lines $x = 2$ and $x = -2$ are the asymptotes.

As $x \to \infty$, $y \to 1^+$ from above

$\quad x \to -\infty$, $y \to 1^+$ from above

This is so because the numerator is greater than the denominator when x is large.

For $-2 < x < 2$, $y < 0$ and the curve is asymptotic to $x = \pm 2$

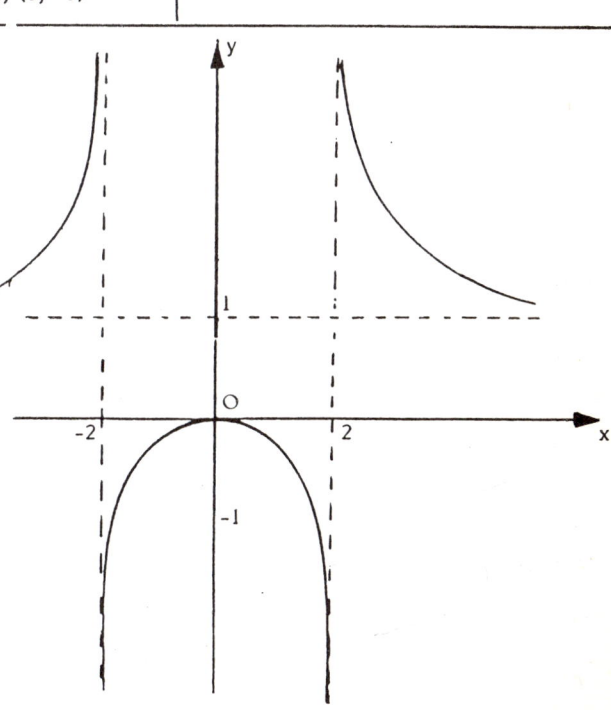

It would be instructive for you to study the sketches of the following curves and reasoning out the shape and critical behaviour of each of them.

Example: (5)

$$y = \frac{x^2}{(x+2)(x-1)}$$

What are the asymptotes?

Why is the RIGHT (TOP) branch approaching $y = 1$ from below?

Why is the LEFT (TOP) branch $\to y = 1$ from above?

Useful points are at
$x = 0$, $x = 2$, $x = 4$, $x = -3$
$x = -1$.

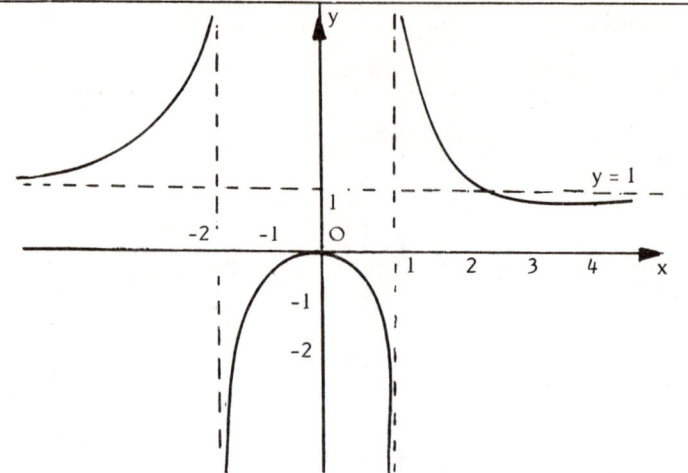

Example: (6)

$$y = \frac{(x+1)(x-1)}{(x+2)(x-2)}$$

What are the asymptotes?

As $x \to \pm \infty$, to which line does the curve approach?

The useful points:

$x = 0, 1, 1.5, -1, -1.5$

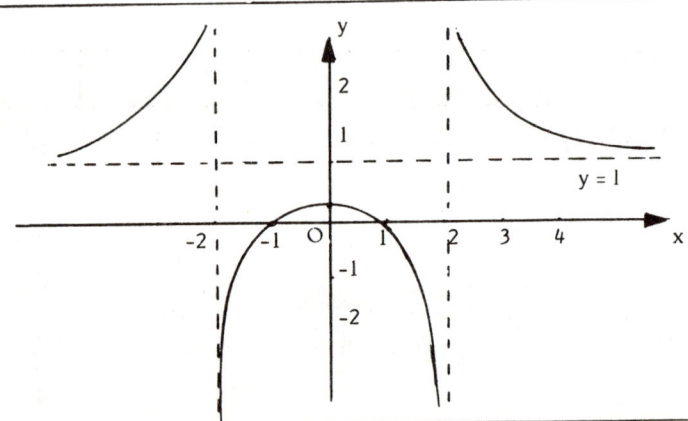

Example: (7)

$$y = \frac{x(x+2)}{x^2 - 1}$$

Questions:
a Asymptotes?
b. After $x = 1$, as $x \to \infty$ what does y approach?
c Before $x = -1$, as $x \to -\infty$, how does y approach 1?
d. As $x \to \pm 1$, what does $y \to$?

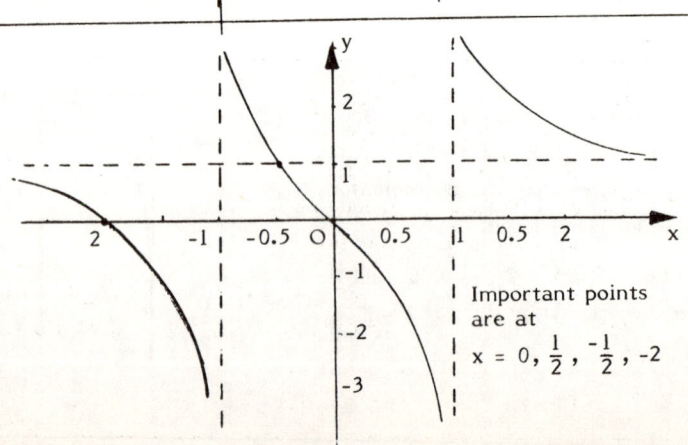

Important points are at
$x = 0, \frac{1}{2}, -\frac{1}{2}, -2$

1.5 Trigonometric Graphs

1. $y = a \sin bx$

   The amplitude $= a$

   The period, $p = \dfrac{2\pi}{b}$

   $f(x) = \sin x$

   $f(-x) = -\sin x$

   $\therefore f(x) = \sin x$ is an odd function.

   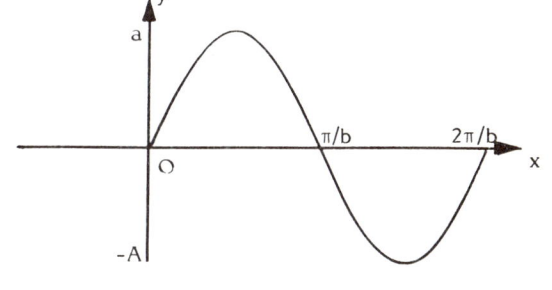

2. $y = A \cos bx$

   Amplitude $= A$

   Period $p = \dfrac{2\pi}{b}$

   $f(x) = \cos x$ is an even function.

   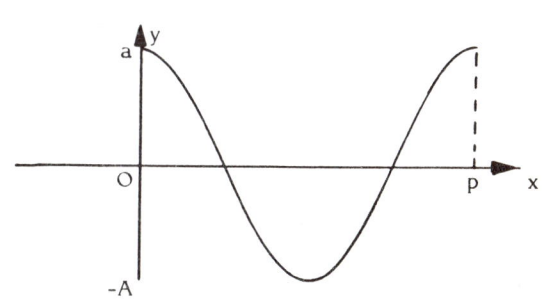

3. $y = \tan x$

   $y \to \infty$ as $x \to (2n - 1)\dfrac{\pi}{2}$

   The asymptotes are at

   $x = (2n - 1)\dfrac{\pi}{2}$,

   $n = 0, \pm 1, \pm 2, \ldots$

   $f(x) = \tan x$ is an odd function.

   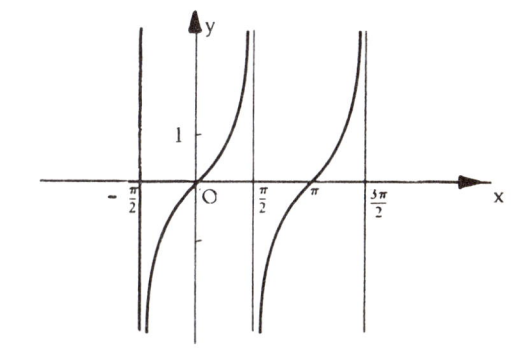

4. (a) $y = \operatorname{cosec} x$, period 2π

      $\operatorname{cosec} x$ is an odd function

      $\operatorname{cosec} x \to \infty$ at $x = n\pi$ ($n = 0, \pm 1, \pm 2, \ldots$)

   (b) $y = \sec x$, period 2π

      $\sec x$ is an even function

      $\sec x \to \infty$ at $x = (2n + 1)\dfrac{\pi}{2}$,   ($n = 0, \pm 1, \ldots$)

   (c) $y = \cot x$ is an odd function,   period π, with asymptotes at

      $x = n\pi$,   ($n = 0, \pm 1, \ldots$)

      The sketches are on the next page.

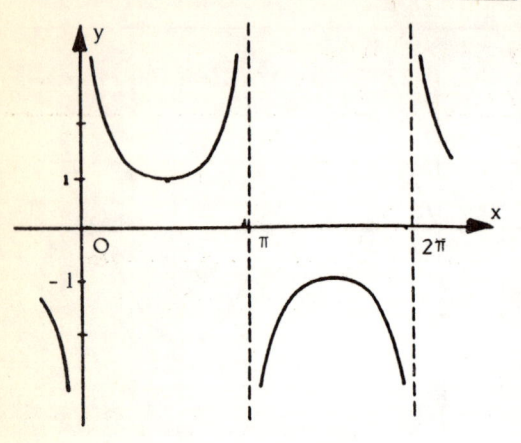

y = cosec x

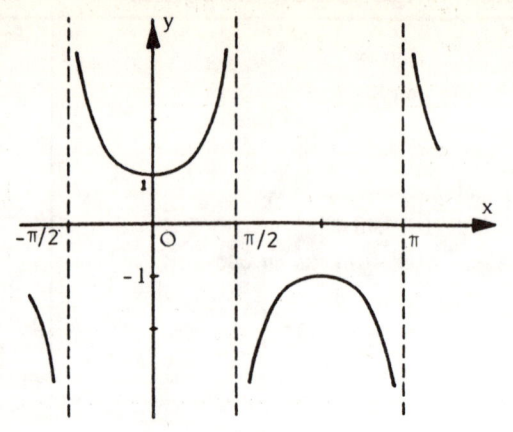

y = sec x

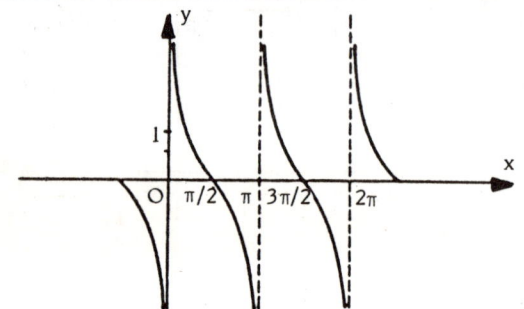

y = cot x

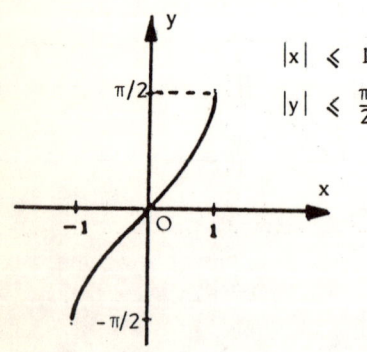

$|x| \leqslant 1$
$|y| \leqslant \frac{\pi}{2}$

y = sin^{-1} x

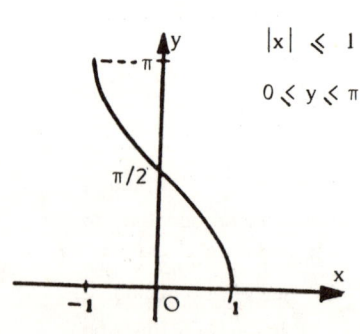

$|x| \leqslant 1$
$0 \leqslant y \leqslant \pi$

y = cos^{-1} x

Example: (1) Sketch the following curves:
(a) $\sin(x+y) = 1$
(b) $y = |\cos x|$, $|x| \leqslant 2\pi$
(c) $y = \sin^2 x$
(d) $y = \cos(\sin^{-1} x)$

Solution:

(a) $\sin(x+y) = 1$

$\therefore x + y = n\pi + (-1)^n \dfrac{\pi}{2}$ is the general solution. $[n = 0, \pm 1, \pm 2, \ldots]$

Now $x + y = K$ represents a series of parallel lines.

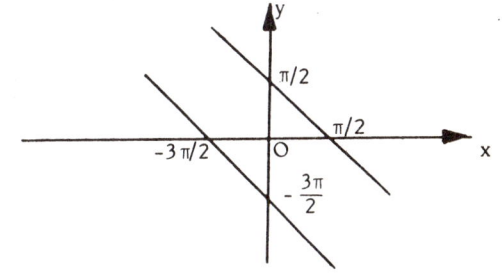

(b) $y = |\cos x|$, $-2\pi \leqslant x \leqslant 2\pi$

The easiest way to draw the sketch of any absolute function is to draw the curve of ordinary function and then draw the REFLECTION of the graph below the x-axis

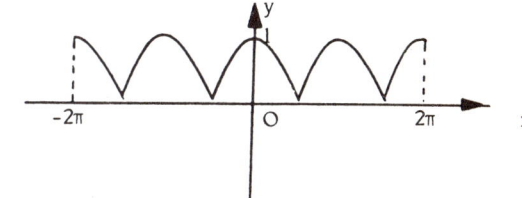

(c) $y = \sin^2 x$

$y \geqslant 0$ for all real x

The greatest value of y is 1

Some points:

$(0, 0)$, $(\dfrac{\pi}{4}, 0.5)$, $(\dfrac{\pi}{2}, 1)$

$(\dfrac{3\pi}{4}, 0.5)$, $(\pi, 0)$ etc.

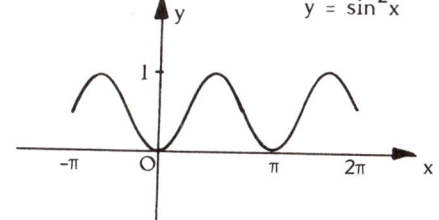

(d) $y = \cos(\sin^{-1} x)$

Here $|x| \leqslant 1$

We simplify the function by replacing $\sin^{-1} x$ by $\cos^{-1} \sqrt{1-x^2}$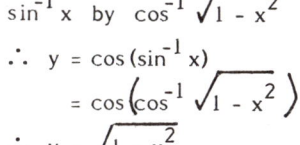

$\therefore y = \cos(\sin^{-1} x)$
$= \cos\left(\cos^{-1}\sqrt{1-x^2}\right)$

$\therefore y = \sqrt{1-x^2}$

$\therefore$ Graph of $y = \cos(\sin^{-1} x)$ is a semi-circle, above x-axis, radius 1, centre O.

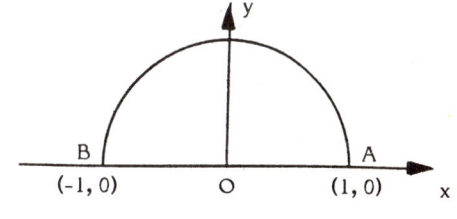

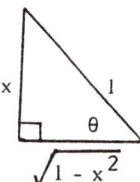

1.6 Exponential Curves

Sketch the following curves:

(a) $y = e^x$

  $y > 0$ for all x

  As $x \to \infty$, $y \to \infty$

  $x \to -\infty$, $y \to 0$

Some points:

(0, 1), (1, e = 2.7), (2, 7.4), (-1, 0.3)

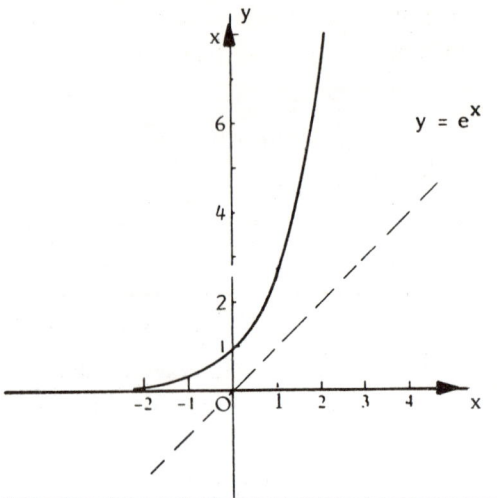

(b) $y = e^{-x^2}$
1. $y > 0$ for all x. A (0, 1)
2. $f(x) = f(-x)$, even function. The graph is symmetric about the x-axis
3. As $x \to \infty$, $y \to 0$
4. $\frac{dy}{dx} = -2x\,e^{-x^2}$ gives a maximum at $x = 0$, $y = 1$
5. $\frac{d^2y}{dx^2} = -2[1 - 2x^2]e^{-x^2} = 0$ gives inflexion at $x = 0.7$ and $x = -0.7$, $y = 0.6$

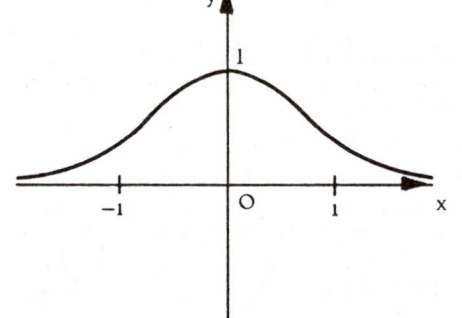

(c) $y = x\,e^{-x}$
1. $y > 0$ for $x > 0$

   $y < 0$ for $x < 0$
2. As $x \to \infty$, $y \to 0$

   As $x \to -\infty$, $y \to -\infty$
3. $\frac{dy}{dx} = e^{-x}(1 - x) = 0$ gives

   $x = 1$, $y = e^{-1} = 0.4$ (Maximum)
4. Some points

   (0, 0), (1, 0.4), (2, 0.26), (-1, -2.7)

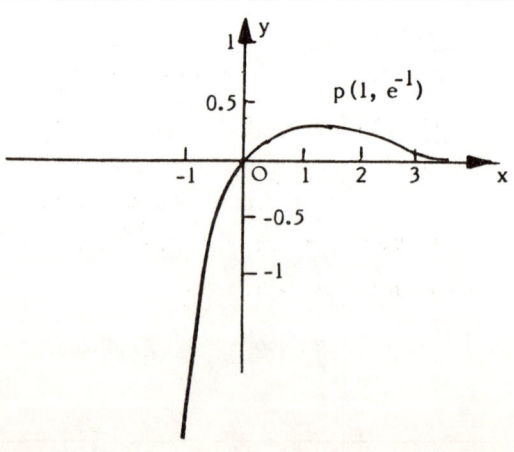

1.7 Drawing Graphs by Composition of Ordinates

(a) <u>Addition or Subtraction of Ordinates</u>

<u>EXAMPLE:</u> (1) Sketch the curve $y = 1 + 2\sin(2x)$, $-\pi \leqslant x \leqslant \pi$.

<u>SOLUTION:</u> We separately sketch $y_1 = 1$ and $y_2 = 2\sin 2x$.

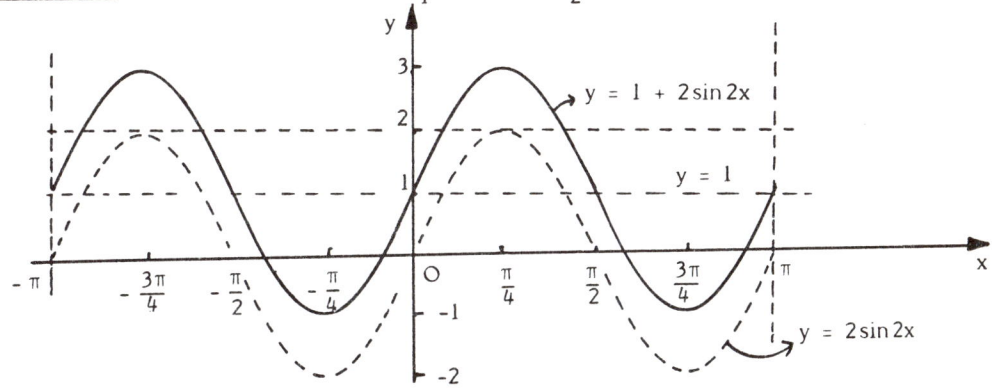

Algebraic addition of ordinates gives us the equation

$$y = y_1 + y_2 = 1 + 2\sin 2x \qquad \ldots (1)$$

By graphical addition we obtain the graph of $y = 1 + 2\sin 2x$, $-\pi \leqslant x \leqslant \pi$, shown by the heavy line.

Note that the amplitude of $y = 2\sin 2x$ is 2 and its period is $\frac{2\pi}{2} = \pi$.

Addition of ordinates must be done at all key points, such as end-points, at the intersections with the axes and the critical points (Maxima, Minima) of both graphs. It is useful to note that the graph of $y = 1 + 2\sin 2x$ is obtained by translating the graph of $y = 2\sin 2x$ one unit upwards, thus preserving all the characteristics of $y = 2\sin 2x$.

<u>EXAMPLE:</u> (2)
Sketch the graph of the function $f(x) = 2\sin x + x$, $0 \leqslant x \leqslant 2\pi$.

<u>SOLUTION:</u> Let $y_1 = 2\sin x$ and $y_2 = x$

The sine graph has an amplitude of 2 units and a period of 2π. $y_2 = x$ is a straight line through the origin. We separately sketch these graphs and by graphical addition at key points $x = 0, \frac{\pi}{2}, \pi, \frac{3\pi}{2}, \pi$, obtain the composite graph of $y = x + 2\sin x$, as shown by the solid line.

(cont.)

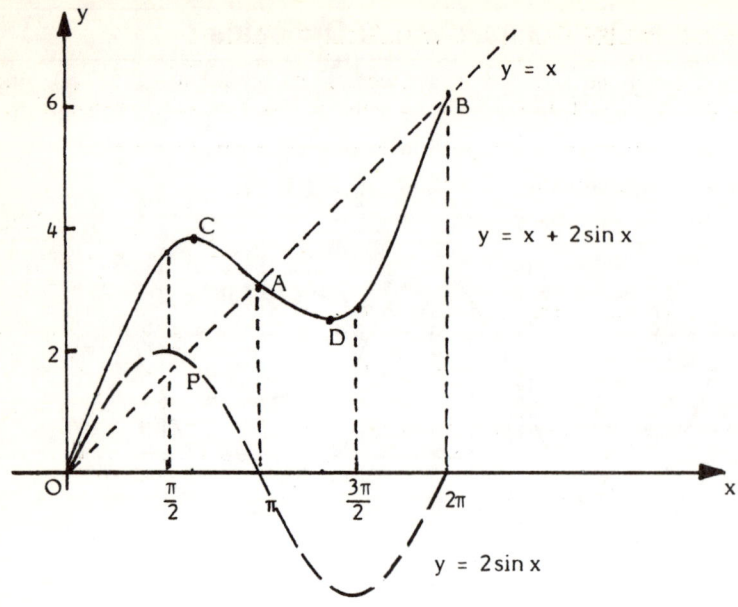

x	0	π/2	π	3π/2	2π
y_2	0	1.57	3.14	4.71	6.28
y_1	0	2	0	-2	0
$y_1 + y_2$	0	3.57	3.14	2.71	6.28

Note that the points of intersection of the required curve $y = x + 2\sin x$ and $y = x$ are where the curve $y = 2\sin x$ cuts the x-axis. So, O, A(π, π), (B$(2\pi, 2\pi)$ are the points on the graph.

Critical Points:

$y = x + 2\sin x$ | The stationary points are given by $1 + 2\cos x = 0$
i.e. $\cos x = -\frac{1}{2}$

$\frac{dy}{dx} = 1 + 2\cos x$ | $\therefore x = \frac{2\pi}{3}$ and $x = \frac{4\pi}{3}$ are stationary points.

$\frac{d^2y}{dx^2} = -2\sin x$ | $f''(\frac{2\pi}{3}) < 0$ and $f''(\frac{4\pi}{3}) > 0$

So C$(\frac{2\pi}{3}, \frac{2\pi}{3} + \sqrt{3})$ is a maximum point.   C(2.1, 3.8)

and D$(\frac{4\pi}{3}, \frac{4\pi}{3} - \sqrt{3})$ is a minimum point.   D(4.2, 2.5)

We have sufficient information to sketch the graph.

Note: $\frac{d^2y}{dx^2} = 0$ gives the point of inflection, i.e. $\sin x = 0$ and $\sin x$ changes sign as x increases through π.

$\therefore x = \pi$ is the point of inflection A(π, π)

(b) **Drawing Graphs by Reflecting Functions in Co-ordinate Axes**

A function $y = -f(x)$ can be graphed by reflecting the graph of $y = f(x)$ in the x-axis. The graph of $y = c - f(x)$ may then be obtained by a suitable translation.

EXAMPLE: Sketch the following curves

(a) $y = -\sin x$ (b) $y = 1 - \sin x$

SOLUTION:

We draw the graph of $y = \sin x$ (dotted line), then reflect it in the x-axis to obtain the graph of $y = -\sin x$ and finally shift it vertically upwards by 1 unit.

The graph of $y = 1 - \sin x$ is shown by the heavy line.

The key points to consider for plotting are

$x = 0, \frac{\pi}{2}, \pi, \frac{3\pi}{2}, 2\pi$

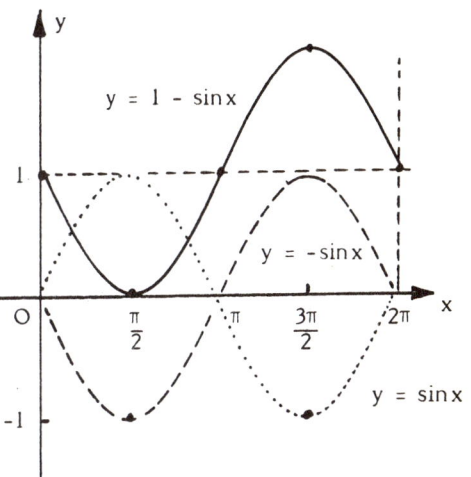

(c) **Graph of $y = |f(x)|$ from the graph of $y = f(x)$**

Since $|f(x)| \geqslant 0$ for all x, all we have to do is to draw the reflection of any part of the curve $y = f(x)$ below the x-axis, in the x-axis, leaving unchanged those parts above the x-axis.

EXAMPLE: Sketch the curves: (a) $y = x^2 - 4$ (b) $y = |x^2 - 4|$

(c) $y = 2 + |x^2 - 4|$

SOLUTION:

(a) $y = y_1 = x^2 - 4$ is a (complete) parabola. (The part below the x-axis is shown by a dotted line)

(b) Reflecting only the part of the parabola below the x-axis, we obtain the graph of $y = y_2 = |x^2 - 4|$

(c) Shifting y_2, 2 units vertically upwards, we sketch the graph of

$y = y_3 = 2 + |x^2 - 4|$

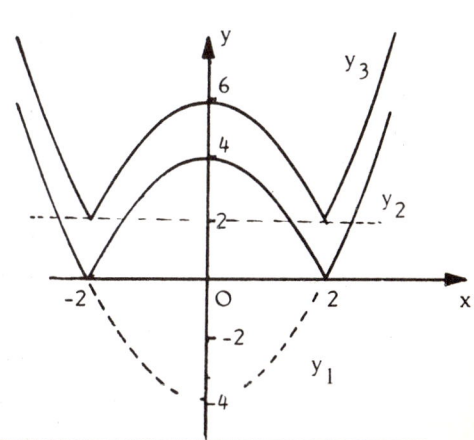

(d) Graph of $y = f(-x)$ by initially graphing $y = f(x)$

$y = f(-x)$ is the reflection of the graph of $y = f(x)$ in the y-axis.

EXAMPLE: (a) Sketch $y = \sqrt{-x}$
(b) Sketch $y = \log_e(-x)$
(c) Sketch $y = \log_e |x|$

Note: The graph of $y = \log_e |x|$ is the graph
$$y = \log_e x, \quad x > 0$$
$$= \log(-x), \quad x < 0$$
i.e. both branches make the graph of $y = \log_e |x|$.

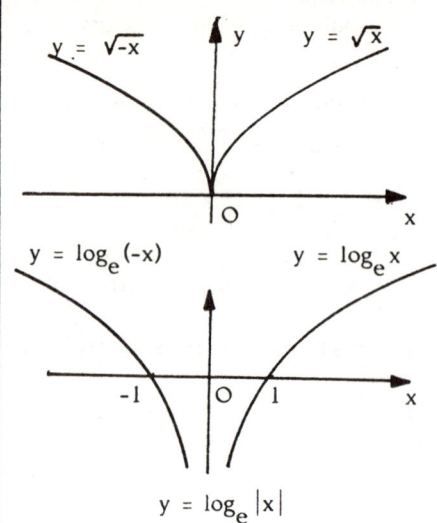

(e) Graph of $y = f(x - a)$ by graphing $y = f(x)$

The graph of $y = f(x - a)$ is obtained by shifting the graph of $y = f(x)$ to the right by a units, if $a > 0$ and to the left by $|a|$ units if $a < 0$.

EXAMPLE:
Sketch the curves   (a) $y = \cos(x - 1)$ (b) $y = \log_e(x + 1)$

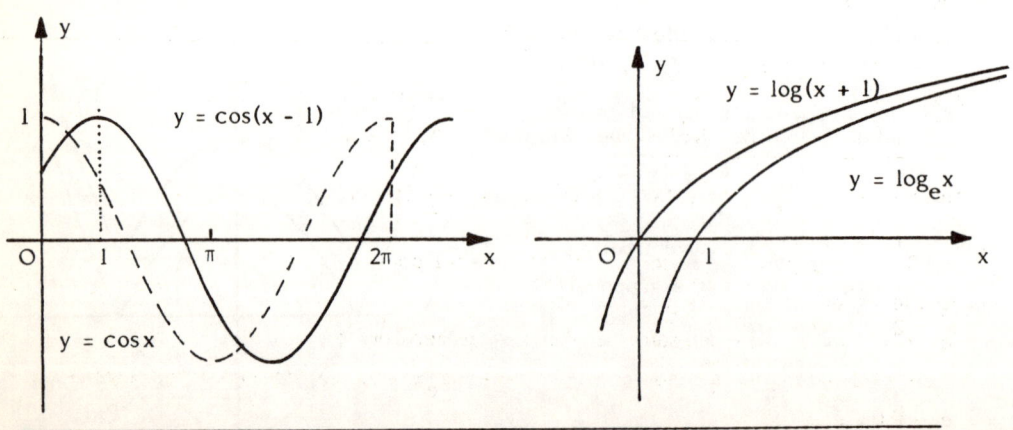

(f) **Graphing the functions by multiplication of ordinates**

EXAMPLE: Sketch $y = xe^{-x}$

We separately sketch the curves $y = y_1 = x$
and $y = y_2 = e^{-x}$
We derive the properties of the graph
$y = y_1 \cdot y_2 = xe^{-x}$ from Fig. 1.
When $x < 0$, $y = xe^{-x} < 0$
$\quad\quad\quad x > 0$, $xe^{-x} > 0$
As $x \to \infty$, $xe^{-x} \to 0$;
As $x \to -\infty$, $xe^{-x} \to -\infty$
$\frac{dy}{dx} = e^{-x}(1-x)$, $\frac{d^2y}{dx^2} = -e^{-x}(2-x)$, the
stationary point $x = 1$ is a maximum.
Some useful points: (0,0), (1, 0.37), (2, 0.3), (-1, -2.7).

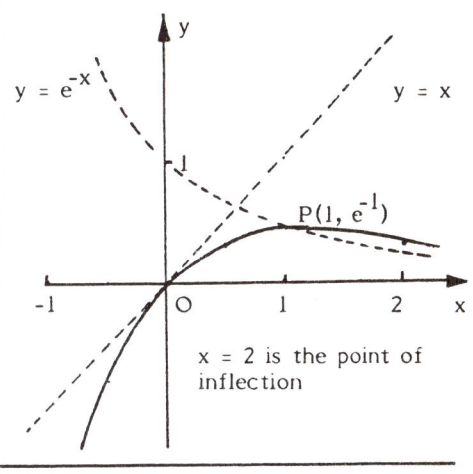

$x = 2$ is the point of inflection

The graph can now be sketched (solid line).

(g) **Graphing the functions by division of ordinates**

Graphing $y = \frac{f(x)}{g(x)}$ by division of ordinates.

EXAMPLE: Sketch $y = \frac{\log_e x}{x}$ by separately sketching
$y = \log_e x$ and $y = x$.

SOLUTION:
$y = \frac{\log_e x}{x}$ exists only for $x > 0$.
A few points:

x	0.5	1	2	e	5
$\log_e x$	-0.7	0	0.7	1	1.6
y	-1.4	0	0.35	0.37	0.32

Asymptote at $x = 0$.
As $x \to \infty$, $y \to 0$.

Critical Points: $\frac{dy}{dx} = \frac{1}{x^2}(x \cdot \frac{1}{x} - \log_e x) = \frac{1}{x^2}(1 - \log_e x)$

$\frac{dy}{dx} = 0 \Rightarrow \log_e x = 1 \Rightarrow x = e$ is the critical point.
Using the graph of $y = \log_e x$, we find:
Since $x^2 > 0$, $\frac{dy}{dx}$ has the same sign as the numerator $N = 1 - \log_e x$.
For $x < e$, $1 - \log_e x > 0$ and for $x > e$, $1 - \log_e x < 0$, so the maximum point is at
$x = e \to P(e, e^{-1})$
The sketch of $y = \frac{\log_e x}{x}$ is shown by the solid line.

(h) Graph of $[f(x)]^n$, $n > 1$ by graphing $f(x)$

Let $y = g(x) = [f(x)]^n$, then $g'(x) = n \cdot f'(x) \cdot [f(x)]^{n-1}$, so all the stationary points and the x-intercepts of $y = f(x)$ are the stationary points of $g(x)$. The following properties of $[f(x)]^n$ may be useful.

1. If $|f(x)| > 1$, then $|g(x)| > |f(x)|$, e.g. $x > 2 \Rightarrow x^2 > 4 \Rightarrow x^2 > x$
2. If $0 < |f(x)| < 1$, then $0 < |g(x)| < |f(x)|$, e.g. $0 < x < \frac{1}{2} \Rightarrow x^2 < x$
3. $[f(x)]^n \geqslant 0$ for all x, if n is even, e.g. $(x^2 - 4)^2 > 0$ for all x
4. If n is odd: (a) $[f(x)]^n > 0$ for $f(x) > 0$, e.g. $(x - 2)^3 > x - 2$ for $x > 2$
   (b) $[f(x)]^n < 0$ for $f(x) < 0$, e.g. $(x - 2)^3 < x - 2$ for $x < 2$
5. Points of Intersection are useful and obtained by solving, $g(x) = f(x)$.

EXAMPLE: (1) Sketch $y = (x^2 - 1)^2$
Le $y = g(x) = (x^2 - 1)^2$, $f(x) = x^2 - 1$
(1) $f'(x) = 0$ and $f(x) = 0$ give
$2x = 0$ and $x^2 - 1 = 0$
So, $x = 0, \pm 1$ are the stationary points.
$g'(x) = 4x(x^2 - 1)$, $g''(x) = 4(3x^2 - 1)$
$g''(0) < 0$, $g''(1) > 0$, $g''(-1) > 0$
So, the maximum occurs at $x = 0$ and minimum occurs at $x = \pm 1$
(2) $g(x) = g(-x)$, so $g(x)$ is symmetric about the y-axis.
(3) $g(x) \geqslant 0$ for all x, $g(x) \to \infty$ as $x \to \pm \infty$
(4) Points of intersection: $(x^2 - 1)^2 = x^2 - 1$ gives $x = \pm 1, \pm \sqrt{2} = \pm 1.4$
(5) Additional points: $(0, 1), (\pm 1, 0), (\pm 2, 1), (\pm 2, 9)$

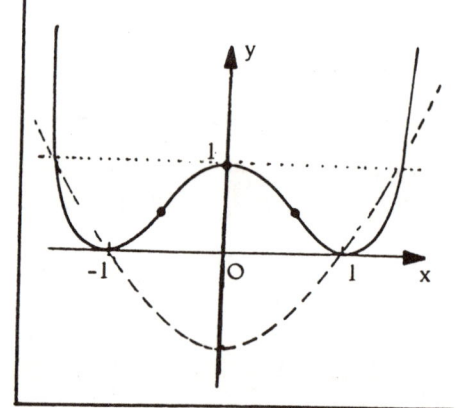

EXAMPLE: (2) Sketch $y = \sin^2 x$
The period of $g(x) = \sin^2 x = \frac{1}{2}(1 - \cos 2x)$ is π.
Let $f(x) = \sin x$.
$g(x) \geqslant 0$ for all x. $g'(x) = 2 \sin x \cos x$
$f(x) = 0$, $f'(x) = 0$ give $\sin x = 0$, $\cos x = 0$
So stationary points are at $x = 0, \pi, 2\pi, \frac{\pi}{2}, \frac{3\pi}{2}, \ldots$
Observe that $\sin^2 x < |\sin x|$ except at the stationary points.
The graph of $g(x)$ can now be sketched with the points (Fig. 1).
$(0, 0), (\frac{\pi}{2}, 1), (\pi, 0), (\frac{3\pi}{2}, 1), (2\pi, 0)$.

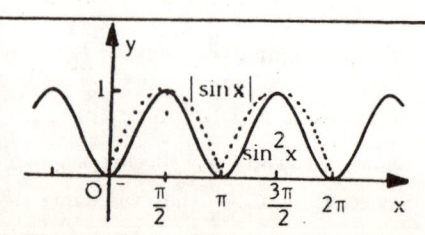

(i) Graphs of the Reciprocal Functions

By using the properties of the reciprocal function $y = \frac{1}{f(x)}$, in relation to the known graph of $y = f(x)$, we can draw the sketch of $y = \frac{1}{f(x)}$.

To sketch $y = \frac{1}{f(x)}$, consider the following:

a. If $y > 0$, then $\frac{1}{y} > 0$ and if $y < 0$, then $\frac{1}{y} < 0$. As y increases $\frac{1}{y}$ decreases.

b. Solve the equation $y = \frac{1}{y}$ i.e. $y = \pm 1$ for the common points of intersection.

c. The asymptotes of $\frac{1}{y}$ are given by $y = 0$.

d. Behaviour of the function as $x \to \pm \infty$

e. Simple points at $x = 0, \pm 1$, etc.

Example: (1)

Sketch $y = \log_e x$ and $y = \frac{1}{\log_e x}$

$x > 0$ for $y = \log_e x$

$y = \log_e x$ is a known graph

$y = \frac{1}{\log_e x}$ is shown by solid line and can be sketched as follows. (base, e, omitted for convenience)

1. The asymptote for $y = \frac{1}{\log x}$ is at $x = 1$

2. The points of intersections are given by solving:
$\log_e x = \frac{1}{\log_e x}$ i.e. $x = e \doteq 2.7$
and $x = e^{-1} = 0.37$

3. As $y = \log x$ increases from 1
$y = \frac{1}{\log x}$ decreases. (both positive)

4. As $x \to 1^+$, $y = \frac{1}{\log x} \to \infty$ and
$x \to 1^-$, $y \to -\infty$.

5. Some useful points $(0.1, -0.4)$, $(0.9, -9.5)$, $(1.1, 10.4)$.

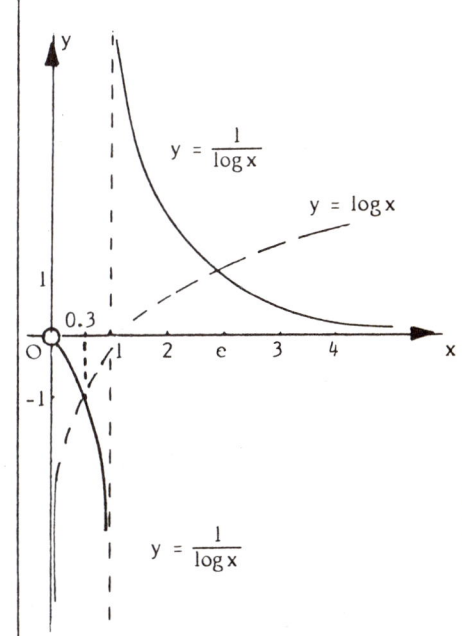

Example: (2) Sketch the curve

$$y = \frac{1}{x^2 - 4}$$

Solution:

$y = x^2 - 4$ is a parabola as shown in the figure. (broken line)

The graphs of both functions

$y = \frac{1}{x^2 - 4}$ and $y = x^2 - 4$

are both positive or both negative.
These two meet at points given by

$$x^2 - 4 = \frac{1}{x^2 - 4}$$

$$x^2 - 4 = \pm 1$$

$$x = \pm \sqrt{5}, \pm\sqrt{3}$$

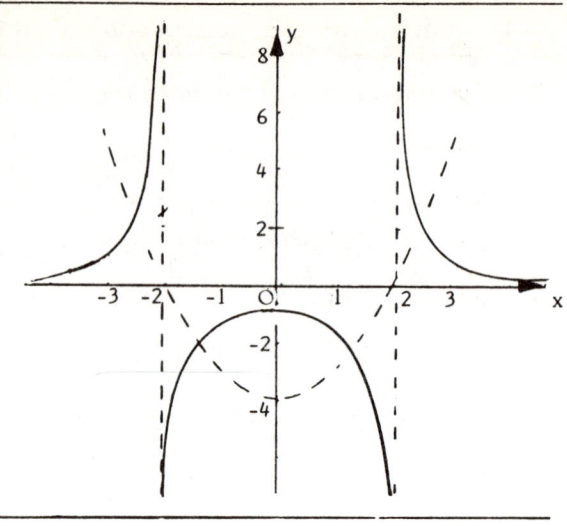

The graph of $y = \frac{1}{x^2 - 4}$ has vertical asymptotes at $x = \pm 2$ and horizontal asymptotes as the x-axis. Also $x = 0$, $y = -\frac{1}{4}$. This is reasonably sufficient information to sketch the graph. (SOLID LINE)

Example: (3) Sketch the curves

$$y = x^3 + 1 \text{ and } y = \frac{1}{x^3 + 1}$$

Solution:

1. Draw the graph: $y = x^3 + 1$
2. Asymptote of $y = \frac{1}{x^3 + 1}$ at $x = -1$
3. $x = 0, y = 1$ is a common point.
4. As $x \to \infty$, $y \to 0$ for
   $y = \frac{1}{x^3 + 1}$
5. As $y > 0$ and increases, $\frac{1}{y} > 0$ and decreases.
6. As $y < 0$ and increases, $\frac{1}{y} < 0$ and decreases.
7. Two graphs intersect at $x = 0$ and $x = -1.2$

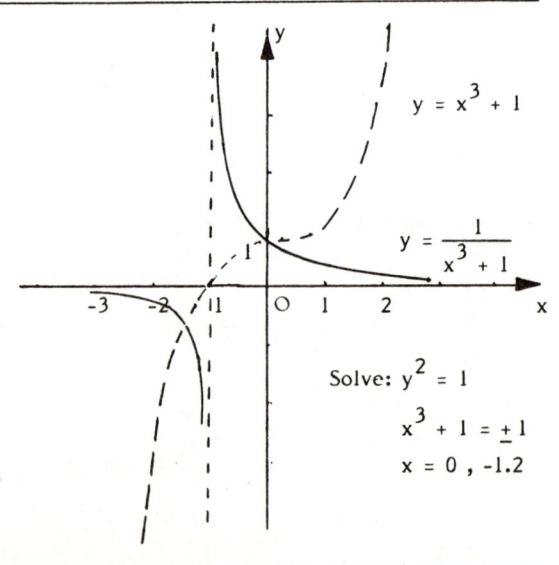

Solve: $y^2 = 1$

$x^3 + 1 = \pm 1$

$x = 0, -1.2$

(j)   Graph of $\sqrt{f(x)}$ by graphing $f(x)$

By noting the following, the sketch of $y = g(x) = \sqrt{f(x)}$ can be developed.

1. $g(x) = \sqrt{f(x)}$ exists only for $f(x) \geq 0$. e.g. $\sqrt{x^2 - 4} \Rightarrow x^2 \geq 4 \Rightarrow x \geq 2$ or $x \leq -2$

2. $g(x) \geq 0$ for all x in the domain of $g(x)$.

3. (a) $\sqrt{f(x)} < f(x)$ if $f(x) > 1$, e.g. $\sqrt{x} < x$ if $x > 1$

    (b) $\sqrt{f(x)} = f(x)$ if $f(x) = 1$

    (c) $\sqrt{f(x)} > f(x)$ if $0 < f(x) < 1$, e.g. $\sqrt{x} > x$ if $0 < x < 1$

4. $\dfrac{dy}{dx} = \dfrac{f'(x)}{2\sqrt{f(x)}}$, so $f'(x) = 0$ gives the location of stationary points and $f(x) = 0$ gives the positions of the vertical tangents.

EXAMPLE:

(a) Sketch the curve $y = f(x) = x^3 - 4x$ and hence sketch

(b) $y = \sqrt{f(x)}$

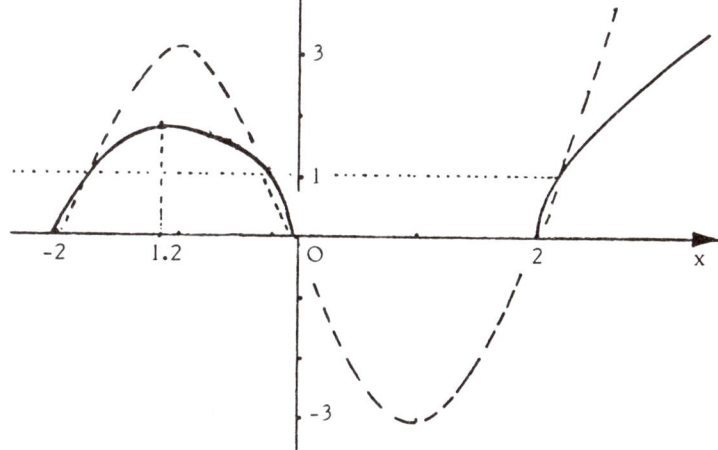

Solution

(a) The graph of $y = f(x) = x^3 - 4x = x(x - 2)(x + 2)$ is as shown in the diagram (broken line).

(b) Let $g(x) = \sqrt{f(x)}$.

The domain of $g(x)$ is given by $f(x) \geq 0$. From the graph of $y = f(x)$, this is $-2 \leq x \leq 0$ or $x \geq 2$. Remembering that:

(i) $g(x) \geq 0$ (ii) $g(x) = \sqrt{f(x)} \leq f(x)$ for $f(x) \geq 1$

(iii) $g(x) > f(x)$ for $0 < f(x) < 1$,

We take the square root of the ordinates of $y = f(x)$ in the domain of $g(x)$. The graph of $y = g(x)$ is shown by the solid line. Verify that the maximum turning point of $f(x)$ and hence $g(x)$ occurs at $x = \sqrt{\dfrac{4}{3}} = 1.15$.

1.8 Implicit Differentiation and Sketching Curves

Consider the function $y = x^2$ and the relation $x^2 + y^2 = 4$.

For $y = x^2$, $\frac{dy}{dx} = 2x$.

But to find $\frac{dy}{dx}$ from $x^2 + y^2 = 4$, where y is not defined explicitly in terms of x, we have two ways of finding $\frac{dy}{dx}$.

(a) $x^2 + y^2 = 4$

Solve for y

$y = \sqrt{4 - x^2}$ or $y = -\sqrt{4-x^2}$

$\therefore \frac{dy}{dx} = \frac{-x}{\sqrt{4-x^2}}$ or $\frac{dy}{dx} = \frac{x}{\sqrt{4-x^2}}$

$= -\frac{x}{y}$ $= -\frac{x}{y}$

(b) We differentiate $x^2 + y^2 = 4$ as it is, term by term.

$\therefore 2x + 2y \frac{dy}{dx} = 0$

$\therefore \frac{dy}{dx} = -\frac{x}{y}$

It is not always possible to solve explicitly for y, as in the example $x^3 + y^3 - 3axy = 0$. For these types of functions, called the implicit functions, we find the derivative by differentiating each term and then solving for $\frac{dy}{dx}$.

Example:

(a) $x^3 + y^3 - 3xy = 0$, find $\frac{dy}{dx}$

Differentiate with respect to x

$3x^2 + 3y^2 \frac{dy}{dx} - 3(x \frac{dy}{dx} + y) = 0$

$\therefore \frac{dy}{dx}(3y^2 - 3x) = 3y - 3x^2$

$\frac{dy}{dx} = \frac{y - x^2}{y^2 - x}$

(b) $x \sin y = 2$, find $\frac{dy}{dx}$

Differentiate with respect to x

$\therefore x \cos y \cdot \frac{dy}{dx} + \sin y = 0$

$\therefore \frac{dy}{dx} = -\frac{\sin y}{x \cos y}$

$= -\frac{\tan y}{x}$

Graphs of $y^2 = f(x)$

EXAMPLE: Sketch $y^2 = x(x-1)(x-2)$

We have $y = \pm \sqrt{x(x-1)(x-2)}$ ... (1)

1. The graph of $g(x) = x(x-1)(x-2)$ shows that $g(x) \geq 0$ for $0 \leq x \leq 1$ or $x \geq 2$. This is the domain of $f(x) = \sqrt{x(x-1)(x-2)}$.

2. Relation (1) shows that the required curve is symmetric about the x-axis. Hence there is a loop in the interval $0 \leq x \leq 1$. As $x \to \infty$, $y \to \pm \infty$.

3. $y^2 = x^3 - 3x^2 + 2x$

   $2y \frac{dy}{dx} = 3x^2 - 6x + 2$ gives the turning point at $x = 0.42$.

4. $\frac{dy}{dx}$ is undefined at $x = 0, 1, 2$, so $x = 0$, $x = 1$, $x = 2$ are the vertical tangents.

5. Intersection with the axes: $x = 0, 1, 2$

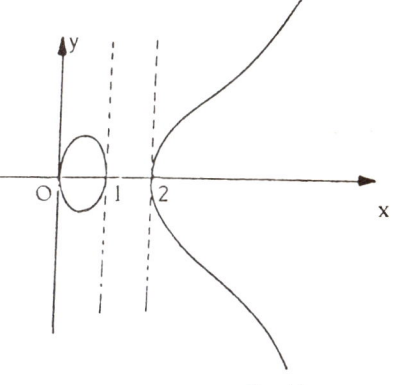

Fig. 40

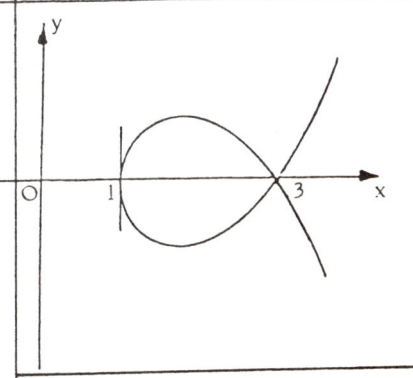

EXAMPLE: Sketch $y^2 = (x-1)(x-3)^2$

We have $y = \pm (x-3)\sqrt{x-1}$ ... (1)

1. The curve is symmetric about the x-axis.

2. Intersection with the x-axis: $x = 1$, $x = 3$

3. The domain is $x \geq 1$. There is a loop between $x = 1$ and $x = 3$, due to symmetry.

4. As $x \to \infty$, $y \to \pm \infty$

5. $2y \frac{dy}{dx} = 2(x-1)(x-3) + (x-3)^2$
   $= (x-3)(3x-5)$

   The possible critical points are $x = 3$ or $\frac{5}{3}$.

   $x = 1$ is the vertical tangent.

1.9 Applications

By using the graphs of functions, we can:

(a) Solve an inequality such as $\cos 2x \geq \frac{1}{2}$ or $2|x| - |x - 2| \geq 1$

(b) Find the number of solutions of an equation, such as $2\sin x = x$ or $x = e^{-x}$ and by application of Newton's formula $x_2 = x_1 - \frac{f(x_1)}{f'(x_1)}$, find a particular root to any required degree of accuracy.

(c) Solve physical and engineering problems involving equations which are either impossible or extremely difficult to solve.

EXAMPLE: (1) Solve for x: $\sin 2x \geq \frac{1}{2}$, $0 \leq x \leq 2\pi$

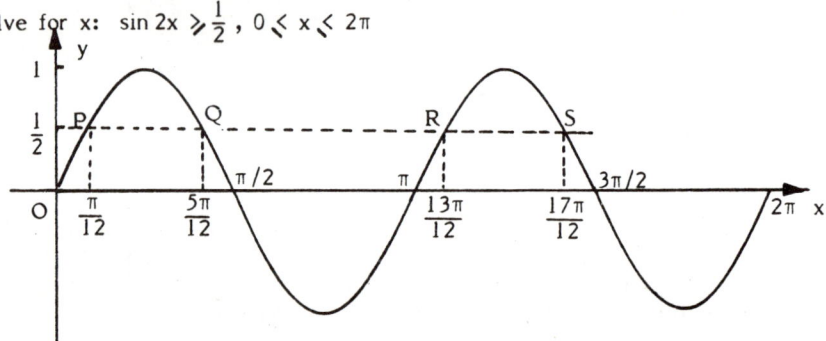

The sketch shows the graph of $y = \sin 2x$ and $y = \frac{1}{2}$. The intersections P, Q, R, S are obtained by solving $\sin 2x = \frac{1}{2} \Rightarrow 2x = \frac{\pi}{6}, \frac{5\pi}{6}, \frac{13\pi}{6}, \frac{17\pi}{6}$ giving $x = \frac{\pi}{12}, \frac{5\pi}{12}, \frac{13\pi}{12}, \frac{17\pi}{12}$

Hence the solution of the inequality $\sin 2x \geq \frac{1}{2}$ is given by $\frac{\pi}{12} \leq x \leq \frac{5\pi}{12}$ or $\frac{13\pi}{12} \leq x \leq \frac{17\pi}{12}$.

EXAMPLE: (2) Solve for x: $2|x| - |x - 2| \geq 2$

To solve this, we draw the graph of $y = 2|x| - |x - 2|$ as follows:

(i) For $x \geq 2$, $y_1 = 2x - (x - 2) = x + 2$

(ii) For $0 < x < 2$, $y_2 = 2x - (x - 2) = 3x - 2$

(iii) For $x \leq 0$, $y_3 = -2x - (x - 2) = -x - 2$

Now draw the line $y = 2$.

This line intersects the graph of $y = 2|x| - |x - 2|$ at P and Q.

At P, $y_3 = 2 \Rightarrow -x - 2 = 2 \Rightarrow x = -4$

At Q, $y_2 = 2 \Rightarrow 3x - 2 = 2 \Rightarrow x = \frac{4}{3} = 1\frac{1}{3}$

Hence the solution of $2|x| - |x - 2| \geq 2$ is given by $x \leq -4$ or $x \geq 1\frac{1}{3}$

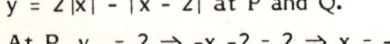

Note that the sharp corners are located where $|x| = 0$ and $|x - 2| = 0$.

EXAMPLE: (3) Find the stationary points of the function $y = f(x) = \frac{(x+1)(x+4)}{x}$.

Sketch the graph and find the domain and range of $f(x)$. Using the graph:

(a) Solve the inequality $\frac{(x+1)(x+4)}{x} \geq 10$

(b) Shade the region R between the line $y = 10$ and the curve $y = \frac{(x+1)(x+4)}{x}$. Find the area of this region R.

(c) Find the volume of revolution when the region R is rotated about the x-axis.

SOLUTION:

$f(x) = \frac{(x+1)(x+4)}{x} = \frac{x^2 + 5x + 4}{x}$

$f(x) = x + 5 + \frac{4}{x}$ ... (1)

$f'(x) = 1 - \frac{4}{x^2}$ ... (2)

$f''(x) = \frac{8}{x^3}$ ... (3)

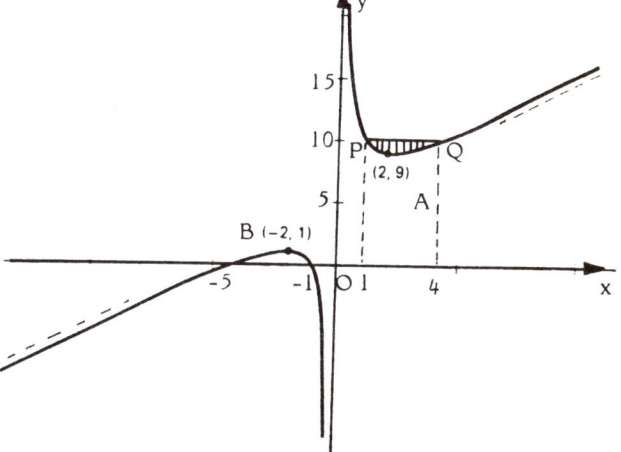

$f'(x) = 0 \Rightarrow x^2 - 4 = 0$, the stationary points are where $x = \pm 2$.

$f''(2) > 0$ and $f''(-2) < 0$

$\therefore$ A(2,9) is the minimum and B(-2,1) is the maximum point on the curve.

(i) Vertical asymptote at $x = 0$.

(ii) Intercepts: $y = 0$ gives the x-intercepts $x = -1, -4$.

(iii) As $|x| \to \infty$, using (1) $f(x) \to x + 5$ (oblique asymptote).

The graph can now be sketched. From the graph, we find that the domain is all real x and the range is $y \leq 1$ or $y \geq 9$.

(a) To solve the inequality $\frac{(x+1)(x+4)}{x} \geq 10$, draw the line $y = 10$. The line cuts the graph at P and Q. Since $x > 0$ for P and Q, $(x+1)(x+4) \geq 10x$
$\therefore x^2 - 5x + 4 \geq 0$ $(x-1)(x-4) > 0 \Rightarrow x \geq 4$ or $0 < x \leq 1$.

(b) Area of the shaded region between the line $y_1 = 10$ and the curve $y_2 = f(x) = x + 5 + \frac{4}{x}$ is given by

$$A = \int_a^b (y_1 - y_2) dx = \int_1^4 [10 - (x + 5 + \frac{4}{x})] dx = [5x - \frac{x^2}{2} - 4\log_e x]_1^4$$

$\therefore A = 5(4-1) - \frac{1}{2}(16-1) - 4(\log 4 - \log 1) = 15 - 7.5 - 8\log_e 2 = 7.5 - 8\log_e 2$ sq.u.

(cont.)

(c) Volume $= \pi \int_a^b (y_1^2 - y_2^2) dx = \pi \int_1^4 [100 - (x + 5 + \frac{4}{x})^2] dx$

$V = \pi \int_1^4 (67 - x^2 - 10x - \frac{16}{x^2} - \frac{40}{x}) dx$

$= \pi [67x - \frac{x^3}{3} - 5x^2 + \frac{16}{x} - 40 \log_e x]_1^4$

$= \pi [67(4 - 1) - \frac{1}{3}(64 - 1) - 5(16 - 1) + (\frac{16}{4} - 16) - 40 \log_e 4]$

$= (93 - 40 \log_e 4) \pi$ c.u.

EXAMPLE: (4) Determine the number of roots of the equation $2\sin x - x = 0$ and find the positive root to 2 decimal places by using Newton's formula

$$x_2 = x_1 - \frac{f(x_1)}{f'(x_1)}$$

SOLUTION:

The graphs of $y = 2\sin x$ and $y = x$ intersect at three points where
$2\sin x = x$
i.e. $2\sin x - x = 0$
At O, $x = 0$
At P, $x \doteq 1.9$ and at Q, $x \doteq -1.9$

So, the equation $2\sin x - x = 0$ has 3 roots.

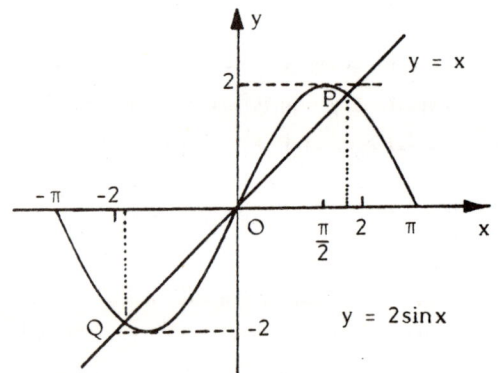

Let $f(x) = 2\sin x - x$ and $x_1 = 1.9$,

then $f'(x) = 2\cos x - 1$.

Substituting $f(1.9) = 0.18141$, $f'(1.9) = 1.8323$ in the formula

$x = x_1 - \frac{f(x_1)}{f'(x_1)} = 1.9 + \frac{0.18141}{-1.8323} = 1.80$ to 2 decimal places.

EXAMPLE: (5)

A rod of length L is hung from a pivot A, attached to the rim of a horizontal circular disc of radius r. The system rotates with a constant angular velocity ω about the vertical axis OD. It can be shown that $(r + L\sin\theta)\omega^2 = g\tan\theta$, where g is the acceleration due to gravity.

Show by a graphical method that, if $0 \leq \theta \leq \frac{\pi}{2}$, then there is just one value of θ which satisfies this relation.

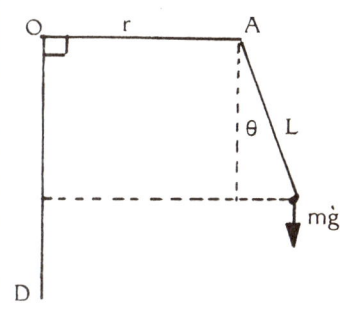

SOLUTION:

We draw the graphs of
$y_1 = \omega^2(r + L\sin\theta)$ and $y_2 = g\tan\theta$.

y_1 is of the form $y_1 = A + B\sin\theta$

where $A = r\omega^2 > 0$, $B = L\omega^2 > 0$

y_1 is obtained by drawing $B\sin\theta$ and then shifting it vertically up by A units.

It is seen that these graphs intersect at only one point P, where $\theta = \theta_1$, so there is just one value of θ, which satisfies the given relation.

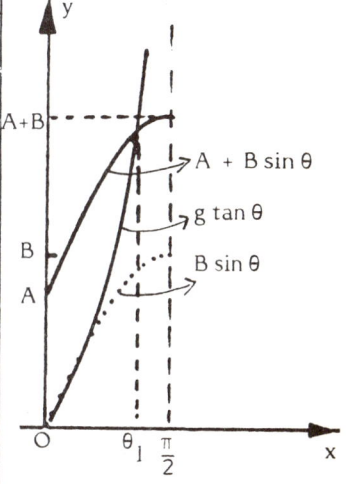

1.10 Miscellaneous Curve Sketching

In this section we sketch the functions involving combinations of trigonometric, exponential, rational and irrational functions. Several or all of the techniques of section 1.2 may be required. A sketch of a function should show the following features:

1. Intercepts
2. Symmetry
3. Asymptotes
4. Critical points
5. Concavity
6. Rise and fall

Do not attempt a scale drawing, unless one is stipulated.

<u>EXAMPLE: (1)</u> Sketch $y = \dfrac{x(x+1)}{x-1}$

<u>SOLUTION:</u>

(i) Intercepts:

$y = 0$ gives the x-intercepts
$x = 0$ and $x = -1$.
$x = 0$ gives $y = 0$

(ii) Symmetry:

$f(-x) \neq f(x), -f(x)$
No symmetry.

(iii) Asymptotes:

Vertical asymptote: $x = 1$
We write $y = x + 2 + \dfrac{2}{x-1}$ (by long division), as $x \to \infty$,
$y \to x + 2$
$\therefore y = x + 2$ is the oblique asymptote.

We work out the rough shape of the curve by separately sketching
$y_1 = x + 2$ and $y_2 = \dfrac{2}{x-1}$
(hyperbola) and then using
$y = y_1 + y_2$.

(iv) Critical points:

$f'(x) = \dfrac{x^2 - 2x - 1}{(x-1)^2}$, $x \neq 1$

The critical points are given by $f'(x) = 0$.
$x^2 - 2x - 1 = 0$ gives $x = 1 \pm \sqrt{2} \doteq -0.4, 2.4$
$f''(x)$ is too complicated, so we use the signs of $f'(x)$. Now $(x-1)^2 > 0$ for all x, $x \neq 1$, so by drawing a parabola given by the numerator $N(x) = x^2 - 2x - 1$, we find:
For $x < -0.4$ or $x > 2.4$, $f'(x) > 0$ i.e. $f(x)$ is increasing
For $-0.4 < x < 1$, $1 < x < 2.4$, $f'(x) < 0$ i.e. $f(x)$ is decreasing
Also the points A(-0.4, 0.2), B(2.4, 5.8) are respectively, the maximum and the miminum points. This is sufficient information for the sketch (solid line).

Signs of f'(x) are given by this graph.

EXAMPLE: (2)   Sketch the curve $y = 2\cos x + \cos 2x$, $0 \leqslant x \leqslant 2\pi$

SOLUTION:

The period of $f(x) = 2\cos x$ is 2π and the period of $g(x) = \cos 2x$ is π, so the function $y = 2\cos x + \cos 2x$ is periodic with period 2π. A few key points are necessary to guide us correctly along the curve. These are:

$$(0, 3), \ (\tfrac{\pi}{2}, -1), \ (\pi, -1), \ (\tfrac{3\pi}{2}, -1), \ (2\pi, 3)$$

Both $f(x)$ and $g(x)$ are continuous curves for all x.

To find the critical points, we have:

$$\tfrac{dy}{dx} = -2\sin x - 2\sin 2x = -2\sin x(1 + 2\cos x)$$

The critical points are given by $\sin x = 0$ or $\cos x = -\tfrac{1}{2}$

These are $(0, 3), (\pi, -1), (2\pi, 3)$ and $(\tfrac{2\pi}{3}, -\tfrac{3}{2}), (\tfrac{4\pi}{3}, -\tfrac{3}{2})$

It is unnecessary to check the nature of these points as we have sufficient points to sketch the curve.

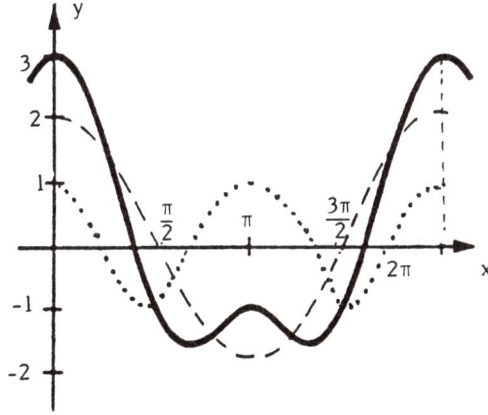

We can also sketch this curve by the addition of ordinates of the curves $f(x) = 2\cos x$ and $g(x) = \cos 2x$ at the selected key points $x = 0, \tfrac{\pi}{4}, \tfrac{\pi}{2}, \tfrac{3\pi}{4}, \ldots, \tfrac{7\pi}{4}, 2\pi$. This is shown in the figure.

EXAMPLE: (3) Sketch the curve $y = \dfrac{1}{1 + \sin x}$

SOLUTION:

(i) Intercepts:
No x-intercept.
The y-intercept is (0, 1)

(ii) $f(-x) \neq f(x), -f(x)$, No symmetry

(iii) Asymptotes:
Vertical asymptotes are where $\sin x = -1$
i.e. at
$x = 2n\pi + \dfrac{3\pi}{2}$, $n = 0, \pm 1, \pm 2, \ldots \Rightarrow (x = \ldots, -\dfrac{\pi}{2}, \dfrac{3\pi}{2}, \dfrac{7\pi}{2}, \dfrac{11\pi}{2}, \ldots)$

(iv) Critical Points: $f'(x) = \dfrac{-\cos x}{(1 + \sin x)^2}$, $\sin x \neq -1$

$f'(x) = 0$ when $\cos x = 0$, giving $x = \ldots, -\dfrac{3\pi}{2}, \dfrac{\pi}{2}, \dfrac{5\pi}{2}, \ldots$ where we exclude those points given by $\sin x = -1$.

v) $f''(x) = \dfrac{\sin x \cdot (1 + \sin x)^2 + 2\cos x (1 + \sin x) \cos x}{(1 + \sin x)^4}$

$f''(x) = \dfrac{\sin x (1 + \sin x) + 2\cos^2 x}{(1 + \sin x)^3}$, now using $\cos^2 x = (1 - \sin x)(1 + \sin x)$

and cancelling $1 + \sin x$, $f''(x) = \dfrac{2 - \sin x}{(1 + \sin x)^2}$

∴ $f''(x) > 0$ for all real x, and the curve is concave up.

(vi) $f(\dfrac{\pi}{2}) = \dfrac{1}{2}$ (All critical points on the line $y = \dfrac{1}{2}$)

(vii) $y > 0$ for all x ($\sin x \neq -1$) and the curve is periodic with a period of 2π.
The principal branch is in the interval $-\dfrac{\pi}{2} < x < \dfrac{3\pi}{2}$. The curve is as shown in the figure.

(viii) A few simple points (0, 1) and (π, 1) are useful in sketching.

EXAMPLE: (4) Sketch the curve $y = \dfrac{1}{1 + \sin x}$ by initially sketching $y = 1 + \sin x$.

SOLUTION:

After sketching $y = \sin x$, we shift the curve 1 unit vertically up.
The asymptotes are where $1 + \sin x = 0$.
These points are easily seen to be
$x = \ldots, -\dfrac{\pi}{2}, \dfrac{3\pi}{2}, \ldots$

The maxima of $y = 1 + \sin x$ are the minima of the reciprocal curve $y = \dfrac{1}{1 + \sin x}$. These are at $x = -\dfrac{3\pi}{2}, \dfrac{\pi}{2}, \dfrac{5\pi}{2}, \ldots$

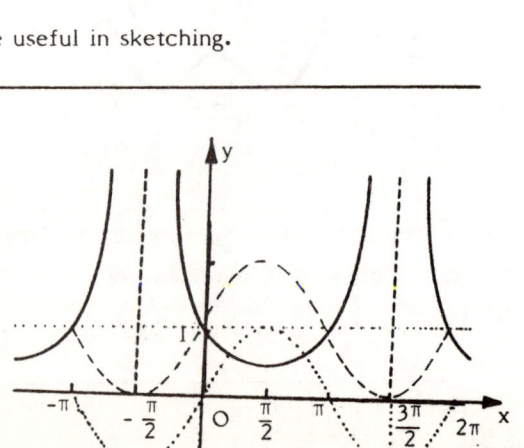

The graph of $y = \dfrac{1}{1 + \sin x}$ can now be sketched. (Heavy line)
A few simple points such as (0, 1), (π, 1) are useful.

EXAMPLE: (5)

Sketch $y^2 = x^2(1 - x^2)$

SOLUTION:

(i) Intercepts:

  $y = 0$ gives the x-intercepts

  $x = 0, \pm 1$

  $x = 0$ gives $y = 0$

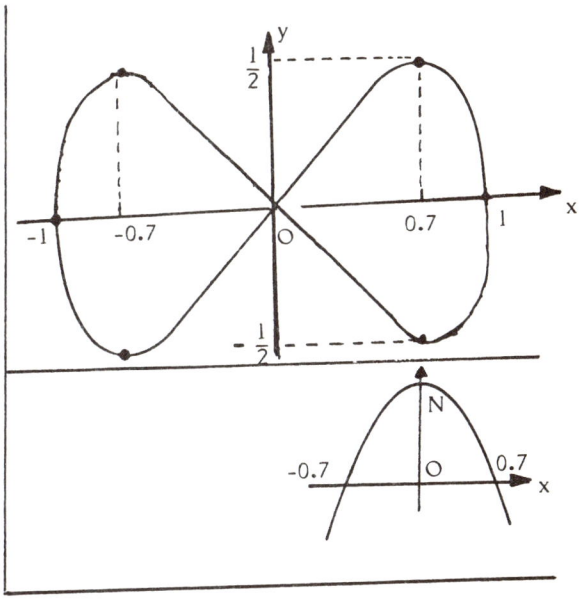

(ii) Symmetry:

  $y = \pm x \sqrt{1 - x^2}$, $-1 \leq x \leq 1$

  So the curve is symmetric about the x-axis.

  Let $y = f(x) = x\sqrt{1 - x^2}$. We shall eventually combine the graph of $y = f(x)$ with the reflection in the x-axis, i.e.

  $y = -x\sqrt{1 - x^2}$ to obtain the

  the required graph of
  $y^2 = x^2(1 - x^2)$.

  Now $f(-x) = -f(x)$, so $y = f(x)$ is point symmetric about 0. Putting these facts together, the curve is symmetric about both axes as well as the origin.

(iii) No asymptotes.

(iv) $f'(x) = \sqrt{1 - x^2} - x^2(1 - x^2)^{-1/2} = \dfrac{1 - 2x^2}{\sqrt{1 - x^2}}$, $x \neq 1, -1$

  The critical points are given by $1 - 2x^2 = 0 \Rightarrow x = \pm \dfrac{1}{\sqrt{2}}$

  Since $\sqrt{1 - x^2} > 0$, the sign of $f'(x)$ depends on the sign of the numerator $N(x) = 1 - 2x^2$ (A parabola) This graph tells us that:

  (a) $f(\dfrac{1}{\sqrt{2}})$ is the minimum, $f(-\dfrac{1}{\sqrt{2}}) = -\dfrac{1}{2}$, $(\dfrac{1}{\sqrt{2}} \doteq 0.7)$

  (b) $f(\dfrac{1}{\sqrt{2}})$ is the maximum, $f(\dfrac{1}{\sqrt{2}}) = \dfrac{1}{2}$.

  (c) The curve is rising for $-\dfrac{1}{\sqrt{2}} < x < \dfrac{1}{\sqrt{2}}$ as $f'(x) > 0$ and falling for

  $-1 \leq x \leq \dfrac{1}{\sqrt{2}}$ and $\dfrac{1}{\sqrt{2}} \leq x \leq 1$

  Also, $f'(x)$ does not exist at $x = \pm 1$, so there are vertical tangents at $x = \pm 1$.

This is sufficient information to sketch the curve which is a double loop, as shown in the diagram.

EXAMPLE: (6)   Sketch $y^2 = \dfrac{(x+1)(x+2)}{x}$

SOLUTION:

We have: $y = \pm \sqrt{\dfrac{(x+1)(x+2)}{x}}$

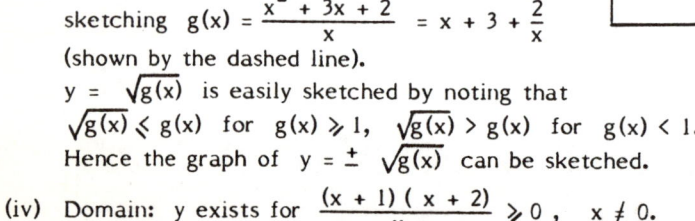

The curve is symmetric about the x-axis.

(i) Intercepts:

  $x \neq 0$, so, no y-intercept
  $y = 0$ gives $x = -1, x = -2$

(ii) Symmetry:

  Let $f(x) = \sqrt{\dfrac{(x+1)(x+2)}{x}}$

  $f(x) \neq f(-x)$
  No symmetry about the y-axis.

(iii) Asymptote at $x = 0$.

  We work out the rough shape by initially sketching $g(x) = \dfrac{x^2 + 3x + 2}{x} = x + 3 + \dfrac{2}{x}$
  (shown by the dashed line).
  $y = \sqrt{g(x)}$ is easily sketched by noting that
  $\sqrt{g(x)} \leq g(x)$ for $g(x) \geq 1$, $\sqrt{g(x)} > g(x)$ for $g(x) < 1$.
  Hence the graph of $y = \pm \sqrt{g(x)}$ can be sketched.

(iv) Domain: y exists for $\dfrac{(x+1)(x+2)}{x} \geq 0$, $x \neq 0$.

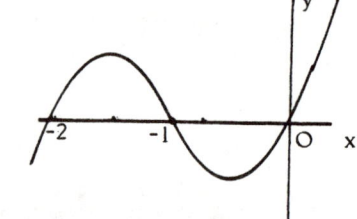

  Multiply by x^2, then $x(x+1)(x+2) > 0$
  The domain is $x > 0$ or $-2 \leq x \leq -1$.
  Since the curve is symmetric about the x-axis, there is a loop in the interval $-2 \leq x \leq -1$.

(v) Critical Points:

  Differentiating $y^2 = \dfrac{x^2 + 3x + 2}{x}$ w.r.t. x:

  $2y \dfrac{dy}{dx} = \dfrac{x(2x+3) - (x^2 + 3x + 2)}{x^2} = \dfrac{x^2 - 2}{x^2}$

  $\therefore \dfrac{dy}{dx} = \dfrac{x^2 - 2}{2x^2 y}$, $x \neq 0, y \neq 0$ i.e. $x \neq 1, -2$.

  Vertical tangents at $x = 0, x = -1, x = -2$

  $\dfrac{dy}{dx} = 0$ gives $x = \pm \sqrt{2}$ as the critical points, i.e. A(1.4, 2.4), B(1.4, -2.4), C(-1.4, 0.4), D(-1.4, -0.4).

  The curve being symmetric about the x-axis, we have altogether 4 critical points. For obvious reasons the maxima and minima occur at both points $x = \sqrt{2}$ and $x = -\sqrt{2}$.

  There are vertical tangents at $x = 0, -1, -2$. This is sufficient information to sketch the curve.

EXAMPLE: (7)   Sketch $y = e^{1/x}$

SOLUTION:

$y = f(x) = e^{1/x}$

$y > 0$ for all real x, $x \neq 0$.

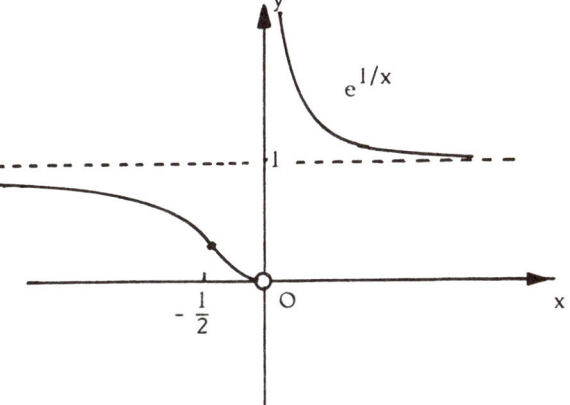

(i) $f(-x) \neq f(x), -f(x)$

No symmetry

(ii) $x \neq 0$, $y \neq 1$

The graph does not intersect the axes.

(iii) As $x \to \pm \infty$, $y \to e^0 = 1$

The horizontal asymptote: $y = 1$.

(iv) Critical Points:

$\frac{dy}{dx} = -\frac{1}{x^2} e^{1/x} < 0$ for all $x, x \neq 0$. So the function is strictly decreasing for either $x > 0$ or $x < 0$.

(v) Behaviour near $x = 0$

As $x \to 0^+$, $y \to e^{\infty} \to \infty$, so the y-axis is a vertical asymptote for the right branch of the curve $(x > 0)$.

As $x \to 0^-$, $y \to e^{-\infty} \to 0$ for the left branch $(x < 0)$

(vi) $f''(x) = \frac{1}{x^4} e^{1/x} + e^{1/x} \cdot \frac{2}{x^3} = \frac{1}{x^3} \cdot e^{1/x} \cdot (2 + \frac{1}{x}) = \frac{e^{1/x}(2x+1)}{x^4}$

$f''(x) > 0$ for $x > -\frac{1}{2}$, $x \neq 0$

$f''(x) < 0$ for $x < -\frac{1}{2}$

So $x = -\frac{1}{2}$ is a point of inflection with the curve concave down for $x < -\frac{1}{2}$ and concave up for $x > -\frac{1}{2}$ but $x \neq 0$.

This is sufficient information for a sketch of $y = e^{1/x}$.

EXAMPLE: (8)

Sketch $y = e^{-x}\cos x$ for $0 \leq x \leq 2\pi$

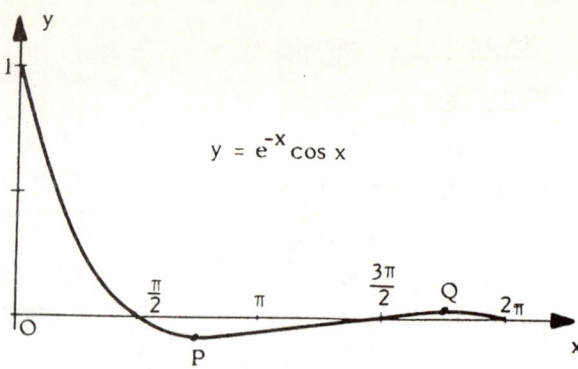

SOLUTION:

(i) Intersections:

$x = 0$, $y = 1$
$y = 0$ gives $\cos x = 0 \Rightarrow x = \frac{\pi}{2}, \frac{3\pi}{2}$

(ii) Symmetry:

$f(x) \neq f(-x), -f(x)$

No symmetry about the y-axis or 0.

(iii) No asymptotes.

(iv) Critical points:

$\frac{dy}{dx} = -e^{-x}\cos x - e^{-x}\sin x$

$= -e^{-x}(\cos x + \sin x)$

$\frac{dy}{dx} = 0$, when $\cos x + \sin x = 0 \Rightarrow \tan x = -1 \Rightarrow x = \frac{3\pi}{4}, \frac{7\pi}{4}$.

$\frac{d^2y}{dx^2} = e^{-x}(\cos x + \sin x + \sin x - \cos x) = 2e^{-x}\sin x$

When $x = \frac{3\pi}{4}$, $\frac{d^2y}{dx^2} > 0$, so y has a minimum at $x = \frac{3\pi}{4}$, $P(\frac{3\pi}{4}, -0.07)$.

When $x = \frac{7\pi}{4}$, $\frac{d^2y}{dx^2} < 0$, so y has a maximum at $x = \frac{7\pi}{4}$, $Q(\frac{7\pi}{4}, 0.003)$.

Also $\frac{d^2y}{dx^2} = 0 \Rightarrow \sin x = 0 \Rightarrow$ The points of inflection at $x = 0, \pi, 2\pi$.

(v) It is useful to draw the basic graphs $y = e^{-x}$ and $y = \cos x$.

From these two we find that $e^{-x}\cos x > 0$ for $0 < x < \frac{\pi}{2}$ and $e^{-x}\cos x < 0$ for $\frac{\pi}{2} < x < \frac{3\pi}{2}$.

The simple points are $(0, 1)$, $(\frac{\pi}{2}, 0)$, $(\pi, -e^{-\pi})$ i.e. $(\pi, -0.04)$, $(\frac{3\pi}{2}, 0)$ and $(2\pi, e^{-2\pi}) = (2\pi, 0.002)$

The sketch is as shown in the diagram.

EXAMPLE: (9)

Sketch $y = \log_e (1 + \cos x)^2$, $-2\pi \leq x \leq 2\pi$

SOLUTION:

(i) Intercepts:

$y = 0$ when $\cos x = 0$, i.e. $x = \pm \frac{\pi}{2}, \pm \frac{3\pi}{2}$

Also $x = 0 \Rightarrow y = \log_e 4$.

(ii) $f(x) = f(-x)$, so the curve is symmetric about the y-axis.

(iii) Asymptotes:

$y \to -\infty$ when $1 + \cos x \to 0$
The asymptotes are $x = \pm \pi$

(iv) $\frac{dy}{dx} = \frac{2(-\sin x)}{1 + \cos x}$, the critical points are given by $\sin x = 0$

$\therefore x = 0, \pm 2\pi$ ($\therefore \cos x \neq -1$, we exclude $x = \pm \pi$)

$\frac{d^2y}{dx^2} = -2 \frac{(1 + \cos x)\cos x + \sin x (\sin x)}{(1 + \cos x)^2} = -2 \frac{(1 + \cos x)}{(1 + \cos x)^2} = \frac{-2}{1 + \cos x}$

For $x = 0, \pm 2\pi$, $\frac{d^2y}{dx^2} < 0$, so the critical points are maximum points.

These are $(0, \log_e 4)$, $(2\pi, \log_2 4)$, $(-2\pi, \log_e 4)$.

Other points are $(\pm \frac{\pi}{2}, 0)$, $(\pm \frac{3\pi}{2}, 0)$

This is sufficient information to draw the sketch.

EXAMPLE: (10)

Sketch the curve $y = \dfrac{(x-1)^2}{(x+1)^3}$

SOLUTION:

(i) Intercepts:

x = 0, y = 1 and y = 0 gives x = 1

(ii) $f(x) \neq f(-x), -f(x)$, so, no symmetry

(iii) Asymptotes:

As $x \to -1^+$, $y \to \infty^+$ and as
$x \to -1^-$, $y \to \infty^-$
x = -1 is the asymptote.
As $x \to +\infty$, $y \to 0^+$
As $x \to -\infty$, $y \to 0^-$. Horizontal asymptote y = 0.

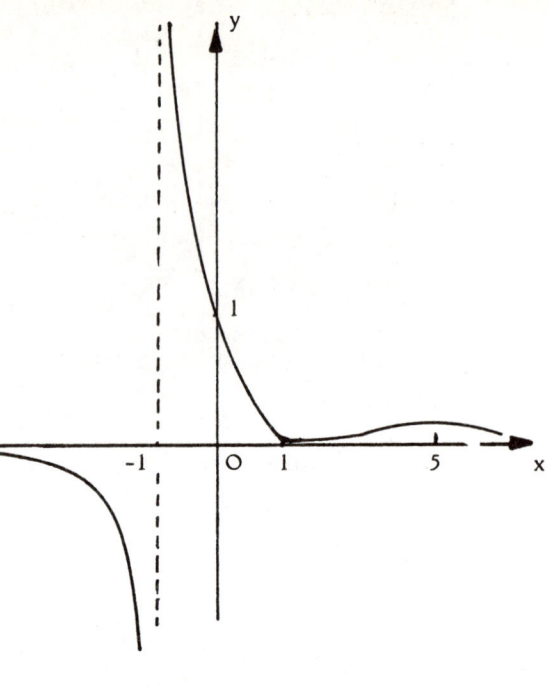

(iv) Critical Points:

$$f'(x) = \dfrac{2(x-1)(x+1)^3 - 3(x+1)^2(x-1)^2}{(x+1)^6}$$

$$= \dfrac{2(x-1)(x+1) - 3(x-1)^2}{(x+1)^4}$$

$\therefore f'(x) = \dfrac{(x-1)(5-x)}{(x+1)^4}$, so the

critical points are $(1, 0), (5, \dfrac{2}{27})$

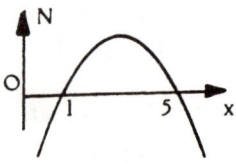

Since $(x+1)^4$ is always > 0, the signs of f'(x) depend on the numerator N = (x - 1)(5 - x).

The graph of N(x) is a parabola as shown in the figure.
This graph indicates that f(1) is the minimum and f(5) is the maximum point.
The sketch can now be drawn with this information.

EXAMPLE: (11)

Sketch $y = \dfrac{(\log_e x)^2}{x}$

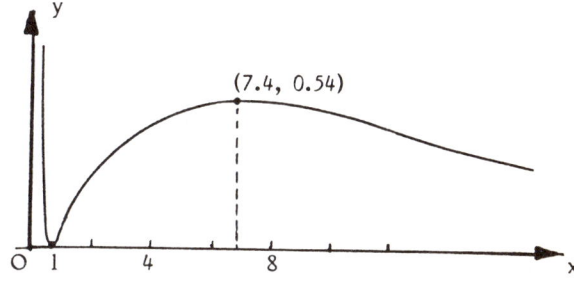

SOLUTION:

(i) Intersections

$x \neq 0$, so, no y-intersection

$y = 0 \Rightarrow \log_e x = 0 \Rightarrow x = 1$

(ii) $f(x) = \dfrac{(\log_e x)^2}{x}$ exists for $x > 0$

$f(x) \geqslant 0$ for all x

(iii) $f(x) \neq f(-x), -f(x)$. No symmetry.

(iv) Asymptotes:

Vertical asymptote $x = 0$

As $x \to \infty$, $y \to 0$

$y = 0$ is the horizontal asymptote. Verify this by taking $x = e^{10}$, whence $f(e^{10}) = \dfrac{100}{e^{10}} \doteq 0$

(v) Critical Points:

$$\frac{dy}{dx} = \frac{x(2\log x)\,1/x - (\log x)^2}{x^2} = \frac{2\log x - (\log x)^2}{x^2} = \frac{\log_e x \,(2 - \log_e x)}{x^2}$$

$\dfrac{dy}{dx} = 0 \Rightarrow \log_e x = 0$ or $\log_e x = 2$

$\therefore x = 1$ and $x = e^2 = 7.4$ are the critical points

For $0 < x < 1$, $\dfrac{dy}{dx} < 0$, so y is decreasing

for $1 < x < e^2$, $\dfrac{dy}{dx} > 0$, y is increasing

$\therefore x = 1$ is the minimum point

$x = e^2$ is the maximum point.

This is sufficient information to sketch the function.

Exercise 1A

1. Sketch the functions $y = f(x)$ and $y = g(x)$, hence by the addition of ordinates, sketch the graph of $y = f(x) + g(x)$:
   (a) $f(x) = x$, $g(x) = \sqrt{x}$
   (b) $f(x) = \sin x$, $g(x) = \cos x$
   (c) $f(x) = x$, $g(x) = \cos x$
   (d) $f(x) = x$, $g(x) = \frac{1}{x}$

2. Sketch separately the functions $y = f(x)$ and $y = g(x)$, hence by the subtraction of ordinates, sketch the graph of $y = f(x) - g(x)$:
   (a) $f(x) = x$, $g(x) = \sqrt{x}$
   (b) $f(x) = \sin x$, $g(x) = \cos x$
   (c) $f(x) = x$, $g(x) = \cos x$
   (d) $f(x) = x$, $g(x) = \frac{1}{x}$

3. Sketch the function $y = f(x)$, hence by reflection in the y-axis, sketch $y = f(-x)$:
   (a) $f(x) = \cos x$
   (b) $f(x) = \sin^{-1} x$
   (c) $f(x) = e^x$

4. Sketch the function $y = f(x)$, hence by translation, sketch $y = f(x + a)$:
   (a) $f(x) = \cos x$, sketch $f(x - 1)$
   (b) $f(x) = e^x$, sketch $f(x + 1)$

5. Sketch $y = f(x)$ and $y = g(x)$, hence sketch $y = f(x) \cdot g(x)$ (any other informaation may be used):
   (a) $f(x) = x$, $g(x) = \cos x$
   (b) $f(x) = x$, $g(x) = \log_e x$

6. Sketch $y = f(x)$ and $y = g(x)$, hence sketch $y = \frac{f(x)}{g(x)}$ (any other information may be used):
   (a) $f(x) = x - 2$, $g(x) = x + 2$
   (b) $f(x) = \sin x$, $g(x) = x$

7. Sketch $y = [f(x)]^2$, given:
   (a) $f(x) = x^2 - 4$
   (b) $f(x) = \log_e x$

8. Sketch $y = f(x)$ and hence $y = \sqrt{f(x)}$:
   (a) $f(x) = x^3$
   (b) $f(x) = \sin x$
   (c) $f(x) = x^2(4 - x^2)$

9. Sketch the following functions by the most appropriate techniques, noting intercepts, asymptotes, critical points, behaviour near $x = 0$, when $x \to \pm \infty$, etc:
   (a) $f(x) = e^{-x} \sin x$
   (b) $f(x) = \left| \frac{1}{2} - \sin(x - 1) \right|$
   (c) $f(x) = x^2 e^{-x}$
   (d) $f(x) = \frac{x(x - 1)}{x - 2}$
   (e) $f(x) = \sqrt{\frac{x(x - 1)}{x - 2}}$
   (f) $f(x) = \frac{x^4}{x^2 - 1}$
   (g) $y^2 = \frac{x^2(2 + x)}{2 - x}$
   (h) $f(x) = (x - 2)^3 + 1$

10. (a) Show that $\dfrac{1}{x-2} - \dfrac{4}{x+3} + 3 = \dfrac{3x^2 - 7}{(x-2)(x+3)}$

(b) Find the vertical and horizontal asymptotes of the curve $y = f(x) = \dfrac{3x^2 - 7}{(x-2)(x+3)}$

(c) Find the turning points and determine their nature.

(d) Sketch the curve.

(e) Using the sketch, solve the inequality $0 < \dfrac{3x^2 - 7}{(x-2)(x+3)} < 3$

(f) Find the area between the curve and the x-axis between their points of intersection.

11. Solve the following inequalities by graphical methods:

(a) Sketch separately the graphs of $y = 2|x - 1|$ and $y = |x + 2|$, hence solve the inequality $2|x - 1| \geqslant |x + 2|$.

(b) Sketch the function $f(x) = \cos 2x$, $0 \leqslant x \leqslant 2\pi$, hence solve the inequality $\cos 2x \leqslant \dfrac{1}{2}$.

12. Sketch the curve $y^2 = x(x - 2)^2$

(a) Find the area of the loop in the exact form.

(b) Find the volume of the solid when the region inside the loop is rotated about the x-axis.

13. The chord AB subtends an angle θ at the centre O of the circle, where $0 < \theta < \pi$

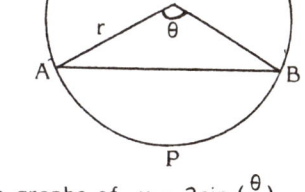

(a) Show that the perimeter p of the minor segment APB is given by $p = 2r \sin\left(\dfrac{\theta}{2}\right) + r\theta$

(b) If p is half of the circumference, prove that $2\sin\left(\dfrac{\theta}{2}\right) = \pi - \theta$

(c) Find θ, in this case, by separately sketching the graphs of $y = 2\sin\left(\dfrac{\theta}{2}\right)$ and $y = \pi - \theta$, $0 < \theta < \pi$.
Give your answer to 1 decimal place.

(d) Using one step of Newton's method, find the value of θ to 2 decimal places.
(Hint: $f(\theta) = 2\sin\left(\dfrac{\theta}{2}\right) + \theta - \pi$)

14. By sketching the graphs of $y = x^2 + 2$ and $y = \dfrac{1}{x}$ on the same axes, find the approximate root of the equation $f(x) = x^3 + 2x - 1 = 0$. Hence, using Newton's method, find to 2 decimal places a better root of $f(x) = 0$.

15. (a) Sketch the function $y = f(x) = \dfrac{3x + 2}{(2x - 1)(x + 3)}$, showing the asymptotes and the points of intersection with the axes.

(b) Express $f(x)$ in partial fractions, i.e. $\dfrac{3x + 2}{(2x - 1)(x + 3)} = \dfrac{A}{2x - 1} + \dfrac{B}{x + 3}$

(c) Shade the region whose area is given by the integral $\displaystyle\int_1^5 f(x)\,dx$. Find this area.

16. By sketching the graphs of $y = e^{-x}$ and $y = x$ on the same axes, find to one decimal place the approximate root of $f(x) = x - e^{-x} = 0$. Hence by using Newton's method, find to 2 decimal places a better root of $f(x) = 0$.

Exercise: 1B

Sketch the following curves, showing the CRITICAL points and labelling the axes carefully. All logarithms are to the base e.

1. (a) $y = |x - 2|$ (b) $y = |2x - 3|$
   (c) $y = x - |x|$ (d) $y = |x| - x$
   (e) $y = |x + 1| + |x - 1|$

2. (a) $|y| = x - 1$ (b) $|x| - |y| = 2$
   (c) $|x| + |y| = 1$ (d) $|y| = |x + 1|$
   (e) $|y - 1| = x$ (f) $|y| = |x| + 1$
   (g) $|x + y| = 2$ (h) $y = |x + 2| + x$

3. For all real values of x, the symbol $[x]$ denotes 'the greatest integer not exceeding x'.
   Sketch the graph of $y = [x]$, $|x| \leqslant 3$

4. Given that $0 < a < b$, draw the sketch of $y = |x - a|$ for $|x| \leqslant b$. Hence evaluate $\int_{-b}^{b} |x - a| \, dx$

5. $y = \max(x, 1 - x)$ where $\max(a, b)$ denotes the greater of the two numbers a and b, i.e.
   $\max(a, b) = a$ if $a > b$
   $ = b$ if $a < b$

6. (a) $y = x + [x]$, $-2 \leqslant x \leqslant 2$
   (b) $y = x - [x]$, where $[x]$ has the meaning given in Exercise (3)

7. (a) $y = 4x^2 - 1$ (b) $y = |4 - x^2|$
   (c) $|y| = 4 - x^2$ (d) $y = (x - 2)^2$

8. (a) $y = x^3 - 2x^2 - 4x + 4$ (b) $y = x(x-1)^3$
   (c) $y = (x^2 - 1)(x^2 + 1)$ (d) $y = \frac{1}{4}(x-2)^2(x^2-1)$
   (e) $y = (x^2 - 1)^2$

9. (a) $y = \frac{x}{x-2}$ (b) $y = \frac{2x-4}{x+2}$
   (c) $y = \frac{2}{(x+1)^2}$ (d) $y = \frac{x}{(x-2)^2}$
   (e) $y = \frac{x^2}{x-1}$ (f) $y = \frac{1}{x^2+1}$
   (g) $y = \frac{1}{(x-2)(x+3)}$ (h) $y = \frac{x^2}{x^2+2}$
   (i) $y = \frac{(x+2)(x-3)}{(x+1)(x-2)}$

10. (a) $y = \frac{x(x+3)}{(x+2)(x-2)}$ (b) $y = \frac{x^2-1}{x^3}$
    (c) $y = \frac{x^2-4}{x+3}$

11. (a) $y^2 = x^3$ (b) $y^2 = 9x(x^2-4)$
    (c) $y^2 = \frac{x^2+1}{x(x-1)}$ (d) $y^2 = \frac{x}{x-1}$
    (e) $y^2 = 4x(x-2)$ (f) $x^2 = \frac{4+y^2}{4-y^2}$

12. (a) $y = \sin^2(2x)$, $(-\pi \leqslant x \leqslant \pi)$ (b) $y = \cos^2(2x)$, $(-\pi \leqslant x \leqslant \pi)$

    (c) $\sin(x + y) = 0$ (d) $\cos(x + y) = 0$

    (e) $y = |\sin x|$, $|x| \leqslant 2\pi$ (f) $y = \sin|x|$, $|x| \leqslant 2\pi$

    (g) $y = \dfrac{\sin x}{x}$ (h) $y = \sin(\sin^{-1} x)$

    (i) $y = \sin^{-1}(\sin x)$ (j) $y = \sin(\cos^{-1} x)$

    (k) $y = \sin^{-1}(\cos x)$ (l) $y = \sqrt{\sin^2 x}$

    (m) $y = \sqrt{\cos^2 x}$

13. (a) $y = e^{x^2}$ (b) $y = xe^x$

    (c) $y = \dfrac{e^x + e^{-x}}{2}$ (d) $y = \dfrac{x - 1}{e^x}$

    (e) $y = \left[\dfrac{1 - x}{1 + x}\right] e^x$ (f) $y = e^{-x} \cos x$

14. (a) $y = \log |x|$ (b) $y = \log_e(x^2 - 1)$

    (c) $y = x \log x$ (d) $y = \dfrac{x}{\log x}$

    (e) $y \sqrt{x} = \log x$ (f) $y = \left|\dfrac{\log x}{x}\right|$

15. (a) $x^2 + 2y^2 - 1 = 2(x + 2y)$ (b) $x^2(y - 1) = y$

    (c) $(x + 3)(y - 2) = 1$ (d) $(x + 2)(y + 1) = 1$

MISCELLANEOUS

16. Determine the domain and the range of the function $y = \log_e (x - x^2)$.
    (a) Find the nature of the turning points and
    (b) Hence sketch the curve $y = \log_e (x - x^2)$

17. A function is defined by $f(x) = \dfrac{e^x - e^{-x}}{e^x + e^{-x}}$.

    (a) Find (i) $\lim\limits_{x \to \infty} f(x)$
        (ii) $\lim\limits_{x \to -\infty} f(x)$

    (b) State the domain and the range of the function.

    (c) Determine the stationary points and their nature and hence sketch the curve $y = f(x)$.

    (d) Determine the inverse function $y = f^{-1}(x)$ and draw the sketch of $y = f^{-1}(x)$.

18. A function is defined by $f(x) = x\sin^{-1}(x^2)$
    (a) State the domain and the range of $f(x)$
    (b) Show that $f(-x) = -f(x)$
    (c) Find $f'(x)$
    (d) Describe the behaviour of $f'(x)$ near $x = 0$ and $x = 1$
    (e) Hence sketch the curve $y = f(x)$

19. Sketch each of the following:
    (a) $y = (x - 1)(x - 2)$
    (b) $y = |(x - 1)(x - 2)|$
    (c) $y = |x - 1|(x - 2)$
    (d) $y = (x - 1)|x - 2|$
    (e) $y = \dfrac{1}{(x - 1)(x - 2)}$

20. A function $f(x) = \dfrac{\log_e x}{x}$, $x > 0$.

   (a) Show that the curve $y = f(x)$ has a maximum at $x = e$ and $y = \dfrac{1}{e}$

   (b) Discuss the behaviour of $f(x)$ near $x = 0$ and when $x \to \infty$

   (c) Sketch the curve $y = f(x)$, by considering the points at $x = 1, 2, 3, \dfrac{1}{e}, 10$

21. Sketch the graph of $f(x) = \dfrac{2x - 8}{(x - 3)(x + 1)}$, showing the points of intersection with the axes, the turning points and asymptotes.

22. Sketch the graph of the function $y = \dfrac{x^2 - x + 1}{(x - 2)^2}$, showing the points of intersection with axes, the turning points and asymptotes.

23. Sketch the graph of $y = \dfrac{2x}{x^2 - 1}$.

24. Prove that the curve $y = x^2 e^{-x}$ has a minimum turning point at $(0, 0)$ and a maximum turning point at $(2, \dfrac{4}{e^2})$. Hence sketch the curve.

25. Sketch the curve $y = \dfrac{x^2}{x^2 - 1}$, showing the vertical and horizontal asymptotes, turning points and inflexions.

26. Sketch the curves $y = 10x e^{-x^2/2}$ and $y = 10 e^{-x^2/2}$ on the same axes, showing the turning and inflexion points.

27. Sketch the curve $y = \dfrac{2x}{1 + x^2}$, showing that it has a minimum at $A(-1, -1)$ and a maximum at $B(1, 1)$ and inflexion at 0.

28. Sketch the curve $y^2 = \dfrac{1}{(x+1)(2-x)}$, showing the vertical and horizontal asymptotes as well as the turning points.

29. Sketch the following curve, showing the critical features:
$y = x^2 - |x|$.

30. Sketch the curve $y^2 = \dfrac{x^2}{x^2 - 4}$, showing the vertical and horizontal asymptotes.

    (Hint: $x = 0, y = 0$ is a point, a lonely point detached from the rest of the graph.)

31. The following curves are of the type $y^2 = f(x)$. Sketch them.
    (a) $y^2 = (x-1)(x-2)^2$ (b) $y^2 = (x-2)^3$
    (c) $y^2 = (x-1)(x-2)(x-3)$ (d) $y^2 = x^2(x+2)$
    (e) $y^2 = x - x^3$

32. Using the properties of the reciprocal functions, sketch the graphs of the following pairs of functions on the same set of axes.
    (a) $y = x - 2$ and $y = \dfrac{1}{x-2}$ (b) $y = x^2 - 4$ and $y = \dfrac{1}{x^2 - 4}$
    (c) $y = 9 - x^2$ and $y = \dfrac{1}{9 - x^2}$ (d) $y = x^3 - 1$ and $y = \dfrac{1}{x^3 - 1}$
    (e) $y = |x| - 2$ and $y = \dfrac{1}{|x| - 2}$ (f) $y = (x-1)(x-2)$ and $y = \dfrac{1}{(x-1)(x-2)}$

33. Use CALCULUS to find the turning points, the sign of $\dfrac{dy}{dx}$ etc. to sketch the following curves:
    (a) $y^2 = x^3 + 1$ (b) $y = \dfrac{x^2}{x^2 + 4}$ (c) $y^2 = x^3$

34. Find the turning points of the curve $y = \dfrac{1}{x} - \dfrac{1}{x^2} - \dfrac{1}{x^3}$ and hence sketch it.

35. Find the turning points of the curve $y = 8x - \dfrac{4}{x^2}$ and hence sketch it.

CHAPTER 2 INTEGRATION

Almost any function $y = f(x)$ can be differentiated, but unfortunately, the reverse process of integration is not only difficult, there is no systematic method for integration. Even worse there are functions which can never be integrated, for example:

$$e^{-x^2}, \quad \frac{\sin x}{x^2}$$

So first we have a standard list of integrals and then learn a few more tricks.
NOTE: All logarithms in this chapter are to the base e.

2.1 Standard Integrals

1. $\dfrac{d}{dx}\left[\dfrac{x^{n+1}}{n+1}\right] = x^n \quad\rightarrow\quad \displaystyle\int x^n\,dx = \dfrac{x^{n+1}}{n+1} + C, \quad n \ne -1.$

2. $\dfrac{d}{dx}\left[\dfrac{(ax+b)^{n+1}}{a(n+1)}\right] = (ax+b)^n \quad\rightarrow\quad \displaystyle\int (ax+b)^n\,dx = \dfrac{(ax+b)^{n+1}}{a(n+1)} + C, \quad n \ne -1.$

3. $\dfrac{d}{dx}\left[\dfrac{\sin(ax+b)}{a}\right] = \cos(ax+b) \quad\rightarrow\quad \displaystyle\int \cos(ax+b)\,dx = \dfrac{\sin(ax+b)}{a} + C$

4. $\dfrac{d}{dx}\left[\dfrac{\cos(ax+b)}{a}\right] = -\sin(ax+b) \quad\rightarrow\quad \displaystyle\int \sin(ax+b)\,dx = -\dfrac{\cos(ax+b)}{a} + C$

5. $\dfrac{d}{dx}\left[\dfrac{\tan(ax+b)}{a}\right] = \sec^2(ax+b) \quad\rightarrow\quad \displaystyle\int \sec^2(ax+b)\,dx = \dfrac{\tan(ax+b)}{a} + C$

6. $\dfrac{d}{dx}\left[\dfrac{e^{ax+b}}{a}\right] = e^{ax+b} \quad\rightarrow\quad \displaystyle\int e^{ax+b}\,dx = \dfrac{e^{ax+b}}{a} + C$

7. $\dfrac{d}{dx}\left[e^{f(x)}\right] = f'(x)e^{f(x)} \quad\rightarrow\quad \displaystyle\int f'(x)e^{f(x)}\,dx = e^{f(x)} + C$

8. $\dfrac{d}{dx}(\log_e x) = \dfrac{1}{x}$ $\quad\rightarrow\quad$ $\displaystyle\int \dfrac{1}{x}\,dx = \log_e x + C$

9. $\dfrac{d}{dx}\left[\log_e f(x)\right] = \dfrac{f'(x)}{f(x)}$ $\quad\rightarrow\quad$ $\displaystyle\int \dfrac{f'(x)}{f(x)}\,dx = \log_e f(x) + C$

10. $\dfrac{d}{dx}\left[\log_e (ax+b)\right] = \dfrac{a}{ax+b}$ $\quad\rightarrow\quad$ $\displaystyle\int \dfrac{1}{ax+b}\,dx = \dfrac{1}{a}\log_e (ax+b) + C$

11. $\dfrac{d}{dx}\left[\sin^{-1}\dfrac{x}{a}\right] = \dfrac{1}{\sqrt{a^2 - x^2}}$ $\quad\rightarrow\quad$ $\displaystyle\int \dfrac{1}{\sqrt{a^2 - x^2}}\,dx = \sin^{-1}\dfrac{x}{a} + C$

12. $\dfrac{d}{dx}\left[\tan^{-1}\dfrac{x}{a}\right] = \dfrac{a}{a^2 + x^2}$ $\quad\rightarrow\quad$ $\displaystyle\int \dfrac{1}{a^2 + x^2}\,dx = \dfrac{1}{a}\tan^{-1}\dfrac{x}{a} + C$

13. $\dfrac{d}{dx}\log_e\left[\dfrac{x-a}{x+a}\right] = \dfrac{2a}{x^2 - a^2}$ $\quad\rightarrow\quad$ $\displaystyle\int \dfrac{1}{x^2 - a^2}\,dx = \dfrac{1}{2a}\log\left[\dfrac{x-a}{x+a}\right] + C$

for $x > a,\ a > 0$

14. $\dfrac{d}{dx}\log_e\left[\dfrac{a+x}{a-x}\right] = \dfrac{2a}{a^2 - x^2}$ $\quad\rightarrow\quad$ $\displaystyle\int \dfrac{1}{a^2 - x^2}\,dx = \dfrac{1}{2a}\log_e\left[\dfrac{a+x}{a-x}\right] + C$

for $x < a,\ a > 0$

15. $\dfrac{d}{dx}\log_e(x + \sqrt{x^2 \pm a^2}) = \dfrac{1}{\sqrt{x^2 \pm a^2}}$ $\quad\rightarrow\quad$ $\displaystyle\int \dfrac{dx}{\sqrt{x^2 \pm a^2}} = \log_e(x + \sqrt{x^2 \pm a^2}) + C$

16. $\dfrac{d}{dx}(a^x) = a^x \cdot \log_e a$ $\quad\rightarrow\quad$ $\displaystyle\int a^x\,dx = \dfrac{a^x}{\log_e a} + C,\quad a > 0$

17. $\dfrac{d}{dx}(\cot x) = -\csc^2 x$ $\quad\rightarrow\quad$ $\displaystyle\int \csc^2 x\,dx = -\cot x + C$

18. $\dfrac{d}{dx}(\sec x) = \sec x \tan x$ $\quad\rightarrow\quad$ $\displaystyle\int \sec x \tan x\,dx = \sec x + C$

19. $\dfrac{d}{dx}(\csc x) = -\csc x \cot x$ $\quad\rightarrow\quad$ $\displaystyle\int \csc x \cot x\,dx = -\csc x + C$

The following two formulas should be noted:

20. $\displaystyle\int \sec x\,dx = \log_e (\sec x + \tan x) + C$

21. $\displaystyle\int \csc x\,dx = -\log_e (\csc x + \cot x) + C$

2.2 Change of Variable: Substitution

We are easily tempted to apply a known method to new situations.

$\int x^2 \, dx = \frac{x^3}{3} + C$, so why not $\int \sin^2 x \, dx = \frac{\sin^3 x}{3} + C$?

Now $\frac{d}{dx}\left[\frac{\sin^3 x}{3}\right] = \sin^2 x \cos x$, not $\sin^2 x$.

Consider $y = e^{x^2}$, then $\frac{dy}{dx} = 2x \, e^{x^2}$.

But given $\int 2x \, e^{x^2} \, dx$, how do we proceed to find such integrals?

The method of substitution, leading to a change of variable, is used to solve such problems. The symbol I will be used to represent the integral in each question.

WORKED EXAMPLES

1. $\int 2x \, e^{x^2} \, dx$

Solution:

Let $u = x^2$

$\therefore \frac{du}{dx} = 2x$

$\therefore I = \int 2x \, e^{x^2} \, dx$

$= \int e^u \frac{du}{dx} \, dx$

$= \int e^u \, du$

$= e^u + C$

$= e^{x^2} + C$

2. $\int \frac{2x}{\sqrt{x^2 - 4}} \, dx$

Solution:

Let $u = x^2 - 4$

$\frac{du}{dx} = 2x$

Substitute for $2x$ and $x^2 - 4$ in terms of u

$\therefore I = \int \frac{1}{\sqrt{u}} \frac{du}{dx} \, dx$

$= \int u^{-1/2} \, du$

$= 2\sqrt{u} + C$

$= 2\sqrt{x^2 - 4} + C$

Thus $\int f(x) \, dx = \int g(u) \, du$ by using either $u = \phi(x)$ or $x = \theta(u)$

In either case $\int g(u) \, du$ is easy to integrate.

Integrate the following:

(3) $\int \dfrac{\sin^{-1} x}{\sqrt{1 - x^2}}\, dx$ (4) $\int \dfrac{e^x}{e^{2x} + 1}\, dx$ (5) $\int \dfrac{1}{x \log_e x}\, dx$

Solution:

(3) $I = \int \dfrac{\sin^{-1} x}{\sqrt{1 - x^2}}\, dx$ Let $u = \sin^{-1} x$

$= \int u \cdot \dfrac{du}{dx} \cdot dx$ $\dfrac{du}{dx} = \dfrac{1}{\sqrt{1 - x^2}}$

$= \int u\, du$

$= \dfrac{u^2}{2} + C$

$= \dfrac{1}{2} (\sin^{-1} x)^2 + C$

(4) $I = \int \dfrac{e^x\, dx}{e^{2x} + 1}$ Let $u = e^x$

$= \int \dfrac{\frac{du}{dx} \cdot dx}{u^2 + 1}$ $\therefore \dfrac{du}{dx} = e^x$

$= \int \dfrac{du}{u^2 + 1}$

$= \tan^{-1} u + C$

$= \tan^{-1}(e^x) + C$

(5) $\int \dfrac{dx}{x \log_e x}$ Let $u = \log x$, $\dfrac{du}{dx} = \dfrac{1}{x}$

$= \int \dfrac{1}{\log x} \cdot \dfrac{1}{x}\, dx$ ← Watch this: → $\dfrac{dx}{x} = du$

$= \int \dfrac{1}{u} \cdot du$

$= \log_e u + C$

$= \log_e (\log_e x) + C$

Exercise 2A (change of variable)

Find the indefinite integrals:

1. (a) $\displaystyle\int 2x(x^2+1)^3\,dx$
   (b) $\displaystyle\int 2x(1-x^2)^4\,dx$
   (c) $\displaystyle\int \frac{4x^3\,dx}{x^4+1}$
   (d) $\displaystyle\int \frac{4x^3\,dx}{(x^4+1)^2}$
   (e) $\displaystyle\int x\sqrt{1-x^2}\,dx$
   (f) $\displaystyle\int \frac{2x\,dx}{1+x^4}$
   (g) $\displaystyle\int \frac{x\,dx}{\sqrt{x^2-1}}$
   (h) $\displaystyle\int \frac{dx}{\sqrt{x}\sqrt{1-\sqrt{x}}}$

2. (a) $\displaystyle\int \cos^2 x\,\sin x\,dx$
   (b) $\displaystyle\int \sin^3 x\,\cos x\,dx$
   (c) $\displaystyle\int \tan^4 x\cdot\sec^2 x\,dx$
   (d) $\displaystyle\int \cot^4 x\,\text{cosec}^2 x\,dx$
   (e) $\displaystyle\int \frac{-\sin x}{\cos^2 x}\,dx$
   (f) $\displaystyle\int (1+\cos x)^4 \sin x\,dx$
   (g) $\displaystyle\int \sec^5 x\,\tan x\,dx$
   (h) $\displaystyle\int (1+\tan x)^2 \sec^2 x\,dx$

3. (a) $\displaystyle\int x^2 e^{x^3}\,dx$
   (b) $\displaystyle\int \frac{e^{-x}\,dx}{1+e^{-2x}}$
   (c) $\displaystyle\int \frac{e^{\sin^{-1}x}}{\sqrt{1-x^2}}\,dx$
   (d) $\displaystyle\int \frac{e^x\,dx}{\sqrt{e^{2x}+1}}$

4. (a) $\displaystyle\int \frac{1}{x}\log x\,dx$
   (b) $\displaystyle\int \frac{1}{x}(\log x)^2\,dx$
   (c) $\displaystyle\int \frac{dx}{x(\log x)^3}$
   (d) $\displaystyle\int \frac{dx}{x(1+\log x)^3}$

5. (a) $\int \sin x \cos x \, e^{\cos 2x} \, dx$ (b) $\int \dfrac{-\sin x \, dx}{1 + \cos^2 x}$

   (c) $\int 2^{\sin x} \cos x \, dx$ (d) $\int \dfrac{e^x}{e^{2x} - 1} \, dx$

6. Evaluate:

   (a) $\int_0^1 2x(x^2 - 3)^3 \, dx$ (b) $\int_0^{\pi/4} \sin^3 x \cos x \, dx$

   (c) $\int_0^3 \dfrac{x \, dx}{\sqrt{x^2 + 16}}$ (d) $\int_2^e \dfrac{dx}{x \log_e x}$

   (e) $\int_0^1 \dfrac{e^x}{e^x + 1} \, dx$ (f) $\int_0^{\pi/2} \dfrac{\cos x \, dx}{(1 + \sin x)^2}$

2.3 Integration by Parts

The reverse process of the product rule $\dfrac{d}{dx}(uv) = u\dfrac{dv}{dx} + v\dfrac{du}{dx}$ is the method of integration by parts.

From the above,

$$u \dfrac{dv}{dx} = \dfrac{d}{dx}(uv) - v \dfrac{du}{dx}$$

$\therefore \int u \cdot \dfrac{dv}{dx} \cdot dx = uv - \int v \dfrac{du}{dx} \cdot dx \quad \ldots (1)$

or, $\int u \, dv = uv - \int v \, du \quad \ldots (2)$

WORKED EXAMPLES

1. $\int x \, e^x \, dx$

   Let $u = x$, $\dfrac{dv}{dx} = e^x$

   $\therefore \dfrac{du}{dx} = 1$, $v = \int e^x \, dx = e^x$

   Using the formula $\int uv' \, dx = uv - \int v u' \, dx$

   $\int x \, e^x \, dx = x e^x - \int e^x \cdot 1 \cdot dx$

   $= x e^x - e^x + C$

2. $\int x \cos x \, dx$

   $u = x$, $\dfrac{dv}{dx} = \cos x$

   $u' = 1$, $v = \int \cos x \, dx$

   $\qquad = \sin x$

   $\therefore \int x \cos x \, dx$

   $= uv - \int v u' \, dx$

   $= x \sin x - \int \sin x \, dx$

   $= x \sin x + \cos x + C$

3. $\int \log x \, dx$

   Write $\int \log x \, dx$ as $\int (\log x) \cdot 1 \, dx$

   and let $u = \log x$, $\dfrac{dv}{dx} = 1$

   $\therefore \dfrac{du}{dx} = \dfrac{1}{x}$, $v = x$

   $\therefore \int \log x \, dx$

   $= uv - \int v u' \, dx$

   $= (\log x) x - \int x \cdot \dfrac{1}{x} \, dx$

   $= x \log x - x + C$

Warning: A bad selection of u or v can lead to a disastrous situation. For example in $\int x \log x \, dx$, if you choose $u = x$, $\dfrac{dv}{dx} = \log x$, then $v = \int \log x \, dx$ is not easy to integrate. Again in $\int x \cdot \cos x \, dx$, if $u = \cos x$, $\dfrac{dv}{dx} = x$, then $v = \dfrac{x^2}{2}$.

$\int x \cos x \, dx = uv - \int u'v \, dx = \dfrac{x^2}{2} \cos x + \dfrac{1}{2} \int x^2 \sin x \, dx$, a situation worse than $\int x \cos x \, dx$.

---

4. $\int e^x \cos x \, dx$

   Let $u = e^x$, $\dfrac{dv}{dx} = \cos x$

   $u' = e^x$, $v = \sin x$

   $\therefore I = \int e^x \cos x \, dx$

   $\quad = uv - \int v u' \, dx$

   $\quad = e^x \sin x - \int e^x \sin x \, dx \qquad \ldots (1)$

   We integrate $\int e^x \sin x \, dx$ by parts again

   $\quad = e^x (-\cos x) - \int e^x (-\cos x) \, dx$

   $\quad = -e^x \cos x + I \qquad$ where $I = \int e^x \cos x \, dx$

   Then from (1)

   $\therefore I = e^x \sin x + e^x \cos x - I$

   $2I = e^x (\sin x + \cos x)$, divide by 2

   $\therefore I = \int e^x \cos x \, dx = \dfrac{1}{2} e^x (\sin x + \cos x) + C$

Note: It is important to note that the given integral may occur while integrating it by parts, but actually this occurrence helps to find the solution, as seen above.

Integrals with x^2 or x^3 require repeated use of the 'integration by parts' method. For example to find:

(5) $\int x^2 \cos x \, dx$ $\qquad u = x^2, \; \frac{dv}{dx} = \cos x$

$= x^2 \sin x - \int 2x \sin x \, dx$ $\qquad u' = 2x, \; v = \sin x$

Again $\int x \sin x \, dx = x(-\cos x) - \int 1 \cdot (-\cos x) \, dx$ $\qquad u = x, \; v' = \sin x$

$\qquad\qquad\qquad\quad = -x \cos x + \sin x$ $\qquad\qquad\qquad\qquad u' = 1, \; v = -\cos x$

$\therefore \int x^2 \cos x \, dx = x^2 \sin x - 2(-x \cos x + \sin x) + C$

$\qquad\qquad\qquad\;\; = x^2 \sin x + 2x \cos x - 2 \sin x + C$

---

(6) Find $\int \sin^{-1} x \, dx$

Write $I = \int (\sin^{-1} x) \cdot 1 \cdot dx$ $\qquad$ Let $u = \sin^{-1} x, \; \frac{dv}{dx} = 1$

$\quad\; = uv - \int v \, u' \, dx$ $\qquad\qquad\qquad\qquad\quad u' = \frac{1}{\sqrt{1-x^2}}, \; v = x$

$\quad\; = x \sin^{-1} x - \int \frac{x \, dx}{\sqrt{1-x^2}}$ $\quad\ldots$ (1)

Now for $\int \frac{x \, dx}{\sqrt{1-x^2}},$ $\qquad\qquad$ Use $u = 1 - x^2, \; \frac{du}{dx} = -2x$

$\qquad\qquad\qquad\qquad\qquad\qquad\qquad\;$ ← or $x \, dx = -\frac{du}{2}$

$\quad\; = -\frac{1}{2} \int \frac{du}{\sqrt{u}}$ $\qquad\qquad\qquad$ [It's easier to substitute

$\qquad\qquad\qquad\qquad\qquad\qquad\qquad\;$ for $x \, dx$, than x itself]

$\quad\; = -\frac{1}{2} \int u^{-1/2} \, du$

$\quad\; = -\sqrt{u}$

$\quad\; = -\sqrt{1-x^2}$

$\therefore \; I = x \sin^{-1} x + \sqrt{1-x^2} + C$ $\qquad$ [from (1)]

So it seems there is no end to the number of tricks you may be required to play in Integration. But that is what makes it so fascinating!

Exercise 2B

Integrate the following:

1. (a) $\int x e^{-x} dx$ (b) $\int x^2 e^x dx$ (c) $\int e^x \sin x \, dx$

2. (a) $\int x \cos 2x \, dx$ (b) $\int x^2 \sin x \, dx$ (c) $\int x^2 \cos x \, dx$

3. (a) $\int x \sec^2 x \, dx$ (b) $\int x \sin^2 x \, dx$ (c) $\int x \csc^2 x \, dx$

4. (a) $\int x^2 \log x \, dx$ (b) $\int \sqrt{x} \log_e x \, dx$ (c) $\int (\log x)^2 dx$

5. (a) $\int \cos^{-1} x \, dx$ (b) $\int \tan^{-1} x \, dx$ (c) $\int x \tan^{-1} x \, dx$

6. (a) $\int \log(x^2 - 1) dx$ (b) $\int e^{-2x} \cos 3x \, dx$ (c) $\int x (\log_e x)^2 dx$

7. (a) $\int x \tan^2 x \, dx$ (Hint: $\tan^2 x = \sec^2 x - 1$)

   (b) $\int x \cos^2 x \, dx$ (Hint: $2\cos^2 x = 1 + \cos 2x$)

8. (a) $\int \sqrt{x^2 + 1} \, dx$ (Hint: Write $\int (\sqrt{x^2 + 1}) \cdot 1 \, dx$)

   (b) $\int \sqrt{4 - x^2} \, dx$

9. Evaluate the following definite integrals:

   (a) $\int_0^1 x e^x dx$ (b) $\int_0^{\pi/2} x \cos x \, dx$ (c) $\int_1^e x \log_e x \, dx$

   (d) $\int_0^{1/2} \sin^{-1} 2x \, dx$ (e) $\int_0^{\pi/2} e^x \cos x \, dx$ (f) $\int_0^{\pi/2} x \sin^2 x \, dx$

10. (a) Use the substitution $y = \frac{2}{3} \sin \theta$ to find $\int_0^{2/3} \sqrt{4 - 9y^2} \, dy$

    (b) Find $\int_0^1 \frac{\sin^{-1} y}{\sqrt{1 + y}} dy$

11. (a) Use integration by parts to show that

$$\int \cos^{-1}\left(\frac{x}{6}\right) dx = x \cos^{-1}\left(\frac{x}{6}\right) - 6\sqrt{1 - \frac{x^2}{36}} + C$$

(b) Show that $\int_0^1 \tan^{-1} u \, du = \frac{\pi}{4} - \frac{1}{2} \log_e 2$

12. Evaluate:

(a) $\int_0^{\pi/3} x \sec^2 x \, dx$ (b) $\int_1^e \log_{10} x \, dx$ (c) $\int_0^{\pi} x \cos x \, dx$

(d) $\int_1^e \log_e x \, dx$ (e) $\int_e^{e^2} x \log_e x \, dx$ (f) $\int_e^{e^4} \frac{dx}{x \log_e x}$

(g) $\int_0^{\pi/4} x \sin 2x \, dx$ (h) $\int_1^e \frac{\log_e x}{x^4} dx$ (i) $\int_0^1 t e^{-2t} dt$

(j) $\int_0^1 u \tan^{-1} u \, du$ (k) $\int_0^{\log 2} t e^{-t} dt$ (l) $\int_0^1 \sin^{-1} t \, dt$

(m) $\int_0^{\pi/4} x \cos^2 x \, dx$ (Hint: $\cos^2 x = \frac{1}{2}(1 + \cos 2x)$)

2.4 Trigonometric Integrals Powers of sinx, cosx, tanx

Using $\sin^2 x = \frac{1}{2}(1 - \cos 2x)$ and $\cos^2 x = \frac{1}{2}(1 + \cos 2x)$, we find:

1. $\int \sin^2 x \, dx = \frac{1}{2} \int (1 - \cos 2x) \, dx = \frac{1}{2}\left(x - \frac{\sin 2x}{2}\right) + C$

2. $\int \cos^2 x \, dx = \frac{1}{2} \int (1 + \cos 2x) \, dx = \frac{1}{2}\left(x + \frac{\sin 2x}{2}\right) + C$

3. $\int \sin^3 x \, dx = \int \sin^2 x \cdot \sin x \, dx$ $\quad u = \cos x$

$= \int (1 - \cos^2 x) \sin x \, dx$ $\quad \frac{du}{dx} = -\sin x$

$= \int -(1 - u^2) \, du$

$= -u + \frac{u^3}{3} + C$

$= -\cos x + \frac{1}{3} \cos^3 x + C$

4. $\int \cos^3 x \, dx = \int (1 - \sin^2 x) \cos x \, dx \qquad \sin x = u$

$\qquad \qquad = \int (1 - u^2) \, du \qquad \qquad \frac{du}{dx} = \cos x$

$\qquad \qquad = u - \frac{u^3}{3} + C$

$\qquad \qquad = \sin x - \frac{1}{3} \sin^3 x + C$

5. Noting $\sin^4 x = (\sin^2 x)^2 = \frac{1}{4}(1 - \cos 2x)^2$

$\int \sin^4 x \, dx = \frac{1}{4} \int (1 - 2\cos 2x + \cos^2 2x) \, dx$

$\qquad \qquad = \frac{1}{4} \int [1 - 2\cos 2x + \frac{1}{2}(1 + \cos 4x)] \, dx$

$\qquad \qquad = \frac{1}{4} [\frac{3}{2} x - \sin 2x + \frac{1}{8} \sin 4x] + C$

6. $\int \cos^5 x \, \sin^2 x \, dx \qquad \qquad u = \sin x$

$\qquad = \int \cos^4 x \cdot \sin^2 x \cdot \cos x \, dx \qquad \frac{du}{dx} = \cos x$

$\qquad = \int (1 - \sin^2 x)^2 \cdot \sin^2 x \cdot \cos x \, dx$

$\qquad = \int (1 - u^2)^2 \cdot u^2 \, du$

$\qquad = \int u^2 (1 - 2u^2 + u^4) \, du$

$\qquad = \frac{u^3}{3} - \frac{2u^5}{5} + \frac{u^7}{7} + C, \quad$ where $u = \sin x$

7. $\int \tan x \, dx = \int \frac{\sin x}{\cos x} \, dx = -\log \cos x + C$

$\qquad \qquad \qquad \qquad = \log \sec x + C$

8. $\int \tan^3 x \, dx = \int \tan^2 x \, \tan x \, dx$

$\qquad \qquad = \int (\sec^2 x - 1) \tan x \, dx \qquad u = \tan x$

$\qquad \qquad = \int \tan x \, \sec^2 x \, dx - \int \tan x \, dx$

$\qquad \qquad = \int u \, du + \log \cos x + C$

$\qquad \qquad = \frac{1}{2} \tan^2 x + \log \cos x + C$

9. $\int \tan^4 x \, dx = \int \tan^2 x \cdot \tan^2 x \, dx$

$\qquad = \int (\sec^2 x - 1) \tan^2 x \, dx$

$\qquad = \int \sec^2 x \tan^2 x \, dx - \int \tan^2 x \, dx$

$\qquad = \int u^2 \, du - \int (\sec^2 x - 1) \, dx \qquad u = \tan x$ for the first integral

$\qquad = \frac{1}{3} \tan^3 x - \tan x + x + C$

10. $\int \sec x \, dx = \int \frac{\sec x (\sec x + \tan x)}{\sec x + \tan x} \, dx$

$\qquad = \int \frac{\sec^2 x + \sec x \tan x}{\tan x + \sec x} \, dx$

$\qquad = \int \frac{f'(x)}{f(x)} \, dx \qquad f(x) = \tan x + \sec x$

$\qquad = \log_e (\tan x + \sec x) + C$

11. $\int \sec^4 x \, dx = \int \sec^2 x (1 + \tan^2 x) \, dx \qquad u = \tan x$

$\qquad = \int (1 + u^2) \, du$

$\qquad = u + \frac{u^3}{3} + C$, where $u = \tan x$

$\qquad = \tan x + \frac{1}{3} \tan^3 x + C$

All the even powers of sec x and cosec x are integrated as above (odd powers by integration by parts).

12. $\int \operatorname{cosec} x \, dx = -\int -\frac{(\operatorname{cosec} x + \cot x) \operatorname{cosec} x}{\operatorname{cosec} x + \cot x} \, dx \qquad \boxed{\int \frac{f'(x)}{f(x)} \, dx = \log f(x)}$

$\qquad = -\log_e (\operatorname{cosec} x + \cot x) + C$

13. $\int \sec^3 x \, dx = \int \sec x \cdot \sec^2 x \, dx \qquad$ Integrate by parts

$\qquad = \sec x \tan x - \int \tan x \sec x \cdot \tan x \, dx$

$\qquad = \sec x \tan x - \int \sec x (\sec^2 x - 1) \, dx$

$\qquad = \sec x \tan x - \int \sec^3 x \, dx + \log (\sec x + \tan x)$

Solve for $\int \sec^3 x \, dx$, then

$\int \sec^3 dx = \frac{1}{2} \sec x \tan x + \frac{1}{2} \log (\sec x + \tan x) + C$

2.5 Use of t = tan(x/2)

Rational Expression in sinx and cosx

Expression of the form $\int \dfrac{dx}{a\cos x + b\sin x + c}$ can only be integrated by special substitution $t = \tan\dfrac{x}{2}$

We have $\dfrac{dt}{dx} = \dfrac{1}{2}\sec^2\dfrac{x}{2} = \dfrac{1}{2}(1+t^2)$, so $dx = \dfrac{2dt}{1+t^2}$

Also $\sin x = \dfrac{2t}{1+t^2}$, $\cos x = \dfrac{1-t^2}{1+t^2}$

WORKED EXAMPLES

(1) Find: $\int \dfrac{1}{3 + 2\cos x}\, dx$

$$I = \int \dfrac{1}{3 + \dfrac{2(1-t^2)}{1+t^2}} \cdot \dfrac{2\,dt}{1+t^2}$$

$$= \int \dfrac{2\,dt}{5 + t^2}$$

$$= \dfrac{2}{\sqrt{5}} \tan^{-1}\left[\dfrac{t}{\sqrt{5}}\right] + C$$

$$= \dfrac{2}{\sqrt{5}} \tan^{-1}\left[\dfrac{\tan^{-1}\dfrac{x}{2}}{\sqrt{5}}\right] + C$$

(2) Find: $\int \dfrac{dx}{\sin x + \cos x}$

$$I = \int \dfrac{1}{\dfrac{2t}{1+t^2} + \dfrac{1-t^2}{1+t^2}} \cdot \dfrac{2\,dt}{1+t^2}$$

$$= \int \dfrac{2\,dt}{1 + 2t - t^2}$$

$$= \int \dfrac{2\,dt}{2 - (1-t)^2}$$

(cont. next page)

$$= \int \frac{-2\,dy}{2 - y^2}, \quad y = 1 - t$$

$$= 2 \int \frac{dy}{y^2 - 2}$$

$$= \frac{2}{2\sqrt{2}} \log \left| \frac{y - \sqrt{2}}{y + \sqrt{2}} \right| + C$$

$$\therefore I = \frac{1}{\sqrt{2}} \log \left| \frac{1 - t - \sqrt{2}}{1 - t + \sqrt{2}} \right| + C$$

$$= \frac{1}{\sqrt{2}} \log_e \left| \frac{1 - \sqrt{2} - \tan\frac{x}{2}}{1 + \sqrt{2} - \tan\frac{x}{2}} \right| + C$$

(3) $\int \frac{\sin\theta}{2 - \cos\theta}\,d\theta$

$$= \int \frac{dU}{U} \qquad\qquad U = 2 - \cos\theta$$

$$= \log_e U + C \qquad\qquad \frac{dU}{d\theta} = \sin\theta$$

$$= \log_e (2 - \cos\theta) + C$$

(4) $\int \frac{\cos x}{3 + 2\cos x}\,dx$

Arrange numerator as $\frac{1}{2}(3 + 2\cos x) - \frac{3}{2}$

$$\therefore I = \int \frac{\frac{1}{2}(3 + 2\cos x) - \frac{3}{2}}{3 + 2\cos x}\,dx$$

$$= \int \left[\frac{1}{2} - \frac{\frac{3}{2}}{3 + 2\cos x} \right] dx$$

$$= \frac{1}{2}x - \frac{3}{2}\cdot\frac{2}{\sqrt{5}} \tan^{-1}\left[\frac{\tan\frac{x}{2}}{\sqrt{5}}\right] + C \quad \text{using example (1)}$$

$$= \frac{x}{2} - \frac{3}{\sqrt{5}} \tan^{-1}\left[\frac{\tan\frac{x}{2}}{\sqrt{5}}\right] + C$$

Exercise 2C

Integrate the following:

1. $\displaystyle\int_0^{\pi/2} \sin^3 x \, dx$
2. $\displaystyle\int_0^{\pi/4} \cos^4 x \, dx$
3. $\displaystyle\int_0^{\pi/4} \tan^4 x \, dx$
4. $\displaystyle\int \sin^2 x \cos^2 x \, dx$
5. $\displaystyle\int \sin^3 x \cos^2 x \, dx$
6. $\displaystyle\int \cos^5 x \sin^2 x \, dx$
7. $\displaystyle\int \sin^{5/2} x \cos x \, dx$
8. $\displaystyle\int \frac{\sin^5 x}{\cos^2 x} \, dx$
9. $\displaystyle\int \cot^3 x \, dx$
10. $\displaystyle\int \operatorname{cosec}^3 x \, dx$
11. $\displaystyle\int \operatorname{cosec}^4 x \, dx$
12. $\displaystyle\int \cos^3 2x \, dx$
13. $\displaystyle\int \tan^3 2x \, dx$
14. $\displaystyle\int \sin^3 2x \, dx$
15. $\displaystyle\int \cos^{2/3} x \sin^5 x \, dx$
16. $\displaystyle\int \sin^4 x \cos^3 x \, dx$
17. $\displaystyle\int \frac{\cos^2 x}{\sin^4 x} \, dx$
18. $\displaystyle\int \frac{\sin^3 x}{\cos^2 x} \, dx$
19. $\displaystyle\int \frac{1}{\cos x} \, dx$
20. $\displaystyle\int \frac{1}{1 - \sin x} \, dx$
21. $\displaystyle\int_0^{\pi/3} \frac{1}{1 + \sin x} \, dx$
22. $\displaystyle\int_0^{\pi/2} \frac{dx}{2 + \cos x}$
23. $\displaystyle\int \frac{dx}{\sin x - \cos x}$
24. $\displaystyle\int \frac{\sin x}{2 + \cos x} \, dx$
25. $\displaystyle\int_0^{\pi/2} \frac{1}{3 + 5\cos x} \, dx$

2.6 Reduction Formulas

A reduction formula is one that reduces the index (usually an integer) of the integrand. By repeated applications the index is reduced to either one or zero. By using the method of integration by parts, we can establish the following reduction formulas:

1. $\int \sin^n x \, dx = -\frac{1}{n} \sin^{n-1} x \cdot \cos x + \frac{(n-1)}{n} \cdot \int \sin^{n-2} x \, dx$

2. $\int \cos^n x \, dx = \frac{1}{n} \cdot \cos^{n-1} x \cdot \sin x + \frac{n-1}{n} \cdot \int \cos^{n-2} x \, dx$

3. $\int \tan^n x \, dx = \frac{\tan^{n-1} x}{n-1} - \int \tan^{n-2} x \, dx$

Solution:

Let $I_n = \int \sin^n x \, dx$, so that $I_{n-2} = \int \sin^{n-2} x \, dx$

Using integration by parts:

$I_n = \int \sin^{n-1} x \cdot \sin x \, dx$

$\quad = \int \sin^{n-1} x \cdot \frac{d}{dx}(-\cos x) \, dx \qquad \qquad [\text{let } u = \sin^{n-1} x \,,\, \frac{dv}{dx} = \sin x]$

$\quad = \sin^{n-1} x \cdot (-\cos x) - \int (n-1) \sin^{n-2} x \cos x \cdot (-\cos x) \, dx$

$\quad = -\cos x \cdot \sin^{n-1} x + (n-1) \int \sin^{n-2}(1 - \sin^2 x) \, dx$

$\quad = -\cos x \cdot \sin^{n-1} x + (n-1) I_{n-2} - (n-1) I_n$

Solve for I_n, then:

$I_n = -\frac{1}{n} \cdot \sin^{n-1} x \cos x + \frac{n-1}{n} I_{n-2}$, where $I_n = \int \sin^n x \, dx$

You can see why these formulae are called the 'REDUCTION formulas'. The index n is reduced to $n-2$ or $n-1$. For the example above, starting with, say, $n = 10$, we shall have $n = 8, 6, 4, 2, 0$, which means you only have to evaluate $\int \sin^0 x \, dx = \int dx$. If n is originally odd, then you have to evaluate only $\int \sin x \, dx$, etc. Proof of $\int \cos^n x \, dx$ is similar.

For $\tan^x dx$, we write $I_n = \int \tan^n x \, dx = \int \tan^{n-2} x (\sec^2 x - 1) dx = \int \tan^{n-2} x \sec^2 x \, dx - I_{n-2}$

$\therefore \quad I_n = \frac{\tan^{n-1} x}{n-1} - I_{n-2}$

WORKED EXAMPLES

1. $\int \sin^6 x \, dx = -\frac{1}{6} \sin^5 x \cos x + \frac{5}{6} I_4$

$\qquad I_4 = -\frac{1}{4} \sin^3 x \cos x + \frac{3}{4} I_2$

$\qquad I_2 = -\frac{1}{2} \sin x \cos x + \frac{1}{2} I_0$

$\qquad I_0 = \int dx = x$

$\therefore \int \sin^6 x \, dx = -\frac{1}{6} \sin^5 x \cos x + \frac{5}{6}(-\frac{1}{4} \sin^3 x \cos x + \frac{3}{4} I_2)$

$\qquad\qquad\qquad = -\frac{1}{6} \sin^5 x \cos x - \frac{5}{24} \sin^3 x \cos x + \frac{5}{8} I_2$

$\qquad\qquad\qquad = -\frac{1}{6} \sin^5 x \cos x - \frac{5}{24} \sin^3 x \cos x + \frac{5}{8}(-\frac{1}{2} \sin x \cos x + \frac{1}{2} I_0)$

$\therefore \int \sin^6 x \, dx = -\frac{1}{6} \sin^5 x \cos x - \frac{5}{24} \sin^3 x \cos x - \frac{5}{16} \sin x \cos x + \frac{5}{16} x$

Since $[\sin^m x \cos^k x]_0^{\pi/2} = 0$, we have

$\int_0^{\pi/2} \sin^6 x \, dx = \frac{5}{16} [x]_0^{\pi/2} = \frac{5\pi}{32}$

So, if the limits are 0 and $\frac{\pi}{2}$, the easier method is:

$\int_0^{\pi/2} \sin^6 x \, dx = \left[-\frac{1}{6} \sin^5 x \cos x\right]_0^{\pi/2} + \frac{5}{6} I_4 = \frac{5 I_4}{6}$

$I_4 = \frac{3}{4} I_2 = \frac{3}{4} \cdot \frac{1}{2} I_0 = \frac{3}{4} \cdot \frac{1}{2} \cdot \frac{\pi}{2}$

$\therefore \int_0^{\pi/2} \sin^6 x \, dx = \frac{5}{6} \cdot \frac{3}{4} \cdot \frac{1}{2} \cdot \frac{\pi}{2} = \frac{5}{32} \cdot \pi$

---

2. $\int_0^{\pi/2} \sin^8 x \, dx = \frac{7}{8} I_6 = \frac{7}{8} \cdot \frac{5}{6} \cdot \frac{3}{4} \cdot \frac{1}{2} \cdot \frac{\pi}{2} = \frac{35\pi}{256}$

You must show that $[\sin^m x \cos^k x]_0^{\pi/2} = 0$. Also remember you can not use this easier method for limits other than 0 and $\frac{\pi}{2}$. For $\int_0^{\pi/3} \sin^6 x$, we must use the long method.

Exercise 2D

Find a formula finding I_n in terms of I_{n-1} : (for examples 1-4)

1. $I_n = \int x^n e^x \, dx$
2. $I_n = \int x^n e^{-2x} \, dx$
3. $I_n = \int (\log_e x)^n \, dx$
4. $I_n = \int \frac{dx}{(x^2 + a^2)^n}$

Find a formula reducing I_n to I_{n-2} : (for examples 5-9)

5. $I_n = \int \cot^n x \, dx$, hence find $\int \cot^6 x \, dx$

6. $I_n = \int \cos^n x \, dx$, hence find (a) $\int \cos^6 x \, dx$ (b) $\int_0^{\pi/2} \cos^8 x \, dx$

7. $I_n = \int \sin^n x \, dx$, hence find (a) $\int_0^{\pi/2} \sin^8 x \, dx$ (b) $\int_0^{\pi/4} \sin^4 x \, dx$

8. $I_n = \int \tan^n x \, dx$, hence find (a) $\int \tan^5 dx$ (b) $\int_0^{\pi/4} \tan^8 x \, dx$

9. $I_n = \int (\sin^{-1} x)^n \, dx$, hence find $\int_0^1 (\sin^{-1} x)^3 \, dx$ (Hint: $x = \sin U$)

10. Show that $U_n = \frac{-2n}{2n+3} U_{n-1}$, if $U_n = \int_{-1}^{0} x^n (1+x)^{1/2} \, dx$, hence evaluate U_3.

11. If $I_n = \int e^{mx} \tan^n x \, dx$, show that
$$I_n = \frac{e^{mx}}{n-1} \tan^{n-1} x - \frac{m}{n-1} \cdot I_{n-1} - I_{n-2}$$

12. Find $\int x^4 e^x \, dx$, using the reduction formula developed in Exercise 1.

13. If $I_n = \int \sec^n x \, dx$, prove that
$$I_n = \frac{\sec^{n-2} x \tan x}{n-1} + \frac{n-2}{n-1} \cdot I_{n-2}$$
Hence, evaluate $\int_0^{\pi/4} \sec^6 dx$

14. Prove: $\int x^n e^{-x} \, dx = -e^{-x} \cdot x^n + n \int x^{n-1} \cdot e^{-x} \, dx$
Hence, find: $\int x^3 e^{-x} \, dx$

2.7 Trigonometric Substitution

Integrals involving expressions like $\sqrt{a^2 + x^2}$, $\sqrt{a^2 - x^2}$ etc. are simplified by substitution. $x = a \tan\theta$, $x = a \sin\theta$, $x = a \cos\theta$ etc.

WORKED EXAMPLES

1. Find $\int \dfrac{1}{\sqrt{a^2 + x^2}} \, dx$

   $x = a \tan\theta$, $\dfrac{dx}{d\theta} = a \sec^2\theta$

   $\therefore \; I = \int \dfrac{a \sec^2\theta \, d\theta}{\sqrt{a^2(1 + \tan^2\theta)}}$

   $= \int \dfrac{a \sec^2\theta \, d\theta}{a \sec\theta}$

   $= \int \sec\theta \, d\theta$

   $= \log_e (\sec\theta + \tan\theta) + C$

   $= \log \left(\dfrac{\sqrt{a^2 + x^2}}{a} + \dfrac{x}{a} \right) + C$

   $= \log \left(\dfrac{\sqrt{a^2 + x^2} + x}{a} \right) + C$

   $= \log (x + \sqrt{a^2 + x^2}) - \log_e a + C$

   $= \log (x + \sqrt{a^2 + x^2}) + K$

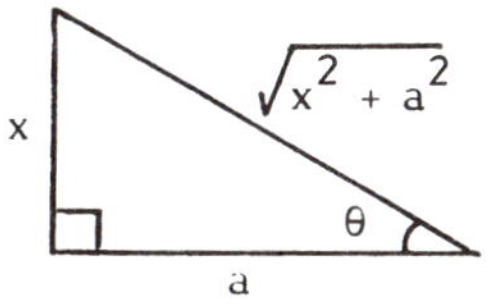

   Fig. 1

2. Find $\int \dfrac{dx}{\sqrt{x^2 - a^2}}$, $x > a > 0$

   Let $x = a \sec\theta$ $\quad \dfrac{dx}{d\theta} = a \sec\theta \tan\theta$

   $\therefore \; I = \int \dfrac{a \sec\theta \tan\theta \, d\theta}{\sqrt{a^2(\sec^2\theta - 1)}} \quad \sec^2\theta = 1 + \tan^2\theta$

   $= \int \sec\theta \, d\theta$

   $= \log (\sec\theta + \tan\theta) + K$

   $\therefore \; I = \log \left(\dfrac{x}{a} + \sqrt{\dfrac{x^2}{a^2} - 1} \right) + K$

   $= \log_e (x + \sqrt{x^2 - a^2}) + C$

[Note: $\log a$ is a constant]

Exercise 2E

Use $x = a\sin\theta$ for $\sqrt{a^2 - x^2}$, $x = a\tan\theta$ for $\sqrt{a^2 + x^2}$ and $x = a\sec\theta$ for $\sqrt{x^2 - a^2}$, to find:

1. $\displaystyle\int \frac{dx}{\sqrt{4 + x^2}}$

2. $\displaystyle\int \frac{dx}{x^2\sqrt{9 - x^2}}$

3. $\displaystyle\int \frac{x^2\,dx}{\sqrt{16 - x^2}}$

4. $\displaystyle\int \frac{\sqrt{4 - x^2}}{x^2}\,dx$

5. $\displaystyle\int \frac{x^2\,dx}{\sqrt{25 - x^2}}$

6. $\displaystyle\int \sqrt{x^2 + a^2}\,dx$

7. $\displaystyle\int \sqrt{a^2 - x^2}\,dx$

8. $\displaystyle\int \frac{x^2\,dx}{\sqrt{x^2 + 4}}$

9. $\displaystyle\int \sqrt{4 + x^2}\,dx$

10. $\displaystyle\int \sqrt{25 - x^2}\,dx$

11. $\displaystyle\int \frac{dx}{(4 + x^2)^{3/2}}$

12. $\displaystyle\int \frac{dx}{x\sqrt{4 - x^2}}$

13. $\displaystyle\int \frac{dx}{x^2\sqrt{x^2 - 4}}$

14. $\displaystyle\int \frac{x}{\sqrt{1 - x^2}}\,dx$

15. $\displaystyle\int \frac{\sqrt{1 - x^2}}{x}\,dx$

16. $\displaystyle\int \frac{x}{(\sqrt{1 - x^2})^3}\,dx$

17. $\displaystyle\int \frac{x^2}{\sqrt{x^2 - 4}}\,dx$

18. $\displaystyle\int \frac{\sqrt{x^2 - a^2}}{x^2}\,dx$

19. $\displaystyle\int \frac{dx}{x\sqrt{x^2 - 4}}$

20. $\displaystyle\int \frac{\sqrt{x^2 + 4}}{x^2}\,dx$

21. $\displaystyle\int \frac{x^2 + 3}{\sqrt{x^2 + 9}}\,dx$

2.8 Integration of Rational Functions

TYPE I: We shall consider the rational function $\dfrac{P(x)}{ax + b}$ where $P(x)$ is a polynomial.

We divide $P(x)$ by $ax + b$ by long division and write

$P(x) = Q(x) + \dfrac{R}{ax + b}$ where $Q(x)$ is a polynomial and R is a constant.

EXAMPLES: Integrate the following:

(a) $\int \frac{2x-1}{2x+1} dx$ (b) $\int \frac{x^3}{x-2} dx$ (c) $\int \frac{x^3-1}{x-1} dx$ (d) $\int_0^1 \frac{x^3}{2x+1} dx$

SOLUTION:

(a) Divide $2x - 1$ by $2x + 1$

$$2x+1 \overline{)\begin{array}{r} 1 \\ 2x-1 \\ 2x+1 \\ \hline -2 \end{array}}$$

$$\therefore \int \frac{2x-1}{2x+1} dx = \int (1 - \frac{2}{2x+1}) dx$$
$$= x - \log_e(2x+1) + C$$

When the denominator is linear, we can divide by inspection. For example,
$$\frac{2x-1}{2x+1} = \frac{2x+1-2}{2x+1} = 1 - \frac{2}{2x+1}$$

(b) $\int \frac{x^3}{x-2} dx$

$$= \int \left[x^2 + 2x + 4 + \frac{8}{x-2} \right] dx$$

$$= \frac{x^3}{3} + x^2 + 4x + 8 \log(x-2) + C$$

$$x-2 \overline{)\begin{array}{r} x^2 + 2x + 4 \\ x^3 \\ x^3 - 2x^2 \\ \hline 2x^2 \\ 2x^2 - 4x \\ \hline 4x \\ 4x - 8 \\ \hline 8 \end{array}}$$

(c) Observe that $x^3 - 1$ can be factorised as $(x-1)(x^2 + x + 1)$

$$\therefore \int \frac{x^3-1}{x-1} dx = \int (x^2 + x + 1) dx = \frac{x^3}{3} + \frac{x^2}{2} + x + C$$

Of course, we can divide $x^3 - 1$ by $x - 1$ and get the same result.

(d) $\int_0^1 \frac{x^3}{2x+1} dx$

$$= \int_1^3 \frac{1}{16} \cdot \frac{(U-1)^3}{U} dU$$

$$= \frac{1}{16} \int_1^3 \frac{U^3 - 3U^2 + 3U - 1}{U} dU$$

$$= \frac{1}{16} \int_1^3 (U^2 - 3U + 3 - \frac{1}{U}) dU$$

$$= \frac{1}{16} \left[\frac{U^3}{3} - \frac{3U^2}{2} + 3U - \log_e U \right]_1^3$$

$$= \frac{1}{16} \left[\frac{8}{3} - \log_e 3 \right]$$

To make division easier, let $U = 2x + 1$
$$\therefore \frac{dU}{dx} = 2 \rightarrow dx = \frac{dU}{2}$$
when $x = 0$, $U = 1$
$x = 1$, $U = 3$
Also $x = \frac{U-1}{2}$

TYPE II: Integral of the form $\int \dfrac{P(x)}{ax^2 + bx + c} \, dx$.

If the degree of $P(x) \geq 2$ we divide $P(x)$ by $ax^2 + bx + c$ and express $\dfrac{P(x)}{ax^2 + bx + c}$ in the form $Q(x) + \dfrac{Bx + D}{ax^2 + bx + c}$

We shall only consider the cases where $ax^2 + bx + c$ is irreducible over the real field, i.e. $ax^2 + bx + c$ cannot be factorised. Method of completing the square and the following integrals are required.

1. $\int \dfrac{dx}{x^2 + a^2} = \dfrac{1}{a} \tan^{-1} \dfrac{x}{a} + C$

2. $\int \dfrac{dx}{x^2 - a^2} = \dfrac{1}{2a} \log_e \left[\dfrac{x - a}{x + a} \right] + C, \quad |x| > a$

3. $\int \dfrac{dx}{a^2 - x^2} = \dfrac{1}{2a} \log_e \left[\dfrac{a + x}{a - x} \right] + C, \quad |x| < a$

EXAMPLES:

(1) $\int \dfrac{dx}{x^2 - 4x + 5}$

$= \int \dfrac{dU}{U^2 + 1}$

$= \tan^{-1} U + C$

$= \tan^{-1}(x - 2) + C$

The quadratic $x^2 - 4x + 5$ is irreducible over the real field, so we complete the square.

$x^2 - 4x + 5 = (x - 2)^2 + 1 = U^2 + 1$

where $U = x - 2$

$\dfrac{dU}{dx} = 1 \rightarrow dx = dU$

(2) $\int \dfrac{2x - 3}{x^2 - 4x + 5} \, dx$

$= \int \dfrac{2x - 4}{x^2 - 4x + 5} \, dx + \int \dfrac{dx}{x^2 - 4x + 5}$

$= \log(x^2 - 4x + 5) + \tan^{-1}(x - 2) + C,$

The derivative of $x^2 - 4x + 5$ is $2x - 4$
We write $2x - 3 = 2x - 4 + 1$

using example (1).

(3) $\displaystyle\int \frac{dx}{x^2 + 6x + 4}$

$= \displaystyle\int \frac{dU}{U^2 - 5}$

$= \dfrac{1}{2\sqrt{5}} \log \left[\dfrac{U - \sqrt{5}}{U + \sqrt{5}} \right] + C$

$= \dfrac{1}{2\sqrt{5}} \log \left[\dfrac{x + 3 - \sqrt{5}}{x + 3 + \sqrt{5}} \right] + C$

The quadratic $x^2 + 6x + 4$ is irreducible

$\therefore\ x^2 + 6x + 4 = (x + 3)^2 - 5$
$\qquad\qquad\qquad\ = U^2 - 5$

where $\quad U = x + 3$

(4) $\displaystyle\int \frac{dx}{2x^2 + 7x + 13}$

$= \dfrac{1}{2} \displaystyle\int \frac{dU}{U^2 + \frac{55}{16}}$

$= \dfrac{4}{2\sqrt{55}}\ \tan^{-1}\left(\dfrac{U}{\sqrt{55}/4}\right) + C$

$= \dfrac{2}{\sqrt{55}}\ \tan^{-1}\left(\dfrac{4x + 7}{\sqrt{55}}\right) + C$

$2x^2 + 7x + 13$ cannot be factorised.

$2x^2 + 7x + 13 = 2\left[x^2 + \dfrac{7}{2}x + \dfrac{13}{2}\right]$

$\qquad\qquad\qquad = 2\left[(x + \dfrac{7}{4})^2 + \dfrac{55}{16}\right]$

$\qquad\qquad\qquad = 2\left[U^2 + \dfrac{55}{16}\right]$

where $\ U = x + \dfrac{7}{4}$

Exercise 2F

Find the integrals:

1. $\displaystyle\int \dfrac{6x}{3x+2}\,dx$

2. $\displaystyle\int \dfrac{x^4}{1-x}\,dx$

3. $\displaystyle\int \dfrac{x^2}{x+1}\,dx$

4. $\displaystyle\int \dfrac{2x-3}{1-2x}\,dx$

5. $\displaystyle\int \dfrac{ax+b}{cx+d}\,dx$

6. $\displaystyle\int \dfrac{x^2}{3x-1}\,dx$

7. $\displaystyle\int \dfrac{dx}{x^2+x+1}$

8. $\displaystyle\int \dfrac{dx}{x^2-x+1}$

9. $\displaystyle\int \dfrac{dx}{x^2+2ax+b}$

10. $\displaystyle\int \dfrac{3\,dx}{9x^2-6x+2}$

11. $\displaystyle\int \dfrac{4x+3}{x^2+2x+3}\,dx$

12. $\displaystyle\int \dfrac{x\,dx}{x^2-x+1}$

13. $\displaystyle\int \dfrac{x\,dx}{x^2+2x-2}$

14. $\displaystyle\int \dfrac{x^2+x+1}{x^2-x+1}\,dx$

Evaluate the following in the exact form:

15. $\displaystyle\int_{2}^{3} \dfrac{dx}{x^2-6x+10}$

16. $\displaystyle\int_{1}^{3} \dfrac{dx}{x^2+2x-1}$

17. $\displaystyle\int_{0}^{1} \dfrac{(x+1)\,dx}{x^2+x+1}$

18. $\displaystyle\int_{-1}^{0} \dfrac{2x+1}{x^2+6x+10}\,dx$

19. $\displaystyle\int_{2}^{4} \dfrac{3\,dx}{x^2+x-2}$

20. $\displaystyle\int_{a}^{b} \dfrac{x^3}{1-x}\,dx \qquad (1 < a < b)$

2.9 Method of Partial Fractions

It is easy to add two fractions.

1. $\dfrac{a}{b} + \dfrac{c}{d} = \dfrac{ad + bc}{bd}$

2. $\dfrac{1}{x-3} - \dfrac{1}{x-2} = \dfrac{x-2-x+3}{(x-3)(x-2)} = \dfrac{1}{(x-3)(x-2)}$

The reverse process of separating a fraction such as $\dfrac{1}{(x-3)(x-2)}$ is not so simple. We shall now study a method of splitting the general rational function $\dfrac{P(x)}{A(x)}$ into its partial fractions.

If the degree of $P(x) \geqslant A(x)$, we first divide $P(x)$ by $A(x)$, and express $\dfrac{P(x)}{A(x)}$ as the sum of a polynomial and a rational function $\dfrac{R(x)}{A(x)}$ where the degree of $R(x) <$ the degree of $A(x)$.

The method of decomposing a rational function $\dfrac{R(x)}{A(x)}$ into partial fractions can be stated as follows:

1. Factorise the denominator.

   For example: $\dfrac{1}{x^3 - 1} = \dfrac{1}{(x-1)(x^2+x+1)}$.

2. A theorem on polynomials ensures that every polynomial $R(x)$ with real coefficients can be factorised into the product of powers of either linear terms of the form $(x-a)^n$ or irreducible quadratics of the form $(x^2 + bx + c)^m$.

We are only required to study cases where $n = 1$ and $m = 1$ i.e. the factors are not repeated.

3. In each partial fraction, the degree of the numerator $<$ the degree of the denominator.

Example: (1)

Find $\int \dfrac{2x - 1}{(x - 2)(x - 3)} \, dx$ by partial fractions.

Solution:

Let $\dfrac{2x - 1}{(x - 2)(x - 3)} = \dfrac{A}{x - 2} + \dfrac{B}{x - 3}$, where A and B are constants

Multiply both sides by $(x - 2)(x - 3)$

$\therefore \quad 2x - 1 = A(x - 3) + B(x - 2) = x(A + B) - 3A - 2B$

This is an identity, so by comparing coefficients of similar terms:

$\quad A + B = 2 \quad$ and $\quad 3A + 2B = 1$

Solve these: $A = -3, \quad B = 5$

$\therefore \int \dfrac{2x - 1}{(x - 2)(x - 3)} \, dx = \int \left[\dfrac{-3}{x - 2} + \dfrac{5}{x - 3} \right] dx$

$\qquad\qquad\qquad\qquad = -3 \log(x - 2) + 5 \log(x - 3) + C$

$\qquad\qquad\qquad\qquad = \log_e \dfrac{(x - 3)^5}{(x - 2)^3} + C$

Example: (2)

Find $\int \dfrac{2x + 3}{(x^2 + 2)(x - 2)} \, dx$

Solution:

Here we have an irreducible quadratic factor $x^2 + 2$, so we write

$\dfrac{2x + 3}{(x - 2)(x^2 + 2)} = \dfrac{A}{x - 2} + \dfrac{Bx + C}{x^2 + 2}$

Multiply both sides by $(x - 2)(x^2 + 2)$

Then $2x + 3 = A(x^2 + 2) + Bx(x - 2) + C(x - 2)$

$\qquad\qquad\quad = x^2(A + B) + x(-2B + C) + (2A - 2C)$

$\therefore \quad A + B = 0, \quad -2B + C = 2 \quad$ and $\quad 2A - 2C = 3$

(cont. next page)

Solve: $A = \frac{7}{6}$, $B = -\frac{7}{6}$, $C = -\frac{1}{3} = -\frac{2}{6}$

$\therefore \int \frac{2x + 3}{(x - 2)(x^2 + 2)} dx = \frac{7}{6} \int \frac{1}{x - 2} dx + \frac{1}{6} \int -\frac{7x - 2}{x^2 + 2} dx$

$\qquad = \frac{7}{6} \int \frac{1}{x - 2} dx - \frac{7}{6} \int \frac{x}{x^2 + 2} dx - \frac{1}{3} \cdot \int \frac{1}{x^2 + 2} dx$

$\qquad = \frac{7}{6} \log(x - 2) - \frac{7}{12} \log(x^2 + 2) - \frac{1}{3\sqrt{2}} \cdot \tan^{-1} \frac{x}{\sqrt{2}} + C$

Example: (3)

$\int \frac{1}{(x - 2)(x + 1)^2} dx$

Solution:

We have a repeated factor $(x + 1)$, 2 times. We write:

$\frac{1}{(x - 2)(x + 1)^2} = \frac{A}{x - 2} + \frac{B}{(x + 1)} + \frac{C}{(x + 1)^2}$

$\therefore \quad 1 = A(x + 1)^2 + B(x + 1)(x - 2) + C(x - 2)$

Here it is easier to use suitable values of x.

Put $x = -1$, $\therefore$ $1 = -3C$, or $C = -\frac{1}{3}$

$\qquad x = 2$, $\qquad 1 = 9A$, $\qquad A = \frac{1}{9}$

$\qquad x = 0$, $\qquad 1 = A - 2B - 2C$, $\quad B = -\frac{1}{9}$

$\therefore \int \frac{1}{(x - 2)(x + 1)^2} dx = \int \left[\frac{1}{9} \frac{1}{(x - 2)} - \frac{1}{9} \frac{1}{(x + 1)} - \frac{1}{3} \frac{1}{(x + 1)^2} \right] dx$

$\qquad = \frac{1}{9} \log(x - 2) - \frac{1}{9} \log(x + 1) + \frac{1}{3} \cdot \frac{1}{(x + 1)} + K$

$\qquad = \frac{1}{9} \log \frac{x - 2}{x + 1} + \frac{1}{3} \frac{1}{(x + 1)} + K$

Example: (4)

$$\int \frac{1}{x^3 - 1} \, dx$$

Solution:

We have $x^3 - 1 = (x - 1)(x^2 + x + 1)$

$\therefore \quad \dfrac{1}{x^3 - 1} = \dfrac{A}{x - 1} + \dfrac{Bx + C}{x^2 + x + 1}$

Multiply by $(x - 1)(x^2 + x + 1)$

Then $1 = A(x^2 + x + 1) + Bx(x - 1) + C(x - 1)$

Put $x = 1$, $\quad 3A = 1 \quad$ or $\quad A = \dfrac{1}{3}$

$\quad\quad x = 0, \quad A - C = 1 \quad$ or $\quad C = -\dfrac{2}{3}$

$\quad\quad x = -1, \quad A + 2B - 2C = 1 \quad$ or $\quad B = -\dfrac{1}{3}$

Hence $\displaystyle \int \frac{1}{x^3 - 1} \, dx = \frac{1}{3} \cdot \int \frac{1}{x - 1} \, dx - \frac{1}{3} \int \frac{x + 2}{x^2 + x + 1} \, dx$

$\quad\quad\quad\quad\quad\quad\quad\quad = \dfrac{1}{3} \log(x - 1) - \dfrac{1}{3} I$, where

$I = \displaystyle \int \frac{x + 2}{x^2 + x + 1} \, dx = \int \frac{\frac{1}{2}(2x + 1) + \frac{3}{2}}{x^2 + x + 1} \, dx$

$\quad\quad\quad\quad\quad\quad = \dfrac{1}{2} \displaystyle \int \frac{2x + 1}{x^2 + x + 1} + \frac{3}{2} \cdot \int \frac{1}{(x + \frac{1}{2})^2 + \frac{3}{4}} \, dx$

$\quad\quad\quad\quad\quad\quad = \dfrac{1}{2} \log(x^2 + x + 1) + \sqrt{3} \tan^{-1}\left[\dfrac{(x + \frac{1}{2})}{\sqrt{3}/2}\right]$

$\therefore \displaystyle \int \frac{1}{x^3 - 1} \, dx = \frac{1}{3} \log(x - 1) - \frac{1}{6} \log(x^2 + x + 1) - \frac{\sqrt{3}}{3} \cdot \tan^{-1} \frac{2x + 1}{\sqrt{3}} + C$

SUMMARY: To integrate $\displaystyle \int \frac{A(x)}{P(x)} \, dx$

1. If degree of $A(x) \geqslant P(x)$, then divide $A(x)$ by $P(x)$
2. If deg. $A(x) <$ deg. $P(x)$, then factorise $P(x)$ completely.
   (a) For each linear factor $(x - a)$, write the corresponding term $\dfrac{A}{x - a}$
   (b) For $(x - a)^n$, write $\dfrac{A}{(x - a)} + \dfrac{B}{(x - a)^2} + \ldots + \dfrac{C}{(x - a)^n}$
3. If $ax^2 + bx + c$ occurs, then write $\dfrac{Ax + B}{ax^2 + bx + c}$

Warning: Do not use A or B twice; all constants must be different.

Exercise 2G

Use the method of PARTIAL FRACTIONS to find:

1. $\displaystyle\int \frac{1}{(x-1)(x-2)}\,dx$

2. $\displaystyle\int \frac{x+2}{(x-1)(x-2)}\,dx$

3. $\displaystyle\int \frac{x^2+2}{(x-1)(x-2)}\,dx$

4. $\displaystyle\int \frac{2x+3}{x^2-7x+12}\,dx$

5. $\displaystyle\int \frac{x^3+5}{x^2+x}\,dx$

6. $\displaystyle\int \frac{x^2}{(x-2)(x+2)(x+3)}\,dx$

7. $\displaystyle\int \frac{1}{(x+1)(x^2+4)}\,dx$

8. $\displaystyle\int \frac{x^3+2}{x(x^2+1)}\,dx$

9. $\displaystyle\int \frac{1}{x(x-1)^2}\,dx$

10. $\displaystyle\int \frac{2x\,dx}{(x-2)^2(x+1)}$

11. $\displaystyle\int \frac{x\,dx}{x^4-1}$

12. $\displaystyle\int \frac{x^3}{x^3-1}\,dx$

13. $\displaystyle\int \frac{dx}{(x+2)^2(x^2+4)}$

14. $\displaystyle\int \frac{dx}{(x^2+1)(x^2+2)}$

15. $\displaystyle\int \frac{x^2-1}{(x-2)(x^2+x+2)}\,dx$

$\left[\text{Hint: let } x^2 = y \text{ only for decomposing } \dfrac{1}{(y+1)(y+2)} \text{ into partial fractions}\right]$

Evaluate the following:

16. $\displaystyle\int_3^4 \frac{dx}{x^2-3x+2}$

17. $\displaystyle\int_1^2 \frac{dx}{x^2(x+2)}$

18. $\displaystyle\int_0^1 \frac{2x\,dx}{(x+2)(x^2+4)}$

19. $\displaystyle\int_0^{\pi/4} \frac{\cos\theta\,d\theta}{2+\sin\theta}$

(Hint: $2+\sin\theta = y$)

20. $\displaystyle\int_0^{\pi/2} \frac{\cos\theta\,d\theta}{\sin^2\theta + 5\sin\theta + 6}$

(Hint: $y = \sin\theta$)

21. $\displaystyle\int \frac{1}{(x^2-1)^2}\,dx$

(Hint: $(x^2-1)^2 = (x+1)^2(x-1)^2$)

22. $\displaystyle\int \frac{1}{1+\sqrt{x}}\,dx$ (Let $U = \sqrt{x}$)

2.10 Completing the Square (Integration)

Integrand of the type involving the irreducible quadratic $ax^2 + bx + c$ over the real field is easily found by completing the square and then using one of the following:

1. $\displaystyle\int \frac{dx}{x^2 + a^2} = \frac{1}{a} \cdot \tan^{-1}\left(\frac{x}{a}\right)$
2. $\displaystyle\int \frac{dx}{\sqrt{x^2 \pm a^2}} = \log(x + \sqrt{x^2 \pm a^2})$
3. $\displaystyle\int \frac{dx}{\sqrt{a^2 - x^2}} = \sin^{-1}\left(\frac{x}{a}\right)$

Example: (1)

Find $\displaystyle\int \frac{1}{x^2 - 4x + 5}\, dx$

Solution:

$x^2 - 4x + 5 = (x-2)^2 + 1 = U^2 + 1^2, \quad U = x - 2$

$\therefore I = \displaystyle\int \frac{dU}{U^2 + 1^2} = \tan^{-1} U + C = \tan^{-1}(x - 2) + C$

Example: (2)

$\displaystyle\int \frac{dx}{\sqrt{4x - x^2}}$

Solution:

$4x - x^2 = -(x^2 - 4x + 4 - 4)$

$\qquad = 4 - (x - 2)^2$

$\qquad = 4 - U^2, \quad U = x - 2$

$\therefore I = \displaystyle\int \frac{dU}{\sqrt{4 - U^2}}$

$\qquad = \sin^{-1} \frac{U}{2} + C$

$\qquad = \sin^{-1} \frac{(x - 2)}{2} + C$

Example: (3) $\quad \int \dfrac{2x + 3}{\sqrt{x^2 + 2x + 3}} \, dx$

Solution:

$x^2 + 2x + 3 = (x + 1)^2 + 2 = U^2 + 2$

Also $\dfrac{d}{dx}(x^2 + 2x + 3) = 2x + 2$

Rearranging:

$$I = \int \dfrac{2x + 2 + 1}{\sqrt{x^2 + 2x + 3}}$$

$$= \int \dfrac{(2x + 2)\,dx}{\sqrt{x^2 + 2x + 3}} + \int \dfrac{1}{\sqrt{(x+1)^2 + 2}} \, dx$$

$$= I_1 + I_2$$

For I_1, let $z = x^2 + 2x + 3$, $\quad \dfrac{dz}{dx} = 2x + 2$

For I_2, let $U = x + 1$

$$\therefore \quad I = \int \dfrac{dz}{\sqrt{z}} + \int \dfrac{dU}{\sqrt{U^2 + 2}}$$

$$= 2\sqrt{z} + \log(U + \sqrt{U^2 + 2}) + C$$

$$\therefore \quad I = 2\sqrt{x^2 + 2x + 3} + \log(x + 1 + \sqrt{x^2 + 2x + 3}) + C$$

Example: (4) $\quad \int \dfrac{x^2}{x^2 - 4x + 6} \, dx$,

Divide out

$I = \int \left[1 + \dfrac{4x - 6}{x^2 - 4x + 6} \right] dx$, $\quad \dfrac{d}{dx}(x^2 - 4x + 6) = 2x - 4$

$$= \int \left[1 + \dfrac{2(2x - 4)}{x^2 - 4x + 6} + \dfrac{2}{(x - 2)^2 + 2} \right] dx, \quad U = x - 2$$

$$= x + 2\log(x^2 - 4x + 6) + 2 \int \dfrac{dU}{U^2 + 2}$$

$$= x + 2\log(x^2 - 4x + 6) + \sqrt{2} \tan^{-1} \dfrac{(x - 2)}{\sqrt{2}} + C$$

Exercise 2H

Find:

1. $\displaystyle\int \frac{1}{x^2 + 2x + 4}\, dx$

2. $\displaystyle\int \frac{2x}{x^2 + 2x + 4}\, dx$

3. $\displaystyle\int \frac{x^2 + 1}{x^2 + 2x + 4}\, dx$

4. $\displaystyle\int \frac{dx}{\sqrt{x^2 + 2x + 4}}$

5. $\displaystyle\int \frac{x\, dx}{\sqrt{x^2 + 2x + 4}}$

6. $\displaystyle\int \frac{dx}{\sqrt{2x - x^2}}$

7. $\displaystyle\int \frac{dx}{2x^2 + x + 5}$

8. $\displaystyle\int \frac{x + 2}{\sqrt{x^2 + x + 1}}\, dx$

9. $\displaystyle\int \frac{x\, dx}{\sqrt{6x - x^2}}$

10. $\displaystyle\int \frac{dx}{\sqrt{2 - x - x^2}}$

11. $\displaystyle\int \frac{x\, dx}{\sqrt{x^4 - 3x^2 + 1}}$

12. $\displaystyle\int \frac{x\, dx}{\sqrt{1 - 2x - x^2}}$

13. $\displaystyle\int \frac{(1 - 2x)\, dx}{\sqrt{x^2 + 2x + 3}}$

14. Show that:

$$\int_0^1 \frac{dx}{\sqrt{x^2 + 2x + 2}} = \log_e \left| \frac{2 + \sqrt{5}}{1 + \sqrt{2}} \right|$$

15. Evaluate:

$$\int_0^1 \frac{dx}{x^2 + 4x + 5}$$

16. $\displaystyle\int_0^{\sqrt{3}} \frac{x + 12}{x^2 + 9}\, dx$

17. $\displaystyle\int_0^1 \frac{dx}{\sqrt{2x - x^2}}$

18. $\displaystyle\int \frac{x+1}{\sqrt{x(1-x)}}\, dx$

19. $\displaystyle\int \sqrt{\frac{1-x}{1+x}}\, dx$ $\left[\text{Hint: } I = \displaystyle\int \frac{1-x}{\sqrt{(1-x)(1+x)}}\, dx = \displaystyle\int \frac{1-x}{\sqrt{1-x^2}}\, dx\right]$

20. $\displaystyle\int \sqrt{\frac{x}{x+2}}\, dx$

2.11 Integration: Special Properties

Use of the following formulas simplifies the work and saves time.

1. $\displaystyle\int_0^a f(x)\, dx = \int_0^a f(a-x)\, dx$

2. $\displaystyle\int_{-a}^a f(x)\, dx = 2\int_0^a f(x)\, dx$, if $f(x) = f(-x)$, i.e. $f(x)$ is an even function.

3. $\displaystyle\int_{-a}^a f(x)\, dx = 0$, if $f(x) = -f(-x)$, i.e. $f(x)$ is an odd function.

Proof:

1. Put $a - x = U$, when $x = 0$, $U = a$
   $x = a$, $U = 0$

∴ RHS $= \displaystyle\int_0^a f(a-x)\, dx = \int_a^0 f(U)(-dU) = -\int_a^0 f(U)\, du = \int_0^a f(U)$

But $\displaystyle\int_0^a f(U)\, du = \int_0^a f(x)\, dx$

LHS $= \displaystyle\int_0^a f(x)\, dx =$ RHS.

2. The graph of an even function is symmetrical about the y-axis, i.e. $f(x) = f(-x)$.

$\therefore \int_{-a}^{a} f(x)\,dx$ = Area PABQ
$\qquad\qquad\quad$ = 2 x Area MOBQ
$\qquad\qquad\quad$ = $2 \int_{0}^{a} f(x)\,dx$

Thus for an even function $\int_{-a}^{a} f(x)\,dx = 2 \int_{0}^{a} f(x)\,dx$

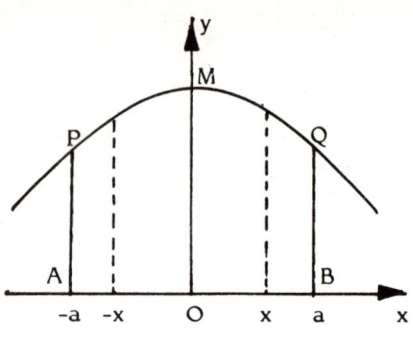

Fig. 2

3. The graph of an odd function has a point symmetry about O.

Area OBA = - Area ODC

$\therefore \int_{-a}^{a} f(x)\,dx = 0$ (as an integral)

Thus for an odd function

$\int_{-a}^{a} f(x)\,dx = 0$

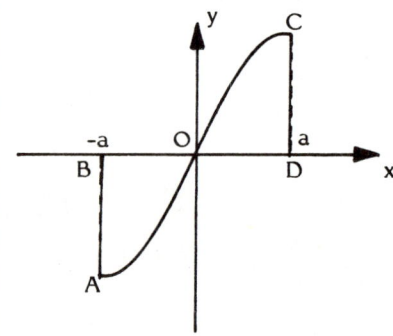

Fig. 3

Note:

Though as a pure integral $\int_{-a}^{a} f(x)\,dx = 0$, if $f(x)$ is odd, we need to be careful if the area bounded by the curve $y = f(x)$ and the x-axis is required. Then we use:

$A = A_1 + A_2 = \left| \int_{-a}^{0} f(x)\,dx \right| + \left| \int_{0}^{a} f(x)\,dx \right| = 2 \left| \int_{0}^{a} f(x)\,dx \right|$

WORKED EXAMPLES

Evaluate:

1. $\int_{-2}^{2} x^2 \, dx$
2. $\int_{-\pi}^{\pi} \sin x \, dx$

Solution:

1. $f(x) = x^2$ is an even function as $f(-x) = (-x)^2 = x^2$

   $\therefore \int_{-2}^{2} x^2 \, dx = 2 \int_{0}^{2} x^2 \, dx = 2 \left[\frac{x^3}{3}\right]_{0}^{2} = \frac{16}{3}$

2. $f(x) = \sin x$ and $f(-x) = \sin(-x) = -\sin x$

   $\therefore f(x)$ is an odd function.

   $\therefore \int_{-\pi}^{\pi} \sin x \, dx = 0$

Note: The area between the curve and x-axis from $x = -\pi$ to $x = \pi$ is given by

$A = 2 \int_{0}^{\pi} \sin x \, dx = 2[-\cos x]_{0}^{\pi}$
$= 2 \times 2$
$= 4$

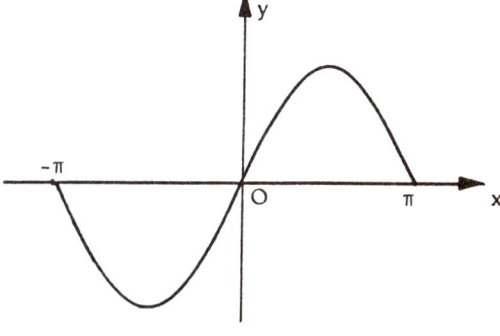

Fig. 4

3. Use the result $\int_{0}^{a} f(x) \, dx = \int_{0}^{a} f(a-x) \, dx$ to evaluate

   (a) $\int_{0}^{\pi/2} \frac{\sin x}{\sin x + \cos x} \, dx$

   (b) $\int_{0}^{2} x^2 \sqrt{(2-x)} \, dx$

Solution:

(a) $I = \int_{0}^{\pi/2} \frac{\sin x}{\sin x + \cos x} \, dx$ ... (1),   Replace x by $\frac{\pi}{2} - x$

$\therefore I = \int_{0}^{\pi/2} \frac{\sin(\pi/2 - x)}{\sin(\pi/2 - x) + \cos(\pi/2 - x)} = \int_{0}^{\pi/2} \frac{\cos x \, dx}{\cos x + \sin x}$ ... (2)

(cont. next page)

Add (1) and (2): $\therefore 2I = \int_0^{\pi/2} \dfrac{\sin x + \cos x}{\sin x + \cos x} dx$

$$= \int_0^{\pi/2} dx$$

$$= \dfrac{\pi}{2}$$

$$\therefore I = \dfrac{\pi}{4}$$

(b) $\int_0^2 x^2 (2-x)^{1/2} dx = \int_0^2 (2-x)^2 [2-(2-x)]^{1/2} dx$

$$= \int_0^2 (4 - 4x + x^2) \cdot x^{1/2} dx$$

$$= \left[\dfrac{8}{3} x^{3/2} - \dfrac{8}{5} x^{5/2} + \dfrac{2}{7} x^{7/2} \right]_0^2$$

$$= \dfrac{128\sqrt{2}}{105}$$

---

4.   Using the property of odd and even functions, evaluate:

(a) $\int_{-1}^{1} \tan^5 x \, dx$ (b) $\int_{-2}^{2} \dfrac{x^3}{x^4 + 1} dx$

Solution:

(a) $f(x) = \tan^5 x$

$\therefore f(-x) = [\tan(-x)]^5$

$\qquad = [-\tan x]^5$

$\qquad = -\tan^5 x$

$\qquad = -f(x)$

$\therefore f(x)$ is an odd function

$\int_{-1}^{1} \tan^5 x \, dx = 0$

(b) $f(x) = \dfrac{x^3}{x^4 + 1}$

$f(-x) = \dfrac{(-x)^3}{(-x)^4 + 1} = \dfrac{-x^3}{x^4 + 1}$

$\therefore f(-x) = -f(x)$

$\therefore f(x)$ is an odd function

$\therefore \int_{-2}^{2} \dfrac{x^3}{x^4 + 1} dx = 0$

Exercise 21

1. Using the properties of the odd and the even functions evaluate:

(a) $\int_{-2}^{2} x^3 \, dx$

(b) $\int_{-\pi/4}^{\pi/4} \cos x \, dx$

(c) $\int_{-1}^{1} \sin^3 x \, dx$

(d) $\int_{-1}^{1} x^2 \tan x \, dx$

(e) $\int_{-1}^{1} (x^2 + x^2 \sin x) \, dx$

(f) $\int_{-3}^{3} \frac{x^5}{x^4 + 1} \, dx$

(g) $\int_{-2}^{2} (x \cos^2 x - 100 x^5 + 2) \, dx$

(h) $\int_{-\pi/2}^{\pi/2} \sin^3 x \cos^4 x \, dx$

2. Prove that $\int_{0}^{a} f(x) \, dx = \int_{0}^{a} f(a - x) \, dx$ and evaluate

(a) $\int_{0}^{\pi/2} \frac{\sqrt{\sin x}}{\sqrt{\sin x} + \sqrt{\cos x}} \, dx$

(b) $\int_{0}^{1} x^3 (1 - x)^6 \, dx$

(c) $\int_{0}^{\pi/2} x \left(\frac{\pi}{2} - x\right) \cos^2 x$

(d) $\int_{0}^{\pi/2} \cos^2 x \, dx$

(e) $\int_{0}^{1} 10100 \, x(1 - x)^{99} \, dx$

3. Using the properties of odd/even functions, evaluate:

(a) $\int_{-1}^{1} \frac{x^2 + x^3 + \sin x}{1 + x^2} \, dx$

(b) $\int_{0}^{\pi} \frac{\sin x \, dx}{a + b \cos^2 x}$, $a > 0$, $b > 0$

4. (a) Show that if $f(x)$ is even and $f'(x)$ exists, then $f'(x)$ is odd.

   (b) If $f(x)$ is odd and continuous for all x, and $b > a > 0$, use a sketch to explain why $\int_{-a}^{b} f(x) \, dx = \int_{a}^{b} f(x) \, dx$

Exercise 2J   (REVISION)

Use any suitable method. Some integrals can be found in more than one way. Integrate the following:

1. $\int \dfrac{x}{\sqrt{x-2}}\, dx$

2. $\int_0^1 x^2 \sqrt{1-x}\, dx$

3. $\int_1^2 \dfrac{e^{2x}}{e^x - 1}\, dx$, using $u = e^x - 1$

4. $\int_1^2 x^4 \sin(x^5)\, dx$

5. $\int \dfrac{\sin 2x}{a^2 + b^2 \sin^2 x}\, dx$
   (Hint: $t = a^2 + b^2 \sin^2 x$)

6. $\int \dfrac{1}{a^2 \cos^2 x + b^2 \sin^2 x}\, dx$
   (Hint: Divide by $\cos^2 x$)

7. $\int \dfrac{dx}{2(1+x)\sqrt{x}}$

8. $\int \dfrac{x}{x^4 + 1}\, dx$ (Hint: $U = x^2$)

9. $\int \dfrac{dx}{1 + e^x}$

10. $\int \dfrac{1 + e^x}{1 - e^x}\, dx$ (Hint: $t = e^x$)

11. $\int_2^3 x^2 \sin x\, dx$

12. $\int x^2 \log x\, dx$

13. $\int x\sqrt{1+x}\, dx$

14. $\int \dfrac{dx}{x^2 \sqrt{1+x^2}}$

15. $\int \dfrac{dx}{x\sqrt{x^2 - 1}}$

16. $\int \dfrac{e^x}{1 + e^{2x}}\, dx$

17. $\int \dfrac{dx}{x^2 + x + 5}$

18. $\int x \sin^{-1} x\, dx$

19. $\int \dfrac{dx}{4x^2 + 4x + 5}$

20. $\int \dfrac{dx}{x^2 + 4x - 5}$

21. $\int \dfrac{dx}{1 + 3x - x^2}$

22. $\int \dfrac{dx}{\sqrt{4x^2 + 4x + 5}}$

23. $\int \dfrac{3x + 2}{4x^2 + 4x + 5}\, dx$

24. $\int \dfrac{3x + 2}{\sqrt{4x^2 + 4x + 5}}\, dx$

25. $\int \dfrac{dx}{5 + 4\sin x}$

26. $\int \dfrac{3\sin x + 2\cos x}{3\cos x + 2\sin x}\, dx$
    [Hint: $3\sin x + 2\cos x \equiv$
    $A(3\cos x + 2\sin x) + B(-3\sin x + 2\cos x)$]

27. $\int \sqrt{\dfrac{a+x}{a-x}}\, dx$ (Hint: multiply by $\sqrt{a+x}$)

28. $\int \sqrt{x^2 - x + 1}\, dx$

29. $\int \dfrac{dx}{2 - 3\cos 2x}$ ($\cos 2x = 1 - 2\sin^2 x$, divide by $\cos^2 x$)

30. $\int \dfrac{dx}{(3\cos x + 2\sin x)^2}$ (Hint: divide by $\cos^2 x$)

31. $\int \dfrac{\cos x}{5 - 3\cos x}\, dx$

32. $\int \cos \sqrt{x}\, dx$ (Hint: $x = t^2$)

33. $\int \dfrac{2x + 5}{x^2 - x - 2}\, dx$

34. $\int \dfrac{x^3}{x^2 - 3x + 2}\, dx$

35. $\int \dfrac{2x\, dx}{(x^2 + 3)(x^2 + 1)}$, $(x^2 = t)$

36. $\int \dfrac{dx}{x - x^3}$ $[x - x^3 = x(1-x)(1+x)]$

37. $\int \dfrac{dx}{1 + 3e^x + 2e^{2x}}$, $(e^x = t)$

38. $\int \dfrac{dx}{(1 + x + x^2 + x^3)}$ (Factorise)

39. $\int \dfrac{\cos x\, dx}{(1 + \sin x)(2 + \sin x)}$

40. $\int \dfrac{dx}{\sin x + \sin 2x}$

(Multiply by $\sin x$, then $t = \cos x$)

41. Show that $\int_0^{\pi/2} \sin^n \theta\, d\theta = \dfrac{n-1}{n} \int_0^{\pi/2} \sin^{n-2} \theta\, d\theta$, and hence show that

$\int_0^{\pi/2} \sin^4 \theta\, d\theta = \dfrac{3\pi}{16}$

42. Apply successively the result of exercise 41 to show that

$\int_0^{\pi/2} \sin^n \theta\, d\theta = \dfrac{(n-1)(n-3)\ldots 4.2}{n(n-2)\ldots 3.1}$ if n is odd

and $= \dfrac{(n-1)(n-3)\ldots 3.1}{n(n-2)\ldots 4.2} \cdot \dfrac{\pi}{2}$ if n is even.

43. Establish the reduction formula (using integration by parts)

$\int x^n \sin bx\, dx = -\dfrac{x^n}{b} \cos bx + \dfrac{n}{b} \int x^{n-1} \cos bx\, dx$,

hence evaluate: $\int_0^{\pi/4} x^2 \sin 2x\, dx$

44. Establish the formula (using integration by parts)

$\int x^n \sin^{-1} x\, dx = \dfrac{x^{n+1}}{n+1} \sin^{-1} x - \dfrac{1}{n+1} \int \dfrac{x^{n+1}}{\sqrt{1-x^2}}\, dx + C$

Hence find $\int_0^1 x \sin^{-1} x\, dx$

45. Establish the reduction formula

$\int \cot^n dx = -\dfrac{\cot^{n-1} x}{n-1} - \int \cot^{n-2} x\, dx$

[Hint: $\cot^n x = \cot^{n-2} x (\csc^2 x - 1)$]

CHAPTER 3 VOLUMES

3.1 Formulas for Volumes

In elementary calculus, we have the following two formulas for calculating the volumes of revolution.

1. The volume of revolution generated by the region bounded by the curve $y = f(x)$, above the x-axis, between $x = a$ and $x = b$ is given by:

$$V = \int_a^b \pi y^2 \, dx \quad \text{(Fig. 1)}$$

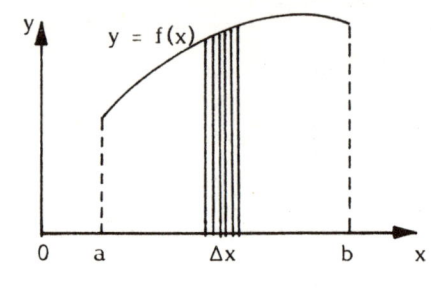

Fig. 1

2. The volume of revolution generated by the region bounded by the curve $x = f(y)$, between $y = a$ and $y = b$ is given by:

$$V = \int_a^b \pi x^2 \, dy \quad \text{(Fig. 2)}$$

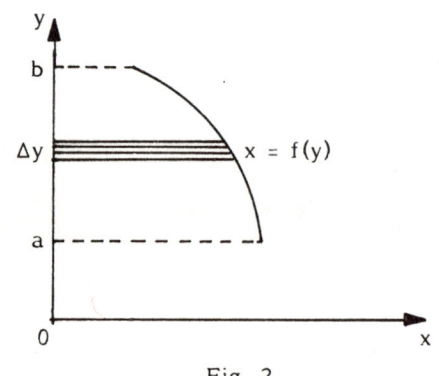

Fig. 2

In many cases, it is necessary to calculate volumes whose boundaries are not surfaces of revolution and hence the two formulas stated above can not be used. For example we cannot find the volume of a pyramid or a doughnut shaped solid by these two formulas.

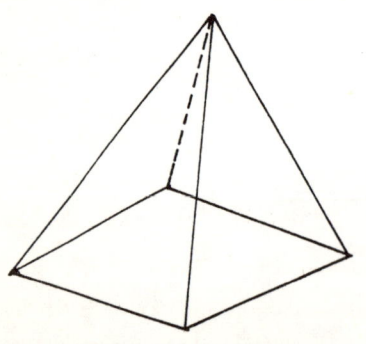

Fig. 3: Pyramid

Fig. 4: Doughnut

In what follows, the formulas for volumes would be derived intuitively by means of simple examples.

The volume of a solid of uniform cross-section A and height h is given by

$$V = A \cdot h$$

If h is very small, we have an element of volume given by

$$\Delta V = A \cdot \Delta z$$

where $h = \Delta z$

Let us calculate the volume of the solid (pyramid) shown in the figure.

We slice the whole pyramid by n planes parallel to the base of pyramid.

Let the distance between two successive planes be Δz.

We find the area $A(z)$ of one of the cross-sections at a distance z from the vertex V. Quite clearly $A(z)$ is a function of z.

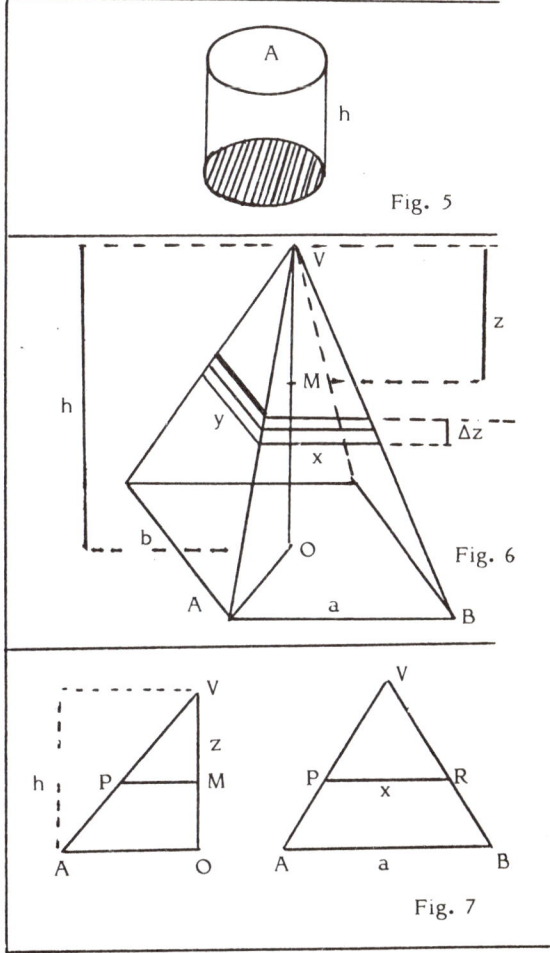

Fig. 5

Fig. 6

Fig. 7

We express $A(z)$ in terms of the sides a and b of the base. From the two similar triangles shown in the diagram, we have:

$$\left. \begin{array}{l} \dfrac{x}{a} = \dfrac{z}{h} \qquad \text{i.e.} \quad x = \dfrac{az}{h} \\ \text{Similarly} \qquad\qquad y = \dfrac{bz}{h} \end{array} \right\} \quad \ldots\ (1)$$

∴   A(z) = area of the rectangular cross-section at P

$$= x \cdot y$$

$$= \frac{za}{h} \cdot \frac{zb}{h} \qquad \text{[from relation (1)]}$$

$$= \frac{abz^2}{h^2}$$

The volume of the pyramid is

$$V = \Sigma \Delta V = \Sigma A(z) \Delta z$$

As $n \to \infty$, $\Sigma \Delta V \to V$ and $\Sigma A(z) \Delta z = \int_0^h A(z) dz$

∴ $$V = \int_0^h A(z) dz$$

$$= \int_0^h \frac{abz^2}{h^2} dz$$

$$= \frac{ab}{h^2} \left[\frac{z^3}{3} \right]_0^h$$

$$= \frac{abh^3}{3h^2}$$

∴ $$V = \frac{1}{3} abh \qquad \ldots (1)$$

Now from solid geometry, we know that the volume of the pyramid is given by

$$V = \frac{1}{3} B \cdot h$$

where B = area of the base = ab

The formula $V = \int_a^b A(z) dz$ used above is quite general and the following general statement can be made: (see diagram above)

The volume of a solid whose cross-sectional area is a continuous function A(z), is given by:

$$V = \int_a^b A(z) dz$$

where z is the distance of the cross-section from the pre-determined point (or a plane). The limits of integration are chosen to include the entire volume. To evaluate V, we must express A(z) and dz in terms of a single variable.

We note that the general formula for the volume $V = \int_a^b A(z)\, dz$ includes the volumes of revolution given by

$$V = \int_a^b \pi y^2 \, dx .$$

In the diagram:

$$z = x$$
$$A(z) = A(x)$$
$$= \text{area of the disc at a distance } x \text{ from the origin}$$
$$= \pi y^2$$

Hence $V = \int_a^b A(z)\, dz = \int_a^b \pi y^2 \, dx .$

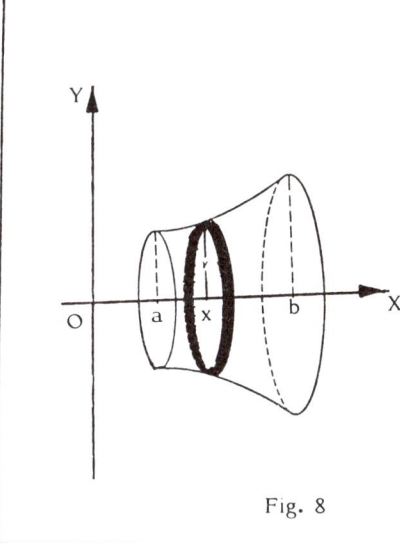

Fig. 8

Note that the volume of revolution given by the last formula is also known as a <u>DISC</u> method.

An Important Method

Finding lengths from the given diagram is of particular interest in calculating the required volume. An elegant method is presented below and you will be asked to derive the same result by using similar triangles.

<u>Example: (1)</u>
Find the length y in terms of h, from the diagram which shows an isosceles trapezium.

<u>Solution:</u>
We observe that:
$$y = 4 \text{ when } h = 0$$
$$y = 12 \text{ when } h = 5$$

Since y is always proportional to h, y is a linear function of h

$\therefore \quad y = mh + b$

Substituting the given values

$$b = 4 \quad \text{and} \quad m = \frac{8}{5}$$

$$y = \frac{8h}{5} + 4$$

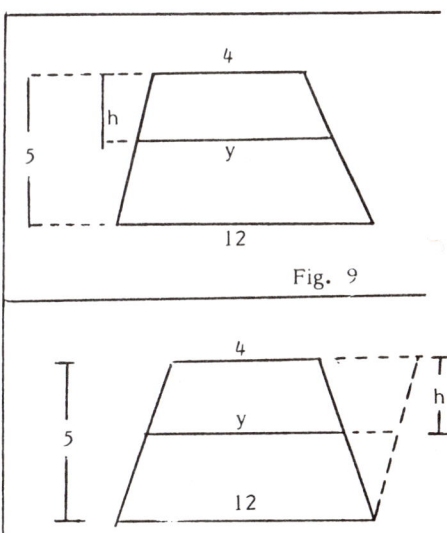

Fig. 9

Fig. 10

Example: (2)

Using the intercept properties of parallel lines, prove the above result. (Fig. 10)

Example: (3)

Find the volume of the block shown in Fig. 3.

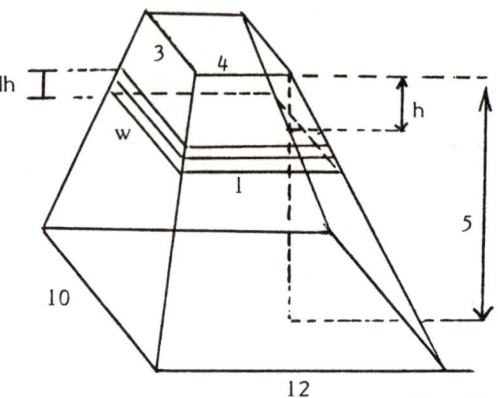

Fig. 11

Solution:

We consider the block to be made up of horizontal laminas of length l, width w and thickness dh.

Hence, $V = \int_0^5 wl\, dh$

$= \int_0^5 (\frac{7h}{5} + 3)(\frac{8h}{5} + 4)\, dh$

$= \frac{4}{25} \int_0^5 (14h^2 + 65h + 75)\, dh$

$= \frac{4}{25} \left[\frac{14h^3}{3} + \frac{65h^2}{2} + 75h \right]_0^5$

$= 283$ to 3 significant figures

$w = \frac{7h}{5} + 3$

$l = \frac{8h}{5} + 4$

The students familiar with the prismoidal formula

$V = \frac{h}{6}(A + B + 4M)$ can verify the result.

$A = 3 \times 4 = 12$

$B = 10 \times 12 = 120$

$M = (\frac{10 + 3}{2})(\frac{12 + 4}{2}) = 208$

$\therefore\ V = \frac{5}{6}(12 + 120 + 208 \times 4) = 283$

Example: (4)

The base of a certain solid is the circle $x^2 + y^2 = 4$.
Each plane section of this solid cut out by a plane perpendicular to the y-axis is an equilateral triangle with one side in the base of the solid. Find the volume.

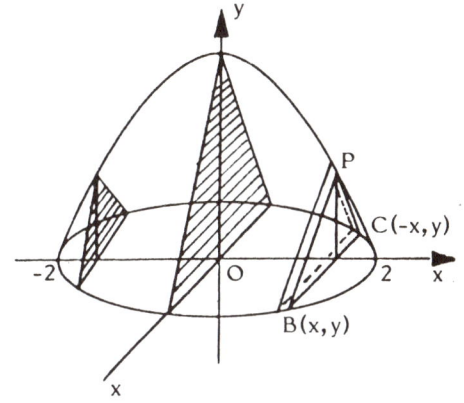

Fig. 12

Solution:

A typical slice is an equilateral triangle PBC.

$$BC = 2x$$
$$\begin{aligned}
A &= \text{Area of } \triangle PCB \\
&= \tfrac{1}{2} PC \cdot PB \sin 60° \\
&= \tfrac{1}{2} \cdot 2x \cdot 2x \cdot \tfrac{\sqrt{3}}{2} \\
&= \sqrt{3}\, x^2
\end{aligned}$$

$$\begin{aligned}
V &= \int_a^b A(x)\, dy \\
&= \int \sqrt{3}\, x^2 \, dy \qquad , \qquad x^2 + y^2 = 4 \\
&= \int_{-2}^{2} \sqrt{3}(4 - y^2)\, dy \qquad \text{The limits are the ends of the diameter.}\\
&= 2 \int_0^2 \sqrt{3}(4 - y^2)\, dy \qquad \text{(Owing to symmetry)}\\
&= 2\sqrt{3} \left[4y - \tfrac{y^3}{3} \right]_0^2 \\
&= \tfrac{32\sqrt{3}}{3}
\end{aligned}$$

Example: (5)

Find the volumes generated when the areas bounded by the given curves and lines are rotated about the x-axis.

(a) $y = x + 1$, $x = 2$, $y = 0$

(b) $y = \cos x$, $x = 0$, $x = \pi$

(c) $y = 2x - x^2$, $y = 0$

Solutions:

Since the rotation is about the x-axis, we use the formula $V = \int_a^b \pi y^2 \, dx$

(a) $y = x + 1$

∴ The limits are $a = -1, b = 2$

∴ $V = \pi \int_{-1}^{2} y^2 \, dx = \pi \int_{-1}^{2} (x^2 + 2x + 1) \, dx$

$= \pi \left[\frac{x^3}{3} + x^2 + x \right]_{-1}^{2}$

$= 9\pi$

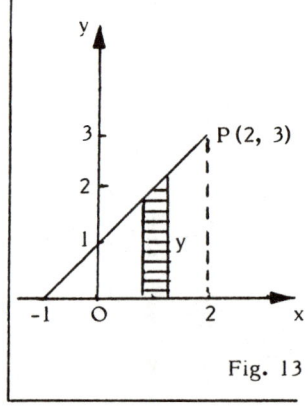

Fig. 13

Verify: V = volume of a cone = $\frac{\pi r^2 h}{3} = \frac{\pi \times 9 \times 3}{3} = 9\pi$

(b) $y = \cos x$, $a = 0$, $b = \pi$

$y^2 = \cos^2 x = \frac{1}{2}(1 + \cos 2x)$

∴ $V = \frac{1}{2} \pi \int_0^{\pi} (1 + \cos 2x) \, dx$

$= \frac{\pi}{2} \left[x + \frac{1}{2} \sin 2x \right]_0^{\pi}$

$= \frac{\pi^2}{2}$

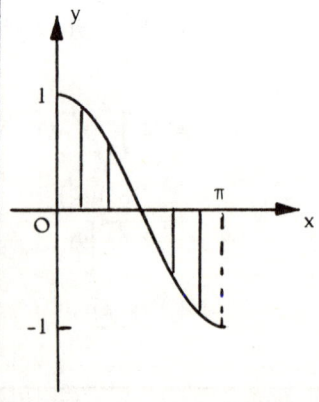

Fig. 14

(c) $y = 2x - x^2$, $y = 0$

Solve these: $x = 0$ or $x = 2$

$$V = \int_0^2 \pi y^2 \, dx$$

$$= \pi \int_0^2 (4x^2 - 4x^3 + x^4) \, dx$$

$$= \pi \left[\frac{4x^3}{3} - x^4 + \frac{x^5}{5} \right]_0^2$$

$$= \frac{16\pi}{15}$$

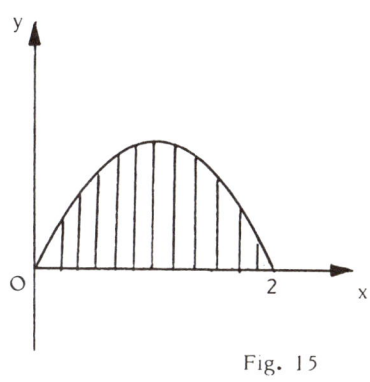

Fig. 15

Example: (6)

Find the volume generated when the area bounded by the curve $y = x^2$, $y = 2$ and $x = 0$ is rotated

(a)   about the y-axis   (b)   about the line $y = 2$

Solution:

(a)   A typical strip is shown and it will generate a volume

$$\Delta V = \pi x^2 \Delta y$$

$$\therefore V = \int_0^2 \pi x^2 \, dy, \quad x^2 = y$$

$$= \pi \int_0^2 y \, dy$$

$$= \pi \left[\frac{y^2}{2} \right]_0^2$$

$$\therefore V = 2\pi$$

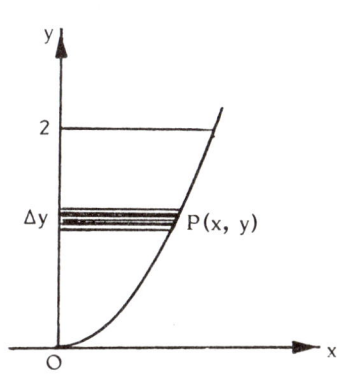

Fig. 16

(b) The typical strip has a radius

$r = y_1 - y_2 = 2 - x^2$

The volume generated when the region OABO is rotated about the line $y = 2$, is given by:

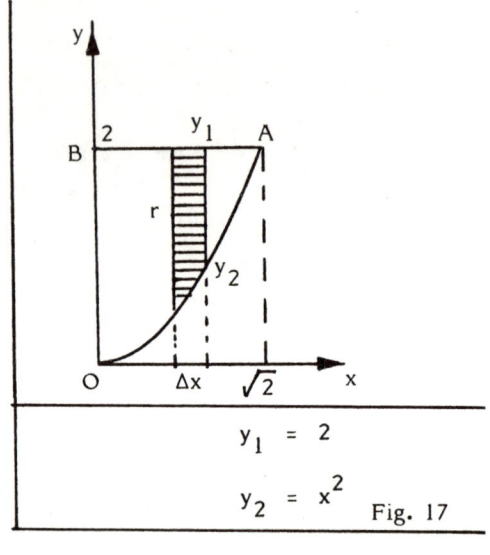

$y_1 = 2$
$y_2 = x^2$
Fig. 17

$$V = \pi \int_0^{\sqrt{2}} r^2 \, dx$$

$$= \pi \int_0^{\sqrt{2}} (2 - x^2)^2 \, dx$$

$$= \pi \int_0^{\sqrt{2}} (4 - 4x^2 + x^4) \, dx$$

$$= \pi \left[4x - \frac{4x^3}{3} + \frac{x^5}{5} \right]_0^{\sqrt{2}}$$

$$= \frac{32\sqrt{2}\,\pi}{15}$$

Note: The rotation is not about the x-axis, hence we can not use

$$V = \int_a^b \pi (y_1^2 - y_2^2) \, dx$$

Exercise 3A

For Exercises 1-10 find the volumes of revolution when the areas bounded by the given curves and lines are rotated about the x-axis.

1. $y = \sqrt{x}$, $x = 0$, $x = 2$
2. $y = x^2 + 1$, $x = 0$, $x = 2$
3. $y = x^2 - x$, $y = 0$
4. $y = \sin x$, $x = 0$, $x = \pi$
5. $y = \cos x$, $x = \frac{\pi}{4}$, $x = \frac{\pi}{2}$
6. $y = \tan x$, $x = 0$, $x = \frac{\pi}{4}$
7. $y = x^2 - 4$, $y = 0$
8. $y = \sin x \cos x$, $y = 0$, $0 \leqslant x \leqslant \frac{\pi}{2}$
9. $y = \log_e x$, $x = 1$, $x = 2$
10. $y = \frac{1}{2}(e^x + e^{-x})$, $x = 0$, $x = 1$

For Exercises 11-15 find the volumes of revolution when the areas bounded by the given curves and lines are rotated about the y-axis.

11. $x + y = 4$, $y = 0$, $y = 2$
12. $y = \sqrt{x}$, $x = 0$, $x = 4$
13. $x = 4 - y^2$, $x = 0$
14. $y = \log_e x$, $x = 1$, $x = 2$ (Hint $x = e^y$)
15. $y = \sin^{-1} x$, $x = 0$, $x = 1$ (Hint $x = \sin y$)

16. The base of a certain solid is the circle $x^2 + y^2 = 9$. If each plane section of the solid cut by a plane perpendicular to the x-axis is :

   (a) a square with one edge in the base of the solid, find the volume of the solid.

   (b) an equilateral triangle with one side in the base of the solid, find the volume.

   (c) a semi-circle with its diameter in the base of the solid, find the volume.

   (d) an isosceles right-angled triangle with the shorter side in the base, find the volume.

   (e) an isosceles right-angled triangle with its hypotenuse in the base, find the volume.

---

17. Find the volume of revolution when the region inside the ellipse $\dfrac{x^2}{a^2} + \dfrac{y^2}{b^2} = 1$ is rotated around the x-axis.

18. A rugby ball has a volume that is the same as the volume generated by rotating the region inside the ellipse $\dfrac{x^2}{25} + \dfrac{y^2}{20} = 1$ about the x-axis. Find the volume of the ball.

---

19. A solid has a base in the shape of an ellipse whose major axis is 12 units and minor axis 8 units. If each section perpendicular to the major axis is an isosceles triangle with altitude 12 units, show that the volume of the solid is 144π.

20. The base of a solid is the circle $x^2 + y^2 = 8x$ and every plane section perpendicular to the x-axis is a rectangle whose height is one third of the distance of the plane of the section from the origin. Show that the volume of the solid is $\dfrac{64\pi}{3}$.

3.2 Volumes: Shell Method

In Section 3.1, the volume of revolution was found by rotating the rectangular strips perpendicular to the axis of revolution. The elementary volume was a disc.

If the rectangular strip is parallel to the axis of revolution, a cylindrical shell is generated. A shell is a solid contained between two parallel concentric surfaces.

To find the element of volume contained in a shell of inner radius, $r = x$ and outer radius, $R = x + \Delta x$, length y, we have

$$\Delta V = \pi (R^2 - r^2) y$$
$$= \pi y (x^2 + 2x\Delta x + \Delta x^2 - x^2)$$
$$= 2\pi xy \cdot \Delta x + \pi y \cdot \Delta x^2$$

As Δx is very small, $(\Delta x)^2$ is negligible.

Hence $\Delta V \doteqdot 2\pi xy \cdot \Delta x$

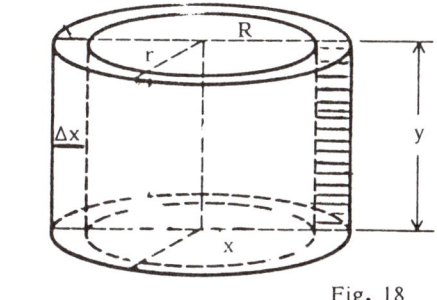

Fig. 18

To find the volume when a region bounded by the curve $y = f(x)$, $a \leqslant x \leqslant b$, and the x-axis, is rotated about the y-axis, we divide the volume into thin cylindrical shells. The cross-section of one typical shell is shown in the diagram. The element of volume is given by

$$\Delta V = 2\pi xy \Delta x$$
$$\therefore V = \int_a^b 2\pi xy \, dx,$$

where limits are chosen to include the entire volume.

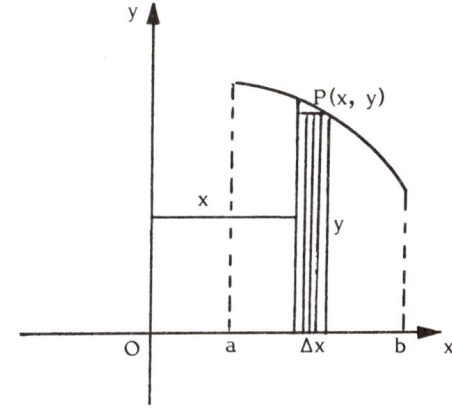

Fig. 19

Example: (1)

The region bounded by the parabola $y = x^2$, the x-axis and the line $x = 2$ is rotated about the y-axis. Find the resulting volume by using the shell method.

Solution:

The volume swept out by the typical strip (height y, breadth Δx) at a distance x from O, is given by

$\Delta V = 2\pi x \cdot y \cdot \Delta x$

The limits of integration are $a = 0$ to $b = 2$

∴ The required volume is

$$V = \int_0^2 2\pi xy \, dx \quad , \quad y = x^2$$

$$= \int_0^2 2\pi x^3 \, dx$$

$$= 8\pi$$

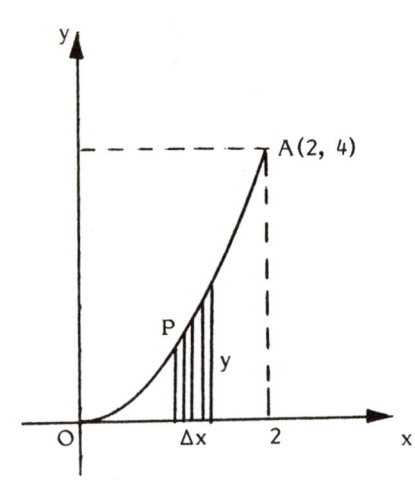

Fig. 20

The method is very general and each example requires a good deal of pre-planning and modification, so let us make it general.

Element of volume $\boxed{\Delta V = \text{Inner circumference} \times \text{Height} \times \text{Thickness}}$

Four usual cases are summarised below.

In each case the region R is rotated about a specified axis.

(a) $V_y = \int_a^b 2\pi x \cdot y \cdot dx$

gives the volume generated when the region R bounded by $y = f(x)$, $x = a$, $x = b$, $y = 0$ is rotated about the y-axis.

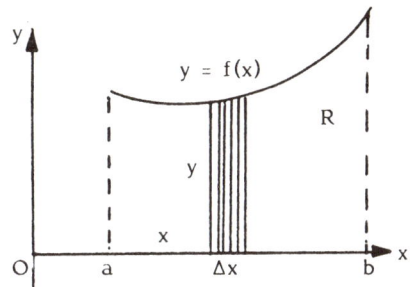

Fig. 21

(b) $V_x = \int_a^b 2\pi y \cdot x \cdot dy$

gives volume when the region bounded by the curve $x = f(y)$, lines $y = a$, $y = b$, $x = 0$ is rotated about the x-axis.

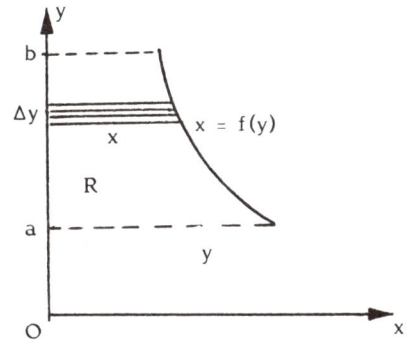

Fig. 22

(c) The region between two curves $y_1 = f(x)$ and $y_2 = g(x)$ is rotated about the y-axis. The volume is given by

$V_y = \int_a^b 2\pi x (y_1 - y_2) dx$

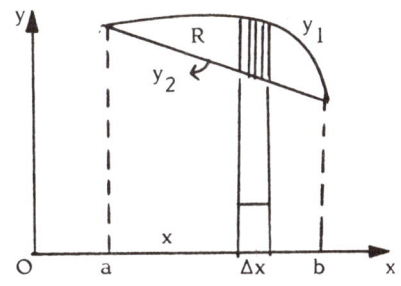

Fig. 23

(d) The region R bounded by the curve $y = f(x)$, $a \leqslant x \leqslant b$, and above the x-axis is rotated about the line $x = c$, where $c > b$, the volume of revolution is given by: $V = \int_a^b 2\pi (c - x) y\, dx$

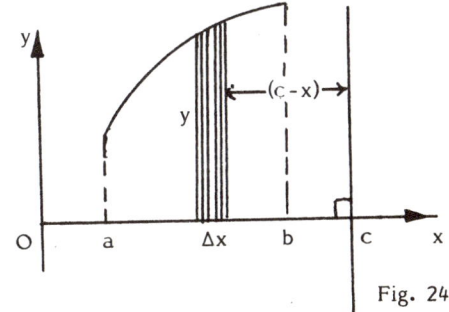

Fig. 24

Example: (2)

Find the volume of the solid formed by rotating the circle $x^2 + y^2 = 4$ about the line $x = 4$.

Solution:

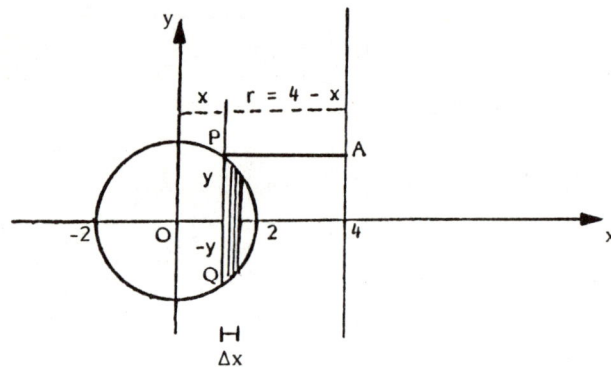

Fig. 25

$x^2 + y^2 = 4$

$y = \sqrt{4 - x^2}$

Volume of cylindrical shell at $P(x, y)$

$\Delta V = 2\pi r h \, \Delta x$

$r = 4 - x \quad$ (PA)

$h = 2y \quad$ (PQ)

Using the shell method for finding the volume, we have:

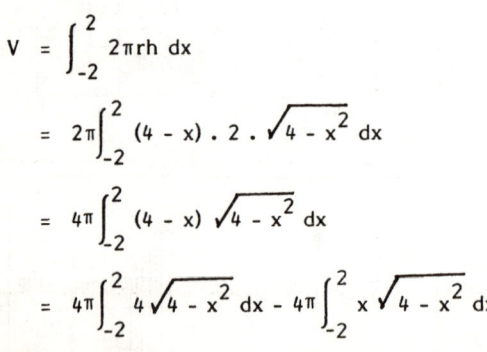

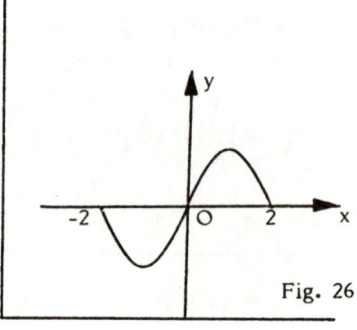

Fig. 26

The second integral is zero, since the function $f(x) = x\sqrt{4 - x^2}$ is an odd function. (See Fig. 26) For the first integral, let $x = 2\sin\theta$

$$V = 16\pi \int_{-\pi/2}^{\pi/2} \sqrt{4 - 4\sin^2\theta} \, (2\cos\theta \, d\theta)$$

$$= 64\pi \int_{-\pi/2}^{\pi/2} \cos^2\theta \, d\theta$$

$$= 32\pi \int_{-\pi/2}^{\pi/2} (1 + \cos 2\theta) \, d\theta$$

$$= 32\pi \left[\theta + \frac{1}{2}\sin 2\theta\right]_{-\pi/2}^{\pi/2}$$

$$= 32\pi^2$$

3.3 Volumes: Washer Method

A washer is a small hollow cylinder (with small height). If the radii of two concentric circles are R and r, and the height of the washer Δy, then the volume of the washer is

$\Delta V = \pi (R^2 - r^2) \Delta y$

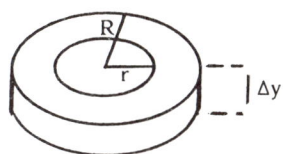

Fig. 27

Example: (1)

Use the washer method of finding the volume generated when the region bounded by the parabola $y = x^2$ and the lines $x = 2$ and $y = 0$ is rotated about the y-axis.

Solution:

A typical strip at $P(x, y)$ in the given region will sweep out a washer of volume $\Delta V = \pi(R^2 - r^2)\Delta y$

$$= \pi(4 - x^2)\Delta y$$

$\therefore$ Required volume $V = \int_0^4 \pi(4 - x^2) dy$

$$= \int_0^4 \pi(4 - y) dy, \quad y = x^2$$

$$= \pi \left[4y - \frac{y^2}{2}\right]_0^4$$

$$= \pi [16 - 8]$$

$$= 8\pi$$

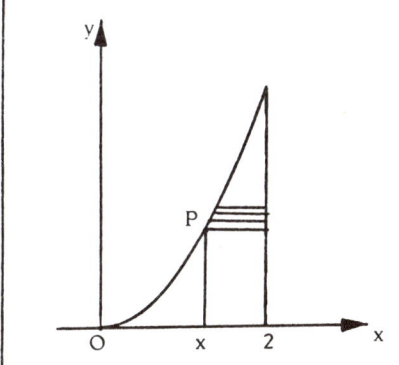

[$r = x$, $R = 2$]

Fig. 28

Exercise 3B

In Exercises 1-5, find the volumes generated when the region bounded by the given curves and lines is rotated about the x-axis.

1. $y = x^2 + 1$, $\quad y = 5$
2. $y = x^2 + 2$, $\quad y = x + 4$
3. $y = 1 - x^2$, $\quad y = 1 - x$
4. $x = 3y - y^2$, $\quad x = 0$
5. $y = x + 2$, $\quad y = 4$, $\quad x = 0$

In Exercises 6-10, find the volumes when the region bounded by the given curves and lines is rotated about the y-axis.

6. $y = x$, $\quad x = 2$, $\quad y = 0$
7. $y = x^2$, $\quad x = 2$, $\quad y = 0$
8. $y = x^3$, $\quad x = 2$, $\quad y = 0$
9. $y = x$, $\quad y = 3x - x^2$
10. $y = \sin x$, $\quad y = 0$, $\quad 0 \leqslant x \leqslant \frac{\pi}{2}$

(Hint: $\int x \sin x \, dx$, integrate by parts)

11. The region bounded by $y = -1$, $y = e^{2x}$, $x = 0$ and $x = 2$ is revolved about the line $y = -1$. Find the volume of the resulting solid.

12. A circle of radius 2 is given by $x^2 + y^2 = 4$ and is revolved about the line $x = 5$. Using the washer method, prove that the resulting volume (called a TORUS) is $40\pi^2$.

(Hint: Simplify your work by remembering that

$$\int_{-2}^{2} \sqrt{4 - x^2} \, dx = \text{area of a semi-circle} = 2\pi \,)$$

3.4 Worked Examples (Miscellaneous)

EXAMPLE: (1) The triangle with vertices A(2,2), B(2,4) and C(4,4) is rotated about (i) the x-axis, (ii) the y-axis, (iii) the line x = 8. Find the volume generated in each case.

SOLUTION

(i) Equation of AC is $y = x$.
Equation of BC is $y = 4$.
The element of volume, $\Delta V = \pi(y_2^2 - y_1^2)\Delta x$
$y_2 = 4$ and $y_1 = x$
Substitute in the formula

$$V = \int_a^b \pi(y_2^2 - y_1^2)\,dx = \pi\int_2^4 (16 - x^2)\,dx$$

$$\therefore V = \pi\left[16x - \frac{x^3}{3}\right]_2^4 = \frac{40\pi}{3}$$

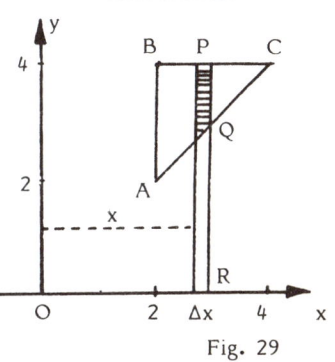
Fig. 29

(ii) $V = \int_2^4 \pi(x_2^2 - x_1^2)\,dy$, $\quad x_2 = y$
$\quad x_1 = 2$

$$= \pi\int_2^4 (y^2 - 4)\,dy$$

$$= \pi\left[\frac{y^3}{3} - 4y\right]_2^4$$

$$= \pi\left[\frac{64}{3} - 16 - \left(\frac{8}{3} - 8\right)\right]$$

$$= \frac{32\pi}{3}$$

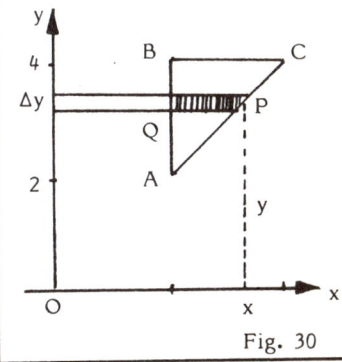
Fig. 30

(iii) $r_2 = PR = 8 - 2 = 6$, $r_1 = QR = 8 - x = 8 - y$ $\quad (y = x)$

$$\therefore V = \int_2^4 \pi(r_2^2 - r_1^2)\,dy$$

$$= \int_2^4 \pi[36 - (8-y)^2]\,dy$$

$$= \pi\int_2^4 (-28 + 16y - y^2)\,dy$$

$$= \pi\left[-28y + 8y^2 - \frac{y^3}{3}\right]_2^4$$

$$= \frac{64\pi}{3}$$

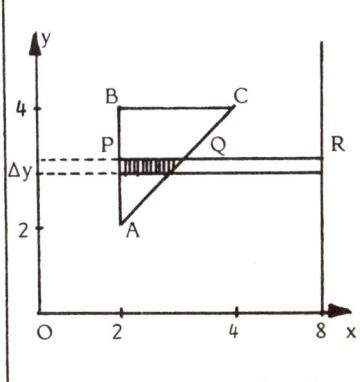
Fig. 31

EXAMPLE (2)

The area bounded by the curve $y = x^2 + 2$ and the line $y = 2x + 5$ is revolved about the x-axis.
Find the volume.

SOLUTION:

$y = x^2 + 2$ ... (1)
$y = 2x + 5$ ... (2)

Solve (1) and (2) for the intersections.

$\therefore x^2 + 2 = 2x + 5$
$x^2 - 2x - 3 = 0$
$(x - 3)(x + 1) = 0$
$x = 3$ or $x = -1$

The element of volume when the region ACBA is rotated about the x-axis is given by:

$\Delta V = \pi (PM^2 - QM^2) \Delta x$ (washer)
$= \pi (y_2^2 - y_1^2) \Delta x$

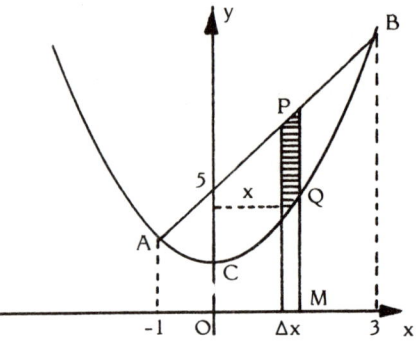

Fig. 32

We substitute $y_1 = x^2 + 2$, $y_2 = 2x + 5$

$\therefore \Delta V = \pi [(2x + 5)^2 - (x^2 + 2)^2]$
$= \pi (4x^2 + 20x + 25 - x^4 - 4x^2 - 4)$
$= \pi (20x - x^4 + 21)$

$\therefore$ Volume $V = \int_a^b \pi (y_2^2 - y_1^2) \, dx$

$= \int_{-1}^{3} \pi (20x - x^4 + 21) \, dx$

$= \pi [10x^2 - \frac{x^5}{5} + 21x]_{-1}^{3}$

$= \pi [(90 - \frac{243}{5} + 63) - (10 + \frac{1}{5} - 21)]$

$= \frac{576\pi}{5}$

EXAMPLE: (3) The cross-sections of a certain solid by planes perpendicular to the x-axis are circles extending from the curve $y = x^2$ to the curve $y = 2 - x^2$. The solid lies between the points of intersection of these curves. Find the volume of this solid.

SOLUTION:

The curves $y = 2 - x^2$ ... (1)

and $y = x^2$ ... (2)

intersect at $A(-1, 1)$ and $B(1, 1)$.

The element of volume at distance x from the origin is given by:

$$\Delta V = \pi r^2 \cdot \Delta x \qquad (\text{disc, radius } r)$$

where $r = \frac{1}{2} PQ = \frac{1}{2}(PM - QM) = \frac{1}{2}(y_2 - y_1)$

$PM = y_2 = 2 - x^2$

$QM = y_1 = x^2$

$\therefore \Delta V = \pi \cdot r^2 \cdot \Delta x$

$\qquad = \pi \cdot \frac{1}{4}(y_2 - y_1)^2 \, \Delta x$

$V = \int_{-1}^{1} dV = \int_{-1}^{1} \frac{\pi}{4}(y_2 - y_1)^2 \, dx \qquad y_2 - y_1 = 2 - x^2 - x^2 = 2(1 - x^2)$

$\qquad = \pi \int_{-1}^{1} (1 - 2x^2 + x^4) \, dx$

$\qquad = 2\pi \int_{0}^{1} (1 - 2x^2 + x^4) \, dx \qquad (\text{owing to the symmetry})$

$\qquad = 2\pi \left[x - \frac{2x^3}{3} + \frac{x^5}{5} \right]_0^1$

$\qquad = 2\pi \left(1 - \frac{2}{3} + \frac{1}{5} \right)$

$\qquad = \frac{16\pi}{15}$

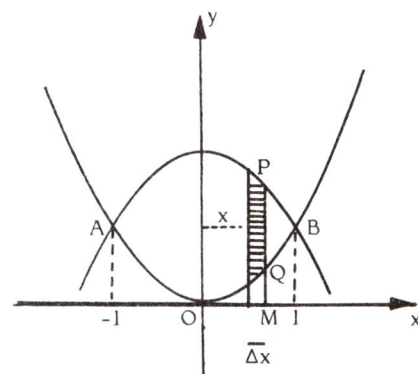

Fig. 33

EXAMPLE: (4) The region bounded by curve $y = 2x - x^2$ and the line $y = x$ is rotated about the y-axis. Find the volume by the method of cylindrical shells.

SOLUTION:

The curve $y = 2x - x^2$ and the line $y = x$ intersect at $O(0,0)$ and $A(1,1)$

We use:

$$V = 2\pi \int_a^b x(y_2 - y_1)\,dx \quad \ldots (1)$$

$y_2 = PR = 2x - x^2$, $\quad y_1 = QR = x$

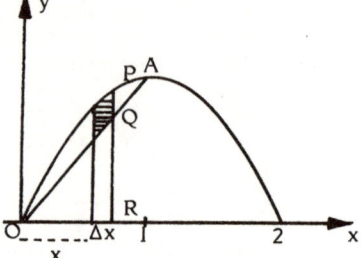

Fig. 34

$$\therefore V = 2\pi \int_0^1 x(2x - x^2 - x)\,dx$$

$$= 2\pi \int_0^1 (x^2 - x^3)\,dx$$

$$= 2\pi \left[\frac{x^3}{3} - \frac{x^4}{4}\right]_0^1$$

$$= 2\pi \left(\frac{1}{3} - \frac{1}{4}\right)$$

$$= \frac{\pi}{6}$$

EXAMPLE: (5) The area bounded by the curve $y^2 = x$ and the line $x = 1$ is revolved about the line $x = 3$. Find the volume generated, by the method of shells.

SOLUTION

$$V = \int_a^b 2\pi(c - x)h\,dx, \quad c = 3, \ y^2 = x$$
$$h = PQ = 2y = 2\sqrt{x}$$

$$= \int_0^1 4\pi(3 - x)\sqrt{x}\,dx$$

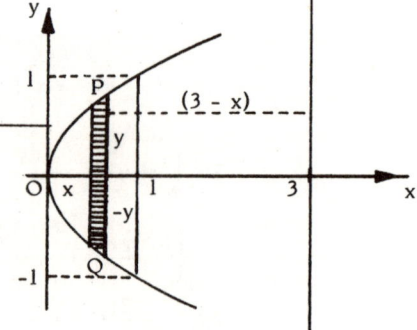

$$= 4\pi \int_0^1 (3x^{1/2} - x^{3/2})\,dx$$

Fig. 35

$$= 4\pi \left[2x^{3/2} - \frac{2}{5}x^{5/2}\right]_0^1$$

$$= 4\pi \left(2 - \frac{2}{5}\right)$$

$$= \frac{32\pi}{5}$$

REVISION : VOLUMES : Exercise 3C

1. (a) On a number plane, shade the region R representing the inequality
   $(x - 4)^2 + y^2 \leq 4$.

   (b) Show that the volume of a right cylindrical shell of height H with inner and outer radii r and r + Δr respectively is given by $2\pi r H \cdot \Delta r$.

   (c) The region R in (a) above is rotated about the y-axis, generating a solid of revolution called a torus. By using the shell method, prove that the volume of this torus is $32\pi^2$.

2. A solid figure has a semi-circular base of radius 4 units. The cross-sections at right angles to the semi-diameter of this base are semi-ellipses. If the semi-minor axis of each ellipse is $\frac{1}{2}$ of the semi-major axis, prove that the volume of the solid is given by $V = \frac{\pi}{4} \int_0^4 (16 - x^2) dx$ and hence find the volume of the solid.

3. The area common to the curves $y = x^2$ and $y^2 = x$ is revolved about the y-axis. Find the volume generated by using:
   (a) the disc method (washer)
   (b) the cylindrical shells.

4. The co-ordinates of the vertices of a triangle PQR are (0, 4), (2, 2) and (-2, 2) respectively. The region PQR is rotated about the
   (a) x-axis   (b) y-axis   (c) line x = 4.
   Find the volume of revolution generated in each case.

5. A certain solid has a semi-circular base of radius 4 units. The cross-sections at right angles to the x-axis are triangles with one leg in the base. If the heights of these triangles are bounded by the arc of the parabola $y = 16 - x^2$, show that the volume of the solid is given by:

   $V = \int_0^4 (16 - x^2)^{3/2} dx$ and hence find V.

6. An electronic valve used in a computer is in the shape of a solid that has a circular base. At a height z above the horizontal base, the horizontal cross-section is a circle of radius R given by the relation

$$R = f(z) = 1 - \frac{z^2}{h^2}.$$

If the height of the solid is h, find the volume of this solid.

7. A frustum of a right circular cone is shown in the diagram.

(a) Prove that $x = r + (\frac{R-r}{h})z$.

(b) Prove that the volume of the frustum is given by
$$V = \frac{\pi h}{3}(R^2 + Rr + r^2).$$

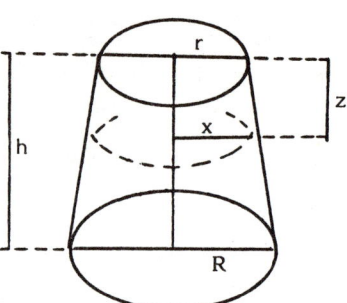

Fig. 36

8. A very large waste container is shown in the diagram.
The top face of the container is a rectangle of sides 3 m and 4 m respectively and the bottom is a rectangle of sides 2 m and 3 m respectively. If the height of the container is 1.5 m, find the volume of this container by integration.

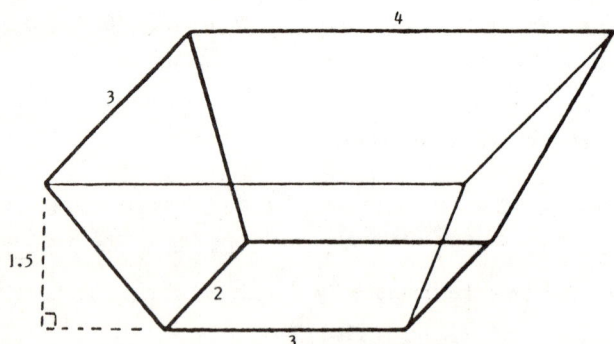

Fig. 37

9. The area bounded by the parabola $y^2 = 4ax$ and the line $x = a$ is rotated about the line $x = a$. Find the volume generated, by using the Shell method.

10. Find the volume of the torus obtained by rotating the area bounded by the circle $x^2 + y^2 = a^2$ about the line $x = c$, $(c > a)$. Use the method of (a) cylindrical shells and (b) disc (washer method).

11. The area bounded by the parabola $y^2 = 4ax$ and the line $x = a$ is rotated about the y-axis. Find the volume by two methods.

12. A ring of altitude $2h$ is generated by revolving about the y-axis the area of the segment bounded by the circle $x^2 + y^2 = a^2$ and the chord of length $2h$ that is parallel to the y-axis. By using the method of shells, show that the volume is given by $\frac{4\pi h^3}{3}$

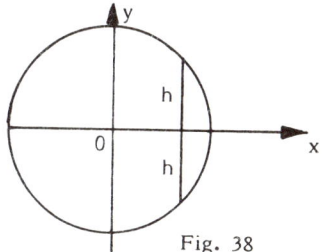

Fig. 38

13. The area enclosed by the ellipse $\frac{x^2}{25} + \frac{y^2}{16} = 1$ is rotated about the line $x = 8$. By using the method of shells, find the volume generated.

14. The ellipse in exercise (13) is revolved about the vertical line through the vertex $A(5,0)$. Find the volume.

15. The triangle ABC formed by the points $A(a,0)$, $B(-a,0)$, $C(0,a)$ is revolved about the line $x = 2a$. Find the volume generated by disc (washer) method.

16. The cross sections of a certain solid by planes perpendicular to the x-axis are circles with diameters extending from the curve $y = x^2$ to the curve $y = 8 - x^2$. The solid lies between the points of intersection of these two curves. Find the volume of this solid.
[Hint: radius r is given by $2r = (8 - x^2) - x^2 = 8 - 2x^2$ and $V = \int_{-2}^{2} A(x)\,dx$, where $A = \pi r^2$]

17. The area bounded by the curve $y = x^2 + 1$ and the line $y = 3 - x$ is revolved about the x-axis. Find the volume of revolution. (Hint: use the washer method)

18. The region bounded by the curves $y = 3x - x^2$ and $y = x$ is rotated about the y-axis. Find the volume by the shell method.

19. The triangle with vertices (a, a), $(a, 2a)$, $(2a, 2a)$ is rotated (a) about the x-axis (b) about the y-axis. Find the volume generated in each case.

20. The area bounded by the curve $y^2 = 4x$ and the line $x = 1$ is revolved about the line $x = 2$. Find the volume generated.

CHAPTER 4 COMPLEX NUMBERS

4.1 Introduction

- Necessity is the mother of invention.

<u>Invented Number Systems:</u> <u>Complex Numbers</u>

Imagination and art of invention were required several times in extending our number system from the counting numbers.

1. The first invented system <u>J</u>: the set of all integers as developed from the counting numbers. In this system we can solve equations such as $x \pm 2 = 0$, in general $x + b = 0$, where b is any integer.

2. The second invented system <u>Q</u>: the set of all rational numbers p/q as developed from the integers. In this system we can solve equations such as $2x - 3 = 0$, in general $ax + b = 0$, where a and b are rational numbers.

3. The third invented system <u>R</u>: the set of all real numbers x as developed from the rational numbers. In this system, we can solve not only the types $x + a = 0$, $ax + b = 0$, but in addition all quadratic equations $ax^2 + bx + c = 0$, $a \neq 0$ and $\Delta = b^2 - 4ac \geq 0$. The roots are not real if $\Delta < 0$. The simple quadratic equation $x^2 + 1 = 0$ or $x^2 + x + 1 = 0$ is impossible to solve with the above mentioned three number systems. There is no real number that satisfies the equation $x^2 + 1 = 0$, since $x = \sqrt{-1}$ does not exist in the real number system R.

A new kind of number has to be invented to handle the roots which are not real. The symbol $\boxed{i = \sqrt{-1}}$ is used with the understanding that $\boxed{i^2 = -1}$. i is called the imaginary number. The roots of $x^2 = -1$ can now be written as
$x^2 = -1 = i^2 \longrightarrow x = \pm i$

Again the roots of $x^2 + 2x + 3 = 0$ can be given as
$x = \dfrac{-2 \pm \sqrt{-8}}{2} = -1 \pm \sqrt{-2} = -1 \pm \sqrt{2}\, i$

Now we come to <u>the fourth invented system</u>, the set of all complex numbers of the form $\boxed{x + iy}$. We shall use a single pronumeral z to define a complex number $x + iy$, i.e.

$$\boxed{z = x + iy}$$

x is called the real part and

y is called the imaginary part of the complex number z.

It is important to note that the imaginary part of a complex number is not imaginary! It is i that is called the imaginary number.

The history of imaginary numbers is very fascinating. The earlier mathematicians thought that such numbers had no practical use (hence the term 'imaginary'), yet complex numbers are of great importance in fields such as Electronics.

A complex number can also be defined by an ordered pair of numbers (x, y), without ever mentioning the imaginary number i, but in this book we shall only work with the binary form $z = x + iy$. However, the computer requires the form (x, y) for multiplication of two complex numbers.

4.2 Operations with Complex Numbers

We have the following definitions:

1. Equality: $a + bi = c + di$ if and only if $a = c$ and $b = d$.
2. Addition: $(a + bi) + (c + di) = (a + c) + (b + d)i$
3. Multiplication: $(a + bi)(c + di) = (ac - bd) + (ad + bc)i$

By using these definitions, we can verify that the complex numbers satisfy all the laws of algebra and hence the complex numbers form a field (denoted by C).

EXAMPLE: (1)   If $x + iy = 3 - 5i$, then $x = 3$, $y = -5$

EXAMPLE: (2)   Find the sum of $2 + 3i$ and $3 + 2i$

SOLUTION: $(2 + 3i) + (3 + 2i) = (2 + 3)i = 5 + 5i$

EXAMPLE: (3)   Find the product of $2 + 5i$ and $3 + 6i$

SOLUTION: $(2 + 5i)(3 + 6i) = (2 \times 3 - 5 \times 6) + (2 \times 6 + 5 \times 3)i = -24 + 27i$

If you ignore the definition of multiplication and expand $(2 + 5i)(3 + 6i)$, i.e. $6 + 15i + 12i + 30i^2$ and put $i^2 = -1$, then the result is $-24 + 27i$, and so you now discover the secret of strange definitions!

Identity elements:

By definition: $(a + bi) + (0 + 0i) = (a + 0) + (b + 0)i = a + bi$

and $(a + bi)(1 + 0i) = (a.1 - b.0) + (a.0 + b.1)i = a + bi$

Thus, the complex number $0 + 0.i$, written as $z = 0$, is the additive identity and $1 + 0.i$ written as $z = 1$, is the multiplicative identity for the set C of complex numbers.

Additive inverse:

We define the additive inverse of the complex number $a + ib$ to be a number $x + iy$ such that:

$$(a + bi) + (x + iy) = 0 + 0 \cdot i$$
$$\therefore (a + x) + (b + y)i = 0 + 0 \cdot i$$

By definition of two equal complex numbers, we have:

$$a + x = 0 \quad \text{and} \quad b + y = 0 \quad \text{giving} \quad x = -a, \ y = -b$$

Hence the additive inverse of $z = a + bi$ is $-a - bi$, i.e. $-z$. Using this, we can now find the difference: (subtraction)

$$(a + bi) - (c + id) = (a + bi) + (-c - di) = (a - c) + (b - d)i \,.$$

Multiplicative inverse:

The multiplicative inverse of the complex number $a + bi \neq 0$ is defined to be a number $x + iy$ such that $(a + bi)(x + iy) = 1 + 0 \cdot i$. By definition of equality,

$$\therefore ax - by = 1$$
$$\text{and} \quad bx + ay = 0$$

We solve these equations for x and y, then

$$x = \frac{a}{a^2 + b^2} \quad \text{and} \quad y = -\frac{b}{a^2 + b^2} \,,$$

hence the multiplicative inverse of $z = a + bi$ is the complex number $z^{-1} = \left[\frac{a}{a^2 + b^2}, \frac{-b}{a^2 + b^2}\right]$. Note that $z \cdot z^{-1} = z \cdot \frac{1}{z} = 1$, $z \neq 0$.

We can now divide a complex number z by another complex number w, but shall use a method used in ex. (6) below, i.e. complex conjugates. We can easily verify that the complex numbers obey all the rules of Algebra and hence they form a complex field C. Further, if $b = 0$, then $a + bi$ reduces to the real number a, hence the set of real numbers R is a subset of the complex numbers C. If $a = 0$, $b \neq 0$, then $a + bi$ reduces to bi, and we call bi a purely imaginary number.

Note that a real number can be written in the form $a + bi$, for example $2 = 2 + 0 \cdot i$. Similarly a purely imaginary number such as $2i$ can also be written as $0 + 2i$.

Calculations with the complex numbers do not require any special rules; wherever i^2 occurs we replace it by -1. Further,

$$i^3 = -i, \quad i^4 = i^2 \times i^2 = (-1)(-1) = 1, \quad i^5 = i^4 \cdot i = i \quad \text{etc.}$$

Complex conjugates:

If two complex numbers differ only in the sign of their imaginary parts, each is called the conjugate of the other. Thus $a + bi$ and $a - ib$ are the conjugate complex numbers. Notation $\bar{z}$ is used for the conjugate of z, i.e. $\bar{z} = a - ib$. Since $z + \bar{z} = (a + bi) + (a - bi) = 2a$, the sum of two conjugate complex numbers is a real number.

EXAMPLE: (4) Find the sum and difference of $3 + 2i$ and $3 - 2i$

SOLUTION: $(3 + 2i) + (3 - 2i) = 6$ and $(3 + 2i) - (3 - 2i) = 4i$

Again the product $z\bar{z} = (a + bi)(a - bi) = a^2 + b^2$, hence the product of two conjugate complex numbers is a non-negative real number.

EXAMPLE: (5) $(3 + 2i)(3 - 2i) = 9 + 4 = 13$

QUOTIENT:

We can simplify the quotient $\dfrac{a + bi}{c + di}$, i.e. divide $a + bi$ by $c + di$ by using the following procedure:

$$\frac{a + bi}{c + di} \cdot \frac{c - di}{c - di} = \frac{(ac + bd) + (bc - ad)i}{c^2 + d^2}$$

$$= \frac{ac + bd}{c^2 + d^2} + \frac{bc - ad}{c^2 + d^2} \cdot i$$

EXAMPLE: (6) Divide $3 + 4i$ by $2 + i$

SOLUTION: $\dfrac{3 + 4i}{2 + i} = \dfrac{(3 + 4i)}{(2 + i)} \cdot \dfrac{(2 - i)}{(2 - i)} = \dfrac{6 + 8i - 3i - 4i^2}{4 + 1} = \dfrac{10 + 5i}{5}$

$\therefore \dfrac{3 + 4i}{2 + i} = 2 + i$

EXAMPLE: (7) If $(x + iy)(2 + 3i) = 5 + 6i$, find x and y.

SOLUTION: Write $x + iy = \dfrac{5 + 6i}{2 + 3i} = \dfrac{5 + 6i}{2 + 3i} \cdot \dfrac{2 - 3i}{2 - 3i} = \dfrac{28 - 3i}{13}$

Equating real and imaginary parts, $x = \dfrac{28}{13}$, $y = -\dfrac{3}{13}$

Alternatively, expanding and equating real and imaginary parts, we find:

$\left. \begin{array}{l} 2x - 3y = 5 \\ 3x + 2y = 6 \end{array} \right]$, solving these: $x = \dfrac{28}{13}$, $y = -\dfrac{3}{13}$

EXAMPLE: (8) Expand (a) $(1 + i)^4$ and (b) $(1 - i)^5$ and simplify in the form $a + ib$.

SOLUTION:

(a) $(1 + i)^4 = 1 + 4i + 6i^2 + 4i^3 + i^4$
$= 1 + 4i - 6 - 4i + 1$
$= -4$

and (b) $(1 - i)^5 = 1 - 5i + 10i^2 - 10i^3 + 5i^4 - i^5$
$= 1 - 5i - 10 + 10i + 5 - i$
$= -4 + 4i$

It is easier to expand by writing $z = 1 + i$
$z^4 = z^2 \cdot z^2 = (1 + i)^2 (1 + i)^2$
$= (2i)(2i) = -4$
Similarly $z^5 = z^2 \cdot z^2 \cdot z$
$= (-2i)(-2i)(1 - i)$
$= -4(1 - i)$ etc.

EXAMPLE: (9) Express $(2 - 3i)^{-1}$ in the form $a + ib$

SOLUTION: $(2 - 3i)^{-1} = \dfrac{1}{(2 - 3i)} \times \dfrac{2 + 3i}{2 + 3i} = \dfrac{2 + 3i}{13} = \dfrac{2}{13} + \dfrac{3}{13} i$

Exercise 4A

Perform the indicated operations and express the answers in the form $a + ib$:

1. $(3 + 2i) + (2 - 3i)$
2. $(5 - 2i) - (3 - 2i)$
3. $(-3 - 4i) - (12 - 5i)$
4. $(3 + 2i) - (3 - 2i)$
5. $(3 + 4i)(2 + i)$
6. $(5 - i)(3 - 4i)$
7. $3i(2 - i)$
8. $(4 - 3i)^2$
9. $(1 + i)^2$
10. $(1 - 3i)^{-2}$
11. $i(2 + i)(2 - i)$
12. $(-4i)(2i)$
13. $\dfrac{1 + i}{1 - i}$
14. $\dfrac{3 + 2i}{5 + 2i}$
15. $\dfrac{3 - 2i}{5i}$
16. $\dfrac{1 + 2i}{i^3}$

Find x and y in each of the following:

17. $3x + 2iy = 12 + 5i$
18. $(2 - 3i) + (x + 2iy) = 5 - 4i$
19. $(x - iy)^2 = 2i$
20. $(x + iy)(3 + 4i) = 2 - 5i$
21. Expand: $(2 + i)^3$ and answer in the form $a + ib$.
22. If $x + iy = 5(\cos 60° - i \sin 60°)$, find x and y in the surd form and hence express (a) $(x + iy)^2$ (b) $\dfrac{1}{x - iy}$ in the form $a + ib$
23. If $z = 2 + i$, evaluate:
    (a) $3z + 4$
    (b) $z^2 - 2z + 3$
    (c) $\dfrac{2z - 1}{2z + 1}$
    (d) $(z - 1)(z^2 + z + 1)$
24. If $z = x + iy$, express each of the following in the form $a + ib$:
    (a) $\bar{z}$
    (b) $\dfrac{1}{z}$
    (c) $\dfrac{z + 1}{z - 1}$
    (d) $z^2 - 1$
25. Solve the following equations for z; express answers in the form $a + ib$:
    (a) $(1 + i)z = 2 - i$
    (b) $\dfrac{2z}{2 + i} + 3 - 2i = (1 - i)z$
    (c) $\dfrac{2}{z} = 1 + i + \dfrac{3}{1 - i}$
    (d) $\dfrac{z + 3}{z - 1} = 2 - 3i$

26. Solve the following equations for z; express answers in the form $a + ib$:

    (a) $z^2 + z + 1 = 0$ (b) $z^2 - 2z + 4 = 0$ (c) $2z^2 - 3z + 2 = 0$ (d) $z + \frac{1}{z} = 2$

27. Find the quadratic equations with roots given below:

    (a) $i, -i$ (b) $1 + i, 1 - i$ (c) $2 + 3i, 2 - 3i$

    (d) $3 + i, 1 + 3i$ (e) $2 + i, \frac{1}{2 + i}$

28. Solve the following pairs of equations for z and w where z and w are complex numbers. Express answers in the form $a + ib$.

    (a) $z + iw = 2 + 3i$
        $z - iw = 2 - 3i$

    (b) $2z + w = 1 + i$
        $z - w = 1 - i$

    (c) $(2 + i)z + (2 - i)w = 1$
        $(2 - i)z + (2 + i)w = 2$

    (d) $z + (1 - i)w = 2i$
        $w + (1 - i)z = 1$

29. Given $z = 2 + i$, evaluate the following in the form $a + ib$:

    (a) $\frac{1}{z}$ (b) z^2 (c) $\frac{1}{z^2}$ (d) $z^2 + \frac{1}{z^2}$ (e) z^3 (f) z^4

    (Hint: $z^3 = z^2 \cdot z$ and $z^4 = z^2 \cdot z^2$)

30. What is the fallacy in the following:

    $\sqrt{-3} \cdot \sqrt{-12} = \sqrt{(-3) \cdot (-12)} = 6$?

    What is the correct answer?

31. Prove the associative law for multiplication of complex numbers:

    $(z_1 \cdot z_2)z_3 = z_1(z_2 \cdot z_3)$ (Hint: Let $z_1 = x_1 + iy_1$ etc.)

32. Prove the commutative law for multiplication: $z_1 z_2 = z_2 z_1$

4.3 Complex Plane (Argand Diagram)

A complex number is an ordered pair (x, y) of real numbers, so if we consider (x, y) to be the cartesian coordinates of a point in a rectangular coordinate system, every complex number (x, y) then corresponds to some point in the coordinate plane. Conversely, every point (x, y) corresponds to some complex number x + iy. Thus there is a one-to-one correspondence between the set of complex numbers and the set of points in the coordinate plane. The plane is called the COMPLEX PLANE or the Argand diagram (J. Argand: 1768-1822).

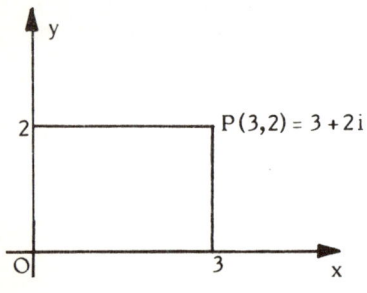 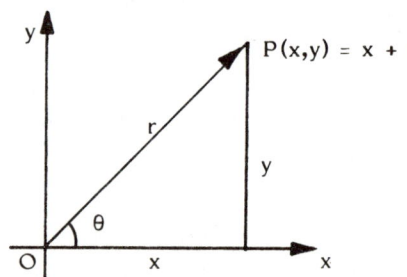

Fig. 1 Fig. 2

The complex number $z = 3 + 2i$ is represented by the point P(3,2) in the coordinate plane (Fig. 1). The x-axis is called the real axis and the y-axis is called the imaginary axis. For $z = x + iy$,

x = real part of z = Re(z)
y = imaginary part of z = Im(z)

In the above example: Re(z) = 3, Im(z) = 2, z = 3 + 2i.

TRIGONOMETRIC FORM OF COMPLEX NUMBERS

A vector is a directed line-segment. We can represent the complex number $z = x + iy$ by the vector drawn from the origin to the point P(x,y) (see Fig. 2). The length of the vector OP is given by:

$$r = OP = \sqrt{x^2 + y^2}$$

r is called the modulus of the complex number $z = x + iy$.
r is denoted by $|z|$, so modulus of z is given by:

$$|z| = r = \sqrt{x^2 + y^2}$$

The direction of the vector OP is given by the angle θ which OP makes with the positive direction of the x-axis. Hence θ is completely determined by the equations:

$$x = r\cos\theta \quad \text{and} \quad y = r\sin\theta$$

The angle θ is called an <u>argument</u> of the complex number $z = x + iy$. The angle θ is measured in radians, but degrees may be used for convenience. Its value is, however, not determined uniquely, since

$$\cos\theta = \cos(\theta \pm 2k\pi) \quad \text{and} \quad \sin\theta = \sin(\theta \pm 2k\pi)$$

where k is an integer. In order to determine θ uniquely, we impose the restriction that

$$-\pi < \theta \leqslant \pi$$

Thus for the complex number $z = x + iy$, we can write its trigonometric form as:

$$z = x + iy = r(\cos\theta + i\sin\theta), \quad -\pi < \theta \leqslant \pi.$$

This is called the modulus-argument form of the complex number z. We abbreviate this to mod-arg(z) for our convenience. Frequently to save the space, we may write:

$$z = r(\cos\theta + i\sin\theta) \quad \text{as} \quad r\text{cis}\,\theta$$

For example $z = 5(\cos 60° + i\sin 60°) = 5\text{cis}\,60°$.

It is strongly recommended that you draw a diagram depicting the complex number $z = x + iy$ to determine the angle θ. The formula $\tan\theta = \frac{y}{x}$ should be used with caution as θ is defined for $-\pi < \theta \leqslant \pi$.

Note carefully that arg z is not defined for $z = 0$.

We have:

Complex number	Cartesian form	Mod-arg form of z
z	$x + iy$ $P(x,y)$	$x = r\cos\theta, \; y = r\sin\theta$ $z = r(\cos\theta + i\sin\theta) = r\text{cis}\,\theta$ $\text{mod}\,z = |z| = r = \sqrt{x^2 + y^2}$ $\arg z = \theta$ where $-\pi < \theta \leqslant \pi$

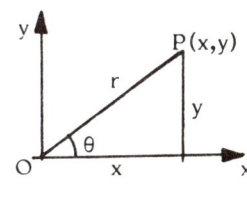

Fig. 3

EXAMPLES

(10) Express $3 + 4i$ in mod-arg form: (Fig. 4)

SOLUTION: $r = \sqrt{3^2 + 4^2} = 5$
$\tan\theta = \frac{4}{3}$ (θ in the first quadrant)
$\theta = 53°$ (to the nearest degree)
$\therefore z = 3 + 4i = 5\operatorname{cis} 53°$

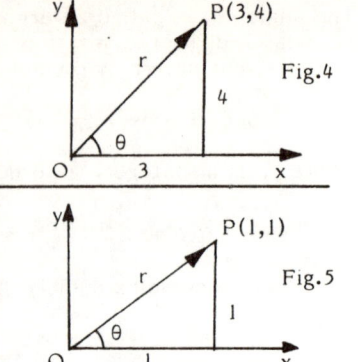
Fig.4

(11). Express $1 + i$ in mod-arg form: (Fig. 5)

SOLUTION: $r = \sqrt{1^2 + 1^2} = \sqrt{2}$
$\therefore \tan\theta = 1$
$\theta = 45°$
$\therefore z = 1 + i = \sqrt{2}(\cos 45° + i\sin 45°)$
$= \sqrt{2}\operatorname{cis}(\pi/4)$

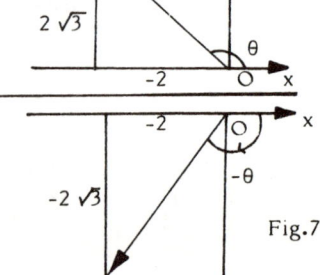
Fig.5

(12) Express $-2 + 2\sqrt{3}i$ in mod-arg form: (Fig. 6)

SOLUTION: $r = \sqrt{(-2)^2 + (2\sqrt{3})^2} = 4$
$\theta = \frac{2\pi}{3}$ from $\tan\theta = -\sqrt{3}$
$\therefore z = -2 + 2\sqrt{3}i = 4\operatorname{cis} 2\pi/3$

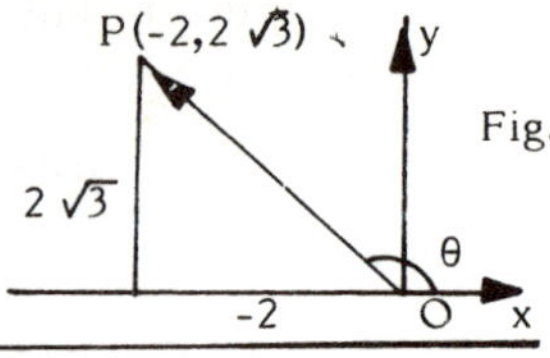

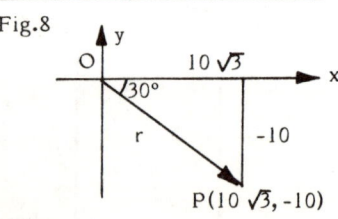
Fig.6

(13) Express $-2 - 2\sqrt{3}i$ in mod-arg form: (Fig. 7)

SOLUTION: $r = \sqrt{(-2)^2 + (-2\sqrt{3})^2} = 4$
$\therefore \theta = -120° = -2\pi/3$ from $\tan\theta = \sqrt{3}$
$\therefore z = 4\operatorname{cis}\left(\frac{-2\pi}{3}\right)$

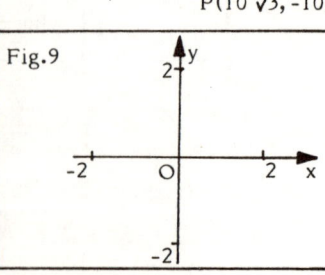
Fig.7

(14) Express $10\sqrt{3} - 10i$ in mod-arg form: (Fig. 8)

SOLUTION: $r = \sqrt{(10\sqrt{3})^2 + (-10)^2} = 20$
$\theta = -30°$ from $\tan\theta = -\frac{1}{\sqrt{3}}$
$\therefore 10\sqrt{3} - 10 = 20\operatorname{cis}(-30°)$ or $20\operatorname{cis}(-\pi/6)$

Fig.8

(15) Express in mod-arg form: (Fig. 9)
(a) 2 (b) $2i$ (c) -2 (d) $-2i$

SOLUTION:
(a) $2 = 2 + 0 \cdot i = 2\operatorname{cis} 0$
(b) $2i = 0 + 2i = 2\operatorname{cis}(\pi/2)$
(c) $-2 = -2 + 0i = 2\operatorname{cis} \pi$
(d) $-2i = 0 - 2i = 2\operatorname{cis}(-\pi/2)$

Fig.9

(16) Express (a) $2\operatorname{cis} 150°$ (b) $5\operatorname{cis} 210°$ in Cartesian form:

(a) $2\operatorname{cis} 150° = 2(\cos 150° + i\sin 150°) = 2(-\frac{\sqrt{3}}{2} + \frac{i}{2}) = -\sqrt{3} + i$

(b) $5\operatorname{cis} 210° = 5(\cos 210° + i\sin 210°) = -\frac{5\sqrt{3}}{2} - \frac{5i}{2}$

Exercise 4B

Convert the following to the mod-arg form:

1. 5
2. -5
3. $5i$
4. $-5i$
5. $2 + 2i$
6. $2 - 2i$
7. $-2 + 2i$
8. $-2 - 2i$
9. $-4\sqrt{2} + 4\sqrt{2}i$
10. $10\sqrt{3} + 10i$
11. $-\frac{1}{2} + \frac{\sqrt{3}}{2}i$
12. $-\frac{5}{2} - \frac{5\sqrt{3}}{2}i$
13. $\frac{1}{1 + i}$
14. $\frac{10}{4 + 3i}$
15. $(1 - i)^2$

Convert the following to the Cartesian form:

16. $5 \operatorname{cis} \pi/2$
17. $10 \operatorname{cis} 0$
18. $4 \operatorname{cis} \pi$
19. $2 \operatorname{cis}(-\pi/2)$
20. $5 \operatorname{cis} -\pi/3$
21. $\sqrt{2} \operatorname{cis} \pi/3$
22. $\sqrt{2} \operatorname{cis} \pi/4$
23. $5 \operatorname{cis}(-5\pi/6)$
24. $10 \operatorname{cis}(-\pi/3)$
25. $4 \operatorname{cis} 2\pi/3$

4.4 Multiplication and Division of Complex Numbers Using Trigonometry

The mod-arg form of complex numbers can be used to advantage in finding products and quotients. The mod-arg form is useful in finding the roots of complex numbers.

MULTIPLICATION: Let $z_1 = r_1(\cos\theta_1 + i\sin\theta_1)$ and $z_2 = r_2(\cos\theta_2 + i\sin\theta_2)$ be any two complex numbers, then:

$$\begin{aligned} z_1 z_2 &= r_1 r_2 (\cos\theta_1 + i\sin\theta_1)(\cos\theta_2 + i\sin\theta_2) \\ &= r_1 r_2 [(\cos\theta_1 \cos\theta_2 - \sin\theta_1 \sin\theta_2) + i(\sin\theta_1 \cos\theta_2 + \cos\theta_1 \sin\theta_2)] \\ &= r_1 r_2 [\cos(\theta_1 + \theta_2) + i\sin(\theta_1 + \theta_2)] \end{aligned} \quad \ldots (1)$$

Thus to multiply two complex numbers, multiply their moduli r_1 and r_2 and add the arguments, θ_1 and θ_2.

We can easily generalise:

$$z_1 z_2 z_3 \ldots z_n = r_1 r_2 r_3 \ldots \operatorname{cis}(\theta_1 + \theta_2 + \theta_3 + \ldots + \theta_n) \quad \ldots (2)$$

Letting $z_1 = z_2 = z_3 = \ldots = z = r\operatorname{cis}\theta$

$$z^n = r^n \operatorname{cis} n\theta = r^n (\cos n\theta + i\sin n\theta) \quad \ldots (3)$$

DIVISION:

To find the quotient $\dfrac{z_1}{z_2} = \dfrac{r_1(\cos\theta_1 + i\sin\theta_1)}{r_2(\cos\theta_2 + i\sin\theta_2)}$

Multiply and divide by the conjugate of $\cos\theta_2 + i\sin\theta_2$, i.e. $(\cos\theta_2 - i\sin\theta_2)$, we have:

$$\begin{aligned} \frac{z_1}{z_2} &= \frac{r_1(\cos\theta_1 + i\sin\theta_1)(\cos\theta_2 - i\sin\theta_2)}{r_2(\cos\theta_2 + i\sin\theta_2)(\cos\theta_2 - i\sin\theta_2)} \\ &= \frac{r_1}{r_2} \cdot \frac{[(\cos\theta_1 \cos\theta_2 + \sin\theta_1 \sin\theta_2) + i(\sin\theta_1 \cos\theta_2 - \sin\theta_2 \cos\theta_1)]}{\cos^2\theta_2 + \sin^2\theta_2} \end{aligned}$$

$$\therefore \quad \frac{z_1}{z_2} = \frac{r_1}{r_2}[\cos(\theta_1 - \theta_2) + i\sin(\theta_1 - \theta_2)] \quad \ldots (4)$$

Thus the modulus of the quotient of two complex numbers is the quotient of their respective moduli and the argument of the quotient is the argument of the numerator minus the argument of the denominator.

From results (1) and (4), we immediately deduce that:

$|z_1 z_2| = r_1 r_2 = |z_1||z_2|$ and $\left|\dfrac{z_1}{z_2}\right| = \dfrac{r_1}{r_2} = \dfrac{|z_1|}{|z_2|}$, but it is not always correct to say that $\arg(z_1 z_2) = \theta_1 + \theta_2$, because the sum $\theta_1 + \theta_2$ may be outside the domain $-\pi < \theta \leqslant \pi$. It may be necessary to add $\pm 2\pi$ to bring the $\arg(z_1 z_2)$ or $\arg(z_1/z_2)$ into this domain. Hence $\arg z_1 z_2 = \arg z_1 + \arg z_2 \pm 2\pi$ (if necessary) and $\arg(z_1/z_2) = \arg z_1 - \arg z_2 \pm 2\pi$ (if necessary).

EXAMPLE: (17) Find the product: $2(\cos 60° + i\sin 60°) \cdot 3(\cos 120° + i\sin 120°)$

SOLUTION: Product = $6[\cos(60° + 120°) + i\sin(60° + 120°)] = 6(\cos 180° + i\sin 180°) = -6$

EXAMPLE: (18)

Find the quotient: $10(\cos 105° + i\sin 105°) \div 2(\cos 45° + i\sin 45°)$

SOLUTION:

$\quad$ QUOTIENT $= 5[\cos(105° - 45°) + i\sin(105° - 45°)] = 5(\cos 60° + i\sin 60°)$

$\therefore$ Quotient $= 5/2 + (5\sqrt{3}/2)i$

EXAMPLE: (19) Find the quotient $[-1/2 - (\sqrt{3}/2)i] \div (1 - i)$ in mod-arg form.

SOLUTION: Change each number to the mod-arg form, then:

$\quad$ QUOTIENT $= \dfrac{1(\cos -120° + i\sin -120°)}{\sqrt{2}(\cos -45° + i\sin -45°)}$

$\qquad\qquad\quad = (1/\sqrt{2})[\cos(-120° - -45°) + i\sin(-120° - -45°)]$

$\qquad\qquad\quad = (1/\sqrt{2})(\cos -75° + i\sin -75°)$

$\quad$ or $\quad = (1/\sqrt{2})(\cos 75° - i\sin 75°)$

EXAMPLE: (20) Solve for r and θ if $r(\cos\theta + i\sin\theta) = \dfrac{2\operatorname{cis} 45° + 3\operatorname{cis} 30°}{4\operatorname{cis} 60° - 3\operatorname{cis} 30°}$

SOLUTION: Numerator = N and Denominator = D

$\quad$ N $= 2(\cos 45° + i\sin 45°) + 3(\cos 30° + i\sin 30°)$

$\quad\;\; = 2\cos 45° + 3\cos 30° + i(2\sin 45° + 3\sin 30°)$

$\quad\;\; = 4.01229 + 2.9142\,i$

Mod-arg form of N = $4.96 \operatorname{cis}(35.99°)$

$\quad$ D $= (4\cos 60° - 3\cos 30°) + i(4\sin 60° - 3\sin 30°)$

$\quad\;\; = -0.59808 + i(1.96410)$

Mod-arg form of D = $2.05 \operatorname{cis} 106.94°$

Hence $r(\cos\theta + i\sin\theta) = 4.96 \operatorname{cis} 35.99° / 2.05 \operatorname{cis} 106.94°$

$\qquad\qquad\qquad\qquad\quad = 2.42 \operatorname{cis}(-70.95°)$

$\therefore\; r = 2.42\quad$ and $\quad \theta = -70.95°$

Exercise 4C

Perform the indicated operation and express the result in the form $a + ib$.

1. $4(\cos 40° + i\sin 40°) \cdot 2(\cos 50° + i\sin 50°)$
2. $5(\cos 120° + i\sin 120°) \cdot 2(\cos 60° + i\sin 60°)$
3. $4(\cos 135° + i\sin 135°) \cdot 3(\cos 90° + i\sin 90°)$
4. $5(\cos 2\pi/3 + i\sin 2\pi/3) \cdot 2(\cos \pi/6 + i\sin \pi/6)$
5. $[2(\cos \pi/3 + i\sin \pi/3)]^2$
6. $[3(\cos \pi/6 + i\sin \pi/6)]^3$
7. $12(\cos 0° + i\sin 0°) \div [6(\cos 120° + i\sin 120°)]$
8. $10(\cos 2\pi/3 + i\sin 2\pi/3) \div [5(\cos \pi/6 + i\sin \pi/6)]$
9. $-10(\cos 2\pi/3 + i\sin 2\pi/3) \div [-5(\cos -\pi/6 + i\sin -\pi/6)]$
10. $6(\cos -2\pi/3 + i\sin -2\pi/3) \div [2(\cos -\pi/3 + i\sin -\pi/3)]$
11. Prove that $[r(\cos\theta + i\sin\theta)]^3 = r^3(\cos 3\theta + i\sin 3\theta)$
12. Change each of the following complex numbers to mod-arg form and perform the indicated operation, giving answers in mod-arg form.

    (a) $\dfrac{1+i}{1-i}$ (b) $\dfrac{(-1+i)}{\sqrt{3}-i}$ (c) $(1+i)(1+\sqrt{3}i)$ (d) $\dfrac{(\sqrt{3}+i)(1-i)}{(1+\sqrt{3}i)(\sqrt{3}-i)}$

13. If $z_1 = 4\operatorname{cis} 120°$ and $z_2 = 2\operatorname{cis} 30°$, find

    (a) $z_1 \cdot z_2$ (b) $\dfrac{z_1}{z_2}$ (c) $(z_1)^2$ (d) $(z_2)^{10}$ and express your answers in the form $a + ib$.

14. Express $z_1 = 1 + \sqrt{3}i$ and $z_2 = \sqrt{3} + i$ in mod-arg form and hence write down the following in $r\operatorname{cis}\theta$ form:

    (a) $(z_1)^5$ (b) $(z_2)^4$ (c) $(z_1 z_2)^5$ (d) $\dfrac{z_1}{z_2}$ (e) $\dfrac{z_2}{z_1}$

15. Express (a) $z_1 + z_2$ (b) $z_1 - z_2$ in mod-arg form if $z_1 = 1 + \sqrt{3}i$, $z = \sqrt{3} + i$ and hence find

    (c) $\dfrac{z_1 + z_2}{z_1 - z_2}$ and   (d) $\left[\dfrac{z_1 + z_2}{z_1 - z_2}\right]^2$ in the form $A + iB$.

4.5 Powers of Complex Numbers: De Moivre's Theorem

For any real number x ($x > 0$), we know that $x^n = x \cdot x \ldots x$ to n factors, if n is a positive integer.
The corresponding result for any complex number $z = a + ib = r(\cos\theta + i\sin\theta)$ is of far-reaching importance and leads to a theorem known as De Moivre's theorem.

Let $z = a + ib = r(\cos\theta + i\sin\theta)$, then by the product rule of two complex numbers
$$z^2 = r^2(\cos\theta + i\sin\theta)(\cos\theta + i\sin\theta) = r^2(\cos 2\theta + i\sin 2\theta)$$
Then $z^3 = z \cdot z^2 = r(\cos\theta + i\sin\theta) \cdot r^2(\cos 2\theta + i\sin 2\theta) = r^3(\cos 3\theta + i\sin 3\theta)$

By successive applications of the product rule, we get:
$$z^4 = r^4(\cos 4\theta + i\sin 4\theta)$$
and so on. These results can be summarised in the following theorem:

Theorem: If n is any positive integer ($n > 0$), then
$$[r(\cos\theta + i\sin\theta)]^n = r^n(\cos n\theta + i\sin n\theta)$$

For $r = 1$, we obtain De Moivre's theorem:
$$(\cos\theta + i\sin\theta)^n = \cos n\theta + i\sin n\theta$$

De Moivre's theorem can also be proved by the method of mathematical induction. (This proof is given in a later section.) It also holds for $n = 0$ and for a negative integer.

EXAMPLE: (21) Find $(1 + i)^6$

SOLUTION: Write $z = 1 + i$ in the mod-arg form.
$z = \sqrt{2}(\cos \pi/4 + i\sin \pi/4)$
$\therefore z^6 = [\sqrt{2}(\cos \pi/4 + i\sin \pi/4)]^6 = (\sqrt{2})^6(\cos 6\pi/4 + i\sin 6\pi/4)$
$\qquad = 8(\cos 3\pi/2 + i\sin 3\pi/2)$
$\qquad = -8i$

EXAMPLE: (22) Evaluate in the form $a + ib$: $(1 + \sqrt{3}i)^4 \div (-1 + \sqrt{3}i)^7$

SOLUTION: We write $z = 1 + \sqrt{3}i = 2(\cos 60° + i\sin 60°)$
$\qquad \omega = -1 + \sqrt{3}i = 2(\cos 120° + i\sin 120°)$
$\therefore z^4 = 2^4(\cos 60° + i\sin 60°)^4 = 16(\cos 240° + i\sin 240°)$ and
$\omega^7 = 2^7(\cos 120° + i\sin 120°)^7 = 128(\cos 840° + i\sin 840°)$
$\qquad = 128(\cos 120° + i\sin 120°)$

Hence $\dfrac{z^4}{\omega^7} = \dfrac{16}{128}[\cos(240° - 120°) + i\sin(240° - 120°)]$
$\qquad = (1/8)(\cos 120° + i\sin 120°)$, i.e. $-1/16 + i(\sqrt{3}/16)$

Exercise 4D

Evaluate in the form $a + ib$, by using De Moivre's theorem:

1. $(\cos 12° + i \sin 12°)^5$
2. $[2(\cos 15° + i \sin 15°)]^6$
3. $(\cos \pi/4 + i \sin \pi/4)^4$
4. $[2(\cos \pi/3 + i \sin \pi/3)]^6$
5. $[\cos(-\pi/4) + i \sin(-\pi/4)]^6$
6. $[2(\cos 2\pi/3 - i \sin 2\pi/3)]^4$
   (Hint: bracketed expression = cis $-2\pi/3$)

Express the following in mod-arg and cartesian form (7 to 14).

7. $(1 + i)^6$
8. $(3 + 4i)^{-2}$
9. $(1 - i)^4$
10. $(\sqrt{3} - i)^4$
11. $(-1 - i)^{10}$
12. $(2 - 2\sqrt{3}i)^{-4}$
13. $(1 + \sqrt{3}i)^4$
14. $(2\sqrt{3} + 2i)^5$

Simplify the following in the form $r \operatorname{cis} \theta$ and wherever possible, express the answers in the form $a + ib$ (15 to 20).

15. $(1 - i)^4 (1 + i)^3$
16. $(1 - \sqrt{3}i)^3 (1 + i)^4$
17. $\dfrac{(1 + \sqrt{3}i)^3}{(1 - i)^4}$
18. $\dfrac{(2 + 2i)^4}{(1 - \sqrt{3}i)^2}$
19. $\dfrac{(2 \operatorname{cis} \pi/6)^4}{(4 \operatorname{cis} \pi/3)^3}$
20. $\dfrac{(3 \operatorname{cis} \pi/12)^5}{[3 \operatorname{cis}(-\pi/36)]^3}$

4.6 Roots of Complex Numbers

Finding a desired root of a non-negative real number is a simple matter. For example:

The two square roots of 4 are ± 2

The cube root of 8 is $(8)^{1/3} = 2$ and so on.

But finding the desired roots of complex numbers is not so simple, as we must use De Moivre's theorem to find the:

three cube roots, four 4th roots, five 5th roots and so on of a complex number $a + ib$.

EXAMPLE: (23)   Find all the cube roots of -1

SOLUTION: We use two methods to find the cube roots.

Method I: If z is a cube root of -1, then

$\therefore \quad z^3 + 1 = 0$, hence $(z + 1)(z^2 - z + 1) = 0$

The three cube roots are $-1, \dfrac{1 \pm \sqrt{3}i}{2}$

Method II: We write $-1 = \cos\pi + i\sin\pi$ and make the expression general by adding $2k\pi$ to the $\arg(-1)$, hence

$-1 = \cos(\pi + 2k\pi) + i\sin(\pi + 2k\pi)$ ... (1)

Now let the required cube root be $R(\cos\phi + i\sin\phi)$

$\sqrt[3]{\cos(\pi + 2k\pi) + i\sin(\pi + 2k\pi)} = R(\cos\phi + i\sin\phi)$

We take the cube of both sides:

$\therefore \quad R^3(\cos 3\phi + i\sin 3\phi) = \cos(\pi + 2k\pi) + i\sin(\pi + 2k\pi)$

Equating the real and imaginary parts:

$R^3 \cos 3\phi = \cos(\pi + 2k\pi)$ and $R^3 \sin 3\phi = \sin(\pi + 2k\pi)$

From these: $R^3 = 1$, i.e., $R = 1$ and $3\phi = \pi + 2k\pi$

$\therefore \quad \phi = \pi/3 + 2k\pi/3$

Hence the cube roots are given by:

$z = (\cos\phi + i\sin\phi) = \cos(\pi/3 + 2k\pi/3) + i\sin(\pi/3 + 2k\pi/3)$

where $k = 0, 1, 2$.

For $k = 3$, the angle is $\pi/3 + 2\pi$ and the corresponding cube-root is the same as the root for $k = 0$. In a similar manner, $k = 4$ produces the same root as $k = 1$ and so on. The three cube roots of $(-1)^{1/3}$ are:

$k = 0$, $\quad z_1 = \cos \pi/3 + i\sin \pi/3 \quad = 1/2 + \sqrt{3}/2 \cdot i$

$k = 1$, $\quad z_2 = \cos \pi + i\sin \pi \quad = -1$

$k = 2$, $\quad z_3 = \cos 5\pi/3 + i\sin 5\pi/3 \quad = 1/2 - \sqrt{3}/2 \cdot i$

These three roots are the same as given by Method I.

The modulus of each root is 1

i.e. $|z_1| = |z_2| = |z_3| = 1$, hence these three distinct cube-roots lie on a circle of radius 1 and centre the origin.

They are equally spaced, the angular distance between any two roots being $360° \div 3 = 120°$.

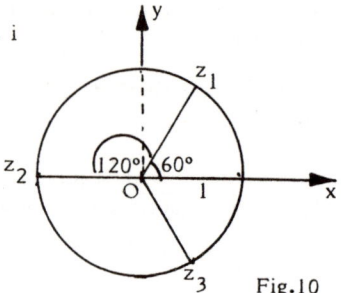

Fig.10

Definition: If n is a positive integer, then $R(\cos\phi + i\sin\phi)$ is an nth root of $r(\cos\theta + i\sin\theta)$ if and only if $R^n(\cos\phi + i\sin\phi)^n = r(\cos\theta + i\sin\theta)$

From this, and using De Moivre's theorem:

$\qquad R^n(\cos n\phi + i\sin n\phi) = r(\cos\theta + i\sin\theta)$

$\therefore \quad r\cos\theta = R^n\cos n\phi \quad$ and $\quad r\sin\theta = R^n\sin n\phi$

By squaring and adding:

$\qquad R^n = r$, hence $\cos\theta = \cos n\phi$ gives $n\phi = \theta + 2k\pi$

Hence $R = r^{1/n}$, $\phi = \dfrac{\theta + 2k\pi}{n}$, where $k = 0, 1, 2, \ldots (n-1)$

We conclude that the n nth roots of the complex number $r(\cos\theta + i\sin\theta)$ have the modulus $r^{1/n}$ and arguments are given by $\dfrac{\theta + 2k\pi}{n}$, $k = 0, 1, 2, \ldots (n-1)$.

EXAMPLE: (24) Find the 4th roots of $-8 + 8\sqrt{3}i$

SOLUTION: Write $-8 + 8\sqrt{3}i = 16(\cos 2\pi/3 + i\sin 2\pi/3) = 16(\cos 120° + i\sin 120°) = z^4$

$\therefore$ The 4th roots are $z = 2[\cos \dfrac{(2k\pi + 2\pi/3)}{4} + i\sin\dfrac{(2k\pi + 2\pi/3)}{4}]$, $k = 0, 1, 2, 3$

The four roots are:

$k = 0$, $\quad z_1 = 2(\cos 30° + i\sin 30°) \quad = \sqrt{3} + 1i$

$k = 1$, $\quad z_2 = 2(\cos 120° + i\sin 120°) \quad = -1 + \sqrt{3}i$

$k = 2$, $\quad z_3 = 2(\cos 210° + i\sin 210°) \quad = -\sqrt{3} - 1 \cdot i$

$k = 3$, $\quad z_4 = 2(\cos 300° + i\sin 300°) \quad = 1 - \sqrt{3} \cdot i$

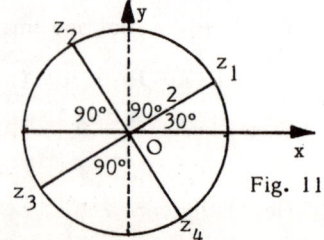

Fig. 11

The points in the Argand diagram that correspond to these four distinct 4th roots are equally spaced (at an angular distance of $360° \div 4 = 90°$) on a circle of radius 2 and centre the origin.

EXAMPLE: (25) Find all 5 roots of $z^5 - 32 = 0$ and show them in an Argand diagram.

SOLUTION: $z^5 = 32 = 32(\cos 0 + i\sin 0) = 32[\cos 2k\pi + i\sin 2k\pi]$

The five fifth roots are given by

$$z = 2[\cos \frac{2k\pi}{5} + i \sin \frac{2k\pi}{5}] \quad \text{where } k = 0, 1, 2, 3, 4.$$

To clearly visualise the roots, we replace π by 180°, then the five roots of $z^5 = 32$ are:

$k = 0, \quad z_1 = 2\text{cis}\, 0° = 2 \quad$ (the only real root)
$k = 1, \quad z_2 = 2\text{cis}\, 72°$
$k = 2, \quad z_3 = 2\text{cis}\, 144°$
$k = 3, \quad z_4 = 2\text{cis}\, 216°$
$k = 4, \quad z_5 = 2\text{cis}\, 288°$

Note that the argument of successive root increases by $360° \div 5$ i.e. 72°. This way you can quickly write down all the roots.

Observing that:
$|z_1| = |z_2| \ldots = |z_5| = 2$, we can show these roots on a circle of radius 2, centre O.

From the diagram:
$z_5 = \bar{z}_2$
$z_4 = \bar{z}_3$

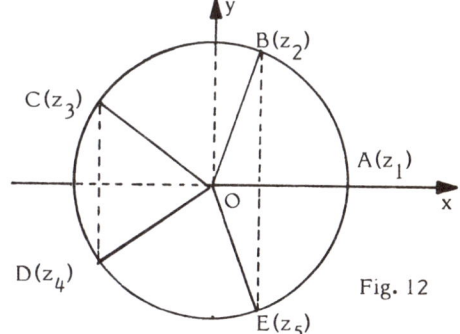

Fig. 12

EXAMPLE: (26) Solve $z^5 = 16\sqrt{2} + 16\sqrt{2}\,i$

SOLUTION: Write $1 + i = \sqrt{2}\,\text{cis}(\pi/4) = \sqrt{2}\,\text{cis}(2k\pi + \pi/4)$

$\therefore \quad z^5 = 32\text{cis}(2k\pi + \pi/4)$

The five 5th roots are given by

$\quad z = 2\text{cis}(\pi/20 + 2k\pi/5)$

The five roots are: $\quad k = 0, 1, 2, 3, 4.$

$z_1 = 2\text{cis}\, 9°$
$z_2 = 2\text{cis}(9° + 72°) = 2\text{cis}\, 81°$
$z_3 = 2\text{cis}(9° + 144°) = 2\text{cis}\, 153°$
$z_4 = 2\text{cis}(9° + 216°) = 2\text{cis}\, 225°$
$z_5 = 2\text{cis}(9° + 288°) = 2\text{cis}\, 297°$

Exercise 4E

1. Find the two square roots of:
   (a) $-16i$
   (b) $2 + 2\sqrt{3}i$
   (c) $-2\sqrt{3} - 2i$
   (d) $4 + 3i$

2. Find all the cube roots of:
   (a) i
   (b) -8
   (c) $27\left(\frac{1}{2} + \frac{\sqrt{3}}{2}i\right)$
   (d) $-8i$

3. Find the four 4th roots of:
   (a) -1
   (b) -16
   (c) $-8 - 8\sqrt{3}i$
   (d) $\frac{1}{2} - \frac{\sqrt{3}}{2}i$

4. Find the five roots of:
   (a) 32
   (b) -32
   (c) $-\frac{\sqrt{3}}{2} + \frac{1}{2}i$
   (d) $32i$

5. Find the solution set for each of the following equations. Express your answers in the form $a + bi$.

   (a) $x^3 - i = 2$
   (b) $x^2 + (3 - i)x - 3i = 0$
   (c) $x^4 + 1 = 0$
   (d) $x^4 + 16i = 0$
   (e) $x^2 - 1 + i = 0$
   (f) $x^6 - 64 = 0$
   (g) $x^4 = \frac{1}{2} - \frac{\sqrt{3}}{2}i$
   (h) $x^2 + i = 0$

4.7 De Moivre's Theorem and its Applications

We have used De Moivre's theorem in finding the powers and the roots of complex numbers. We now prove it by the method of induction and consider some further applications.

De Moivre's theorem is:

$$\text{For any integer } n, \ (\cos\theta + i\sin\theta)^n = \cos n\theta + i\sin n\theta \qquad \ldots (1)$$

Proof: For $n = 0$, $(\cos\theta + i\sin\theta)^0 = 1 = \cos 0 + i\sin 0$

For $n = 1$, $\cos\theta + i\sin\theta = \cos\theta + i\sin\theta$

So the theorem is true for $n = 0$ and $n = 1$. We assume it true for $n = k$, a positive integer, so:

$$(\cos\theta + i\sin\theta)^k = \cos k\theta + i\sin k\theta \qquad \ldots (2)$$

Multiply both sides of (2) by $\cos\theta + i\sin\theta$, then

$$(\cos\theta + i\sin\theta)^{k+1} = (\cos k\theta + i\sin k\theta)(\cos\theta + i\sin\theta)$$

$$= (\cos k\theta \cos\theta - \sin k\theta \sin\theta) + i(\sin k\theta \cos\theta + i\cos k\theta \sin\theta)$$

$$= \cos(k+1)\theta + i\sin(k+1)\theta$$

This proves that the theorem is true for $n = k + 1$, if it is true for $n = k$. Since it is true for $n = 1$, then it is true for $n = 2$ and so on for all positive integers n.

The theorem is also true when n is a negative integer.
Let $n = -m$, where m is a positive integer.

$$\therefore \ (\cos\theta + i\sin\theta)^n = (\cos\theta + i\sin\theta)^{-m} = \frac{1}{(\cos\theta + i\sin\theta)^m} = \frac{1}{\cos m\theta + i\sin m\theta}$$

by using the theorem for positive integer m.

Now $\dfrac{1}{\cos m\theta + i\sin m\theta} = \dfrac{(\cos m\theta - i\sin m\theta)}{(\cos m\theta + i\sin m\theta)(\cos m\theta - i\sin m\theta)} = \dfrac{\cos m\theta - i\sin m\theta}{1}$

Finally $\cos m\theta - i\sin m\theta = \cos(-n\theta) - i\sin(-n\theta) = \cos n\theta + i\sin n\theta$.

Hence the theorem is true for negative integers.

DERIVATION OF TRIGONOMETRIC FORMULA

By application of both De Moivre's theorem and binomial expansion, we can find:

(a) $\cos n\theta$ and $\sin n\theta$ in terms of powers of $\sin\theta$ and $\cos\theta$.

(b) $\cos^n\theta$ and $\sin^n\theta$ in terms of multiple angles (2θ, 3θ, etc.)

For (a) and (b) we shall need the following:

Let $z = \cos\theta + i\sin\theta$, then:
$z^n = \cos n\theta + i\sin n\theta$ and $z^{-n} = \cos n\theta - i\sin n\theta$.

Adding, $\quad z^n + z^{-n} = 2\cos n\theta \quad \ldots (1)$

Subtracting, $z^n - z^{-n} = 2i\sin n\theta \quad \ldots (2)$

For $n = 1$, $\quad z + \dfrac{1}{z} = 2\cos\theta$, $\quad z - \dfrac{1}{z} = 2i\sin\theta$

$n = 2$, $\quad z^2 + \dfrac{1}{z^2} = 2\cos 2\theta$, $\quad z^2 - \dfrac{1}{z^2} = 2i\sin 2\theta$, etc.

EXAMPLE: (27) Express (a) $\cos 4\theta$ in terms of $\cos\theta$
(b) $\sin 4\theta$ in terms of $\cos\theta$ and $\sin\theta$
(c) $\tan 4\theta$ in terms of $\tan\theta$.

SOLUTION: We use $c = \cos\theta$ and $s = \sin\theta$ to simplify our work.

By De Moivre's theorem:

$\cos 4\theta + i\sin 4\theta = (\cos\theta + i\sin\theta)^4 = (c + is)^4$

$\qquad = c^4 + 4c^3 is + 6c^2 i^2 s^2 + 4c i^3 s^3 + i^4 s^4$

$\qquad = c^4 - 6c^2 s^2 + s^4 + i(4c^3 s - 4cs^3)$

(Note that $i^2 = -1$, $i^3 = -i$, $i^4 = 1$, etc.)

Equating real and imaginary parts:

(a) $\cos 4\theta = c^4 - 6c^2 s^2 + s^4 = c^4 - 6c^2(1-c^2) + (1-c^2)^2$,

using $\cos^2\theta = 1 - \sin^2\theta$

$\therefore \cos 4\theta = 8\cos^4\theta - 8\cos^2\theta + 1$

(b) $\sin 4\theta = 4c^3 s - 4cs^3 = 4\cos^3\theta\sin\theta - 4\sin^3\theta\cos\theta$

We note that $\sin 4\theta$ cannot be expressed in terms of $\sin\theta$ alone.

(c) $\tan 4\theta = \dfrac{\sin 4\theta}{\cos 4\theta} = \dfrac{4c^3 s - 4cs^3}{c^4 - 6c^2 s^2 + s^4}$

Divide both the numerator and the denominator by c^4 remembering $\sin\theta/\cos\theta = \tan\theta$,

we have: $\tan 4\theta = \dfrac{4\tan\theta - 4\tan^3\theta}{1 - 6\tan^2\theta + \tan^4\theta}$

EXAMPLE: (28)

(a) If $z = \cos\theta + i\sin\theta$, show that:

    (i) $z^n + \dfrac{1}{z^n} = 2\cos n\theta$ (ii) $z^n - \dfrac{1}{z^n} = 2i\sin n\theta$

(b) Express the following in terms of $\cos n\theta$ or $\sin n\theta$

    (i) $\cos^4\theta$ (ii) $\sin^4\theta$ (iii) $\sin^3\theta$

SOLUTION:

(a) $z = \cos\theta + i\sin\theta$

      $\dfrac{1}{z} = z^{-1} = \cos\theta - i\sin\theta$

By De Moivre's theorem:

$\therefore \quad z^n = \cos n\theta + i\sin n\theta, \quad \dfrac{1}{z^n} = z^{-n} = \cos n\theta - i\sin n\theta$

Adding: $\quad z^n + \dfrac{1}{z^n} = 2\cos n\theta \quad\quad\quad \ldots\text{(i)}$

Subtracting: $\quad z^n - \dfrac{1}{z^n} = 2i\sin n\theta \quad\quad \ldots\text{(ii)}$

(b) (i) $(2\cos\theta)^4 = \left(z + \dfrac{1}{z}\right)^4 = \left(z^4 + \dfrac{1}{z^4}\right) + 4\left(z^2 + \dfrac{1}{z^2}\right) + 6$

$\therefore \quad 16\cos^4\theta = 2\cos 4\theta + 8\cos 2\theta + 6 \quad$ [using results (a)(i) n = 4, 2]

$\quad\quad \cos^4\theta = \dfrac{1}{8}(\cos 4\theta + 4\cos 2\theta + 3)$

(ii) $(2i\sin\theta)^4 = \left(z - \dfrac{1}{z}\right)^4 = \left(z^4 + \dfrac{1}{z^4}\right) - 4\left(z^2 + \dfrac{1}{z^2}\right) + 6$

$\therefore \quad 16\sin^4\theta = 2\cos 4\theta - 8\cos 2\theta + 6 \quad$ [in (a)(i) n = 4, 2]

$\quad\quad \sin^4\theta = \dfrac{1}{8}(\cos 4\theta - 4\cos 2\theta + 3)$

(iii) $(2i\sin\theta)^3 = \left(z - \dfrac{1}{z}\right)^3$,   expand and rearrange.

$\quad\quad\quad\quad\quad\quad = \left(z^3 - \dfrac{1}{z^3}\right) - 3\left(z - \dfrac{1}{z}\right) \quad$ [in (a)(ii) n = 3, 1]

$\therefore \quad -8i\sin^3\theta = 2i\sin 3\theta - 6i\sin\theta$

$\quad\quad \sin^3\theta = \dfrac{1}{4}(3\sin\theta - \sin 3\theta)$

Exercise 4F

1. Express (a) $\cos 3\theta$ (b) $\sin 3\theta$ in terms of $\cos\theta$ and $\sin\theta$, hence express $\tan 3\theta$ in terms of $\tan\theta$

2. Express (a) $\cos 5\theta$ (b) $\sin 5\theta$ in terms of $\cos\theta$ and $\sin\theta$, hence express $\tan 5\theta$ in terms of $\tan\theta$

3. Express (a) $\cos 6\theta$ (b) $\sin 6\theta$ in terms of $\cos\theta$ and $\sin\theta$ and hence express $\tan 6\theta$ in terms of $\tan\theta$

4. Express (a) $\cos^3\theta$ (b) $\sin^3\theta$ in terms of multiples of θ

5. Express (a) $\cos^5\theta$ (b) $\sin^5\theta$ in terms of multiples of θ and hence integrate (c) $\int \cos^5\theta \, d\theta$ (d) $\int \sin^5\theta \, d\theta$

6. Express (a) $\cos^6\theta$ (b) $\sin^6\theta$ in terms of multiples of θ, and hence integrate (c) $\int_0^{\pi/2} \cos^6\theta \, d\theta$ (d) $\int_0^{\pi/2} \sin^6\theta \, d\theta$

7. Find the constants p, q, r and s if: (a) $\cos^7\theta = p\cos 7\theta + q\cos 5\theta + r\cos 3\theta + s$ and hence evaluate: (b) $\int_0^{\pi/2} \cos^7\theta \, d\theta$

8. Find the constants p, q, r, s if: (a) $\sin^7\theta = p\sin 7\theta + q\sin 5\theta + r\sin 3\theta + s\sin\theta$, and hence evaluate: (b) $\int_0^{\pi/2} \sin^7\theta \, d\theta$

9. Show that $(1 + \cos\theta + i\sin\theta)^n = 2^n \cos^n\left(\frac{\theta}{2}\right) \left[\cos n\frac{\theta}{2} + i\sin n\frac{\theta}{2}\right]$, where n is a positive integer

10. Prove the following:

    (a) $\cot 4\theta = \dfrac{1 - 6\tan^2\theta + \tan^4\theta}{4\tan\theta - 4\tan^3\theta} = \dfrac{\cot^4\theta - 6\cot^2\theta + 1}{4\cot^3\theta - 4\cot\theta}$

    (b) $\cot 5\theta = \dfrac{1 - 10\tan^2\theta + 5\tan^4\theta}{5\tan\theta - 10\tan^3\theta + \tan^5\theta} = \dfrac{\cot^5\theta - 10\cot^3\theta + 5\cot\theta}{5\cot^4\theta - 10\cot^2\theta + 1}$

4.8 Square Roots of a Complex Number

We usually use De Moivre's theorem to find the roots of a complex number; but there is also a special requirement to obtain the square roots in the form $a + ib$.

Two methods of obtaining the square roots are:

1. We convert $z^2 = a + ib$ to mod-arg form and use De Moivre's theorem to solve $z^2 = a + ib$.
2. We assume the solution $z = x + iy$ and hence solve two simultaneous equations involving x and y.

METHOD I: Using De Moivre's theorem.

EXAMPLE: (29) Find the two square roots of $2 + 2\sqrt{3}i$

Let $z^2 = 2 + 2\sqrt{3}i = 4(\cos \pi/3 + i\sin \pi/3) = 4[\cos(2k\pi + \pi/3) + i\sin(2k\pi + \pi/3)]$

By De Moivre's theorem:

$$z = 2\left[\cos\left(\frac{2k\pi + \pi/3}{2}\right) + i\sin\left(\frac{2k\pi + \pi/3}{2}\right)\right], \quad k = 0, 1.$$

The two roots are:

$z_1 = 2(\cos \pi/6 + i\sin \pi/6) = \sqrt{3} + i$
$z_2 = 2(\cos 7\pi/6 + i\sin 7\pi/6) = -\sqrt{3} - i$

Verify that, $[\pm(\sqrt{3} + i)]^2 = 2 + 2\sqrt{3}i$

METHOD II:

Let $z = x + iy$, then
$$z^2 = a + ib$$
$$\therefore \quad x^2 - y^2 + 2ixy = a + ib$$
Equating real and imaginary parts.
$x^2 - y^2 = a$ and $2xy = b$, then:
$(x^2 + y^2)^2 = (x^2 - y^2)^2 + 4x^2y^2 = a^2 + b^2$
$\therefore x^2 + y^2 = \sqrt{a^2 + b^2}$ as $x^2 + y^2 > 0$
Finally we solve
$x^2 - y^2 = a$ and $x^2 + y^2 = \sqrt{a^2 + b^2}$
for x and y.

EXAMPLE: (30)

Find the square roots of $7 + 6\sqrt{2}i$

SOLUTION: Let $(x + iy)^2 = 7 + 6\sqrt{2}i$
$\therefore x^2 - y^2 = 7$ and $2xy = 6\sqrt{2}$
Now $(x^2 + y^2)^2 = (x^2 - y^2)^2 + 4x^2y^2$
$ = 49 + 72$
$ = 121$
$\therefore x^2 + y^2 = 11$ ... (1)
and $x^2 - y^2 = 7$ ... (2)
Solving (1) and (2):
$x = \pm 3$, $y = \pm\sqrt{2}$
We check $xy = 6\sqrt{2}$ for the proper combination of x and y.
The required roots are:
$\pm(3 + \sqrt{2}i)$

Exercise 4G

1. Find the square roots of the following in the form $x + iy$.
   - (a) $3 + 4i$
   - (b) $3 - 4i$
   - (c) $5 + 2\sqrt{6}i$
   - (d) $7 - 6\sqrt{2}i$
   - (e) $5 + 12i$
   - (f) $8 + 6i$
   - (g) i
   - (h) $-8i$

2. Solve the following equations, expressing the answers in the form $x + iy$.
   - (a) $z^2 = -15 + 8i$
   - (b) $z^2 = 1 + \sqrt{3}i$
   - (c) $z^2 = 2i$

3. Use the formula $z = (-b \pm \sqrt{b^2 - 4ac})/2a$ to express the roots of the following equations in $x + iy$ form:
   - (a) $z^2 - (1 - 4i)z - (5 - i) = 0$ (Hint: $\sqrt{5 - 12i} = 3 - 2i$)
   - (b) $z^2 + (2 + 4i)z - 11 - 2i = 0$ (Hint: $\sqrt{8 + 6i} = 3 + i$)
   - (c) $z^2 + (4 + 2i)z + (3 + 2i) = 0$
   - (d) $z^2 + (4 - 2i)z + 6 = 0$

4. Write each of the following in the form $a + ib$.
   (Take $\sqrt{z}$ to mean the square root whose real part > 0)
   - (a) $\dfrac{1 + i}{\sqrt{8 + 6i}}$
   - (b) $\sqrt{\dfrac{5 - 12i}{5 + 12i}}$
   - (c) $1 + z + z^2$ where $z = \sqrt{8 + 6i}$

5. Prove the following:
   - (a) $\sqrt{a + bi} + \sqrt{a - bi} = \sqrt{2(\sqrt{a^2 + b^2} + a)}$
   - (b) $\sqrt{a + bi} - \sqrt{a - bi} = i\sqrt{2(\sqrt{a^2 + b^2} - a)}$

6. If $x + iy = \sqrt{\dfrac{a + ib}{c + id}}$, prove that $(x^2 + y^2)^2 = \dfrac{a^2 + b^2}{c^2 + d^2}$.

7. Simplify: $\dfrac{\sqrt{5 + 12i}}{\sqrt{5 + 12i}} + \dfrac{\sqrt{5 - 12i}}{\sqrt{5 - 12i}}$

4.9 Properties of Conjugate Complex Numbers

$\bar{z} = x - iy$ is the conjugate of $z = x + iy$.
If the point $P(x,y)$ represents $z = x + iy$ in the complex plane, then $Q(x,-y)$ is the reflection of P in the x-axis and hence $\bar{z}$ is the reflection of z in the x-axis. Note that $x + iy$ is the conjugate of $x - iy$. We have:

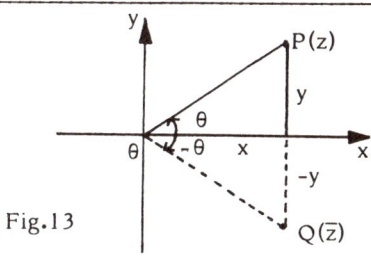

Fig.13

1. $|z| = |\bar{z}| = \sqrt{x^2 + y^2}$ 2. $\arg \bar{z} = -\arg z$ 3. $z\bar{z} = x^2 + y^2 = |z|^2 = |\bar{z}|^2$
4. $z + \bar{z} = 2x$ (a real number)   5. $z - \bar{z} = 2iy$ (a purely imaginary number)

Further, for two complex numbers z_1 and z_2 we prove the following properties:

6. $\overline{z_1 + z_2} = \bar{z}_1 + \bar{z}_2$ 7. $\overline{z_1 - z_2} = \bar{z}_1 - \bar{z}_2$ 8. $\overline{z_1 z_2} = \bar{z}_1 \cdot \bar{z}_2$

9. $\overline{\left(\dfrac{z_1}{z_2}\right)} = \dfrac{\bar{z}_1}{\bar{z}_2}$ 10. $z^{-1} = \dfrac{\bar{z}}{|z|^2}$

Proof: Let $z_1 = a + ib$ and $z_2 = c + id$, then

(a) $z_1 + z_2 = a + ib + c + id$
  $= (a + c) + i(b + d)$
  $\therefore \overline{z_1 + z_2} = (a + c) - i(b + d)$
  $= (a - ib) + (c - id)$
  $= \bar{z}_1 + \bar{z}_2$

(b) $z_1 - z_2 = a + ib - c - id$
  $= (a - c) + i(b - d)$
  $\therefore \overline{z_1 - z_2} = (a - c) - i(b - d)$
  $= (a - ib) - (c - id)$
  $= \bar{z}_1 - \bar{z}_2$

(c) $z_1 \cdot z_2 = (a + ib)(c + id)$
  $= (ac - bd) + i(bc + ad)$
  $\therefore \overline{z_1 \cdot z_2} = (ac - bd) - i(bc + ad)$
  $= (a - ib)(c - id)$
  $= \bar{z}_1 \cdot \bar{z}_2$

(d) We have
  $\dfrac{z_1}{z_2} = \dfrac{(ac + bd) - i(ad - bc)}{c^2 + d^2}$ (see Section 4.2, example 5)

  Again, $\dfrac{\bar{z}_1}{\bar{z}_2} = \dfrac{(a - ib)}{(c - id)} = \dfrac{(a - ib)(c + id)}{(c - id)(c + id)}$
  $= \dfrac{(ac + bd) + i(ad - bc)}{c^2 + d^2}$, hence
  $\overline{\left(\dfrac{z_1}{z_2}\right)} = \dfrac{\bar{z}_1}{\bar{z}_2}$

(e) $z^{-1} = \dfrac{1}{z} = \dfrac{\bar{z}}{z\bar{z}} = \dfrac{\bar{z}}{|z|^2}$, using property (3)

We easily generalise, but shall not prove that:

11. $\overline{z_1 + z_2 + z_3 + \ldots + z_n} = \bar{z}_1 + \bar{z}_2 + \ldots + \bar{z}_n$

12. $\overline{z_1 w_1} + \overline{z_2 w_2} + \ldots + \overline{z_n w_n} = \bar{z}_1 \cdot \bar{w}_1 + \bar{z}_2 \cdot \bar{w}_2 + \ldots + \bar{z}_n \cdot \bar{w}_n$

In particular, if w is real, then using $\bar{w} = w$, we have

13. $\overline{z_1 w_1} + \overline{z_2 w_2} + \ldots + \overline{z_n w_n} = w_1 \bar{z}_1 + w_2 \bar{z}_2 + \ldots + w_n \bar{z}_n$

We shall use the properties (9), (10) and (11) in the next chapter on Polynomials.

EXAMPLE: (31): If $z = 4 + 3i$, express the following in $a + ib$ form:

(a) $\bar{z}$ (b) $z + \bar{z}$ (c) $z - \bar{z}$ (d) $z\bar{z}$ (e) z^{-1}

SOLUTION:

(a) $\bar{z} = 4 - 3i$ (b) $z + \bar{z} = 4 + 3i + 4 - 3i = 8$ (c) $z - \bar{z} = 4 + 3i - (4 - 3i) = 6i$

(d) $z\bar{z} = (4 + 3i)(4 - 3i)$ (e) $z^{-1} = \dfrac{1}{z} = \dfrac{\bar{z}}{z\bar{z}} = \dfrac{\bar{z}}{|z|^2} = \dfrac{4 - 3i}{25} = \dfrac{4}{25} - \dfrac{3}{25}i$, using (d).

$\quad = 16 + 9$

$\quad = 25 \qquad$ Note that $z^{-1} \neq \bar{z}$ in general, even though $\arg z^{-1} = \arg \bar{z}$.

EXAMPLE: (32) If $x + iy = \sqrt{\dfrac{a + ib}{c + id}}$, prove that $(x^2 + y^2)^2 = \dfrac{a^2 + b^2}{c^2 + d^2}$

SOLUTION: We square both sides and write

$\omega = (x + iy)(x + iy) = \dfrac{a + ib}{c + id} \qquad \ldots (1)$

Using, $\overline{z_1 \cdot z_2} = \dfrac{\bar{z}_1}{\bar{z}_2}$ and $\overline{\left(\dfrac{z_1}{z_2}\right)} = \dfrac{\bar{z}_1}{\bar{z}_2}$,

$\bar{\omega} = (x - iy)(x - iy) = \dfrac{a - ib}{c - id} \qquad \ldots (2)$

Multiplying (1) and (2) and using $(x + iy)(x - iy) = x^2 + y^2$, etc.

$(x^2 + y^2)(x^2 + y^2) = \dfrac{a^2 + b^2}{c^2 + d^2}$, hence the required result.

Exercise 4H

1. Given (a) $z = 1 + 2i$ (b) $z = 3 - i$, find and sketch the following:
   (i) $\bar{z}$ (ii) $z + \bar{z}$ (iii) $z - \bar{z}$ (iv) $z \cdot \bar{z}$ (v) $|z|$ (vi) $|\bar{z}|$ (vii) z^{-1}

2. If $x + iy = (a + ib)^2$, then without finding x and y, prove that
   $x^2 + y^2 = (a^2 + b^2)^2$

3. If $a + ib = \dfrac{(x + i)^2}{2x - i}$, prove that $a^2 + b^2 = \dfrac{(x^2 + 1)^2}{4x^2 + 1}$

4. If $x + iy = \sqrt{\dfrac{1 + i}{1 - i}}$, show that $x^2 + y^2 = 1$

5. If $a = \cos\alpha + i\sin\alpha$, $b = \cos\beta + i\sin\beta$, $c = \cos\gamma + i\sin\gamma$ and $a + b + c = 0$,
   then prove that: $\dfrac{1}{a} + \dfrac{1}{b} + \dfrac{1}{c} = 0 \qquad$ (Hint: $\dfrac{1}{a} = \dfrac{\bar{a}}{|a|^2}$ etc.)

6. If $(a + ib)^{1/3} = x + iy$, prove that: $4(x^2 - y^2) = \dfrac{a}{x} + \dfrac{b}{y}$
   [Hint: $(a + ib) = (x + iy)^3$, equate real and imaginary parts, substitute in $\dfrac{a}{x} + \dfrac{b}{y}$]

7. Find θ, $0 \leqslant \theta \leqslant 2\pi$, if $\dfrac{3 + 2i\sin\theta}{1 - 2i\sin\theta}$ is purely imaginary.

8. Prove that $(1 - \cos\theta + 2i\sin\theta)^{-1} = \dfrac{1 - 2i\cot(\theta/2)}{5 + 3\cos\theta}$

4.10 The Complex Roots of Unity

The equations of the form $z^n = a + ib$ give rise to n roots which are equally spaced on a circle of radius r, where r is the modulus of any root. In the special case where $z^n = 1$, then $r = 1$, i.e. all of the roots lie on a circle of radius 1, centre the origin ($x^2 + y^2 = 1$).

In the chapter on Polynomials, we shall learn that the complex roots of $z^n - 1 = 0$ (if any) must occur in conjugate pairs.

We shall also show that if ω is a complex root of $z^n - 1 = 0$ with the smallest positive argument, then the n roots of $x^n - 1 = 0$ are:
$1, \omega, \omega^2, \ldots, \omega^{n-1}$ and consequently, the sum of the roots is given by
$1 + \omega + \omega^2 + \ldots + \omega^{n-1} = 0$.

EXAMPLE: (33) Solve $z^3 - 1 = 0$

SOLUTION: Factorise $z^3 - 1 = 0$, then
$(z - 1)(z^2 + z + 1) = 0$. The three roots are:
$z_1 = 1$, $z_2 = \frac{-1}{2} + \frac{\sqrt{3}}{2}i$, $z_3 = -\frac{1}{2} - \frac{\sqrt{3}}{2}i$
Let $\omega = z_2 = -\frac{1}{2} + \frac{\sqrt{3}}{2}i$, then
$\omega^2 = \frac{1}{4} - 2 \cdot \frac{1}{2} \cdot \frac{\sqrt{3}}{2}i - \frac{3}{4} = -\frac{1}{2} - \frac{\sqrt{3}}{2}i = z_3$

Thus $1, \omega$ and ω^2 are the three roots of $z^3 - 1 = 0$

We find $z_1 + z_2 + z_3 = -\dfrac{\text{coefficient of } z^2}{\text{coefficient of } z^3} = 0$

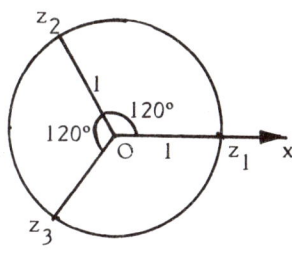

Fig. 14

Alternatively $1 + \omega + \omega^2 = z_1 + z_2 + z_3 = 1 - \frac{1}{2} + \frac{\sqrt{3}}{2}i - \frac{1}{2} - \frac{\sqrt{3}}{2}i = 0$

The roots of $z^3 - 1 = 0$ lie on the circle $x^2 + y^2 = 1$. The roots are equally spaced with angular separation between any two roots equal to $360 \div 3 = 120°$. We observe that $z_3 = \bar{z}_2$.

EXAMPLE: (34) Solve $z^4 - 1 = 0$

SOLUTION: $(z - 1)(z + 1)(z^2 + 1) = 0$.

The four roots are: $1, -1, i, -i$

Let $\omega = i$, then
$\omega^2 = -1$
$\omega^3 = i^3 = -i$

Again, $1 + \omega + \omega^2 + \omega^3 = 1 + i - 1 - i = 0$

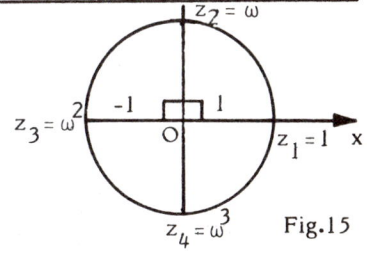

Fig.15

The roots lie on the circle $x^2 + y^2 = 1$, the angular separation between any two consecutive roots being $360 \div 4 = 90°$.
We also observe that $z_4 = \bar{z}_2$.

EXAMPLE: (35) If ω is a complex root of the equation $x^7 - 1 = 0$, then show that the other complex roots are ω^2, ω^3, ω^4, ω^5 and ω^6. Also prove that $1 + \omega + \omega^2 + \omega^3 + \omega^4 + \omega^5 + \omega^6 = 0$.

SOLUTION: $\quad z^7 = 1 = \cos 2k\pi + i\sin 2k\pi \quad \ldots (1)$

Let $z = r(\cos\theta + i\sin\theta)$ be a root of $z^7 - 1 = 0$, then by De Moivre's theorem:
$$z^7 = r^7 (\cos 7\theta + i\sin 7\theta) \quad \ldots (2)$$

From (1) and (2), equating the real and the imaginary parts:
$$r^7 \cos 7\theta = \cos(2k\pi) \quad \text{and} \quad r^7 \sin 7\theta = \sin 2k\pi$$

By squaring and adding, $r^{14} = 1$, hence $r = 1$ since $r > 0$

$\therefore \quad \cos 7\theta = \cos 2k\pi$, whence $7\theta = 2k\pi$

$\therefore \quad \theta = \dfrac{2k\pi}{7}$, where $k = 0, 1, 2, \ldots, 6$

The seven roots of unity are given by:

$z_1 = \cos 0 + i\sin 0 = 1 \qquad\qquad z_2 = \cos 2\pi/7 + i\sin 2\pi/7$

$z_3 = \cos 4\pi/7 + i\sin 4\pi/7 \qquad\quad z_4 = \cos 6\pi/7 + i\sin 6\pi/7$

$z_5 = \cos 8\pi/7 + i\sin 8\pi/7 \qquad\quad z_6 = \cos 10\pi/7 + i\sin 10\pi/7$

$z_7 = \cos 12\pi/7 + i\sin 12\pi/7$

Now we apply De Moivre's theorem, in reverse order, i.e.

$\cos n\theta + i\sin n\theta = (\cos\theta + i\sin\theta)^7$ to each of the above complex roots.

Let $z_2 = \omega = \cos 2\pi/7 + i\sin 2\pi/7$

$z_3 = \cos 4\pi/7 + i\sin 4\pi/7 = (\cos 2\pi/7 + i\sin 2\pi/7)^2 = \omega^2$

$z_4 = \cos 6\pi/7 + i\sin 6\pi/7 = (\cos 2\pi/7 + i\sin 2\pi/7)^3 = \omega^3$ and so on,

hence, $z_5 = \omega^4$, $z_6 = \omega^5$, $z_7 = \omega^6$.

To prove that $1 + \omega + \omega^2 + \ldots + \omega^6 = 0$, we note that the sum of the roots of $z^7 - 1 = 0$ is zero, because: $z_1 + z_2 + \ldots + z_7 = \dfrac{-\text{coef. of } z^6}{\text{coef. of } z^7}$, hence substituting for z_1, z_2, etc. we have: $1 + \omega + \omega^2 + \ldots + \omega^6 = 0$.

Observations: The roots of $z^n - 1 = 0$ are given by:

(1) $z = \cos\dfrac{2k\pi}{n} + i\sin\dfrac{2k\pi}{n}$, where $k = 0, 1, 2, \ldots, (n-1)$.

(2) If n is even, two roots of $z^n - 1 = 0$ are real, i.e. ± 1.

(3) If n is odd, only one root of $z^n - 1 = 0$, i.e. $z = 1$ is real.

(4) If one complex root is called ω, then the entire set of roots is given by: $1, \omega, \omega^2, \ldots, \omega^{n-1}$.

(5) $1 + \omega + \omega^2 + \ldots + \omega^{n-1} = 0$, either by using the sum of the roots of $z^n - 1 = 0$ or summing up by observing that this sum is a geometric series, with sum $= \dfrac{1 - \omega^n}{1 - \omega} = \dfrac{1 - 1}{1 - \omega} = 0$, since $\omega^n = 1$, $\omega \neq 1$.

Exercise 4I

1. If ω is a complex cube root of unity (i.e. a root of $z^3 = 1$), prove that ω^2 is also a complex cube root of unity. Further prove that:
   (a) $1 + \omega + \omega^2 = 0$ (b) $\dfrac{1}{1+\omega} + \dfrac{1}{1+\omega^2} = 1$ (c) $(1+\omega)^3 = -1$ (d) $(1+\omega^2)^5 = -\omega^2$

2. ω is a complex root of the equation $z^3 - 1 = 0$. Form a quadratic equation whose roots are given by $\alpha = 2 + \omega$ and $\beta = 2 + \omega^2$.

3. If ω is the complex cube root of unity, show that:
   (a) $(1 + \omega - \omega^2)^3 - (1 - \omega + \omega^2)^3 = 0$ (b) $\dfrac{a + b\omega + c\omega^2}{c + a\omega + b\omega^2} = \omega^2$
   (c) $\dfrac{a + b\omega + c\omega^2}{b + c\omega + a\omega^2} = \omega$

4. If $x = a + b$, $y = a\omega + b\omega^2$, $z = a\omega^2 + b\omega$, where $1, \omega, \omega^2$ are the cube roots of unity, prove that:
   (a) $x + y + z = 0$ (b) $(a + b\omega + c\omega^2)(a + b\omega^2 + c\omega) = a^2 + b^2 + c^2 - ab - bc - ca$

5. If $1, \omega, \omega^2$ are the three cube roots of unity, prove that
   $(a + b + c)(a + b\omega + c\omega^2)(a + b\omega^2 + c\omega) = a^3 + b^3 + c^3 - 3abc$.

6. If ω is a complex root of $z^5 - 1 = 0$, show that ω^2, ω^3 and ω^4 are the other complex roots.
   (a) Prove that $1 + \omega + \omega^2 + \omega^3 + \omega^4 = 0$.
   (b) Find the quadratic equations whose roots are $\alpha = \omega + \omega^4$ and $\beta = \omega^2 + \omega^3$ (Hint: use $\omega^5 = 1$ to reduce ω^6 and ω^7)
   (c) Show the roots of $z^5 - 1 = 0$ in an Argand diagram.
   (d) Find the area of the pentagon formed by the roots.

7. If ω is a complex root of $z^6 - 1 = 0$ with the smallest positive argument, then show that the other roots are $\omega^2, \omega^3, \omega^4, \omega^5$. Prove that:
   (a) $1 + \omega + \omega^2 + \omega^3 + \omega^4 + \omega^5 = 0$.
   (b) Find all the roots in the form $a + ib$ and indicate these roots in an Argand diagram. Find the area of the hexagon formed by the roots.
   (c) Find the two quadratic equations whose roots are
       (i) ω and ω^5 (ii) ω^2 and ω^4
   (d) Using part (c), show that
       (i) $z^6 - 1 = (z - 1)(z + 1)[(z - \omega)(z - \omega^5)][(z - \omega^2)(z - \omega^4)]$
           $= (z^2 - 1)(z^2 + z + 1)(z^2 - z + 1)$
       (ii) The roots of $z^4 + z^2 + 1 = 0$ are $\omega, \omega^2, \omega^4$ and ω^5

8. Show that if ω is one complex root of the equation $z^n - 1 = 0$, then
   (a) $z^n - 1 = (z - 1)(z - \omega)(z - \omega^2) \ldots (z - \omega^{n-1})$
   (b) Deduce from part (a) that:
   $z^{n-1} + z^{n-2} + \ldots + z + 1 = (z - \omega)(z - \omega^2) \ldots (z - \omega^{n-1})$
   (c) $(1 - \omega)(1 - \omega^2) \ldots (1 - \omega^{n-1}) = n$

9. Prove by mathematical induction that for any real θ,
   $\cos n\theta + i \sin n\theta = (\cos\theta + i\sin\theta)^n$
   (a) Find the 6 sixth roots of 1, expressing each in the form $a + ib$.
   (b) Using part (a), find the four roots of $z^4 + z^2 + 1 = 0$ and show their positions in an Argand diagram.

4.11 Miscellaneous: Factorisation over the Complex Field

Consider the factorisation of $z^3 - 1 = 0$ over C. $z^3 - 1 = (z - 1)(z^2 + z + 1)$
Now $z^2 + z + 1$ has no real linear factors, but over C we can write
$z^2 + z + 1 = (z - \alpha)(z - \beta)$ where $\alpha = \dfrac{-1 + \sqrt{3}i}{2}$, $\beta = \dfrac{-1 - \sqrt{3}i}{2}$

Thus it appears that we can factorise expressions of the form $z^n - 1$, $z^n + 1$ and (by extension) $z^{n-1} + z^{n-2} + ... + 1$, into either: (a) real quadratic factors or (b) complex linear factors.

EXAMPLE: (36) Factorise $z^6 - 1$ into real quadratic and real linear factors, hence factorise $z^4 + z^2 + 1$.

SOLUTION: We solve the corresponding equation $z^6 - 1 = 0$
$z^6 = 1 = \cos(2k\pi) + i\sin(2k\pi)$, hence the six sixth roots are given by
$z = \cos(2k\pi/6) + i\sin(2k\pi/6)$, $k = 0, 1, 2, 3, 4, 5$. i.e.
$z_1 = \cos 0 + i\sin 0 = 1$, $z_4 = -1$
$z_2 = \cos \pi/3 + i\sin \pi/3$, $z_5 = \cos 4\pi/3 + i\sin 4\pi/3 = \cos 2\pi/3 - i\sin 2\pi/3$
$z_3 = \cos 2\pi/3 + i\sin 2\pi/3$, $z_6 = \cos 5\pi/3 + i\sin 5\pi/3 = \cos \pi/3 - i\sin \pi/3$

We find that $z_6 = \bar{z}_2$ and $z_5 = \bar{z}_3$, hence:
$z_2 + z_6 = z_2 + \bar{z}_2 = 2\cos \pi/3$ and $z_3 + z_5 = z_3 + \bar{z}_3 = 2\cos 2\pi/3$
Also $z_2 z_6 = z_2 \bar{z}_2 = 1$, $z_3 z_5 = z_3 \bar{z}_3 = 1$

Now $z^6 - 1 = (z - z_1)(z - z_2)(z - z_3)(z - z_4)(z - z_5)(z - z_6)$
$= (z - 1)(z + 1)[(z - z_2)(z - z_6)][(z - z_3)(z - z_5)]$
$= (z - 1)(z + 1)[z^2 - (z_2 + z_6) + z_2 z_6][z^2 - (z_3 + z_5) + z_3 z_5]$
$= (z - 1)(z + 1)[z^2 - 2\cos(\pi/3) z + 1][z^2 - 2\cos(2\pi/3) z + 1]$

Since $z^6 - 1 = (z^2 - 1)(z^4 + z^2 + 1)$, we at once have:
$z^4 + z^2 + 1 = \dfrac{z^6 - 1}{z^2 - 1} = [z^2 - 2\cos(\pi/3) z + 1][z^2 - 2\cos(2\pi/3) z + 1]$

EXAMPLE: (37) Solve $z^6 + 1 = 0$. Express the roots in the form $a + ib$. Show these roots in an Argand diagram. Factorise $z^6 + 1$ into real quadratic factors.

SOLUTION: $z^6 = -1 = \cos(\pi + 2k\pi) + i\sin(\pi + 2k\pi)$, hence the six sixth roots are given by $z = \text{cis} \dfrac{\pi + 2k\pi}{6}$, where $k = 0, 1, 2, 3, 4, 5$.

$z_1 = \text{cis} \pi/6 = \sqrt{3}/2 + i/2$ | $z_4 = \text{cis} 7\pi/4 = -\sqrt{3}/2 - i/2$
$z_2 = \text{cis} \pi/2 = 0 + i$ | $z_5 = \text{cis} 3\pi/2 = 0 - i$
$z_3 = \text{cis} 5\pi/6 = -\sqrt{3}/2 + i/2$ | $z_6 = \text{cis} 11\pi/2 = \sqrt{3}/2 - i/2$

We have $z_6 = \bar{z}_1$, hence $z_1 + z_6 = z_1 + \bar{z}_1 = \sqrt{3}$, $z_1 z_6 = 1$
and $z_5 = \bar{z}_2$, $z_2 + z_5 = z_2 + \bar{z}_2 = 0$, $z_2 z_5 = 1$
and $z_4 = \bar{z}_3$, $z_3 + z_4 = z_3 + \bar{z}_3 = -\sqrt{3}$, $z_3 z_4 = 1$

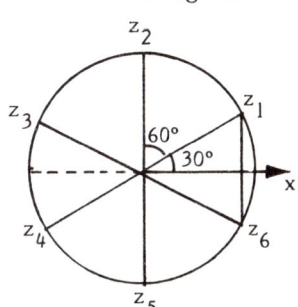

Fig.16

The factors of $z^6 + 1$ are:
$$z^6 + 1 = [(z - z_1)(z - z_6)][(z - z_2)(z - z_5)][(z - z_3)(z - z_4)]$$
$$= [z^2 - (z_1 + z_6)z + z_1 z_6][z^2 - (z_2 + z_5)z + z_2 z_5][z^2 - (z_3 + z_4)z + z_3 z_4]$$
$$= (z^2 - \sqrt{3}z + 1)(z^2 + 1)(z^2 + \sqrt{3}z + 1)$$
$$= (z^2 + 1)(z^2 - \sqrt{3}z + 1)(z^2 + \sqrt{3}z + 1)$$

We could have easily arrived at this result by writing:
$$z^6 + 1 = (z^2+1)(z^4 - z^2 + 1) = (z^2+1)[(z^2+1)^2 - 3z^2] = (z^2+1)(z^2 - \sqrt{3}z + 1)(z^2 + \sqrt{3}z + 1).$$

So why waste time? This is not so, as the algebraic identities that we have just established can be used to derive numerous trigonometrical relations. See the next example.

EXAMPLE: (38) Factorise $z^5 + 1$ into real linear and quadratic factors and hence deduce that $4\sin\frac{\pi}{10}\cos\frac{\pi}{5} = 1$

SOLUTION: The roots of $z^5 = -1$ are given by $z = \text{cis}\frac{\pi + 2k\pi}{5}$, $k = 0, 1, 2, 3, 4$.
The five fifth roots are:
$z_1 = \cos\pi/5 + i\sin\pi/5$; $z_4 = \cos 7\pi/5 + i\sin 7\pi/5 = \cos(3\pi/5) - i\sin(3\pi/5) = \bar{z}_2$
$z_2 = \cos 3\pi/5 + i\sin 3\pi/5$; $z_5 = \cos 9\pi/5 + i\sin 9\pi/5 = \cos\pi/5 - i\sin\pi/5 = \bar{z}_1$
$z_3 = -1$ $z_1 + z_5 = z_1 + \bar{z}_1 = 2\cos\pi/5$, $z_1 z_5 = z_1 \bar{z}_1 = 1$
$\quad\quad\quad z_2 + z_4 = z_2 + \bar{z}_2 = 2\cos 3\pi/5$, $z_2 z_4 = z_2 \bar{z}_2 = 1$, hence:
$$z^5 + 1 = (z - z_3)(z - z_1)(z - z_5)(z - z_2)(z - z_4)$$
$$= (z + 1)[z^2 - (z_1 + \bar{z}_1)z + z_1\bar{z}_1][z^2 - (z_2 + \bar{z}_2)z + z_2\bar{z}_2]$$

$\therefore z^5 + 1 = (z + 1)[z^2 - 2\cos(\pi/5)z + 1][z^2 - 2\cos(3\pi/5)z + 1]$ ... (1)
Now $z^5 + 1 = (z + 1)(z^4 - z^3 + z^2 - z + 1)$ ... (2),
hence: $(z^2 - 2\cos(\pi/5)z + 1)[z^2 - 2\cos(3\pi/5)z + 1] = z^4 - z^3 + z^2 - z + 1$ ... (3)
Compare the coefficient of z^2 on both sides of identity (3), then
$\quad\quad 4\cos\pi/5 \cos 3\pi/5 + 1 + 1 = 1$
$\therefore 4\cos(\pi/5)\cos(3\pi/5) = -1$, now $\cos 3\pi/5 = \sin\left[\frac{\pi}{2} - \frac{3\pi}{5}\right] = -\sin\frac{\pi}{10}$, hence:
$\quad\quad 4\sin(\pi/10)\cos(\pi/5) = 1$

SOLUTION TO THE EQUATIONS

(1) $z^{n-1} + z^{n-2} + ... + 1 = 0$ and (2) $z^{n-1} - z^{n-2} + z^{n-3} - ... + ... - z + 1 = 0$

We can change these into the form $z^n \mp 1 = 0$, as follows
$z^{n-1} + z^{n-2} + z^{n-3} + ... + z + 1 = \frac{z^n - 1}{z - 1}$ and $z^{n-1} - z^{n-2} + z^{n-3} - ... - z + 1 = \frac{z^n + 1}{z + 1}$
We solve the equations $z^n - 1 = 0$ and $z^n + 1 = 0$, and remove
the real root 1 from the roots of $z^n - 1 = 0$, and
the real root -1 from the roots of $z^n + 1 = 0$,   (n is odd)
to obtain the roots of equations (1) and (2) respectively.

EXAMPLE: (39)

(a) Solve $z^4 + z^3 + z^2 + z + 1$
(b) $z^4 - z^3 + z^2 - z + 1 = 0$

SOLUTION:

(a) We change $z^4 + z^3 + z^2 + z + 1 = 0$
to $\dfrac{z^5 - 1}{z - 1} = 0$, $z \neq 1$

Hence $z^5 - 1 = 0$ whose roots are given by:
$z = \text{cis}(2k\pi/5)$, $k = 0, 1, 2, 3, 4, 5$.

We omit the root $z = 1$, then the roots of $z^4 + z^3 + z^2 + z + 1 = 0$ are given by:
$z = \text{cis}(2k\pi/5)$, $k = 1, 2, 3, 4$.

(b) We change $z^4 - z^3 + z^2 - z + 1 = 0$
to $\dfrac{z^5 + 1}{z + 1} = 0$, $z \neq -1$

The roots of the given equation are given by:
$z = \text{cis}\left[\dfrac{\pi + 2k\pi}{5}\right]$

where $k = 0, 1, 3, 4$, since we must remove the root $z = -1$ given by $k = 2$

Exercise 4J

1. Resolve $z^5 - 1$ into the real linear and quadratic factors. Hence prove that $\cos\dfrac{2\pi}{5} + \cos\dfrac{4\pi}{5} = -\dfrac{1}{2}$.

2. Resolve $z^5 + 1$ into the real linear and quadratic factors. Hence prove that $\cos\dfrac{\pi}{5} + \cos\dfrac{3\pi}{5} = \dfrac{1}{2}$.

3. Find the roots of $z^4 + 1 = 0$ and show them in an Argand diagram. Resolve $z^4 + 1$ into real real quadratic factors and deduce that:
$\cos 2\theta = 2(\cos\theta - \cos\pi/4)(\cos\theta - \cos 3\pi/4)$

4. Find the roots of $z^6 + 1 = 0$, and hence resolve $z^6 + 1$ into real quadratic factors; deduce that $\cos 3\theta = 4(\cos\theta - \cos\pi/6)(\cos\theta - \cos\pi/2)(\cos\theta - \cos 5\pi/6)$

5. Show that the roots of $(z - 1)^4 + (z + 1)^4 = 0$ are $\pm i\cot(\pi/8)$ and $\pm i\cot(3\pi/8)$

6. Show that the roots of (a) $(z - 1)^6 + (z + 1)^6 = 0$ are $\pm i\cot\pi/12$, $\pm i\cot 5\pi/12$, $\pm i$

7. Solve the following equations:
   (a) $z^3 + z^2 + z + 1 = 0$
   (b) $z^5 + z^4 + z^3 + z^2 + z + 1 = 0$
   (c) $z^4 - z^2 + 1 = 0$
   (d) $z^4 + z^2 + 1 = 0$
   [Hint: $z^6 + 1 = (z^2 + 1)(z^4 - z^2 + 1)$]
   [Hint: $z^6 - 1 = (z^2 - 1)(z^4 + z^2 + 1)$]

4.12 Geometric Representation of Complex Numbers

We have remarked that the complex number $z = x + iy$ may be considered an ordered pair (x, y) of real numbers and further that (x, y) can be regarded as the coordinates of a point in a coordinate plane. Conversely a point in the coordinate plane corresponds to a complex number $x + iy$.
We call such a plane an Argand diagram or the complex plane.

Three complex numbers

$z_1 = 3 + 2i$, $z_2 = -2 + 1i$ and $z_3 = 0 - 2i$

are represented in the plane by points
$P(3,2)$, $Q(-2,1)$ and $R(0,-2)$ respectively.

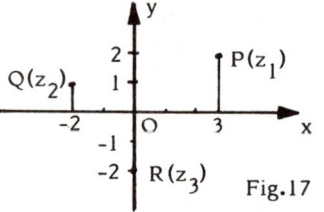

Fig.17

Any relation between points in a plane can be regarded as a relation between corresponding complex numbers and vice versa. For example, the locus of a set of points satisfying the equation $x^2 + y^2 = a^2$ (a circle, radius a, centre at the origin) can be stated as either $z\bar{z} = a^2$ or $|z| = a$ where $z = x + iy$. Many more locus problems can be solved by the use of complex variable $z = x + iy$. Here we are killing two birds with one stone! Instead of two variables x and y we work with only one variable z. Not only that, but by equating real and imaginary parts of the equation, we obtain a complete set of solutions.

Addition:

Let the complex numbers $z_1 = x_1 + iy_1$ and
$z_2 = x_2 + iy_2$ be represented by the points A
and B respectively on the Argand plane.
Complete the parallelogram OACB. Then the
mid-points of AB and OC are the same. But
the mid-point of AB is $P\left[\dfrac{x_1 + x_2}{2}, \dfrac{y_1 + y_2}{2}\right]$,
so the coordinates of C are $(x_1 + x_2, y_1 + y_2)$.

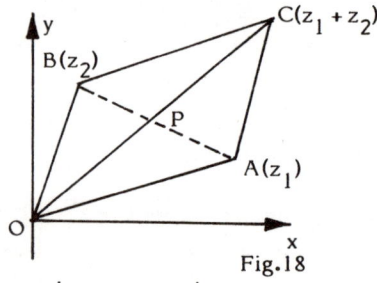

Fig.18

Thus the point C corresponds to the sum of the complex numbers z_1 and z_2, i.e. $z_1 + z_2 = (x_1 + x_2) + i(y_1 + y_2)$.

Subtraction:

We first represent $-z_1$ by D, so that AD is
bisected at O. Complete the parallelogram
OBCD, then the point C represents the
complex number $z_2 + (-z_1)$ i.e. $z_2 - z_1$
Since OA = OD = BC and OA || BC,
OABC is a parallelogram, and hence OC is
parallel to AB. The coordinates of
C are $(x_2 - x_1, y_2 - y_1)$.

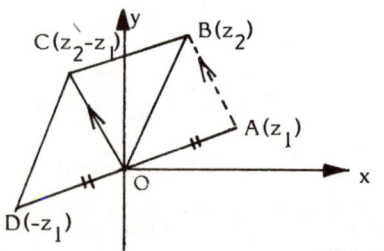

Fig.19

We also note that the length of the segment AB is given by

$AB = |z_2 - z_1| = \sqrt{(x_2 - x_1)^2 + (y_2 - y_1)^2}$

It is advisable to draw a diagram and then calculate $\arg(z_2 - z_1)$

EXAMPLE: (40)

The complex numbers $z_1 = 4 + 2i$ and $z_2 = 1 + 4i$ are represented by points A and B respectively in the plane.
$z_1 + z_2 = 4 + 2i + 1 + 4i = 5 + 6i$
The end-point C of the diagonal OC of the parallelogram OACB represents the sum $z = z_1 + z_2 = 5 + 6i$
C is the point (5,6)

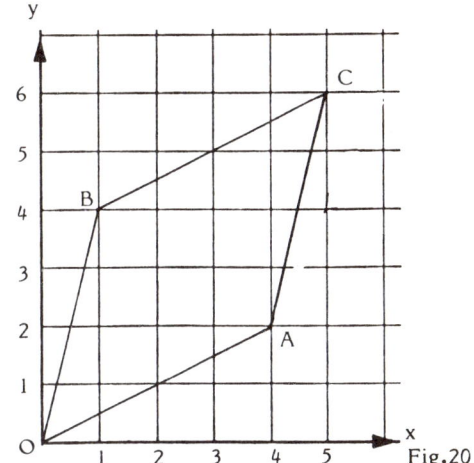
Fig.20

EXAMPLE: (41)

$A(z_1)$ represents $z_1 = 2 + i$
$B(z_2)$ represents $z_2 = 1 + 3i$
$D(-z_2)$ represents $-z_2 = -1 - 3i$
$z = z_1 - z_2 = (2 - 1) + (1 - 3)i = 1 - 2i$
Let $C(1,-2)$ represent $z = 1 - 2i$

From the scaled diagram we find that C is the end-point of the diagonal of parallelogram OACD where D is given by $-z_2$

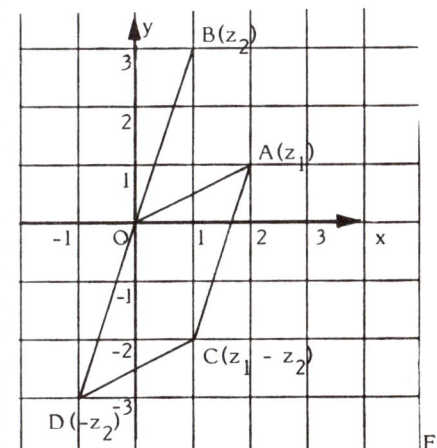
Fig.21

EXAMPLE: (42)

$z_1 = -2$ and $z_2 = 3 + 2i$
Find the following:
(a) $z = z_2 - z_1$ (b) $\mod(z_2 - z_1)$ (c) $\arg(z_2 - z_1)$

SOLUTION:

Let $A(-2,0)$ and $B(3,2)$ represent the complex numbers z_1 and z_2 respectively; then:

(a) $z = z_2 - z_1 = 3 + 2i - (-2) = 5 + 2i$
∴ $C(5,2)$ represents the difference $z_2 - z_1$ where OC || and = to AB

(b) $\mod(z_2 - z_1) = |z_2 - z_1| = \sqrt{25 + 4} = \sqrt{29}$

(c) $\arg(z_2 - z_1) = \theta = \angle COX = \angle BAX$ where $\tan\theta = \frac{2}{5}$

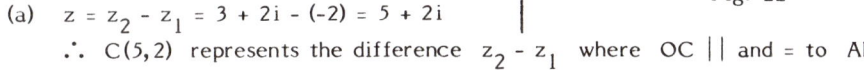
Fig. 22

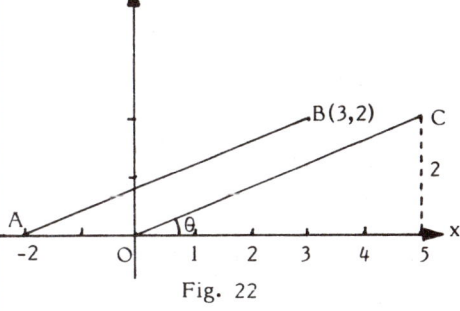
Fig. 23

EXAMPLE: (43)

Prove that the diagonals of a rhombus intersect at right angles.

SOLUTION:

For simplicity we represent the vertices of the rhombus by the complex numbers 0, z_1, $z_1 + z_2$ and z_2 where $|z_1| = |z_2| \neq 0$
C represents $z_1 + z_2$ and D represents $z_2 - z_1$ such that OD is $\parallel$ and $=$ to AB. Our geometrical proposition is equivalent to saying that

$$\arg \frac{z_2 - z_1}{z_2 + z_1} = \pm \frac{\pi}{2}, \text{ i.e. } \omega = \frac{z_2 - z_1}{z_2 + z_1} \text{ is}$$

purely imaginary. This would be so if $\omega + \bar{\omega} = 0$.

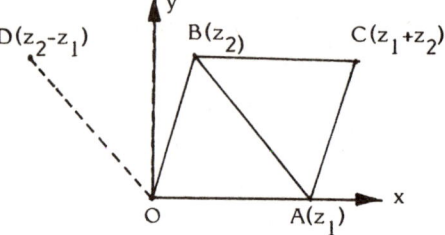

Fig. 24

We find that $\omega + \bar{\omega} = \dfrac{z_2 - z_1}{z_2 + z_1} + \dfrac{\bar{z}_2 - \bar{z}_1}{\bar{z}_2 + \bar{z}_1} = \dfrac{2(z_2 \bar{z}_2 - z_1 \bar{z}_1)}{(z_2 + z_1)(\bar{z}_2 + \bar{z}_1)}$

Now $z_2 \bar{z}_2 = |z_2|^2$, $z_1 \bar{z}_1 = |z_1|^2$, and given that $|z_1| = |z_2|$, then $\omega + \bar{\omega} = 0$

TRIANGULAR INEQUALITY

We prove the inequality

$|z_1 + z_2| \leqslant |z_1| + |z_2|$

Proof: In $\triangle$OAC, using the fact that the sum of two sides of a triangle $\geqslant$ the third side, we have:

OC $\leqslant$ OA + AC

$\therefore |z_1 + z_2| \leqslant |z_1| + |z_2|$,

because AC = OB = $|z_2|$ and OA = $|z_1|$.
The only time inequality holds is when $\arg z_1 = \arg z_2 = \theta$ (Fig. 26)

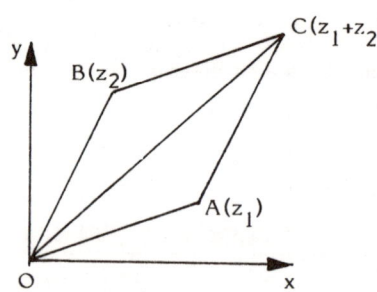

Fig. 25

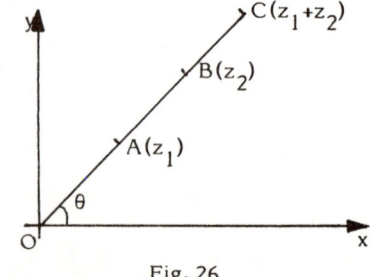

Fig. 26

Exercise 4K

Perform the indicated operations graphically. Use graph paper.

1. $(2 + 3i) + (2 + 2i)$
2. $(3 - i) + (5 + 2i)$
3. $(3) + (-2 - 3i)$
4. $(-1 + 3i) + (2i)$
5. $(3 - 2i) - (1 + i)$
6. $(6 + 4i) - (3 - 2i)$
7. $(-1) - (-3 + 5i)$
8. $(2i) - (-3 + i)$
9. Given that $z = x + iy$, $z_1 = x_1 + iy_1$, P is the point $P(x,y)$ and A is the point (x_1, y_1), draw the sketch of the directed line segment AP in the Argand diagram, if $z - z_1$ is equal to:
   (a) $z - 3$ (b) $z + 3$ (c) $z + 2i$ (d) $z - 1 + 2i$ (e) $z + 2 + 3i$

10. Find the modulus and argument of each of the complex numbers z and ω,
    $z = \dfrac{1 + i}{1 - i}$ and $\omega = \dfrac{\sqrt{2}}{1 - i}$

    Plot the points representing z, ω and $z + \omega$ on an Argand diagram. Deduce from the diagram that $\tan \dfrac{3\pi}{8} = \sqrt{2} + 1$.

11. The points P and Q are represented by the complex numbers $z = 1 - 3i$ and $\omega = -3 + 4i$ respectively. Find a point R on the real axis such that PRQ is a right-angled triangle.

12. The points A, B, C and D in the Argand diagram represent the numbers $1 + 2i$, 3, $5 + 2i$, $3 + 4i$ respectively. Prove that ABCD is a square. Find the complex number representing the intersection of the diagonals.

13. If $|z| = |w|$, prove that $\dfrac{z + \omega}{z - \omega}$ is purely imaginary. By drawing a suitable diagram, give a geometrical interpretation of the result.

14. Prove that for any two complex numbers z_1 and z_2
    $|z_1 + z_2| \geqslant |z_1| - |z_2|$, assuming $|z_1| > |z_2|$. When does the equality sign hold?

15. Prove that $|z_1 - z_2|^2 + |z_1 + z_2|^2 = 2|z_1|^2 + 2|z_2|^2$

    Give a geometrical interpretation of the result.

4.13 Product and Quotient: Rotation

We now give the graphical representation of multiplication and division of complex numbers.

Let B and C be the points representing the complex numbers. Let A be the point (1, 0) $z_1 = r_1 \text{cis}\theta_1$ and $z_2 = r_2 \text{cis}\theta_2$ respectively. Construct $\angle POC$ equal to θ_1. Construct $\angle OCP$ equal to $\angle OAB$. Triangles OAB and OCP are similar, hence their sides are proportional.

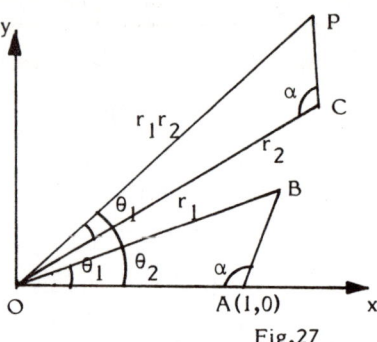

Fig.27

$\dfrac{OP}{OB} = \dfrac{OC}{OA}$ and this gives $OP = r_1 r_2$. Hence point P represents the complex number $r_1 r_2 \text{cis}(\theta_1 + \theta_2)$ which is the product of $r_1 \text{cis}\theta_1$ and $r_2 \text{cis}\theta_2$.

Although similar graphical representation can be given to division, it is not very elegant and of no practical use. Let us now turn our attention to a very important application of i as an operator that rotates a directed line segment.

(a) ROTATION OF A POINT A(z) THROUGH +90°

In the product $z_1 z_2 = r_1 r_2 [\cos(\theta_1 + \theta_2) + i\sin(\theta_1 + \theta_2)]$, let $z_1 = i$, $z_2 = z$, then $\theta_1 = \dfrac{\pi}{2}$ and we write $\theta_2 = \theta$, then $iz = r[\cos(\theta + \dfrac{\pi}{2}) + i\sin(\theta + \dfrac{\pi}{2})]$

The above results mean that when we multiply z by i, we rotate the point A(z) through a positive angle of 90° about O.

If $z = x + iy$, after rotation through 90°, we have $iz = i(x + iy) = -y + ix$

Note that $|z| = |iz| = r$

Similar interpretations are given to the powers of i as follows:

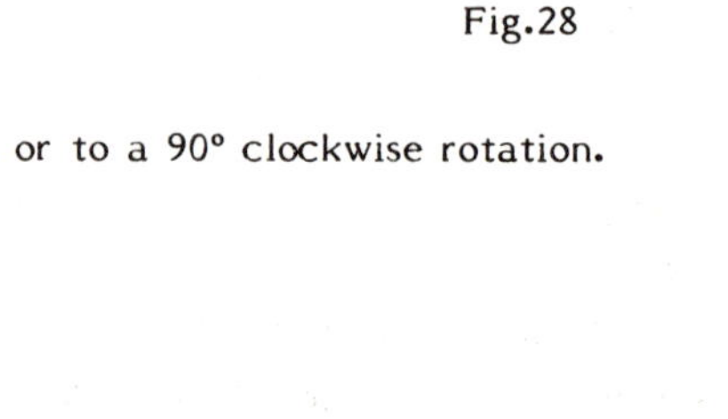

i^2 corresponds to 180° counterclockwise rotation
i^3 corresponds to 270° counterclockwise rotation, or to a 90° clockwise rotation.

Fig.28

EXAMPLE: (44)

P is the point P(3,2) in the Argand diagram representing the complex number $z = 3 + 2i$. OP is rotated about the origin through $+90°$. Find the complex number represented by the new position of P in the plane.

SOLUTION:

$z = 3 + 2i$

$iz = i(3 + 2i) = -2 + 3i$

$\therefore$ New position of P is A(-2, 3)

A represents the complex number

$z_1 = -2 + 3i$, $|z_1| = |z| = \sqrt{13}$

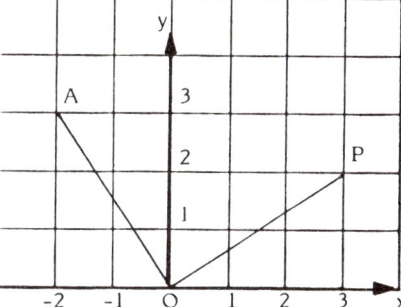

Fig.29

EXAMPLE: (45)

OABC is a square in an Argand diagram. The point A represents the complex number $z = \sqrt{3} + i$. Find the complex numbers represented by B and C in the form $a + ib$.

SOLUTION:

A represents $z = \sqrt{3} + i$, C represents iz

and B represents $z + iz$.

Hence C represents $i(\sqrt{3} + i)$, i.e. $-1 + \sqrt{3}i$,

B represents $\sqrt{3} + i + i(\sqrt{3} + i)$, i.e.

$\sqrt{3} - 1 + (\sqrt{3} + 1)i$.

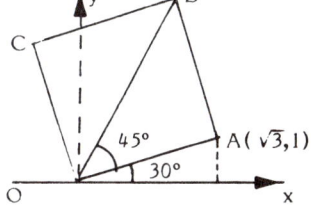

Fig.30

EXAMPLE: (46)

P is the point (2,3) in the Argand diagram representing the complex number $z = 2 + 3i$. The segment OP is rotated through $+60°$, and P now occupies the position of the point Q. Find the coordinates of Q.

SOLUTION:

We use $z_1 z_2 = r_1 r_2 [\cos(\theta_1 + \theta_2) + i\sin(\theta_1 + \theta_2)]$

Let $z_1 = 2 + 3i$ and $z_2 = \cos 60° + i\sin 60°$, then:

multiplying $2 + 3i$ by $\cos 60° + i\sin 60°$ is equivalent to rotating the length OP through $+60°$.

Let Q be the point (x, y), then

$x + iy = (2 + 3i)(\cos 60° + i \sin 60°) = (2 + 3i)\left[\dfrac{1}{2} + \dfrac{\sqrt{3}}{2}i\right]$

$\qquad = 1 - \dfrac{3\sqrt{3}}{2} + i\left(\dfrac{3}{2} + \sqrt{3}\right)$

$\therefore$ Q is the point $\left[1 - \dfrac{3\sqrt{3}}{2}, \dfrac{3}{2} + \sqrt{3}\right]$

Exercise 4L

1. P is the point in the Argand diagram and represents the complex number $1 + 2i$. The segment OP is rotated through (a) $+30°$ (b) $+45°$ (c) $+90°$. Find the complex number that represents the point occupied by P after each rotation is completed.

2. The point A in an Argand diagram represents the complex number $1 + i$. Find the complex number represented by B if OBA is an equilateral triangle.

3. OPQR is a square in an Argand diagram, where O is the origin. The point P represents the complex number z given by $z = r(\cos 30° + i \sin 30°)$. Find the complex numbers represented by Q and R.

4. OABC is a rhombus in an Argand diagram, where O is the origin. The point A is $(1,2)$. If $\angle BOA = 30°$, and B is in the second quadrant, find the complex numbers representing the points B and C.

5. PQRS is a square in an Argand diagram, where P, Q, R and S represent the numbers $2 + i$, $3 + 2i$, $2 + 3i$ and $1 + 2i$ respectively. This square is rotated anticlockwise about O through $+90°$. Find the complex numbers that correspond to the new positions occupied by the points P, Q, R and S respectively.

4.14 Locus Problems with the Complex Variable z

From our study of the co-ordinate geometry, we know that $y = f(x)$ or $f(x,y) = c$ represents a locus of a point $P(x,y)$, satisfying a certain condition. Since $z = x + iy$, as x and y vary, z varies and hence z may describe a curve in an Argand plane.

(a) **CIRCLE** $x^2 + y^2 = r^2$

Let $P(z = x + iy)$ be on the circle $x^2 + y^2 = r^2$.
Now $|z| = \sqrt{x^2 + y^2} = r$
Thus $|z| = r$ represents a circle of radius r and the centre $O(0,0)$. We can also write $z\bar{z} = r^2$ as the equation of the circle $x^2 + y^2 = r^2$.

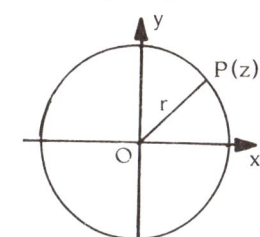

Fig.31

(b) **CIRCLE** $(x-a)^2 + (y-b)^2 = r^2$

If $P(z)$ is a typical point on the circle, centre $C(a + ib)$, radius r, then $PC = r$
i.e. $|z - \omega| = r$, where $\omega = a + ib$

Thus $|z - \omega| = r$, represents a circle with the centre at $C(\omega = a + ib)$ and radius r.

Using the result $z\bar{z} = |z|^2$, we can write this equation as: $(z - \omega)(\bar{z} - \bar{\omega}) = r^2$
i.e. $z\bar{z} - \omega\bar{z} - \bar{\omega}z + \omega\bar{\omega} = r^2$ (There is some advantage in writing the equation of a circle in this manner).

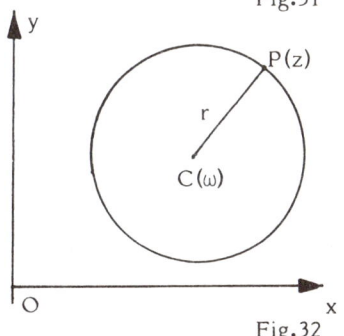

Fig.32

EXAMPLES: (47)

Write the equations of the following circle in the form $|z| = r$ or $|z - \omega| = r$:

(a) $x^2 + y^2 = 4$ (b) $(x - 1)^2 + (y - 2)^2 = 4$ (c) $x^2 + y^2 - 4x - 6y = 0$

SOLUTION:

(a) $x^2 + y^2 = 4$
$|z| = 2$

(b) $(x - 1)^2 + (y - 2)^2 = 4$, centre is (1,2)
$\omega = 1 + 2i$
We write $|z - \omega| = 2$
or $|z - 1 - 2i| = 2$

(c) $x^2 + y^2 - 4x - 6y = 0$
$(x - 2)^2 + (y - 3)^2 = 13$, centre is $C(2,3)$, radius $= \sqrt{13}$
We write $|z - (2 + 3i)| = \sqrt{13}$ as the equation of this circle.

Exercise 4M

1. Express the equations of the circles in the form $|z| = r$:
   (a) $x^2 + y^2 = 1$ (b) $x^2 + y^2 = 9$ (c) $x^2 + y^2 = \frac{1}{4}$ (d) $2x^2 + 2y^2 = 1$

2. Express the following equations in the form $z\bar{z} = r^2$:
   (a) $x^2 + y^2 = 25$ (b) $x^2 + y^2 = 64$ (c) $ax^2 + ay^2 = 1$ (d) $3x^2 + 3y^2 = 5$

3. Express the equations in cartesian form, stating the radius and the centre of each circle.
   (a) $|z| = 4$ (b) $|2z| = 1$ (c) $z\bar{z} = 25$ (d) $4z\bar{z} = 1$

4. Express the equations in the cartesian form, describing each locus.
   (a) $|z - 2| = 1$ (b) $|z + 2| = 3$ (c) $|z - 3i| = 2$ (d) $|z + 2i| = 5$
   (e) $|2z| = |z - 1|$ (f) $|z - (2 + i)| = 2$

5. Express the following equations of circles in the form $|z - \omega| = r$
   (a) $x^2 + y^2 - 2x - 2y$
   (b) $x^2 + y^2 + 2x + 4y + 1 = 0$
   (c) $x^2 + y^2 + x + 3y = 0$
   (d) $2x^2 + 2y^2 + 4x + 3y + 1 = 0$

6. Show that the following equations represent circles in an Argand diagram. State their centres and radii.
   (a) $(z - 2)(\bar{z} - 2) = 4$
   (b) $(z - \omega)(\bar{z} - \bar{\omega}) = 1$, where $\omega = 1 + i$
   (c) $(z - 2 + 3i)(\bar{z} - 2 - 3i) = 4$
   (d) $(z - 1 - i)(\bar{z} - 1 + i) = 9$

4.15 Miscellaneous Locus Problems (Including Inequations)

EXAMPLE: (48)

Draw a neat sketch of points satisfying the following conditions:
(a) $Re(z) = 3$ (b) $Im(z) > 2$

SOLUTION:
(a) $Re(z) = 3$, $z = x + iy$
  $Re(x + iy) = 3$
  $\therefore x = 3$
The locus is the vertical line $x = 3$

(b) $Im(z) > 2$, $z = x + iy$
  $\therefore y > 2$
The locus is a half-plane above the line $y = 2$

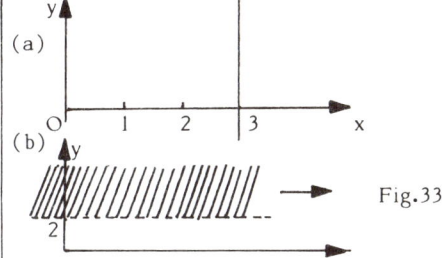

Fig.33

EXAMPLE: (49)

Sketch the curve $|z| = 2$

SOLUTION:

$|z|$ is the distance of a point from the origin, so the locus of $|z| = 2$ is a circle of radius 2, centre $O(0,0)$.

The cartesian equation of this circle is

$x^2 + y^2 = 4$

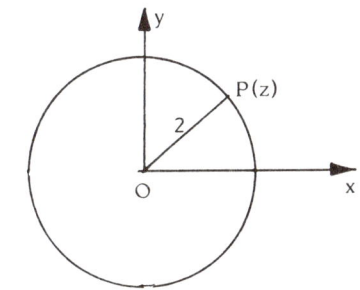

Fig.34

EXAMPLE: (50)

Describe the locus $|z - 2 + 3i| = 3$

SOLUTION:

Write: $|z - (2 - 3i)| = 3$ ... (1)

We know that the equation of the form $|z - w| = r$, represents a circle. Hence (1) represents a circle of radius 3 and centre $(2,-3)$ whose cartesian equation is

$(x - 2)^2 + (y + 3)^2 = 9$

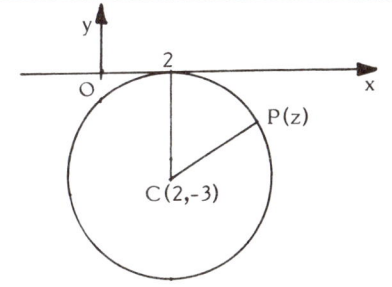

Fig.35

EXAMPLE: (51)

Sketch the region defined by $|z - 2 + 3i| \leq 3$.

SOLUTION:

From example (50) this region is the set of points within and on the boundary of the circle, radius 3, centre $(2,-3)$.

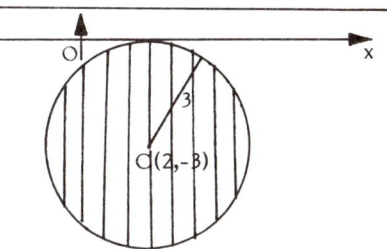

Fig.36

EXAMPLE: (52)

Describe the loci of z if
(a) $|z - 2| = |z + 1 - i|$
(b) $|z - 2| < |z + 1 - i|$

SOLUTION:

(a) $P(z)$ where $z = x + iy$

We have:
$$|z - 2| = |z - (-1 + i)| \quad \ldots (1)$$

Let A be $(2,0)$ and
B be $(-1,1)$

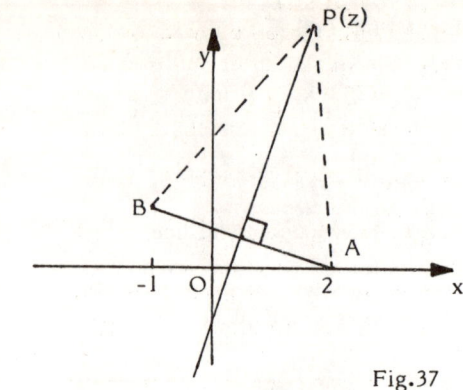

Fig. 37

The relation (1) says that $PA = PB$ for all positions of P and from plane geometry we know that the locus of P is then the perpendicular bisector of AB.

(b) $|z - 2| < |z - (-1 + i)|$

represents a set of points closer to $A(2,0)$ than $B(-1,1)$. Hence the locus of $P(z)$ is the region on the right hand side of the perpendicular bisector of AB, excluding the bisector itself.

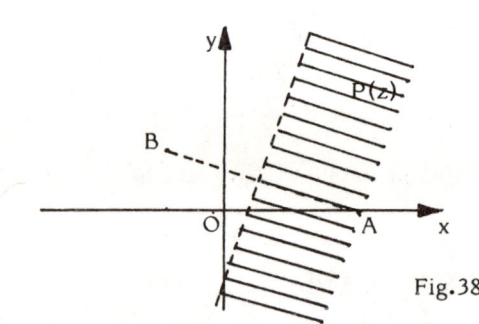

Fig. 38

EXAMPLE: (53) (may be deferred until after Chapter 6)

Describe the locus
$|z - 2| + |z + 2| = 6$

SOLUTION:

Here $A(2,0)$, $B(-2,0)$
we have $PA + PB = 6$ (given).
This is the condition for the locus of z to be an ellipse.

The locus of P is an ellipse.
The foci are $(\pm 2, 0)$.
The centre is O.

Length of semi-major axis is 3
Length of semi-minor axis is $\sqrt{5}$

Equation of the ellipse is $\dfrac{x^2}{9} + \dfrac{y^2}{5} = 1$

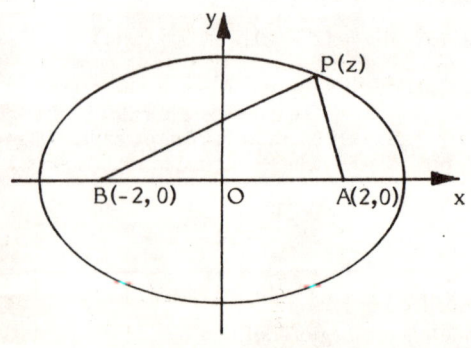

Fig. 39

EXAMPLE: (54)

Sketch the region defined by: (a) $0 \leqslant \arg z \leqslant \frac{\pi}{3}$ (b) $|z| \leqslant 2$ and $0 \leqslant \arg z \leqslant \frac{\pi}{4}$

SOLUTION:

(a) $\arg z = \frac{\pi}{3} = 60°$

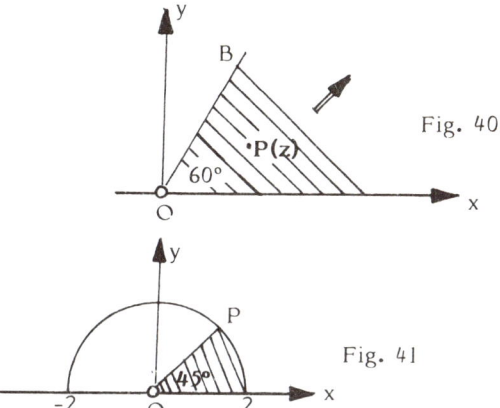

Fig. 40

Locus of $P(z)$ satisfying
$0 \leqslant \arg z \leqslant \pi/3$ is the set of points within the angular region $\angle POX = 60°$ (shaded) including the boundaries, excluding the origin.

$\arg z$ is not defined for $z = 0$

(b) $|z| \leqslant 2$ and $0 \leqslant \arg z \leqslant \pi/4$

The region shaded is within the circle of radius 2, centre 0, restricted in the sector $0 \leqslant \arg z \leqslant 45°$, excluding the origin O.

Fig. 41

EXAMPLE: (55)

Find the locus of ω if $\omega = \frac{z-1}{z}$, given $|z| = 2$

SOLUTION:

We eliminate z from $\omega = \frac{z-1}{z}$ by using $|z| = 2$

Solve for z, then $z\omega = z - 1$ so $z(\omega - 1) = -1$ and $z = \frac{1}{1 - \omega}$

$\therefore |z| = \frac{1}{|1 - \omega|}$, but $|1 - \omega| = |\omega - 1|$ and $|z| = 2$, then

$|\omega - 1| = \frac{1}{2}$

Hence the locus of ω is a circle of radius $\frac{1}{2}$ and centre $(1,0)$. The cartesian equation of the circle is $(x - 1)^2 + y^2 = \frac{1}{4}$

EXAMPLE: (56)

Find the locus of z if $\omega = \frac{z-2}{z}$, given that ω is purely imaginary.

SOLUTION:

$\omega = \frac{z-2}{z} = 1 - \frac{2}{z}$, $z = x + iy$

$\therefore \omega = 1 - \frac{2\bar{z}}{z\bar{z}} = 1 - \frac{2(x - iy)}{x^2 + y^2}$

$\therefore \omega = 1 - \frac{2x}{x^2 + y^2} + \frac{2iy}{x^2 + y^2}$

Now if ω is purely imaginary, then $Re(\omega) = 0$

$\therefore 1 - \frac{2x}{x^2 + y^2} = 0$

$\therefore x^2 + y^2 - 2x = 0$

$(x - 1)^2 + y^2 = 1$ or $|z - 1| = 1$

Hence locus of z is a circle of radius 1, centre $(1,0)$.

EXAMPLE: (57)

Describe the locus given by the equation $|z + 2| = 2|z - 2 + i|$

SOLUTION:

Let $z = x + iy$, then the given equation becomes:

$|x + iy + 2| = 2|x + iy - 2 + i|$

$|(x + 2) + iy| = 2|(x - 2) + i(y + 1)|$

or $\sqrt{(x + 2)^2 + y^2} = 2\sqrt{(x - 2)^2 + (y + 1)^2}$

squaring both sides and simplifying:

$3x^2 + 3y^2 - 20x + 8y + 16 = 0.$ Divide by 3

$x^2 + y^2 - \frac{20}{3}x + \frac{8}{3}y + \frac{16}{3} = 0.$ Complete the squares.

$\left(x - \frac{10}{3}\right)^2 + \left(y + \frac{4}{3}\right)^2 = \frac{100}{9} + \frac{16}{9} - \frac{16}{3} = \frac{68}{9}$

So the locus is a circle, centre $\left(\frac{10}{3}, -\frac{4}{3}\right)$, radius $\frac{\sqrt{68}}{3}$

EXAMPLE: (58)

Sketch on an Argand diagram the locus given by the equation:

$\arg(z - 2) - \arg(z + 2) = \frac{\pi}{3}$

SOLUTION:

$\arg(z - 2) = \angle PBx = \theta$, B(2, 0)

$\arg(z + 2) = \angle PAx = \phi$, A(-2, 0)

Now $\theta - \phi = \frac{\pi}{3}$, so $\angle APB = \frac{\pi}{3}$

The locus of z, as represented by the point P, is thus the major arc of the circle with AB as a chord. This chord AB subtends an angle of at the circumference. By symmetry, we find the centre on the y-axis. Now angle $\angle ACB = 120°$.

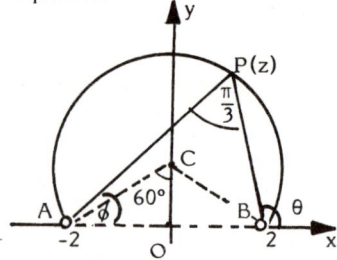

Fig. 42

(Points A and B are excluded from the locus)

$\cos 30° = \frac{2}{r}$ gives $r = 2\sec 30° = 2 \cdot \frac{2}{\sqrt{3}} = \frac{4}{\sqrt{3}}$

$CO = 2\tan 30° = \frac{2}{\sqrt{3}}$

Hence the centre is $(0, \frac{2}{\sqrt{3}})$ and radius is $\frac{4}{\sqrt{3}}$

The cartesian equation of the circle is

$x^2 + \left(y - \frac{2}{\sqrt{3}}\right)^2 = \frac{16}{3}$

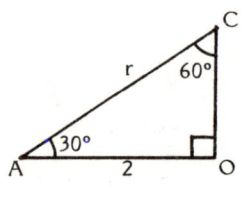

Fig. 43

Exercise 4N

1. Find the Cartesian equation of the following curves, and sketch and describe them (Exercises l, m and n may be postponed until after Chapter 6):

(a) $|z| = 2$ (b) $|z - 2| = 3$ (c) $|z + 2| = 3$

(d) $|z - i| = 2$ (e) $|z + 2i| = 3$ (f) $|z + 2 - 3i| = 2$

(g) $|z| = |z - 1|$ (h) $|z - 2| = |z + i|$

(i) $|z + 2 - 3i| = |z + 2 + i|$ (j) $|z - 2i| = 2|z + 1|$

(k) $|z + 2 - 3i| = 2|z + 2 + i|$ (l)* $|z - 1| + |z + 1| = 4$

(m)* $|z - i| + |z + i| = 4$ (n)* $|z| + |z - 1| = 4$

2. Sketch the following curves after giving their Cartesian equations. Describe the curves.

(a) $\arg z = \pi/3$ (b) $\arg z = -\pi/4$ (c) $\arg(z + 2) = 5\pi/6$

(d) $\arg z = \pi/2$ (e) $\arg z = \pi$ (f) $\arg(z + 2i) = \pi/3$

3. Sketch the following regions in the complex plane, showing whether the boundaries are included or not.

(a) $|z| < 2$ (b) $|z| \geqslant 3$ (c) $|z - i| > 2$

(d) $|z - 2| < 3$ (e) $|z + 2 + 3i| < 2$ (f) $2 < |z - 1| \leqslant 3$

(g) $2 \leqslant |z + 2 - i| \leqslant 4$ (h) $\arg z \leqslant \pi/3$ (i) $\pi/3 \leqslant \arg z \leqslant \pi/2$

(j) $-\pi/2 < \arg z < \pi/6$ (k) $\arg(z + 2) \leqslant \pi/6$ (l) $|z - 3i| > |z + 2|$

4. Sketch the following regions of the complex plane, showing carefully the boundaries (included or not).

(a) $|z| \leqslant 3$ and $0 \leqslant \arg z \leqslant \pi/3$ (b) $|z| \leqslant 2$ and $\pi/6 \leqslant \arg z \leqslant 2\pi/3$

(c) $2 \leqslant |z| \leqslant 4$ and $\operatorname{Re}(z) \geqslant 1$ (d) $2 \leqslant |z| \leqslant 3$ and $\operatorname{Im}(z) \geqslant 1$

(e) $1 \leqslant |z| \leqslant 3$ and $0 \leqslant \arg z \leqslant \pi/2$

5. For the following, describe the locus of the complex number w, where z is restricted as indicated.

(a) $w = z - 2$, $|z| = 3$ (b) $w = \dfrac{z - 2}{z}$, $|z| = 1$

(c) $w = \dfrac{z - 2i}{1 - z}$, $|z| = 2$ (d) $w = \dfrac{z - 2 + i}{z + 2 - i}$, $|z| = 1$

6. Find the locus of z if:

(a) $w = \dfrac{z - 1}{z}$ and w is purely real

(b) $w = \dfrac{z - i}{z - 2}$ and w is purely imaginary

(c) $w = \dfrac{z - 2}{z + 2}$ and $\arg w = \dfrac{\pi}{3}$

Exercise 40 (REVISION)

1. For the complex number $z = x + iy$, find the locus of z. Describe it and draw a neat sketch, if:

   (a) $\arg(z - 2) = \pi/3$ (b) $|z| = z + \bar{z} + 2$ (c) $z\bar{z} - 4(z + \bar{z}) = 10$

   (d) $\arg\left[\dfrac{z - 2}{z - 1}\right] = \pi/2$ (e) $|z + 1| + |z - 1| = 3$

2. The points z_1, z_2 and z_3 are three complex numbers that lie on a circle passing through the origin. Prove that the points which represent $1/z_1$, $1/z_2$ and $1/z_3$ are collinear.

3. (a) Express $\sqrt{5 - 12i}$ in the form $a + ib$.

   (b) Hence or otherwise, find the locus of the point which represents z on the Argand diagram, if $|z^2 - 5 + 12i| = |z - 3 + 2i|$.

4. (a) If x and y are real, solve the equation $\dfrac{iy}{1 + ix} - \dfrac{3y + 4i}{3x + y} = 0$

   (b) Show that the locus of the point $z = x + iy$ is

   (i) a straight line if $\dfrac{z + i}{z + 2}$ is purely real

   (ii) a circle if $\dfrac{z + i}{z + 2}$ is purely imaginary.
   Find the centre and radius of this circle.

5. Given $z_1 = 3 + 4i$ and $z_2 = -3 - 4i$

   (a) Draw a neat sketch of the locus specified by $|z - z_1| = |z - z_2|$.
   Find the Cartesian equation of the locus of z.

   (b) Show that the locus of a point represented by the complex number $z = x + iy$ and obeying the condition $|z - z_1| = 3|z - z_2|$ is a circle.
   Find its centre and radius.

6. P is a variable point on the line $x = 4$ and OPQR is a rectangle in which the length of OP is twice the length of OR. Find the locus of S in Cartesian form, where S is the point of intersection of the diagonals.

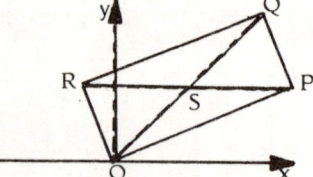

7. Given that $(1 + 4i)p - 3q = 3 + 5i$, find if:
   (a) p and q if p and q are real
   (b) p and q if p and q are complex conjugates.

8. Draw neat sketches of the loci represented by the equations $|z - 2| = 2$ and $|z - 2i| = 2$. Find the complex numbers for the points represented by the intersections of these loci.

9. The point A in an Argand diagram represents the complex number $3 + 4i$. Find the complex number represented by B if OBA is an equilateral triangle. Also find the point D if OABD is a rhombus. (All rotations are anti-clockwise.)

10. (a) The complex number z is given by $z = 1 + \dfrac{1+i}{1-i}$

　　　Find　(i) $\operatorname{Re}(z)$　(ii) $\operatorname{Im}(z)$　(iii) $|z|$　(iv) $\arg z$

　(b) Draw a neat labelled sketch to indicate the locus of the complex number z.
　　　(i) $|z - 3 + i| = 2$　(ii) $\operatorname{Re}(z - iz) \geq 1$

　(c) Determine the locus of the complex number z if
　　　$\arg(z - 1) = \dfrac{\pi}{6} + \arg(z + 4)$. Sketch the locus on an Argand diagram.

　(d) Shade on the Argand diagram the region for which
　　　$\dfrac{2\pi}{3} < \arg z < \pi$　and　$|z| \leq 2$

　　　For part (d), choose a point in the region (above) and label it P. Suppose P represents the complex number z. Then label clearly the points A, B, C, D and E which represent $\bar{z}$, $-z$, iz, z^2 and $z + 2$.

11. (a) $OPQR$ is a square in an Argand diagram where O is the origin. The point P is given by $z = r(\cos\theta + i\sin\theta)$. Find the complex numbers represented by Q and R.

　(b) If $\theta = 30°$, $r = 1$ in part (a) and the square $OPQR$ is now rotated through $60°$ (anti-clockwise direction) to become $OP'Q'R'$, find the complex numbers represented by P', Q' and R' in the mod-arg form.

12. (a) Calculate the modulus and argument of the
　　　(i) sum of the roots
　　　(ii) product of the roots
　　　of the equation $(4 - 3i)z^2 - (3 - 2i)z + 5 + 2i = 0$

　(b) Show that the point representing $\sin\pi/3 + i\cos\pi/3$ in the Argand diagram lies on the circle of radius 1 and the centre at $(\sqrt{3}, 0)$.

　(c) If t is real and $z = \dfrac{2 + it}{2 - it}$ show that as t varies the locus of z is a circle. Find the radius and the centre.

13. (a) Draw the sketch (on an Argand diagram) of the region in which z lies if both $|z - (2 + i)| \leq 4$ and $\pi/6 \leq \arg(z - 1 - i) \leq \pi/2$ are satisfied.

　(b) The complex numbers $z_1 = -\sqrt{3} - i$, $z_2 = \sqrt{3} - i$ and $z_3 = 2i$ are represented by the points P, Q and R respectively. Show that the triangle PQR is an equilateral triangle.

14. (a) Complex numbers $z_1 = \dfrac{p}{1 + 2i}$ and $z_2 = \dfrac{r}{1 + i}$ where p and r are real. Find p and r, if $z_1 - z_2 = 4i$.

　(b) The complex number z satisfies the equation $\arg(z + 2) = \pi/4$.
　　　(i) Sketch the locus of point P which represents z.
　　　(ii) Find the modulus and argument of z when $|z|$ is the minimum.
　　　(iii) Hence find z in the form $x + iy$ when $|z|$ is the minimum.

15. (a) Calculate the modulus and argument of the complex number which represents the product of the roots of the equation
$(4 + 3i)z^2 - (1 - i)z + (2 + i) = 0$.

(b) Find the two square roots of $3 + 4i$ and sketch them in an Argand diagram.

16. (a) Find all six roots of -1, expressing each in the form $x + iy$ and show them on a circle in an Argand diagram.

(b) Solve $z^2 + 16 = -30i$ completely.

17. The point P (which represents $z = x + iy$) moves in a straight line parallel to the imaginary axis. Prove that the point Q which represents z^2 moves in a certain parabola. Find the focus. Also describe the locus of Q when P moves on the imaginary axis.

18. (a) Prove that $\dfrac{z_1 + z_2}{z_1 - z_2}$ is purely imaginary if $|z_1| = |z_2|$

(b) Show that the points represented by the complex numbers z_1, z_2 and $\dfrac{z_1 - 2iz_2}{1 - 2i}$ form the vertices of a right-angled triangle.

(Hint: $\arg\left[\dfrac{z_1 - z_3}{z_2 - z_3}\right] = \dfrac{\pi}{2}$, where $z_3 = \dfrac{z_1 - 2iz_2}{1 - 2i}$)

19. Let $z = x + iy$ and $w = u + iv = (z - 1)^2 + 2$ be complex numbers in an Argand diagram. Show that as z moves along the y-axis from $O(0,0)$ to $A(0,2)$ the point w moves along an arc of a certain parabola. Find the corresponding points on this parabola and the Cartesian equation of the parabola.

20. (a) For the complex number $z = r(\cos\theta + i\sin\theta)$, given that $r = 5$, $\theta = \dfrac{\pi}{3}$, find the modulus and argument of (i) z^2 (ii) $\bar{z}$ (iii) $1/z$ (iv) iz

(b) If $z_1 = 4 + 3i$ and $|z_2| = 10$, find the
(i) maximum value (ii) minimum value of $|z_1 + z_2|$
(iii) express the corresponding values of z_2 in the form $x + iy$

21. (a) Find the modulus and argument of $z = \dfrac{\sqrt{3} + i}{1 + i}$. Find the smallest positive integer, n, such that z^n is real; hence find z^n for this value of n.

(b) Sketch the circle whose Cartesian equation is $(x - 2)^2 + y^2 = 4$. The point A represents the complex number $z = r(\cos\theta + i\sin\theta)$.
(i) Express $|z|$ in terms of θ if A lies on the given circle.
(ii) Find $\left|\dfrac{1}{z}\right|$ and $\arg\left(\dfrac{1}{z}\right)$ if A lies on the circle.
(iii) Show that as A moves on the circle, the point P representing $1/z$ lies on a certain line.

22. The complex numbers $z = x + iy$ and $w = u + iv$ are related so that $w = z - \frac{1}{z}$. Show that:

$$u = x - \frac{x}{x^2 + y^2} \quad \text{and} \quad v = y + \frac{y}{x^2 + y^2}$$

Find the locus of w if (a) $|z| = 2$ (b) $|z| = 1$.
Describe each locus geometrically.

23. Find r and θ if $r(\cos\theta + i\sin\theta) = \dfrac{3\operatorname{cis}45° + 2\operatorname{cis}30°}{5\operatorname{cis}60° - 4\operatorname{cis}30°}$

24. Solve the equations: (a) $\dfrac{z^3 + 1}{z^3 - 1} = i$ (b) $z^2 = i\bar{z}$

25. The four complex numbers u, v, w and z are represented on the complex plane by points P, Q, R and S respectively. If $u + w = v + z$ and $u - w = i(v - z)$, determine the possible shapes of the quadrilateral $PQRS$.

26. (a) Show that $\dfrac{z^9 - 1}{z^3 - 1} = z^6 + z^3 + 1$

(b) Prove that:
$z^6 + z^3 + 1 = (z^2 - 2z\cos\frac{2\pi}{9} + 1)(z^2 - 2z\cos\frac{4\pi}{9} + 1)(z^2 - 2z\cos\frac{8\pi}{9} + 1)$

(c) Deduce from (b) that:
$2\cos3\theta + 1 = 8(\cos\theta - \cos\frac{2\pi}{9})(\cos\theta - \cos\frac{4\pi}{9})(\cos\theta - \cos\frac{8\pi}{9})$

27. (a) Factorise $z^3 + 1$ into linear and quadratic factors with real coefficients.

(b) Prove that $z^5 + 1 = (z + 1)(z^2 - 2z\cos\frac{\pi}{5} + 1)(z^2 - 2z\cos\frac{3\pi}{5} + 1)$

(c) By observing that $z^{15} + 1 = (z^3)^5 + 1$, prove that
$z^{15} + 1 = (z+1)(z^2 - z + 1)(z^6 - 2z^3\cos\frac{\pi}{5} + 1)(z^6 - 2z^3\cos\frac{3\pi}{5} + 1)$

28. Show that if $|\omega| = 1$ and $\operatorname{Re}(\omega) = -\frac{1}{2}$, then $\omega^3 = 1$

29. Prove that $\dfrac{1 + \sin\theta + i\cos\theta}{1 + \sin\theta - i\cos\theta} = \sin\theta + i\cos\theta$ and deduce that
$\left[1 + \sin\frac{\pi}{5} + i\cos\frac{\pi}{5}\right]^5 + i\left[1 + \sin\frac{\pi}{5} - i\cos\frac{\pi}{5}\right]^5 = 0$

30. Express $\left[1 + i\tan\frac{4k+1}{4m}\pi\right]^m$ in the form $a + ib$, where m and k are integers.

CHAPTER 5 POLYNOMIALS

5.1 Introduction

In 3U Mathematics, we learned many important properties of polynomials in the real variable x. In this chapter we shall study these properties and a few more theorems about polynomials over the complex field C. Let us first revise some of the important work on polynomials.

The general nth degree polynomial function of a real variable x is of the form:

$$P(x) = a_n x^n + a_{n-1} x^{n-1} + a_{n-2} x^{n-2} + \ldots + a_1 x + a_0, \quad a_n \neq 0$$

where the coefficients $a_0, a_1, \ldots$ are real, and n is a non-negative integer.

OPERATIONS ON POLYNOMIALS

When two or more polynomials are added, subtracted or multiplied, the result is another polynomial. The division of one polynomial P(x) by another polynomial A(x) may or may not be exact. When P(x) is divided by A(x), we can write the identity:

$$P(x) = Q(x) \cdot A(x) + R(x)$$

where, P(x) is called the dividend,
Q(x) is called the quotient,
A(x) is called the divisor,
R(x) is called the remainder.   [deg R(x) < deg A(x)]

If R(x) = 0, P(x) is exactly divisible by A(x), then Q(x) and A(x) are called the factors of P(x).

THE REMAINDER AND FACTOR THEOREMS

In the division of P(x) by A(x), if A(x) is a linear polynomial x - a, then the degree of R(x) must be zero, i.e. R(x) is a constant. We write:

$$P(x) = (x - a) Q(x) + R$$

Substitute x = a, then

$$P(a) = 0 \cdot Q(a) + R$$
$$\therefore R = P(a).$$

So, the remainder theorem is:
If P(x) is divided by (x - a), the remainder is P(a). Further, if P(a) = 0, then x - a is a factor of P(x), and conversely, if x - a is a factor of P(x) then P(a) = 0. The result is known as the factor theorem. A value of x, such that P(x) = 0, is called a ZERO of the polynomial P(x) or a root of equation P(x) = 0. For example, x = 2 is a zero of $P(x) = x^3 - 8$.

EXAMPLE (1) Find the remainder when $P(x) = 2x^3 - 3x^2 - 4x - 6$ is divided by $A(x) = x - 2$

SOLUTION:

$$\begin{array}{r}
2x^2 + x - 2 \\
x - 2 \overline{\smash{)}\, 2x^3 - 3x^2 - 4x - 6} \\
\underline{2x^3 - 4x^2} \\
x^2 - 4x \\
\underline{x^2 - 2x} \\
-2x - 6 \\
\underline{-2x + 4} \\
-10
\end{array}$$

If we only want the remainder, we use:

$R = P(2) = 16 - 12 - 8 - 6 = -10$

The remainder is -10. We can write $P(x) = (x - 2)(2x^2 + x - 2) - 10$

EXAMPLE (2) Show that $x + 3$ is a factor of $x^3 - 3x + 18$ and hence find the other factors.

SOLUTION: We have $P(x) = x^3 - 3x + 18$, $x - a = x + 3$, so $a = -3$ and $P(-3) = -27 + 9 + 18 = 0$.

Since $P(-3) = 0$, $x + 3$ is a factor of $P(x)$ we divide $P(x)$ by $x + 3$ to find other factors.

$$\begin{array}{r}
x^2 - 3x + 6 \\
x + 3 \overline{\smash{)}\, x^3 + 0 \cdot x^2 - 3x + 18} \\
\underline{x^3 + 3x^2} \\
-3x^2 - 3x \\
\underline{-3x^2 - 9x} \\
6x + 18 \\
\underline{6x + 18} \\
0
\end{array}$$

Observe that the missing term x^2 is arranged as $0 \cdot x^2$. This is important and reduces the chance of errors. The other factor of $P(x)$ is $x^2 - 3x + 6$. (Irreducible over the R-field)

EXAMPLE (3) Find the values of the constant m if the polynomial $P(x) = 4x^3 - m^2x^2 - 4mx + 64$ is divisible by $x + 1$, hence find the other factors of $P(x)$

SOLUTION: $P(x) = 4x^3 - m^2x^2 - 4mx + 64$ is divisible by $x + 1$, i.e. $x - (-1)$

∴ $P(-1) = 0$ gives $-4 - m^2 + 4m + 64 = 0$

∴ $m^2 - 4m - 60 = 0$, i.e. $(m - 10)(m + 6) = 0$

∴ $m = 10$ or $m = -6$

For $m = 10$, $P(x) = 4x^3 - 100x^2 - 40x + 64 = 4(x^3 - 25x^2 - 10x + 16)$

Divide $x^3 - 25x^2 - 10x + 16$ by $x + 1$, then

$P(x) = 4(x + 1)(x^2 - 26x + 16)$, ($x^2 - 26x + 16$ is irreducible over R-field)

For $m = -6$, $P(x) = 4x^3 - 36x^2 + 24x + 64 = 4(x^3 - 9x^2 + 6x + 16)$

Divide $x^3 - 9x^2 + 6x + 16$ by $x + 1$, then

$P(x) = 4(x + 1)(x^2 - 10x + 16) = 4(x + 1)(x - 2)(x - 8)$

EXAMPLE: (4) Given that $x = 2$ is a root of $x^3 - 4x^2 + 14x - 20 = 0$, find the other roots.

SOLUTION:

Divide $x^3 - 4x^2 + 14x - 20$ by $x - 2$

$\therefore (x^3 - 4x^2 + 14x - 20) = (x - 2)(x^2 - 2x + 10)$

$\therefore$ The equation is $(x - 2)(x^2 - 2x + 10) = 0$

$\therefore x = 2$ (given root) or $x^2 - 2x + 10 = 0$, i.e. $x = \dfrac{2 \pm \sqrt{-36}}{2} = 1 \pm 3i$

Observe that the complex roots $1 + 3i$ and $1 - 3i$ are conjugate. We shall later prove that the complex roots of a real polynomial occur in conjugate pairs.

EXAMPLE: (5) Solve: $x^3 - 3x^2 + 4x - 2 = 0$.

SOLUTION:

The constant term $2 = 2 \times 1$. This suggests we try $x = \pm 2, \pm 1$ for the roots.

Let $P(x) = x^3 - 3x^2 + 4x - 2$

$\therefore P(2) = 8 - 12 + 8 - 2 \neq 0$

$P(1) = 1 - 3 + 4 - 2 = 0$

$\therefore x = 1$ is a root of $P(x) = 0$

Divide $P(x)$ by $x - 1$

$\therefore P(x) = (x - 1)(x^2 - 2x + 2)$

The roots of $P(x) = 0$ are $1, \dfrac{2 \pm \sqrt{-4}}{2}$, i.e. $1, 1 \pm i$

Again observe that the complex roots occur in a pair of conjugates.

Exercise 5A

Perform the following divisions, and check the remainder by using the remainder theorem.

1. $(x^3 - 2x^2 + 3x - 1) \div (x - 2)$
2. $(x^4 - 2x^2 + 3x - 2) \div (x + 2)$
3. $(x^4 + 2x^3 + 2x^2 - 2x - 3) \div (x^2 - 1)$
4. $(2x^3 - x^2 + x - 1) \div (x - 1)$

In each of the following, decide whether $A(x)$ is a factor of $P(x)$.

5. $P(x) = x^4 - 2x^3 + x^2 + x - 6$, $A(x) = x - 2$
6. $P(x) = 2x^3 - 3x + 1$, $A(x) = x + 1$
7. $P(x) = x^3 + 2x^2 - x + 6$, $A(x) = x + 3$
8. $P(x) = 5x^3 + 7x^2 + 3x - 1$, $A(x) = x + 3$

Find the remainder of the following without actually dividing, i.e. use the remainder theorem.

9. $P(x) = 4x^3 - 3x^2 - x + 7$, $A(x) = x + 2$
10. $P(x) = 5x^4 - 2x^3 + x + 8$, $A(x) = x + 3$
11. $P(x) = 2x^4 - 4x^2 + 5$, $A(x) = 2x + 1$
12. $P(x) = x^3 - ax^2 + bx + 2$, $A(x) = x - 2$

Find values of k such that $A(x)$ is a factor of $P(x)$.

13. $P(x) = x^4 - 3kx^3 + 3x - 1$, $A(x) = x - 1$
14. $P(x) = x^3 - kx^2 + 4x - 4$, $A(x) = x - 2$
15. $P(x) = x^3 - 3x^2 - 6kx + 8k$, $A(x) = x - 2$
16. $P(x) = x^4 + kx^3 + 7x + 21$, $A(x) = x + 3$

Use the factor theorem to find the value of k that makes $A(x)$ a factor of $P(x)$ and hence find the zeros of $P(x)$.

17. $P(x) = 3x^3 - 12x^2 - 11x - k$, $A(x) = x - 5$
18. $P(x) = 2x^3 - 6x^2 + kx + 4$, $A(x) = x - 2$
19. $P(x) = kx^3 + x^2 - 8x + 6$, $A(x) = x - 1$
20. $P(x) = x^4 + x^3 + kx^2 + 4x - 24$, $A(x) = x + 3$

5.2 Zeros of a Polynomial/Multiple Roots

Rational or Integral Zeros

We use the formula $x = \dfrac{-b \pm \sqrt{b^2 - 4ac}}{2a}$ (or factorise by inspection) to find the zeros of a second degree polynomial $P(x) = ax^2 + bx + c$, but it is generally very difficult to find the zeros of higher degree polynomials such as $3x^4 + 2x^3 - x^2 + 7$. This is because some, or even all the zeros of a polynomial may not be integers, e.g. $x^2 + 2 = 0$ has no real zeros, let alone integer ones. The following theorem is very useful in finding rational zeros (if any), though we shall mainly be concerned with zeros which are integers.

Theorem:

Let $P(x) = a_n x^n + a_{n-1} x^{n-1} + \ldots + a_1 x + a_0$ be a polynomial with integer coefficients. If $x = \dfrac{r}{s}$, where $\dfrac{r}{s}$ is in its lowest terms, is a rational zero of $P(x)$, then r must be a factor of a_0 and s must be a factor of a_n.

Proof: Since $x = \dfrac{r}{s}$ is a zero of $P(x)$, then $P(\dfrac{r}{s}) = 0$.

$\therefore\ a_n (\dfrac{r}{s})^n + a_{n-1} (\dfrac{r}{s})^{n-1} + \ldots + a_1 (\dfrac{r}{s}) + a_0 = 0$.

Multiplying both sides by s^n and rearranging:

$a_n r^n + a_{n-1} r^{n-1} \cdot s + \ldots + a_1 r \cdot s^{n-1} = -a_0 s^n$

Or, $r(a_n r^{n-1} + a_{n-1} r^{n-2} \cdot s + \ldots + a_1 s^{n-1}) = -a_0 s^n$ ... (1)

The relation (1) shows that r is a factor of $a_0 s^n$. But r cannot be factor of s^n as r and s have no common factor, hence r must be a factor of a_0. In the same manner, we can prove that s is a factor of a_n. Further, if $a_n = 1$, $P(x)$ is monic and the zeros of $P(x)$ are integers as s must be a factor of 1.

EXAMPLE: Find all the zeros of $P(x) = x^3 + 2x^2 - 3x - 6$
SOLUTION:

Since $P(x)$ is monic, the integral zeros must be the factors of the constant term -6. All the possible factors are $\pm 1, \pm 2, \pm 3, \pm 6$. We find that only $x = -2$ satisfies $P(x) = 0$, so -2 is a zero of $P(x)$.
$P(x)$ is of degree 3 and therefore has 3 zeros.
The other two zeros must be irrational or complex. To find these, we divide $P(x)$ by $x + 2$.
$\therefore P(x) = (x + 2)(x^2 - 3)$
Hence the zeros of $P(x)$ are: $-2, \pm \sqrt{3}$.

It is possible that $P(x)$ has no integral zeros, as the following example shows.

EXAMPLE: Show that $P(x) = x^4 - x^2 - 2x + 6$ has no rational zeros.
SOLUTION:

All the possible factors of 6 are: $\pm 1, \pm 2, \pm 3, \pm 6$.
None of these numbers satisfy $P(x) = 0$, hence $P(x)$ has no integral zeros. Since a fourth degree polynomial must have 4 zeros (see section 5.3, theorem 3), we conclude that the zeros of $P(x)$ are either irrational or complex.

EXAMPLE: Find all the roots of $5x^3 + 28x^2 + 10x - 3 = 0$
SOLUTION:

Let $P(x) = 5x^3 + 28x^2 + 10x - 3 = 0$.
To make our work easier, we transform this equation so that the leading term has a coefficient equal to 1.
Observing that the coefficient of x^3 is 5, we multiply the equation by 25 and then put $y = 5x$.
$\therefore (5x)^3 + 28(5x)^2 + 50(5x) - 75 = 0$
Or $y^3 + 28y^2 + 50y - 75 = 0$ ... (1)
By testing the possible factors of 75 i.e. $\pm 1, \pm 3, \pm 5, \pm 15, \pm 25, \pm 75$, we find that $y = -3$ is a root of (1), hence
$P(y) = (y + 3)(y^2 + 25y - 25)$
The roots of (1) are: $y = -3, \dfrac{-25 \pm 5\sqrt{29}}{2}$

Using $x = \dfrac{y}{5}$, the roots of the given equation are:
$x = \dfrac{-3}{5}, \dfrac{-5 \pm \sqrt{29}}{2}$

Multiple Roots

Consider the polynomial $P(x) = (x - 2)^2 (x^2 + 5x + 6)$

$x = 2$ is called a double root of the equation $P(x) = 0$. Similarly for $P(x) = (x - 2)^3 (x + 2)$, $x = 2$ is called a triple root of $P(x) = 0$. In general, we call b, a multiple root of order r if
$$P(x) = (x - b)^r Q(x), \qquad Q(b) \neq 0.$$
We also speak of a root of multiplicity r.

Theorem: If $x = b$ is a root of multiplicity r of the real polynomial equation $P(x) = 0$, then $x = b$ is also a root of the derived polynomial equation $\frac{dP}{dx} = 0$ of multiplicity $(r - 1)$.

Proof:
Let $P(x) = (x - b)^r \cdot Q(x)$, where $Q(b) \neq 0$.

$\therefore \quad \frac{dP}{dx} = r(x - b)^{r-1} Q(x) + \frac{dQ}{dx} \cdot (x - b)^r$

$\qquad\qquad = (x - b)^{r-1} \left[r Q(x) + (x - b) \frac{dQ}{dx} \right]$

$\qquad\qquad = (x - b)^{r-1} S(x)$, where $S(b) \neq 0$, $S(x)$ is the polynomial in the bracket.

This clearly shows that $x = b$ is a root of multiplicity $(r - 1)$ of the derived equation $\frac{dP}{dx} = 0$.

EXTENSION:

If $(x - a)^r$ is a factor of $P(x)$, then
1. $(x - a)^{r-1}$ is a factor of $\frac{dP}{dx}$
2. $(x - a)^{r-2}$ is a factor of $\frac{d^2P}{dx^2}$ and so on.

EXAMPLE: (6) Show that $\frac{dP}{dx}$ has a zero of multiplicity 2 if $P(x) = (x - 2)^3 (x^2 + 2)$

SOLUTION: $\frac{dP}{dx} = 3(x - 2)^2 (x^2 + 2) + 2x(x - 2)^3$

$\qquad\qquad = (x - 2)^2 [3(x^2 + 2) + 2x(x - 2)]$

$\therefore \quad \frac{dP}{dx}$ has $x = 2$ as a double root

EXAMPLE: (7) Solve the equation $x^3 - 3x - 2 = 0$, given that it has a double root.

SOLUTION:

Let $P(x) = x^3 - 3x - 2$

$\frac{dP}{dx} = 3x^2 - 3 = 3(x - 1)(x + 1) = 0$ gives $x = \pm 1$

The possibilities for the double root are 1 and -1

Now $P(1) = 1 - 3 - 2 \neq 0$ and $P(-1) = -1 + 3 - 2 = 0$

$\therefore$ $x = -1$ is a double root of $P(x) = x^3 - 3x - 2 = 0$

Divide out $x^3 - 3x - 2$ by $(x + 1)^2$, i.e. $x^2 + 2x + 1$, then $x^3 - 3x - 2 = (x + 1)^2(x - 2)$

$\therefore$ The roots of $x^3 - 3x - 2 = 0$ are $-1, -1, 2$

EXAMPLE: (8) Show that:

(a) $x^2 + px + q = 0$ has a double root, if $p^2 = 4q$
(b) $x^3 + px + q = 0$ has a double root, if $4p^3 + 27q^2 = 0$

SOLUTION:

(a) Let $P(x) = x^2 + px + q$, then $\frac{dP}{dx} = 2x + p$

$\frac{dP}{dx} = 0$ gives $2x + p = 0$, hence $x = -\frac{p}{2}$ is a double root of $x^2 + px + q = 0$.

Substituting $x = -\frac{p}{2}$ in the equation,

$\frac{p^2}{4} - \frac{p^2}{2} + q = 0$ whence $p^2 = 4q$

We can check this condition for $x^2 + px + q = 0$ by using $\Delta = p^2 - 4q = 0$ for equal roots.

(b) $P(x) = x^3 + px + q$, then $\frac{dP}{dx} = 3x^2 + p = 0$ gives $x^2 = -\frac{p}{3}$

For x to be real, $p \leq 0$.

To avoid irritating fractional powers, we write the original equation $x(x^2 + p) = -q$ as

$x^2(x^2 + p)^2 = q^2$, now put $x^2 = -\frac{p}{3}$.

$\therefore$ $-\frac{p}{3}(-\frac{p}{3} + p)^2 = q^2$ which gives $4p^3 + 27q^2 = 0$

Exercise 5B

Find the real roots of the following equations, given that each equation has a double root:

1. $x^3 - 7x^2 + 11x - 5 = 0$
2. $x^3 - 2x^2 - 4x + 8 = 0$
3. $x^3 - 2x^2 - 15x + 36 = 0$
4. $x^4 + x^3 + x + 1 = 0$

5. Find the real roots of each equation, given that each has a triple root:

   (a) $P(x) = x^4 + 2x^3 - 12x^2 + 14x - 5 = 0$

   (b) $P(x) = x^4 - 6x^3 + 12x^2 - 10x + 3 = 0$

   [Hint: $\frac{d^2P}{dx^2} = 0$ and $P(x) = 0$ have a common root]

6. Find the point where the tangent to the curve

   (a) $y = x^3 - 2x^2 + 3$ at $x = 2$

   (b) $y = x^3 - 2x^2 + 1$ at $x = 1$

   meets the curve again at Q. Find the coordinates of Q.

7. Find the values of k such that each of the following equations has a double root:

   (a) $P(x) = x^3 + 6x^2 + 9x + k = 0$

   (b) $P(x) = x^3 + 3x^2 - 24x + k = 0$

   Find the roots of $P(x) = 0$ for each value of k.

8. Find all the roots of the following equations. First find all the integral roots, then by division of $P(x)$ find the other roots.

   (a) $x^3 - x^2 - 4x + 4 = 0$

   (b) $x^3 + 2x^2 - 5x - 6 = 0$

   (c) $2x^3 - 9x^2 + 7x + 6 = 0$

   (Hint: Multiply by 4, let $y = 2x$)

   (d) $x^4 + x^3 - 7x^2 - 13x - 6 = 0$

   (e) $x^3 - 4x^2 + x + 6 = 0$

   (f) $x^4 - 6x^3 - x^2 + 34x + 8 = 0$

   (g) $4x^3 - 11x^2 + x + 1 = 0$
   (Hint: multiply by 16, $y = 4x$)

   (h) $4x^3 - 5x - 2 = 0$
   (Hint: $y = 2x$)

   (i) (Solve for $\tan \theta$ only): $\tan^4 \theta - 2\tan^3 \theta - 13\tan^2 \theta + 14\tan \theta + 24 = 0$

9. Prove the theorem:

   If $x = r$ is an integral zero of the monic polynomial

   $P(x) = x^n + a_{n-1}x^{n-1} + \ldots + a_0$, then r must be a factor of a_0.

5.3 Polynomials over the Complex Field

A polynomial such as $x^2 + 4$ has no real factors. Using $i^2 = -1$, we can factorise $x^2 + 4$.

$$x^2 + 4 = x^2 - 4i^2 = (x - 2i)(x + 2i)$$

Thus a real polynomial with no real factors can be factorised over the complex field. We shall now study several theorems which are essential for the factorisation of polynomials.

You might wonder whether every polynomial has a zero. The following theorem answers this question.

Theorem 1: The Fundamental Theorem of Algebra

If $P(x)$ is a polynomial of degree $n \geqslant 1$, then $P(x)$ has at least one zero over the complex field.

The proof is beyond the scope of this book. It was first proved by the German mathematician Gauss in 1799, when he was 22.

From this theorem and the factor theorem, it follows that if $P(x)$ is a polynomial of degree $n \geqslant 1$, then there is at least one number c_1 such that:

$$P(x) = (x - c_1) Q_1(x)$$

If we repeat the process on the polynomial $Q_1(x)$, we get:

$$P(x) = (x - c_1)(x - c_2) Q_2(x)$$

If we repeat the process n times, we obtain the following:

Theorem 2: If $P(x)$ is a polynomial of degree $n \geqslant 1$, then there exist n numbers $c_1, c_2, ..., c_n$ (not necessarily distinct) such that

$$P(x) = a_n (x - c_1)(x - c_2) ... (x - c_n)$$

where $a_n \neq 0$ is the leading coefficient.

Theorem 2 ensures that every polynomial of degree $n \geqslant 1$ can be completely factorised into n linear factors. Each of the numbers $c_1, c_2, ... c_n$ is a zero of $P(x)$ and hence a root of the equation $P(x) = 0$.

Now let $P(c) = 0$, then:

$$P(c) = a_n (c - c_1)(c - c_2) ... (c - c_n) = 0$$

This is possible only if c is one of the numbers $c_1, c_2, ..., c_n$. So it follows from theorem 2 that:

Theorem 3: A polynomial $P(x)$ of degree $n \geqslant 1$ has at most n distinct zeros.

This ensures that the equation $P(x) = 0$ has at most n distinct roots.

EXAMPLE: (9) The polynomial $P(x) = (x - 2)^3 (x - 3)(x + 1)$ has 5 zeros, $2, 2, 2, 3, -1$. Here 2 is a zero of multiplicity 3.

EXAMPLE: (10) The polynomial $P(x) = x^3 - 1 = (x - 1)(x^2 + x + 1)$ has 3 zeros: $1, \dfrac{-1 \pm \sqrt{3}i}{2}$

Observe that the complex zeros of the polynomial $x^3 - 1$ are a pair of conjugates. An important fact about the complex zeros of $P(x)$ with real coefficients is given in the following theorem.

Theorem 4: If $a + ib$ is a complex zero of the polynomial $P(x)$ of degree $n \geqslant 1$, having real coefficients, then $a - ib$ is also a zero of $P(x)$.

It follows that if $a + ib$ is a root of $P(x) = 0$, then so is $a - ib$.

There are two methods of proving this theorem.

Method I: <u>Using the properties of complex conjugates</u>

We shall need the following properties of conjugates.

If z_1 and z_2 are two complex numbers and m is a real number, then:

(a) $\overline{(z_1 + z_2)} = \bar{z}_1 + \bar{z}_2$

(b) $\overline{mz_1} = m\bar{z}_1$

(c) $\overline{z_1^n} = (\bar{z}_1)^n$

Let $z = a + ib$ be a complex zero of $P(x) = a_n x^n + \ldots + a_0$

$\therefore a_n z^n + a_{n-1} z^{n-1} + \ldots + a_0 = 0$, hence:

$\overline{a_n z^n + a_{n-1} z^{n-1} + \ldots + a_0} = \bar{0} = 0$

By property (a):

$\overline{a_n z^n} + \overline{a_{n-1} z^{n-1}} + \ldots + \overline{a_1 z} + \overline{a_0} = 0$

By property (b):

$a_n \overline{z^n} + a_{n-1} \overline{z^{n-1}} + \ldots + a_1 \bar{z} + a_0 = 0$

By property (c):

$a_n (\bar{z})^n + a_{n-1} (\bar{z})^{n-1} + \ldots + a_1 \bar{z} + a_0 = 0$

But the L.H.S. of the above equation is $P(\bar{z})$

This completes the proof. The requirement that $P(x)$ have real coefficients is essential.

Verify that $x = -2i$ is a root of $x^2 + 2xi = 0$ but $x = 2i$ is not.

Alternative Proof:

Let $z = a + ib$ be a complex zero of the polynomial $P(x)$ with real coefficients.

We use $\bar{z} = a - ib$, $z + \bar{z} = 2a$, $z\bar{z} = a^2 + b^2$ to form the product:

$$(x - z)(x - \bar{z}) = x^2 - (z + \bar{z})x + z\bar{z} = x^2 - 2ax + a^2 + b^2$$

If $P(x)$ is divided by $x^2 - 2ax + a^2 + b^2$, the remainder must be of degree < 2. Hence,

$$P(x) = [x^2 - 2ax + a^2 + b^2] Q(x) + mx + n$$
$$= [x - (a + bi)][x - (a - bi)] Q(x) + mx + n$$

Since $a + ib$ is a zero of $P(x)$, $P(a + ib) = 0$. Substituting $x = a + ib$, gives:

$$0 = 0 + m(a + ib) + n$$

$\therefore \quad (am + n) + bmi = 0 = 0 + 0 \cdot i$

Comparing the real and imaginary parts separately, $am + n = 0$ and $bm = 0$ and hence $m = 0$ and $n = 0$. $\quad (b \ne 0)$

Thus, $P(x) = [x - (a + ib)][x - (a - ib)] Q(x)$

Hence $P(a - ib) = 0$, i.e. $a - ib$ is also a zero of $P(x)$.

WORKED EXAMPLES

EXAMPLE: (11) Factorise over the complex field $\mathbb{C}$

(a) $x^2 + 2x + 3$ $\qquad$ (b) $4x^2 + 3x + 2$

SOLUTION: By completing the square

$$\begin{aligned}
\text{(a)} \quad x^2 + 2x + 3 &= (x^2 + 2x + 1) + 2 \\
&= (x + 1)^2 + 2 \qquad [i^2 = -1] \\
&= (x + 1)^2 - 2i^2 \\
&= [x + 1 + \sqrt{2}i][x + 1 - \sqrt{2}i]
\end{aligned}$$

$$\begin{aligned}
\text{(b)} \quad 4x^2 + 3x + 2 &= 4\left[\left(x + \tfrac{3}{8}\right)^2 + \tfrac{23}{64}\right] \\
&= 4\left[x + \tfrac{3}{8} + \tfrac{\sqrt{23}}{8}i\right]\left[x + \tfrac{3}{8} - \tfrac{\sqrt{23}}{8}i\right]
\end{aligned}$$

EXAMPLE: (12) Factorise over the complex field C

(a) $x^4 - 1$ (b) $x^3 + 3x^2 - x - 3$ (c) $x^3 - 1$

SOLUTION:

(a) $x^4 - 1 = (x^2 - 1)(x^2 + 1)$
$= (x - 1)(x + 1)(x - i)(x + i)$

(b) Let $P(x) = x^3 + 3x^2 - x - 3$. The constant $3 = 3 \times 1$, so we try $\pm 1, \pm 3$

∴ $P(1) = 1 + 3 - 1 - 3 = 0$

∴ $x - 1$ is a factor of $P(x)$

Divide $P(x)$ by $x - 1$

∴ $P(x) = (x - 1)(x^2 + 4x + 3) = (x - 1)(x + 1)(x + 3)$

It must be remembered that R is a subset of C.

(c) $x^3 - 1 = (x - 1)(x^2 + x + 1) = (x - 1)\left[\left(x + \frac{1}{2}\right)^2 + \frac{3}{4}\right]$

∴ $x^3 - 1 = (x - 1)(x + \frac{1}{2} + \frac{\sqrt{3}}{2}i)(x + \frac{1}{2} - \frac{\sqrt{3}}{2}i)$

EXAMPLE: (13) Show that $x = 1 + i$ is a zero of the polynomial
$P(x) = x^3 + 2x^2 - 6x + 8$ and hence factorise $P(x)$ completely over C.

SOLUTION:

$P(x) = x^3 + 2x^2 - 6x + 8$

We know that if $1 + i$ is a zero of $P(x)$ with real coefficients, then $1 - i$ is also a zero of $P(x)$. We form the product:

$(x - z)(x - \bar{z})$ where $z = 1 + i$, $\bar{z} = 1 - i$, $z + \bar{z} = 2$, $z\bar{z} = 2$

$= x^2 - (z + \bar{z})x + z\bar{z}$

$= x^2 - 2x + 2$

Divide $P(x)$ by $x^2 - 2x + 2$

∴ $P(x) = (x + 4)(x^2 - 2x + 2) = (x + 4)(x - 1 - i)(x - 1 + i)$

Note: If $z = a + ib$ is a zero of real $P(x)$, then $\bar{z} = a - ib$ is also a zero of $P(x)$. It is easier to divide $P(x)$ by $(x - z)(x - \bar{z}) = x^2 - 2ax + a^2 + b^2$, than by $x - a - ib$.

Exercise 5C

Factorise the following quadratics over the complex field C.

1. $x^2 + 4$
2. $x^2 + c^2$
3. $x^2 + 5$
4. $x^2 + x + 1$
5. $x^2 + 3x + 5$
6. $3x^2 + 2x + 1$
7. $4x^2 - x + 1$
8. $2x^2 + 1$

One zero of the polynomial $P(x)$ is given, find the other zeros over the complex field C.

9. $P(x) = x^3 - 3x^2 + 4x - 4$; $x = 2$
10. $P(x) = 2x^3 - 2x^2 - x - 6$; $x = 2$
11. $P(x) = x^3 + x^2 - 7x + 65$; $x = 2 - 3i$
12. $P(x) = 2x^3 - 5x^2 + 6x - 2$; $x = 1 - i$
13. $P(x) = x^4 - 2x^3 - 7x^2 + 26x - 20$; $x = 2 + i$
14. $P(x) = x^4 + 3x^3 - x^2 - 13x - 10$; $x = -2 - i$
15. $P(x) = 2x^4 + 11x^3 + 20x^2 + 7x - 10$; $x = i - 2$

Factorise completely over the complex field:

16. $x^4 + 3x^2 + 4$ [Hint: $P(x) = (x^2 + 2)^2 - x^2$]
17. $x^4 + 16$ [Hint: $P(x) = (x^2 + 4)^2 - 8x^2$]
18. $x^4 + x^2 + 1$ [Hint: $P(x) = (x^2 + 1)^2 - x^2$]
19. $x^6 - 1$ [Hint: $P(x) = (x^2 - 1)(x^4 + x^2 + 1)$]

20. Evaluate the following in the form $a + ib$.

    (a) $P(x) = x^3 + x^2 + x + 1$ for $x = 1 - i$

    [Hint: Write $P(x) = x^2(x + 1) + (x + 1)$ and substitute]

    (b) $P(x) = x^4 - 2x^3 + x^2 - 3x + 2$ for $x = 1 + i$

    [Hint: $P(x) = x^2(x^2 - 2x) + x^2 - 3x + 2$]

5.4 Relation between Roots and Coefficients of P(x) = 0

In 3U Mathematics we have studied the relations between the roots and coefficients of polynomials equations $P(x) = 0$ of degrees 2, 3 and 4.

1. $ax^2 + bx + c = 0$, $\alpha + \beta = -\dfrac{b}{a}$, $\alpha\beta = \dfrac{c}{a}$

2. $ax^3 + bx^2 + cx + d = 0$,
$$\alpha + \beta + \gamma = -\dfrac{b}{a}$$
$$\alpha\beta + \beta\gamma + \gamma\alpha = \dfrac{c}{a}$$
$$\alpha\beta\gamma = -\dfrac{d}{a}$$

3. $ax^4 + bx^3 + cx^2 + dx + e = 0$
$$\alpha + \beta + \gamma + \delta = -\dfrac{b}{a}, \quad \Sigma\alpha\beta = \dfrac{c}{a}, \quad \Sigma\alpha\beta\gamma = -\dfrac{d}{a}, \quad \alpha\beta\gamma\delta = \dfrac{e}{a}$$

The following two theorems are used in establishing the relation between the coefficients and the roots of the polynomial equation.

$$P(x) = a_n x^n + a_{n-1} x^{n-1} + \dots + a_1 x + a_0 = 0 .$$

Theorem (5): If a polynomial $P(x)$ of degree $n \geqslant 1$ vanishes for more than n values of x, it is the zero polynomial, i.e. $a_n = a_{n-1} = \dots = a_0 = 0$.

Referring to the theorem (3), i.e. a polynomial of degree n cannot have more than n distinct zeros, we find that the assumption that $P(x)$ is not the zero polynomial contradicts the fact that the polynomial vanishes for more than n values of x. Hence $P(x)$ is the zero polynomial.

EXAMPLE: (14) Show that $a = b = c = 0$ if $P(x) = ax^2 + bx + c$ vanishes for $x = m, n, r$ (3 distinct values)

SOLUTION:

We have: $am^2 + bm + c = 0$ ... (1)
$an^2 + bn + c = 0$ ... (2)
$ar^2 + br + c = 0$ ... (3)

Subtracting, we get: $a(m^2 - n^2) + b(m - n) = 0$, $m \neq n$
$a(m + n) + b = 0$ ... (4)
Similarly $a(n + r) + b = 0$ ... (5)

Subtracting (5) from (4): $a(m - r) = 0$, $m \neq r$
$\therefore a = 0$, then from (4): $b = 0$, then from (1): $c = 0$

Theorem (6): If two polynomials, each of the degree n, $P(x) = \Sigma a_n x^n$ and $Q(x) = \Sigma b_n x^n$ have equal values for more than n values of x, then:
$$a_n = b_n, \quad a_{n-1} = b_{n-1}, \quad \ldots \quad a_0 = b_0.$$

Proof: We write $R(x) = P(x) - Q(x) = \Sigma (a_n - b_n) x^n$

Now $R(x)$ is a polynomial of degree n and it vanishes for more than n values of x, hence by the theorem (3):
$$a_n - b_n = 0, \quad a_{n-1} - b_{n-1}, \quad \ldots \quad a_0 - b_0 = 0.$$
This proves the theorem.

RELATION BETWEEN ROOTS OF $P(x) = 0$

Let $x_1, x_2, \ldots, x_n$ be the n roots of $P(x) = 0$. We divide out $P(x)$ by the leading coefficient a_n and write the identity:

$$x^n + \frac{a_{n-1}}{a_n} x^{n-1} + \frac{a_{n-2}}{a_n} x^{n-2} + \ldots + \frac{a_0}{a_n} = (x - x_1)(x - x_2) \ldots (x - x_n)$$

R.H.S. $= x^n - (\Sigma x_1) x^{n-1} + (\Sigma x_1 x_2) x^{n-2} + \ldots + (-1)^n x_1 x_2 \ldots x_n$.

comparing coefficients on each side.

(1) $S_1 = $ Sum of the roots $= x_1 + x_2 + \ldots + x_n = -\dfrac{a_{n-1}}{a_n}$

(2) $S_2 = $ Sum of products of roots taken two at a time. $= x_1 x_2 + x_1 x_3 + \ldots = +\dfrac{a_{n-2}}{a_n}$

… and so on.

(n) $S_n = $ Product of all roots $= x_1 x_2 \ldots x_n = (-1)^n \dfrac{a_0}{a_n}$

These relations also help us to write down the equation whose roots $x_1, x_2, \ldots, x_n$ are given.

$$x^n - S_1 x^{n-1} + S_2 x^{n-2} + \ldots + (-1)^n S_n = 0$$

The relation for S_1 is frequently needed in many problems of solving polynomial equations.

$$S_1 = \text{Sum of the roots} = x_1 + x_2 + \ldots + x_n = -\frac{\text{coeff. of } x^{n-1}}{\text{coeff. of } x^n} = -\frac{a_{n-1}}{a_n}$$

WORKED EXAMPLES

EXAMPLE: (15) If α, β, γ are the roots of $x^3 - 2x^2 + x + 3 = 0$, evaluate:

(a) $\alpha^2 + \beta^2 + \gamma^2$ (b) $\alpha^3 + \beta^3 + \gamma^3$ (c) $\alpha^4 + \beta^4 + \gamma^4$

SOLUTION:

We have: $\alpha + \beta + \gamma = 2$, $\alpha\beta + \beta\gamma + \gamma\alpha = 1$, $\alpha\beta\gamma = -3$

(a) $\alpha^2 + \beta^2 + \gamma^2 = (\alpha + \beta + \gamma)^2 - 2(\alpha\beta + \beta\gamma + \gamma\alpha) = 4 - 2 = 2$

(b) A formula to convert $\Sigma\alpha^3$ in terms of $\Sigma\alpha$ and $\Sigma\alpha\beta$ is very difficult, so we try a simple trick:

Re-write the equation as $x^3 = 2x^2 - x - 3$ and substitute $x = \alpha, \beta, \gamma$ and add:

$\therefore \alpha^3 + \beta^3 + \gamma^3 = 2(\alpha^2 + \beta^2 + \gamma^2) - (\alpha + \beta + \gamma) - 3 - 3 - 3$

$= 2 \times 2 - 2 - 9$

$= -7$

By using the formula, we can verify that

$\Sigma\alpha^3 = (\Sigma\alpha) \cdot (\Sigma\alpha^2 - \Sigma\alpha\beta) + 3\alpha\beta\gamma = 2(2-1) - 9 = -7$

(c) There is no known formula that relates $\Sigma\alpha^4$ with $\Sigma\alpha$ etc. so we proceed as follows:

Multiply the given equation by x and write: $x^4 = 2x^3 - x^2 - 3x$

Substitute α, β, γ and add:

$\therefore \Sigma\alpha^4 = 2\Sigma\alpha^3 - \Sigma\alpha^2 - 3\Sigma\alpha = 2 \cdot (-7) - 2 - 3(2) = -22$

EXAMPLE: (16) Solve $P(x) = x^4 - 3x^3 - 6x^2 + 28x - 24 = 0$, given that $P(x) = 0$ has a root of multiplicity 3.

SOLUTION:

Since $P(x)$ has a root of multiplicity 3, $P(x)$, $\frac{dP}{dx}$ and $\frac{d^2P}{dx^2}$ have a common zero.

Now $\frac{dP}{dx} = 4x^3 - 9x^2 - 12x + 28$ and $\frac{d^2P}{dx^2} = 12x^2 - 18x - 12$

Solving $12x^2 - 18x - 12 = 0 \rightarrow (x-2)(2x+1) = 0$

$\therefore x = 2$ or $x = -\frac{1}{2}$

Since $P(-\frac{1}{2}) \neq 0$, $P(2) = 0$, $x = 2$ is the triple root of $P(x) = 0$

Now the sum of the roots is:

$2 + 2 + 2 + x_4 = 3$, so $x_4 = -3$, hence the roots are:

2, 2, 2 and -3

Transformation of Polynomial Equations:

1. The equation whose roots are the reciprocals of the roots of a given equation, is obtained by putting $x = \frac{1}{y}$ in the given equation.
2. The equation whose roots are those of a given equation multiplied by a constant m, is obtained by putting $x = \frac{y}{m}$ in the given equation.
3. The equation whose roots differ by a constant k from the roots of a given equation is obtained by putting $x = y + k$ ($k > 0$ or $k < 0$) in the given equation.
4. The equation whose roots are the squares of the roots of a given equation is obtained by putting $x = \sqrt{y}$ in the given equation.

EXAMPLE: If α, β, γ are the roots of $2x^3 + 3x^2 + x - 5 = 0$, form the equation whose roots are:

(a) $\frac{1}{\alpha}, \frac{1}{\beta}, \frac{1}{\gamma}$ (b) $2\alpha, 2\beta, 2\gamma$ (c) $2 + \alpha, 2 + \beta, 2 + \gamma$

(d) $\alpha - 2, \beta - 2, \gamma - 2$ (e) $\alpha^2, \beta^2, \gamma^2$ (f) $-\alpha, -\beta, -\gamma$

SOLUTION:

(a) Let $y = \frac{1}{x}$, since $x = \alpha, \beta, \gamma,$ $y = \frac{1}{\alpha}, \frac{1}{\beta}, \frac{1}{\gamma}$.

Put $x = \frac{1}{y}$ (from $y = \frac{1}{x}$) in the given equation $2x^3 + 3x^2 + x - 5 = 0$

$\therefore \frac{2}{y^3} + \frac{3}{y^2} + \frac{1}{y} - 5 = 0$ giving $2 + 3y + y^2 - 5y^3 = 0$

The required equation is: $5x^3 - x^2 - 3x - 2 = 0$.

(b) Let $y = 2x$, since $x = \alpha, \beta, \gamma$, $y = 2\alpha, 2\beta, 2\gamma$

From $2x = y$, we put $x = \frac{y}{2}$ in the given equation, $2x^3 + 3x^2 + x - 5 = 0$

$\therefore \frac{2y^3}{8} + \frac{3y^2}{4} + \frac{y}{2} - 5 = 0$

Multiplying by 4, $y^3 + 3y^2 + 2y - 20 = 0$

So, the required equation is $x^3 + 3x^2 + 2x - 20 = 0$.

(c) Let $y = 2 + x$, since $x = \alpha, \beta, \gamma,$ $y = 2 + \alpha, 2 + \beta, 2 + \gamma$

Substituting $x = y - 2$ in the given equation, $2x^3 + 3x^2 + x - 5 = 0$

$2(y-2)^3 + 3(y-2)^2 + (y-2) - 5 = 0$

This simplifies to $2y^3 - 9y^2 + 13y - 11 = 0$, hence the required equation is: $2x^3 - 9x^2 + 13x - 11 = 0$

(d) Let $y = x - 2$, then substituting $x = y + 2$ in the given equation:

$2(y + 2)^3 + 3(y + 2)^2 + (y + 2) - 5 = 0$ which simplifies to:

$2y^3 + 15y^2 + 37y + 25 = 0$

$\therefore 2x^3 + 15x^2 + 37x + 25 = 0$ is the required equation.

(e) Let $y = x^2$ then putting $x = \sqrt{y}$, we obtain the equation whose roots are $\alpha^2, \beta^2, \gamma^2$.

$\therefore 2y^{3/2} + 3y + \sqrt{y} - 5 = 0$

To remove the radical signs, we write:

$3y - 5 = -\sqrt{y}(2y + 1)$, $(y^{3/2} = y\sqrt{y})$

Squaring both sides:

$9y^2 - 30y + 25 = y(4y^2 + 4y + 1)$, which simplifies to: $4y^3 - 5y^2 + 31y - 25 = 0$

$\therefore 4x^3 - 5x^2 + 31x - 25 = 0$ is the required equation.

(f) Let $y = -x$, then putting $x = -y$ we obtain the equation whose roots are $-\alpha, -\beta, -\gamma$.

$\therefore -2y^3 + 3y^2 - y - 5 = 0$, hence the required equation is

$2x^3 - 3x^2 + x + 5 = 0$.   (Compare this with the original equation)

Exercise 5D

1. If α, β, γ are the roots of $x^3 - 2x^2 - 3x + 1 = 0$, evaluate:

   (a) $\alpha^2 + \beta^2 + \gamma^2$ (b) $\alpha^3 + \beta^3 + \gamma^3$ (c) $\alpha^4 + \beta^4 + \gamma^4$

2. If α, β, γ are the roots of $x^3 - 5x - 1 = 0$, evaluate

   (a) $\alpha^{-1} + \beta^{-1} + \gamma^{-1}$ (b) $\alpha^5 + \beta^5 + \gamma^5$ (c) $(\alpha + \beta - \gamma)(\beta + \gamma - \alpha)(\gamma + \alpha - \beta)$
   (Hint: $\alpha + \beta + \gamma = 0$)

3. If $\alpha, \beta, \gamma, \delta$ are the roots of $x^4 + x^3 + 2x^2 + 3x + 4 = 0$, evaluate

   (a) $\alpha + \beta + \gamma + \delta$ (b) $\alpha\beta + \alpha\gamma + \alpha\delta + \beta\gamma + \beta\delta + \gamma\delta$

   (c) $\alpha^2 + \beta^2 + \gamma^2 + \delta^2$

4. Solve the equation $x^3 - 3x^2 - 6x + 8 = 0$, given that the roots are in geometric progression.
   [Hint: Let the roots be $\frac{a}{r}$, a, ar]

5. Solve the equation $x^4 + 2x^3 - 21x^2 - 22x + 40 = 0$, given that the roots are in arithmetic progression. [Hint: Let the roots be $a - 3d, a - d, a + d, a + 3d$]

6. If $x^4 + 4x^3 + mx^2 + nx + 9 = (x^2 + bx + c)^2$ for all values of x, find all possible values of b and c and the corresponding values of m and n.

7. Find the condition satisfied by p, q, r if the roots of $x^3 + px^2 + qx + r = 0$ are in arithmetic progression.

8. Solve the equation $6x^3 - 17x^2 - 5x + 6 = 0$, given that the product of two of its roots is -2.

9. The equation $x^4 + 2x^3 - 3x^2 - 4x + 4 = 0$ has a double root. Solve the equation completely.

10. The roots α, β, γ of the equation $x^3 + bx^2 + 12x + 4 = 0$ are such that $\alpha^{-1}, \beta^{-1}, \gamma^{-1}$ are in arithmetic progression. Find b and solve the equation.
    [Hint: Let $x = \frac{1}{u}$, then $4u^3 + 12u^2 + bu + 1 = 0$ has roots $\frac{1}{\alpha}, \frac{1}{\beta}$ and $\frac{1}{\gamma}$ which are in arithmetic progression]

11. If α, β, γ are the roots of $x^3 + 2x^2 - 2x + 3 = 0$, form the equation whose roots are:

   (a) $\frac{2}{\alpha}, \frac{2}{\beta}, \frac{2}{\gamma}$ (b) $2\alpha, 2\beta, 2\gamma$ (c) $\alpha + 1, \beta + 1, \gamma + 1$

   (d) $\alpha - 2, \beta - 2, \gamma - 2$ (e) $\alpha^2, \beta^2, \gamma^2$ (f) $\frac{\alpha}{2}, \frac{\beta}{2}, \frac{\gamma}{2}$

12. If α, β, γ are the roots of $2x^3 + 3x^2 - x - 1 = 0$, form the equation whose roots are:

   (a) $\alpha + 2, \beta + 2, \gamma + 2$ (b) $\frac{1}{\alpha+2}, \frac{1}{\beta+2}, \frac{1}{\gamma+2}$ (c) $\alpha^2, \beta^2, \gamma^2$
   (Hint: use (a))

13. If α, β, γ are the roots of $x^3 + bx + c = 0$, form the equation whose roots are:

   (a) $2\alpha, 2\beta, 2\gamma$ (b) $\beta + \gamma - \alpha, \gamma + \alpha - \beta, \alpha + \beta - \gamma$ (Hint: $\alpha + \beta + \gamma = 0$)

   (c) $\frac{1}{\alpha+\beta}, \frac{1}{\beta+\gamma}, \frac{1}{\gamma+\alpha}$ (Hint: let $y = \frac{1}{\alpha+\beta} = \frac{1}{-\gamma} = -\frac{1}{x}$ etc.)

14. If α, β, γ are the roots of $x^3 + bx^2 + cx + d = 0$, form the equation whose roots are $\alpha^{-1}, \beta^{-1}, \gamma^{-1}$ and hence evaluate   (a) $\alpha^{-1} + \beta^{-1} + \gamma^{-1}$

   (b) $\alpha^{-1}\beta^{-1} + \beta^{-1}\gamma^{-1} + \gamma^{-1}\alpha^{-1}$ (c) $\alpha^{-2} + \beta^{-2} + \gamma^{-2}$
   [Hint: $p^2 + q^2 + r^2 = (p+q+r)^2 - 2(pq + qr + rp)$]

15. If $\alpha, \beta, \gamma, \delta$ are the roots of $x^4 - x^2 + 2x + 3 = 0$, form the equation whose roots are:

   (a) $2\alpha, 2\beta, 2\gamma, 2\delta$ (b) $\alpha^{-1}, \beta^{-1}, \gamma^{-1}, \delta^{-1}$ (c) $\alpha^2, \beta^2, \gamma^2, \delta^2$

16. α, β, γ are the roots of $x^3 - 2x + 3 = 0$

   (a) Form the equation whose roots are $\alpha^2, \beta^2, \gamma^2$

   (b) Using the result of (a), now form the equation with roots $\alpha^2 + 1, \beta^2 + 1, \gamma^2 + 1$.

   (c) Hence evaluate $(\alpha^2 + 1)(\beta^2 + 1)(\gamma^2 + 1)$

5.5 Miscellaneous (Worked Examples)

EXAMPLE: (18) For what real values of c is $z - ci$ a factor of
$P(z) = z^4 - z^3 + 9z^2 - 4z + 20$? Hence solve $P(z) = 0$, $c \neq 0$.

SOLUTION: By the factor theorem:

$P(ci) = 0$ gives $c^4 + c^3 i - 9c^2 - 4ci + 20 = 0$

$\therefore c^4 - 9c^2 + 20 + i(c^3 - 4c) = 0$

Equating the real and imaginary parts:

$c^4 - 9c^2 + 20 = 0$ and $c^3 - 4c = 0$

i.e. $(c^2 - 5)(c^2 - 4) = 0$ and $c(c - 2)(c + 2) = 0$

Now $c \neq 0$ and $c^2 = 5$ satisfy one but not both equations

$\therefore$ only $c^2 = 4$, i.e. $c = \pm 2$ satisfies both

We divide $P(z)$ by $(z + 2i)(z - 2i)$, i.e. $z^2 + 4$

$\therefore P(z) = (z^2 + 4)(z^2 - z + 5)$

$\therefore$ The roots of $P(z) = 0$ are: $\pm 2i$, $\dfrac{1 \pm \sqrt{19}\, i}{2}$

EXAMPLE: (19) If α, β and γ are the roots of $x^3 + bx + c = 0$, find the equation whose roots are α^2, β^2 and γ^2.

SOLUTION: **METHOD I**

We have $\quad \alpha + \beta + \gamma = 0$

$\qquad\qquad \alpha\beta + \beta\gamma + \gamma\alpha = b$

$\qquad\qquad \alpha\beta\gamma = -c$

Let $x_1 = \alpha^2$, $x_2 = \beta^2$, $x_3 = \gamma^2$, then

$S_1 = \Sigma x_1 = \alpha^2 + \beta^2 + \gamma^2 = (\Sigma\alpha)^2 - 2\Sigma\alpha\beta = -2b$

$S_2 = \Sigma x_1 x_2 = \Sigma \alpha^2 \beta^2 \quad\quad = (\Sigma\alpha\beta)^2 - 2\Sigma\alpha\beta^2\gamma$

$\qquad\qquad\qquad\qquad\qquad\quad = (\Sigma\alpha\beta)^2 - 2\alpha\beta\gamma\,\Sigma\alpha$

$\qquad\qquad\qquad\qquad\qquad\quad = b^2$

$S_3 = x_1 x_2 x_3 = \alpha^2 \beta^2 \gamma^2 \quad = c^2$

The required equation is

$x^3 - S_1 x^2 + S_2 x - S_3 = 0$, i.e. $x^3 + 2bx^2 + b^2 x - c^2 = 0$

SOLUTION: METHOD II

Let $y = x^2$

This transformation will give us an equation whose roots are α^2, β^2 and γ^2.
To minimise the calculation, we write:

$$x(x^2 + b) = -c$$

Substitute $x = \sqrt{y}$

$\therefore \sqrt{y}(y + b) = -c$. Squaring

$y(y^2 + 2by + b^2) = c^2$ or $y^3 + 2by^2 + b^2y - c^2 = 0$ is the equation whose roots are α^2, β^2, γ^2. This method is much superior to and easier than the other method.

EXAMPLE: (20) When a polynomial $P(x)$ is divided by $x - 1$ the remainder is 2, when divided by $x - 2$ the remainder is 3. Find the remainder when $P(x)$ is divided by $(x - 1)(x - 2)$.

SOLUTION:

The degree of the remainder is less than that of the divisor. When the divisor is $(x - 1)(x - 2)$, the remainder must be of the form $ax + b$, hence
Let $P(x) = (x - 1)(x - 2) Q(x) + ax + b$ ... (1)
Given that $P(1) = 2$, $P(2) = 3$, we now have: $2 = a + b$ and $3 = 2a + b$
Solving these, we get $a = 1$, $b = 1$, hence the remainder is $x + 1$.

EXAMPLE: (21) If $z = \cos\theta + i\sin\theta$, prove that $z^n + z^{-n} = 2\cos n\theta$, hence solve the equation $3z^4 - z^3 + 4z^2 - z + 3 = 0$.

SOLUTION:

$z = \cos\theta + i\sin\theta$
$z^n = \cos(n\theta) + i\sin(n\theta)$ and $z^{-n} = \cos(n\theta) - i\sin(n\theta)$
$\therefore z^n + \dfrac{1}{z^n} = 2\cos(n\theta)$ ... (1)

The equation is: (rearrange)
$3(z^4 + 1) - (z^3 + z) + 4z^2 = 0$. Divide by z^2, then: $3(z^2 + \dfrac{1}{z^2}) - (z + \dfrac{1}{z}) + 4 = 0$.
Using (1) with $n = 2$ and $n = 1$, we now have:
$6\cos 2\theta - 2\cos\theta + 4 = 0$,   using $\cos 2\theta = 2\cos^2\theta - 1$
$6(2c^2 - 1) - 2c + 4 = 0$ $\qquad\qquad = 2c^2 - 1$
$\therefore 6c^2 - c - 1 = 0$
$(2c - 1)(3c + 1) = 0$ gives $c = \dfrac{1}{2}$ or $-\dfrac{1}{3}$
If $\cos\theta = \dfrac{1}{2}$, $\sin\theta = \pm\dfrac{\sqrt{3}}{2}$, $-\pi < \theta \leqslant \pi$
and $\cos\theta = -\dfrac{1}{3}$, $\sin\theta = \pm\dfrac{\sqrt{8}}{3}$
$\therefore$ The roots are: $\dfrac{1}{2}(1 \pm \sqrt{3}\,i)$, $\dfrac{1}{3}(-1 \pm \sqrt{8}\,i)$

Exercise 5E (REVISION AND MISCELLANEOUS)

1. Factorise the following polynomials over (a) R (b) C
   (a) $x^3 - 8$ (b) $x^4 - 16$ (c) $x^3 + 1$

2. Factorise the following polynomials over C.
   (a) $x^2 + 4$ (b) $x^2 + 8x + 8$
   (c) $x^2 - 4x + 6$ (d) $x^3 + 3x^2 + 4x + 12$
   (e) $x^4 + 4x^2 + 3$ (f) $x^3 + x^2 - 4x - 24$

3. For each of the following, find a polynomial of lowest degree, having the given zeros.
   (a) $2 + i$, $2 - i$ (b) $3 + 4i$, $3 - 4i$
   (c) -2, $2 + i$, $2 - i$ (d) 3, $1 + i$
   (e) $1 - \sqrt{2}$, $1 + \sqrt{2}$, $1 + i$ (f) $4 - i$, $3 + i$

4. For the following polynomials, one zero is given. Find the remaining zeros.
   (a) $P(x) = x^3 - 7x^2 + 17x - 15$, $x = 3$
   (b) $P(x) = x^3 - 7x^2 + 17x - 15$, $x = 2 - i$
   (c) $P(x) = x^4 - 3x^3 + 6x^2 + 2x - 60$, $x = 1 - 3i$
   (d) $P(x) = 2x^3 - 13x^2 + 32x - 13$, $x = 3 - 2i$

5. Factorise the following over C, by using the factor theorem:
   (a) $x^3 + x^2 + x + 1$ (b) $x^3 - x^2 - 4x - 6$
   (c) $x^3 - 3x^2 + 7x - 5$ (d) $2x^3 - 2x^2 - x - 6$

6. Solve the following over C. (Factor theorem is useful)
   (a) $x^3 + 1 = 0$ (b) $x^4 - 16 = 0$
   (c) $x^4 - 4 = 0$ (d) $x^4 + 3x^2 + 2 = 0$
   (e) $x^4 - 7x^3 + 18x^2 - 22x + 12 = 0$

7. Given $P(x) = x^4 - 5x^3 + 4x^2 + 3x + 9 = 0$ has a root of multiplicity 2, solve the equation completely.

8. Given $1 - i$ is a root of the equation $z^2 - (c - 2i) z + 3 + ib = 0$ where b and c are real. Find b and c. [Hint: $\alpha + \beta = -b/a$, and use $\alpha\beta = c/a$]

9. If $z = \cos\theta + i\sin\theta$, prove (by using De Moivre's theorem) that:
   $$z^n + z^{-n} = 2\cos n\theta$$
   Hence solve $2z^4 + 3z^3 + 5z^2 + 3z + 2 = 0$

10. If $mx^3 + nx^2 + p = 0$ has a double root, prove that $27m^2 p = -4n^3$.
    [Use $P(x) = \frac{dP}{dx} = 0$ have a common root]

11. (a) Use Mathematical Induction to prove that
   $(\cos\theta + i\sin\theta)^n = \cos n\theta + i\sin n\theta$, for positive integers n.
   (b) Solve $x^6 = -1$, giving answers in $A + iB$ form.
   (c) Find the four roots of $x^4 - x^2 + 1 = 0$ and show them on an Argand diagram.

12. (a) Show that $x - 3 + 2i$ is a factor of the polynomial
   $P(x) = x^3 - 9x^2 + 31x - 39$ and hence decompose $P(x)$ over
   (i) field R   (ii) field C.
   (b) $P(x) = 2x^5 - 13x^4 + 24x^3 + 8x^2 - 64x + 48$ has a root of multiplicity 4, find the roots.

13. Given that $\cot\theta = y + 1$ and α and β are the roots of $z^2 - 2z + 2 = 0$,
   prove that: $\dfrac{(y + \alpha)^n - (y + \beta)^n}{\alpha - \beta} = \dfrac{\sin n\theta}{(\sin\theta)^n}$

14. Solve $x^5 = 1$ by De Moivre's theorem and indicate roots on a circle of radius 1 in an Argand diagram. Express the roots in the $\text{cis}\,\theta$ form.
   Find the area of the regular pentagon formed by the five points representing these roots.
   Solve the equation $x^4 + x^3 + x^2 + x + 1 = 0$.
   Deduce that $\cos\dfrac{2\pi}{5}$ and $\cos\dfrac{4\pi}{5}$ are the roots of $4x^2 + 2x - 1 = 0$.

15. Given that $2 - i$ is a root of the equation $3x^3 - 10x^2 + 7x + 10 = 0$, solve the equation completely.

16. Solve $z^4 + z^2 + 1 = 0$, giving all the four roots in $r\,\text{cis}\,\theta$ form, $-\pi < \theta \leq \pi$.

17. Find K if $P(x) = x^3 - 6x^2 + 9x + K$ has a root of multiplicity 2.

18. One root of $x^2 + (1 - i)x + K = 0$ is $2 + 3i$.
   Find the other root of this equation and the value of K in the form $a + ib$.

19. (a) Solve $\tan 4\theta = 1$, $0 \leq \theta \leq \pi$
   (b) Prove that $\tan 4\theta = \dfrac{4\tan\theta - 4\tan^3\theta}{1 - 6\tan^2\theta + \tan^4\theta}$
   (Hint: Find $\sin 4\theta$ and $\cos 4\theta$ from the $(\text{cis}\,\theta)^4$ expansion)
   (c) Using parts (a) and (b) and $z = \tan\theta$, find the roots of
   $z^4 + 4z^3 - 6z^2 - 4z + 1 = 0$.
   (d) Using (c) find:
   (i) $\tan\dfrac{\pi}{16} + \tan\dfrac{5\pi}{16} + \tan\dfrac{9\pi}{16} + \tan\dfrac{13\pi}{16}$
   (ii) $\tan^2\dfrac{\pi}{16} + \tan^2\dfrac{5\pi}{16} + \tan^2\dfrac{9\pi}{16} + \tan^2\dfrac{13\pi}{16}$

20. Using the method of finding the square-roots of a complex number, find the roots of the following equations in the form $A + iB$, where A, B are real.
    (a) $z^2 + 3iz + 2 = 0$
    (b) $z^2 + (2+3i)z - \frac{1}{2} - 2i = 0$
    (c) $z^2 - (4+2i)z + 6 + 8i = 0$
    (d) $z^2 = 3 - 4i$
    (e) $z^2 + (4+2i)z + 3 + 2i = 0$
    (f) $z^2 - (3+i)z + 4 + 3i = 0$

21. (a) Show that the roots of $z^2 + 2z + 3 = 0$ lie outside the circle $|z| = 1$
    (b) Show that the roots of $z^2 + z + 1 = 0$ lie on the circle $|z| = 1$
    (Hint: Consider the modulus of each root)

22. Prove that $z = 1 - i$ is the root of $P(z) = z^4 - 6z^3 + 15z^2 - 18z + 10 = 0$. Find the other roots.
    [Hint: Dividing $P(z)$ by $z - (1 - i)$, you can show that the remainder is zero, but this involves very awkward division, so a better method is to divide by
    $[(z - 1) + i][(z - 1) - i] = (z - 1)^2 - i^2 = z^2 - 2z + 2$.
    This not only proves that $z = 1 - i$ is a root, but also gives all the remaining roots in one simple division.]

23. Solve
    (a) $z^4 - 2z^2 + 4 = 0$
    (b) $(x - 1)^6 + (x + 1)^6 = 0$
    (c) $2z^2 = 1 + i$
    (d) $z^4 - 30z^2 + 289 = 0$

24. Solve $x^8 + 1 = 0$, express each root in the form $r \operatorname{cis} \theta$ and then $A + iB$. Decompose $x^8 + 1$ into real quadratic factors and deduce that
    $\cos 4\theta = 8\left[\cos\theta - \cos\frac{\pi}{8}\right]\left[\cos\theta - \cos\frac{3\pi}{8}\right]\left[\cos\theta - \cos\frac{5\pi}{8}\right]\left[\cos\theta - \cos\frac{7\pi}{8}\right]$

25. $z = 1 - i$ is a root of $z^3 + az^2 + bz + 6 = 0$, where a and b are real. Find a and b and all the roots of the equation.

26. $z = -\frac{1}{2} - i\frac{\sqrt{3}}{2}$ is a root of $z^4 + 2z^3 + z^2 - 1 = 0$. Find all the other roots.

27. Find m and n such that $x = 3$ is a double root of $x^4 + mx^3 + 13x^2 + nx - 36 = 0$.

28. Show that the polynomial $x^n + mx - b = 0$ has a multiple root provided
    $\left(\frac{m}{n}\right)^n + \left(\frac{b}{n-1}\right)^{n-1} = 0$. Find this root.

29. If the equation $x^3 + 3mx + n = 0$ has a double root, then prove that $n^2 = -4m^3$, and that this root is $-\frac{n}{2m}$.

30. Solve $x^4 - 6x^3 + 12x^2 - 10x + 3 = 0$ given that the equation has a root of multiplicity 3.

31. Solve $z^2 + 2\sqrt{2}\,iz + 2\sqrt{3}\,i = 0$; express the roots in the form $A + iB$.

32. If the polynomial $x^3 + 3mx^2 + 3nx + r = 0$ has a double root, prove that:
$(mn - r)^2 = 4(m^2 - n)(n^2 - mr)$.

33. Given that the roots of $4x^3 - 24x^2 + 45x - 26 = 0$ are in arithmetic progression, find them.

34. If α, β, γ are the roots of $x^3 - x - 1 = 0$ find the equation whose roots are $\dfrac{1+\alpha}{1-\alpha}, \dfrac{1+\beta}{1-\beta}, \dfrac{1+\gamma}{1-\gamma}$ [Hint: $y = \dfrac{1+x}{1-x}$ where $x = \alpha, \beta, \gamma$]

35. When a polynomial $P(x)$ is divided by $(x - 3)$, the remainder is 5 and when divided by $x - 4$, the remainder is 9. Find the remainder when $P(x)$ is divided by $(x - 3)(x - 4)$.

CHAPTER 6   CONIC SECTIONS

6.1   Introduction

The subject of conic sections had been studied by ancient Greek mathematicians (200 B.C.). In recent times, it has acquired an added importance in space explorations. The safest and the most economical path to the planet Mars is an elliptical orbit, called 'the Hohmann ellipse'. (The Hohmann ellipse is an ideal trajectory requiring a minimum of energy for a journey between any two planets, named after the German engineer who calculated it in 1925.)

The conic sections are a family of curves obtained by cutting a right circular cone by a plane at various inclinations to the axis of the cone.

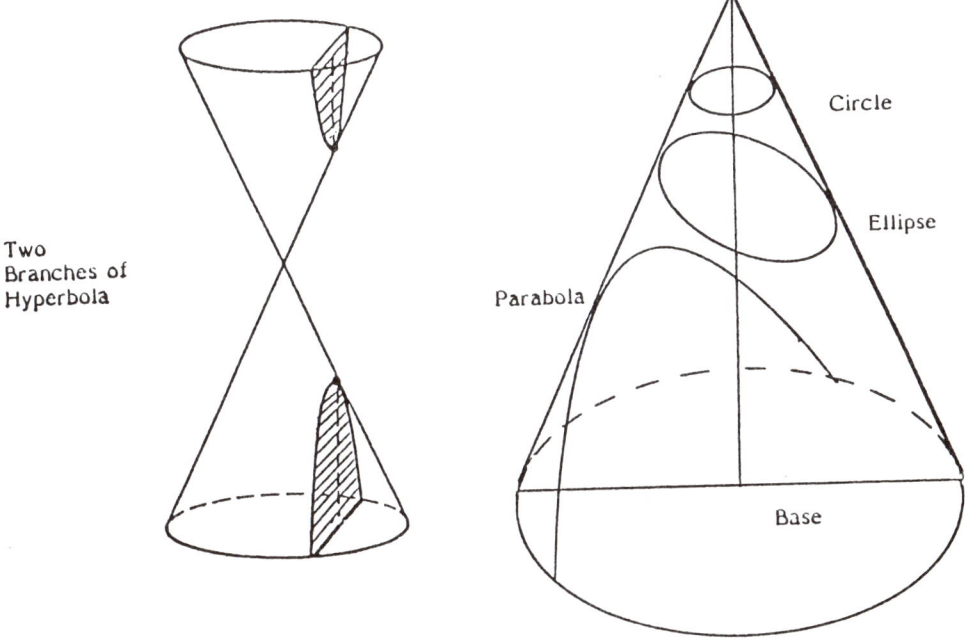

Fig. 1   Fig. 2

If the slice is parallel to the base, the curve is a circle, if the slice is parallel to the slant side of cone, the curve is a parabola; between these two, we have an ellipse. Finally, any other cut (intersecting also the mirror image of the cone) produces a hyperbola.

We shall only study the CENTRAL CONICS ellipse and hyperbola and their properties. The case of the parabola has been studied previously (3U Mathematics).

Definition:

A conic is the locus of a point P which moves in a plane so that its distance from a given point S and its distance from a fixed line, d, always are in the same ratio, i.e.

$$\frac{PS}{PM} = e$$

The fixed point, S, is called the focus

The fixed line, d, is called the directrix

The ratio, e, is called the eccentricity

If $e = 1$, $PS = PM$, the conic is a parabola

$\quad e < 1$, $PS < PM$, the conic is an ellipse

$\quad e > 1$, $PS > PM$, the conic is a hyperbola.

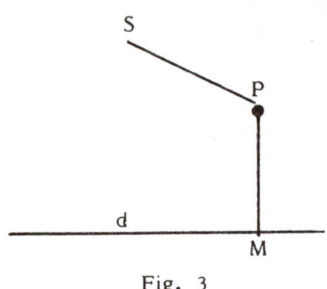

Fig. 3

6.2 Ellipse (e < 1): (Focus and Directrix Definition)

Let $P(x, y)$ be any point on ellipse.

S is the focus, ZM is the directrix.

Draw SZ ⊥ the directrix, and mark the points A and A' on this line so that

$$\frac{SA}{AZ} = e, \qquad \frac{SA'}{A'Z} = e$$

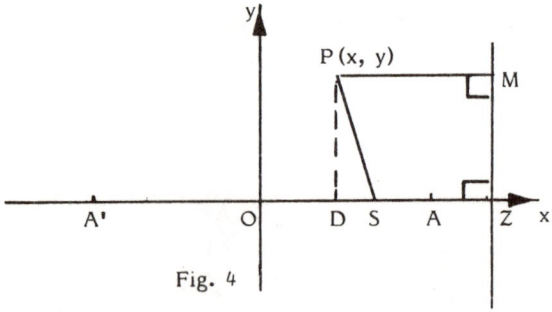

Fig. 4

By definition, A and A' are on the ellipse. O is the mid-point of AA'. Take the rectangular axes at O, as shown.

$\qquad$ Let $AA' = 2a$; $\qquad S(c, 0)$, then

$\qquad SA = e \cdot AZ \quad$ and $\quad SA' = e A'Z$

$\therefore \quad SA' + SA = A'A = 2a \qquad \ldots (1)$

and $\qquad SA' - SA = e(A'Z - AZ) = 2ae \quad \ldots (2)$

Adding and subtracting:

$\qquad SA = a(1 - e)$, $\quad SA' = a(1 + e)$

Then $\qquad c = OS = OA - SA = a - a(1 - e) = ae$

and $\quad OZ = OA + AZ = a + \frac{1}{e}(a - ae) = \frac{a}{e}$

$\therefore\ S$ is $(c, 0) = (ae, 0)$

Z is $(\frac{a}{e}, 0)$, $\qquad PM = OZ - OD = \frac{a}{e} - x$

Now $\quad \frac{PS}{PM} = e \quad$ (by definition),

$\therefore\ SP^2 = e^2\ (PM^2)$

$(x - ae)^2 + y^2 = e^2 (\frac{a}{e} - x)^2$

$(x - ae)^2 + y^2 = (a - ex)^2$

$(1 - e^2) x^2 + y^2 = a^2(1 - e^2)$

Let $\quad b^2 = a^2(1 - e^2)$, then divide by $a^2(1 - e^2)$

$\therefore\ \frac{x^2}{a^2} + \frac{y^2}{b^2} = 1 \quad \ldots (3)$

Equation (3) is the equation of the ellipse in standard form.

The point S is called the focus of the ellipse and the line $x = \frac{a}{e}$ is the directrix. By symmetry of the equation of ellipse, we infer that it has two foci $S(ae, 0)$ and $S'(-ae, 0)$ and two directrices (See Fig. 5)

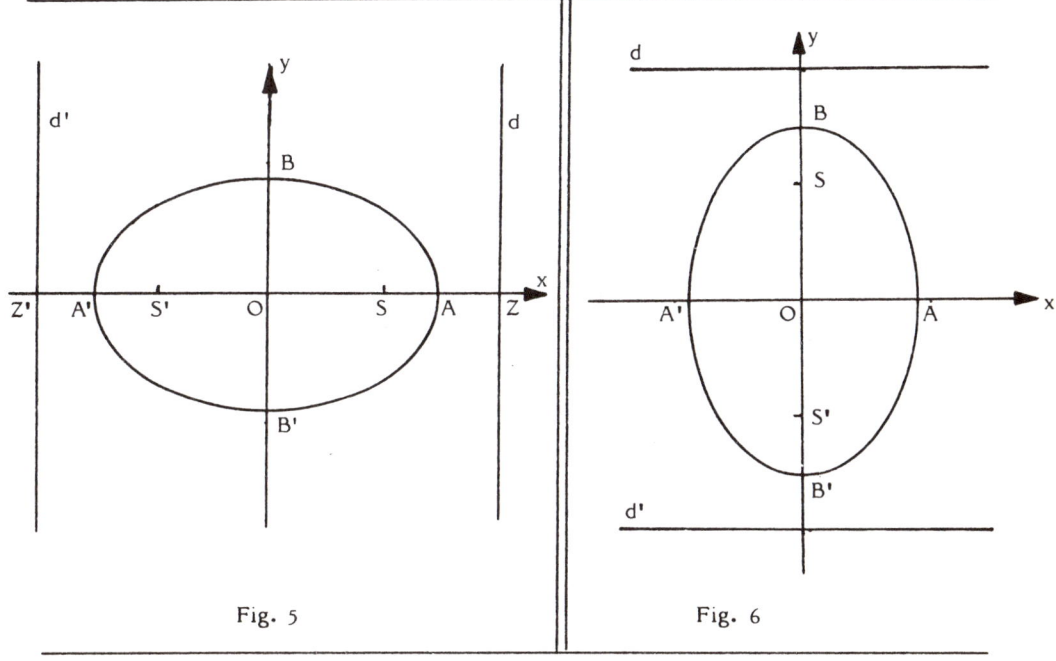

Fig. 5   Fig. 6

Important Features of the Ellipse:

The ellipse $\dfrac{x^2}{a^2} + \dfrac{y^2}{b^2} = 1$ has the following properties. (Fig. 5)

1. The curve is symmetric about both axes.
2. The major axis $AA' = 2a$, $A(a, 0)$, $A'(-a, 0)$
3. The minor axis $BB' = 2b$, $B(0, b)$, $B'(0, -b)$

Note that since $b^2 = a^2(1 - e^2)$, $e < 1$, then $b < a$.

4. The centre of the ellipse is at $O(0, 0)$
5. Foci: $S(ae, 0)$, $S'(-ae, 0)$
6. Equation of two directrices are $x = \pm \dfrac{a}{e}$

If the foci are at $S(0, be)$ and $S(0, -be)$, the standard form of the equation of the ellipse is $\dfrac{x^2}{a^2} + \dfrac{y^2}{b^2} = 1$, with $a^2 = b^2(1 - e^2)$, $a < b$

and its properties are: (see Fig. 6)

1. The major axis is along the y-axis, $BB' = 2b$
2. The minor axis is along the x-axis, $AA' = 2a$
3. The foci are given by $(0, \pm be)$ with centre $O(0, 0)$
4. The directrices are $y = \pm \dfrac{b}{e}$

WORKED EXAMPLES

Find the eccentricity, foci, directrices of the following ellipses:

(1) $\dfrac{x^2}{25} + \dfrac{y^2}{9} = 1$

Solution: (see Fig. 5)

$a = 5$, $b = 3$

$b^2 = a^2(1 - e^2)$

$\therefore 9 = 25(1 - e^2)$

$\therefore e = \dfrac{4}{5}$

∴ The foci are $(\pm ae, 0) = (\pm 4, 0)$

The directrices are $x = \pm \dfrac{a}{e} = \pm \dfrac{25}{4}$

(2) $\dfrac{x^2}{9} + \dfrac{y^2}{25} = 1$

Solution: (see Fig. 6)

For this ellipse, the major axis is along the y-axis.

$a = 3, \quad b = 5$

$a^2 = b^2(1 - e^2)$

$9 = 25(1 - e^2)$ gives $e = \dfrac{4}{5}$

The foci are $(0, \pm be) = (0, \pm 4)$

The directrices are: $y = \pm \dfrac{b}{e} = \pm \dfrac{25}{4}$

Exercise 6A

Find: (a) the centre   (b) the eccentricity   (c) the foci
(d) the lengths of axes   (e) the equations of directrices
for the following ellipses:

1. $\dfrac{x^2}{16} + \dfrac{y^2}{9} = 1$
2. $\dfrac{x^2}{9} + \dfrac{y^2}{16} = 1$
3. $\dfrac{x^2}{36} + \dfrac{y^2}{25} = 1$
4. $\dfrac{x^2}{16} + \dfrac{y^2}{36} = 1$
5. $\dfrac{x^2}{25} + \dfrac{y^2}{10} = 1$
6. $\dfrac{x^2}{12} + \dfrac{y^2}{48} = 1$
7. $4x^2 + y^2 = 4$
8. $4x^2 + 9y^2 = 1$
9. $9x^2 + 4y^2 - 36 = 0$
10. $x^2 + 2y^2 - 1 = 0$

Find the equations of the ellipses described as follows.

11. Foci on the x-axis, centre $(0, 0)$, $a = 4$, $b = 2$
12. Foci on the y-axis, centre $(0, 0)$, $a = 2$, $b = 5$
13. Foci $(\pm 4, 0)$, $b = 3$
14. Foci $(0, \pm \sqrt{5})$, $a = 3$
15. Centre $(0, 0)$, the length of major axis = 10 and length of the minor axis = 6
16. Centre $(0, 0)$, minor axis = 12, focus $(0, 4)$.
17. Eccentricity $e = \dfrac{2}{3}$, major axis = 12

6.3 The Hyperbola

Starting with the definition $\frac{PS}{PM} = e$, $e > 1$ for the hyperbola and using the following diagram, you can easily derive the standard equation of the hyperbola as:

$$\frac{x^2}{a^2} - \frac{y^2}{b^2} = 1$$

where $b^2 = a^2(e^2 - 1)$

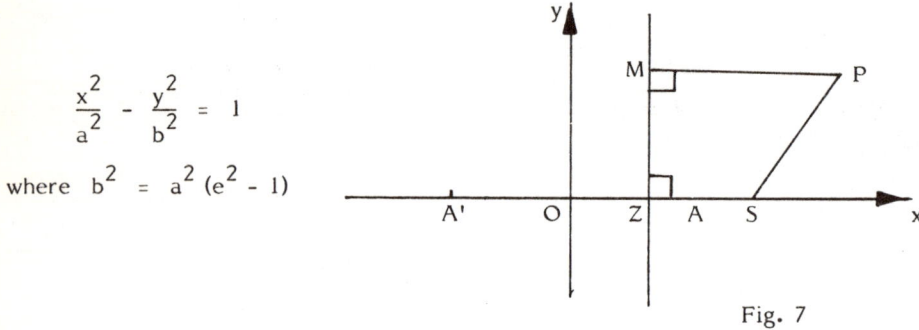

Fig. 7

The hyperbola $\frac{x^2}{a^2} - \frac{y^2}{b^2} = 1$

has the following properties (see Fig. 8)

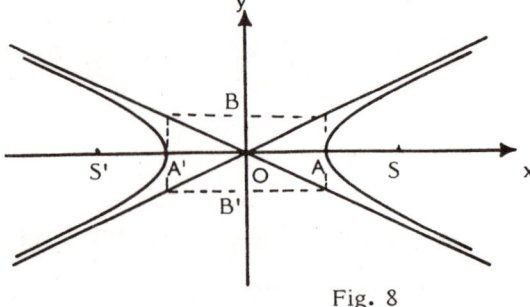

Fig. 8

1. It is symmetric about both axes.
2. The <u>transverse axis</u> is the line segment joining the vertices A (a, 0), A' (- a, 0) and AA' = 2a.
3. The <u>foci</u> are S (ae, 0), A' (-ae, 0), centre O (0, 0)
4. The <u>conjugate axis</u> is the segment BB', where B (0, b) and B' (0, -b)
5. The equations of <u>two directrices</u> are $x = \pm \frac{a}{e}$
6. The <u>asymptotes</u> are: $y = \pm \frac{b}{a} \cdot x$

The rectangle through the vertices A, A', B and B', is very useful in drawing the graph of the hyperbola. Also draw the asymptotes $y = \pm \frac{b}{a} x$ through the corners of this rectangle. The hyperbola fits nicely between the two asymptotes.

The hyperbola given by $\frac{y^2}{a^2} - \frac{x^2}{b^2} = 1$ is shown in Fig. 9 with all the important details.

1. It is symmetric with respect to both axes.
2. The foci are on the y-axis, $S(0, ae)$, $S'(0, -ae)$.
3. The transverse axis $AA' = 2a$, $A(0, a)$, $A'(0, -a)$.
4. The conjugate axis $BB' = 2b$, $B(b, 0)$, $B'(-b, 0)$.
5. The directrices are $y = \pm \frac{a}{e}$.
6. The asymptotes are: $y = \pm \frac{a}{b} x$

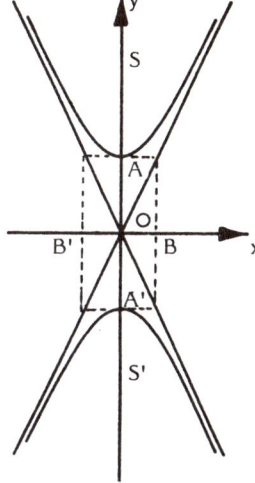

Fig. 9

WORKED EXAMPLES

1. Find the foci, directrices, asymptotes and vertices of the following hyperbolas and hence sketch them.

   (a) $\frac{x^2}{16} - \frac{y^2}{25} = 1$ (See Fig. 10)

   (i) $a = 4$, $b = 5$

   $c^2 = a^2 e^2 = a^2 + b^2$

   $\therefore c = \sqrt{41}$ or $c = -\sqrt{41}$

   $\therefore$ The foci are $(\pm \sqrt{41}, 0)$

   (ii) The directrices are $x = \pm \frac{a}{e}$

   But $c = ae$

   $\sqrt{41} = 4 \cdot e$ or $e = \frac{\sqrt{41}}{4}$

   $\therefore$ the directrices are $x = \pm \frac{16}{\sqrt{41}}$

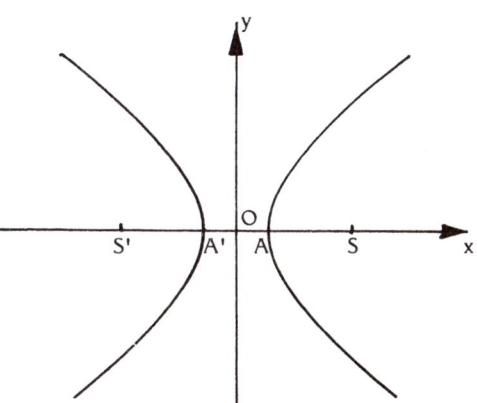

Fig. 10

(iii) The vertices are
A (4, 0), A' (-4, 0),

(iv) The asymptotes are $y = \pm \frac{5}{4} x$

(b) $\frac{y^2}{9} - \frac{x^2}{16} = 1$ (See Fig. 11)

$a = 3, \quad b = 4$

$c^2 = a^2 + b^2 = a^2 e^2$

$\therefore c = 5, \quad e = \frac{5}{3}$

If we put $y = 0$, we have $x^2 = -16$ and this shows that the foci lie on the y-axis.

$\therefore$ the foci are $(0, \pm 5)$
and vertices $(\pm 0, 3)$

The directrices are

$y = \pm \frac{9}{5}$

The asymptotes are

$y = \pm \frac{3}{4} x$

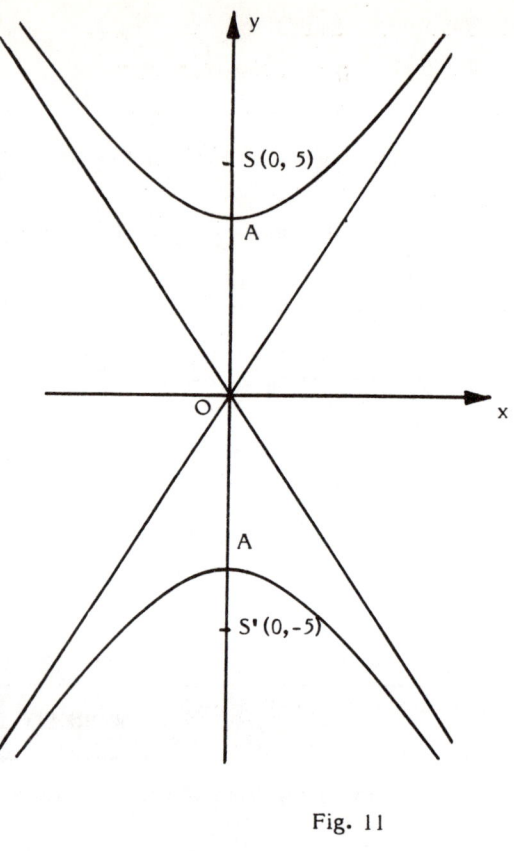

Fig. 11

Exercise 6B

1. For the following hyperbolas, find the foci, directrices and vertices and sketch them:

   (a) $\frac{x^2}{25} - \frac{y^2}{16} = 1$ (c) $x^2 - 4y^2 = 1$

   (b) $\frac{y^2}{16} - \frac{x^2}{25} = 1$ (d) $4x^2 - y^2 = 4$

2. Find the angle between the asymptotes of the hyperbola $\frac{x^2}{a^2} - \frac{y^2}{b^2} = 1$

3. Draw an accurate sketch of $x^2 - y^2 = a^2$.
   Find the angle between the asymptotes.
   [The curve given by $x^2 - y^2 = a^2$ is called a RECTANGULAR HYPERBOLA]

6.4 Shape of the Conics

We can study the variation of the shapes of conics in general by varying the eccentricity e or changing the ratio b/a.

Eccentricity

For $0 < e < 1$, the conic is an ellipse and $e = \dfrac{c}{a}$, where c is the focal distance given by
$c = \sqrt{a^2 - b^2}$, $a > b > 0$.

If we keep a fixed and vary c over the interval $0 \leqslant c \leqslant a$, the resulting ellipses vary in shape, as shown in the diagram.

For $e = 0$, i.e. $b = a$, the shape is circular.

As e increases, the shape becomes flatter and when e is nearly 1, the ellipse reduces towards a line-segment.

$e = 0$
$c = 0$

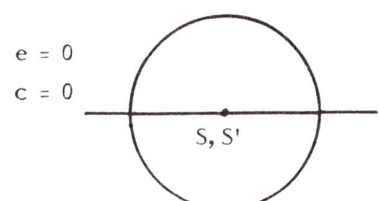

$e = 0.86$

$e = 0.95$

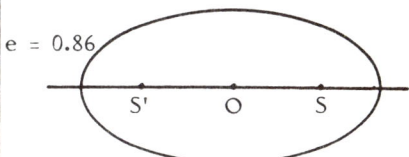

$e = 0.97$

$e \simeq 1$

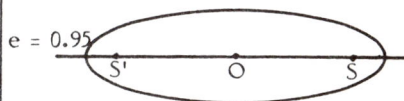

The orbit of a planet around the sun is elliptical in shape, but the orbits of most of the planets are nearly circular, as can be seen from the table of eccentricities.

Planet	e
Neptune	0.01
Earth	0.02
Jupiter	0.05
Mercury	0.21

The varying shape of an ellipse can also be examined by changing the ratio $b : a$, as shown below.

(cont)

b/a = 5/3
b/a = 1
b/a = 3/5
b/a = 1/4

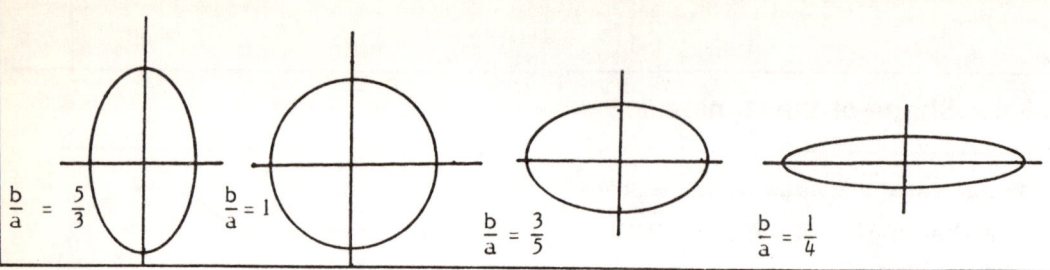

Finally, we examine the variation of the shape of conics as e varies from zero to a very large value.

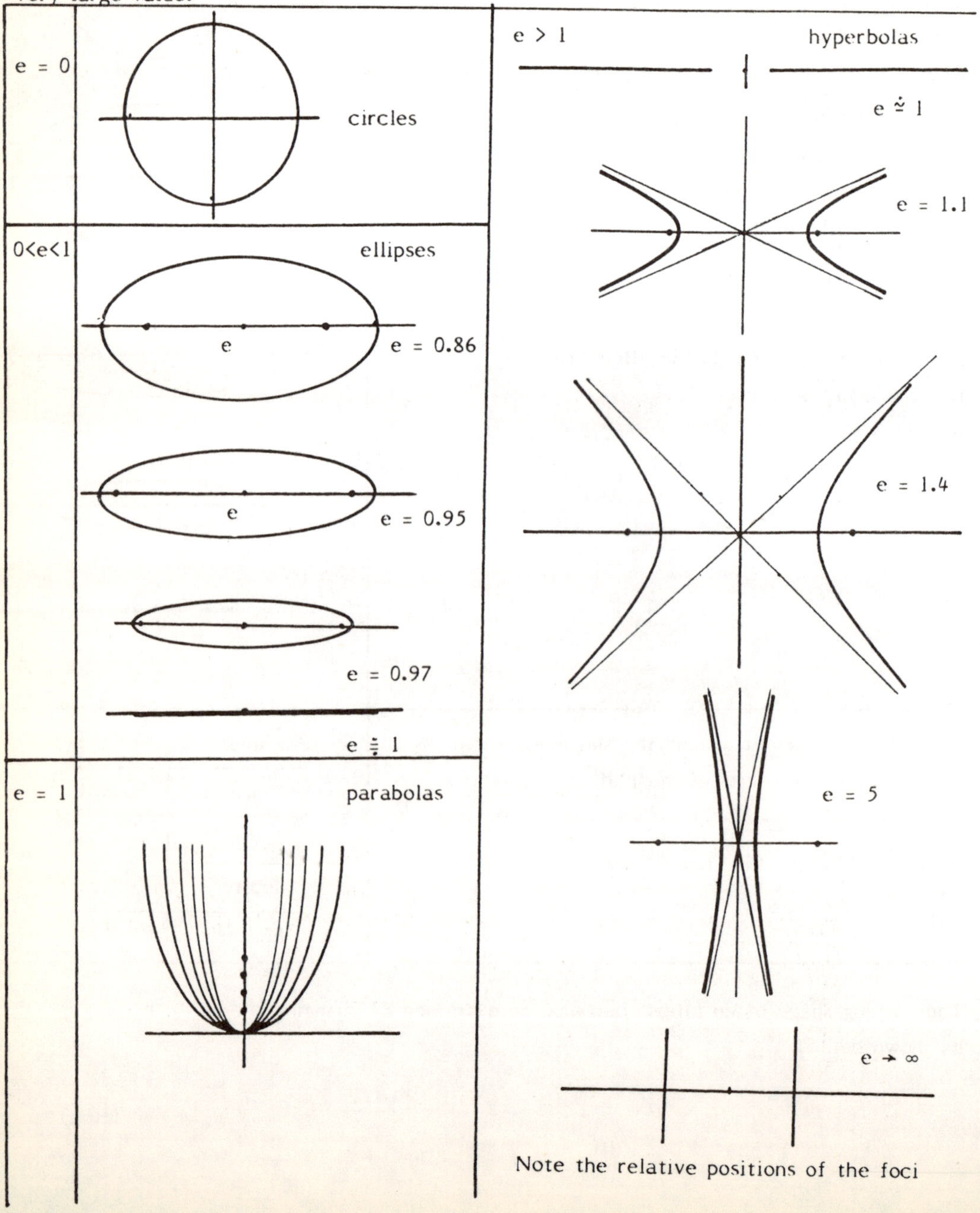

e = 0
circles
0<e<1
ellipses
e
e = 0.86
e
e = 0.95
e = 0.97
e ≑ 1
e = 1
parabolas
e > 1
hyperbolas
e ≑ 1
e = 1.1
e = 1.4
e = 5
e → ∞
Note the relative positions of the foci

6.5 Parametric Equations of the Circle and the Ellipse

Consider a circle with centre at the origin and radius a.
Let $P(x,y)$ be a point on the circle and $\angle POx = \theta$.
We have the relations:
$x = a\cos\theta$, $y = a\sin\theta$.
The point $(a\cos\theta, a\sin\theta)$ lies on the circle
$x^2 + y^2 = a^2$ for all values of θ. We restrict θ
in the range $0 \leq \theta < 2\pi$, in order to have one-one
correspondence between a point and its parameter.

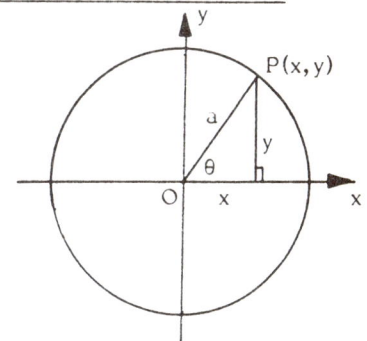

$x = a\cos\theta$, $y = a\sin\theta$ are called the parametric
equations of the circle.

Parametric Equations of an Ellipse: Auxiliary Circle

Consider now the equations:
$x = a\cos\theta$, $y = b\sin\theta$.
It is easy to show that the point
$(a\cos\theta, b\sin\theta)$ lies on the ellipse
$\dfrac{x^2}{a^2} + \dfrac{y^2}{b^2} = 1$, for all values of θ,
$0 \leq \theta < 2\pi$.
i.e. $\dfrac{a^2\cos^2\theta}{a^2} + \dfrac{b^2\sin^2\theta}{b^2} = 1$

or $\cos^2\theta + \sin^2\theta = 1$, which is true.
$x = a\cos\theta$, $y = b\sin\theta$ are then the
parametric equations of the ellipse $\dfrac{x^2}{a^2} + \dfrac{y^2}{b^2} = 1$

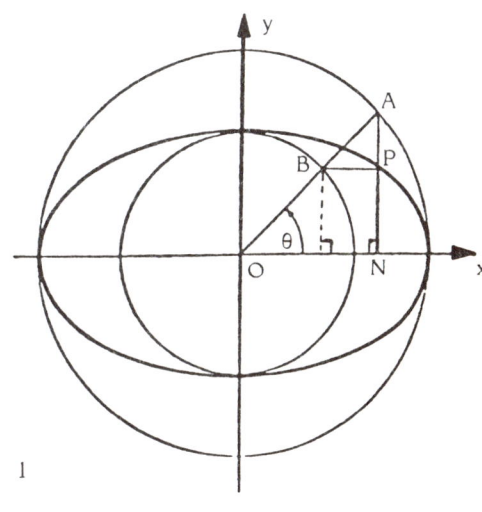

and θ is called the eccentric angle and it has a
geometric meaning as shown in the diagram. It can be shown that the ellipse can be
constructed, point by point, by using the parametric equations as follows:
we draw two concentric circles with radii a and b, a > b. These are
called the major and minor AUXILIARY circles, respectively. To determine a point
P on the ellipse, draw a line through O making any angle θ with the positive
x-axis.

Let A and B be the points of intersection of this line with the auxiliary circles. Through A draw a line parallel to the y-axis, and through B draw a line parallel to the x-axis. These lines intersect at P where

$x = ON = OA\cos\theta = a\cos\theta$

$y = NP = OB\sin\theta = b\sin\theta$

The point $P(a\cos\theta, b\sin\theta)$ is usually referred to as $P(\theta)$, or 'the point θ', on the ellipse.

It is worth noting that $\frac{PN}{AN} = \frac{b\sin\theta}{a\sin\theta} = \frac{b}{a}$, a constant for all positions of P. This fact alone is sufficient to determine a point on the ellipse by reducing each y-coordinate of the auxiliary circle $x^2 + y^2 = a^2$ in the ratio $b : a$.

6.6 Equations of the Chord, Tangent and Normal to the Ellipse

We consider the ellipse with general point $(a\cos\theta, b\sin\theta)$. The gradient of the line joining the points ϕ and θ is

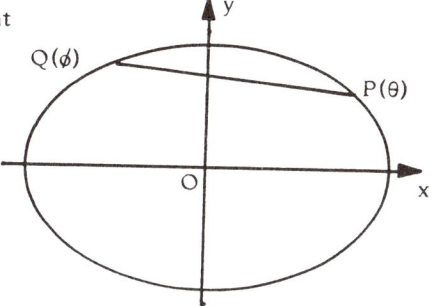

$$m = \frac{b\sin\phi - b\sin\theta}{a\cos\phi - a\cos\theta}$$

$$= \frac{2b\cos(\frac{\phi+\theta}{2})\sin(\frac{\phi-\theta}{2})}{-2a\sin(\frac{\phi+\theta}{2})\sin(\frac{\phi-\theta}{2})}$$

$$\therefore m = \frac{-b\cos(\frac{\phi+\theta}{2})}{a\sin(\frac{\phi+\theta}{2})} \quad \text{or} \quad -\frac{b}{a}\cot(\frac{\theta+\phi}{2})$$

The equation of the chord is then:

$$y - b\sin\theta = \frac{-b\cos(\frac{\phi+\theta}{2})}{a\sin(\frac{\phi+\theta}{2})} \cdot (x - a\cos\theta)$$

or $\quad \frac{x}{a}\cos(\frac{\theta+\phi}{2}) + \frac{y}{b}\sin(\frac{\theta+\phi}{2}) = \cos\theta\cos(\frac{\theta+\phi}{2}) + \sin\theta\sin(\frac{\theta+\phi}{2})$

This simplifies to: $\quad \frac{x}{a}\cos(\frac{\theta+\phi}{2}) + \frac{y}{b}\sin(\frac{\theta+\phi}{2}) = \cos(\frac{\theta-\phi}{2})$

The equation of the tangent at θ is obtained by letting $\phi = \theta$ in the equation above, giving:

$$\frac{x}{a}\cos\theta + \frac{y}{b}\sin\theta = 1$$

Alternative Method:

The gradient of the tangent at the point $P(x_1, y_1)$ is obtained by differentiating $\frac{x^2}{a^2} + \frac{y^2}{b^2} = 1$.

$$\therefore \frac{2x}{a^2} + \frac{2y}{b^2}\frac{dy}{dx} = 0 \quad \text{and} \quad \frac{dy}{dx} = \frac{-b^2 x_1}{a^2 y_1} \quad \text{at } P.$$

The equation of the tangent is $\quad y - y_1 = \frac{-b^2 x_1}{a^2 y_1}(x - x_1)$

$$\therefore \frac{xx_1}{a^2} + \frac{yy_1}{b^2} = \frac{x_1^2}{a^2} + \frac{y_1^2}{b^2}$$

But $\quad \frac{x_1^2}{a^2} + \frac{y_1^2}{b^2} = 1$, as $P(x_1, y_1)$ lies on the ellipse.

(cont)

So, the equation of the tangent is:

$$\frac{xx_1}{a^2} + \frac{yy_1}{b^2} = 1$$

Substituting $x_1 = a\cos\theta$, $y_1 = b\sin\theta$, we have

$$\frac{x\cos\theta}{a} + \frac{y\sin\theta}{b} = 1$$

as the equation of the tangent at $P(\theta)$, in the form obtained above.

Equation of the Normal

We have $\frac{dy}{dx} = \frac{-b^2 x_1}{a^2 y_1}$, so the equation of the normal at $P(x_1, y_1)$ is

$$y - y_1 = \frac{a^2 y_1}{b^2 x_1}(x - x_1)$$

$$\therefore \frac{b^2}{y_1}(y - y_1) = \frac{a^2}{x_1}(x - x_1), \text{ which simplifies to:}$$

$$\boxed{\frac{a^2 x}{x_1} - \frac{b^2 y}{y_1} = a^2 - b^2}$$

Finally, substituting $x_1 = a\cos\theta$, $y_1 = b\sin\theta$, this equation becomes:

$$\boxed{\frac{ax}{\cos\theta} - \frac{by}{\sin\theta} = a^2 - b^2} \quad \text{or} \quad \boxed{ax\sec\theta - by\csc\theta = a^2 - b^2}$$

Note: The corresponding results for the circle $x^2 + y^2 = a^2$ are easily obtained, either by substituting $b = a$ in the above results or deriving them as above.
We have: for the circle $x^2 + y^2 = a^2$, at $P(x_1 = a\cos\theta, y_1 = a\sin\theta)$.
The equation of the tangent:

$$\boxed{xx_1 + yy_1 = a^2} \quad\quad \boxed{x\cos\theta + y\sin\theta = a}$$

The equation of the normal at $P(x_1, y_1)$ or $P(a\cos\theta, a\sin\theta)$:

$$\boxed{xy_1 - yx_1 = 0} \quad\quad \boxed{x\sin\theta - y\cos\theta = 0}$$

6.7 Parametric Equations of the Hyperbola

It is easy to verify that $x = a\sec\theta$, $y = b\tan\theta$ are the parametric equations of the hyperbola $\frac{x^2}{a^2} - \frac{y^2}{b^2} = 1$. We can also derive the parametric equations of the hyperbola by using the auxiliary circle $x^2 + y^2 = a^2$, as shown in the adjacent diagram.

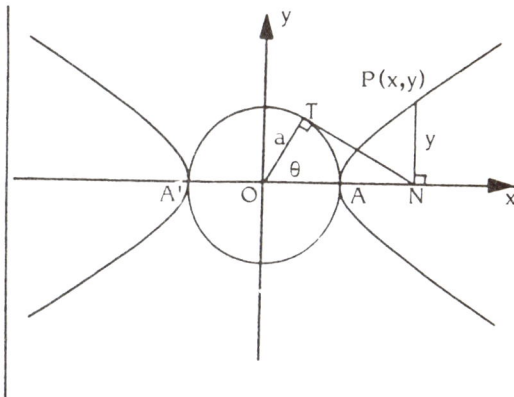

The point T lies on the circle, where $\angle TOx = \theta$ and the tangent to the circle at T meets the x-axis at N. $PN \perp Ox$, with $P(x, y)$ on the hyperbola.

Now $x = ON$ and from the right-angled $\triangle OTN$, $\cos\theta = \frac{OT}{ON}$.

So, $ON = OT\sec\theta = a\sec\theta$.

$\therefore x = a\sec\theta$

By substituting $x = a\sec\theta$ into $\frac{x^2}{a^2} - \frac{y^2}{b^2} = 1$, we find $\sec^2\theta - \frac{y^2}{b^2} = 1$, i.e. $y^2 = b^2(\sec^2\theta - 1)$.

$\therefore y = b\tan\theta$ since $y > 0$ in the first quadrant.

We note that: $\frac{-\pi}{2} < \theta < \frac{\pi}{2}$ for the right-hand branch

and $\frac{\pi}{2} < \theta < \frac{3\pi}{2}$ for the left-hand branch.

1. The equation of the chord joining the points $P(a\sec\theta, b\tan\theta)$ and $Q(a\sec\phi, b\tan\phi)$ is

    $\frac{x}{a}\cos\tfrac{1}{2}(\theta - \phi) - \frac{y}{b}\sin\tfrac{1}{2}(\theta + \phi) = \cos\tfrac{1}{2}(\theta + \phi)$

2. The equation of the tangent at $P(x_1, y_1)$ is:

    $\frac{xx_1}{a^2} - \frac{yy_1}{b^2} = 1$,

    or at $P(a\sec\theta, b\tan\theta)$ is: $\frac{x\sec\theta}{a} - \frac{y\tan\theta}{b} = 1$

3. The equation of the normal at $P(x_1, y_1)$ is:

    $\frac{xa^2}{x_1} + \frac{yb^2}{y_1} = a^2 + b^2$

    or, at $P(a\sec\theta, b\tan\theta)$ is: $xa\cos\theta + yb\cot\theta = a^2 + b^2$

6.8 A Special (Rectangular) Hyperbola $xy = c^2$

$x = ct$, $y = \dfrac{c}{t}$ are the parametric equations of $xy = c^2$

We have $y = \dfrac{c^2}{x}$

$\dfrac{dy}{dx} = \dfrac{-c^2}{x^2}$

Substitute $x = ct$

$\therefore \dfrac{dy}{dx} = \dfrac{-1}{t^2}$

Hence, the equation of the tangent at $P(ct, \dfrac{c}{t})$ is given by:

$$y - \dfrac{c}{t} = -\dfrac{1}{t^2}(x - ct)$$

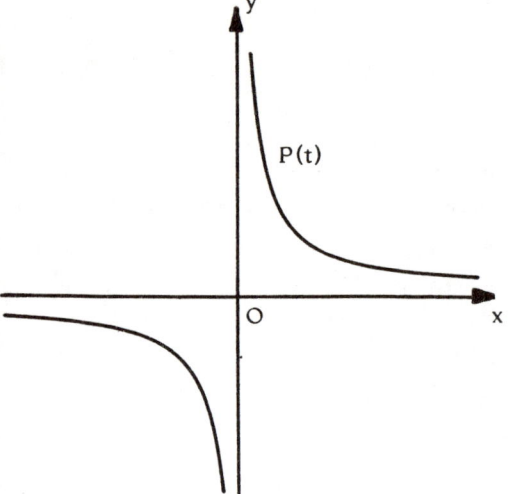

or $\boxed{x + t^2 y = 2ct}$

The tangent has gradient $-\dfrac{1}{t^2}$, and so the gradient of the normal is t^2. The equation of the normal is $y - \dfrac{c}{t} = t^2(x - ct)$, i.e. $\boxed{t^3 x - ty = c(t^4 - 1)}$

The equation of the chord PQ with $P(cp, \dfrac{c}{p})$ and $Q(cq, \dfrac{c}{q})$ is given by

$$y - \dfrac{c}{p} = \dfrac{\dfrac{c}{p} - \dfrac{c}{q}}{cp - cq}(x - cp).$$

This simplifies to $\boxed{x + pqy = c(p + q)}$

By solving the equations of two tangents at P and Q, namely: $x + p^2 y = 2pc$ and $x + q^2 y = 2qc$, we find the point of intersection of these to be

$$R\left(\dfrac{2cpq}{p+q}, \dfrac{2c}{p+q}\right).$$

The following results are left as an exercise to the reader.

1. The equation of the chord joining $P(x_1, y_1)$ and $Q(x_2, y_2)$ is:

$$y - y_1 = \dfrac{-c^2}{x_1 x_2}(x - x_1)$$

2. The point of intersection of the normals at $P(cp, \dfrac{c}{p})$ and $Q(cq, \dfrac{c}{q})$ is given by:

$$x = \dfrac{cqp(p^2 + q^2 + pq) + c}{pq(p+q)}, \quad y = \dfrac{cp^3 q^3 + c(p^2 + pq + q^2)}{pq(p+q)}$$

Though the coordinates look formidable, it is a basic and interesting exercise in algebraic manipulation!

EXAMPLES:

Find the equations of the tangents and the normals to the following curves at the given points:

(1) $\dfrac{x^2}{4} + \dfrac{y^2}{12} = 1$, $P(-1,3)$ (2) $x = 2\cos\theta$, $y = 3\sin\theta$ at $\theta = \dfrac{\pi}{4}$

(3) $x^2 - 2y^2 = 1$, $P(-3,2)$ (4) $x = \sqrt{2}\sec\theta$, $y = 2\tan\theta$ at $\theta = \dfrac{\pi}{4}$

SOLUTION: (T = tangent, N = normal)

(1) $3x^2 + y^2 = 12$

$\therefore\ 6x + 2y\dfrac{dy}{dx} = 0$

At $P(-1,3)$, $\dfrac{dy}{dx} = 1$

The equations of the tangent and the normal are:

$y - 3 = x + 1$, i.e. $y = x + 4$ ... (T)

and $y - 3 = -(x + 1)$, i.e. $y = -x + 2$ ... (N)

(2) $\dfrac{dy}{dx} = \dfrac{dy/d\theta}{dx/d\theta} = \dfrac{3\cos\theta}{-2\sin\theta}$

For $\theta = \dfrac{\pi}{4}$, $\dfrac{dy}{dx} = -\dfrac{3}{2}$.

The required equations are:

$P(\theta) = (2\cos\theta, 3\sin\theta)$

$P(\pi/4) = (\sqrt{2}, 3/\sqrt{2})$

$\therefore\ y - \dfrac{3}{\sqrt{2}} = -\dfrac{3}{2}(x - \sqrt{2})$, i.e.

$3x + 2y = 6\sqrt{2}$ ... (T)

and $y - \dfrac{3}{\sqrt{2}} = \dfrac{2}{3}(x - \sqrt{2})$, i.e.

$4x - 6y = -5\sqrt{2}$ ... (N)

We can find these by using the cartesian equation of the ellipse

$\dfrac{x^2}{4} + \dfrac{y^2}{9} = 1$ at $P(\sqrt{2}, \dfrac{3}{\sqrt{2}})$

(3) $x^2 - 2y^2 = 1$, $P(-3,2)$

$\therefore\ 2x - 4y\dfrac{dy}{dx} = 0$

$\dfrac{dy}{dx} = -\dfrac{3}{4}$ at P

The required equations are:

$y - 2 = -\dfrac{3}{4}(x + 3)$ and

$y - 2 = \dfrac{4}{3}(x + 3)$

i.e. $3x + 4y + 1 = 0$ ... (T)

$4x - 3y + 18 = 0$ ... (N)

(4) $x = \sqrt{2}\sec\theta$, $y = 2\tan\theta$, $\theta = \dfrac{\pi}{4}$

$P(x_1, y_1) = P(2,2)$ for $\theta = \dfrac{\pi}{4}$

$\dfrac{dy}{dx} = \dfrac{2\sec^2\theta}{\sqrt{2}\sec\theta\tan\theta} = \dfrac{\sqrt{2}\sec\theta}{\tan\theta}$

At $\theta = \dfrac{\pi}{4}$, $\dfrac{dy}{dx} = 2$

The required equations are:

$y - 2 = 2(x - 2)$

and $y - 2 = -\dfrac{1}{2}(x - 2)$, i.e.

$y = 2x - 2$ ... (T)

and $x + 2y = 6$ ... (N)

We can also find these equations from the cartesian equation of the hyperbola

$\dfrac{x^2}{2} - \dfrac{y^2}{4} = 1$ at $P(2,2)$

Exercise 6C

Find the equations of the tangents and the normals to the following curves at the points indicated:

1. $2x^2 + y^2 = 6$ P $(1,2)$
2. $3x^2 + 2y^2 = 5$ P $(-1,1)$
3. $x = 3\sin\theta$, $y = 2\cos\theta$ P $(\theta = \pi/3)$
4. $x = 4\cos\theta$, $y = 3\sin\theta$ P $(\theta = \pi/4)$
5. $3x^2 - 4y^2 = 24$ P $(4, -\sqrt{6})$
6. $x^2 - 2y^2 = 2$ P $(-2,1)$
7. $3x^2 - 2y^2 = 1$ P $(1,-1)$
8. $x = 2\sec\theta$, $y = 3\tan\theta$ P $(\theta = \pi/4)$
9. $x = \sec\theta$, $y = \tan\theta$ P $(\theta = \pi/3)$
10. $xy = c^2$ (c is constant)   P $(ct, \frac{c}{t})$

11. Find the (two) equations of the tangents of gradient $\frac{1}{2}$ to the ellipse $x^2 + 6y^2 = 15$.

12. The point $P(x = 3, y > 0)$ lies on the ellipse $\frac{x^2}{25} + \frac{y^2}{9} = 1$. Find the equations of the tangent and the normal at P. Also find the coordinates of the point in which this tangent intersects the directrix corresponding to the focus S.

13. Find the equations of the tangent and the normal at $P(9,-3)$ on the hyperbola $\frac{x^2}{54} - \frac{y^2}{18} = 1$. The normal meets the curve again in Q. Find the coordinates of the point of intersection of the tangents at P and Q.

14. The line $y = 2x - 4$ intersects the curve $\frac{x^2}{3} - \frac{y^2}{2} = 1$ at P and Q. Find the coordinates of the point of intersection R of the tangents at P and Q. What is the angle between the normals at P and Q?

15. Prove that the line $x + y = 5$ is a tangent to the ellipse $9x^2 + 16y^2 = 144$. Find the coordinates of the point of contact.

16. Show that the line $3x + 4y = 10$ is a normal to the hyperbola $2x^2 - 3y^2 = 5$ and find the point at which the line is normal.

17. Find the equations of the tangents to the hyperbola $2x^2 - 3y^2 = 6$ which are parallel to the line $x + y = 0$. Also find the points of contact.

18. Show that the line $lx + my + n = 0$ touches the

    (a) ellipse $\dfrac{x^2}{a^2} + \dfrac{y^2}{b^2} = 1$, if $a^2l^2 + b^2m^2 = n^2$

    (b) hyperbola $\dfrac{x^2}{a^2} - \dfrac{y^2}{b^2} = 1$, if $a^2l^2 - b^2m^2 = n^2$.

19. The tangent at $P(x_1, y_1)$ on the hyperbola $\dfrac{x^2}{a^2} - \dfrac{y^2}{b^2} = 1$, $x_1 > 0$, intersects the directrix at Q. S is the focus (ae, 0). Prove that PSQ is a right angle.

20. Find the equations of the four tangents common to the hyperbola $x^2 - 2y^2 = 4$ and the circle $x^2 + y^2 = 1$. Find the points of contact of these tangents with the circle.

[Hint: Let $xx_1 + yy_1 = 1$ be a tangent to $x^2 + y^2 = 1$ at $P(x_1, y_1)$]

6.9 Miscellaneous Problems on Conics

1. Find the equation of the tangent at $P(x_1, y_1)$ to the ellipse $\dfrac{x^2}{a^2} + \dfrac{y^2}{b^2} = 1$. Find the point $Q(X, 0)$ where this tangent meets the x-axis, and prove that $Xx_1 = a^2$. Find the point $R(0, Y)$ where the tangent meets the y-axis. Show that the locus of a point $T(X, Y)$ is given by the equation $\dfrac{a^2}{x^2} + \dfrac{b^2}{y^2} = 1$.

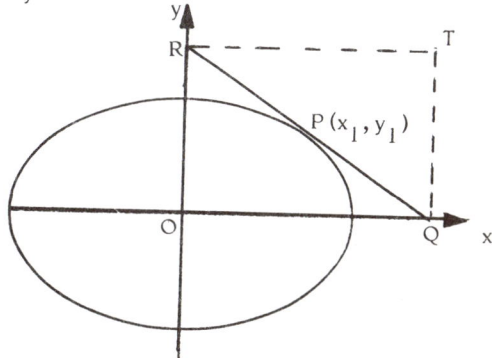

Solution:

The equation of the tangent at $P(x_1, y_1)$ is

$$\dfrac{xx_1}{a^2} + \dfrac{yy_1}{b^2} = 1. \quad \text{(Prove it)}$$

Substituting for $Q(X, 0)$,

$$\dfrac{Xx_1}{a^2} = 1$$

∴ $Xx_1 = a^2$ or $x_1 = \dfrac{a^2}{X}$ .... (1)

Similarly $\quad Yy_1 = b^2 \quad$ or $\quad y_1 = \dfrac{b^2}{Y} \quad \ldots$ (2)

To find the locus of T(X, Y), we eliminate x_1 and y_1 by using:

$$\dfrac{x_1^2}{a^2} + \dfrac{y_1^2}{b^2} = 1$$

$\therefore \quad \dfrac{a^4}{X^2 a^2} + \dfrac{b^4}{Y^2 b^2} = 1$

Hence the locus of R is given by the equation

$$\dfrac{a^2}{x^2} + \dfrac{b^2}{y^2} = 1.$$

---

2. Find the equations of the tangent and normal to the hyperbola $3x^2 - y^2 = 3$ at $P(4, 3\sqrt{5})$. The tangent meets the x-axis in M and the normal meets the y-axis in N, find the length MN.

Solution:

There is no need to remember the equations of the tangent and normal.

$\quad 3x^2 - y^2 = 3 \qquad$ Differentiating

$\quad 6x - 2y \dfrac{dy}{dx} = 0 \quad$ or $\quad \dfrac{dy}{dx} = \dfrac{3x}{y}$

At $P(4, 3\sqrt{5})$, $\dfrac{dy}{dx} = \dfrac{4}{\sqrt{5}}$

$\therefore$ Equation of the tangent at $P(4, 3\sqrt{5})$ is $\quad y - 3\sqrt{5} = \dfrac{4}{\sqrt{5}} (x - 4)$

or $\quad 4x - \sqrt{5}y = 1 \qquad \ldots$ (1)

For M, put $y = 0$.

$\therefore$ M is $M(\dfrac{1}{4}, 0)$

The equation of the normal is

$\qquad y - 3\sqrt{5} = -\dfrac{\sqrt{5}}{4} (x - 4) \qquad [m_1 m_2 = -1]$

or $\quad \sqrt{5}x + 4y = 16\sqrt{5} \qquad \ldots$ (2)

For N, put x = 0

∴ N is (0, 4√5)

∴ MN = $\sqrt{\frac{1}{16} + 80}$ = $\frac{\sqrt{1281}}{4}$

---

3. Find the equation of the normal at $P(a\sec\theta, b\tan\theta)$ to the hyperbola $\frac{x^2}{a^2} - \frac{y^2}{b^2} = 1$.

This normal intersects the x and y axes at Q and R respectively. M(X, Y) is the mid-point of QR. Find the equation of the locus of M as P varies on the hyperbola.

Solution:

The equation of the normal at P is

$ax\sin\theta + by = (a^2 + b^2)\tan\theta$. (Prove it)

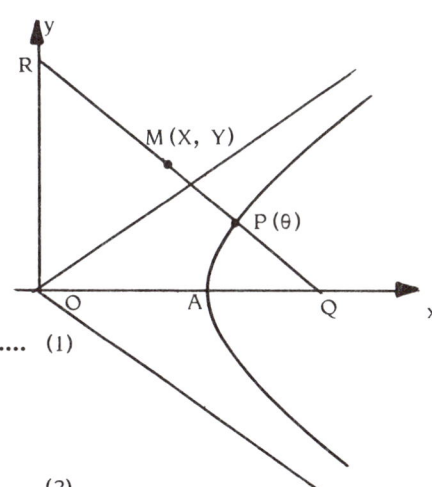

Put y = 0 at Q

∴ $x = \frac{(a^2 + b^2)\tan\theta}{a\sin\theta} = \frac{(a^2 + b^2)\sec\theta}{a}$ .... (1)

Again at R, put x = 0.

∴ $y = \frac{(a^2 + b^2)\tan\theta}{b}$ .... (2)

∴ M(X, Y), being the mid-point of RQ, is

$X = \frac{1}{2a}(a^2 + b^2)\sec\theta$, $Y = \frac{1}{2b}(a^2 + b^2)\tan\theta$

Eliminate θ to find the locus of M

∴ $(2aX)^2 - (2bY)^2 = (a^2 + b^2)^2 (\sec^2\theta - \tan^2\theta)$

or $4a^2X^2 - 4b^2Y^2 = (a^2 + b^2)^2$ is the equation of the locus of M. (Another hyperbola)

Note: If b = a, then the original curve is $x^2 - y^2 = a^2$ and the locus of M is also $x^2 - y^2 = a^2$ i.e. the same curve!

4. The tangent at $P(a\sec\theta, b\tan\theta)$ on the hyperbola $\frac{x^2}{a^2} - \frac{y^2}{b^2} = 1$ intersects the axes Ox and Oy at M and N respectively. Prove that as P varies on the hyperbola, the locus of a point Q is given by $\frac{a^2}{x^2} - \frac{b^2}{y^2} = 1$, where $OMQN$ is a rectangle.

SOLUTION:

The equation of the tangent at
$P(a\sec\theta, b\tan\theta)$ is $\frac{x}{a}\sec\theta - \frac{y}{b}\tan\theta = 1$
at N, $x = 0$, $y = -b\cot\theta$, at M, $y = 0$, $x = a\cos\theta$
$\therefore Q(x,y)$ is $(a\cos\theta, -b\cot\theta)$
$\therefore$ The equation of the locus of Q, by eliminating θ, is:
$x = a\cos\theta$, $y = -b\cot\theta$
$\frac{a}{x} = \sec\theta \qquad \frac{b}{y} = -\tan\theta$
$\therefore \frac{a^2}{x^2} - \frac{b^2}{y^2} = \sec^2\theta - \tan^2\theta = 1$
i.e. $\frac{a^2}{x^2} - \frac{b^2}{y^2} = 1$

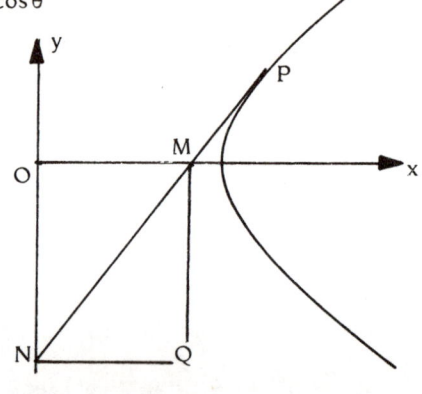

5. The tangent to the hyperbola $xy = c^2$ at the point $P(ct, \frac{c}{t})$ intersects the axes in Q and R and the normal at P intersects the line $y = x$ in S. Prove that $PQ = PR = PS$.

SOLUTION:

The equation of the tangent at $P(ct, \frac{c}{t})$ is
$x + yt^2 = 2ct$
$\therefore Q$ is $(2ct, 0)$
$\quad R$ is $(0, \frac{2c}{t})$

We find that P is the mid-point of RQ.
$\therefore PR = PQ \qquad \ldots (1)$
Now the equation of the normal at P is
$y - \frac{c}{t} = t^2(x - ct)$
Or $t^3x - ty = c(t^4 - 1) \qquad \ldots (2)$

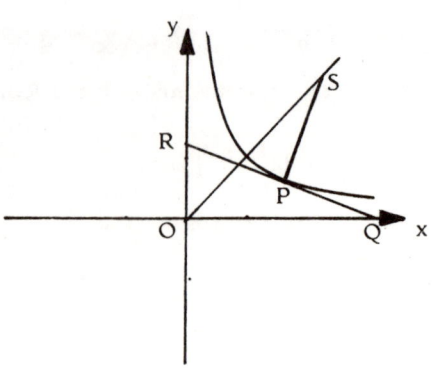

(Solution continued next page)

Solving $y = x$ and equation (2) for S, we have

$$x(t^3 - t) = c(t^4 - 1)$$

$$\therefore x = \frac{c(t^4 - 1)}{t^3 - t} = \frac{c(t^2 + 1)}{t} \qquad (t^2 \neq 1)$$

$$\therefore S \text{ is } \left[\frac{c}{t}(t^2 + 1), \frac{c}{t}(t^2 + 1)\right]$$

$$\therefore SP^2 = \left[\frac{c}{t}(t^2 + 1) - ct\right]^2 + \left[\frac{c}{t}(t^2 + 1) - \frac{c}{t}\right]^2 = \frac{c^2}{t^2} + c^2 t^2$$

$$\therefore SP = \sqrt{\frac{c^2}{t^2} + c^2 t^2} \qquad \ldots (3)$$

Now $PQ^2 = (ct - 2ct)^2 + \left(\frac{c}{t} - 0\right)^2 = c^2 t^2 + \frac{c^2}{t^2}$

$$\therefore PQ = \sqrt{c^2 t^2 + \frac{c^2}{t^2}} \qquad \ldots (4)$$

From (1), (3) and (4): $PQ = PR = PS$.

Exercise 6D

Find the equations of the (a) tangent and (b) normal to the following curves at the points given:

1. $\dfrac{x^2}{25} + \dfrac{y^2}{16} = 1$, $P(\tfrac{5}{2}, 2\sqrt{3})$

2. $x^2 + 4y^2 = 1$, at $x = \tfrac{1}{2}$

3. $x^2 - 2y^2 = 2$, at $x = 2$

4. $x = 4\cos\theta$, $y = 3\sin\theta$, $\theta = \tfrac{\pi}{4}$

5. $x = 5\sec\theta$, $y = 4\tan\theta$, $\theta = \tfrac{\pi}{4}$

6. Show that the equation of the normal to the ellipse $\dfrac{x^2}{a^2} + \dfrac{y^2}{b^2} = 1$

   (a) at $P(x_1, y_1)$ is $\dfrac{x - x_1}{b^2 x_1} = \dfrac{y - y_1}{a^2 y_1}$

   (b) at $P(a\cos\theta, b\sin\theta)$ is $ax\sin\theta - by\cos\theta = (a^2 - b^2)\sin\theta\cos\theta$.

7. Show that the equation of the tangent to the hyperbola

   $\dfrac{x^2}{a^2} - \dfrac{y^2}{b^2} = 1$ at $P(x_1, y_1)$ is $\dfrac{xx_1}{a^2} - \dfrac{yy_1}{b^2} = 1$

   and at the point $(a\sec\theta, b\tan\theta)$ is $\dfrac{x}{a}\sec\theta - \dfrac{y}{b}\tan\theta = 1$.

8. Show that the equation of the normal to the hyperbola $\dfrac{x^2}{a^2} - \dfrac{y^2}{b^2} = 1$

   (a) at $P(x_1, y_1)$ is $\dfrac{a^2}{x_1} \cdot x + \dfrac{b^2}{y_1} \cdot y = a^2 + b^2$

   (b) at $P(a\sec\theta, b\tan\theta)$ is $ax\cos\theta + by\cot\theta = a^2 + b^2$.

9. P is any point on the ellipse $\dfrac{x^2}{a^2} + \dfrac{y^2}{b^2} = 1$, with foci S and S', prove that

   $PS + PS' = 2a$.

10. $P(x, y)$ is any point on the hyperbola $\frac{x^2}{a^2} - \frac{y^2}{b^2} = 1$ with foci S and S', prove that $|PS' - PS| = 2a$.

11. Find the equations of the tangent and normal to

    (a) the ellipse $\frac{x^2}{9} + \frac{y^2}{4} = 1$ at $x = 1$

    (b) the hyperbola $x^2 - y^2 = 4$ at $x = 3$.

12. Find the equations of two tangents to the ellipse $16x^2 + 25y^2 = 400$ which are parallel to the line $y = x + 2$.

13. The tangent to the hyperbola $\frac{x^2}{16} - \frac{y^2}{9} = 1$ at $P(4\sqrt{2}, 3)$ meets the asymptotes of the hyperbola at A and B. Show that P is the mid-point of AB. Find the length of AB in the exact form.

14. Find the equation of the tangent to the curve whose parametric equations are $x = 2\cos\theta$ and $y = 3\sin\theta$ at $\theta = \frac{\pi}{3}$. This tangent meets the x-axis in A and y-axis in B. Find the length AB.

15. Show that the equation of the normal to the ellipse $\frac{x^2}{a^2} + \frac{y^2}{b^2} = 1$ at $P(a\cos\theta, b\sin\theta)$ is given by $ax\sin\theta - by\cos\theta = (a^2 - b^2)\sin\theta\cos\theta$. The normal at P meets the x-axis at M and N is the foot of the perpendicular PN to the x-axis. Prove that $MN = \frac{b^2\cos\theta}{a}$.

16. The tangent to the hyperbola $\frac{x^2}{a^2} - \frac{y^2}{b^2} = 1$ at $P(a\sec t, b\tan t)$ meets the asymptotes in A and B. Prove that P is the mid-point of AB.

17. The chord through the focus $S(ae, 0)$ of the ellipse $\frac{x^2}{a^2} + \frac{y^2}{b^2} = 1$, at right angles to the x-axis meets the ellipse at $P(a\cos\theta, b\sin\theta)$. The normal at P passes through the end-point B' of the minor axis, of the ellipse. Prove that:

    (a) $\cos\theta = e$ and $\sin\theta = \sqrt{1 - e^2}$

    (b) equation of the normal at P is $ax\sin\theta - by\cos\theta = (a^2 - b^2)\sin\theta\cos\theta$

    (c) $e^4 + e^2 - 1 = 0$. Hence, find e in the exact form.

18. The ellipse $\frac{x^2}{a^2} + \frac{y^2}{b^2} = 1$ intersects the x-axis at A and A'. Find the co-ordinates of A and A'. Write down the equations of the tangents at A, A' and $P(x_1, y_1)$. Let the tangents at A and P intersect in Q and those at A' and P at Q'. Prove that the product AQ.A'Q' is independent of the position of P.

19. Show that the condition for the line $y = mx + c$ to be a tangent to the ellipse $\frac{x^2}{a^2} + \frac{y^2}{b^2} = 1$ is $c^2 = a^2m^2 + b^2$. Prove that the pair of tangents from the point P(4, 5) to the ellipse $\frac{x^2}{25} + \frac{y^2}{16} = 1$ are at right angles to one another.

20. Show that the tangent to the ellipse $\frac{x^2}{a^2} + \frac{y^2}{b^2} = 1$ at $P(x_1, y_1)$ has the equation $\frac{xx_1}{a^2} + \frac{yy_1}{b^2} = 1$. This tangent meets the x-axis at T. PN is perpendicular to the x-axis, and the normal at P meets the x-axis at G. Show that OT × NG = b^2, where O is the centre of the ellipse.

21. The line $y = mx + c$ is a tangent to the hyperbola $\frac{x^2}{25} - \frac{y^2}{16} = 1$. Show that $c^2 = 25m^2 - 16$. The tangents from $P(x_1, y_1)$ to this hyperbola meet at right angles. Prove that the locus of P is the circle $x^2 + y^2 = 9$.

22. $P(a\sec\theta, b\tan\theta)$ and $Q(a\sec\phi, b\tan\phi)$ are two points on the hyperbola $\frac{x^2}{a^2} - \frac{y^2}{b^2} = 1$, such that $\theta + \phi = 90°$. Find the co-ordinates of the mid-point R of PQ and hence show that the locus of R is given by $\frac{x^2}{a^2} - \frac{y^2}{b^2} = \frac{y}{b}$.

23. $P(x_1, y_1)$ is a point on the hyperbola $\frac{x^2}{25} - \frac{y^2}{16} = 1$. Prove that the equation of the tangent at P is $16xx_1 - 25yy_1 = 400$.

   (a) Find the co-ordinates of the point G at which this tangent cuts the x-axis.

(b) Hence prove that $\dfrac{SP}{S'P} = \dfrac{SG}{S'G}$ where S and S' are the foci of the hyperbola.

24. Show that the normal to the ellipse $\dfrac{x^2}{a^2} + \dfrac{y^2}{b^2} = 1$ at $P(x_1, y_1)$ is given by

$$a^2 y_1 x - b^2 x_1 y = (a^2 - b^2) x_1 y_1 .$$

(a) This normal meets the x-axis at G. Prove that $GS = e \cdot PS$ and $GS' = e \, PS'$, where S and S' are the foci of the ellipse.

(b) Hence prove that $\dfrac{PS}{PS'} = \dfrac{GS}{GS'}$.

25. Write down the equation of the normal at $P(5\cos\theta, 3\sin\theta)$ to the ellipse $\dfrac{x^2}{25} + \dfrac{y^2}{9} = 1$.

This normal cuts the x-axis and the y-axis at G and H respectively. Show that the locus of the mid-point of GH is another ellipse with the same eccentricity as the first. Sketch both ellipses on the same co-ordinate axes.

26. Show that the gradient of the line joining the points $P(ct_1, \dfrac{c}{t_1})$ and $Q(ct_2, \dfrac{c}{t_2})$ on the hyperbola $xy = c^2$ is $\dfrac{-1}{t_1 t_2}$. The points P, Q, R lie on this hyperbola. The line through P perpendicular to QR meets the line through Q perpendicular to PR at M. Prove that M lies on the hyperbola $xy = c^2$.

27. Show that the line $y = mx + c$ is a tangent to the ellipse $\dfrac{x^2}{a^2} + \dfrac{y^2}{b^2} = 1$ if $c^2 = a^2 m^2 + b^2$. Hence obtain the quadratic equation satisfied by m, where m is the gradient of the tangent from the external point $P(x_1, y_1)$. Find the locus of P if the two tangents from P are at right angles.

28. Find the equation of the normal at $P(x_1, y_1)$ to the hyperbola $\dfrac{x^2}{a^2} - \dfrac{y^2}{b^2} = 1$.

PN is perpendicular to the x-axis, and this normal meets the x-axis at G. Show that $NG : ON = b^2 : a^2$, where $O(0, 0)$.

29. Show that the equations of the tangent and the normal to the hyperbola $\frac{x^2}{a^2} - \frac{y^2}{b^2} = 1$ at $P(a\sec\theta, b\tan\theta)$ are respectively:

(a) $bx\sec\theta - ay\tan\theta = ab$, and

(b) $by\sec\theta + ax\tan\theta = (a^2 + b^2)\sec\theta\tan\theta$.

The tangent and the normal cut the y-axis at M and N respectively. Show that the circle on MN as diameter passes through the foci of the hyperbola.

30. (a) Show that $ab = 2c^2$ if the ellipse $\frac{x^2}{a^2} + \frac{y^2}{b^2} = 1$ touches the hyperbola $xy = c^2$.

(b) $P(x_1, y_1)$ moves on the line $y = mx$ and $Q(x_2, y_2)$ moves on the line $y = -mx$. Find the co-ordinates of R, the mid-point of PQ, in terms of x_1, x_2 and m. Show that the locus of R is a certain ellipse, if PQ = 2K, where K is a constant.

31. Show that for all values of θ, the point $P(4\cos\theta, 3\sin\theta)$ lies on the ellipse and find the equation of this ellipse.

(a) Find the equations of the tangents at the points P and $Q(-4\sin\theta, 3\cos\theta)$.

(b) Find the point of intersection, T, of these tangents and show that as θ varies, the locus of T is the ellipse $9x^2 + 16y^2 = 288$.

32. The ordinate at $P(a\sec\theta, b\tan\theta)$ meets the asymptote of the hyperbola $\frac{x^2}{a^2} - \frac{y^2}{b^2} = 1$ at Q. The normal at P meets the x-axis at G. Prove that GQ is perpendicular to the asymptote.

(Hint: $ax\tan\theta + by\sec\theta = (a^2 + b^2)\sec\theta\tan\theta$ is the equation of the normal.)

33. Prove that the equation of the tangent to the hyperbola $x^2 - y^2 = c^2$ at $P(x_1, y_1)$ is $xx_1 - yy_1 = c^2$. This tangent meets the lines $y = x$ and $y = -x$ at Q and R respectively. Prove that area of $\triangle OQR$ is constant.

34. Show that $P(a\cos\theta, a\sin\theta)$ lies on the circle $x^2 + y^2 = a^2$. If $P(\theta)$ and $Q(\phi)$ are two points on the circle $x^2 + y^2 = a^2$, prove that the locus of the mid-point of PQ is the line $y = \sqrt{3}x$ given that $\theta + \phi = \frac{2\pi}{3}$ for all positions of P and Q.

35. Simplify $\cos\left(\theta + \frac{\pi}{2}\right)$ and $\sin\left(\theta + \frac{\pi}{2}\right)$. Show that if $P(r_1\cos\theta, r_1\sin\theta)$ and $Q\left[r_2\cos\left(\theta + \frac{\pi}{2}\right), r_2\sin\left(\theta + \frac{\pi}{2}\right)\right]$ lie on the hyperbola $\frac{x^2}{a^2} - \frac{y^2}{b^2} = 1$, then $\frac{1}{r_1^2} + \frac{1}{r_2^2} = \frac{1}{a^2} - \frac{1}{b^2}$, where O is the centre. Deduce that if OP is perpendicular to OQ, then $r_1^{-2} + r_2^{-2}$ is independent of the positions of P and Q.

36. The normal at $P(a\sec\theta, b\tan\theta)$ to the hyperbola $\frac{x^2}{a^2} - \frac{y^2}{b^2} = 1$ meets the x-axis at G, and PN is perpendicular to the x-axis. Prove that $OG : ON = e^2$, where O is (0, 0).

37. $P(x_1, y_1)$ is any point on the ellipse $\frac{x^2}{a^2} + \frac{y^2}{b^2} = 1$. Find the equation of the tangent at P. A line drawn from the centre $O(0, 0)$ parallel to the tangent at P, meets the ellipse at Q. Prove that the area of $\triangle OPQ$ is independent of the position of P. Find the area of $\triangle OPQ$.

38. Find the area of the largest rectangle that can be inscribed in the ellipse $9x^2 + 25y^2 = 225$.

39. A conic is a rectangular hyperbola with eccentricity $\sqrt{2}$, focus (2, 0) and directrix $x = 1$. Prove that the equation of this hyperbola is $x^2 - y^2 = 2$. Sketch the hyperbola with its asymptotes.
    (a) Find the equation of the normal to this hyperbola at a point $P(x_1, y_1) = (\sqrt{2}\sec\phi, \sqrt{2}\tan\phi)$.
    (b) This normal meets the x-axis at $Q(X, 0)$ and the y-axis at $R(0, Y)$. Show that the locus of a point $M(X, Y)$ is given by $x^2 - y^2 = 8$, as P varies.

40. The tangent at $P(a\cos\theta, b\sin\theta)$ to the ellipse $\frac{x^2}{a^2} + \frac{y^2}{b^2} = 1$ cuts the axes at M and N. Show that M and N are $(a\sec\theta, 0)$ and $(0, b\csc\theta)$ respectively. Find the minimum value of the area of $\triangle OMN$ and the corresponding co-ordinates of P.

41. AB is a chord of the curve $xy = c^2$, where A is $(cp, \frac{c}{p})$ and B is $(cq, \frac{c}{q})$. Find the equation of the chord AB. AB meets the coordinate axes in M and N and R is the mid-point of AB. Show that $OR = MR = NR$.

42. Show that the locus of the foot of the perpendicular drawn from the origin to the tangent to the curve $xy = c^2$ at the point $P(ct, \frac{c}{t})$ is given by $(x^2 + y^2)^2 = 4c^2 xy$.

43. Find the locus of the mid-points of chords of the curve $xy = c^2$ drawn parallel to the line $lx + my = 0$.

44. A tangent at $P(ct, \frac{c}{t})$ to the hyperbola $xy = c^2$ intersects the axes in A and B and O is the origin. Prove that the area of triangle OAB is independent of the position of P on the curve $xy = c^2$.

45. The tangents to $xy = c^2$ at $A(cp, \frac{c}{p})$ and $B(cq, \frac{c}{q})$ intersect at R. If the chord AB touches the curve $xy = 4c^2$, show that the locus of R is given by $4xy = c^2$.

46. A variable chord PQ of the hyperbola $xy = c^2$ where P is (x_1, y_1) and Q is (x_2, y_2), is such that $|x_2 - x_1| = 2c$. Prove that the locus of the mid-point of PQ is given by the equation $x^2 y = c^2 (x + y)$.

47. $P(cp, \frac{c}{p})$, $Q(cq, \frac{c}{q})$ are two points on the conic $xy = c^2$. Show that the gradient of PQ is $\frac{-1}{pq}$. If PQ subtends a right angle at a third point $R(cr, \frac{c}{r})$ on the conic, prove that the tangent at R is perpendicular to PQ.

48. $P(cp, \frac{c}{p})$ and $Q(cq, \frac{c}{q})$ are variable points on the conic $xy = c^2$. Prove that the tangents at P and Q intersect at $T(\frac{2cpq}{p+q}, \frac{2c}{p+q})$. Hence prove that if $pq = k$, a constant, then the locus of T is a straight line passing through the origin.

49. PQ is a variable chord of the hyperbola $xy = 16$, where P is $(4p, \frac{4}{p})$ and Q is $(4q, \frac{4}{q})$.

Prove the following:

(a) The equation of the chord PQ is $x + pqy = 4(p + q)$

(b) The equation of the tangent at P is $x + p^2 y = 8p$

(c) The point of intersection of the tangents at P and Q is $T(\frac{8pq}{p+q}, \frac{8}{p+q})$

(d) If the chord PQ passes through the point $R(0, 8)$, show that the locus of T is a straight line, $x = 4$.

50. $P(x_1, y_1)$ is a point on the rectangular hyperbola $x^2 - y^2 = a^2$. S and S' are the foci. Prove the following:

(a) The eccentricity $e = \sqrt{2}$

(b) $|PS| = a - \sqrt{2} x_1$, $|S'P| = a + \sqrt{2} x_1$

(c) $PS \cdot PS' = OP^2$, where O is the origin.

6.10 Tangents and the Chord of Contact

Many properties of the two central conics, the ellipse and hyperbola, are so common that it is convenient and instructive to treat them as one by writing the equation in the form

$$\frac{x^2}{A} + \frac{y^2}{B} = 1 \qquad \ldots (1)$$

where $A = a^2$ and $B = b^2$ for the ellipse but $B = -b^2$ for the hyperbola.

The tangent at $P(x_1, y_1)$ is $\dfrac{xx_1}{A} + \dfrac{yy_1}{B} = 1$ ... (2)

To find the condition for a line to touch the conic, the line:

$$lx + my + n = 0$$

must have the form of the tangent (1). Comparing coefficients:

$$\frac{x_1/A}{l} = \frac{y_1/B}{m} = \frac{-1}{n}$$

$$\therefore \quad x_1 = \frac{-Al}{n}, \quad y_1 = \frac{-Bm}{n}$$

But $P(x_1, y_1)$ lies on the conic (1), so that:

$$\frac{Al^2}{n^2} + \frac{Bm^2}{n^2} = 1, \text{ which simplifies to:}$$

$$Al^2 + Bm^2 = n^2 \qquad \ldots (2)$$

This is the condition for the line $lx + my + n = 0$ to be a tangent to the conic

$$\frac{x^2}{A} + \frac{y^2}{B} = 1.$$

If the equation of the tangent is expressed in the form $y = mx + b$, the condition becomes:

$$Am^2 + B = b^2 \qquad \ldots (3)$$

This is left as an exercise to the student.

Chord of Contact:

The chord PQ, joining the points of the contact of tangents drawn to the conic from an external point $T(x_1, y_1)$, is called the chord of contact.

Let $P(x_2,y_2)$ and $Q(x_3,y_3)$ be the points of contact of tangents drawn to the conic from $T(x_1,y_1)$. The tangent at (x_2,y_2) to the conic $\dfrac{x^2}{A} + \dfrac{y^2}{B} = 1$ is $\dfrac{xx_2}{A} + \dfrac{yy_2}{B} = 1$ and $T(x_1,y_1)$ lies on it, so

$$\dfrac{x_1 x_2}{A} + \dfrac{y_1 y_2}{B} = 1 \qquad \ldots (1)$$

Similarly, for the tangent at $Q(x_3,y_3)$,

$$\dfrac{x_1 x_3}{A} + \dfrac{y_1 y_3}{B} = 1 \qquad \ldots (2)$$

(1) and (2) clearly indicate that the points P and Q lie on the line

$$\dfrac{xx_1}{A} + \dfrac{yy_1}{B} = 1 \qquad \ldots (3)$$

which is therefore the equation of the chord of contact of $T(x_1,y_1)$.

Though the equation of the C.O.C. is the same form as that of a tangent, it must be remembered that $T(x_1,y_1)$ does not lie on the conic.

The method shown above can be used to find the equation of a chord of contact to any conic, i.e. a parabola $x^2 = 4ay$, a circle $x^2 + y^2 = a^2$, a hyperbola $xy = c^2$ etc. It is left as an exercise for the student to prove the following: (Chord of contact = COC)

1. The equation of the COC, from $P(x_1,y_1)$, to a circle $x^2 + y^2 = a^2$ is $xx_1 + yy_1 = a^2$.

2. The equation of the COC, from $P(x_1,y_1)$, to a parabola $x^2 = 4ay$ is $xx_1 = 2a(y + y_1)$

3. The equation of the COC, from $P(x_1,y_1)$, to a rectangular hyperbola $x^2 - y^2 = a^2$ is $xx_1 - yy_1 = a^2$.

4. The equation of the COC, from $P(x_1,y_1)$, to a (special) rectangular hyperbola $xy = c^2$ is $xx_1 + yy_1 = 2c^2$.

6.11 Geometric Properties of the Ellipse

The standard equation of the ellipse is $\frac{x^2}{a^2} + \frac{y^2}{b^2} = 1$; Centre O.

Foci: $S(ae, 0)$, $S'(-ae, 0)$

Directrices: $x = \pm \frac{a}{e}$

Length of semi-major axis = a
Length of semi-minor axis = b
Vertices: $(\pm a, 0)$, $(0, \pm b)$

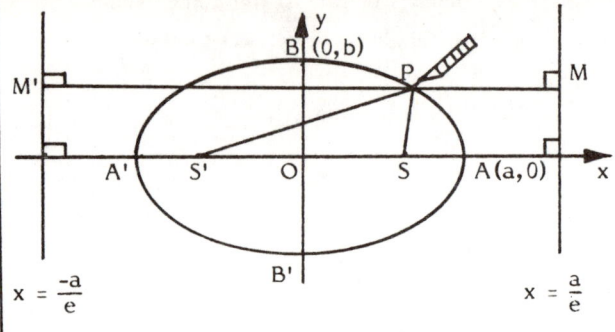

The following properties of the ellipse are proved here:

1. The sum of the focal lengths is a constant, i.e. $SP + S'P = 2a$

   We have $\frac{PS}{PM} = e$ and $\frac{PS'}{PM'} = e$ (Definition)

   $\therefore PS + PS' = e(PM + PM') = e \cdot MM'$

   But MM' = The distance between two directrices = $\frac{2a}{e}$.

   $\therefore PS + PS' = e \cdot \frac{2a}{e} = 2a$, which is a constant

   This fact gives us a fast, accurate (and inexpensive) method of drawing the ellipse.

   A thread of length 2a, fastened at S and S' is kept tightly stretched by a pencil at P. As the pencil moves, it traces out an ellipse. (See the diagram above)

---

2. (a) The normal at P bisects the angle between SP and S'P.
   (b) The tangent at P is equally inclined to SP and S'P.

   These properties are equivalent and we only have to prove one of them. A purely algebraic method is too laborious, so we use the following geometric result. (The proof is given in the appendix)

   If AM is the internal (external) bisector of $\angle BAC$ of $\triangle ABC$, then

   $\frac{AB}{AC} = \frac{BM}{MC} \quad (= \frac{BM'}{M'C})$

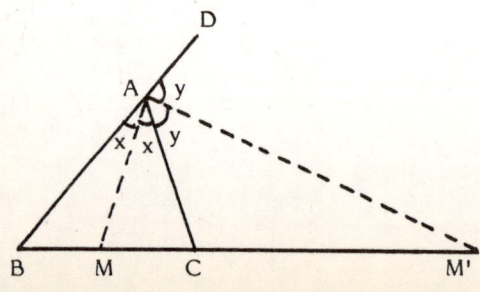

The normal at $P(x_1, y_1)$ is

$$\frac{xa^2}{x_1} - \frac{yb^2}{y_1} = a^2 - b^2 = a^2 e^2, \text{ and meets}$$

the x-axis, where $y = 0$, in $G(e^2 x_1, 0)$

Then, $SG = OS - OG = ae - e^2 x_1 = e(a - ex_1)$

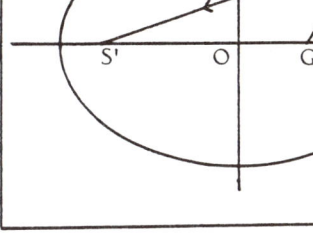

Now $\dfrac{SP}{PM} = e$ (definition)

$\therefore$ $SP = e \cdot PM = e(NM - NP) = e(\dfrac{a}{e} - x_1)$

$\therefore$ $SP = a - ex_1$ (Note: this result is very useful)

$\therefore$ $SG = e \cdot SP$

Similarly $S'G = e \cdot S'P$

$\therefore$ $\dfrac{SG}{S'G} = \dfrac{SP}{S'P}$

$\therefore$ PG bisects the $\angle SPS'$

Thus, the normal at P bisects the angle between SP and S'P.

(b)   Since the normal PG $\perp$ the tangent T'PT,

     $\angle GPT' = \angle GPT$ (both are 90°)   and $\angle S'PG = \angle GPS$

$\therefore$ $\angle GPT' - \angle S'PG = \angle GPT - \angle GPS$

$\therefore$ $\angle T'PS' =. \angle TPS$

Hence, the tangent at P is equally inclined to SP and S'P.

This is the reflecting property of the ellipse. A ray of light or a sound wave originating from the focus S, will be reflected through the other focus S'.

---

3.   The chord of contact from a point on a directrix is a focal chord.

    <u>Proof:</u>

    Let $T(x_1, y_1)$ be a point on the directrix,

    so that $x_1 = \dfrac{a}{e}$.

    The equation of the chord of contact

    is $\dfrac{xx_1}{a^2} + \dfrac{yy_1}{b^2} = 1$.

    For PQ, this becomes $\dfrac{x}{ea} + \dfrac{yy_1}{b^2} = 1$.

    PQ meets the x-axis where $y = 0$, i.e.

    $x = ae$, which is the focus $S(ae, 0)$.

    Hence the result.

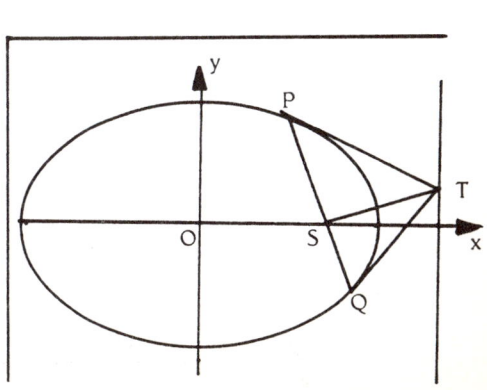

4. That part of the tangent between the point of contact and the directrix subtends a right angle at the corresponding focus.

Proof:

Using the diagram from property 3, we have to prove $\angle PST = 90°$.

The tangent at $P(x_2, y_2)$ is $\dfrac{xx_2}{a^2} + \dfrac{yy_2}{b^2} = 1$ and this meets the directrix in $T(\dfrac{a}{e}, k)$, where

$$\dfrac{x_2}{ae} + \dfrac{ky_2}{b^2} = 1$$

$$\therefore \; aeky_2 = b^2(ae - x_2) = a^2(1 - e^2)(ae - x_2) \quad \ldots (1)$$

The gradient of SP is $m = \dfrac{y_2}{x_2 - ae}$

The gradient of ST is $m' = \dfrac{k}{\dfrac{a}{e} - ae} = \dfrac{ke}{a(1 - e^2)}$

$$\therefore \; mm' = \dfrac{y_2}{x_2 - ae} \cdot \dfrac{ke}{a(1 - e^2)} = \dfrac{aeky_2}{a^2(1 - e^2)(x_2 - ae)}$$

Using (1), we have, $mm' = -1$

$\therefore \; \angle PST = 90°$ and this proves the result.

The ellipse possesses a wealth of useful and interesting properties. Some of these follow simply from the definition and others can be proved by co-ordinate geometry and plane geometry. The reader who masters the general techniques of proving these properties will have no trouble in proving the same properties when particular values of a and b are used.

6.12 Geometric Properties of the Hyperbola

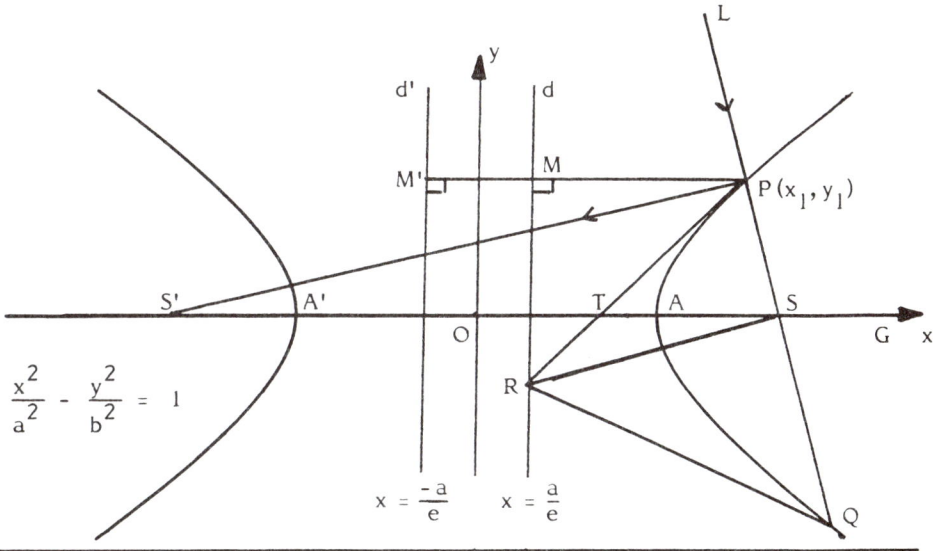

Many properties of the hyperbola are similar to those of the ellipse, so to avoid repetition, the properties are stated without proof. It would be instructive for the reader to supply the proofs referring, if necessary, to the corresponding results for the ellipse.

1. The difference of focal distances is constant.

   $S'P - SP = 2a$, if P is on the branch near S, and

   $SP - S'P = 2a$, if P is on the other branch

   i.e. $|SP - S'P| = 2a$

2. The tangent at P bisects the angle SPS' internally and hence the normal at P bisects $\angle SPS'$ externally.

   (Using the equation of the tangent at P, find the co-ordinate of T and hence prove that $\dfrac{ST}{S'T} = \dfrac{SP}{S'P}$.)

   This is the reflection property of the hyperbola. A ray LP of light directed towards the focus S of a hyperbolic mirror, is reflected towards the other focus S'.

3. The chord of contact from a point on the directrix is a focal chord.

   In the figure, RP, RQ are tangents from R on the directrix.

4. That part of the tangent between the point of contact and the directrix subtends a right angle at the corresponding focus ($\angle PSR = 90°$).

6.13 Properties of the Rectangular Hyperbola

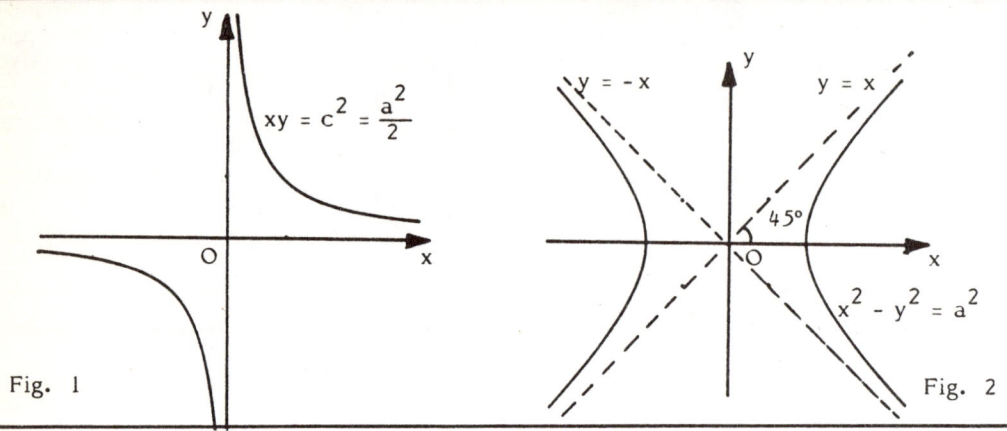

Fig. 1 Fig. 2

In this section we investigate the geometric properties of two special hyperbolas $x^2 - y^2 = a^2$ and $xy = c^2$.

If $b = a$, then the equation $\dfrac{x^2}{a^2} - \dfrac{y^2}{b^2} = 1$ reduces to $x^2 - y^2 = a^2$ and the asymptotes are $y = \pm x$, i.e. $x + y = 0$ and $x - y = 0$, which are perpendicular to each other. A hyperbola whose asymptotes are perpendicular is called a RECTANGULAR hyperbola (Fig. 2).

The reader is familiar with the equation $y = \dfrac{k}{x}$, i.e. $xy = k$, which represents a hyperbola (Fig. 1) with the axes as asymptotes. Thus $xy = c^2$ is also a rectangular hyperbola, but the reader who is not satisfied by this reasoning should refer to two explanations given in the appendix, where it is shown that the hyperbola $xy = \dfrac{a^2}{2}$ is obtained by rotating the hyperbola $x^2 - y^2 = a^2$ through 45° about the origin. We write $c^2 = \dfrac{a^2}{2}$, to simplify our work.

The eccentricity of both hyperbolas is given by $b^2 = a^2(e^2 - 1)$ and with $b = a$, this gives $e = \sqrt{2}$. Obviously most of the properties of hyperbolas $\dfrac{x^2}{a^2} - \dfrac{y^2}{b^2} = 1$, $x^2 - y^2 = a^2$ and $xy = c^2$ are the same, but a few peculiar to $xy = c^2$ are given below with proofs. In science and engineering, it is the form $xy = k$ which is useful rather than $x^2 - y^2 = a^2$. The law connecting the pressure and volume of a perfect gas under constant temperature is $pv = k$, and in electricity the law connecting the current C, the resistance R and the E.M.F. V is given by $CR = V$.

6.14 Geometric Properties of the Rectangular Hyperbola $xy = c^2$

1. The area of the triangle bounded by a tangent and the asymptotes is a constant.

   Proof:
   The equation of the tangent at any point $P(ct, \frac{c}{t})$ on the conic $xy = c^2$ is:
   $$x + t^2 y = 2ct$$
   This meets the axes where
   $$OA = x = 2ct, \quad OB = y = \frac{2c}{t}$$

   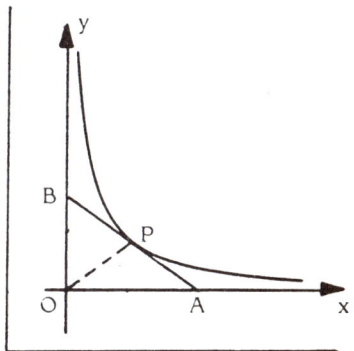

   $\therefore$ Area of the $\triangle OAB = \frac{1}{2} OA \cdot OB$
   $$= \frac{1}{2} \cdot 2ct \cdot \frac{2c}{t} = 2c^2 = \text{a constant.}$$

2. The length of the intercept, cut off from a tangent by the asymptotes, equals twice the distance of the point of contact from the intersection of the asymptotes.

   Proof:
   In the diagram, we want to prove $AB = 2OP$. Using the previous example:
   $P(ct, \frac{c}{t})$, $A(2ct, 0)$, $B(0, \frac{2c}{t})$

   $\therefore \quad AB^2 = 4c^2 t^2 + \frac{4c^2}{t^2} = 4c^2(t^2 + \frac{1}{t^2})$ ... (1)

   $\quad OP^2 = c^2 t^2 + \frac{c^2}{t^2} = c^2(t^2 + \frac{1}{t^2})$ ... (2)

   From (1) and (2):
   $$AB^2 = 4OP^2 \quad \text{which gives} \quad AB = 2OP.$$

Worked Examples: Geometric Properties

EXAMPLE: (1)

Find the equation of the tangent to the ellipse $5x^2 + 9y^2 = 45$ at the point $P(2, \frac{5}{3})$. Find the coordinates of the foci S and S'. SV and $S'V'$ are the perpendiculars to the tangent at P. Prove that: V and V' lie on the circle $x^2 + y^2 = 9$ and $SV \cdot S'V' = 5$.

SOLUTION:

The equation of the ellipse is $\frac{x^2}{9} + \frac{y^2}{5} = 1$.

The equation of the tangent at $P(2, \frac{5}{3})$ is

$\frac{2x}{9} + \frac{5y}{15} = 1$. [using $\frac{xx_1}{a^2} + \frac{yy_1}{b^2} = 1$]

or $2x + 3y = 9$ ... (1)

We have $a^2 = 9$, $b^2 = 5$, then $a^2e^2 = a^2 - b^2$ gives $ae = 2$, so the foci are: $S(2, 0)$ and $S'(-2, 0)$.

$SV \perp$ to the tangent (1), so the equation of SV is $3x - 2y = 6$ ... (2)

Solving (1) and (2), we find $V(\frac{36}{13}, \frac{15}{13})$

$S'V' \perp$ to the tangent (1) and its equation is $3x - 2y = -6$ ... (3)

Solving (1) and (3): $V'(0, 3)$

$V'(0, 3)$ obviously satisfies the equation $x^2 + y^2 = 9$.

Substituting for V in the L.H.S. of this equation:

L.H.S. $= \frac{36^2}{13^2} + \frac{15^2}{13^2} = \frac{1}{13^2} \cdot 3^2 \cdot (12^2 + 5^2) = \frac{3^2 \times 13^2}{13^2} = 9 = $ R.H.S., and

hence both V and V' lie on the auxiliary circle $x^2 + y^2 = 9$.

Now $SV^2 = (\frac{36}{13} - 2)^2 + (\frac{15}{13})^2 = (\frac{10}{13})^2 + (\frac{15}{13})^2 = \frac{325}{169}$

and $S'V'^2 = (-2)^2 + (3)^2 = 13$

$\therefore SV^2 \cdot S'V'^2 = \frac{325}{169} \cdot 13 = 25$ giving $SV \cdot S'V' = 5$

This example is a particular case of the general property of the ellipse $\frac{x^2}{a^2} + \frac{y^2}{b^2} = 1$, i.e. V and V' lie on the auxiliary circle $x^2 + y^2 = a^2$ and $SV \cdot S'V' = b^2$. For this example $a^2 = 9$, $b^2 = 5$.

EXAMPLE: (2): Prove that the portion of the tangent at $P(x_1, y_1)$ to the hyperbola $\frac{x^2}{a^2} - \frac{y^2}{b^2} = 1$ intercepted by the asymptotes is bisected at the point of contact.

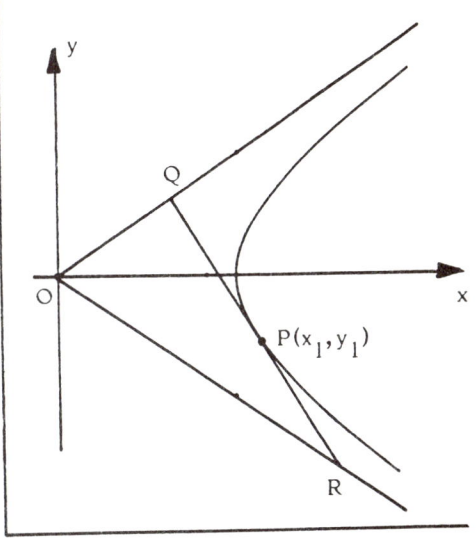

SOLUTION:

The equation of the tangent at $P(x_1, y_1)$ is

$$\frac{xx_1}{a^2} - \frac{yy_1}{b^2} = 1 \qquad \ldots (1)$$

Let R and Q be the intersections of the tangent with the asymptotes.
We find the quadratic equation which gives the ordinates of R and Q. The equation of the asymptotes is $\frac{x^2}{a^2} - \frac{y^2}{b^2} = 0.$ $\qquad \ldots (2)$

From (1) $\quad \frac{xx_1}{a^2} = 1 + \frac{yy_1}{b^2} \quad$ or $\quad x = \frac{a^2}{x_1}(1 + \frac{yy_1}{b^2})$

Substituting into (2): $\frac{a^2}{x_1^2}(1 + \frac{2yy_1}{b^2} + \frac{y^2 y_1^2}{b^4}) - \frac{y^2}{b^2} = 0$

Re-arranging: $y^2 (\frac{a^2 y_1^2}{b^4 x_1^2} - \frac{1}{b^2}) + \frac{2yy_1 a^2}{b^2 x_1^2} + \frac{a^2}{x_1^2} = 0$

This equation gives the ordinates of R and Q.
Let $M(X, Y)$ be the mid-point of RQ.
If the roots are y_1 and y_2, then:

$$Y = \frac{y_1 + y_2}{2} = -\frac{y_1 a^2}{b^2 x_1^2} \div \left(\frac{a^2 y_1^2 - b^2 x_1^2}{b^4 x_1^2}\right) = \frac{-a^2 b^2 y_1}{a^2 y_1^2 - b^2 x_1^2}$$

Since $P(x_1, y_1)$ lies on the conic, $a^2 y_1^2 - b^2 x_1^2 = -a^2 b^2$

$\therefore Y = y_1$

Then using (1), since $M(X, Y)$ lies on the tangent, we have $\frac{Xx_1}{a^2} - \frac{y_1^2}{b^2} = 1$

But $\frac{x_1^2}{a^2} - \frac{y_1^2}{b^2} = 1$ so $\frac{Xx_1}{a^2} = \frac{x_1^2}{a^2}$ giving $X = x_1$

Thus $M(X, Y) = (x_1, y_1)$ which proves the result.

Exercise 6E: PROPERTIES OF CONICS

1. The tangent at $P(x_1, y_1)$ to the ellipse $9x^2 + 16y^2 = 144$ meets the directrices at T and T' respectively. S and S' are the foci. Prove that $\angle PST$ and $\angle PS'T'$ are both right angles.

2. Show that the equation of the normal to the ellipse $16x^2 + 25y^2 = 400$ at the point $P(x_1, y_1)$ is $25x_1 y - 16 x_1 y = 9 x_1 y_1$.
   (a) The normal meets the x-axis at G. Prove that $GS = e \cdot PS$ and $GS' = e \cdot PS'$, where S and S' are the foci.
   (b) Hence prove that $\dfrac{PS}{PS'} = \dfrac{GS}{GS'}$ and that PG bisects the $\angle S'PS$.

3. V and V' are the feet of the perpendiculars from S and S' respectively to the tangent at $P(x_1, y_1)$ to the ellipse $4x^2 + 9y^2 = 36$. Prove that:
   (a) $SV \cdot S'V' = 4$
   (b) V and V' lie on the auxiliary circle $x^2 + y^2 = 9$.

4. M is the mid-point of a variable chord PQ of the ellipse $16x^2 + 25y^2 = 400$, where P is (x_1, y_1) and Q is (x_2, y_2). Prove that the product of the gradients of PQ and OM is constant.

5. NP is the ordinate of a point $P(x_1, y_1)$ on the ellipse $b^2 x^2 + a^2 y^2 = a^2 b^2$. The tangent at P meets the x-axis at A. Prove that $ON \cdot OA = a^2$, where O is the origin.

6. $P(x_1, y_1)$ is a point on the ellipse $\dfrac{x^2}{a^2} + \dfrac{y^2}{b^2} = 1$ and Q is the point on the circle $x^2 + y^2 = a^2$ having the same abscissa. Prove that the tangents at P and Q meet on the x-axis.

7. The tangent at a point $P(x_1, y_1)$ on the hyperbola $16x^2 - 25y^2 = 400$ meets the directrix at T. Show that $\angle PST = 90°$, where S is the corresponding focus.

8. NP is the ordinate of a point $P(x_1, y_1)$ on the hyperbola $\dfrac{x^2}{a^2} - \dfrac{y^2}{b^2} = 1$. The tangent at P meets the x-axis at T. Prove that $ON \cdot OT = a^2$, where O is the origin.

9. $P(x_1, y_1)$ is a point on the hyperbola $\dfrac{x^2}{a^2} - \dfrac{y^2}{b^2} = 1$ with the focus at S. If PS is parallel to the asymptote, prove that the directrix, the asymptote and the tangent at P are concurrent.

10. PQ is a chord of a hyperbola $9x^2 - 16y^2 = 144$ passing through S. The tangents at P and Q intersect at T. Prove that T lies on the directrix corresponding to the focus S.

11. Prove that the point of intersection T of the tangents at $P(cp, \frac{c}{p})$ and $Q(cq, \frac{c}{q})$ on the hyperbola $xy = c^2$ is given by $T(\frac{2cpq}{p+q}, \frac{2c}{p+q})$. OT produced meets the chord PQ at R. Prove that PQ is bisected at R.

12. Prove that the portion of the tangent at $P(1,-1)$ to the hyperbola $3x^2 - 2y^2 = 1$ intercepted between the asymptotes is bisected at the point of contact.

    (Hint: Use the equations of asymptotes $3x^2 - 2y^2 = 0$ and the tangent $3x + 2y = 1$ to find a quadratic in either x or y.)

CHAPTER 7 ELEMENTARY PARTICLE DYNAMICS

7.1 Introduction

Dynamics is the branch of Mechanics (Physics) that deals with the conditions under which bodies move. The other branch of mechanics is called STATICS, which deals with bodies at rest or under equilibrium under the action of some forces.

Two branches of Dynamics are called:

1. KINETICS: Kinetics is the study of effects produced by forces acting on the bodies in motion.

2. KINEMATICS: This deals with the motion of the body without regard to the cause, effect or result of the motion. So far in our work, we have done just that, i.e. the motion of a particle in straight line, the motion of a projectile, the SHM etc. We discussed the motion in terms of the position, velocity, time, acceleration. It did not matter which forces caused this motion.

We shall now introduce "the elements of KINETICS" which relate the forces with the motion of the body. This not only enhances our knowledge of the subject, but we can now solve a wide variety of motion problems, such as the motion in a RESISTING medium, the motion in a circle etc.

Remembering that the 4-Unit Mathematics syllabus requires us to study not only the harder new topics, but also 3U-Maths harder motion problems, we shall first completely summarize the previous work, then revise with harder 3U problems, and then extend to the required new topics.

7.2 Laws of Motion — Force

In everyday life we use force to pull or push an object. In this chapter we study the cause-effect relation between the observed motion and the system of forces.

Newton (1642-1727), one of the most famous and greatest scientists, formulated laws of motion after studying the motion problems which involve application of natural (gravitational) or mechanical (push, pull, friction) forces.

Newton's First Law of Motion. (Inertia)

A body remains in a state of rest, or of uniform motion in a straight line (a constant velocity, no external force) in the absence of a force.

A force is an invisible entity, it is recognised only by its effect, so it is a CONCEPT. A heavier object requires a greater force to move than a lighter object, hence we say a heavier object has greater inertia.

The First Law introduces us to the idea of a Force and mass (inertia), i.e. the definition of what is a force.

Newton's Second Law of Motion

This law relates the change in velocity i.e. acceleration with the magnitude of the force that produced the motion. It states that:

A force acting on a body produces an acceleration which is proportional to the magnitude of the force and this acceleration is in the direction of the force.

The mathematical form of the second law is:

$$\text{Force} = \text{Mass} \times \text{Acceleration}$$
$$F = ma$$

The mass m is a measure of the amount of material and hence the inertia of the body.

In the SI units:

Mass is in kilograms (kg)

Acceleration is in $m.s^{-2}$

Thus a force of 1 N acts on an object of mass of 1 kg, the object accelerates by $1\ m.s^{-2}$.

Mass and Weight of a Body

The weight is the force acting on an object of mass m, due to gravity.

The value of g, the acceleration due to gravity is $9.8\ m.s^{-2}$ (at earth's surface).

$\therefore$ Weight = m × g

$W\ (\text{newtons}) = m(kg) \times g\ (m.s^{-2})$

A weight of 1 kg is equal to 9.8 N.

Never confuse the weight with the mass.

Weight is a force and hence a vector, but mass is a scalar quantity.

Newton's Third Law of Motion:

This law states that the force exerted by one body on another body i.e. action force, is equal to the force exerted by the second body on the first, the reaction force, and they are opposite in direction.

When you kick a football, you are applying a force on the football, and at the same time, the ball's reaction applies an equal force to your foot, it hurts!

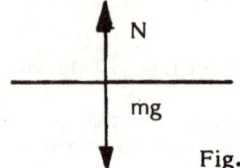

Fig. 1

A body of mass m lying on a horizontal smooth surface is pressing the table with a downward force of its weight, but at the same time the equal and opposite force N acts on the body. This force is the reaction in the direction at right angles to the surface.

WORKED EXAMPLES

EXAMPLE 1:

A body of mass 10 kg is suspended by a string from a ceiling.
Find the tension in the string.

SOLUTION:

You need not show the entire system, only the forces acting on the particle.

The two forces acting on the particle are the tension T, upwards and the gravitational force mg, downwards.

We use Newton's second law:

The resultant force = mass × acceleration.

$\therefore$ $T - mg = m \times 0$, because the system is at rest, hence,
acceleration = 0

$\therefore$ $T = mg$
  $= 10 \times 9.8$ $m = 10$ kg, $g = 9.8$ m.s^{-2}
  $= 98$ kg.m.s^{-2}
  $= 98$ N   (1 N = 1 kg.m.s^{-2})

Fig. 2

EXAMPLE 2:

A particle of mass 20 kg is suspended by two strings. Calculate the tensions in the strings, shown in the diagram. (Acceleration due to gravity $g = 10$ m.s^{-2}).

SOLUTION:

The forces acting on the particle P are the two tensions T_1 and T_2 and the gravitational force mg.

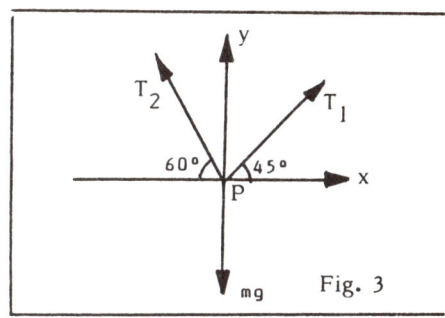

Fig. 3

We select the rectangular coordinate system at P and decompose (resolve) the system of forces into the horizontal components F_x and the vertical components, F_y

$$\Sigma F_x = T_1 \cos 45° - T_2 \cos 60°$$

$$\Sigma F_y = T_1 \sin 45° + T_2 \sin 60° - mg$$

The upward components are considered positive and downward components negative.

Since there is no acceleration in any direction, we have:

$$\Sigma F_x = 0 \text{ and } \Sigma F_y = 0$$

$$\therefore T_1 \cos 45° - T_2 \cos 60° = 0 \text{ and} \quad \text{.... (1)}$$

$$T_1 \sin 45° + T_2 \sin 60° - mg = 0 \quad \text{.... (2)}$$

Remembering, $\cos 45° = \sin 45°$, subtract (1) from (2)

$$\therefore T_2 (\sin 60° + \cos 60°) = mg$$

substitute $m = 20$, $g = 10$

$$T_2 = \frac{200}{\sin 60° + \cos 60°} = 146 \text{ N}$$

From (1):

$$T_1 \cos 45° = T_2 \cos 60°$$

$$\therefore T_1 = \frac{146 \cos 60°}{\cos 45°} = 104 \text{ N}$$

Note: It is very important that:

1. A free-body diagram is drawn, showing all the forces on the particle.
2. The proper resolution of each force into two components at right angles to each other is shown.

   The two perpendicular directions need not always be the HORIZONTAL and the VERTICAL directions.

3. If there is no acceleration, i.e. the system is at rest, only then is:

   $\Sigma F_x = 0$ and $\Sigma F_y = 0$.

   Normally write, $F_x = m.a_x$ and $F_y = m.a_y$, and then substitute for a_x and a_y, for each problem.

EXAMPLE 3:

A truck of mass 3 tonnes is descending an inclined plane at a speed of 20 m/s. Find the retarding force R, necessary to stop the truck in 30 m. (Angle of the incline is 10°).

SOLUTION:

The forces on the truck are:

Normal reaction N, perpendicular to plane.

Retardation force R, along the incline.

mg, force due to gravity.

Angle of incline = 10°

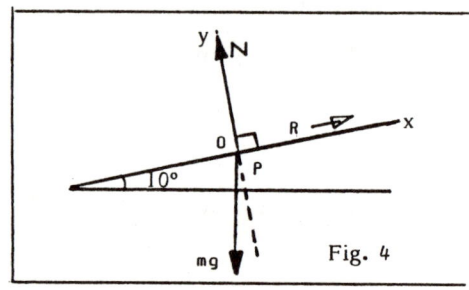

Fig. 4

Resolving the forces along and at right-angles to the plane:

$\Sigma F_x = R - mg \sin 10°$ ... (1)

and $\Sigma F_y = N - mg \cos 10°$ ... (2)

Now the net force on the truck is along the incline, given by m.a, where a is the retardation to be calculated using:

$v^2 = u^2 + 2ax$ given $u = 20$ m/s

∴ $0 = 20^2 + 30 \times 2a$ $x = 30$m

∴ $a = -6\frac{2}{3}$ m.s^{-2}

∴ $\Sigma F_x = ma = 3000 \times \frac{20}{3} = 20000$ N

From (1), $20000 = R - 3000 \times 10 \sin 10°$, giving $R = 25200$ N.

Exercise 7A

In the following examples, take $g = 10$ m.s^{-2}

1. A particle of mass 10 kg is suspended by two strings of length 3 m and 4 m attached to two points at the same level 5 m apart. Find the tensions in the strings.

2. The combined air and road resistance of a car in motion is proportional to v^2, where v is its speed. When the engine is disengaged the car moves down an incline making an angle $\sin^{-1}(1/30)$ with the horizontal, with a velocity of 30 m/s. Find the force required to drive the car up the incline with a steady speed of 24 m/s, given that the mass of the car is 1200 kg.

3. A truck of mass M is driven up a road inclined at an angle θ to the horizontal. After its speed has reached u m/s the engine continues to exert a constant force of F newtons. If the resistance R is constant, find the time taken to reach the velocity v m/s.

4. A car of mass 1500 kg is moving at 60 km/h; when the brakes are applied with a braking force of 12000 N.
    Find: (a) the acceleration
    (b) the time taken by the car to stop
    (c) the distance travelled before coming to rest.

5. A body of mass m is pulled up a smooth incline making an angle θ with the horizontal, and has an acceleration f. Find the force F that pulls the body.

6. A mass of 10 kg is pulled along the horizontal by a chain making an angle of 30° with the horizontal. If the tension in the chain is 50N, find the acceleration of the body and the magnitude of the normal reaction.

7. A smooth block of mass 2 kg slides down an incline making an angle of $\tan^{-1}(3/4)$ with the horizontal. Find the acceleration and the magnitude of the normal reaction.

8. A truck of mass 2000 kg starts to climb an incline of angle given by
    $\theta = \sin^{-1}(1/10)$. The total resistive force is 2000 N.
    Find the retardation it experiences.

9. Find the magnitude of the braking force to stop a car of mass 1200 kg in 20 m when it is travelling at 60 km/h (a) on a horizontal road (b) down an incline of an angle
    $\sin^{-1}(1/40)$.

CHAPTER 8 MOTION PROBLEMS IN TWO DIMENSIONS

We shall first completely summarise the results of various types of motion studied so far in 3U Mathematics, then revise the harder problems of simple harmonic motion and projectile motion, then embark on 4U Motion.

8.1 Introduction: Motion in a Straight Line

Displacement = x

Velocity = $v = \dfrac{dx}{dt} = \dot{x}$

Time = t

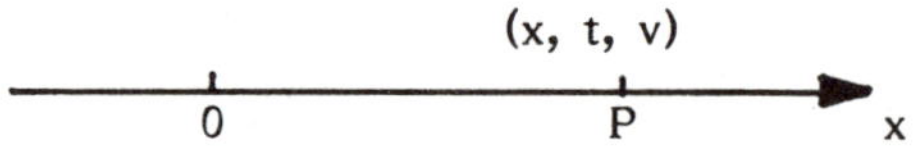

Acceleration $a = \ddot{x} = \dfrac{d^2x}{dt^2} = \dfrac{d}{dx}\left(\dfrac{v^2}{2}\right) = v\dfrac{dv}{dx}$

Fig. 1

For <u>constant</u> acceleration <u>ONLY</u>, the equations of motion are:

u = initial velocity

a = constant acceleration

1. $v = u + at$
2. $v^2 = u^2 + 2ax$
3. $x = ut + \dfrac{1}{2}at^2$

Do not use these formulas for the variable acceleration

<u>Method of Solution</u> (variable acceleration)

1. Given $\ddot{x} = f(t)$, integrate

   $\dot{x} = \int f(t)dt = g(t) + c$

   $x = \int g(t)dt + ct$

2. Given $\ddot{x} = f(x)$, use $\dfrac{d}{dx}\left(\dfrac{v^2}{2}\right) = f(x)$ and integrate.

3. Given $\ddot{x} = f(v)$, use $v\frac{dv}{dx} = f(v)$, and integrate

For VERTICAL MOTION under gravity only replace a, by, g acceleration due to gravity. x may be replaced by y.

1. $y = ut - \frac{1}{2}gt^2$
2. $v = u - gt$
3. $v^2 = u^2 - 2gy$

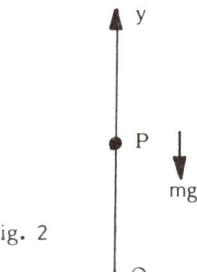

Fig. 2

For downward vertical motion under gravity, assuming the object falls from the rest, we have: (u = 0)

$y = \frac{1}{2}gt^2$

$v = gt$

$v^2 = 2gy$

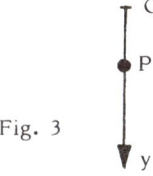

Fig. 3

8.2 Simple Harmonic Motion (Revision)

Definition:

A particle M on a straight line is said to perform a SHM if its displacement x satisfies the differential equation

$\frac{d^2x}{dt^2} = -n^2x$

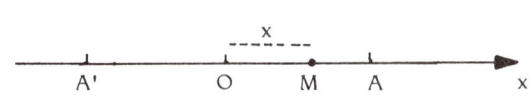

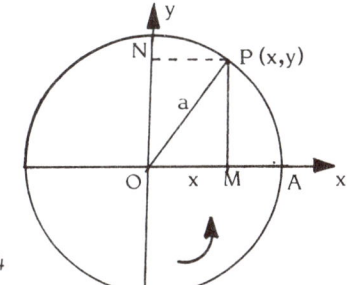

Fig. 4

The acceleration is always directed towards, and proportional to the displacement from the centre.

1. The general solution of $\frac{d^2x}{dt^2} = -n^2x$ is

$x = a\cos(nt + \alpha)$, where a is the amplitude of the SHM, n and α are constants.

2. If the motion starts at A, where $x = +a$, $t = 0$.
   substitute in $x = a \cos(nt + \alpha)$
   $\therefore a = a \cos \alpha$
   $\cos \alpha = 1$ giving $\alpha = 0$
   $\therefore x = a \cos nt$

3. $x = A \cos(nt) + B \sin(nt)$ is also a general solution.

Details of the motion:

Let $x = a \cos(nt + \alpha)$ be the solution of $\ddot{x} = -n^2 x$.

(i) The greatest displacement given by the function $x = a \cos(nt + \alpha)$ is $|x| = a$ and is called the <u>amplitude</u> of SHM.

(ii) The period of SHM is $T = \dfrac{2\pi}{n}$

(iii) The velocity $v = \dfrac{dx}{dt} = -an \sin(nt + \alpha)$

The maximum velocity is $v = \pm an$.

$v = + an$ for the particle moving to the right.

$v = - an$ for the particle moving to the left.

(iv) We have: $x^2 + \dfrac{v^2}{n^2} = a^2$

or $v^2 = n^2(a^2 - x^2)$

Since $v^2 \geq 0$, then $|x| \leq a$

The graph of v^2 shows that v is greatest at $x = 0$ and $v = 0$ at $x = \pm a$.

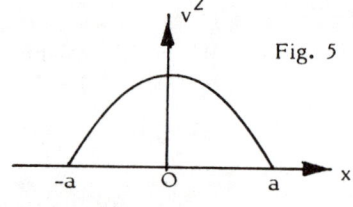

Fig. 5

Hence the particle oscillates between two extreme positions $x = \pm a$. This is why it is also called an oscillatory motion ($-a \leq x \leq a$).

(v.) It is instructive to see that the SHM is closely related to a circular motion of a point P(x,y), centre O(0,0), radius a. (See Fig. 4)

We have: $\theta = nt$

$$x = a \cos nt \quad , \quad y = a \sin nt$$
$$\dot{x} = -na \sin nt \quad , \quad \dot{y} = an \cos nt$$
$$\ddot{x} = -an^2 \cos nt \quad , \quad \ddot{y} = -an^2 \sin nt$$
$$\ddot{x} = -n^2 x \quad , \quad \ddot{y} = -n^2 y$$

∴ Both components of vector OP perform S.H.M. We study more of this in the chapter on CIRCULAR MOTION.
As the point P moves on a circle from initial position at A(x = a), its projection M on the x-axis moves toward O.

M is at A' (x = -a) when P is halfway round the circle. As P continues to describe the negative half of the circle, our point M retraces its path towards the initial point A. Thus as P moves on a circle, its foot of perpendicular PM, i.e. M describes to and fro motion about the centre of attraction, O.

EXAMPLE: (1)

A particle P is in the x - y plane and its coordinates satisfy the equations
$$\frac{d^2x}{dt^2} = -n^2 x \quad \text{and} \quad \frac{d^2y}{dt^2} = -n^2 y.$$
When P is at (5,0), $t = 0$, $\frac{dx}{dt} = 0$, $\frac{dy}{dt} = 4n$

Prove that the locus of P is the ellipse $\frac{x^2}{25} + \frac{y^2}{16} = 1$
Sketch the graph of the locus.

SOLUTION:

$$\frac{d^2x}{dt^2} = -n^2 x$$

∴ $\frac{d}{dx}\left(\frac{v^2}{2}\right) = -n^2 x.$ Integrating

$\frac{v^2}{2} = -\frac{1}{2} n^2 x^2 + c$

at $x = 5$, $v = \frac{dx}{dt} = 0$ ∴ $c = \frac{25}{2} n^2$

∴ $v^2 = n^2 (25 - x^2)$

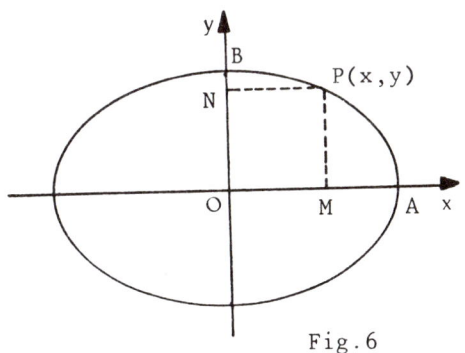

Fig. 6

$\frac{dx}{dt} = -n\sqrt{25 - x^2}$, of negative sign because at A velocity is towards O.

$$n \frac{dt}{dx} = \frac{-1}{\sqrt{25 - x^2}}$$

$$\cos^{-1} \frac{x}{5} = nt + \alpha$$

For $t = 0$ and $x = 5$, we find $\alpha = 0$

$\therefore x = 5 \cos nt$. Similarly, $y = 4 \sin nt$.

we write these as: $\cos nt = x/5$

$\sin nt = y/4$

$$\therefore \frac{x^2}{25} + \frac{y^2}{16} = 1$$

Hence the locus of P is an ellipse. (Shown in Fig. 6) with centre at (0,0) and semi-axes 5 and 4.

Exercise 8A

1. The rise and fall of the tide at a certain port may be considered as simple harmonic, the time difference between successive high tides being 10 hours. The harbour entrance has a depth of 20 m at high tide and 8 m at low tide.

   If the low tide occurs at 10.00 a.m. on a certain day, find the earliest time that a cargo ship requiring a minimum depth of 15 m of water can pass through the entrance.

2. The acceleration of a body moving along the x-axis is given by

   $$\frac{d}{dx}\left(\frac{v^2}{2}\right) = -x \text{ for } x \leqslant 1$$

   $$= 2 - x \text{ for } x > 1.$$

   (a) Show that the quantity $\frac{1}{2}\left(\frac{dx}{dt}\right)^2 + f(x)$ is a constant of motion, where

   $$f(x) = \frac{x^2}{2} \text{ or } \frac{1}{2}(x - 2)^2 \text{ according as } x \leqslant 1 \text{ or } x > 1.$$

   (b) When $t = 0$, $x = 0$ and the initial velocity of the body is 1/3 in the positive direction. Determine the extreme points of the subsequent motion, hence prove that the motion is S.H.M.

   (c) If in Exercise (b), $v = 2$, find the extreme points of the motion. Explain whether the motion now is SHM or not.

3. Show that $x = r\cos(\omega t + \emptyset)$ where $r, \omega, \emptyset$ are constants, is a solution of
$$\frac{d^2x}{dt^2} = -\omega^2 x.$$

A small naval target rises and falls with SHM of period 10 seconds; the height of the waves from the crest to trough is 2 m.

At a horizontal range of 2000 m a gun is fired so that the target would be hit provided it remains stationary in its highest position. The horizontal component of velocity is 1000 m/s. Show that the target would be missed by a vertical height of approximately 0.69 m.

4. A particle moves in a straight line Ox and its equation of motion is
$$\frac{d^2x}{dt^2} = 9 - 9x.$$

Prove that the displacement at time t is given by

$x = 1 + \frac{5}{3}\cos(3t - 127°)$, given that $v = 4$ m/s, when $x = t = 0$.

What is the centre of oscillation?

Find the amplitude and the maximum velocity.

5. The velocity v of a particle moving along the x-axis is given by
$v^2 = 12 + 8x - 4x^2$, where x is the distance from the origin O.

Prove that the motion is SHM and find

(a) the amplitude

(b) the centre of oscillation

(c) the period.

6. P, Q and R are three points on the x-axis such that PQ = QR = 2 m. A particle performs a SHM along the x-axis and is observed to have the velocities of 12, 10 and 6 m/s at P, Q and R respectively. Taking the origin at the centre of oscillation, find

(a) the constant n in the equation $\ddot{x} = -n^2 x$

(b) the distance of P from the centre

(c) the amplitude.

8.3 Motion of a Projectile (Revision)

A particle is projected from a point O in a vertical plane, at an angle of θ to the horizontal, with velocity v.

The only acceleration acting on the particle is due to gravity, hence the equations of the motion are:

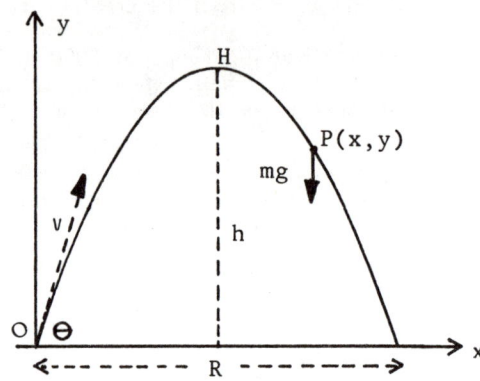

Fig. 7

$$\frac{d^2x}{dt^2} = 0 \quad \text{and} \quad \frac{d^2y}{dt^2} = -g$$

Initially, $x = 0 = y = t$, $v_1 = v \cos \theta$ (horizontal component)

$v_2 = v \sin \theta$ (vertical component)

Integration gives

$$\frac{dx}{dt} = v \cos \theta \qquad \frac{dy}{dt} = v \sin \theta - gt \qquad \ldots (1)$$

$$x = (v \cos \theta) t \qquad y = (v \sin \theta) t - \tfrac{1}{2} gt^2 \qquad \ldots (2)$$

Eliminate t from (2):

The path of the projectile is a parabola

$$y = x \tan \theta - \frac{gx^2 \sec^2 \theta}{2v^2} \qquad \ldots (3)$$

From (2), the time of flight when $y = 0$, $t = T$.

$$\therefore T = \frac{2v \sin \theta}{g} \qquad \ldots (4)$$

From $x = (v \cos \theta) T$, the horizontal range $R = OA$, is

$$R = v \cos \theta \cdot 2v \frac{\sin \theta}{g} = \frac{v^2 \sin 2\theta}{g} . \qquad \ldots (5)$$

The range is the maximum when $\theta = 45°$, $R_{max} = \dfrac{v^2}{g}$. ... (6)

At the highest point H, velocity $\dfrac{dy}{dt}$ (vertical) $= 0$.

$\therefore$ from (1) $t = v \dfrac{\sin \theta}{g}$, hence the maximum height from (2) is

$$h = \dfrac{v^2 \sin^2 \theta}{2g} \qquad \ldots (7)$$

From (5): $R = \dfrac{v^2 \sin 2\theta}{g}$.

Since $\sin 2(90° - \theta) = \sin 2\theta$, there are two angles of projection θ and $90° - \theta$, which give the same horizontal range R. It is easy to see that these two directions are equally inclined to the direction given by $\theta = 45°$.

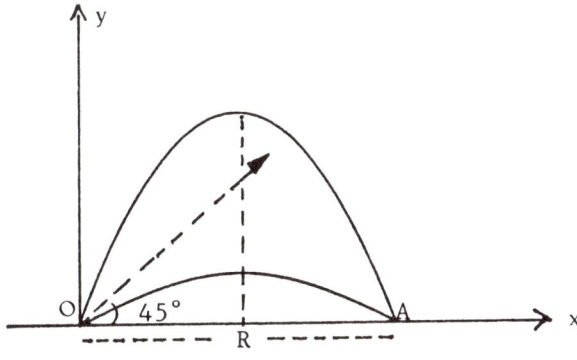

Fig. 8

There is no need to memorise the above results.

Start from: $\ddot{x} = 0$ and $\ddot{y} = -g$.

The formulas of motion are different from those given above when the initial conditions are different. For example, the projectile may have been fired at a height, say, a, above the horizontal ground, in that case the component y is given by:

$$y = a + (v \sin \theta) t - \dfrac{1}{2} gt^2$$

EXAMPLE: (1)

A particle is projected in a vertical plane at right angles to a wall of height, h, standing on horizontal ground at a distance, c, from the point of projection O. It just clears the wall at the highest point of its path. Prove that:

(a) the speed v of projection is given by $v^2 = \dfrac{g}{2h} (c^2 + 4h^2)$

(b) the angle θ of projection is $\tan^{-1} \dfrac{2h}{c}$.

SOLUTION:

Starting with axes at O and

$\frac{d^2x}{dt^2} = 0$ and $\frac{d^2y}{dt^2} = -g$

We can show that

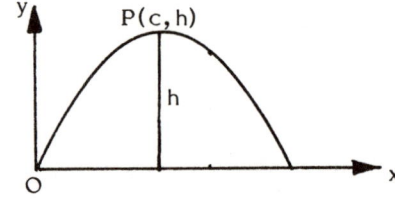

Fig. 9

$x = (v \cos \theta) t$ ... (1)

$\frac{dy}{dt} = v \sin \theta - gt$ ... (2)

$y = (v \sin \theta) t - \frac{gt^2}{2}$ ... (3)

At the highest point, $\dot{y} = 0$, hence $t = \frac{v \sin \theta}{g}$ ... (4)

Substitute $t = \frac{v \sin \theta}{g}$ in (1) at $P(c, h)$.

$\therefore c = v \cos \theta \cdot \frac{v \sin \theta}{g} = \frac{v^2}{g} \sin \theta \cos \theta$ ... (5)

Substitute $y = h$ and $t = v \frac{\sin \theta}{g}$ in (3)

$\therefore h = v \sin \theta \cdot \frac{v \sin \theta}{g} - \frac{g}{2} \cdot \left(\frac{v \sin \theta}{g}\right)^2 = \frac{1}{2} \cdot \frac{v^2}{g} \cdot \sin^2 \theta$ ... (6)

Divide (6) by (5): $\tan \theta = \frac{2h}{c}$ or $\theta = \tan^{-1} \frac{2h}{c}$

From (5):

$c^2 = \frac{v^4}{g^2} \cos^2 \theta \sin^2 \theta$

$= \frac{v^4}{g^2} (1 - \sin^2 \theta) \cdot \sin^2 \theta$ $\left[\text{from (6)} \quad \sin^2 \theta = \frac{2gh}{v^2}\right]$

$\therefore c^2 = \frac{v^4}{g^2} \left(1 - \frac{2gh}{v^2}\right) \cdot \frac{2gh}{v^2}$

This simplifies to $v^2 = \frac{g}{2h} (c^2 + 4h^2)$.

Exercise 8B

1. A stone of mass m is projected with velocity 30 m/s from a point at the foot of an inclined plane making an angle of 30° to the horizontal. The path of the projectile can be assumed to be in the vertical plane containing the line of the greatest slope of the inclined plane. If the angle of projection $\alpha > 30°$, for what values of α will the stone strike the inclined plane:
   (a) horizontally? (b) at right angles?

2. Prove that the range R on a horizontal plane of a particle projected at an angle θ to the horizontal and velocity v is given by: $R = \dfrac{v^2 \sin 2\theta}{g}$
   where g is the acceleration due to gravity in $m.s^{-2}$
   Also prove that the equation of the path of the projectile can be written as:
   (a) $gx^2 \tan^2\theta - 2v^2 x \tan\theta + (2v^2 y + gx^2) = 0$
   (b) At what angle must a body be projected with a speed of $50\ m.s^{-1}$ to just clear a wall 10 m high at a distance of 60 m from the point of projection.
   (Hint: use part (a) with $v = 50$, $y = 10$, $x = 60$, $g = 10$. Find two answers)

3. A stone is projected with an initial velocity v_1 in a vertical plane at an angle θ to the horizontal and hits the ground at a point A. Another stone is projected with an initial velocity v_2 at the same angle of projection, but $v_2 > v_1$.
   Let $B(x_2, y_2)$ and $C(x_1, y_1)$ be two points on the respective paths of flights at the same time t. Show that the gradient of segment BC is independent of time t.

   When the second stone just clears a wall of height h, the first stone hits the ground at A. If the wall stands at point D on the level ground, prove that $AD = h \cot\theta$.

   Further show that
   $\tan(-\emptyset) = \tan\theta - \dfrac{gT}{v_2 \cos\theta}$, where $\emptyset$ is the angle made by the downward flight of the faster stone with the horizontal, and T is the time of flight for the slower stone.

   Hence show that $v_2(\tan\theta + \tan\emptyset) = 2v_1 \tan\theta$.

4. The nozzle of a water hose is at a point O on the horizontal ground. The water comes out of the nozzle with speed U m/s. Neglecting the air-resistance, prove that the water can reach the wall at a distance d from O, if $U^2 > gd$, where g is the acceleration due to gravity.

   If $U^2 = 4gd$, also prove that the maximum height that can be reached by the jet on this wall is given by $\frac{15d}{8}$.

5. A missile is fired from O with initial velocity U at an angle α with the horizontal. Prove that it describes a parabola of focal length $\frac{U^2 \cos^2 \alpha}{2g}$.

   Also prove that any point $P(x,y)$ within and on the circle $x^2 + y^2 = \frac{v^4}{g^2}$ is in danger of being hit by the missile. (g m.s^{-2} is the acceleration due to gravity).

6. A stone is projected upwards at an angle θ to the horizontal. Find an expression for the velocity v at time t in terms of g, t and the initial velocity U.

   If the stone at time t is moving in a direction perpendicular to the initial velocity, show that $t = \frac{U}{g} \csc \theta$ and that the stone's speed is given by $v = U \cot \theta$.

7. A body is projected with speed U from a height h, above a horizontal plane, at an angle θ to the horizontal. Show that the range R on the horizontal is given by

   $$gR^2 \sec^2 \theta - 2U^2 R \tan \theta - 2hU^2 = 0$$

   Further show that the maximum range R_1 is given by

   $$R_1 = \frac{U}{g} \sqrt{U^2 + 2hg}$$

   and the corresponding angle of projection is given by

   $$\tan \theta = \frac{U^2}{gR_1}.$$

   Hence prove that $h = R_1 \cot 2\theta$.

8. A particle is projected from a point O with velocity v at an angle θ to the horizontal. It passes through the point P(x,y) in the vertical plane through O where (x,y) are the co-ordinates of P with respect to the rectangular axes at O.

   Prove that $y = x \tan \theta - \dfrac{gx^2 \sec^2 \theta}{2v^2}$.

   If $x = 20$ m, $y = 10$ m, $g = 10$ m.s^{-2}, $v = 20$ m/s, find the two values of $\tan \theta$ and using, $t = \tan \theta$ and $\sin 2\theta = \dfrac{2t}{1+t^2}$, prove that the ratio of two ranges is $\dfrac{5}{3}$.

9. A particle is projected with velocity v at an angle θ to the horizontal. Show that by suitable choice of axes, the equation of the path of the projectile is

   $$y = x \tan \theta - \dfrac{gx^2 \sec^2 \theta}{2v^2}.$$

   Prove the following:

   (a) There are two possible directions of projection given by $\tan \theta_1$ and $\tan \theta_2$ for a given range R.

   (b) $\tan \theta_1 + \tan \theta_2 = \dfrac{2v^2}{gR}$ and $\tan \theta_1 \tan \theta_2 = 1$.

   (c) Let T_1 and T_2 be the times of flights corresponding to angles of projections θ_1 and θ_2.

   Prove that $\dfrac{T_1}{T_2} = \dfrac{\sin \theta_1}{\sin \theta_2}$.

   (d) From (b) prove that $\theta_1 + \theta_2 = 90°$.

   (e) $R = R_1 \sin 2\theta$, where R_1 is the maximum range.

   (f) If $\dfrac{T_1}{T_2} = \dfrac{2}{1}$, then $\dfrac{R}{R_1} = \dfrac{4}{5}$ [Hint: $\sin 2\theta = \dfrac{2t}{1+t^2}$].

10. Two particles P and Q are projected from the same point O with the same velocity 25 m/s. They both strike the horizontal plane through O at the point A, 60 m from O. P reaches A before Q. Show that:

    (a) the angle of projection of P is $\tan^{-1} \dfrac{3}{4}$ and that of Q is $\tan^{-1} \dfrac{4}{3}$.

    (b) the time of flight of P is 3 seconds.

    (c) the distance between P and Q at the instant P reaches A is $15\sqrt{2}$ m.

    (d) the ratio of the maximum heights reached by P and Q is $\dfrac{9}{16}$.

8.4 Resisted Motion: Other Laws of Motion

In our previous studies of motion, we neglected the effect of air-resistance or air-friction. A body moving in a fluid experiences a resistance which tends to stop the motion. In many cases of motion, the resistance is an important consideration. Cars, planes and boats are streamlined so as to reduce the frictional drag and improve fuel economy.

The air or fluid resistance on an object depends on its:

(i) shape   (ii) size (exposed area)   (iii) speed.

For example, a sky-diver with an unopened parachute falls quite rapidly, but the descent is slowed when the parachute opens. The parachute encounters greater resistance due to its shape and size. A sky-diver can enjoy a free fall (without an open parachute) by employing a spread-eagle position to increase the air resistance and prolong the time of fall.

Air or fluid resistance also depends on the speed of the object. The greater the speed, the greater the air resistance. We shall mostly be concerned with motion for which the resistance is proportional to the speed v or v^2.

Contrary to our perception of resistance, it is quite beneficial to us. Actually it is the road friction that makes car driving possible! Sky-diving is pleasant and possible because the air-resistance helps to slow the descent. Though streamlined cars cost more, they are at least pleasing to our eyes, if not to our purse!

EXAMPLE : (1)

A particle of mass m moves along the x-axis. It experiences a resistive force R given by $R = kv$, where k is a constant and v is the velocity at any time t and position x. Discuss the motion.

SOLUTION:

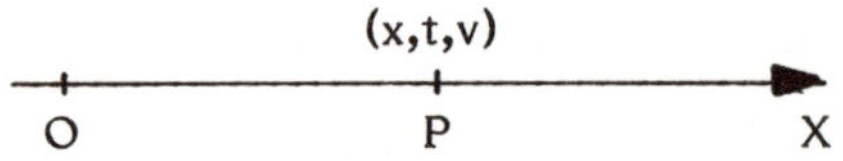

Fig. 10

The equation of motion at time t is given by

$$m \cdot \frac{dv}{dt} = -kv \qquad (F = ma)$$

We attach a negative sign because the resistance opposes the motion.

$$\therefore \frac{dv}{dt} = -\frac{k}{m} \cdot v$$

Integrating $\int \frac{dv}{v} = -\int \frac{k}{m} \cdot dt$

$$\log_e v = -\frac{kt}{m} + A$$

or $v = B\, e^{-kt/m}$, where B is a constant.

If $v = v_0$ at $t = 0$, then $B = v_0$

$$\therefore v = v_0 e^{-kt/m}$$

As $t \to \infty$ the function $e^{-t} \to 0$ and hence $v \to 0$

Further $v = \dfrac{dx}{dt} = v_0 e^{-kt/m}$

$\therefore$ The distance travelled in time t is

$$x = \int_0^t v_0 e^{-kt/m} \, dt = -\dfrac{v_0 m}{k} \left[e^{-kt/m} \right]_0^t$$

or $x = \dfrac{m}{k} v_0 \left[1 - e^{-kt/m} \right]$

Again as $t \to \infty$, $x \to \dfrac{mv_0}{k}$ i.e. it moves with decreasing velocity towards the limiting position $x_t = \dfrac{mv_0}{k}$.

EXAMPLE : (2)

A particle of mass m falls under gravity from rest in a medium with the resistive force given by $R(v) = kv$. Discuss the motion.

SOLUTION:

We take the initial position as the origin and x-axis along the direction of motion. The equation of motion at time t is:

$$m \dfrac{dv}{dt} = mg - mkv$$

$\therefore \quad \dfrac{dv}{dt} = g - kv \quad$ or $\quad dt = \dfrac{dv}{g-kv}$

$\therefore \quad \int_0^t dt = \int_0^v \dfrac{dv}{g-kv}$

$\therefore \quad t = -\dfrac{1}{k} \left[\log_e (g - kv) \right]_0^v$

$\therefore \quad t = -\dfrac{1}{k} [\log(g - kv) - \log(g)] = -\dfrac{1}{k} \log_e \left(1 - \dfrac{kv}{g} \right)$

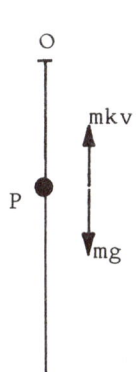

Fig. 11

We can solve this equation for v

$$\therefore \quad e^{-kt} = 1 - \frac{kv}{g}$$

$$\therefore \quad v = \frac{g}{k}(1 - e^{-kt}) \quad \ldots (1)$$

As $t \to \infty$, $v \to \frac{g}{k}$

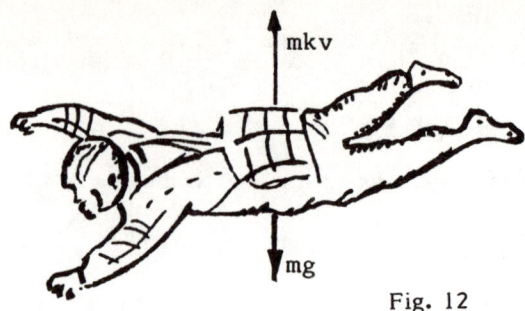

Fig. 12

$v_T = \frac{g}{k}$ is called the terminal velocity and the particle continues to travel with constant velocity v_T. This happens when the resisting force mkv balances the gravitational force on the particle, i.e.

$$mkv = mg \quad \text{or} \quad v = \frac{g}{k}$$

[Have you ever wondered how a team of sky-divers frolic (in the sky) with their parachutes not open! From above you see that a sky-diver should enjoy a free fall until his weight balances the resistive force, thereafter his parachute must open, and with good luck the diver should then enjoy his fall with the reduced terminal velocity. Terminal velocity before the parachute opens is about 200 km/h and it is 40 km/h after the parachute opens.]

Further $v = \frac{dx}{dt} = \frac{g}{k}(1 - e^{-kt})$ from (1)

$$\therefore \quad x = \frac{gt}{k} + \frac{g}{k^2} e^{-kt} + c$$

When $t = 0$, $x = 0$, this gives $c = -\frac{g}{k^2}$

hence $x = \frac{gt}{k} - \frac{g}{k^2}(1 - e^{-kt})$.

EXAMPLE : (3)

A particle of unit mass is thrown vertically upwards with a velocity of U into the air and encounters a resistance kv^2. Find the greatest height h achieved by the particle and the corresponding time.

SOLUTION:

Equation of motion is

$$v \frac{dv}{dx} = -g - kv^2$$

$$\int \frac{v dv}{g + kv^2} = - \int dx$$

$$\therefore \quad x = -\frac{1}{2k} \log_e (g + kv^2) + c$$

When $x = 0$, $v = U$, this gives $c = \frac{1}{2k} \log_e (g + kU^2)$

$$\therefore \quad x = \frac{1}{2k} \log_e \frac{g + kU^2}{g + kv^2} \quad \ldots (1)$$

For the greatest height, $x = h$, $v = 0$

$$\therefore \quad h = \frac{1}{2k} \log (1 + \frac{k}{g} U^2) \quad \ldots (2)$$

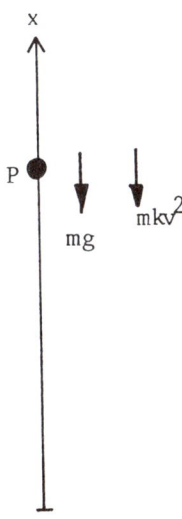

Fig. 13

For the corresponding time, we use:

$$\frac{dv}{dt} = -g - kv^2 \quad \text{or} \quad \frac{dt}{dv} = \frac{-1}{g + kv^2}$$

$$\therefore \quad t = \int \frac{-dv}{g + kv^2} = -\frac{1}{k} \int \frac{dv}{\frac{g}{k} + v^2} , \quad \left[\int \frac{dv}{A^2 + v^2} = \frac{1}{A} \tan^{-1} \left(\frac{v}{A}\right), \text{ where } A = \sqrt{\frac{g}{k}} \right]$$

$$\therefore \quad t = -\frac{1}{k} \cdot \frac{1}{\sqrt{g/k}} \left[\tan^{-1} \sqrt{\frac{k}{g}} \cdot v \right]_U^0$$

$$= \frac{1}{\sqrt{gk}} \tan^{-1} \left(\sqrt{\frac{k}{g}} \cdot U \right)$$

EXAMPLE : (4)

A particle is thrown vertically upwards with speed U in a medium with resistance R = mkv, where m is the mass of the particle and k is a constant. Find the greatest height h reached and the corresponding time.

SOLUTION:

Selecting the origin as the point of projection, the equation of motion is

$$m.v.\frac{dv}{dx} = -mg - mkv$$

$$\therefore \int \frac{v\,dv}{g + kv} = -\int dx$$

$$\therefore x = -\int \frac{\frac{1}{k}(g + kv) - \frac{g}{k}}{g + kv} \cdot dv$$

$$= -\int \left(\frac{1}{k} - \frac{g}{k} \cdot \frac{1}{g + kv} \right) dv$$

$$x = -\frac{v}{k} + \frac{g}{k^2} \log_e (g + kv) + c$$

When $x = 0$, $v = U$, hence $0 = -\frac{U}{k} + \frac{g}{k^2} \log(g + kU) + c$

$$x = \frac{1}{k}(U - v) - \frac{g}{k^2} \log\left(\frac{g + kU}{g + kv} \right) \quad \ldots (1)$$

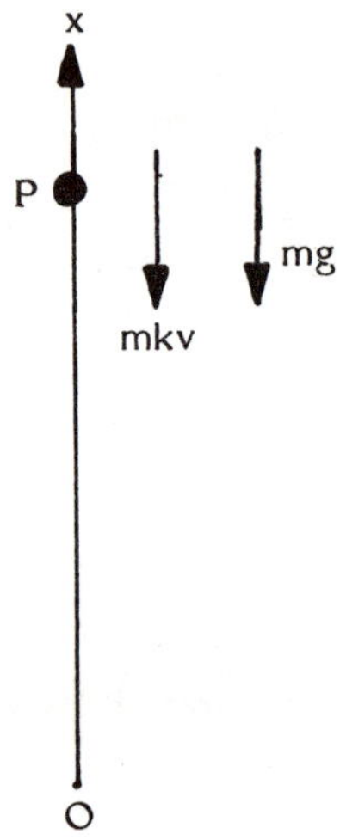

Fig. 14

At the greatest height, $v = 0$, $x = h$

$$\therefore h = \frac{U}{k} - \frac{g}{k^2} \log\left(1 + \frac{kU}{g} \right) \quad \ldots (2)$$

To find the time, we use

$$\frac{dv}{dt} = -g - kv \qquad \text{or} \qquad \frac{dt}{dv} = \frac{-1}{g + kv}$$

$$\therefore t = -\int_U^0 \frac{dv}{g + kv} = \frac{1}{k} \log\left(1 + \frac{kU}{g} \right) \quad \ldots (3)$$

EXAMPLE : (5)

A body is projected vertically upwards from the earth's surface with velocity U. The acceleration of a particle in space is given by kx^{-2}, towards the centre of the earth, where x is the distance of the body from the centre of the earth.

Given that the acceleration is g at the earth's surface, prove that the velocity v at time t is given by

$$v^2 = U^2 - 2gR^2\left(\frac{1}{R} - \frac{1}{x}\right)$$

where R is the radius of the earth.

If $U^2 = 2gR$, find $\frac{dx}{dt}$ in terms of x and show that the body will reach a distance 8R from the earth's surface in 2.72 hours.

Also find the velocity of ESCAPE, i.e. the velocity U of projection so that the body never returns to the earth.

(R = 6400 km, g = 10 m.s^{-2}).

SOLUTION:

Selecting the axes as shown, the equation of motion is

$$m.v.\frac{dv}{dx} = -\frac{mk}{x^2} \qquad \ldots (1)$$

and $g = \frac{k}{R^2}$ (given) at x = R ... (2)

$\therefore \quad k = gR^2$, hence

$$v\frac{dv}{dx} = -\frac{gR^2}{x^2}$$

Integrating, $\frac{v^2}{2} = \frac{gR^2}{x} + C$

At x = R, v = U, so $C = \frac{U^2}{2} - gR$

$\therefore \quad v^2 = U^2 - 2gR^2\left(\frac{1}{R} - \frac{1}{x}\right) \qquad \ldots (3)$

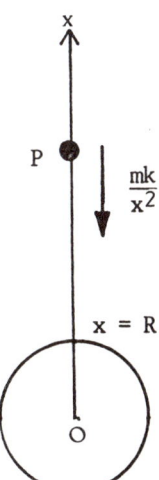

Fig. 15

If $U^2 = 2gR$ then from (3), $v^2 = \dfrac{2gR^2}{x}$

$\therefore \quad v = \dfrac{dx}{dt} = + \sqrt{2gR} \cdot x^{-1/2}$ (sign + as $v \uparrow$ from O)

$$\dfrac{dt}{dx} = \dfrac{x^{1/2}}{R\sqrt{2g}}$$

For $x = 8R + R = 9R$ (from the centre) time taken is

$$t = \int_R^{9R} \dfrac{x^{1/2}}{\sqrt{2gR}} \, dx = \dfrac{1}{\sqrt{2gR}} \cdot \dfrac{2}{3} \left[x^{3/2} \right]_R^{9R}$$

$$= \dfrac{2}{3} \cdot \dfrac{1}{\sqrt{2gR}} \cdot (27 \, R\sqrt{R} - R\sqrt{R})$$

$$= \dfrac{52}{3} \cdot \sqrt{\dfrac{R}{2g}}$$

For $R = 6.4 \times 10^6$ m, $g = 10$ m.s^{-2}, $t = 2.72$ hours

Finally, the particle never returns if $x \to \infty$, hence from (3)

$$v^2 = U^2 - 2gR \qquad \text{(since } \dfrac{1}{x} \to 0\text{)}$$

The body never returns if $v^2 \geqslant 0$.

$\therefore \quad U^2 > 2gR$

$\quad U > \sqrt{2gR}$

$\therefore \quad$ U must be slightly greater than $\sqrt{2 \times 10 \times 6.4 \times 10^6}$

i.e. $\quad U > 11300$ m/s

$\quad U > 11.3$ km/s

$\therefore \quad$ The escape velocity $= 12$ km/s

Exercise 8C

1. A particle of unit mass falls vertically from rest in a medium with resistive force $R = kv$, where v is the velocity of the particle at time t. (k is a constant).

   Find the velocity v and hence show that the terminal velocity is given by $\frac{g}{k}$.

2. A particle of unit mass falls from rest in a medium with resistive force $R = kv^2$, where k is a constant. Prove that the distance x fallen when the velocity is v, is given by:
   $$x = \frac{1}{2k} \log_e \left(\frac{g}{g - kv^2} \right).$$
   Find the distance fallen when it reaches half of its terminal velocity.
   (Hint: The terminal velocity is given by $g - kv^2 = 0$, i.e. $v = \sqrt{g/k}$).

3. An object is projected vertically upwards with initial velocity U from the earth's surface. The acceleration obeys the law given by
   $$\frac{d^2x}{dt^2} = -\frac{k}{x^2}$$
   where x is the distance of the particle from the centre of the earth whose radius is R.

   Given the acceleration is g when $x = R$, show that velocity v in any position is given by:
   $$v^2 = U^2 - 2gR^2 \left(\frac{1}{R} - \frac{1}{x} \right).$$
   Hence show that $U = 12$ km/h for the escape velocity. (i.e. the object does not return to the earth). ($R = 6400$ km, $g = 10$ m.s^{-2})
   (Hint: $x \to \infty$ for escape from the earth and $v^2 > 0$)

4. A particle moves under gravity in a resistive medium with the resistance $R = kv$, where v is the velocity in any position and k is a constant. The particle is projected vertically upwards with velocity $U = \frac{g}{k}$. Show that at any time the expressions for the velocity v and position x are given by:
   $$v = U(2e^{-kt} - 1) \quad \text{and} \quad x = \frac{U}{k}(2 - 2e^{-kt} - kt).$$
   Find the greatest height achieved by the particle.
   (Hint: $v = 0$ for the greatest height).

5. A particle of mass m is projected vertically upwards under gravity with velocity U m/s. The resistive force is $R(v) = mkv^2$ at any time t and position x. Show that the expression for x is given by:

$$x = \frac{1}{2k} \log_e \left[\frac{g + kU^2}{g + kv^2} \right]$$

Show that the greatest height H is given by:

$$H = \frac{1}{2k} \log_e \left[1 + \frac{kU^2}{g} \right]$$

6. A body of mass m falls from rest in a medium with resistive force $R = kv$, where k is the coefficient of air resistance and v is the speed of the object. (k is a constant.) Prove that the distance x fallen when the velocity is v, is given by:

$$x = -\frac{mv}{k} - \frac{m^2 g}{k^2} \log_e \left[1 - \frac{kv}{mg} \right]$$

Find the terminal velocity for a falling 70 kg sky-diver, if $k = 14$ and $g = 10$ m.s^{-2}. Express your answer in km/h.

7. A ball of mass m is thrown vertically upwards with velocity U. The air resistance is $f(v) = kv^2$, at a distance x when velocity is v.

(i) Draw a neat sketch of the motion, showing the forces acting at a distance x from the point of projection.

(ii) Show that $x = \frac{1}{2k} \log_e \left[\frac{g + kU^2}{g + kv^2} \right]$

(iii) Show that the greatest height achieved is

$$H = \frac{1}{2k} \log_e \left[1 + \frac{k}{g} \cdot U^2 \right]$$

(iv) Draw a neat sketch of the downward motion of this ball after it reaches the greatest height H. Show that the distance y fallen when velocity is W, is given by

$$y = \frac{1}{2k} \log_e \left[\frac{g}{g - kW^2} \right]$$

(v) Deduce from (iv) that the terminal velocity V is given by $V^2 = \frac{g}{k}$, and that H can also be given by:

$$H = \frac{1}{2k} \log_e \left[\frac{g}{g - kW^2} \right] \quad \text{where}$$

W is the velocity when $y = H$ for downward motion.

(vi) From (iii) and (v) deduce that $\frac{1}{U^2} + \frac{1}{V^2} = \frac{1}{W^2}$

8. A particle is thrown vertically upwards where the air resistance is given by $R = 0.01\,mv^2$. If the velocity of projection is 60 m/s, find the

   (a) time to reach the highest point

   (b) greatest height H.

9. A particle falling from rest in a vertical line in a medium with resistance kv^2 per unit mass, k is a constant, v is the velocity at any time and position x, prove that it acquires a speed

   $$\left[\sqrt{1 - e^{-2kh}}\right] v_T$$

   in falling through a distance h, where v_T is the terminal velocity given by $\sqrt{\dfrac{g}{k}}$.

   A particle projected upwards in the same medium with initial speed v_I and returns to the point of projection with speed v_R.

   Prove that $v_R^{-2} = v_I^{-2} + v_T^{-2}$.

10. An object of mass 20 kg experiences a resistive force, in newtons, of one-fifth of the square of its velocity in m/s, when it moves through the air.

    This object is projected vertically upwards from a point O with velocity of 30 m/s and reaches the highest point H in time T.

    Given $g = 10\,m.s^{-2}$, find

    (a) the time T

    (b) the distance OH.

11. A particle of unit mass moves in a straight line against a resistance R given by $R = v(1 + v^2)$, where v is the velocity of the particle at a distance x metres from the origin. Prove that $x = \tan^{-1} v_0 - \tan^{-1} v$, where v_0 is the initial velocity at the origin. Use the formula

    $$\tan^{-1} A - \tan^{-1} B = \tan^{-1}\left[\frac{A - B}{1 + AB}\right]$$ to show that:

    $$v = \frac{v_0 - \tan x}{1 + v_0 \tan x}$$

12. A particle of unit mass travels in a straight line against the resisting force $f(v) = v(1 + v^2)$. Its initial velocity is c m/s at the origin. Show that the time t, when velocity is v, is given by:

$$t = \frac{1}{2} \log \left[\frac{1 + v^{-2}}{1 + c^{-2}} \right].$$

Find v^2 as a function of t and hence the limiting value of v at $t \to \infty$.

13. A particle of mass m moves along a straight line under the action of a constant (propelling) force P, and a resistive force mkv, where k is a constant, v is the speed at any time t. Show that if the speed increases from 2 m/s to 4 m/s over a time interval of 5 seconds,

(a) $P = 2km \left[\dfrac{2e^{5k} - 1}{e^{5k} - 1} \right]$.

(b) Find the corresponding distance moved.

(c) Find the propelling force P for $k = 0.5$.

14. The acceleration due to gravity at a distance r from the earth's centre is directed towards the centre and equal to $\dfrac{k}{r^2}$ when $r > R$, equal to kr when $r < R$ and equal to g when $r = R$. Imagine a narrow tunnel along a diameter XY of the earth and the particle is projected from X with initial velocity U towards Y. (R = radius of earth).

If $U^2 < 2gR$, prove that the motion is oscillatory and the amplitude is given by

$$\frac{R}{1 - \dfrac{U^2}{2gR}}.$$

15. A particle is projected vertically upwards from the surface of the earth with initial velocity U. The acceleration due to gravity at a distance x from the centre of the earth is given by $\dfrac{k}{x^2}$, directed towards the centre. Prove that the rocket will escape from the earth provided $U^2 \geq 2gR$, where g is the acceleration due to gravity at earth's surface and R is the earth's radius. Further, if $U^2 = 2gR$, show that the time to achieve the height R above the earth's surface is approximately equal to $0.273 \sqrt{R}$, given $g = 10$ m.s^{-2}.

16. A body of mass m is released from a height h above the ground and it experiences a resistive force R given by $R = 0.1\, mv^2$, where v is the velocity achieved by the body at time t.

    If the object falls from rest under gravity ($g = 10\, m.s^{-2}$)

    Find: (i) the terminal velocity U (i.e. velocity as $t \to \infty$).

    (ii) the height h if the velocity is 0.5U just before the body strikes the ground.

17. A ball of mass, m, is descending vertically in a tank of fluid (under constant gravity). The resistive force is kv per unit mass, where v is the speed and k, a constant.

    (i) Draw a motion diagram at time t and write down the equation of motion using $F = m \cdot \dfrac{dv}{dt}$

    (ii) Write down an expression for time t taken by the ball to acquire the velocity v from rest and hence show that:

    $$v = \dfrac{g}{k}(1 - e^{-kt})$$

    (iii) Find the terminal velocity v_T. If $g = 10$ and $k = 0.2$, draw the graph of v against t.

18. A particle P of unit mass is projected from a point O with velocity U at an angle θ to the horizontal. The particle moves under gravity and each component of its velocity experiences a resistance k times the magnitude of the component. By considering the rectangular axes Ox and Oy and the particle has components v_x and v_y of the velocity v at time t:

    (a) Draw a diagram of the motion of P

    (b) Write down the equations of motion in the form:

    $$\dfrac{d}{dt}(v_x) = \ldots \quad \text{and} \quad \dfrac{d}{dt}(v_y) = \ldots$$

    (c) Prove that $v_x = U\cos\theta\, e^{-kt}$ and $v_y = \dfrac{1}{k}(g + kU\sin\theta)e^{-kt} - \dfrac{g}{k}$

    (d) Prove: $x = \dfrac{U}{k}\cos\theta(1 - e^{-kt})$

    $$y = \dfrac{(kU\sin\theta + g)}{k^2} \cdot (1 - e^{-kt}) - \dfrac{gt}{k}.$$

19. A projectile is fired vertically upwards from the earth's surface with velocity U m/s. The retardation due to gravity is given by the law $\frac{k}{x^2}$ where x is the distance of the projectile from the centre of the earth, and k is a constant. The acceleration due to gravity on the earth's surface is g. The earth's radius is R.

    Neglecting the air resistance, show that if $U^2 = gR$, then the projectile reaches the height R above the earth's surface. Show further that the time for this journey is

    $$\left[\frac{\pi}{2} + 1\right]\sqrt{\frac{R}{g}} .$$

20. An object of mass m is thrown vertically upwards in a medium with a resistance $R = \frac{mv}{k}$, where v is the velocity of the object and k is a constant.

    Given $t = 0 = x$ and the initial velocity is $k(c - g)$, where c is a constant and g is the acceleration due to gravity, x is the distance travelled in time t.

    (a) Draw a neat sketch of the motion and the forces acting at a point P, distance x from the origin. Hence write down the equation of the motion.

    (b) Find the time taken by the object to reach the highest point H and find the height of H above the point of projection.

    (c) The object falls to its original position with the same law of resistance. Will the time of descent be the same as that of ascent? Give your reasons.

CHAPTER 9 CIRCULAR MOTION

9.1 Introduction

The study of circular motion is of great importance in science and engineering. The orbit of the earth around the sun, or the moon around the earth, can be considered circular for practical calculations. The safe speed on a circular section of a highway or railway track is governed by the laws of circular motion. We shall also study the problems related to circular motion, such as conical pendulum and banked tracks.

In solving the motion problems, we often require resolution of the forces in two perpendicular directions OX and OY. These directions need not always be the horizontal and the vertical. Study the following examples of two resolved parts of the force F.

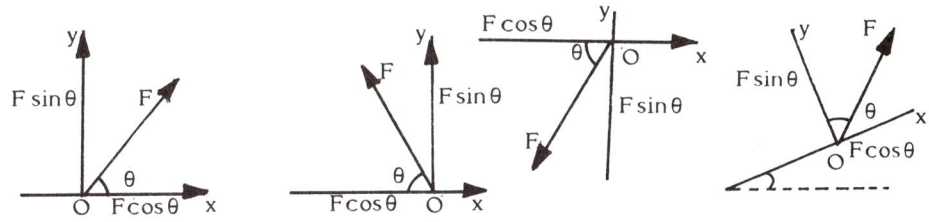

Fig. 1

We shall study the dynamical problems, in which Newton's laws have to be used, namely

(1) $F = ma$ ($m\ddot{x}$ or $m\ddot{y}$)

(2)   Force of action = Force of reaction

To solve any dynamical problem,

1. Resolve all the forces acting on the system in two perpendicular directions.
2. Then using $F = m\ddot{x}$ and $F = m\ddot{y}$:
   $m\ddot{x} = \Sigma X - \Sigma Fx$ and $m\ddot{y} = \Sigma Y - \Sigma Fy$
3. Substitute known values in (2) and solve for the unknown (velocity, force etc.)

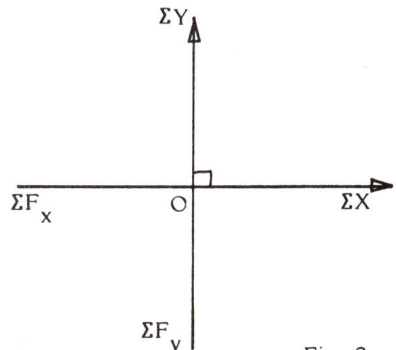

Fig. 2

9.2 Angular Velocity: Period

For a point moving in a straight line, its velocity is defined as the rate of change of its displacement.

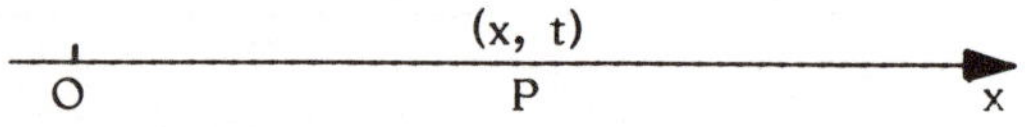

Fig. 3

$v = \dfrac{dx}{dt}$ in m/s where $x = f(t)$

Linear acceleration of a particle is given by $a = \dfrac{d^2x}{dt^2}$ in $m.s^{-2}$.

When a point moves on a curve, we talk about its angular velocity, i.e. the rate of change of its angular displacement, as defined below.

ANGULAR VELOCITY of a point about a given point

Let O be the given point, and OX a line through O of fixed direction.
Suppose P moves in the plane containing OX and $\angle POX = \theta$ at any time t.
The anticlockwise rotation is considered positive and the clockwise rotation negative.
The angular velocity ω (omega) of the moving point P about O is defined as the rate of change of θ, i.e.

$$\omega = \dot{\theta} = \dfrac{d\theta}{dt}$$

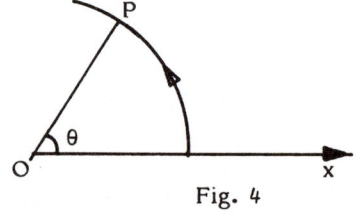

Fig. 4

The unit of angular velocity is the radian/s and is abbreviated as rad/s. Angular velocity is a vector and when the direction is not significant we speak of angular speed. It must be remembered that as defined above ω is a variable, i.e. a function of t. In most of our applications in circular motion, ω is a constant, i.e. a uniform angular velocity. In a later section, we shall talk about the angular acceleration of a point, about a given point.

EXAMPLE: (1)

A point P moves on a circle with uniform angular velocity of $\frac{\pi}{3}$ rad/s. Show the positions of P for t = 0, 1, 2, 3, 4, 5, 6. What is the time taken by the point P to describe the circle once completely?

SOLUTION: $\frac{\pi}{3} = 60°$.

We have:

t	0	1	2	3	4	5	6
θ	0	$\frac{\pi}{3}$	$\frac{2\pi}{3}$	π	$\frac{4\pi}{3}$	$\frac{5\pi}{3}$	2π

Time to describe the circle once completely is 6 s.

$$T = \frac{\text{Angular displacement}}{\text{Angular speed}} = \frac{2\pi}{\pi/3} = 6 \text{ s}$$

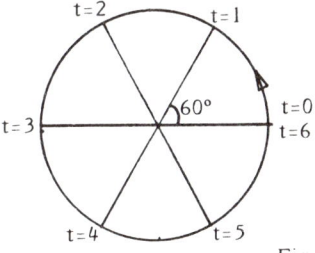

Fig. 5

9.3 Circular Motion: Tangential Velocity

Suppose a particle moves in a circle of radius r (anticlockwise) and sweeps out angle θ in time t.

Let it describe a small arc PQ in time Δt.

arc PQ = r × Δθ

Then v, the tangential velocity at P is given by:

$$v = \frac{d}{dt}(\text{arc PQ}) = \frac{d}{dt}(r \cdot \Delta\theta) = r\frac{d\theta}{dt} \text{ as } \Delta t \to 0$$

Now the angular velocity is $\omega = \frac{d\theta}{dt}$, hence:

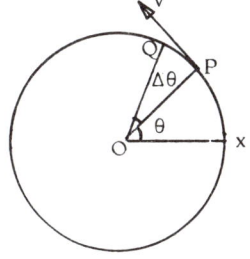

Fig. 6

$$\boxed{v = r\omega} \qquad \ldots (1)$$

The angular velocity ω is usually defined in radians per second, but if the radius of the orbit is extremely large as in planetary motion, ω may be defined in radians per hour or a day or even a year.

It should be remembered that ω is a variable in formula (1), but most of our work deals with the constant angular velocity and hence constant tangential velocity. In that case, at time t,

θ = angular velocity × time

$$\boxed{\theta = \omega t} \qquad \ldots (2)$$

It is usual to describe ω as revolutions per second or minute or hour etc.

EXAMPLE: (2) Convert the angular velocity $\omega = 50$ revolutions per second to radians per second.

SOLUTION: Since 1 rev = 2π radians

$\omega = 50$ rps = $50 \times 2\pi = 100\pi$ rad/s

EXAMPLE: (3) A satellite moves in a circular orbit with 20 revolutions per day. Describe ω in rad/s.

SOLUTION: $\omega = 20$ rpd = $\dfrac{20 \times 2\pi}{24}$ radians per hour

$= \dfrac{5\pi}{3 \times 60}$ rad/min

$= \dfrac{\pi}{36 \times 60}$ rad/s

$= \dfrac{\pi}{2160}$ rad/s

EXAMPLE: (4) A wheel of radius 2 m revolves at 1200 rounds per minute. Find:
(a) its angular velocity
(b) the tangential velocity of a point on the wheel.

SOLUTION: (a) $\omega = 1200$ rpm = $\dfrac{1200 \times 2\pi}{60}$ rad/s = 40π rad/s.

(b) $v = r\omega = 2 \times 40\pi = 80\pi = 251$ m/s.

THE PERIOD:

The period T of a circular motion with constant angular velocity ω is defined to be the time for one revolution.

$\therefore T = \dfrac{\text{angular displacement in one revolution}}{\text{angular velocity}}$

i.e. $\boxed{T = \dfrac{2\pi}{\omega}}$

EXAMPLE: (5) An artificial satellite travels in a circular orbit of radius 9000 km. If the period is 90 minutes, find the angular and the tangential velocity in km/h.

SOLUTION:

$T = \dfrac{2\pi}{\omega}$, given $T = 90$ min = 1.5 h

(a) $\omega = \dfrac{2\pi}{T} = \dfrac{2\pi}{1.5}$ rad/h = 4.19 rad/h

(b) $v = r \times \omega = 9000 \times 4.19 = 37900$ km/h

Exercise 9A

1. A particle on a disc rotating with a uniform angular speed of 4 revolutions per second is 0.2 m from the centre of the disc. Find:
   (a) the tangential speed v of the particle
   (b) the angle through which it rotates in 0.4 s.

2. A car travels halfway around a circular track in 12 s. What is the angular speed of the car? If the radius of the track is 100 m, find the velocity of the car in km/h, to the nearest km/h.

3. A motor shaft has a speed of 240 revolutions per minute. Find its angular speed in rad/s.

4. Find the average angular speed in rad/s of the earth's
   (a) rotation about its axis. (Hint: period is 24 h)
   (b) revolution about the sun. (Assuming a circular orbit and a period of 1 year = 365.25 days)

5. Find the tangential speed of the earth at the equator due to its rotation about its axis, given that the radius of the equatorial circle is 6440 km.
   [Use exercise 4(a)]

6. Find the tangential speed of the earth due to its revolution about the sun, given that the radius of the earth's orbit around the sun is 1.5×10^8 km.
   [Hint: use exercise 4(b)]

7. What is the angular speed of the particle in a circular path of radius 5 m and a tangential velocity of 100 km/h?

8. A belt is wrapped around a pulley that is 0.4 m in diameter. If the pulley rotates at 240 revolutions per minute, what is the linear velocity in m/s of the belt?

9. An aeroplane propeller whose blades are 1.5 m long is rotating at 2400 revolutions per minute.
   (a) Express the angular speed in rad/s
   (b) Find the angular displacement in 4 s
   (c) Find the linear speed of a point on the end of a blade.

10. An artificial satellite travels in a circular orbit of radius 10000 km. If the period is 2 h, find the angular speed in rad/h and the tangential speed in km/h of the satellite.

11. The average distance of the moon from the centre of the earth is 3.85×10^5 km and the period of the moon's revolution about the earth is 27.3 days. Find the angular speed in rad/h and the linear speed of the moon in km/h.

9.4 Acceleration of a Particle Rotating in a Circle

The diagram shows a particle P moving anticlockwise on a circle.

At time t, P is (x, y)

$\angle POX = \theta$

ω = angular velocity (constant)

v = tangential velocity

$\omega = \dfrac{d\theta}{dt}$ = a constant, so $\dfrac{d\omega}{dt} = 0$

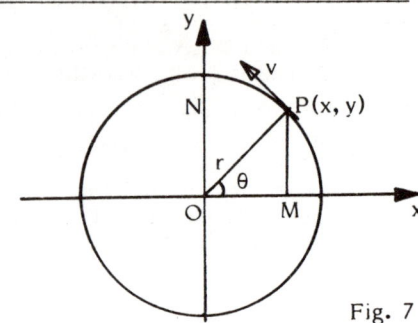

Fig. 7

The horizontal component	The vertical component
$x = r\cos\theta$	$y = r\sin\theta$
The horizontal velocity	The vertical velocity
$\dfrac{dx}{dt} = -r\sin\theta \dfrac{d\theta}{dt} = -r\omega\sin\theta$	$\dfrac{dy}{dt} = r\cos\theta \dfrac{d\theta}{dt} = r\omega\cos\theta$
The horizontal acceleration	The vertical acceleration
$\dfrac{d^2x}{dt^2} = -r\omega\cos\theta \cdot \dfrac{d\theta}{dt} = -r\omega^2\cos\theta$	$\dfrac{d^2y}{dt^2} = -r\omega\sin\theta \cdot \dfrac{d\theta}{dt} = -r\omega^2\sin\theta$
$\therefore \ddot{x} = -r\omega^2\cos\theta$	$\ddot{y} = -r\omega^2\sin\theta$

The resultant acceleration

$$a = \sqrt{\ddot{x}^2 + \ddot{y}^2}$$
$$= \sqrt{(-r\omega^2\cos\theta)^2 + (-r\omega^2\sin\theta)^2}$$
$$= r\omega^2 \sqrt{\cos^2\theta + \sin^2\theta}$$
$$= r\omega^2$$

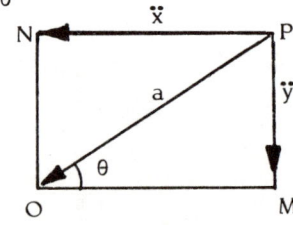

Fig. 8

The direction is towards the centre O, along the radius PO of the circle.

Thus the acceleration of a point moving in a circle with angular velocity ω is

$$a = r\omega^2$$

But $v = r\omega$, so $a = r\omega^2 = r \cdot \dfrac{v^2}{r^2} = \dfrac{v^2}{r}$

$$\therefore \boxed{a = r\omega^2 = \dfrac{v^2}{r}}$$

At a later stage, we shall derive the expression for acceleration when ω is a variable.

9.5 Uniform Circular Motion

As proved before, the acceleration of a particle moving on a circle is given by:

$$a = \frac{v^2}{r} \quad \text{or} \quad a = r\omega^2,$$

directed along the radius, towards the centre.

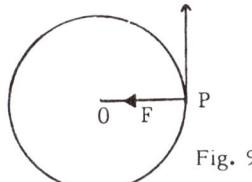

Fig. 9

By Newton's first two laws, there must be a resultant force that causes this motion and its magnitude must be given by

$$\boxed{F = ma = \frac{mv^2}{r}} \quad \text{or} \quad \boxed{F = mr\omega^2}$$

where m is the mass of the particle and this force must act along the radius directed towards the centre. This force is called the CENTRIPETAL FORCE (centre seeking force).

EXAMPLE: (6)

Find the tension in the string when a stone of mass 5 kg is rotating at 50 rpm, the stone is tied at one end of the string and the other end is fixed at point O. The length of the string is 2m. (rpm = revolutions per minute)

SOLUTION:

$\omega = 50 \text{ rpm} = \frac{50 \times 2\pi}{60}$ rad/s, m = 5 kg, r = 2 m

$\therefore \omega = \frac{5\pi}{3}$ rad/s.

The only force acting on the particle is the tension T along the string, hence:

$T = \text{centripetal force} = mr\omega^2$
$\quad = 5 \times 2 \times 25\pi^2/9$
$\quad = 274 \text{ N}$

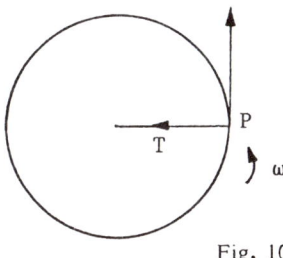

Fig. 10

EXAMPLE: (7)

A string of length 2 m is attached at one end to a fixed point O on a horizontal table, while the other end is attached to a heavy particle of mass m kg. Find the speed v in m/s of the rotation of the particle, given that the tension in the string is n times the weight of the particle.

SOLUTION:

The reaction N = mg is of no concern to us.

$\therefore$ Tension T = centripetal force

$\therefore \quad \frac{mv^2}{r} = n \times mg$ (given)

$\therefore \quad v = \sqrt{rng}$, r = 2

$\therefore \quad = \sqrt{2ng}$ m/s

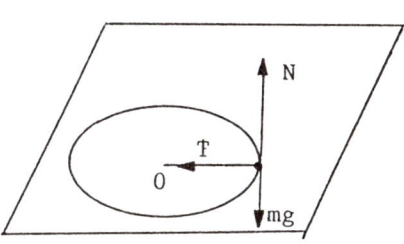

Fig. 11

Exercise 9B

(Take $g = 9.8$ m.s^{-2}, for the following problems)

1. A particle moves on a horizontal circle of radius 2 m with uniform linear speed of 10 m/s. Find the centripetal acceleration required for this motion.

2. A ball of mass 0.5 kg is rotated at the end of an inelastic string in a horizontal circle at 5 m/s. If the length of the string is 2 m, find the centripetal force exerted by the string on the ball.

3. Find the centripetal force on a car of mass 1500 kg travelling around a circular track of radius 75.0 m at a speed of 45.0 km/h.

4. A flywheel of radius 0.4 m rotates with the uniform angular speed of 40π rad/s. Find the centripetal acceleration of a point on the rim of the wheel.

5. The earth rotates on its axis at an angular speed of 1 revolution per 24 h. Find:
   (a) the linear velocity in m/s of a point on the equator where the radius of the earth is 6400 km.
   (b) the centripetal acceleration of a point on the equator.

6. A curve of radius 250 m is planned in a highway. The expected legal limit is 90 km/h. Find the centripetal force of the road on the car of mass 1200 kg.

7. An earth's satellite at a distance of 36000 km above the earth's surface is called synchronous satellite because it and the earth have the same period. Find:
   (a) the angular speed of the satellite in rad/s and rad/h
   (b) the linear speed of the satellite in km/h if the radius of the earth is 6400 km
   (c) the centripetal force required to keep the satellite in the orbit if it has a mass of 1000 kg.

8. A communication satellite in a circular orbit at an altitude of 500 km above the earth's surface makes one revolution in 95 minutes. Given that the radius of the earth is 6400 km, find the centripetal acceleration of the satellite.

9.6 Conical Pendulum

A particle of mass m is attached to one end of a light inelastic string of length l, the other fixed at O.

The particle P moves in a horizontal circle, so that the string describes a cone whose vertical axis passes through the centre C of the circle.

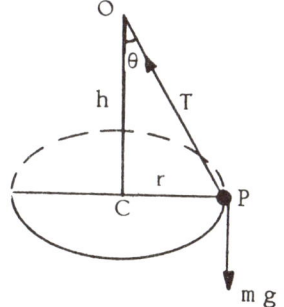

Fig. 12

Suppose that the particle moves with velocity v, then the resultant force is along PC and resolving the forces as shown, we now have

$$T\sin\theta = \text{centripetal force} = \frac{mv^2}{r} \quad \ldots (1)$$

and $\quad T\cos\theta = mg \quad \ldots (2)$

Divide (1) and (2): $\tan\theta = \dfrac{v^2}{rg} \quad \ldots (3)$

Now $\tan\theta = \dfrac{r}{h}$ and $v = r\omega$

$\therefore \quad \dfrac{r^2\omega^2}{rg} = \dfrac{r}{h}$

$\therefore \quad \omega = \sqrt{\dfrac{g}{h}} \quad \ldots (4)$

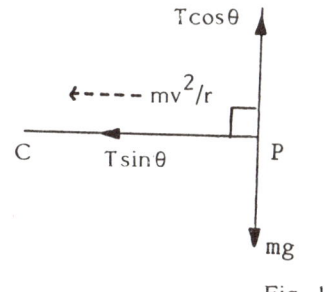

Fig. 13

Hence the period $T = \dfrac{2\pi}{\omega} = 2\pi\sqrt{\dfrac{h}{g}} \quad \ldots (5)$

The period is independent of the mass m and depends only on h, the vertical distance of the circle of rotation below the point of suspension O.

Note that $\omega = \sqrt{\dfrac{g}{h}}$ depends only on h.

SUMMARY (CONICAL PENDULUM)

1. $\tan\theta = \dfrac{v^2}{rg}$
2. $v^2 = rg\tan\theta$
3. $T = 2\pi\sqrt{\dfrac{h}{g}}$
4. $\omega = \sqrt{\dfrac{g}{h}}$

EXAMPLE: (8)

A disc of radius 2 m rotates in a horizontal circle about a vertical axis AB. A light string PQ of length 1 m tied at the rim of the disc at P, and carries a mass of 2 kg at Q. The disc rotates uniformly such that PQ is inclined at an angle of 45° to the vertical. Find:

(a) the speed of the mass at Q
(b) the tension in the string. (g = 9.8 m.s^{-2})

SOLUTION:

The forces acting at Q are:

Tension T in the string
Weight m acting vertically downwards
Resolving at Q along the horizontal and the vertical directions:

$T\cos\theta = mg$ ... (1)

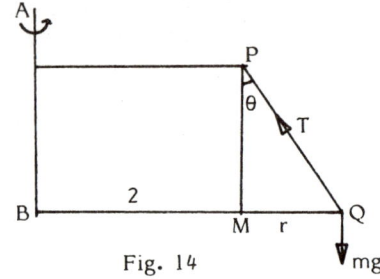
Fig. 14

The unbalanced component must supply the necessary centripetal force $\frac{mv^2}{r}$ for the circular motion of the mass at Q, where v is the tangential speed of Q and
r = BQ = 2 + 1 . sin θ

∴ $T\sin\theta = \frac{mv^2}{r}$ ... (2)

Divide (2) by (1): then

$\tan\theta = \frac{v^2}{gr}$

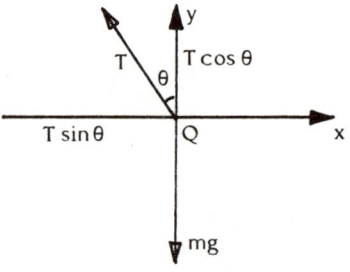
Fig. 15

Given θ = 45°, r = 2 + sin 45°,   g = 9.8

v^2 = gr tan θ = 9.8 x (2 + sin 45°) tan 45°

(a) ∴ v = 5.15 m/s

(b) Using $T\cos\theta = mg$
    T = mg sec θ = 2 x 9.8 x sec 45° = 27.7 N

Exercise 9C

(Take g = 9.8 m.s^{-2}, for the following problems)

1. A mass of 3 kg is attached to one end of a light inelastic string of length 1 m, the other end of which is tied to a fixed point O. If the mass is rotated in a horizontal circle and the string makes an angle of 25° with the downward direction of the vertical, find
   (a) the speed v of the mass in m/s
   (b) the tension T of the string in newtons.

2. A mass of 0.5 kg is suspended from a fixed point O by means of a light rod of length 1 m. The mass is rotated in a horizontal circle and the rod makes an angle of 30° with the downward direction of the vertical. Find:
   (a) the linear velocity of the mass
   (b) the period
   (c) the tension in the rod.

3. A horizontal disc of radius 1 m is free to rotate about a vertical axis AB as shown in the figure. PQ is a light rod of length 1.2 m pivoted to the rim of the disc at P and carrying a mass of 3 kg at Q. The disc is rotated uniformly, so that PQ is inclined at an angle 30° to the vertical. Calculate:
   (a) the speed of the mass at Q in m/s
   (b) the tension in the rod.

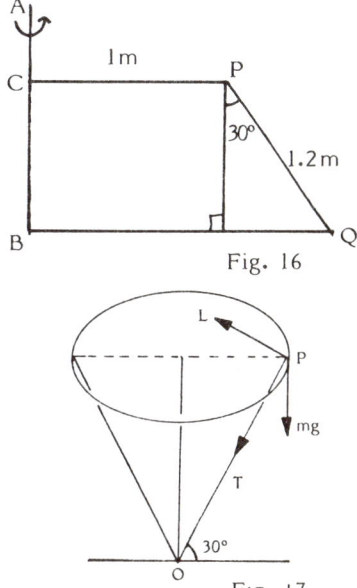

Fig. 16

Fig. 17

4. A model plane of mass 5 kg attached to the end of an inelastic wire of length 20 m flies in a horizontal circle of elevation 30°, while the other end of the wire is held fixed. If the lift (force) L acts at right angles to the wire and L is twice the weight of the plane, find:
   (a) the speed of the plane in m/s
   (b) the tension in the wire in newtons.

5. A train is moving around a circular track of radius 800 m at a uniform speed of 80 km/h. A light inelastic wire is attached to the roof of the carriage and has a small package attached at the other end. Find the angle of inclination of the wire with the vertical. (Hint: The radius of the circle described by the package is approximately the same as that of the circular track.)

9.7 Banked Tracks

The tendency of a vehicle to skid outwards (along the tangential path) as it rounds the curve on a horizontal roadway is opposed by the friction between the road and the tyres (see Fig. 18). The friction is the only force providing the centripetal acceleration as the vehicle travels along the circular path. This frictional force is never sufficient to keep the vehicle in the circular path. If the road is suitably banked, the upward thrust of the road on the vehicle then provides the required centripetal force. Banking means the outer edge is raised above the level of the inner edge of the road (see Fig. 19).

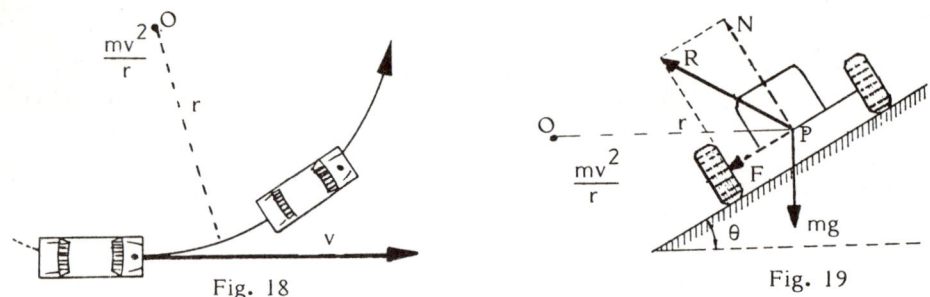

Fig. 18   Fig. 19

We shall now show that it is possible to choose a banking angle θ such that the lateral friction force is zero.

In Fig. 19, R is the reaction of the road on the vehicle of mass m, as it travels along the curve of radius r at a speed v. We resolve R into two components:

(i) the friction force F (side thrust), parallel to the slope
(ii) force N, normal to the road surface.

The resulting acceleration of the vehicle has a magnitude $\frac{v^2}{r}$ and is directed towards O, the centre of the circular path.

By resolving the forces at P, along and perpendicular to the slope, we have:

force along the slope = mass × acceleration along the slope.

$$F + mg\sin\theta = \frac{mv^2}{r}\cos\theta$$

$$\therefore F = \frac{mv^2}{r}\cos\theta - mg\sin\theta$$

Resolving along the perpendicular to the slope, $N = mg\cos\theta - \frac{mv^2}{r}\sin\theta$.

By choosing θ such that the side thrust F is zero, we eliminate the tendency of the vehicle to skid either up or down the slope.

The proper angle of banking for speed v is obtained from

$$\frac{mv^2}{r}\cos\theta - mg\sin\theta = 0 \qquad \text{i.e.} \qquad \boxed{\tan\theta = \frac{v^2}{gr}}$$

The frictional force acting parallel to the slope is called the lateral thrust. For a railway track the use of the correct banking angle θ (obtained by raising the outer rail above the inner one) ensures that there is no lateral thrust between the rail and the wheel flanges, thus reducing the wear on both (rails and wheels). Even when F = 0, the friction force between the tyres and the road (acting parallel to the direction of motion) provides the tractive force on the vehicle.

WORKED EXAMPLES ON BANKED TRACKS

EXAMPLE: (9)

A section of a road is in the form of an arc of a circle of radius 1000 m. Find the banking angle θ if the road is designed to carry traffic at a speed of 25 m/s. ($g = 9.8$ m.s^{-2})

SOLUTION:

The forces on the vehicle are its weight mg and the reaction N (exerted by the road) at right angles to OP. The acceleration of the vehicle is $\frac{v^2}{r}$, horizontally towards the centre of the curve.

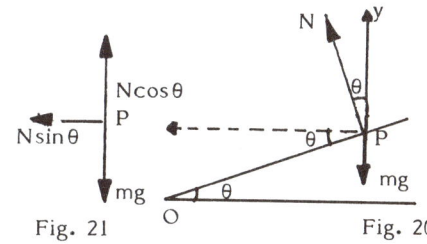

Fig. 21   Fig. 20

Resolving along OP:

$mg \sin\theta = \frac{mv^2}{r} \cos\theta$

$\therefore \tan\theta = \frac{v^2}{rg}$ ... (1)

Substituting $v = 25$ m/s, $g = 9.8$ m.s^{-2}, $r = 1000$ m,

$\tan\theta = \frac{625}{1000 \times 9.8}$ gives $\theta = 3.65°$

Alternatively we can resolve along the horizontal PX and the vertical PY, then:

$N \sin\theta = \frac{mv^2}{r}$ and $N \cos\theta = mg$, hence $\tan\theta = \frac{v^2}{rg}$

EXAMPLE: (10)

A train is travelling around a horizontal curve with uniform speed of 60 km/h. The radius of the curve is 400 m. The rails are 1.5 m apart. Find the elevation h of the outer above the inner rail if there is no lateral force on the rails.

SOLUTION:

Using the same explanation as in the previous example, resolving along AB, we have:

$mg \sin\theta = \frac{mv^2}{r} \cos\theta$, hence $\tan\theta = \frac{v^2}{rg}$

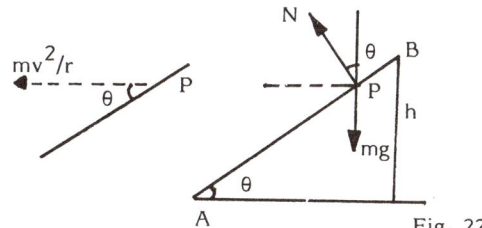

Fig. 22

Now $v = 60$ km/h $= \frac{50}{3}$ m/s, $r = 400$ m, $g = 9.8$ m.s^{-2}, we find $\theta = 4.05°$

Then $h = AB \sin\theta = 1.5 \sin 4.05° = 0.106$ m

Exercise 9D

1. A section of the highway is in the form of an arc of a circle of radius 250 m. Assuming the average speed of cars on the highway to be 60 km/h, find the angle at which the highway should be banked.   ($g = 9.8$ m.s^{-2})

2. A section of the road is in the form of an arc of a circle of radius r. The road is banked at an angle θ, so that a car of mass m travelling at speed v has no tendency to side slip.
   (a) Show that the resultant force on the car is given by $mg\tan\theta$.
   (b) Show that $v^2 = rg\tan\theta$ and hence calculate the banking angle θ, given $v = 80$ km/h, $g = 9.8$ m.s^{-2} and $r = 500$ m. Give your answer in degrees with one decimal place.   ($g = 9.8$ m.s^{-2})

3. A car is travelling around a circular section of the highway which is banked at an angle of 12°. The radius of the curve is 200 m. Find the maximum safe velocity v of the car, so that it does not slip. Express your answer to the nearest km/h.   ($g = 9.8$ m.s^{-2})

4. A train is travelling around a circular curve of radius 200 m with the proper safe speed of 50 km/h. The rails are 1 m apart. Find the banking angle θ of the curve and the elevation h of the outer rail above the inner rail, if there is no side force on the rails.   ($g = 9.8$ m.s^{-2})

5. A cycling track is in the form of a circle of radius 100 m. The proper safe speed for this track is 40 km/h. Find the banking angle to 2 decimal places.   ($g = 9.8$ m.s^{-2})

6. A bobsled track has a hairpin curve of radius 16 m. The curve is banked at 72°. What is the maximum safe speed in km/h for the curve, assuming no frictional forces?   ($g = 9.8$ m.s^{-2})

9.8 Components of Acceleration (Variable Angular Velocity)

Suppose a particle P moves on a circle $x^2 + y^2 = r^2$ and at time t let:
$\angle POX = \theta$, $\omega = d\theta/dt$, $P(x, y)$
$\therefore x = r\cos\theta$ and $y = r\sin\theta$
Differentiating with respect to time t:
$\dot{x} = -r\sin\theta \frac{d\theta}{dt} = -r\omega\sin\theta$, $\dot{y} = r\cos\theta \frac{d\theta}{dt} = r\omega\cos\theta$

$\therefore$ velocity $v = \sqrt{\dot{x}^2 + \dot{y}^2} = r\omega$ ... (1)

$\ddot{x} = -r\omega\cos\theta \frac{d\theta}{dt} - r\sin\theta \cdot \frac{d\omega}{dt} = -r\omega^2\cos\theta - r\dot{\omega}\sin\theta$ ... (2)

$\ddot{y} = -r\omega\sin\theta \frac{d\theta}{dt} + r\cos\theta \cdot \frac{d\omega}{dt} = -r\omega^2\sin\theta + r\dot{\omega}\cos\theta$ ... (3)

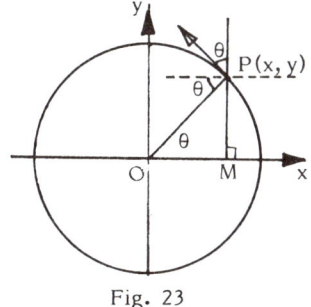

Fig. 23

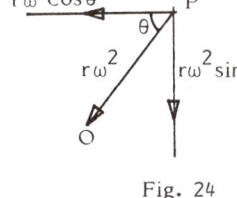

Fig. 24

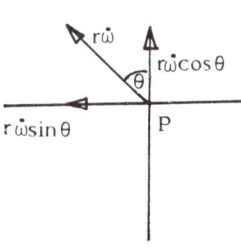

Fig. 25

From equations (2) and (3) and the diagrams showing the resolved parts of two accelerations $r\omega^2$ and $r\dot{\omega}$, we infer that the acceleration of a point moving on a circle has two components:

The tangential component $= r\dot{\omega}$
The normal component $= r\omega^2$ or $\frac{v^2}{r}$ (towards the centre)

EXAMPLE: (11) A point P moves on a circle $x^2 + y^2 = 16$ with uniform angular velocity of 2 rad/s. A is the point (2,0). If $\angle POA = \theta$, $\angle PAX = \phi$ find the angular speed of P about A when $\theta = 0$ and when $\theta = \frac{\pi}{2}$.

SOLUTION: Noting that $\angle OPA = \phi - \theta$,
$\angle PAO = 180° - \phi$ using the sine rule in $\triangle POA$:
$\frac{\sin(\phi - \theta)}{2} = \frac{\sin(180° - \phi)}{4}$
$\therefore 2\sin(\phi - \theta) = \sin\phi$
$\therefore$ Differentiating with respect to time t:
$2\cos(\phi - \theta) \cdot (\dot{\phi} - \dot{\theta}) = (\cos\phi)\dot{\phi}$ ... (1)
Angular velocity of P about A is $\dot{\phi}$.

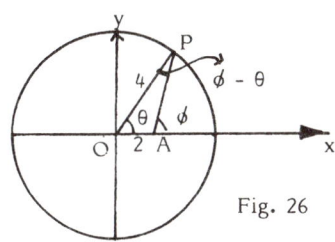

Fig. 26

(cont. on the next page)

When $\theta = 0$, $\phi = 0$, $\dot{\theta} = 2$, then from (1): using $\cos 0 = 1$, $2(\dot\phi - 2) = \dot\phi$ or $\dot\phi = 4$ rad/s.

Again, when $\theta = \frac{\pi}{2}$, ϕ is obtuse, P is at B(0,4), $\tan\phi = -\frac{4}{2} = -2$.

Using equation (2):

$2\cos(\phi - 90°)(\dot\phi - 2) = \dot\phi \cos\phi$

Now $\cos(\phi - 90°) = \sin\phi$, hence dividing by $\cos\phi$,

$2\tan\phi(\dot\phi - 2) = \dot\phi$

Put $\tan\phi = -2$ and solve for $\dot\phi$:

∴ $\dot\phi = 1.6$ rad/s

∴ Angular velocity of P about A when $\theta = \frac{\pi}{2}$ is 1.6 rad/s.

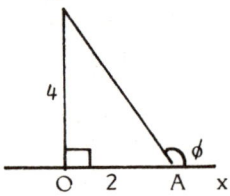

Fig. 27

EXAMPLE: (12)

A car is travelling at 60 km/h and its wheel has a radius of 0.25 m. Find the speed u m/s of the highest point of the wheel.

SOLUTION:

$v = 60$ km h^{-1} = 16.7 m.s^{-1}

The angular velocity of a point on the rim about the centre is given by
$\omega = v/r = 16.7/0.25 = 66.7$ rad h^{-1}

The situation at time t is shown in the diagram with P(x,y) on the circle. Assuming P to be at O at t = 0, the distance travelled by the wheel is OB and this is equal to the arc BP, i.e. OB = $r\theta$.

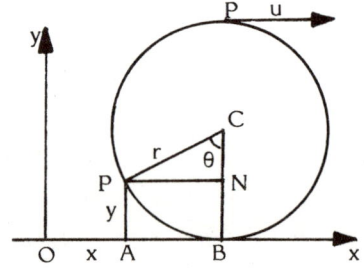

Fig. 28

∴ $x = OB - AB = r\theta - r\sin\theta$, $y = BC - NC = r - r\cos\theta$

∴ $\dot{x} = r(\dot\theta - \dot\theta\cos\theta) = r\omega(1 - \cos\theta)$, $\dot{y} = r\omega\sin\theta$

∴ velocity u of P at any time t is given by:

$$u^2 = \dot{x}^2 + \dot{y}^2 = r^2\omega^2[(1 - \cos\theta)^2 + \sin^2\theta] = 2r^2\omega^2(1 - \cos\theta)$$

Now $1 - \cos\theta = 2\sin^2\frac{\theta}{2}$

∴ $u = 2r\omega\sin\frac{\theta}{2}$

The direction of the velocity of P if desired is given by $\tan\phi = \frac{\dot{y}}{\dot{x}} = \frac{\sin\theta}{1-\cos\theta}$

Substituting for the velocity of the highest point, i.e. $\theta = \pi$, $\omega = 66.7$, $r = 0.25$, the required velocity $u = 2 \times 0.25 \times 66.7 \times \sin\frac{\pi}{2} = 33.4$ m/s.

Exercise 9E (ANGULAR VELOCITY)

1. A point is moving in a circle. Prove that its angular velocity about the centre of the circle is double its angular velocity about any fixed point on the circumference.

2. A point P is moving in a circle of centre O, with uniform angular velocity ω. N is the foot of the perpendicular to a fixed diameter of the circle. Show that the acceleration of N is given by $\omega^2 \cdot ON$ and is directed towards the centre.

3. A point P moves with uniform velocity u along Ox. A is a point on the line $y = b$, and PA = r. Show that the angular velocity of P about A is given by $\dfrac{bu}{r^2}$.

   [Hint: $X = PM = b\cot\theta$, $\dfrac{dX}{dt} = u$, $\dfrac{d\theta}{dt} = \omega$]

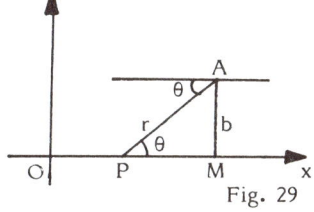
Fig. 29

4. A point P is moving (anti-clockwise) in a circle given by $x^2 + y^2 = a^2$, with uniform angular velocity ω. A is the point (r, 0), r > a. If ∠POX = θ, ∠PAX = φ,

   (a) prove that $r\sin\phi = a\sin(\phi - \theta)$

   (b) prove that the angular velocity of P about A is given by:
   $$\dfrac{d\phi}{dt} = \dfrac{a\omega\cos(\phi - \theta)}{a\cos(\phi - \theta) - r\cos\phi}$$

   Hence find the angular velocity of P about A, when P is at B(a, 0) and C(0, a).

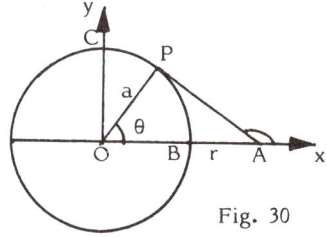
Fig. 30

5. A point P moves on the circle $x^2 + y^2 = 25$ with uniform angular velocity of 1 rad/s. A is the point (3, 0). If ∠POA = θ, find the angular speed of P about A when $\theta = 0$ and when $\theta = \dfrac{\pi}{2}$.

6. A car is travelling at 80 km/h and its wheel has a radius of 0.3 m. Find the speed of the highest point of the wheel.

7. A train is travelling at 60 km/h and a wheel has a radius of 0.4 m. Find the magnitude and direction of the velocity of a point 0.2 m above the rail.

9.9 Miscellaneous (Worked Examples on Circular Motion)

EXAMPLE: (13)

A 15 cm record rotates at an angular speed of 33 rev/min. Find

(a) its angular velocity in rad/s
(b) the speed of a point P on the rim of this record
(c) the acceleration (centripetal) of the point P.

SOLUTION:

(a) $\omega = 33$ rpm $= \frac{33 \times 2\pi}{60} = \frac{11\pi}{10}$ rad/s $= 3.46$ rad/s

(b) $v = r \times \omega = 0.15 \times 11\pi/10 = 0.518$ m/s

(c) $a = r\omega^2 = 0.15 \times \left(\frac{11\pi}{10}\right)^2 = 1.79$ m.s^{-2}

EXAMPLE: (14)

A particle of mass 5 g is rotating in a circular path of radius 1 m with a speed of 2 m/s. Find:

(a) the angular velocity, ω, in rad/s
(b) the centripetal acceleration, a, in m.s^{-2}
(c) the tension in the string, in newtons.

SOLUTION:

(a) $\omega = \frac{v}{r} = \frac{2}{1} = 2$ rad/s

(b) $a = r\omega^2 = 1 \times 2^2 = 4$ m.s^{-2}

(c) The tension T in the string supplies the centripetal force.

$\therefore \quad T = m \cdot r\omega^2 = 0.005 \times 1 \times 2^2 = 0.020$ N

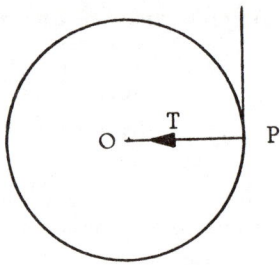

Fig. 31

EXAMPLE: (15)

The force of attraction between the earth and an artificial satellite in circular orbit around the earth is given by

$$F = \frac{GMm}{(R+h)^2}$$

where G is the gravitational constant, M is the mass of the earth, m is the mass of satellite, R is the radius of earth, and h = the height of the orbit above the earth's surface.

A 1000 kg satellite is circling the earth at 1000 km above the surface of the earth ($g = 10$ m.s^{-2} at the earth's surface). Find:

(a) the gravitational force acting on the satellite.
(b) the speed (constant) v of the satellite
(c) the period (given R = 6400 km)

SOLUTION:

Given R = radius of earth = 6400 km

h = satellite's height above the earth = 1000 km

g = 10 m.s^{-2} at the earth's surface

R + h = 7400 km

We have: $F = \dfrac{GMm}{(R+h)^2}$

For h = 0, F = mg

∴ $\dfrac{GMm}{R^2} = mg$

∴ $GM = gR^2$ ... (1)

When at height h, let $F = mg_h$

∴ $mg_h = \dfrac{GMm}{(R+h)^2}$

∴ $g_h = \dfrac{gR^2}{(R+h)^2}$

$= \dfrac{10 \times (6400 \times 10^3)^2}{(7400 \times 10^3)^2}$

$= 7.48$ m.s^{-2}

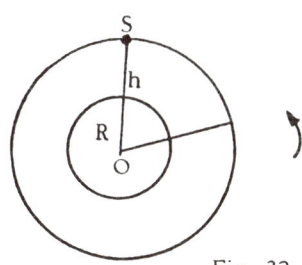

Fig. 32

∴ (a) The gravitational force on the satellite is

$F = m \times g_h = 1000 \times 7.48$

$= 7480$ N

(b) We must have

mg_h = centripetal force = $\dfrac{mv^2}{r}$

where r = R + h

∴ $v^2 = rg_h = (R+h) \cdot g_h$

$= 7400 \times 10^3 \times 7.48$

∴ $v = 7.44 \times 10^3$ m/s

(c) The period $T = \dfrac{2\pi}{\omega} = \dfrac{2\pi r}{v}$

∴ $T = \dfrac{2\pi \times 7400 \times 10^3}{7440}$

$= 6250$ s

$= 1.74$ h

EXAMPLE: (16)

A stone is rotated in a vertical circle of radius 2 m at a constant angular velocity of 30 rad/s, by a string about a pivot 4 m above horizontal ground. Consider the rotation to be clockwise. The string breaks at the highest point of the circle. Find the distance from the pivot, A, to the point B, where the stone hits the ground.
($g = 10$ m.s^{-2})

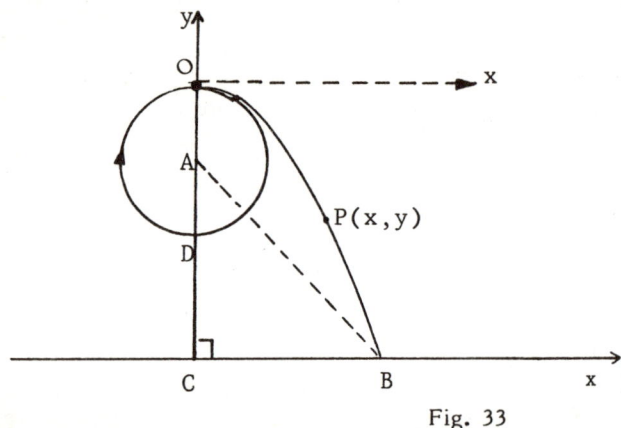

Fig. 33

SOLUTION:

Given: $\omega = 30$ rad/s

Radius = AO = AD = 2 m   OC = 2 + 2 + 2 = 6 m

CD = 2 m

The stone flies off horizontally at O, with velocity

$v = r \times \omega = 2 \times 30 = 60$ m/s.

Thereafter it travels freely under gravity, so describes a parabolic arc OPB
Equations of motion are

$$x = 60t, \quad y = -\tfrac{1}{2}gt^2 \quad \text{(Axes at O, as shown)}$$

At B, $y = -6$ and $g = 10$ m.s^{-2}

$\therefore \quad t^2 = 1.2 \quad \text{or} \quad t = \sqrt{1.2}$ s

Now substitute in $x = 60t$, $x = BC$

$\therefore \quad BC = 60 \times \sqrt{1.2}$

$AB^2 = AC^2 + BC^2 = 4^2 + 60^2 \times 1.2$

$\therefore \quad AB = 65.8$ m

Exercise 9F

1. A satellite moves in a circular orbit of radius 8000 km, making 12 revolutions per day. Find:
   (a) the velocity v in km/h.
   (b) the centripetal force acting on the satellite, if the mass of the satellite is 500 kg.

2. A flywheel of radius 1 m makes 500 revolutions per minute. Find:
   (a) the angular velocity, ω, in rad/s.
   (b) the tangential velocity, v, in m/s of a point on the rim.
   (c) the acceleration of a point on the rim.

3. An artificial satellite of the earth travels in a circular orbit of radius 36000 km. If the period is 12 hours, find the angular velocity, in rad/h, and the speed v in km/h.

4. Find the tension in the string when a stone of mass 10 kg is rotating at 60 rpm, the stone is tied at one end of the string and the other end is fixed at point O. The length of the string is 1 m. (rpm = revolutions per minute)

5. A string of length 1 m is attached at one end to a fixed point O on a table, while the other end is attached to a heavy particle of mass 2 kg. Find the speed v in m/s of the rotation of the particle, given that the tension in the string is 4 times the weight of the particle. ($g = 10$ m.s^{-2})

6. The force of attraction between the earth and its artificial satellite in circular orbit is given by $F = \dfrac{GMm}{x^2}$, where x is the distance of the satellite from the earth's centre, G is a constant, M is the earth's mass, m is the satellite's mass. A 500 kg satellite is circling the earth at 4000 km above the surface of the earth. If the radius of the earth is 6400 km, find:
   (a) the gravitational force acting on the satellite given $g = 10$ m.s^{-2} at the earth's surface
   (b) the velocity v in km/h of the satellite
   (c) the period in hours.

7. A mass of 10 kg is rotated in a horizontal circle of radius 0.25 m on the end of a string 2 m long. Find the greatest number of rev/min, if the string can just sustain a tensile force of 5000 N. ($g = 10$ m.s^{-2})

8. A smooth circular disc of radius 0.25 m rotates in a horizontal plane with angular velocity $\omega = 10$ rad/s about a vertical axis through the centre O. A particle of mass m is attached at P by light inelastic strings to points M and N on the ends of a diameter of the disc, such that MP = 0.4 m, NP = 0.3 m and both strings remain taut. Find the tension in the string NP, and the mass m if the tension in MP is 20 N.

9. A particle of mass m is attached to a fixed point O by a string of length 1 metre and by another string of the same length to a small ring of mass M which can slide on a smooth vertical wire through O. If m describes a horizontal circle with constant angular velocity ω, prove that its depth below O is
$$\left(\frac{m + 2M}{m\omega^2}\right)g$$

10. A particle of mass 5 kg is whirled around at the end of a string 1 m long. It describes a horizontal circle with 36 rev/min. Find the tension in the string and the angle of inclination of the string with the vertical. ($g = 10$ m.s^{-2})

11. The (water) drops shaken off the rim of a rotating umbrella meet the ground in a circle of radius r metres. The rim is a circle of diameter 1 m and is 1.5 m above the ground. It is rotating with an angular velocity of 4π rad/s. Find the radius r. ($g = 10$ m.s^{-2})

12. One end of a light inelastic string of length 1 m is attached to the rim of a horizontal disk of radius 2 m and the other end carries a mass of 5 kg. If the maximum tension in the string may not exceed 300 N, find the maximum angular velocity ω in rad/s and the corresponding inclination of the string to the vertical. ($g = 10$ m.s^{-2})

13. A train travelling at 80 km/h is rounding a curve of radius 500 m. Determine the banking angle, θ, of the track with the horizontal, so that the sideways thrust on the flanges of the wheels would not derail the train. ($g = 10$ m.s^{-2})

14. A stone is rotated with an angular velocity of 5 rad/s in a vertical circle of radius 4 m and centre 10 m above the ground. It breaks off the string when it makes an angle of 30° with the vertical in the positive quadrant. If the motion is clockwise, find the distance from the centre to the point where the stone hits the ground.

15. A truck is travelling around a section of a circular track which is banked at an angle of 16°, and has radius 80 m. Find the velocity, so that the truck does not slip. ($g = 10$ m.s^{-2})

16. Two particles are connected by a string passing through a hole in a smooth table, one particle being on the table, the other underneath. If the masses of both particles are equal, find the velocity v of the particle on the table moving on a circle of radius 2 m, so that the other remains at rest. ($g = 10$ m.s^{-2})

17. An object of mass 1 kg is attached to a string of length 8 m to a fixed point P. It is set rotating with velocity v in a horizontal circle of radius r. Given that the centre is 5 m vertically beneath P, find r and v (given $g = 10$ m.s^{-2})

18. The orbit of the earth around the sun can be assumed to be a circle of radius 1.5×10^{11} m described with uniform angular velocity ω radians per second. Given that 1 year = 365.25 days, find
    (a) ω, in radians per second
    (b) the earth's acceleration towards the sun in m.s^{-2}.

19. The moon makes a complete revolution of the earth in 27.3 days with a nearly circular orbit of radius 3.85×10^8 m. Find:
    (a) the acceleration of the moon towards the earth
    (b) the linear velocity, v m/s, of the moon.

20. A mass of 12 kg at C is connected by light rods to sleeves P and Q which revolve freely about the vertical axis PQ, such that $\angle P = 60°$ and $\angle Q = 30°$.
   (a) Given that PQ = 4 m, show that the radius of the circular path of rotation of C is $\sqrt{3}$ m.
   (b) Find the tensions in the rods PC and QC when the mass makes 120 revolutions per minute.

21. A satellite of mass m revolves in a circular orbit of radius r about a spherical planet of mass M and radius R. It is known that force of attraction between two bodies of masses m_1 and m_2 is given by $F = \dfrac{Gm_1 m_2}{x^2}$, where x is the distance between the centres of the bodies. Show that the period T of revolution of the satellite is given by $\dfrac{2\pi r}{R}\sqrt{\dfrac{r}{k}}$, where k is the force per unit mass at the planet's surface due to its own gravity.

22. A light inextensible string of length 3 metres is threaded through a smooth vertical ring which is free to turn. The string carries a particle at each end. One particle, P, of mass m is at rest at a distance of 1 metre below the ring, while the other particle B of mass M is rotating in a horizontal circle whose centre is P. Show that the velocity, v, of B in terms of m and M, is given by

   $\sqrt{\dfrac{(M+m)g}{M}}$

23. A satellite S is circling the earth at a height 35800 km above the earth's surface, with a period of 1 day. Calculate orbital speed of this satellite. (R = 6400 km, the radius of the earth). Give your answer in km/h.

24. A point P is moving in a circle with an angular velocity ω in an anti-clockwise direction. If the radius of the circle is r metres,
   (a) show that the speed of P is given by $r\omega$
   (b) M and N are the points of projection of P on the coordinate axes with O as the origin. Prove that both M and N execute simple harmonic motion as P rotates about O.

25. A massless rod of length L is hung from pivot A, attached to a rim of a horizontal circular disc of radius r.
   An object of mass m is attached at the other end B of the rod. AB makes an angle θ with the vertical when the disc rotates with constant angular velocity ω about the vertical axis through O.
   (a) Show that $BD = R = r + L\sin\theta$
   (b) Prove that $(r + L\sin\theta)\omega^2 = g\tan\theta$, where $g\ m.s^{-2}$ is the acceleration due to gravity.
   (c) Prove that the speed, v, of the object B is given by
   $v^2 = g\tan\theta\ (r + L\sin\theta)$
   (d) Find the speed of B when $\theta = 45°$, $g = 10\ m.s^{-2}$, $L = 1$ m, $r = 5$ m.

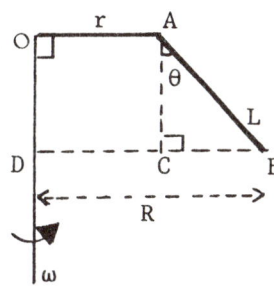

Fig. 34

Chapter 10 Harder 3 Unit Topics

10.1 Harder Trigonometry

We shall need the following formulas:

1. $\sin(A \pm B) = \sin A \cos B \pm \cos A \sin B$
2. $\cos(A \mp B) = \cos A \cos B \pm \sin A \sin B$
3. $\tan(A \pm B) = \dfrac{\tan A \pm \tan B}{1 \mp \tan A \tan B}$
4. $\sin A + \sin B = 2\sin\left(\dfrac{A+B}{2}\right)\cos\left(\dfrac{A-B}{2}\right)$
5. $\sin A - \sin B = 2\cos\left(\dfrac{A+B}{2}\right)\sin\left(\dfrac{A-B}{2}\right)$
6. $\cos A + \cos B = 2\cos\left(\dfrac{A+B}{2}\right)\cos\left(\dfrac{A-B}{2}\right)$
7. $\cos B - \cos A = 2\sin\left(\dfrac{A+B}{2}\right)\sin\left(\dfrac{A-B}{2}\right)$
8. $\sin(180° - A) = \sin A$
9. $\cos(180° - A) = -\cos A$
10. If $\sin x = \sin \alpha$, then $x = n\pi + (-1)^n \alpha$
11. If $\cos x = \cos \alpha$, then $x = 2n\pi \pm \alpha$
12. $\sin 2x = 2\sin x \cos x$
13. $\cos 2x = 2\cos^2 x - 1$
    $= 1 - 2\sin^2 x$
    $= \cos^2 x - \sin^2 x$

Worked Examples

1. Prove that: $\dfrac{\sin B + \sin C}{\sin B - \sin C} = \tan\left(\dfrac{B+C}{2}\right) \cot\left(\dfrac{B-C}{2}\right)$

Solution:

$$\text{L.H.S.} = \dfrac{2\sin\left(\dfrac{B+C}{2}\right)\cos\left(\dfrac{B-C}{2}\right)}{2\cos\left(\dfrac{B+C}{2}\right)\sin\left(\dfrac{B-C}{2}\right)}$$

$$= \tan\left(\dfrac{B+C}{2}\right)\cot\left(\dfrac{B-C}{2}\right)$$

$$= \text{R.H.S.}$$

2. If $A + B + C = 180°$, prove that:
$$\sin 2A + \sin 2B + \sin 2C = 4\sin A \sin B \sin C$$

Solution:
L.H.S. $= 2\sin(A + B)\cos(A - B) + 2\sin C \cos C$
Now $A + B + C = 180°$, so $\sin(A + B) = \sin(180° - C) = \sin C$
and $\cos C = \cos(180° - A - B) = -\cos(A + B)$
$\therefore$ L.H.S. $= 2\sin C \cdot \cos(A - B) - 2\sin C \cdot \cos(A + B)$
$= 2\sin C [\cos(A - B) - \cos(A + B)]$
$= 2\sin C (2\sin A \sin B)$
$= 4\sin A \sin B \sin C$

---

3. Show that $\cos^6\theta - \sin^6\theta = \cos 2\theta (1 - \frac{1}{4}\sin^2 2\theta)$

Solution:
Using $a^3 - b^3 = (a - b)(a^2 + ab + b^2)$, $a = \sin^2\theta$, $b = \cos^2\theta$
L.H.S. $= (\cos^2\theta - \sin^2\theta)(\cos^4\theta + \cos^2\theta \sin^2\theta + \sin^4\theta)$
Now $\cos^2\theta - \sin^2\theta = \cos 2\theta$
and $\cos^4\theta + \cos^2\theta \sin^2\theta + \sin^4\theta = (\cos^2\theta + \sin^2\theta)^2 - \cos^2\theta \sin^2\theta = 1 - \cos^2\theta \sin^2\theta$
$\therefore$ L.H.S. $= \cos 2\theta (1 - \cos^2\theta \sin^2\theta)$
Again, $\sin 2\theta = 2\sin\theta\cos\theta$, so $\sin^2\theta\cos^2\theta = \frac{1}{4}\sin^2 2\theta$
$\therefore$ L.H.S. $= \cos 2\theta (1 - \frac{1}{4}\sin^2 2\theta)$ = R.H.S.

---

4. (a) Solve the equation $\sin 2\theta = \cos 3\theta$, $0° \leqslant \theta \leqslant 360°$
   (b) Show that $\cos 3\theta = 4\cos^3\theta - 3\cos\theta$
   (c) Using the parts (a) and (b), show that $\sin 18° = \frac{\sqrt{5} - 1}{4}$

Solution:

(a) $\cos 3\theta = \sin 2\theta = \cos(90° - 2\theta)$
$\therefore 3\theta = 360° \cdot n \pm (90° - 2\theta)$
$\therefore 5\theta = 360° \cdot n + 90°$ ... (1)
or $\theta = 360° \cdot n - 90°$ ... (2)
For (1), $n = 0, 1, 2, 3, 4$ ($0 \leqslant 5\theta \leqslant 5 \cdot 360°$)
Dividing by 5,
$\theta = 72° \cdot n + 18°$, $n = 0, 1, 2, 3, 4$
$= (18°, 90°, 162°, 234°, 306°)$
From (2), $\theta = 270°$ for $n = 1$.
Hence the complete solution is:
$\theta = (18°, 90°, 162°, 234°, 270°, 306°)$

(b) We use:
$\cos(A + B) = \cos A \cos B - \sin A \sin B$
Put $A = \theta$, $B = 2\theta$, then:
$\cos 3\theta$
$= \cos\theta \cos 2\theta - \sin\theta \sin 2\theta$
$= \cos\theta(2\cos^2\theta - 1) - 2\sin\theta \cdot \sin\theta\cos\theta$
$= 2\cos^3\theta - \cos\theta - 2\cos\theta(1 - \cos^2\theta)$
$= 4\cos^3\theta - 3\cos\theta$

(cont)

(c) Using (b), the given equation becomes:
$4\cos^3\theta - 3\cos\theta = 2\sin\theta\cos\theta$
Now $\theta = 18°$ is a root of this equation, so $\cos\theta \neq 0$
and hence: $4\cos^2\theta - 3 = 2\sin\theta$
$\therefore 4(1 - \sin^2\theta) - 3 = 2\sin\theta$
Or $4\sin^2\theta + 2\sin\theta - 1 = 0$ which gives $\sin\theta = \dfrac{\pm\sqrt{5} - 1}{4}$
Since $\sin 18° > 0$, we have: $\sin 18° = \dfrac{\sqrt{5} - 1}{4}$
Note: We can evaluate $\cos 18°$ by using $\cos^2 18° + \sin^2 18° = 1$

---

5. (a) Using $\tan(A + B) = \dfrac{\tan A + \tan B}{1 - \tan A \tan B}$, prove that
$$\tan(x + y + z) = \dfrac{\tan x + \tan y + \tan z - \tan x \tan y \tan z}{1 - (\tan x \tan y + \tan y \tan z + \tan z \tan x)}$$

(b) Hence show that $\tan 3x = \dfrac{3t - t^3}{1 - 3t^2}$, where $t = \tan x$

(c) Show that $\tan(\dfrac{\pi}{12})$ is a root of the equation $t^3 - 3t^2 - 3t + 1 = 0$

(d) Solve the equation $t^3 - 3t^2 - 3t + 1 = 0$

Solution:
(a) Put $A = x$, $B = y + z$ in the formula $\tan(A + B) = \dfrac{\tan A + \tan B}{1 - \tan A \tan B}$

$\therefore \tan(x + y + z) = \dfrac{\tan x + \tan(y + z)}{1 - \tan x \tan(y + z)} = \dfrac{\tan x + \dfrac{\tan y + \tan z}{1 - \tan y \tan z}}{1 - \dfrac{\tan x(\tan y + \tan z)}{1 - \tan y \tan z}}$

This simplifies to:
$\tan(x + y + z) = \dfrac{\tan x + \tan y + \tan z - \tan x \tan y \tan z}{1 - (\tan x \cdot \tan y + \tan y \cdot \tan z + \tan z \cdot \tan x)}$

(b) Put $z = y = x$ in the result (a), then:
$\tan 3x = \dfrac{3\tan x - \tan^3 x}{1 - 3\tan^2 x} = \dfrac{3t - t^3}{1 - 3t^2}$, $t = \tan x$

(c) Put $x = \dfrac{\pi}{12}$, i.e. $3x = \dfrac{\pi}{4}$, then: $\tan(\dfrac{\pi}{4}) = \dfrac{3t - t^3}{1 - 3t^2}$

Now $\tan(\dfrac{\pi}{4}) = 1$, so this simplifies to: $t^3 - 3t^2 - 3t + 1 = 0$ ... (1)

Hence $t = \tan(\dfrac{\pi}{12})$ is a root of the equation (1).

(d) The constant term 1 suggests we try $t = \pm 1$ as the possible roots of (1).
$t = -1$ satisfies the equation, hence either by inspection or long division, we have:
$t^3 - 3t^2 - 3t + 1 = (t + 1)(t^2 - 4t + 1) = 0$
So, the roots are $t = -1$, $\dfrac{4 \pm \sqrt{12}}{2}$ i.e. -1, $2 \pm \sqrt{3}$. Observing that $0 < \tan(\dfrac{\pi}{12}) = \tan 15° < 1$, we have $\tan 15° = 2 - \sqrt{3}$.

Exercise 10A

For questions 1 to 5 prove that:

1. (a) $8\sin^2\theta\cos^2\theta = 1 - \cos 4\theta$, hence
   (b) $32\cos^2\theta\sin^4\theta = 2 - \cos 2\theta - 2\cos 4\theta + \cos 6\theta$

2. (a) $\cos^8\theta - \sin^8\theta = \cos 2\theta\,(1 - \tfrac{1}{2}\sin^2 2\theta)$
   (b) $\cos^6\theta + \sin^6\theta = \tfrac{1}{4}(1 + 3\cos^2 2\theta)$

3. $\tan(\tfrac{\pi}{4} + \tfrac{\theta}{2}) = \sqrt{\dfrac{1 + \sin\theta}{1 - \sin\theta}} = \sec\theta + \tan\theta$

4. $(2\cos\theta + 1)(2\cos\theta - 1)(2\cos 2\theta - 1)(2\cos 4\theta - 1) = 2\cos 8\theta + 1$

5. $\csc\theta + \csc 2\theta + \csc 4\theta + \cot 4\theta = \cot(\tfrac{\theta}{2})$

6. If $A + B + C = 180°$, prove that:
   (a) $\cos 2A + \cos 2B + \cos 2C = -1 - 4\cos A\cos B\cos C$
   (b) $\cos^2 A + \cos^2 B - \cos^2 C = 1 - 2\sin A\sin B\cos C$

7. If $A + B + C = 90°$, prove that:
   (a) $\sin 2A + \sin 2B + \sin 2C = 4\cos A\cos B\cos C$
   (b) $\sin^2 A + \sin^2 B + \sin^2 C = 1 - 2\sin A\sin B\sin C$

8. Solve the following equations: $0 \leqslant \theta \leqslant 2\pi$
   (a) $\sin 4\theta = \cos 2\theta$ (b) $\sin 3\theta = \sin 2\theta$

9. Solve the following equations: $0° \leqslant \theta \leqslant 360°$
   (a) $4\sin 2\theta - 3\cos 2\theta = 1$
   (b) $\sin 5\theta - \sin 3\theta + \sin\theta = 0$

10. Show that $\cos 3\theta = 4\cos^3\theta - 3\cos\theta$
    Put $x = 2\cos\theta$ in the equation $x^3 - 3x = \sqrt{2}$ and show that the equation reduces to $\cos 3\theta = \dfrac{1}{\sqrt{2}}$
    (a) Hence solve the equation $x^3 - 3x - \sqrt{2} = 0$, giving your answer in the exact form, $x = 2\cos\theta$
    (b) Prove that: $\cos(\tfrac{\pi}{12}) + \cos(\tfrac{9\pi}{12}) + \cos(\tfrac{17\pi}{12}) = 0$
    (Do not use a calculator)

11. (a) Show that $\sin(A + B) - \sin(A - B) = 2\cos A\sin B$
    (b) Show that $2\sin x\,(\cos 2x + \cos 4x + \cos 6x) = \sin 7x - \sin x$
    (c) Deduce that $\cos(\tfrac{2\pi}{7}) + \cos(\tfrac{4\pi}{7}) + \cos(\tfrac{6\pi}{7}) = \tfrac{-1}{2}$
    (d) Prove that $\cos(\tfrac{\pi}{7}) + \cos(\tfrac{3\pi}{7}) + \cos(\tfrac{5\pi}{7}) = \tfrac{1}{2}$

10.2 3 Unit Co-ordinate Geometry: Circles (Harder Problems)

No new theories or ideas are required to solve problems on circles. The following basic properties of circles will be very useful.

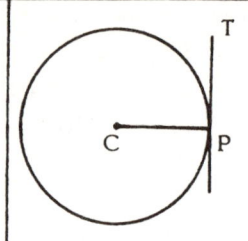

(i) A tangent and the radius at the point of contact are at right angles.
(ii) An angle in a semi-circle is a right angle.
(iii) A line is a tangent if its distance from the centre of the circle is equal to the radius.

---

1. Equation of a Circle

$$(x - h)^2 + (y - k)^2 = r^2 \qquad \ldots (1)$$

is the standard form of the equation of a circle centred at the point C(h, k) and radius r.

$$x^2 + y^2 = r^2 \qquad \ldots (2)$$

is the equation of a circle centred at the origin and radius r.

2. The General Equation

$$x^2 + y^2 + 2gx + 2fy + c = 0 \qquad \ldots (3)$$

where g, f and c are constants, is called the general equation. By completing the squares in x and y, we have:

$$(x + g)^2 + (y + f)^2 = g^2 + f^2 - c$$

This equation has the standard form of the circle with centre at (-g, -f) and radius $\sqrt{g^2 + f^2 - c}$.

Finally the equation:

$$Ax^2 + Ay^2 + Bx + Cy + D = 0 \qquad \ldots (4)$$

when divided by A, reduces to the general form (3), so, (4) is also a general equation of a circle.

EXAMPLE: (1)

Find the centre and the radius of the circles:

(a) $x^2 + y^2 - ax - by = 0$

(b) $3x^2 + 3y^2 + 5x + 12y = 0$

SOLUTION:

(a) Completing the squares, we have:
$$(x - \frac{a}{2})^2 + (y - \frac{b}{2})^2 = \frac{a^2 + b^2}{4}$$
So, the centre is $C(\frac{a}{2}, \frac{b}{2})$

and the radius is $\frac{1}{2}\sqrt{a^2 + b^2}$

(b) Dividing the equation by 3,
$$x^2 + y^2 + \frac{5x}{3} + 4y = 0$$
$$\therefore (x + \frac{5}{6})^2 + (y + 2)^2 = \frac{169}{36}$$
$\therefore$ The centre is $(\frac{-5}{6}, -2)$

and the radius is $\frac{13}{6}$

EXAMPLE: (2)

Find the equation of the circle through the points $(0, 0)$, $(4, 8)$, $(9, 9)$.

SOLUTION:

The given points must satisfy the equation of the circle:
$$x^2 + y^2 + 2gx + 2fy + c = 0 \quad \ldots (1)$$
$\therefore$ $c = 0$, $16 + 64 + 8g + 16f = 0$ and $81 + 81 + 18g + 18f = 0$

These simplify to: $g + 2f = -10$ and $g + f = -9$

Solving for f and g: $g = -8$, $f = -1$

Hence the required equation is $x^2 + y^2 - 16x - 2y = 0$

EXAMPLE: (3)

Find the equation of the circle which touches both axes and passes through the point $A(1, 2)$.

SOLUTION:

Let $(x - h)^2 + (y - k)^2 = r^2 \quad \ldots (1)$

be the equation of the circle.

$A(1, 2)$ satisfies this equation, so
$(1 - h)^2 + (2 - k)^2 = r^2 \quad \ldots (2)$

Since the circle is tangential to both axes, the centre (h, k) must be at a distance equal to the radius from each axis.

$\therefore$ $h = k = r$ and from (2):

$(1 - r)^2 + (2 - r)^2 = r^2$, which simplifies to: $r^2 - 6r + 5 = 0$.

$\therefore$ $r = 1$ or 5

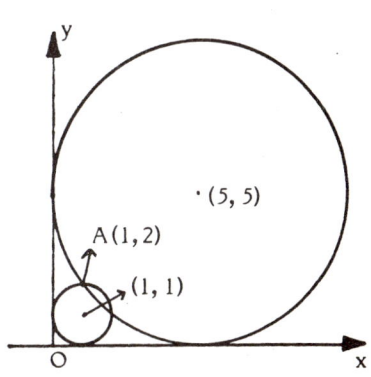

Thus, there are two circles, satisfying the given conditions, i.e.

$(x - 1)^2 + (y - 1)^2 = 1$ and $(x - 5)^2 + (y - 5)^2 = 25$

3. <u>Equation of a Circle having AB as Diameter</u>

Let A be (h, k) and B be (h', k'), and $P(x, y)$ be any point on the required circle. We use the fact that the angle APB in the semicircle is a right angle.

m = gradient of AP = $\dfrac{y - k}{x - h}$

m' = gradient of BP = $\dfrac{y - k'}{x - h'}$

Since AP $\perp$ BP, $mm' = -1$ and this gives:

$$\boxed{(x - h)(x - h') + (y - k)(y - k') = 0}$$

as the equation of the required circle.

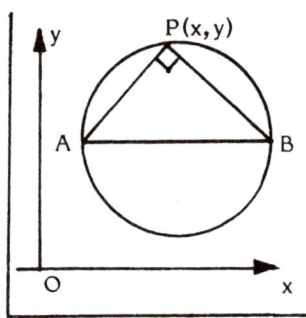

EXAMPLE: (4)

Find the equation of the circle on AB as diameter where A is $(2, 3)$ and B is $(4, 5)$.

SOLUTION:

The required equation is obtained by substituting for $A(2, 3)$ and $B(4, 5)$ in the equation above, i.e.

$(x - 2)(x - 4) + (y - 3)(y - 5) = 0$

or $x^2 + y^2 - 6x - 8y + 23 = 0$

As a check, we find that the centre $(3, 4)$ is the mid-point of AB.

4. Tangents to a Circle

We use the fact that the tangent is perpendicular to the radius at the point of contact.
Consider the equation of the circle
$$x^2 + y^2 + 2gx + 2fy + c = 0. \qquad \ldots (1)$$
The centre is $(-g, -f)$.
If $P(x_1, y_1)$ is a point on the circle, then m = gradient

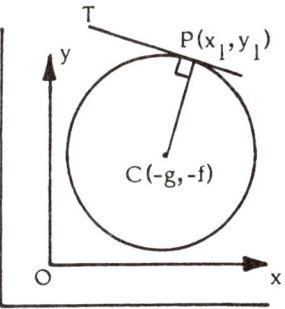

of $CP = \dfrac{y_1 + f}{x_1 + g}$ and the gradient of the tangent PT is then $m' = \dfrac{-1}{m} = -\dfrac{x_1 + g}{y_1 + f}$

The equation of the tangent is $y - y_1 = -\dfrac{x_1 + g}{y_1 + f} \cdot (x - x_1)$

Or $(y - y_1)(y_1 + f) = -(x_1 + g)(x - x_1)$

$\therefore xx_1 + yy_1 + g(x + x_1) + f(y + y_1) = x_1^2 + y_1^2 + 2gx_1 + 2fy_1$

Now $P(x_1, y_1)$ lies on the circle (1), so $x_1^2 + y_1^2 + 2gx_1 + 2fy_1 + c = 0$
Hence the equation of the tangent is

$$\boxed{xx_1 + yy_1 + g(x + x_1) + f(y + y_1) + c = 0}$$

The reader is advised not to memorise this equation, but derive the result for each question.

It will be instructive to prove the following results:

1. The equation of the tangent at $P(x_1, y_1)$ to the circle $x^2 + y^2 = a^2$ is $xx_1 + yy_1 = a^2$ and at $P(a\cos\theta, a\sin\theta)$ is $x\cos\theta + y\sin\theta = a$.

2. Prove that $\dfrac{dy}{dx} = -\dfrac{x + g}{y + f}$ from the equation (1) and hence derive the equation of the tangent at $P(x_1, y_1)$ to the circle $x^2 + y^2 + 2gx + 2fy + c = 0$.

EXAMPLE: (5)
Find the equation of the tangent at $A(-1, 3)$ to the circle $x^2 + y^2 - 8x + 7y - 39 = 0$.

SOLUTION: The centre is $C(4, \dfrac{-7}{2})$. A is $(-1, 3)$

The gradient of $CA = \dfrac{3 + 7/2}{-1 - 4} = \dfrac{-13}{10}$

The tangent is perpendicular to the radius, so the slope of the tangent is $\dfrac{10}{13}$ and hence its equation is $y - 3 = \dfrac{10}{13}(x + 1)$, which simplifies to $10x - 13y + 49 = 0$.

Alternative method:
We find the gradient of the tangent by differentiating the given equation:
$\therefore 2x + 2y\dfrac{dy}{dx} - 8 + 7\dfrac{dy}{dx} = 0$. At $(-1, 3)$, $\dfrac{dy}{dx} = \dfrac{10}{13}$ etc.

Exercise 10B

1. Find the equation of the circle passing through the points:
   (a) $(1, 0)$, $(0, -1)$, $(0, 0)$ (b) $(-1, 3)$, $(2, 2)$, $(1, 4)$

2. Find the centre and the radius of the following circles:
   (a) $x^2 + y^2 + 2x - 4y + 1 = 0$ (b) $8x^2 + 8y^2 - 12x + 20y = 1$

3. Find the equation of the circle whose centre is on the x-axis and which passes through the points $(0, 3)$ and $(4, 1)$.

4. Find the equation of the circle whose centre is at the point $C(-3, -4)$ and which is tangential to the line $3x + 4y = 20$.

5. Find the equation of the circle through the point $A(-1, 2)$ and which is tangential to both axes.

6. Find the equation of the circle centred on the line $y = 2x$, which passes through the point $A(-2, 4)$ and is tangential to the x-axis.

7. Show that the chord whose equation is $x - 3y + 8 = 0$ subtends a right angle at the centre of the circle $9x^2 + 9y^2 - 18x + 6y = 170$.

8. Show that $A(1, 1)$ lies on the circle $x^2 + y^2 + 4x + 6y - 12 = 0$. Find the co-ordinates of B, if AB is a diameter of the circle.

9. Find the equation of the circle passing through the origin and making intercepts a and b on the x- and y-axis respectively.

10. Find the intercept made on the x-axis by the circle which has AB as diameter, where A is $(0, -1)$ and B is $(2, 3)$.

11. Find the equations of the tangents to the following circles at the points indicated:
    (a) $x^2 + y^2 - 6x - 2y - 3 = 0$, $(5, 4)$
    (b) $(x - 1)^2 + (y + 2)^2 = 5$, $(3, -3)$
    (c) $x^2 + y^2 - 4x + 2y = 20$, $(5, 3)$

12. Show that the line $y = mx + b$ is a tangent to the circle $x^2 + y^2 = a^2$, if $b = \pm a \sqrt{1 + m^2}$.

13. Find the equations of the two tangents to the circle $x^2 + y^2 - 2x - 6y + 6 = 0$ which pass through the point $P(-1, 2)$. Use $lx + my + n = 0$. (Warning: do not use $y = mx + b$)

14. Write down the equations of the circles on AB as diameter where:
    (a) $A(4, -8)$, $B(3, 5)$ (b) $A(a, b)$, $B(b, a)$
    (c) $A(a, a)$, $B(-a, -a)$

15. Show that the circles $x^2 + y^2 = 4$ and $x^2 + y^2 + 6x - 8y + 16 = 0$ touch externally.

10.3 Plane Geometry: Circles (Harder Problems)

EXAMPLE: (1)

ABC is an equilateral triangle, inscribed in a circle. X is a point on the minor arc BC.

Prove that: (i) △BDX ||| △ACX

(ii) XB + XC = XA

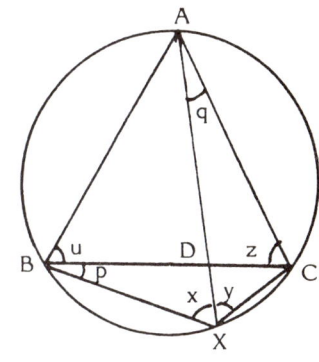

SOLUTION:

Given: △ABC is equilateral
Prove: (i) △BDX ||| △ACX   (ii) XB + XC = XA

Proof: We have,

(i) u = z = 60°   (△ABC is equilateral)

   x = z and y = u (∠s in the same segments on arcs AB and AC respectively)

   Then, in △BDX and △ACX:

   x = y = 60°

   p = q   (∠s in the same segment, arc CX)

   ∠BDX = ∠ACX   (∠ sum of a △ being 180°)

   ∴ △BDX ||| △ACX

(ii) $\frac{XB}{XA} = \frac{BD}{AC}$ giving XB . AC = XA . BD   ... (1)

   Similarly we can prove that △CDX ||| △ABX and the corresponding result
   XC . AB = XA . CD   ... (2)

   Adding (1) and (2):

   XB . AC + XC . AB = XA (BD + CD) = XA . BC

   Now △ABC being equilateral, AB = BC = CA, so, removing the common length, we have the required result:

   XB + CX = XA .

298

EXAMPLE: (2)

In the diagram, AD and BE are perpendicular to BC and AC respectively. Prove that:
(a) HDCE is a cyclic quadrilateral on HC as diameter
(b) AH = AK

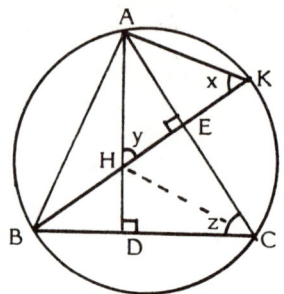

Given:	AD ⊥ BC, BE ⊥ AC
Prove:	(a) HDCE is a cyclic quadrilateral
	(b) AH = AK
Proof:	∠HEC = 90° (BE ⊥ AC)
(a)	∠HDC = 90° (AD ⊥ BC)

∴ E and D are on the circle with HC as diameter.
Hence, HDCE is a cyclic quadrilateral on HC as diameter.

(b)   y = z   (Ext. ∠ of cyc. quad. HDCE = Internal opp. ∠)
      x = z   (∠s in the segment, arc AB)
   ∴ x = y
   ∴ △AHK is isosceles
   ∴ AH = AK

EXAMPLE: (3)

In the diagram, BC is a fixed chord of a circle, A is a variable point on the major arc on the chord BC.
BD ⊥ AC and CE ⊥ AB. Prove that:

(a) BCDE is a cyclic quadrilateral on a circle with BC as diameter.

(b) as A varies, the segment ED has constant length.

(c) the locus of the mid-point of ED is a circle whose centre is the mid-point of BC.

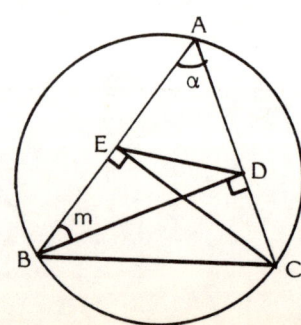

SOLUTION:

Given: BC is a fixed chord, BD $\perp$ AC, CE $\perp$ AB

Prove:
(a) BCDE is a cyclic quadrilateral
(b) ED has constant length
(c) Locus of mid-point of ED is a circle.

Proof:

(a) $\angle$BEC and $\angle$BDC are both 90°.   (BD $\perp$ AC, CE $\perp$ AB)

$\therefore$ E and D lie on the circle whose diameter is BC.

$\therefore$ BCDE is a cyclic quadrilateral.

(b) Since chord BC is of constant length, it subtends a constant angle, say α, at the circumference of the given circle.

Now m = $\angle$ABD = 90° - α (BD $\perp$ AD)

Since α is constant, m is also constant.

Using the fact that equal chords subtend equal angles at the circumference of a circle, we conclude that for various positions of chord ED on the fixed circle, (on BC as diameter) ED must be of constant length.

(c) Let P and M be the mid-points of ED and BC respectively.

Join MP and MD.

M is the centre of the circle BCDE.

$\therefore$ MP $\perp$ ED

$\therefore$ MP^2 = MD^2 - PD^2 = $r^2 - s^2$

Now r = MD = MC = $\frac{1}{2}$BC = a constant

s = PD = $\frac{1}{2}$ED which is a constant

$\therefore$ MP^2 is a constant

Hence, the locus of P is a circle with the centre at the mid-point of BC and the radius

$\frac{1}{2}\sqrt{BC^2 - ED^2}$

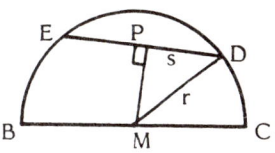

Exercise 10C: PLANE GEOMETRY: CIRCLES (HARDER PROBLEMS)

1. In Fig. 1, if PQ is parallel to RS, prove that PQ = RS.

2. In Fig. 2, P is any point on a diameter AB of a circle; QPR is a chord such that $\angle APQ = 45°$, prove that $AB^2 = 2PQ^2 + 2PR^2$.

3. In Fig. 3, O is the centre of the circle, prove that a + b = c.

4. Two lines OAB, OCD cut a circle at A, B and C, D. If OB = BD, prove OC = CA.

5. ABCD is a quadrilateral inscribed in a circle. BA and CD when produced meet at P. O is the centre of the circle PAC. Prove that BD is perpendicular to OP. (See Fig. 4)

6. Two circles ARPB, AQSB intersect at A and B. PAQ and RAS are straight lines. PR and SQ are produced to meet at M. Prove that MPBQ is a cyclic quadrilateral. (See Fig. 5)

7. AB is a chord of a circle. The tangents at A and B meet at T. AP is drawn perpendicular to AB. TP is drawn perpendicular to TA. Prove that PT is equal to the radius of the circle. (See Fig. 6)

8. Two circles of radii 3 cm and 12 cm touch each other externally. Find the length of their common tangents.

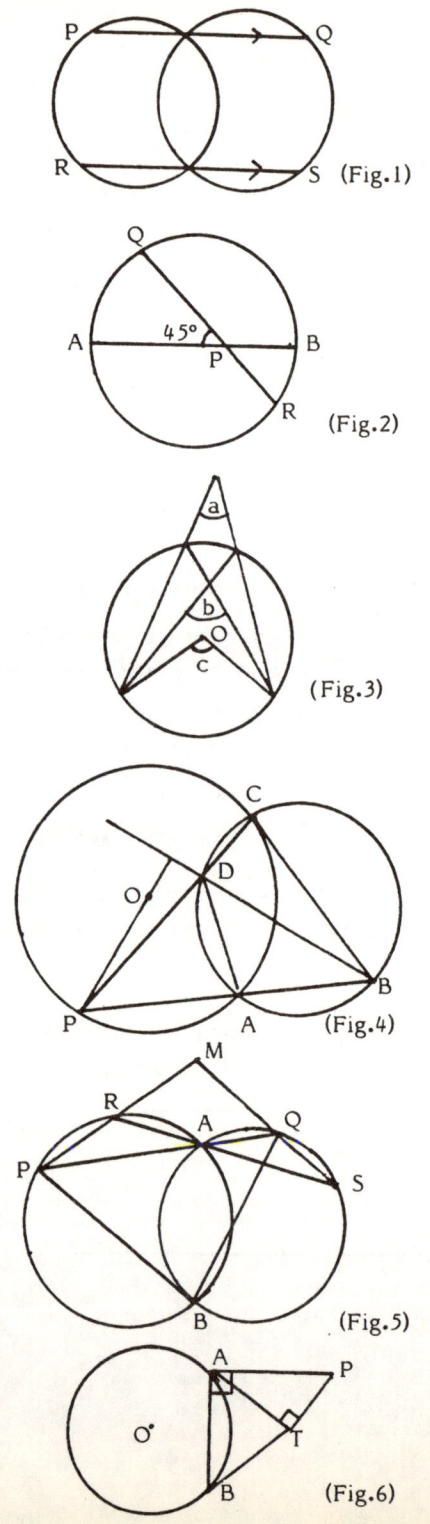

9. In Fig. 7, two tangents from T (to the circle) meet the two tangents from D (to the same circle) at A and C, as shown. Prove that AT - CD = TC - AD.

10. The altitudes PM and QN of an acute-angled triangle PQR meet at H. PM produced cuts the circle PQR at A. Prove that HM = MA. (Hint: Join AQ) (See Fig. 8)

11. AD is an altitude of the triangle ABC, inscribed in a circle. DP is drawn parallel to BA and meets the tangent at A at P. Prove ∠CPA = 90°. (See Fig. 9) (Hint: Show that x = y = z)

12. AB is a diameter of a circle, AC is any chord. M is the mid-point of the arc BC. Prove that AC is perpendicular to the tangent at M.

13. In Fig. 10, three circles intersect at P. Prove that AB is parallel to DC. (Hint: Join PF and PE)

14. In Fig. 11, O is the centre, TP is the tangent and TC bisects ∠OTP, prove that ∠TCP = 45°. (Hint: Join AP)

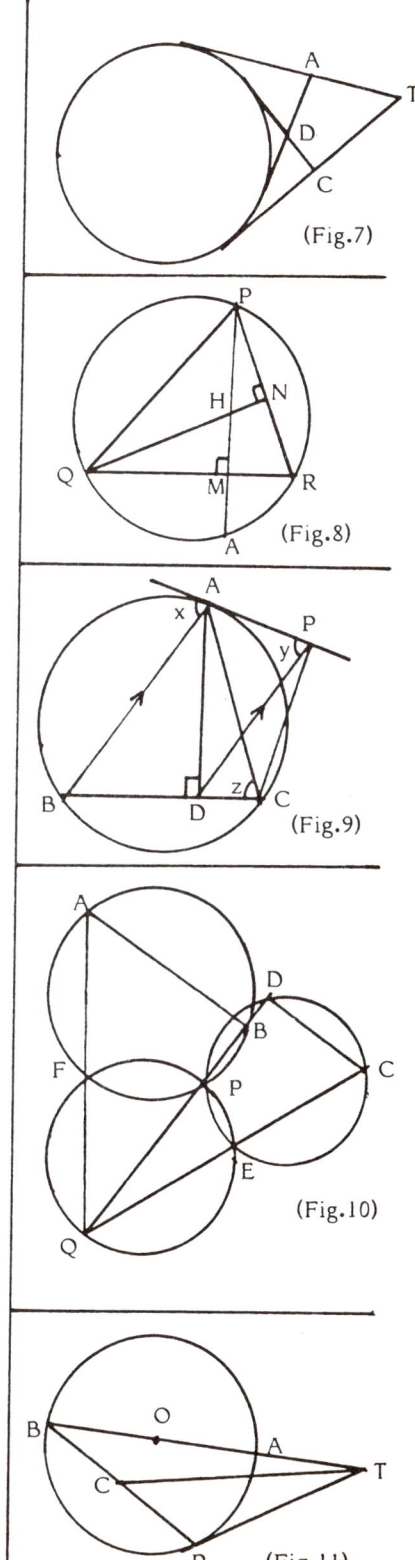

(Fig.7)

(Fig.8)

(Fig.9)

(Fig.10)

(Fig.11)

15. Prove that the quadrilateral formed by the angle bisectors of a cyclic quadrilateral is also cyclic. (Fig. 11)

16. If the two non-parallel sides of a trapezium are equal, prove that the trapezium is cyclic (Fig. 12)

17. Prove that the angle bisectors of the angles formed by producing opposite sides of a cyclic quadrilateral intersect at right angles. (Fig. 13)
(We have to prove $\angle FMP = 90°$
Hint: Produce FM as shown and prove $\triangle FDE \;|||\; \triangle FBN$

18. The bisectors of the opposite angles $\angle P$ and $\angle R$ of a cyclic quadrilateral meet the circle at A and B as shown. Prove that AB is a diameter of the circle. (Fig. 14)

19. Two circles intersect at A and B. A straight line PAQ cuts the circles at P and Q. The tangents at P and Q intersect at T. Prove that PBQT is a cyclic quadrilateral. (See Fig. 15)
(Hint: Join AB, x = y etc.)

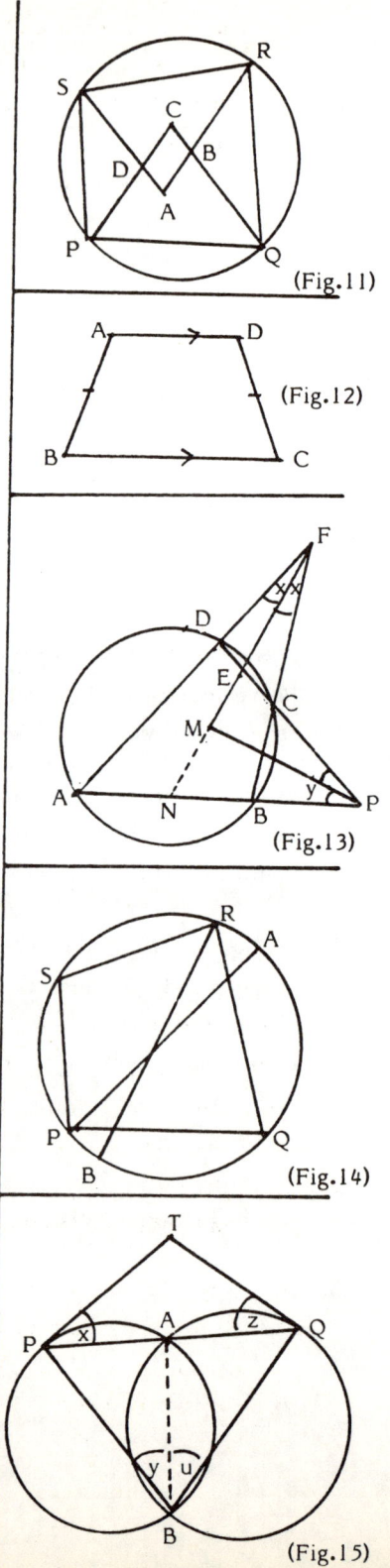

(Fig.11)

(Fig.12)

(Fig.13)

(Fig.14)

(Fig.15)

20. AB and CD are parallel tangents to a circle, centre O. APC is another tangent at P. Prove that ∠AOC is a right angle.
    (See Fig. 16)

21. (a) In Fig. 17 CP is a tangent and CAB is any secant. Prove that

    $CP^2 = CA \cdot CB$

    (Hint: Join AP, show that △PCA, △BCP are similar)

    (b) In Fig. 18 PQ is a common tangent to the two circles, and CAB is a common secant. Prove that CP = CQ.
    [Hint: Use the result (a)]

22. PQ and RS are the common tangents to two circles intersecting at A and B. AB produced either way meets the tangents in M and N as shown. (Fig. 19)   Prove:

    (a) $MP^2 = MA \cdot MB$ and $RN^2 = NB \cdot NA$
    (b) PM = MQ   (See question 21)
    (c) PQ = RS   (Hint: △OEC ≡ △OFC)
    (d) MA = BN   (Hint: MP = RN)

23. P is any point on the circle ABC. PL, PM, PN are the perpendiculars to the sides BC, CA and AB respectively of △ABC. Prove that the points L, M, N are collinear. (Fig. 20)

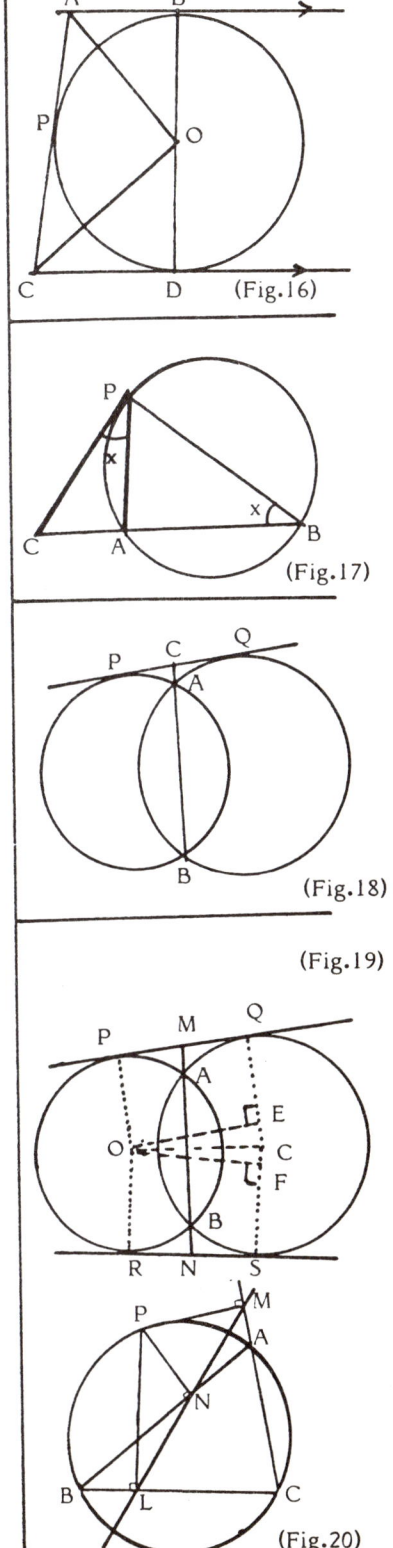

24. In the diagram, two fixed circles intersect at A and B. Prove that ∠PMQ is of constant size for all positions of Q. (Fig. 21)

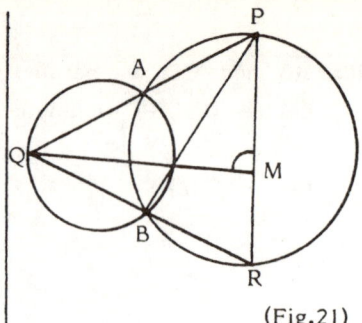

(Fig.21)

25. ABCD is a quadrilateral inscribed in a circle. X, Y, Z, W are the mid-points of the arcs AB, BC, CD and DA respectively. Prove that XZ ⊥ YW.

26. In Fig. 22, two fixed circles intersect at A and B. P is a variable point on one circle. PA and PB when produced meet the other circle at M and N respectively. Prove that MN is of constant length.

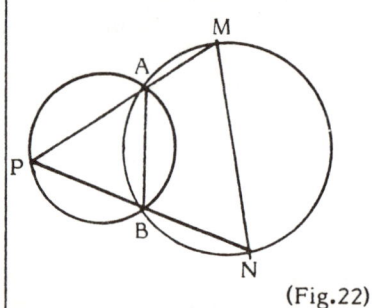

(Fig.22)

27. In the diagram (Fig. 23), △ABC is inscribed in a circle. AD, BE, CF are the altitudes of △ABC. H, the point of intersection of the altitudes, is called the ORTHOCENTRE of the triangle. Prove that:

(a) ∠BHF = ∠BAC
(b) ∠BHC + ∠BAC = 180°
(c) △AEF ||| △ABC
(d) △BDF ||| △EDC
(e) AD bisects ∠FDE
(f) ∠EDF = 180° − 2∠BAC
(g) If BC is fixed and A varies remaining on the major arc on BC, find the locus of H.   [Hint: Use part (b)]
(h) BFEC is a cyclic quadrilateral lying on the circle on BC as diameter.

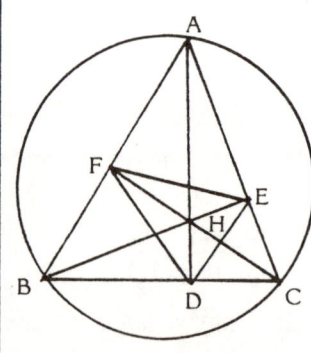

(Fig.23)

10.4 Inequalities

Definition: $x > y$ if and only if $x - y > 0$.

On a real number line this means x lies to the right of y.

Worked Examples

1. Prove that $\frac{a+b}{2} \geq \sqrt{ab}$, if a and b are positive real numbers.

Solution: Consider $(\frac{a+b}{2})^2 - ab$

Now $(\frac{a+b}{2})^2 - ab = \frac{1}{4}(a^2 + 2ab + b^2) - ab = \frac{1}{4}(a-b)^2 \geq 0$

$\therefore \frac{a+b}{2} \geq \sqrt{ab}$, for $a > 0$, $b > 0$, and equality when $a = b$.

2. Given that $x + y = c$, prove that $\frac{1}{x} + \frac{1}{y} \geq \frac{4}{c}$ for $x > 0$, $y > 0$.

Solution: From example (1), $a + b \geq 2\sqrt{ab}$ ... (1)

Put $a = \frac{1}{x}$, $b = \frac{1}{y}$, then: $\frac{1}{x} + \frac{1}{y} \geq \frac{2}{\sqrt{xy}}$ ... (2)

Using (1), $\sqrt{xy} \leq \frac{x+y}{2}$ and putting $x + y = c$

$\sqrt{xy} \leq \frac{c}{2}$ or $\frac{1}{\sqrt{xy}} \geq \frac{2}{c}$

$\therefore$ From (2), $\frac{1}{x} + \frac{1}{y} \geq \frac{4}{c}$

3. If x, y, z are positive real numbers, prove the following:

   (a) $x^2 + y^2 \geq 2xy$ (b) $\frac{x}{y} + \frac{y}{x} \geq 2$ (c) $x^3 + y^3 + z^3 \geq 3xyz$

   (d) $\frac{x+y+z}{3} \geq (xyz)^{1/3}$

(cont)

Solution:

(a) Consider $x^2 + y^2 - 2xy = (x - y)^2$

$\therefore \quad x^2 + y^2 - 2xy \geq 0$

$\therefore \quad x^2 + y^2 \geq 2xy$

(b) Divide the result in part (a) by xy, then:

$\dfrac{x}{y} + \dfrac{y}{x} \geq 2$

(c) We have $x^3 + y^3 = (x + y)(x^2 + y^2 - xy)$

From (a), $x^2 + y^2 - xy \geq xy$

$\therefore \quad x^3 + y^3 \geq (x + y)xy$

$\geq xyz \left(\dfrac{x}{z} + \dfrac{y}{z}\right)$

Similarly $y^3 + z^3 \geq xyz \left(\dfrac{y}{x} + \dfrac{z}{x}\right)$, $z^3 + x^3 \geq xyz \left(\dfrac{z}{y} + \dfrac{x}{y}\right)$

Adding these:

$2(x^3 + y^3 + z^3) \geq xyz \left[\left(\dfrac{x}{z} + \dfrac{y}{z}\right) + \left(\dfrac{y}{x} + \dfrac{z}{x}\right) + \left(\dfrac{z}{y} + \dfrac{x}{y}\right)\right]$

$\geq xyz \left[\left(\dfrac{x}{y} + \dfrac{y}{x}\right) + \left(\dfrac{y}{z} + \dfrac{z}{y}\right) + \left(\dfrac{z}{x} + \dfrac{x}{z}\right)\right]$

Now using (b):

$2(x^3 + y^3 + z^3) \geq xyz(2 + 2 + 2)$

Hence $x^3 + y^3 + z^3 \geq 3xyz$

(d) From (c), we have: $a^3 + b^3 + c^3 \geq 3abc$

Put $a^3 = x$, $b^3 = y$, $c^3 = z$, then:

$x + y + z \geq 3 x^{1/3} \cdot y^{1/3} \cdot z^{1/3}$

Hence $\dfrac{x + y + z}{3} \geq (xyz)^{1/3}$, equality for $x = y = z$.

The general result for a set of n positive numbers $x_1, x_2, \ldots, x_n$ is

$\dfrac{x_1 + x_2 + \ldots + x_n}{n} \geq (x_1 x_2 \ldots x_n)^{1/n}$

i.e. Arithmetic Mean $\geq$ Geometric Mean

Exercise 10D

1. (a) Show that, for $a > 0$, $b > 0$, $c > 0$,
   $$a^2 + b^2 + c^2 \geq ab + bc + ca.$$
   (b) Hence show that $a^2 + b^2 + c^2 \geq 3(abc)^{2/3}$
   [Hint: Use worked example 3(d)]
   (c) Prove that $(a + b + c)^2 \geq 3(ab + bc + ca)$

2. Prove that for $x, y, z \geq 0$, $x + y + z \geq [3(xy + yz + zx)]^{1/2}$
   (Hint: Use question 1c)

3. Prove that for $a, b, c, d \geq 0$, $\dfrac{a + b + c + d}{4} \geq (abcd)^{1/4}$
   (Hint: Let $x = \dfrac{a + b}{2}$, $y = \dfrac{c + d}{2}$, then use worked example 1 repeatedly)

4. A rectangular box of sides a, b, c has a constant surface area S. Using the formulas $S = 2(ab + bc + ca)$ and $V = abc$ (volume), prove that:
   (i) $V^{2/3} \leq \dfrac{S}{6}$ (ii) V is a maximum when the box is a cube.
   (Hint: Let $x = ab, y = bc, z = ca$, then use worked example 3d)

5. If $x, y > 0$, prove that $\dfrac{1}{2}(x^3 + y^3) \geq \left(\dfrac{x + y}{2}\right)^3$
   (Hint: Show that L.H.S. − R.H.S. ≥ 0)

6. For any real numbers x, y, z, u, prove that:
   $(x^2 + y^2)(z^2 + u^2) \geq (xz + yu)^2$
   (Hint: Show that L.H.S. − R.H.S. ≥ 0)

7. For any real numbers x, y, z, a, b, c, prove that:
   $(x^2 + y^2 + z^2)(a^2 + b^2 + c^2) \geq (ax + by + cz)^2$

10.5 Method of Mathematical Induction

Worked Examples

1. (i) Show that for each positive integer n, there are unique positive integers a_n and b_n such that $(1 + \sqrt{3})^n = a_n + \sqrt{3} \cdot b_n$

   (ii) Hence show that $a_n^2 - 3b_n^2 = 2^n \cdot (-1)^n$

Solution:

(i) For $n = 1$, L.H.S. $= 1 + \sqrt{3}$; R.H.S. $= a_1 + \sqrt{3} \cdot b_1$
$\therefore a_1 = 1$, $b_1 = 1$ which are unique integers.
Assume that $(1 + \sqrt{3})^k = a_k + \sqrt{3} \cdot b_k$, where k is a positive integer. ... (1)
Then $(1 + \sqrt{3})^{k+1} = (1 + \sqrt{3})(1 + \sqrt{3})^k = (1 + \sqrt{3})(a_k + \sqrt{3} \cdot b_k)$, using (1).
$\therefore (1 + \sqrt{3})^{k+1} = (a_k + 3b_k) + \sqrt{3}(a_k + b_k) = a_{k+1} + \sqrt{3} \cdot b_{k+1}$,
where $a_{k+1} = a_k + 3b_k$ and $b_{k+1} = a_k + b_k$.
Since a_k and b_k are unique integers, so are a_{k+1} and b_{k+1}. Thus the statement is true for $n = k + 1$.
Since true when $n = 1$, the statement is also true for $n = 2$.
Since true when $n = 2$, the statement is also true for $n = 3$, and so on, the statement is true for all positive integral values of n.

Rather than repeating the foregoing three lines, in the subsequent examples we will say "by the principle of induction, the statement is true for each positive integer n".

(ii) To prove: $a_n^2 - 3b_n^2 = (-1)^n \cdot 2^n$

For $n = 1$, L.H.S. $= a_1^2 - 3b_1^2 = 1 - 3 = -2$, using part (i).
Also R.H.S. $= -1 \cdot 2 = -2$, so the statement is true for $n = 1$. Assuming it to be true for $n = k$, we have:
$$a_k^2 - 3b_k^2 = (-1)^k \cdot 2^k \quad \ldots (2)$$
Then, $a_{k+1}^2 - 3b_{k+1}^2 = (a_k + 3b_k)^2 - 3(a_k + b_k)^2$, using part (i).

This simplifies to $-2(a_k^2 - 3b_k^2)$ and using (2), we have:
$$a_{k+1}^2 - 3b_{k+1}^2 = -2 \cdot (-1)^k \cdot 2^k = 2^{k+1}(-1)^{k+1}$$

Hence the statement is true for $n = k + 1$ and, by the principle of induction, the statement is true for each positive integer n.

2. (a) Show that for $n > 0$, $2n + 3 > 2\sqrt{(n+1)(n+2)}$

   (b) Hence, by induction prove that $\sum_{1}^{n} \dfrac{1}{\sqrt{r}} > 2(\sqrt{n+1} - 1)$

Solution: We have:

(a) $(2n+3)^2 - 4(n+1)(n+2) = 4n^2 + 12n + 9 - 4(n^2 + 3n + 2) = 1 > 0$

   $\therefore$ $(2n+3)^2 > 4(n+1)(n+2)$

   $(2n+3) > 2\sqrt{(n+1)(n+2)}$

(b) $S(n) = 1 + \dfrac{1}{\sqrt{2}} + \dfrac{1}{\sqrt{3}} + \ldots + \dfrac{1}{\sqrt{n}} > 2(\sqrt{n+1} - 1)$ ... (1)

   For $n = 1$, L.H.S. $= 1$ and R.H.S. $= 2(\sqrt{2} - 1) \doteq 0.8$

   So, the statement is true for $n = 1$.

   Assume it is true for $n = k$, where k is a positive integer, then:

   $1 + \dfrac{1}{\sqrt{2}} + \ldots + \dfrac{1}{\sqrt{k}} > 2(\sqrt{k+1} - 1)$

   We add $\dfrac{1}{\sqrt{k+1}}$ on both sides, then

   $S(k+1) > 2\sqrt{k+1} + \dfrac{1}{\sqrt{k+1}} - 2 = \dfrac{2k + 3 - 2\sqrt{k+1}}{\sqrt{k+1}}$

   Using part (a), $S(k+1) > \dfrac{2\sqrt{(k+1)(k+2)} - 2\sqrt{k+1}}{\sqrt{k+1}}$

   This simplifies to $S(k+1) > 2(\sqrt{k+2} - 1) = 2(\sqrt{(k+1)+1} - 1)$

   So, the statement is true for $n = k+1$ and by the principle of induction, it is true for all positive integers.

---

3. Prove by induction that:

   $\sin x + \sin 2x + \sin 3x + \ldots + \sin nx = \dfrac{\sin(\frac{nx}{2}) \sin(\frac{n+1}{2})x}{\sin(\frac{x}{2})}$

Solution: For $n = 1$, L.H.S. $= \sin x$, R.H.S. $= \dfrac{\sin(\frac{x}{2}) \sin x}{\sin(\frac{x}{2})} = \sin x$

So the statement is true for $n = 1$.

Assume it is true for $n = k$, where k is a positive integer, then:

$S(k) = \sin x + \sin 2x + \ldots + \sin kx = \dfrac{\sin(\frac{kx}{2}) \cdot \sin(\frac{k+1}{2})x}{\sin(\frac{x}{2})}$

Adding the next term $\sin(k+1)x$,

(cont)

$$S(k+1) = \frac{\sin(\frac{k+1}{2})x \cdot \sin(\frac{kx}{2})}{\sin(\frac{x}{2})} + \sin(k+1)x$$

Now $\sin(k+1)x = 2\sin(\frac{k+1}{2})x \cdot \cos(\frac{k+1}{2})x$

$$\therefore S(k+1) = \sin(\frac{k+1}{2})x \left[\frac{\sin(\frac{kx}{2})}{\sin(\frac{x}{2})} + 2\cos(\frac{k+1}{2})x \right] \quad \ldots (1)$$

Bracketed expression =

$$\frac{\sin(\frac{kx}{2}) + 2\cos(\frac{k+1}{2})x \cdot \sin\frac{x}{2}}{\sin(\frac{x}{2})}$$

$$= \frac{\sin(\frac{kx}{2}) + \sin(\frac{k+2}{2})x - \sin(\frac{kx}{2})}{\sin(\frac{x}{2})}$$

$$\boxed{\begin{array}{l} \text{We use} \\ 2\cos A \sin B \\ = \sin(A+B) - \sin(A-B) \end{array}}$$

$$= \frac{\sin(\frac{k+2}{2})x}{\sin(\frac{x}{2})}$$

$$\therefore S(k+1) = \frac{\sin(\frac{k+1}{2})x \cdot \sin(\frac{k+2}{2})x}{\sin(\frac{x}{2})}$$

Thus the statement is true for $n = k + 1$ and, by the principle of induction, it is true for all positive integers.

Exercise 10E

Use mathematical induction to prove the results in questions 1 to 5.

1. $\frac{x^n - 1}{x - 1} = x^{n-1} + x^{n-2} + \ldots + x + 1, \quad x \neq 1$

2. $\frac{1}{1 \cdot 3} + \frac{1}{2 \cdot 4} + \frac{1}{3 \cdot 5} + \ldots + \frac{1}{n(n+2)} = \frac{n}{2n+1}$

3. $1 + \frac{1}{1+2} + \frac{1}{1+2+3} + \ldots + \frac{1}{1+2+3+\ldots+n} = \frac{2n}{n+1}$

4. A sequence $\{t_n\}$ is defined so that
   $t_{n+2} = 6t_{n+1} - 5t_n$ and $t_1 = 2, \; t_2 = 6$.
   Prove that $t_n = 5^{n-1} + 1$.

5. $1^2 \cdot 2 + 2^2 \cdot 2^2 + 3^2 \cdot 2^3 + \ldots + n^2 \cdot 2^n = (n^2 - 2n + 3)2^{n+1} - 6$

(cont)

6(i)(a) Show that $\frac{1}{n} - \frac{1}{n+1} = \frac{1}{n(n+1)}$ and $\frac{1}{(n+1)^2} < \frac{1}{n(n+1)}$

(b) Using (a) and the method of induction, prove that:
$$S_n = \sum_{1}^{n} \frac{1}{r^2} \leq 2 - \frac{1}{n+1} \text{ for } n \geq 1$$

(c) Show $1.45 \leq S_{99} \leq 1.99$

(ii) Using the method of induction, prove that for each positive integer n there are unique positive integers a_n and b_n such that
$$(1 + \sqrt{2})^n = a_n + \sqrt{2} \cdot b_n.$$
Prove that $a_n^2 - 2b_n^2 = (-1)^n$

7. Prove by induction that $(1 + x)^n \geq 1 + nx, \; x > -1$

8. If $u_1 = 2, \; u_2 = 3$ and $u_{n+2} = 3u_{n+1} - 2u_n$, prove by induction that $u_n = 2^{n-1} + 1$.

9. Assuming the triangular inequality $|b + c| \leq |b| + |c|$, prove by induction that:
$$|x_1 + x_2 + x_3 + \ldots + x_n| \leq |x_1| + |x_2| + \ldots + |x_n|$$

10. Prove by induction that $x^n + y^n$ is divisible by $x + y$ for all odd positive integers n.

11. Prove by induction that $2n^3 - 3n^2 + n + 31 \geq 0$.

12. Using the results $^nC_0 = \; ^nC_n = 1$ and $^{n+1}C_r = \; ^nC_{r-1} + \; ^nC_r$, prove by induction the binomial theorem:
$$(1 + x)^n = \; ^nC_0 + \; ^nC_1 x + \; ^nC_2 x^2 + \ldots + \; ^nC_r x^r + \ldots + \; ^nC_n x^n.$$

13. (a) Show that $\dfrac{\sin(\frac{3x}{2}) - \sin(\frac{x}{2})}{2\sin(\frac{x}{2})} = \cos x$

(b) Prove by induction that:
$$\cos x + \cos 2x + \cos 3x + \ldots + \cos nx = \frac{\sin(\frac{2n+1}{2})x}{2\sin(\frac{x}{2})} - \frac{1}{2}$$

10.6 Properties of Integrals

1. **Piecewise Functions**

Let $f(x) = g(x)$, if $a \leqslant x \leqslant c$
$ = h(x)$, if $c < x \leqslant b$

Then $\int_a^b f(x)\,dx = \int_a^c g(x)\,dx + \int_c^b h(x)\,dx$

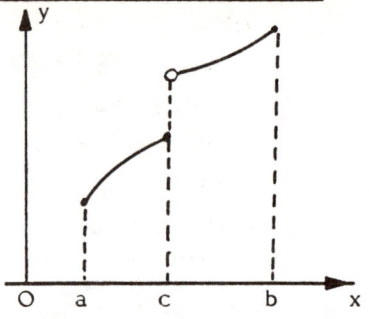

EXAMPLE: (1)

Evaluate $\int_{-1}^{1} f(x)\,dx$, where $f(x) = |x|$, $-1 \leqslant x \leqslant 1$.

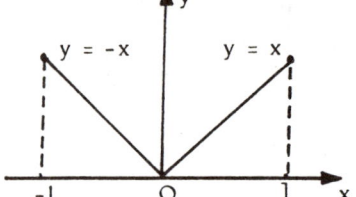

SOLUTION:

$f(x) = |x|$, $-1 \leqslant x \leqslant 1$

$\therefore f(x) = -x$ for $-1 \leqslant x \leqslant 0$
$ = x$ for $0 < x \leqslant 1$

$\therefore \int_{-1}^{1} f(x)\,dx = \int_{-1}^{0} (-x)\,dx + \int_{0}^{1} x\,dx = \left[-\frac{x^2}{2}\right]_{-1}^{0} + \left[\frac{x^2}{2}\right]_{0}^{1} = \frac{1}{2} + \frac{1}{2} = 1$

EXAMPLE: (2)

If $f(x) = \sin x$ for $-\pi \leqslant x \leqslant 0$
$ = x$ for $0 < x \leqslant \pi$,

(a) Evaluate $\int_{-\pi}^{\pi} f(x)\,dx$

(b) Find the area between the curve $y = f(x)$ and the x-axis, $-\pi \leqslant x \leqslant \pi$.

SOLUTION:

(a) As an integral

$\int_{-\pi}^{\pi} f(x)\,dx = \int_{-\pi}^{0} \sin x\,dx + \int_{0}^{\pi} x\,dx$

$= [-\cos x]_{-\pi}^{0} + \left[\frac{x^2}{2}\right]_{0}^{\pi}$

$= -2 + \frac{\pi^2}{2}$

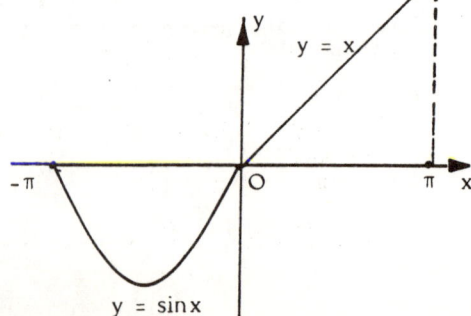

(b) We observe that part of the required area is below the x-axis, so we proceed as follows:

The required area $A = -\int_{-\pi}^{0} \sin x\,dx + \int_{0}^{\pi} x\,dx$

Using part (a), $A = 2 + \frac{\pi^2}{2}$ Sq. u.

EXAMPLE: (3)

The function $F(x)$ is defined as $F(x) = \int_0^x f(t)\,dt$
where $f(t) = 2 - t, \quad 0 \leq t \leq 4$
$\qquad\quad = t - 6, \quad 4 < t \leq 8$

(a) Sketch the graph of the function $f(t)$
(b) Find and determine the nature of the stationary points of the curve $y = F(x)$
(c) Sketch the curve $y = F(x)$; hence find the area between the curve $y = F(x)$ and the x-axis.

(a)

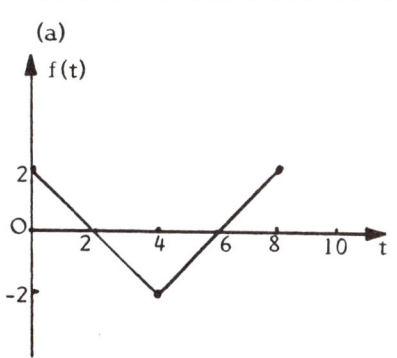

(b) $F(x) = \int_0^x f(t)\,dt, \quad 0 \leq t \leq 8$

$\therefore F'(x) = f(x) \qquad \ldots (1)$

The stationary points of $F(x)$ are given by $f(x) = 0$.

$\therefore 2 - x = 0, \quad 0 \leq x \leq 4$
or $x - 6 = 0, \quad 4 < x \leq 8$

So the stationary points are where $x = 2$ and $x = 6$.

From (1), $F''(x) = f'(x)$

Now $f'(x) = -1, \quad 0 \leq x \leq 4$
and $\quad f'(x) = 1, \quad 4 < x \leq 8$

$\therefore F''(2) < 0$ and $F''(6) > 0$

Hence $A(2, F(2))$ is a maximum point and $B(2, F(6))$ is a minimum turning point.

$F(2) = \int_0^2 f(t)\,dt = \int_0^2 (2-t)\,dt$

$\therefore F(2) = [2t - \frac{t^2}{2}]_0^2 = 2$

$F(6) = \int_0^4 (2-t)\,dt + \int_4^6 (t-6)\,dt$

$\therefore F(6) = [2t - \frac{t^2}{2}]_0^4 + [\frac{t^2}{2} - 6t]_4^6$

$\qquad = 0 + -2$
$\qquad = -2$

$\therefore$ A is $(2, 2)$, B is $(6, -2)$

(c) $F(x) = \int_0^x (2-t)\,dt, \quad 0 \leq t \leq 4$

$\qquad = \int_4^x (t-6)\,dt, \quad 4 < t \leq 8$

$\therefore F_1(x) = 2x - \frac{x^2}{2}, \quad 0 \leq x \leq 4$

$F_2(x) = \frac{x^2}{2} - 6x + 16, \quad 4 < x \leq 8$

$F(x) = 0$ gives the intersections with the x-axis, i.e.

$x = 0, 4, 8$

The sketch of $y = F(x)$ is as shown in the diagram.

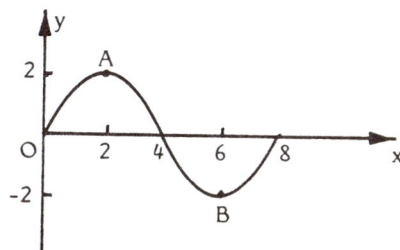

The required area

$A = \int_0^4 (2x - \frac{x^2}{2})\,dx + - \int_4^8 (\frac{x^2}{2} - 6x + 16)\,dx$

$\qquad = \frac{16}{3} - (-\frac{16}{3}) \qquad = \frac{32}{3}$ sq.u.

2. Inequalities involving Integrals

Many important inequalities such as:

1. $\frac{1}{2} + \frac{1}{3} + \frac{1}{4} + \ldots + \frac{1}{n} \leq \log_e n$

2. $1^3 + 2^3 + \ldots + n^3 \leq \frac{n^4}{3}$, etc. can be proved by using the following property of the integral $\int_a^b f(x)\,dx$.

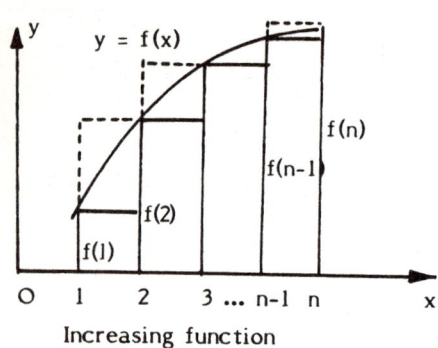
Increasing function

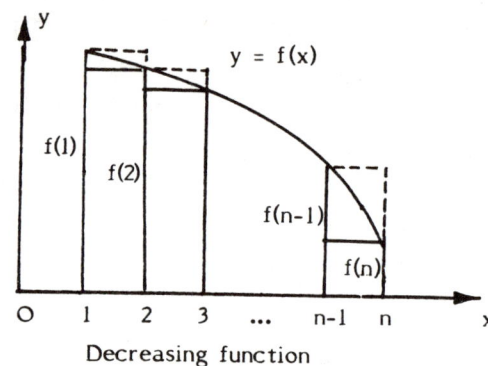
Decreasing function

Using the diagrams we obtain the following inequalities:

1. For $f(x)$ increasing:

Area of inner rectangles $\leq \int_1^n f(x)\,dx \leq$ Area of outer rectangles

$f(1) + f(x) + \ldots + f(n-1) \leq \int_1^n f(x)\,dx \leq f(2) + f(3) + \ldots + f(n)$

2. For $f(x)$ decreasing:

$f(2) + f(3) + \ldots + f(n) \leq \int_1^n f(x) \leq f(1) + f(2) + \ldots + f(n-1)$

EXAMPLE: (1) Prove the inequality: $\frac{1}{2} + \frac{1}{3} + \frac{1}{4} + \ldots + \frac{1}{n} \leq \log_e n$

SOLUTION: Let $f(x) = \frac{1}{x}$, $1 \leq x \leq n$

The L.H.S. of the inequality is a lower sum for the integral

$\int_1^n \frac{1}{x}\,dx = \log_e n$, then using:

$\therefore f(2) + f(3) + \ldots + f(n) \leq \int_1^n f(x)\,dx$

$\therefore \frac{1}{2} + \frac{1}{3} + \ldots + \frac{1}{n} \leq \log_e n$.

Note that the function $f(x)$ is chosen by replacing n by x in the general term of the given series.

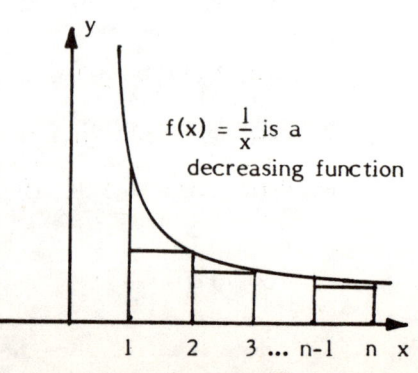
$f(x) = \frac{1}{x}$ is a decreasing function

Exercise 10F

Find the integral of the function $f(x)$ on the stated interval:
1. On $[0, 5]$, $f(x) = x + 2$ if $0 \leq x \leq 2$ and $f(x) = 4$, $2 < x \leq 5$
2. On $[0, 2]$, $f(x) = |x - 1|$
3. On $[-\pi, \pi]$, $f(x) = |\sin x|$
4. On $[-\pi, \pi]$, $f(x) = \cos x$, $-\pi \leq x \leq 0$,
   $\qquad\qquad\qquad\quad = x$, $\qquad\;\; 0 < x \leq \pi$

5. The graph of the function
   $f(t) = 1 - t, \; 0 \leq t \leq 2$
   $\qquad = t - 3, \; 2 < t \leq 5$
   is shown in the diagram.

   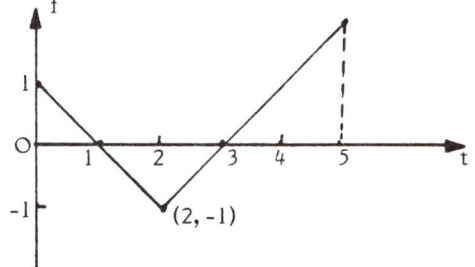

   The function $h(x)$ is defined as:
   $$h(x) = \int_0^x f(t)\,dt, \; 0 \leq x \leq 5$$

   (a) Find the function $h(x)$ over the intervals $0 \leq x \leq 2$ and $2 < x \leq 5$

   (b) Find all the turning points of the function $h(x)$ and hence sketch it.

   (c) Find $\int_0^5 h(x)\,dx$

   (d) Find the area between the curve $y = h(x)$, the x-axis for $0 \leq x \leq 5$

Sketch the function $f(x)$ and prove the following inequalities:

6. $f(x) = \frac{1}{x}$: $1 + \frac{1}{2} + \frac{1}{3} + \ldots + \frac{1}{n-1} \geq \log_e n$

7. $f(x) = \frac{1}{\sqrt{x}}$: $\frac{1}{\sqrt{2}} + \frac{1}{\sqrt{3}} + \ldots + \frac{1}{\sqrt{n}} \leq 2(\sqrt{n} - 1)$

8. $f(x) = \sqrt{x}$: $\sqrt{1} + \sqrt{2} + \ldots + \sqrt{n} \geq \int_0^n \sqrt{x}\,dx = \frac{2}{3} n \sqrt{n}$

9. $f(x) = x^2$: $1^2 + 2^2 + \ldots + (n-1)^2 \leq \frac{n^3}{3} \leq 1^2 + 2^2 + \ldots + n^2$

10. $f(x) = \frac{1}{1 + x^2}$: Subdivide the interval $[0, 1]$ into n equal parts. By considering the values of $f(x)$ at $x = 0, \frac{1}{n}, \frac{2}{n}, \ldots, \frac{r}{n}, \ldots, \frac{n}{n}$, prove that:

    $\frac{1}{n} \sum_{r=1}^{n} \frac{n^2}{n^2 + r^2} \leq \frac{\pi}{4}$. (Hint: $\frac{n^2}{n^2 + r^2} = \frac{1}{1 + (r/n)^2}$)

Appendix 1

Bisector of an Angle of a Triangle

Theorem: The bisector (internal or external) of an angle of a triangle divides the opposite side (internally or externally) in the ratio of the sides containing the angle bisected.

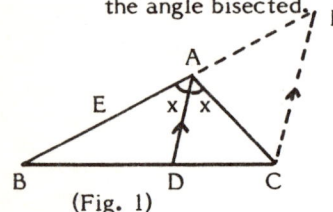
(Fig. 1)

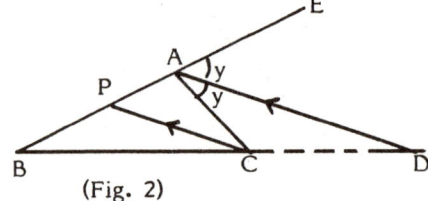
(Fig. 2)

Given: AD bisects ∠BAC, internally, in Fig. (1), externally in Fig. (2), and cuts BC (produced) at D.

Prove: $\dfrac{BD}{DC} = \dfrac{AB}{AC}$

Construction: Through C draw CP parallel to DA to cut BA (produced) at P.

Proof: Take any point E on AB in Fig. (1) and on BA produced in Fig. (2).

Then: ∠EAD = ∠APC (AD // PC, corresponding ∠s)
        ∠DAC = ∠ACP (AD // PC, alt. ∠s)
But, ∠EAD = ∠DAC (given)
∴   ∠APC = ∠ACP , so AP = AC

Since AD // PC, $\dfrac{BD}{DC} = \dfrac{BA}{AP}$

But   AP = AC , ∴ $\dfrac{BD}{DC} = \dfrac{BA}{AC}$

Corollary: If the base BC is divided internally (or externally) at D in the ratio AB : AC, then AD bisects the angle BAC internally (or externally).

The proof is similar to that of the theorem above.

Appendix 2

Rectangular Hyperbola: $xy = c^2$

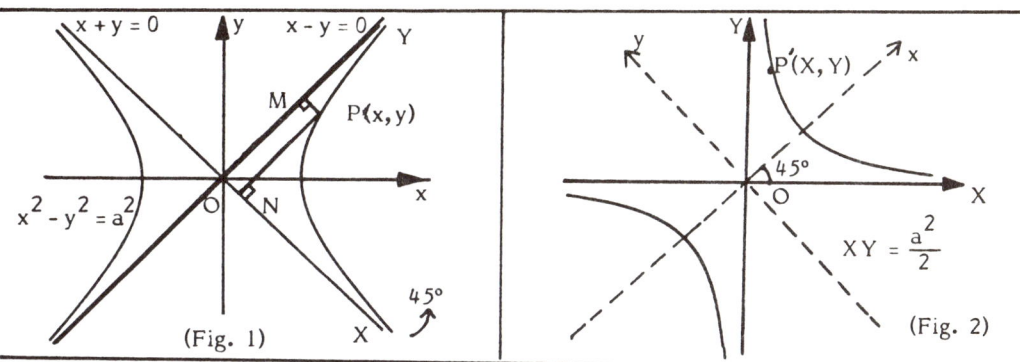

(Fig. 1)   (Fig. 2)

Consider the rectangular hyperbola: $\quad x^2 - y^2 = a^2 \qquad \ldots (1)$

Its asymptotes are the two perpendicular lines

$\qquad x - y = 0 \quad$ and $\quad x + y = 0 \quad$ (Fig. 1)

Let $X = PM$ and $Y = PN$ be the perpendicular distances of any point $P(x,y)$ on the conic, from these asymptotes.

$$\therefore \quad X = \frac{x-y}{\sqrt{2}} \quad \text{and} \quad Y = \frac{x+y}{\sqrt{2}} \qquad \left[d = \frac{ax_1 + by_1 + c}{\sqrt{a^2 + b^2}} \right] \quad \ldots (2)$$

$$\therefore \quad XY = \frac{x^2 - y^2}{2} = \frac{a^2}{2}, \text{ as } P(x,y) \text{ is on the conic.}$$

Putting $c^2 = \frac{a^2}{2}$, the equation of the rectangular hyperbola $x^2 - y^2 = a^2$ referred to its asymptotes as co-ordinate axes is $XY = c^2$.

Alternatively, using complex numbers and taking $P(x,y)$ as any point on the conic $x^2 - y^2 = a^2$, let $X + iY$ represent the point $P'(X,Y)$ after OP is rotated anticlockwise through $45°$.

$$\therefore \quad X + iY = \text{cis}(\tfrac{\pi}{4}) \cdot (x + iy) = \frac{1}{\sqrt{2}}(1+i)(x+iy) = \frac{x-y}{\sqrt{2}} + \frac{x+y}{\sqrt{2}} i$$

$$\therefore \quad X = \frac{x-y}{\sqrt{2}} \quad \text{and} \quad Y = \frac{x+y}{\sqrt{2}}$$

The effect of the rotation used in this method is shown in Fig. 2 - where the orientation of the hyperbola and its asymptotes is that of the familiar type $xy = c^2$.

Answers

(All answers are given to three significant figures)

Chapter 1: Curve Sketching Exercise 1A

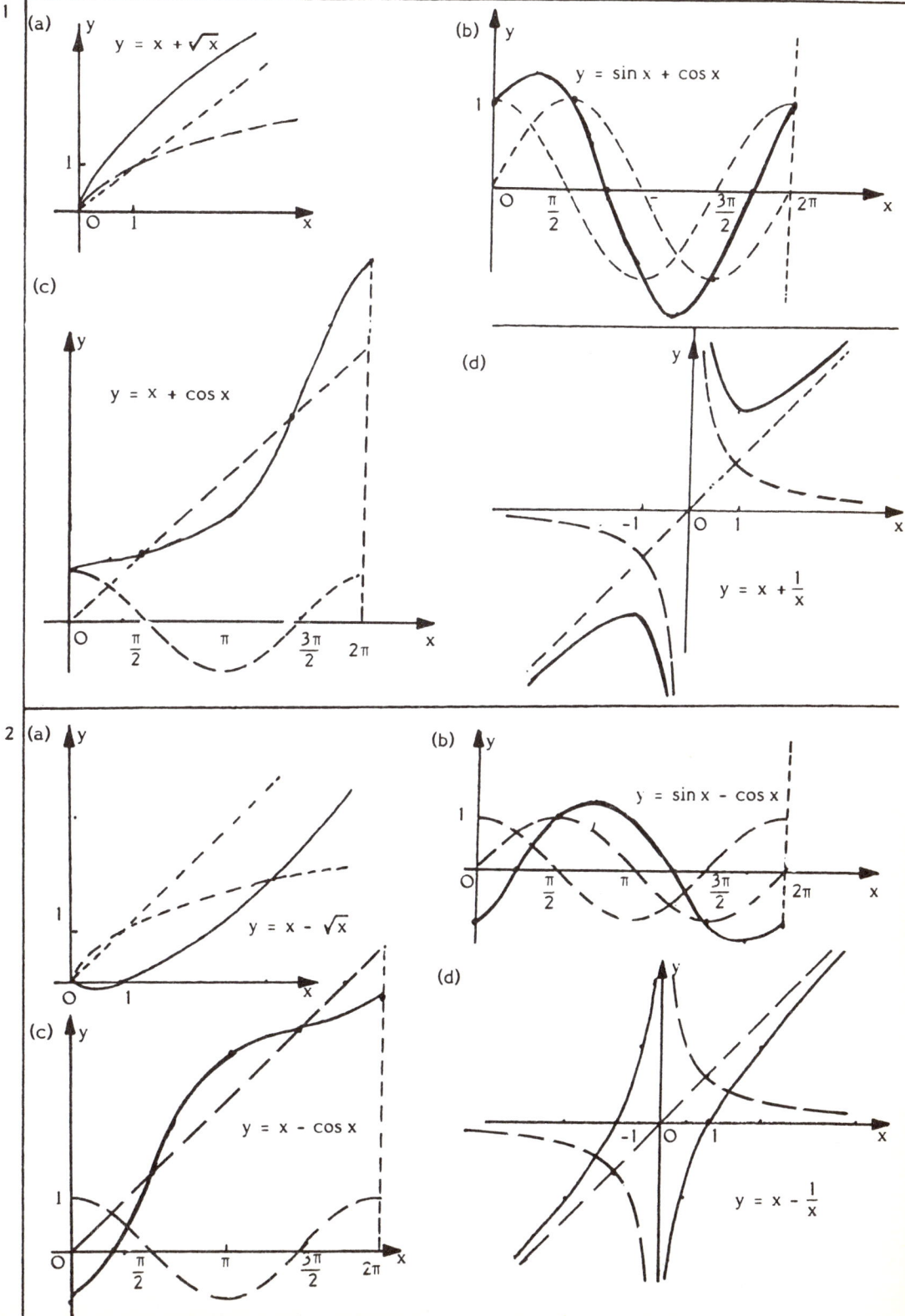

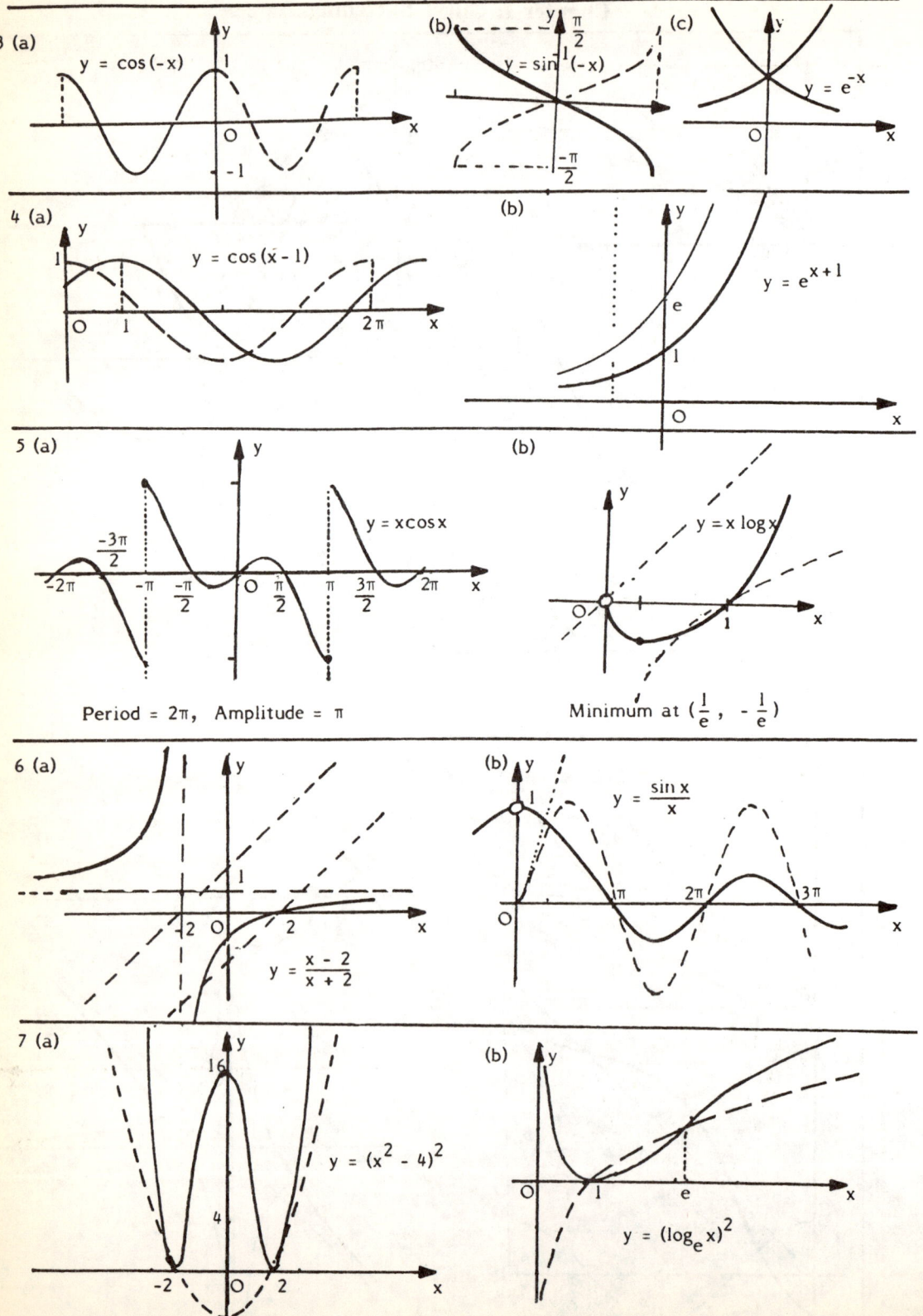

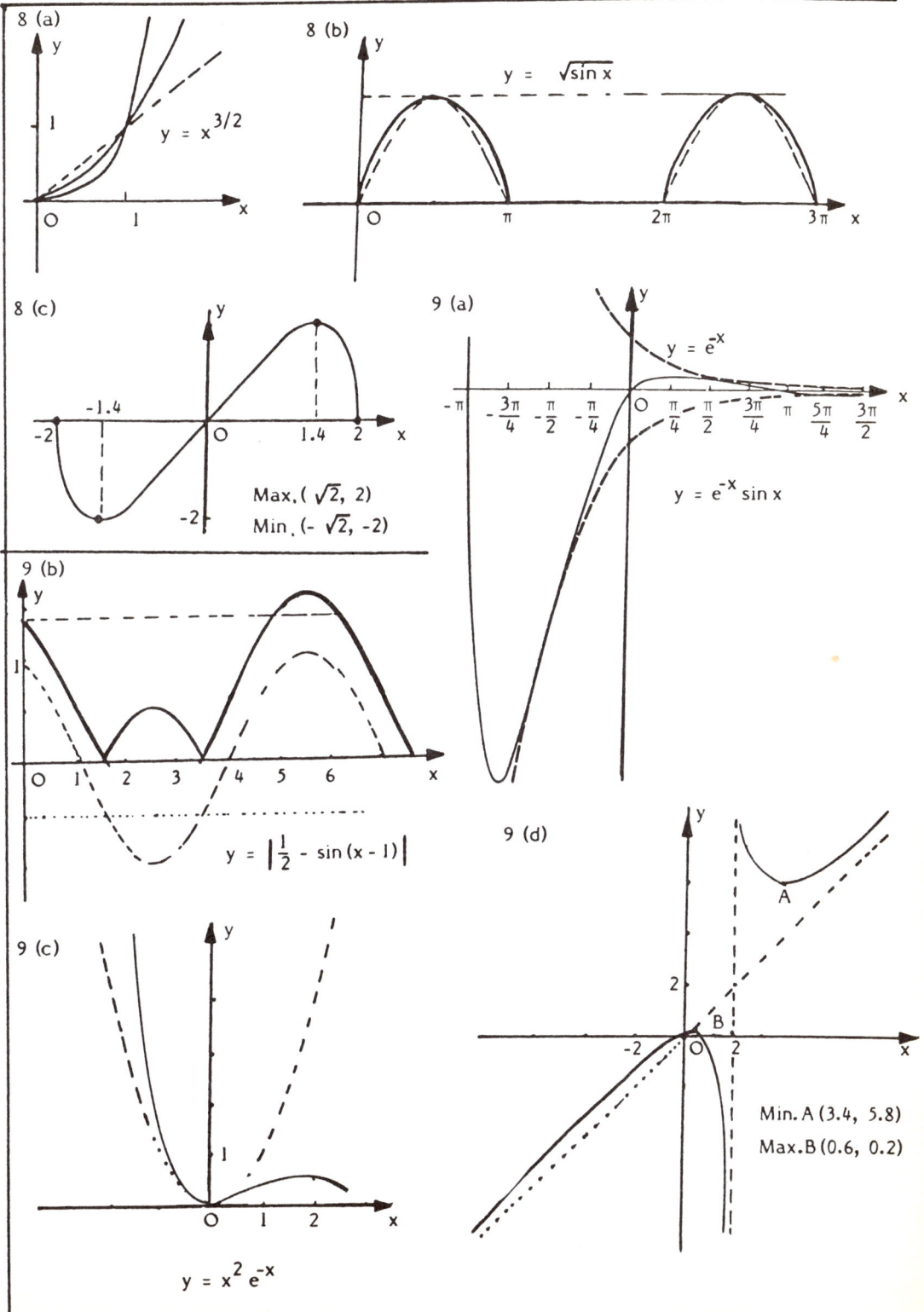

9 (e)
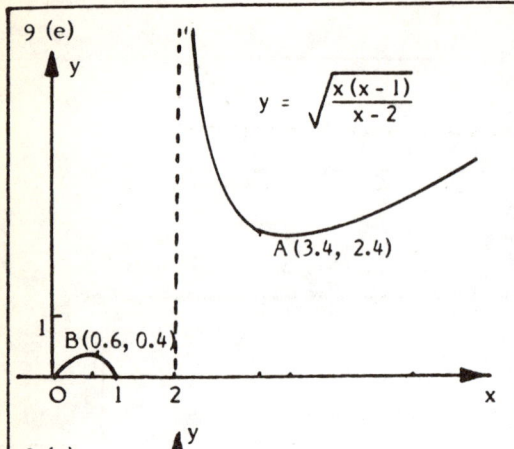

9 (f)
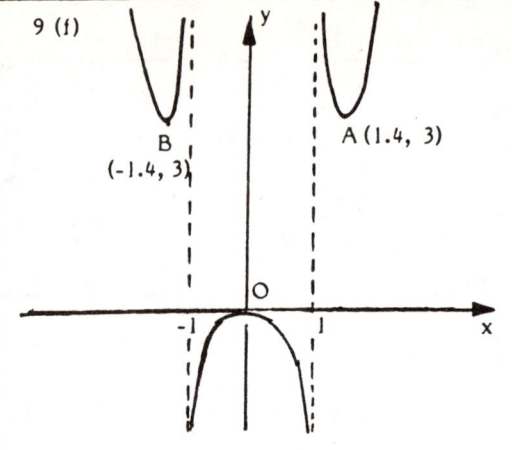

9 (g)
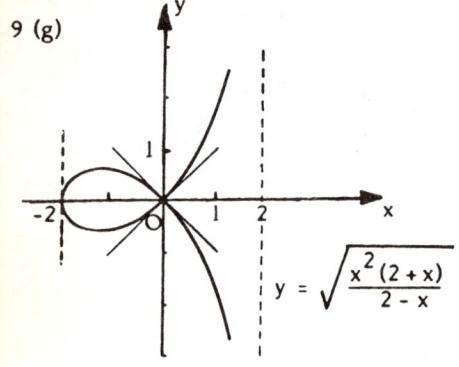

9 (h)
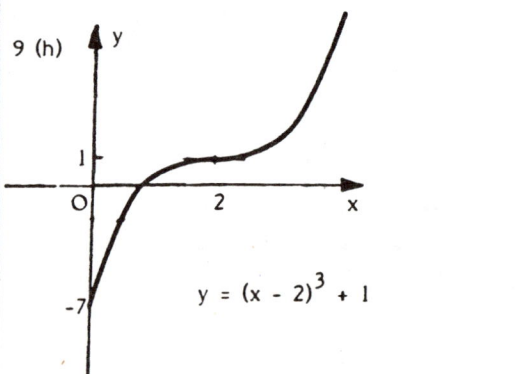

10
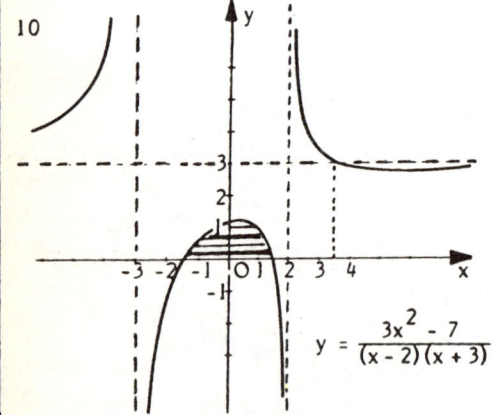

(b) $x = -3$, $x = 2$
(c) Max. $(\frac{1}{3}, \frac{6}{5})$, Min. $(7, \frac{14}{5})$
(d) See the graph above
(e) $x < |\frac{7}{3}|$ or $x > 3\frac{2}{3}$
(f) 2.66

11 (a)
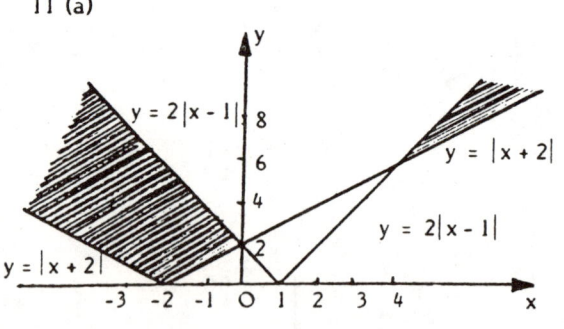

$x \leqslant 0$ or $x \geqslant 4$

11 (b)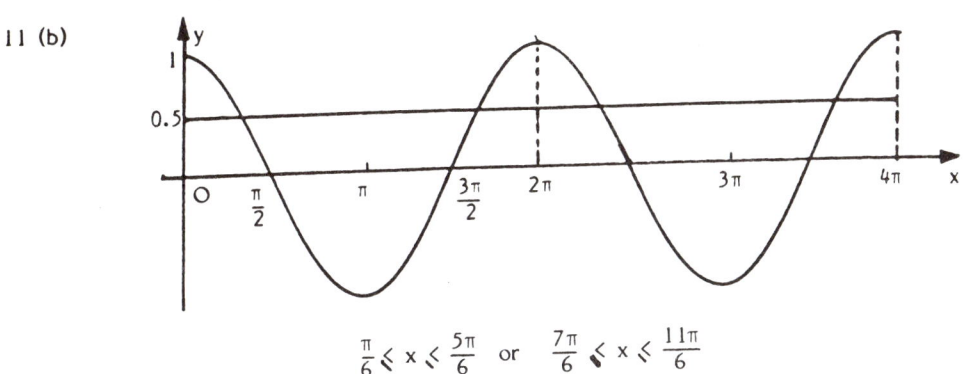

$\frac{\pi}{6} \leq x \leq \frac{5\pi}{6}$ or $\frac{7\pi}{6} \leq x \leq \frac{11\pi}{6}$

12 (a) $\frac{32\sqrt{2}}{15}$ (b) $\frac{4\pi}{3}$

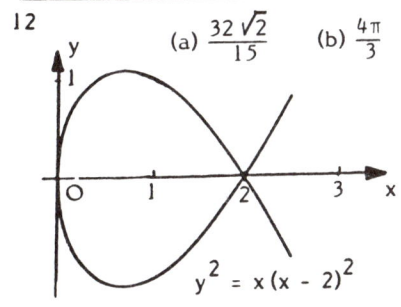

13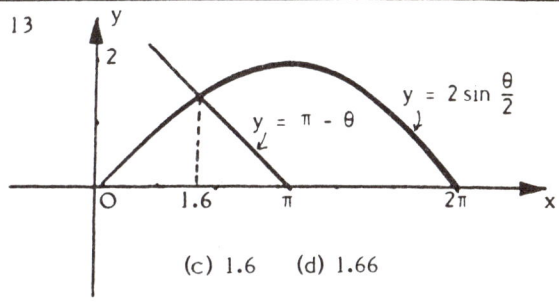

(c) 1.6 (d) 1.66

14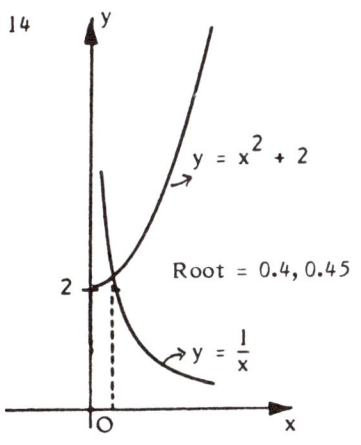

15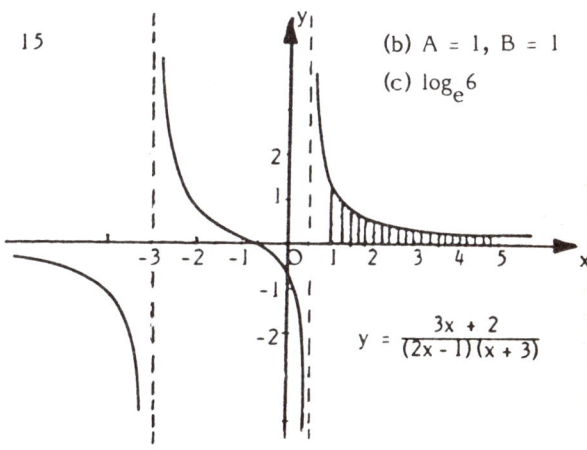

(b) $A = 1$, $B = 1$
(c) $\log_e 6$

16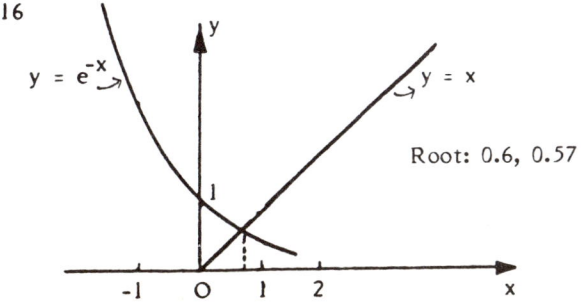

Root: 0.6, 0.57

Exercise 1B

1.
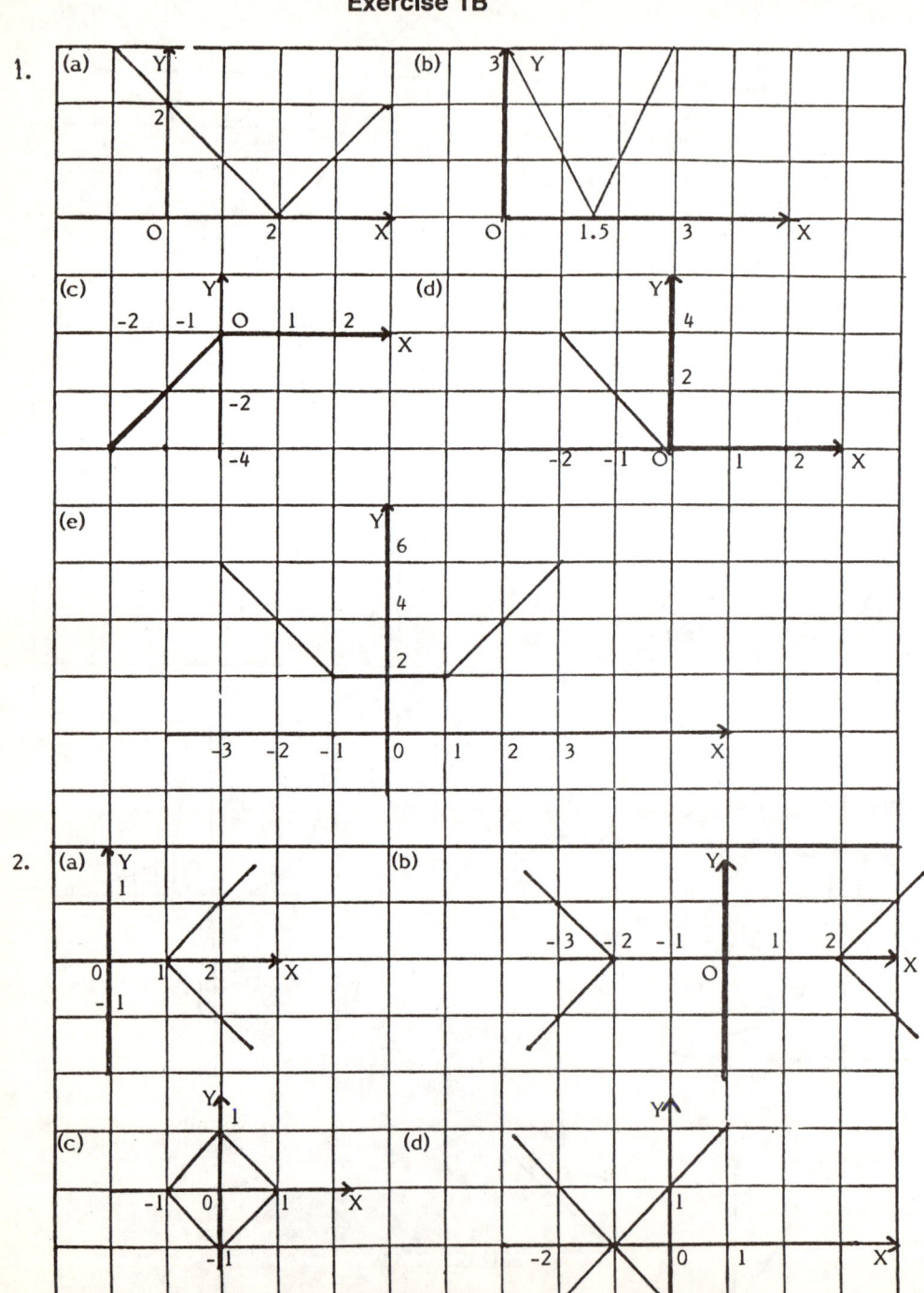

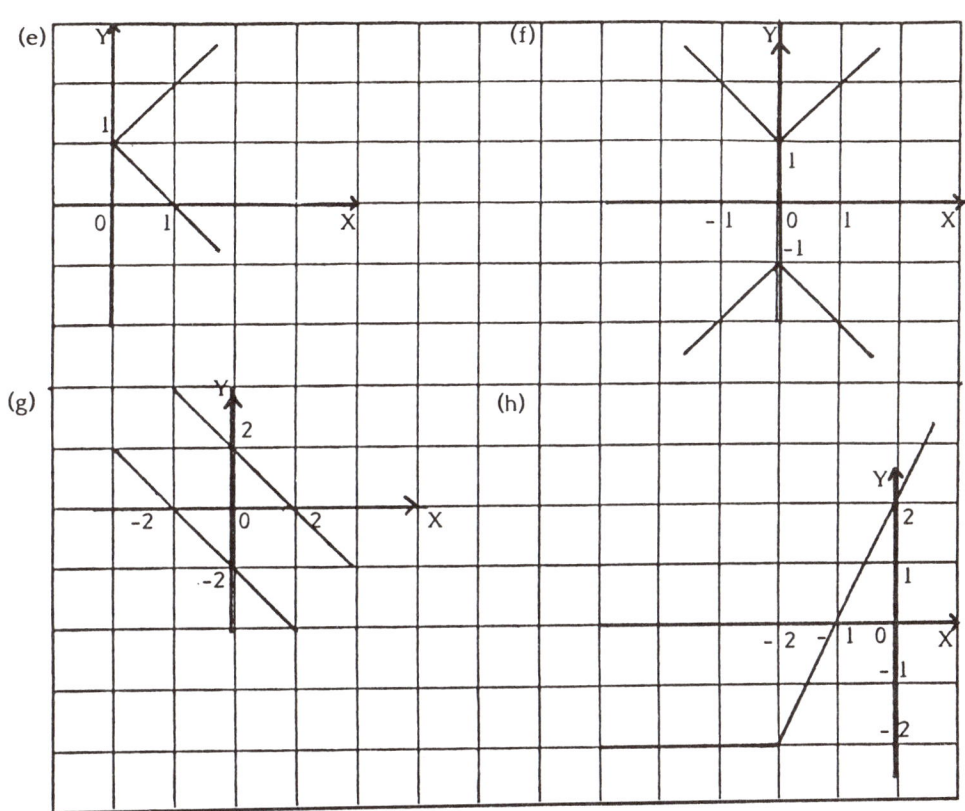

3.

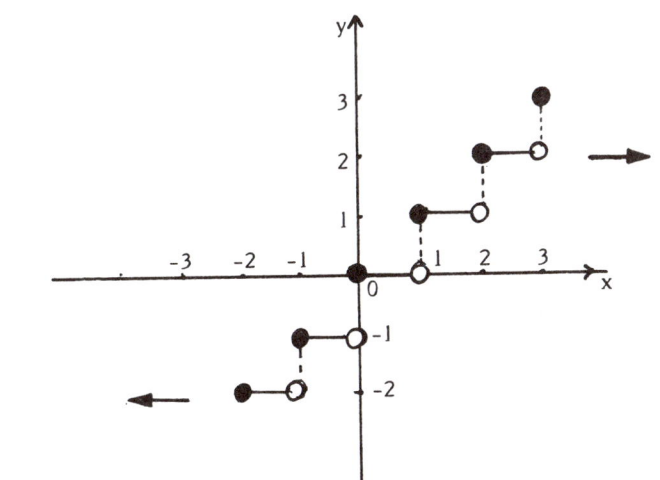

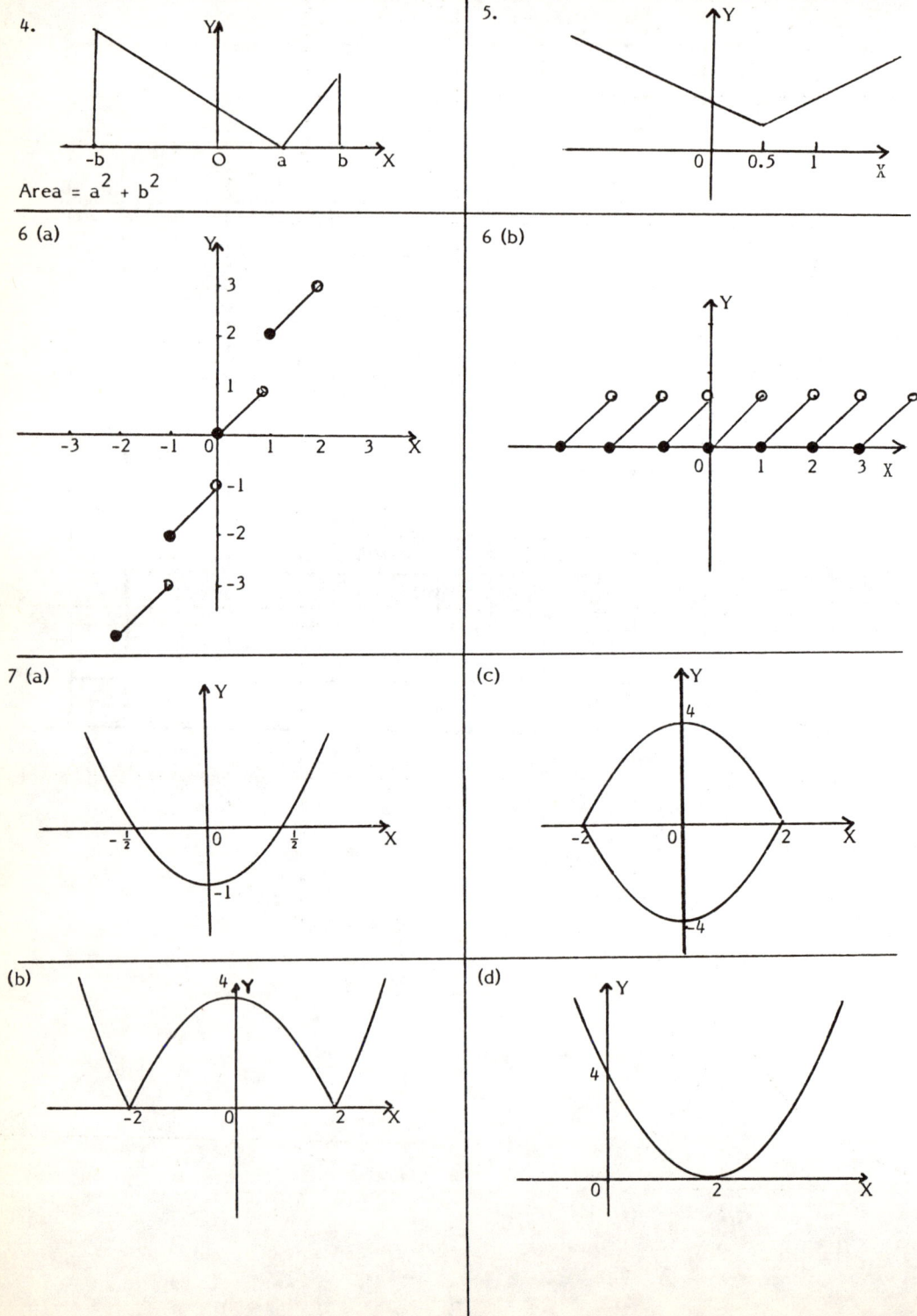

4. Area = $a^2 + b^2$

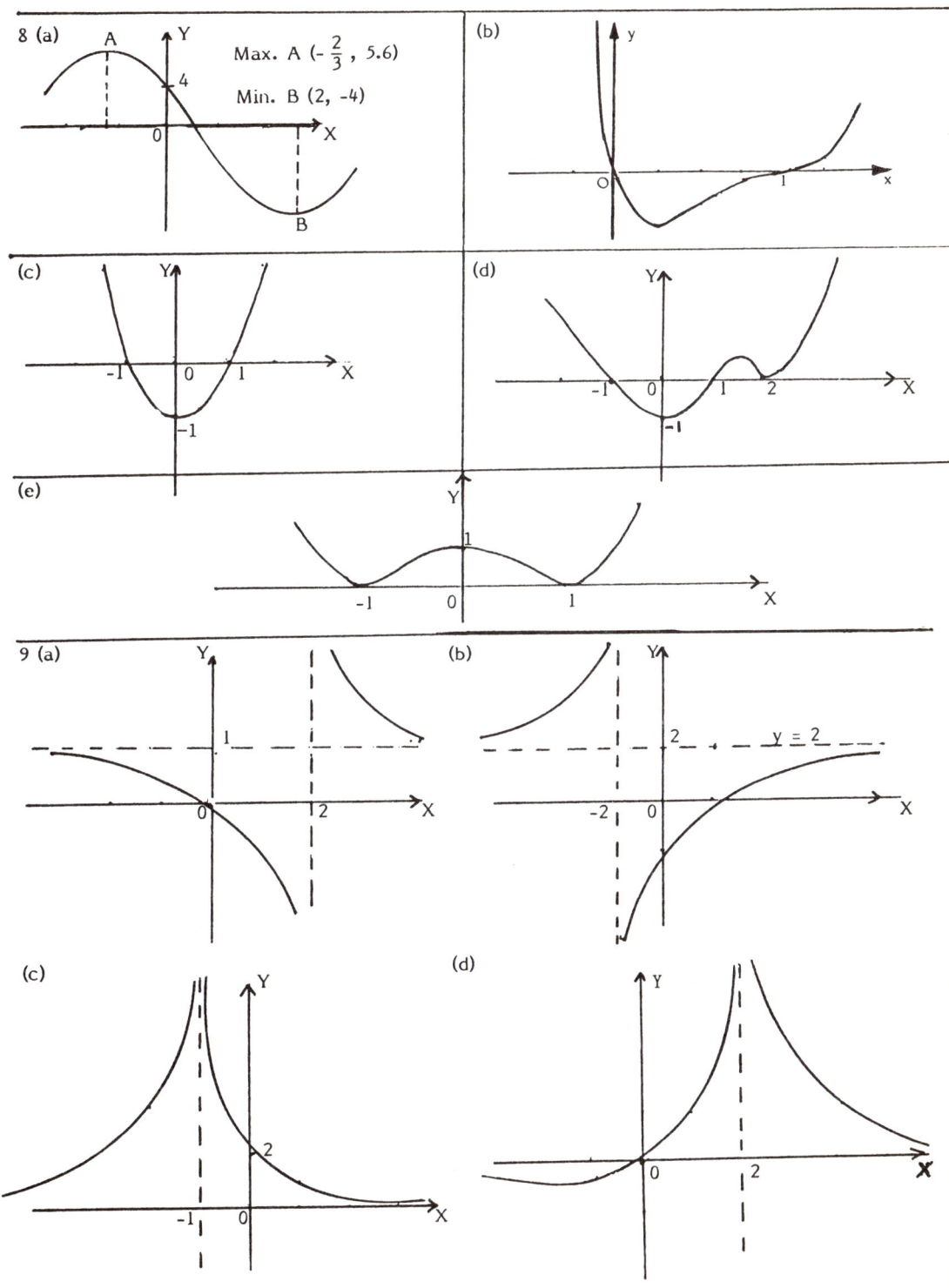

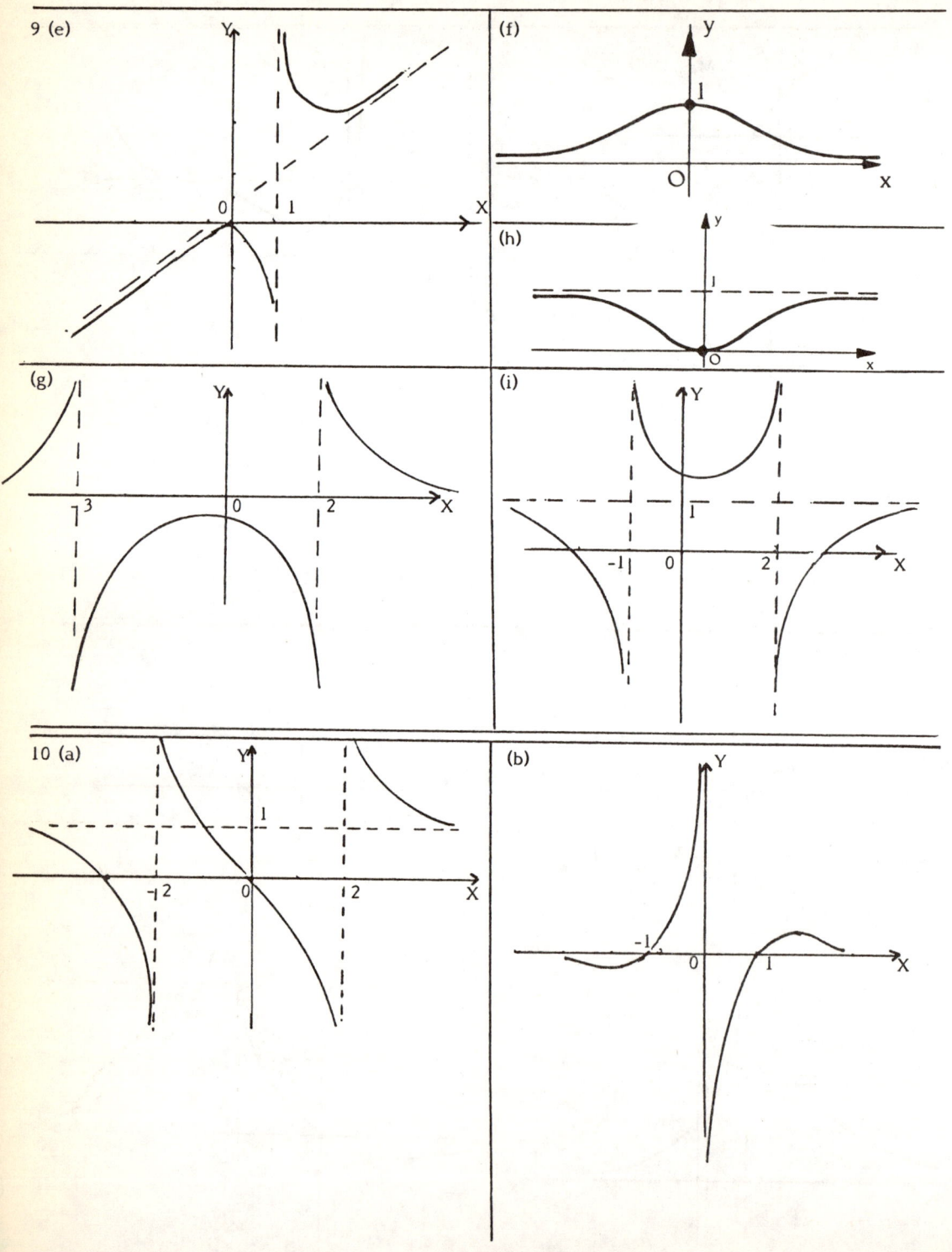

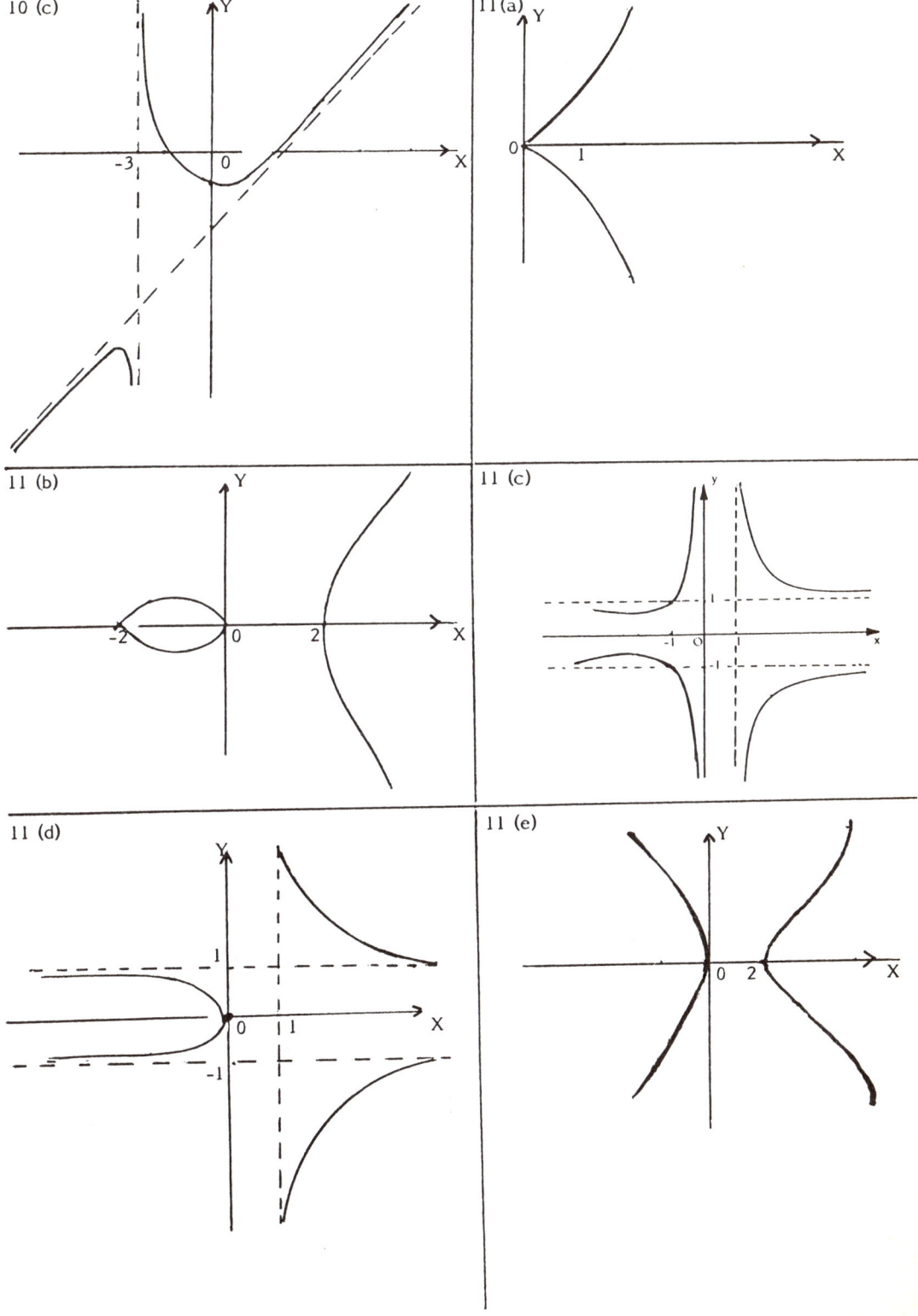

11 (f)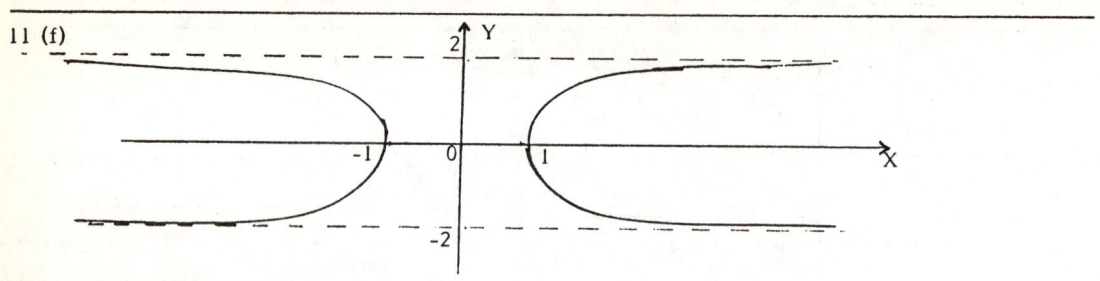

12 (a) See Section 1.5, page 11, Example (c)

(b)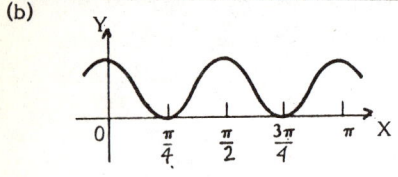

(c)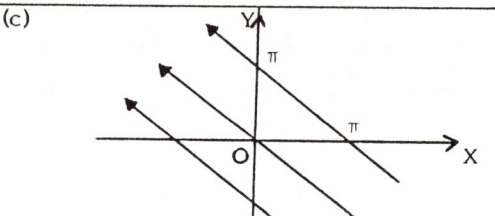

(d)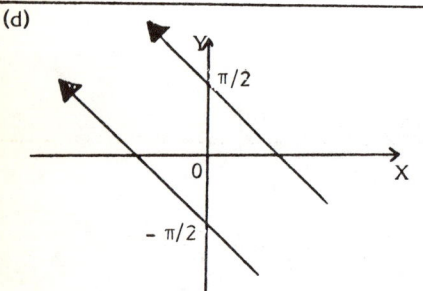

(e)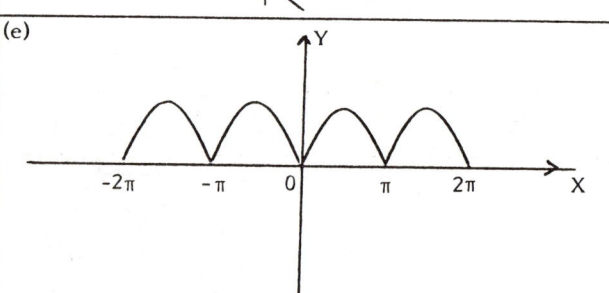

(f)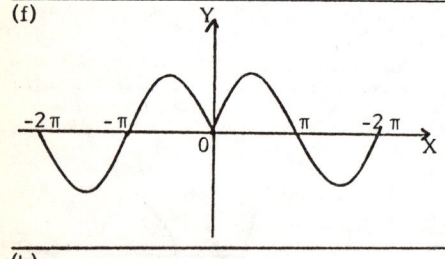

(g)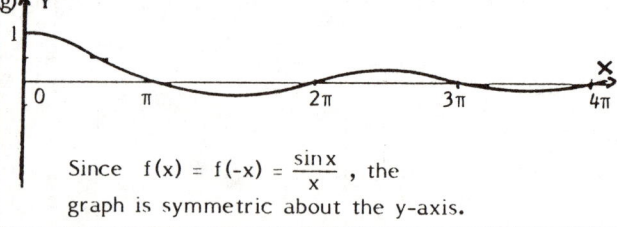

Since $f(x) = f(-x) = \frac{\sin x}{x}$, the graph is symmetric about the y-axis.

(h)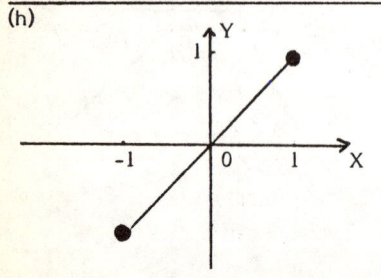

(i)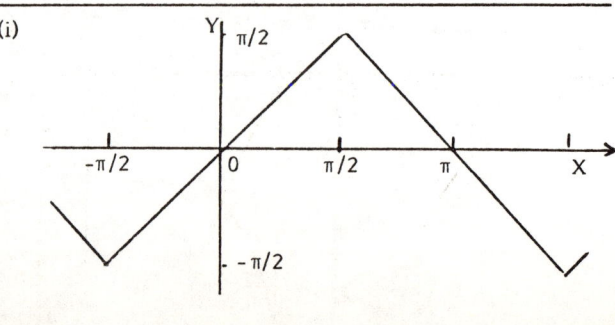

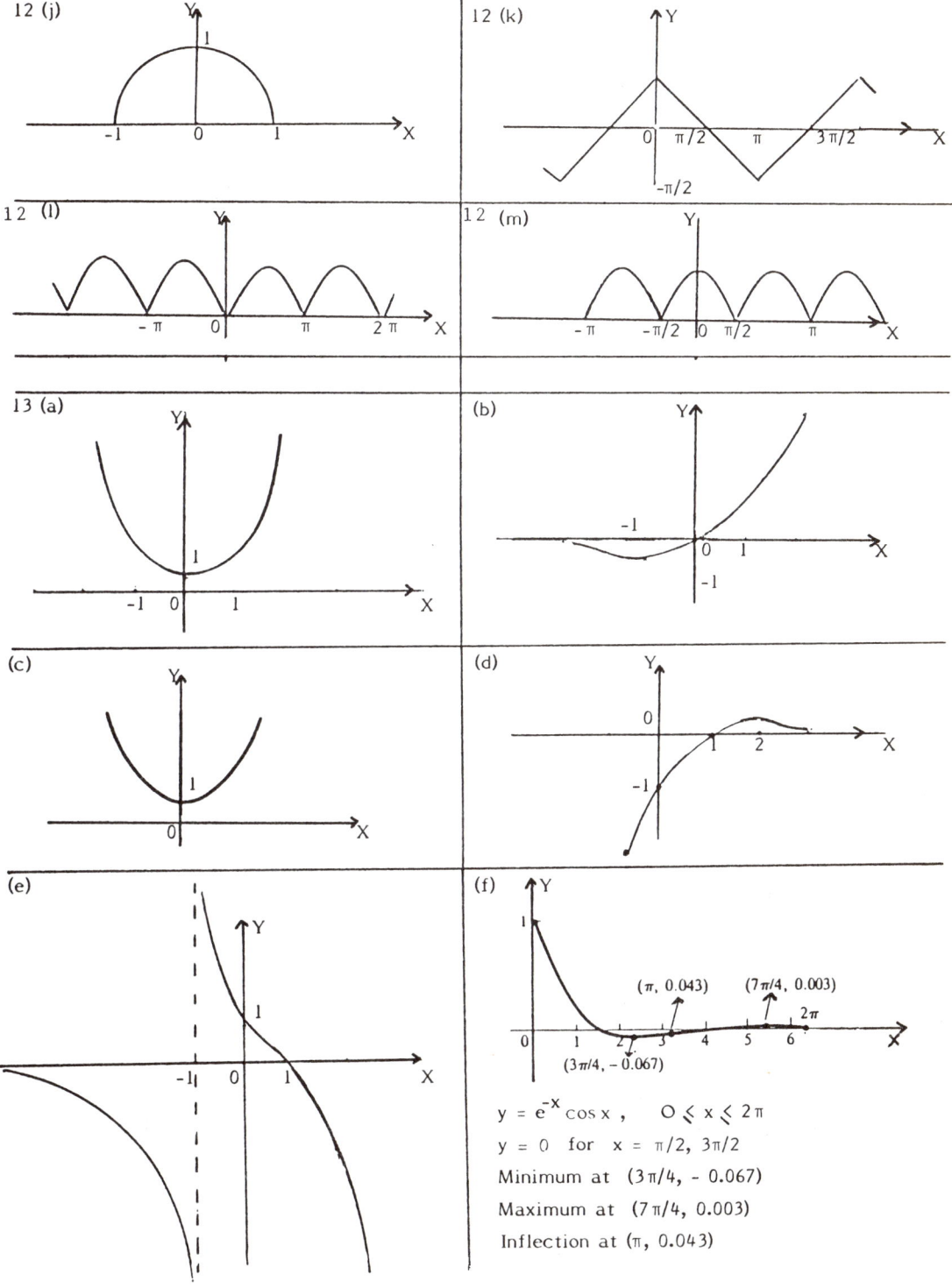

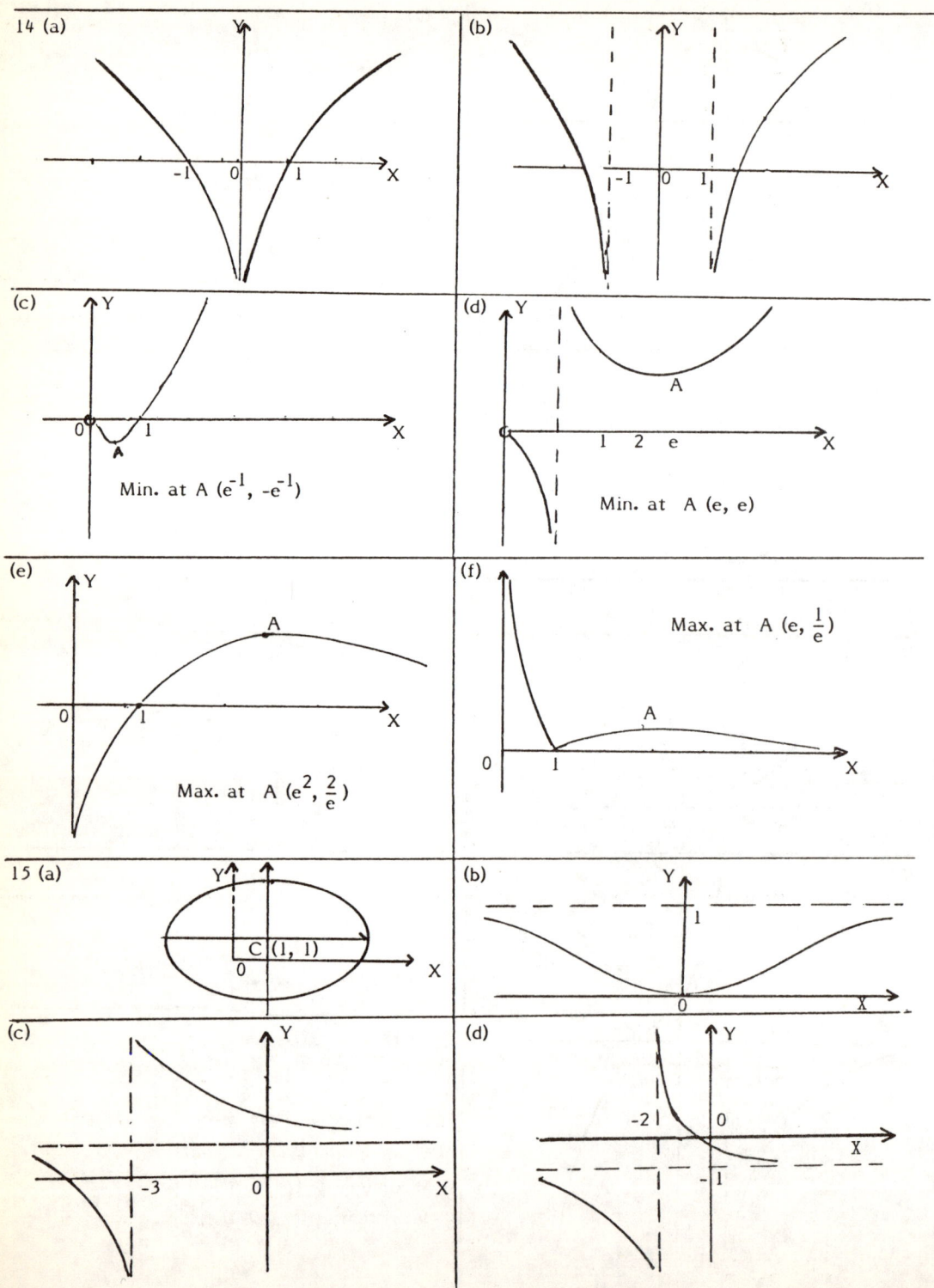

16.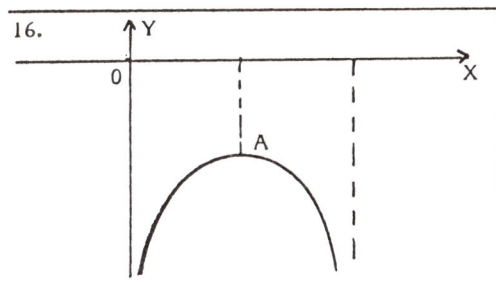

$0 < x < 1$, $y \leq -1.39$

( ) Minimum $A(\frac{1}{2}, -1.39)$

Asymptptes at $x = 0$ and
$x = 1$

17 (c)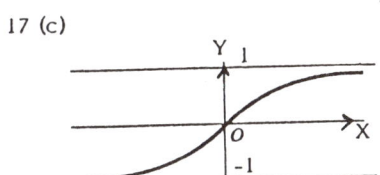

(d)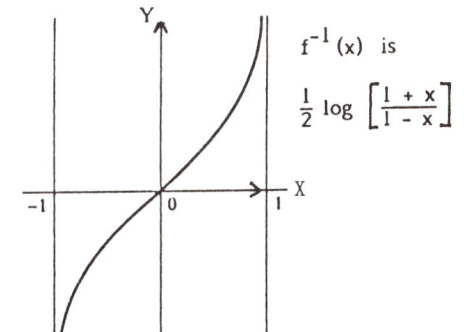

$f^{-1}(x)$ is

$\frac{1}{2} \log \left[\frac{1+x}{1-x}\right]$

(a) 1, -1
(b) All real x, $|y| < 1$
(c) Inflexion at $x = 0$.

18. (e)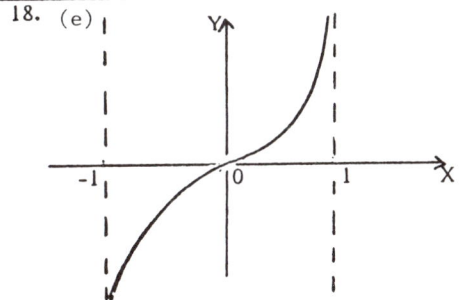

(a) $|x| \leq 1$

(c) $\frac{dy}{dx} = \frac{2x^2}{\sqrt{1-x^4}} + \sin^{-1}(x^2)$

(d) Inflexion at $x = 0$

$\frac{dy}{dx}$ does not exist at $x = \pm 1$

19. (a)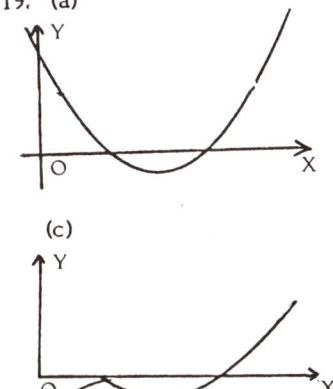

(b)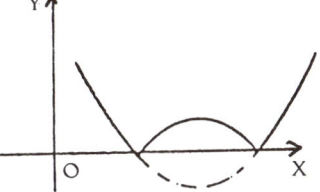

(c)

(d)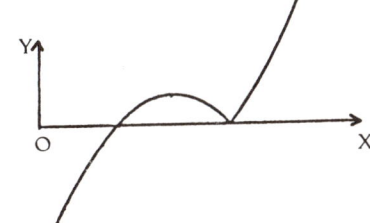

20.
(c)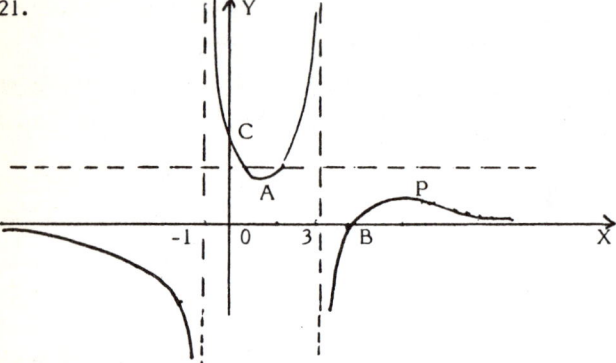

(a) Max. at $A(e, \frac{1}{e})$

(b) Asymptote at $x = 0$
$y \to 0$ as $x \to \infty$.
$y \to -\infty$ as $x \to 0$.

21.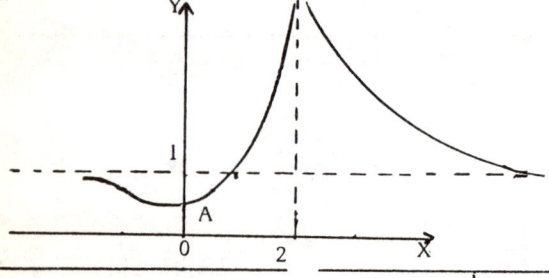

Intersections with axes.
$B(4, 0)$, $C(0, \frac{8}{3})$ $y \to 0$ as $x \to \pm \infty$
Min. at $A(1.8, 0.7)$
Max. at $P(6.6, 0.2)$

22.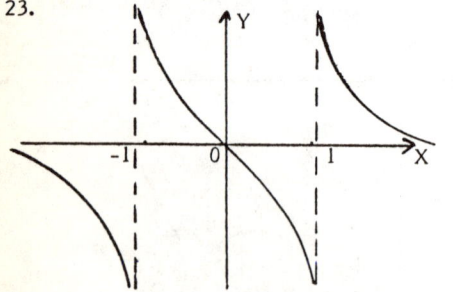

Asymptote at $x = 2$
Min. at $A(0, \frac{1}{4})$

23.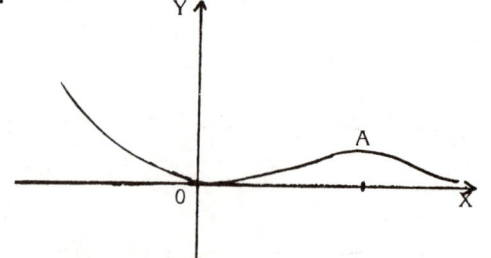

24.

Min. at $O(0, 0)$
Max. at $A(2, \frac{4}{e^2})$
$y \to 0$ as $x \to +\infty$
$y \to \infty$ as $x \to -\infty$.

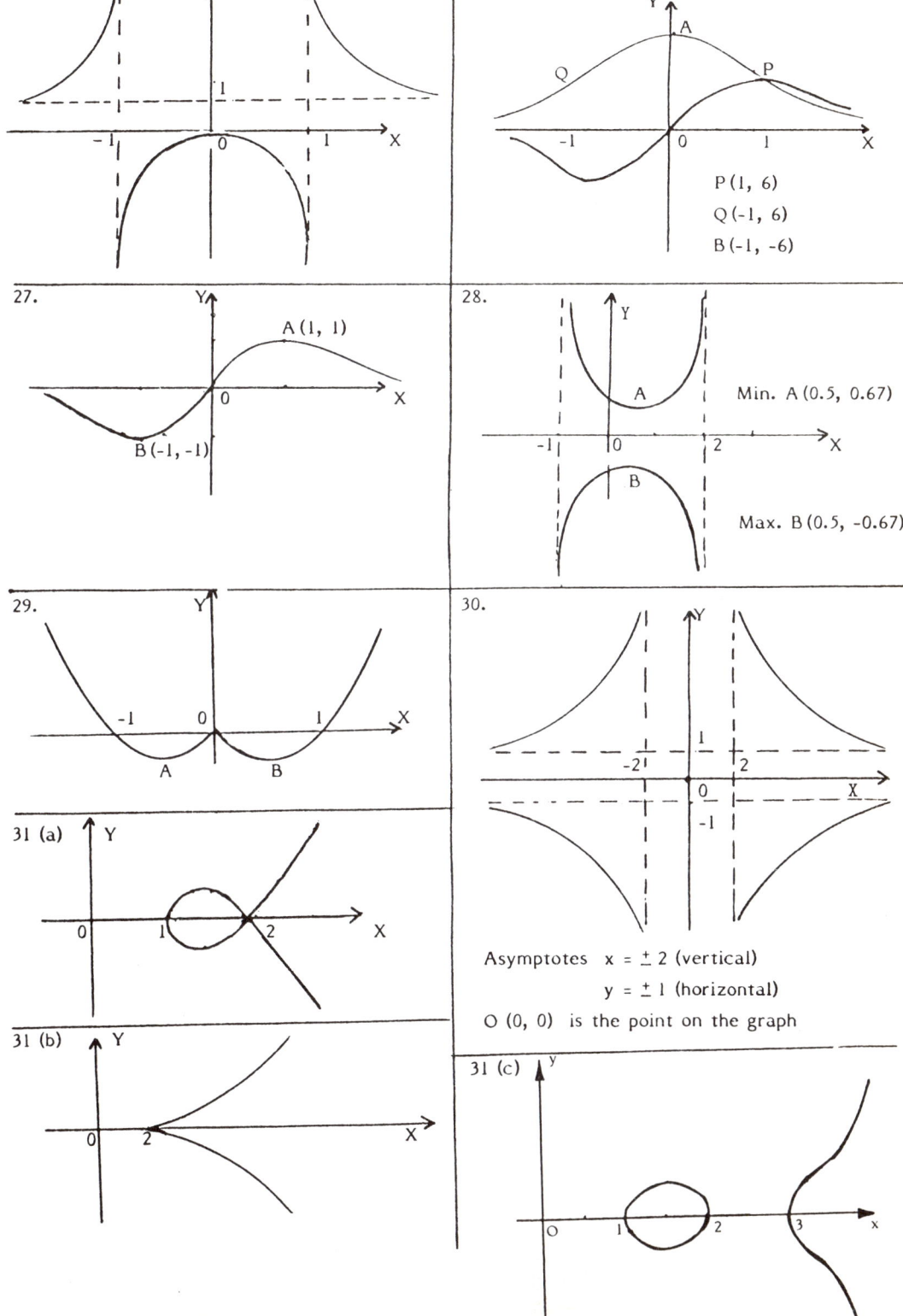

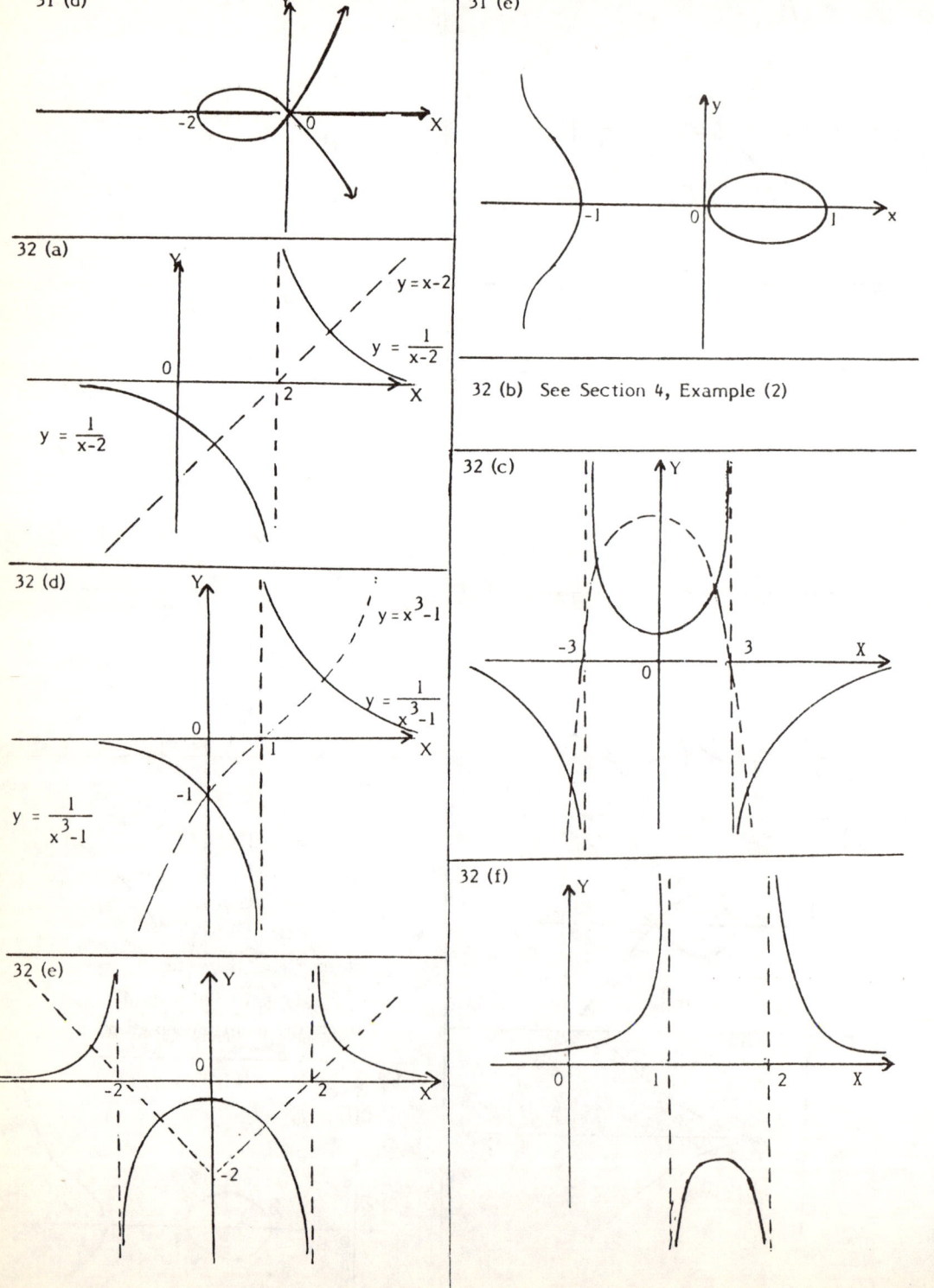

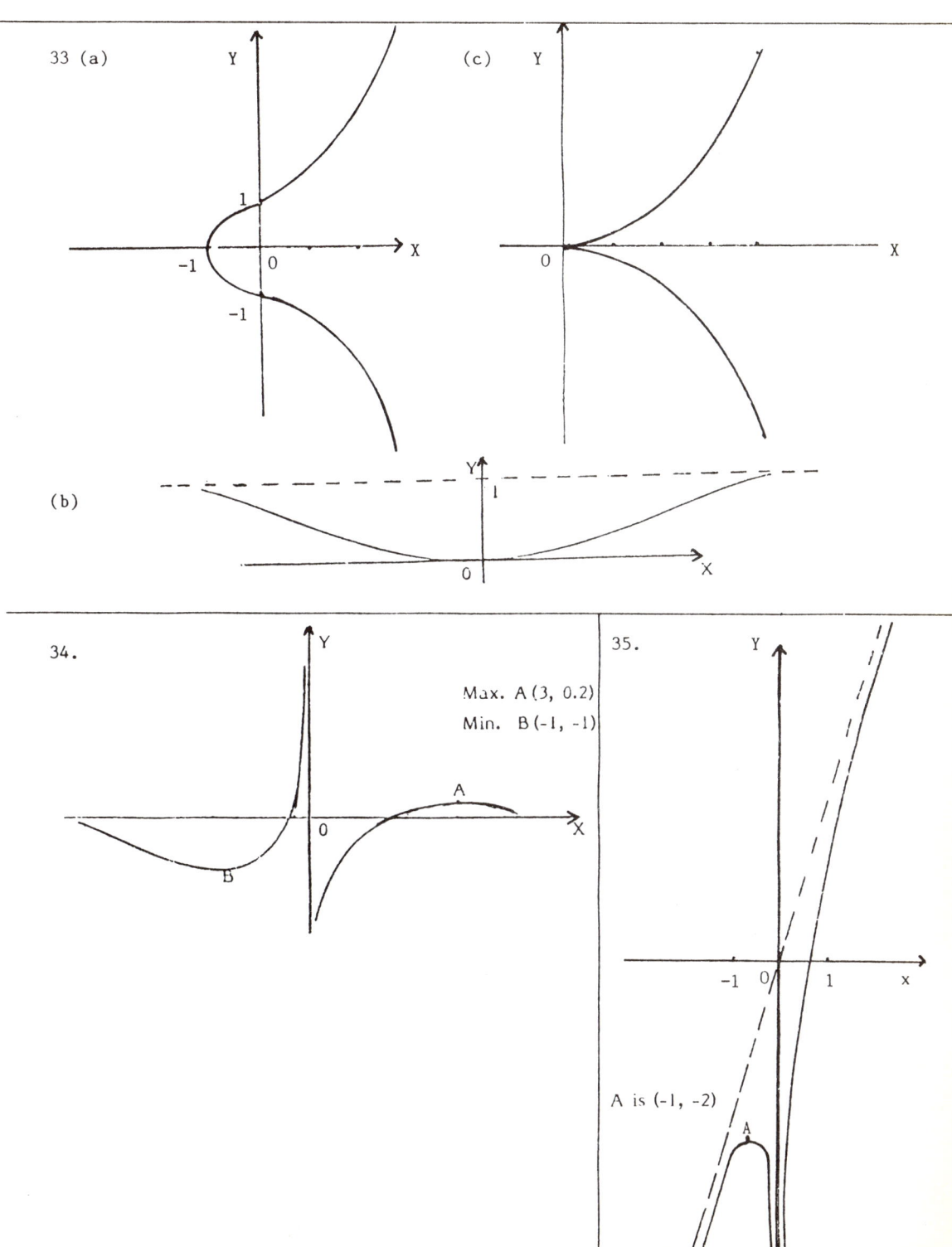

CHAPTER 2 INTEGRATION

Exercise 2A (constant omitted)

1. (a) $\dfrac{(x^2+1)^4}{4}$ (b) $\dfrac{-(1-x^2)^5}{5}$ (c) $\log_e(x^4+1)$

   (d) $-(x^4+1)^{-1}$ (e) $-\dfrac{1}{3}(1-x^2)^{3/2}$ (f) $\tan^{-1}(x^2)$

   (g) $\sqrt{x^2-1}$ (h) $-4\sqrt{1-\sqrt{x}}$

2. (a) $-\dfrac{\cos^3 x}{3}$ (b) $\dfrac{1}{4}\sin^4 x$ (c) $\dfrac{1}{5}\tan^5 x$

   (d) $-\dfrac{1}{5}\cot^5 x$ (e) $\dfrac{-1}{\cos x}$ (f) $-\dfrac{1}{5}(1+\cos x)^5$

   (g) $\dfrac{1}{5}\sec^5 x$ (h) $\dfrac{1}{3}(1+\tan x)^3$

3. (a) $\dfrac{1}{3}e^{x^3}$ (b) $-\tan^{-1}(e^{-x})$ (c) $e^{\sin^{-1}x}$

   (d) $\log_e(e^x + \sqrt{e^{2x}+1})$

4. (a) $\dfrac{1}{2}(\log_e x)^2$ (b) $\dfrac{1}{3}(\log x)^3$ (c) $-\dfrac{1}{2}(\log x)^{-2}$

   (d) $\dfrac{(1+\log x)^{-2}}{-2}$

5. (a) $-\dfrac{1}{4}e^{\cos 2x}$ (b) $\tan^{-1}(\cos x)$ (c) $\dfrac{2^{\sin x}}{\log_e 2}$

   (d) $\dfrac{1}{2}\log\left[\dfrac{e^x-1}{e^x+1}\right]$

6. (a) $-16\dfrac{1}{4}$ (b) $\dfrac{1}{16}$ (c) 1

   (d) 0.367 (e) 0.62 (f) $\dfrac{1}{2}$

Exercise 2B   (constant omitted)

---

1. (a) $e^{-x}(-x - 1)$ (b) $e^x(x^2 - 2x + 2)$ (c) $\frac{1}{2}e^x(\sin x - \cos x)$

2. (a) $\frac{1}{2}x \sin 2x + \frac{1}{4}\cos 2x$ (b) $-x^2 \cos x + 2x \sin x + 2\cos x$

   (c) $x^2 \sin x + 2x \cos x - 2 \sin x$

3. (a) $x \tan x + \log \cos x$ (b) $\frac{x^2}{4} - \frac{x}{4}\sin 2x - \frac{1}{8}\cos 2x$

   (c) $-x \cot x + \log \sin x$

4. (a) $\frac{x^3}{3}\log x - \frac{x^3}{9}$ (b) $\frac{2}{3}x^{3/2}(\log x - \frac{2}{3})$ (c) $x[(\log x)^2 - 2\log x + 2]$

5. (a) $x \cos^{-1} x - \sqrt{1 - x^2}$ (b) $x \tan^{-1} x - \frac{1}{2}\log(x^2 + 1)$

   (c) $\frac{x^2}{2}\tan^{-1} x - \frac{1}{2}x + \frac{1}{2}\tan^{-1} x$

6. (a) $x \log(x^2 - 1) - 2x - \log\left[\frac{x-1}{x+1}\right]$ (b) $\frac{3}{13}e^{-2x}(\sin 3x - \frac{2}{3}\cos 3x)$

   (c) $\frac{x^2}{2}(\log x)^2 - \frac{x^2}{2}\log x + \frac{x^2}{4}$ or $\frac{x^2}{2}[(\log x)^2 - \log x + \frac{1}{2}]$

7. (a) $x \tan x + \log \cos x - \frac{x^2}{2}$ (b) $\frac{x^2}{4} + \frac{x}{4}\sin 2x + \frac{1}{8}\cos 2x$

8. (a) $\frac{1}{2}\left[(x\sqrt{x^2+1}) + \log(x + \sqrt{x^2+1})\right]$ (b) $\frac{1}{2}x\sqrt{4 - x^2} + 2\sin^{-1}\frac{x}{2}$

9. (a) 1 (b) $\frac{\pi}{2} - 1$ (c) $\frac{e^2}{4} + \frac{1}{4}$

   (d) $\frac{\pi}{4} - \frac{1}{2}$ (e) $\frac{1}{2}(e^{\pi/2} - 1)$ (f) $\frac{\pi^2 + 4}{16}$

10. (a) $\frac{\pi}{3}$ (b) $\sqrt{2\pi} - 4$

12. (a) $\frac{\pi}{\sqrt{3}} - \log 2$ (b) $\frac{1}{\log_e 10}$ or $\log_{10} e$ (c) -2

    (d) 1 (e) $\frac{e^2}{4}(3e^2 - 1)$ (f) $\log_e 4$

    (g) $\frac{1}{4}$ (h) $\frac{1 - 4e^{-3}}{9}$ (i) $-\frac{3}{4}e^{-2} + \frac{1}{4}$

(j) $\frac{\pi}{4} - \frac{1}{2}$ (k) $\frac{1}{2}(1 - \log 2)$ (l) $\frac{\pi}{2} - 1$

(m) $\frac{\pi^2 + 4\pi - 8}{64}$

Exercise 2C
---

1. $\frac{2}{3}$

2. $\frac{1}{4} + \frac{3\pi}{32}$

3. $\frac{\pi}{4} - \frac{2}{3}$

4. $\frac{x}{8} - \frac{\sin 4x}{32}$

5. $\frac{\cos^5 x}{5} - \frac{\cos^3 x}{3}$

6. $\frac{U^7}{7} - \frac{2U^5}{5} + \frac{U^3}{3}$, $(U = \sin x)$

7. $\frac{2}{7} U^{7/2}$, $(U = \sin x)$

8. $-\frac{U^3}{3} + 2U + \frac{1}{U}$, $(U = \cos x)$

9. $-\frac{\cot^2 x}{2} - \log \sin x$

10. $\frac{1}{2}(\log \tan \frac{x}{2} - \csc x \cot x)$

11. $-U - \frac{U^3}{3}$ $(U = \cot x)$

12. $\frac{1}{2}\sin 2x - \frac{1}{6}\sin^3 2x$

13. $\frac{1}{4}\tan^2 2x + \frac{1}{2}\log \cos 2x$

14. $-\frac{1}{2}\cos 2x + \frac{1}{6}\cos^3 2x$

15. $-\frac{3}{5}U^{5/3} + \frac{6}{11}U^{11/3} - \frac{3}{17}U^{17/3}$, $(U = \cos x)$

16. $\frac{U^5}{5} - \frac{U^7}{7}$, $(U = \sin x)$

17. $-\frac{1}{3}\cot^3 x$

18. $U + \frac{1}{U}$, $(U = \cos x)$

19. $\log(\sec x + \tan x)$

20. $\frac{2}{1 - \tan(x/2)}$ or $\tan x + \sec x$

21. $\sqrt{3} - 1$

22. $\pi/3\sqrt{3}$

23. $\frac{1}{\sqrt{2}} \log\left[\frac{t + 1 - \sqrt{2}}{t + 1 + \sqrt{2}}\right]$, $t = \tan\left[\frac{x}{2}\right]$

24. $-\log(2 + \cos x)$

25. $\frac{1}{4}\log 3$

Exercise 2D
---

1. $e^x x^n - n I_{n-1}$

2. $-\frac{1}{2} x^n e^{-2x} + \frac{n}{2} I_{n-1}$

3. $x(\log x)^n - n I_{n-1}$

4. $\frac{1}{a^2(2n-2)} \left[\frac{x}{(x^2 + a^2)^{n-1}} + (2n - 3) I_{n-1}\right]$

5. (i) $\dfrac{-U^{n-1}}{n-1} - I_{n-2}$ (ii) $-\dfrac{U^5}{5} + \dfrac{U^3}{3} - U - x$, ($U = \cot x$)

6. (a) $\dfrac{C^5 S}{6} + \dfrac{5C^3 S}{24} + \dfrac{15CS}{48} + \dfrac{15x}{48}$, [$C = \cos x$, $S = \sin x$]

   (b) $\dfrac{35\pi}{256}$

7. (a) $\dfrac{35\pi}{256}$ (b) $\dfrac{3\pi}{32} - \dfrac{1}{4}$

8. (a) $\dfrac{t^4}{4} - \dfrac{t^2}{2} - \log\cos x$, ($t = \tan x$)   (b) $\dfrac{\pi}{4} - \dfrac{76}{105}$

9. (a) $I_n = U^n \sin U + n U^{n-1}\cos U - n(n-1) I_{n-2}$, where $x = \sin U$ (b) $\dfrac{\pi^3}{8} - 3\pi + 6$

10. $-\dfrac{32}{315}$

11. - - -

12. $e^x (x^4 - 4x^3 + 12x^2 - 24x + 24)$ 13. $\dfrac{28}{15}$ 14. $-e^{-x}(x^3 + 3x^2 + 6x + 6)$

Exercise 2E

1. $\log(x + \sqrt{x^2 + 4})$ 2. $-\dfrac{\sqrt{9 - x^2}}{9x}$ 3. $8\sin^{-1}\left(\dfrac{x}{4}\right) - \dfrac{x}{2}\sqrt{16 - x^2}$

4. $-\dfrac{\sqrt{4 - x^2}}{x} - \sin^{-1}\dfrac{x}{2}$ 5. $\dfrac{25}{2}\sin^{-1}\dfrac{x}{5} - \dfrac{x}{2}\sqrt{25 - x^2}$

6. $\dfrac{x}{2}\sqrt{a^2 + x^2} + \dfrac{a^2}{2}\log(x + \sqrt{x^2 + a^2})$ 7. $\dfrac{a^2}{2}\sin^{-1}\dfrac{x}{a} + \dfrac{x}{2}\sqrt{a^2 - x^2}$

8. $\dfrac{x}{2}\sqrt{x^2 + 4} - 2\log(x + \sqrt{x^2 + 4})$ 9. $\dfrac{x}{2}\sqrt{4 + x^2} + 2\log(x + \sqrt{4 + x^2})$

10. $\dfrac{25}{2}\sin^{-1}\dfrac{x}{5} + \dfrac{x}{2}\sqrt{25 - x^2}$ 11. $\dfrac{x}{4}(4 + x^2)^{-1/2}$

12. $-\dfrac{1}{2}\log\left[\dfrac{\sqrt{4 - x^2} + 2}{x}\right]$ 13. $\dfrac{\sqrt{x^2 - 4}}{4x}$ 14. $-\sqrt{1 - x^2}$

15. $\log\left(\dfrac{1 - \sqrt{1 - x^2}}{x}\right) + \sqrt{1 - x^2}$
    or $-\log\left(\dfrac{1 + \sqrt{1 - x^2}}{x}\right) + \sqrt{1 - x^2}$ 16. $(1 - x^2)^{-1/2}$

17. $\dfrac{x}{2}\sqrt{x^2 - 4} + 2\log(x + \sqrt{x^2 - 4})$ 18. $\log(x + \sqrt{x^2 - a^2}) - \dfrac{\sqrt{x^2 - a^2}}{x}$

19. $\dfrac{1}{2}\sec^{-1}\left(\dfrac{x}{2}\right)$ 20. $-\dfrac{\sqrt{x^2 + 4}}{x} + \log\left|\sqrt{x^2 + 4} + x\right|$

21. $\dfrac{x}{2}\sqrt{x^2 + 9} - \dfrac{9}{2}\log(\sqrt{x^2 + 9} + x)$

Exercise 2F

1. $2x - \frac{4}{3} \log(3x+2)$
2. $\frac{x^4}{4} - \frac{x^3}{3} - \frac{x^2}{2} - x - \log(x-1)$
3. $\frac{x^2}{2} - x + \log(x+1)$
4. $-x + \log(1-2x)$
5. $\frac{ax}{c} + \frac{bc-ad}{c^2} \log(cx+d)$
6. $\frac{1}{18}(3x^2+2x) + \frac{1}{27}\log(3x-1)$
7. $\frac{2}{\sqrt{3}} \tan^{-1}\left(\frac{2x+1}{\sqrt{3}}\right)$
8. $\frac{2}{\sqrt{3}} \tan^{-1}\left(\frac{2x-1}{\sqrt{3}}\right)$
9. $\frac{1}{\sqrt{b-a^2}} \tan^{-1} \frac{x+a}{\sqrt{b-a^2}}$ if $b - a^2 > 0$, $\frac{-1}{x+a}$ if $b = a^2$

   and $\frac{1}{2\sqrt{a^2-b}} \log\left[\frac{x+a-\sqrt{a^2-b}}{x+a+\sqrt{a^2-b}}\right]$ if $b < a^2$

10. $\tan^{-1}(3x-1)$
11. $2\log(x^2+2x+3) - \frac{1}{\sqrt{2}} \tan^{-1}\left(\frac{x+1}{\sqrt{2}}\right)$
12. $\frac{1}{2}\log(x^2-x+1) + \frac{1}{\sqrt{3}} \tan^{-1}\left(\frac{2x-1}{\sqrt{3}}\right)$
13. $\frac{1}{2}\log(x^2+2x-2) - \frac{1}{2\sqrt{3}}\log\left[\frac{x+1-\sqrt{3}}{x+1+\sqrt{3}}\right]$
14. $x + \log(x^2-x+1) + \frac{2}{\sqrt{3}} \tan^{-1} \frac{2x-1}{\sqrt{3}}$
15. $\frac{\pi}{4}$
16. $\frac{1}{2\sqrt{2}} \log \frac{(3+\sqrt{2})^2}{7}$
17. $\frac{\log 3}{2} + \frac{\pi}{6\sqrt{3}}$
18. $\log 2 - 5\tan^{-1}\left(\frac{1}{7}\right)$
19. $\log 2$
20. $\frac{1}{3}(a^3-b^3) + \frac{1}{2}(a^2-b^2) + (a-b) + \log\left(\frac{a-1}{b-1}\right)$

Exercise 2G

1. $\log\left[\frac{x-2}{x-1}\right]$
2. $\log\left[\frac{(x-2)^4}{(x-1)^3}\right]$
3. $x + 6\log(x-2) - 3\log(x-1)$
4. $-9\log(x-3) + 11\log(x-4)$
5. $\frac{x^2}{2} - x + 5\log x - 4\log(x+1)$
6. $\frac{1}{5}\log(x-2) - \log(x+2) + \frac{9}{5}\log(x+3)$
7. $\frac{1}{5}\log(x+1) - \frac{1}{10}\log(x^2+4) + \frac{1}{10}\tan^{-1}\frac{x}{2}$
8. $x + 2\log x - \log(x^2+1) - \tan^{-1} x$
9. $\log\left(\frac{x}{x-1}\right) - \frac{1}{x-1}$
10. $\frac{2}{9}\log(x-2) - \frac{2}{9}\log(x+1) - \frac{4}{3}\left(\frac{1}{x-2}\right)$
11. $\frac{1}{4}\log(x^2-1) - \frac{1}{4}\log(x^2+1)$
12. $x + \frac{1}{3}\log(x-1) - \frac{1}{6}\log(x^2+x+1) - \frac{1}{\sqrt{3}}\tan^{-1}\frac{2x+1}{\sqrt{3}}$

13. $\frac{1}{16} \log (x + 2) - \frac{1}{8(x + 2)} - \frac{1}{32} \log (x^2 + 4)$ 14. $\tan^{-1} x - \frac{1}{\sqrt{2}} \tan^{-1} \frac{x}{\sqrt{2}}$

15. $\frac{3}{8} \log (x - 2) + \frac{5}{16} \log (x^2 + x + 2) + \frac{9}{8\sqrt{7}} \tan^{-1} \frac{2x + 1}{\sqrt{7}}$

16. $\log \left(\frac{4}{3}\right)$ 17. $\frac{1}{4} + \frac{1}{4} \log \left(\frac{2}{3}\right)$

18. $-\frac{1}{2} \log \frac{3}{2} + \frac{1}{4} \log \frac{5}{4} + \frac{1}{2} \tan^{-1} \frac{1}{2}$ 19. $\log \left(1 + \frac{1}{2\sqrt{2}}\right)$

20. $\log \left(\frac{9}{8}\right)$ 21. $\frac{1}{4} \log \left(\frac{x + 1}{x - 1}\right) - \frac{x}{2(x^2 - 1)}$

22. $2\sqrt{x} - 2 \log (1 + \sqrt{x})$

Exercise 2H

1. $\frac{1}{\sqrt{3}} \tan^{-1} \left(\frac{x + 1}{\sqrt{3}}\right)$ 2. $\log (x^2 + 2x + 4) - \frac{2}{\sqrt{3}} \tan^{-1} \left(\frac{x + 1}{\sqrt{3}}\right)$

3. $x - \log (x^2 + 2x + 4) - \frac{1}{\sqrt{3}} \tan^{-1} \left(\frac{x + 1}{\sqrt{3}}\right)$ 4. $\log (U + \sqrt{U^2 + 3})$, $U = x + 1$

5. $\sqrt{x^2 + 2x + 4} - \log [x + 1 + \sqrt{x^2 + 2x + 4}]$ 6. $\sin^{-1} (x - 1)$

7. $\frac{2}{\sqrt{39}} \tan^{-1} \frac{4x + 1}{\sqrt{39}}$ 8. $\sqrt{x^2 + x + 1} + \frac{3}{2} \log (x + \frac{1}{2} + \sqrt{x^2 + x + 1})$

9. $-\sqrt{6x - x^2} + 3 \sin^{-1} \left(\frac{x - 3}{3}\right)$ 10. $\sin^{-1} \left(\frac{2x + 1}{3}\right)$

11. $\frac{1}{2} \log (x^2 - \frac{3}{2} + \sqrt{x^4 - 3x^2 + 1})$ 12. $-\sqrt{1 - 2x - x^2} - \sin^{-1} \left(\frac{x + 1}{\sqrt{2}}\right)$

13. $-2\sqrt{U} + 3 \log (x + 1 + \sqrt{U})$, $U = x^2 + 2x + 3$ 15. $\tan^{-1} 3 - \tan^{-1} 2$

16. $\frac{2\pi}{3} + \frac{1}{2} \log \frac{4}{3}$ 17. $\frac{\pi}{2}$ 18. $-\sqrt{x - x^2} + \frac{3}{2} \sin^{-1} (2x - 1)$

19. $\sin^{-1} x + \sqrt{1 - x^2}$ 20. $\sqrt{x^2 + 2x} - \log (x + 1 + \sqrt{x^2 + 2x})$

Exercise 2I

1. (a) 0 (b) $\sqrt{2}$ (c) 0 (d) 0

   (e) $\frac{2}{3}$ (f) 0 (g) 8 (h) 0

2. (a) $\frac{\pi}{4}$ (b) $\frac{1}{840}$ (c) $\frac{\pi^3}{96}$ (d) $\frac{\pi}{4}$ (e) 1

3. (a) $2 - \frac{\pi}{2}$ (b) $\frac{2}{\sqrt{ab}} \tan^{-1} \sqrt{\frac{b}{a}}$

Exercise 2J

1. $\frac{2}{3}(x-2)^{3/2} + 4(x-2)^{1/2} + c$
2. $\frac{16}{105}$
3. $e^2 - e + \log(1+e)$

4. -0.059
5. $\frac{1}{b^2} \log(a^2 + b^2 \sin^2 x)$
6. $\frac{1}{ab} \tan^{-1}\left(\frac{b}{a} \tan x\right)$

7. $\tan^{-1}(\sqrt{x})$
8. $\frac{1}{2} \tan^{-1} x^2$
9. $x - \log(1 + e^x)$

10. $x - 2\log(1 - e^x)$
11. 3.3
12. $\frac{x^2}{3} \log x - \frac{x^3}{9}$

13. $\frac{2}{5}(1+x)^{5/2} - \frac{2}{3}(1+x)^{3/2}$
14. $-\frac{\sqrt{1+x^2}}{x}$
15. $\sec^{-1} x$

16. $\tan^{-1} e^x$
17. $\sqrt{\frac{4}{19}} \tan^{-1}\left(\frac{2x+1}{\sqrt{19}}\right)$

18. $y = \frac{x^2}{2} \sin^{-1} x + \frac{x}{4}\sqrt{1-x^2} - \frac{1}{4}\sin^{-1} x$
19. $\frac{1}{4} \tan^{-1}\left(x + \frac{1}{2}\right)$

20. $\frac{1}{6} \log\left[\frac{x-1}{x+5}\right]$
21. $\frac{1}{\sqrt{13}} \log\left[\frac{\sqrt{13} - 3 + 2x}{\sqrt{13} + 3 - 2x}\right]$

22. $\frac{1}{2} \log\left[x + \frac{1}{2} + \sqrt{\left(x+\frac{1}{2}\right)^2 + 1}\right]$
23. $\frac{3}{8} \log(4x^2 + 4x + 5) + \frac{1}{8} \tan^{-1}\left(x + \frac{1}{2}\right)$

24. $\frac{3}{4}\sqrt{4x^2 + 4x + 5} + \frac{1}{4} \log\left[x + \frac{1}{2} + \sqrt{\left(x+\frac{1}{2}\right)^2 + 1}\right]$

25. $\frac{2}{3} \tan^{-1}\left[\frac{4 + 5\tan x/2}{3}\right]$
26. $\frac{12x}{13} - \frac{5}{13} \log(3\cos x + 2\sin x)$

27. $a \sin^{-1} \frac{x}{a} - \sqrt{a^2 - x^2}$
28. $\frac{2x-1}{4}\sqrt{P} + \frac{3}{8} \log\left(\frac{2x-1}{2} + \sqrt{P}\right)$, $P = x^2 - x + 1$

29. $\frac{1}{2\sqrt{5}} \log \frac{\sqrt{5}\tan x - 1}{\sqrt{5}\tan x + 1}$
30. $-(4\tan x + 6)^{-1}$

31. $-\frac{x}{3} + \frac{5}{6} \tan^{-1}\left(2\tan \frac{x}{2}\right)$
32. $2\sqrt{x} \sin\sqrt{x} + 2\cos\sqrt{x}$

33. $3\log(x-2) - \log(x+1)$
34. $\frac{x^2}{2} + 3x + 8\log(x-2) - \log(x-1)$

35. $\frac{1}{2} \log\left[\frac{x^2 + 1}{x^2 + 3}\right]$
36. $\frac{1}{2} \log\left[\frac{x^2}{1 - x^2}\right]$

37. $x + \log(1 + e^x) - 2\log(1 + 2e^x)$
38. $\frac{1}{2} \log(x+1) - \frac{1}{4} \log(x^2 + 1) + \frac{1}{2} \tan^{-1} x$

39. $\log(1 + \sin x) - \log(2 + \sin x)$

40. $\frac{1}{6} \log(1 - \cos x) + \frac{1}{2} \log(1 + \cos x) - \frac{2}{3} \log(1 + 2\cos x)$

43. $\frac{\pi}{8} - \frac{1}{4}$
44. $\frac{\pi}{8}$

CHAPTER 3 VOLUMES

Exercise 3A

(1) 2π

(2) $\dfrac{206\pi}{15}$

(3) $\dfrac{\pi}{30}$

(4) $\dfrac{\pi^2}{2}$

(5) $\dfrac{\pi^2 - 2\pi}{8}$

(6) $\pi\left(1 - \dfrac{\pi}{4}\right)$

(7) $\dfrac{512\pi}{15}$

(8) $\dfrac{\pi^2}{16}$

(9) $2\pi\left[(\log 2)^2 - 2\log 2 + 1\right]$

(10) $\dfrac{\pi}{4}\left[\dfrac{e^2}{2} - \dfrac{e^{-2}}{2} + 2\right]$

(11) $\dfrac{56\pi}{3}$

(12) $\dfrac{128\pi}{5}$

(13) $\dfrac{512\pi}{15}$

(14) $4\pi\log 2 - 1.5\pi$

(15) $\dfrac{\pi^2}{4}$

(16) (a) 144 (b) $36\sqrt{3}$ (c) 18π
     (d) 72   (e) 36

(17) $\dfrac{4\pi\, ab^2}{3}$

(18) $\dfrac{400\pi}{3}$

Exercise 3B

(1) $\dfrac{1088\pi}{15}$

(2) $\dfrac{162\pi}{5}$

(3) $\dfrac{\pi}{5}$

(4) $\dfrac{27\pi}{2}$

(5) $\dfrac{40\pi}{3}$

(6) $\dfrac{16\pi}{3}$

(7) 8π

(8) $\dfrac{64\pi}{5}$

(9) $\dfrac{8\pi}{3}$

(10) 2π

(11) $\dfrac{\pi}{4}(e^8 + 4e^4 + 3)$

Exercise 3C

(2) $\dfrac{32\pi}{3}$

(3) $\dfrac{3\pi}{10}$

(4) $\dfrac{64\pi}{3}$

(b) $\dfrac{8\pi}{3}$

(c) 32π

(5) 48π

(6) $\dfrac{8\pi h}{15}$

(8) $13.25\ m^3$

(9) $\dfrac{32\pi a^3}{15}$

10. $2\pi^2 a^2 c$ 11. $\dfrac{16\pi a^3}{5}$ 13. $320\pi^2$ 14. $200\pi^2$

15. $4\pi a^3$ 16. $\dfrac{512\pi}{15}$ 17. $\dfrac{117\pi}{5}$ 18. $\dfrac{8\pi}{3}$

19. (a) $\dfrac{5\pi a^3}{3}$ (b) $\dfrac{4\pi a^3}{3}$ 20. $\dfrac{112\pi}{15}$

CHAPTER 4 COMPLEX NUMBERS

Exercise 4A

1. $5 - i$ 2. 2 3. $-15 + i$
4. $4i$ 5. $2 + 11i$ 6. $11 - 23i$
7. $3 + 6i$ 8. $7 - 24i$ 9. $2i$
10. $-\dfrac{2}{25} + \dfrac{3}{50}i$ 11. $5i$ 12. 8
13. i 14. $\dfrac{19 + 4i}{29}$ 15. $-\dfrac{2}{5} - \dfrac{3}{5}i$
16. $-2 + i$ 17. $x = 4,\; y = \dfrac{5}{2}$ 18. $x = 3,\; y = -\dfrac{1}{2}$
19. $(x = 1, y = -1)$ or $(x = -1, y = 1)$ 20. $x = -\dfrac{14}{25},\; y = -\dfrac{23}{25}$
21. $2 + 11i$ 22. $x = \dfrac{5}{2},\; y = -5\dfrac{\sqrt{3}}{2}$ (a) $-\dfrac{25}{2} - \dfrac{25}{2}\sqrt{3}\, i$
(b) $\dfrac{1}{10} - \dfrac{\sqrt{3}}{10}i$ 23. (a) $10 + 3i$ (b) $2 + 2i$
(c) $\dfrac{19 + 4i}{29}$ (d) $1 + 11i$ 24. (a) $x - iy$
(b) $\dfrac{x - iy}{x^2 + y^2}$ (c) $\dfrac{x^2 + y^2 - 1 - 2yi}{(x - 1)^2 + y^2}$ (d) $x^2 - y^2 - 1 + 2xyi$
25. (a) $\dfrac{1}{2} - \dfrac{3}{2}i$ (b) $\dfrac{9}{2} + \dfrac{7}{2}i$ (c) $\dfrac{2}{5} - \dfrac{2}{5}i$

25. (d) $\frac{7}{5} + \frac{6}{5}i$ 26. (a) $-\frac{1}{2} \pm \frac{\sqrt{3}}{2}i$ (b) $1 \pm \sqrt{3}i$

(c) $\frac{3}{4} \pm \frac{\sqrt{7}i}{4}$ (d) 1 27. (a) $x^2 + 1 = 0$

(b) $x^2 - 2x + 2 = 0$ (c) $x^2 - 4x + 13 = 0$ (d) $x^2 - (4 + 4i)x + 10i = 0$

(e) $5x^2 - (12 + 4i)x + 5 = 0$ 28. (a) $z = 2, w = 3$

(b) $z = \frac{2}{3}, w = -\frac{1}{3} + i$ (c) $z = \frac{3}{8} + \frac{i}{4}, w = \frac{3}{8} - \frac{i}{4}$ (d) $z = 1 + i, w = -1$

29. (a) $\frac{2}{5} - \frac{1}{5}i$ (b) $3 + 4i$ (c) $\frac{3}{25} - \frac{4}{25}i$ (d) $\frac{78}{25} + \frac{96}{25}i$

(e) $2 + 11i$ (f) $-7 + 24i$

30. -6, Rule $\sqrt{a} \cdot \sqrt{b} = \sqrt{ab}$ is not defined for the imaginary numbers.

Exercise 4B

1. $5 \text{cis } 0$
2. $5 \text{cis } \pi$
3. $5 \text{cis } \pi/2$
4. $5 \text{cis}(-\pi/2)$
5. $2\sqrt{2} \text{cis}(\pi/4)$
6. $2\sqrt{2} \text{cis}(-\pi/4)$
7. $2\sqrt{2} \text{cis}(3\pi/4)$
8. $2\sqrt{2} \text{cis}(-3\pi/4)$
9. $8 \text{cis}(3\pi/4)$
10. $20 \text{cis}(\pi/6)$
11. $\text{cis}(2\pi/3)$
12. $5 \text{cis}(-2\pi/3)$
13. $\frac{1}{\sqrt{2}} \text{cis}(-\pi/4)$
14. $2 \text{cis}(\theta)$ where $\tan\theta = -\frac{3}{4}$ and θ in 4th quadrant
15. $2 \text{cis}(-\pi/2)$
16. $5i$
17. 10
18. -4
19. $-2i$
20. $\frac{5}{2} - \frac{5\sqrt{3}}{2}i$
21. $\sqrt{2}\left(\frac{1}{2} + \frac{\sqrt{3}}{2}i\right)$
22. $1 + i$
23. $5\left(-\frac{\sqrt{3}}{2} - \frac{1}{2}i\right)$
24. $5(1 - \sqrt{3}i)$
25. $2(-1 + \sqrt{3}i)$

Exercise 4C

1. $8i$
2. -10
3. $-6\sqrt{2}(1 + i)$
4. $-5\sqrt{3} + 5i$
5. $-2 + 2\sqrt{3}i$
6. $27i$
7. $-1 - \sqrt{3}i$
8. $2i$
9. $-\sqrt{3} + i$
10. $\frac{3}{2}(1 - \sqrt{3}i)$
11.
12. (a) $\text{cis}(\pi/2)$ (b) $\frac{1}{\sqrt{2}} \text{cis} \frac{7\pi}{12}$
    (c) $2\sqrt{2} \text{cis}\left(\frac{7\pi}{12}\right)$ (d) $\frac{\sqrt{2}}{2} \text{cis}(-\pi/4)$ 13. (a) $-4\sqrt{3} + 4i$ (b) $2i$
    (c) $-8 - 8\sqrt{3}i$ (d) $512 - 512\sqrt{3}i$
14. $z_1 = 2 \text{cis}(\pi/3), z_2 = 2 \text{cis}(\pi/6)$ (a) $32 \text{cis}(-\pi/3)$ (b) $16 \text{cis}(2\pi/3)$
    (c) $1024 \text{cis}(\pi/2)$ (d) $\text{cis}(\pi/6)$ (e) $\text{cis}(-\pi/6)$
15. (a) $z_1 + z_2 = \sqrt{2}(1 + \sqrt{3}) \text{cis}(\pi/4)$ (b) $z_1 - z_2 = \sqrt{2}(\sqrt{3} - 1) \text{cis}(3\pi/4)$
    (c) $-(2 + \sqrt{3})i$ (d) $-7 - 4\sqrt{3}$

Exercise 4D

1. $\frac{1}{2} + \frac{\sqrt{3}}{2} i$ 2. $64 i$ 3. -1 4. 64
5. i 6. $-8 - 8\sqrt{3} i$ 7. $8 \operatorname{cis}(-\pi/2), -8i$
8. $\frac{1}{25} \operatorname{cis}\theta$, where $\tan\theta = \frac{-24}{-7}$ (θ in 3rd quadrant) $-\frac{7}{625} - \frac{24}{625} i$
9. $4 \operatorname{cis}(\pi), -4$ 10. $16 \operatorname{cis}(-2\pi/3), -8 - 8\sqrt{3}$ 11. $32 \operatorname{cis}(\pi/2), 32i$
12. $\frac{1}{256} \operatorname{cis}(-2\pi/3), \frac{1}{512}(-1 - \sqrt{3} i)$ 13. $16 \operatorname{cis}(-2\pi/3), -8 - 8\sqrt{3} i$
14. $512(-\sqrt{3} + i), 1024 \operatorname{cis}(5\pi/6)$ 15. $8\sqrt{2} \operatorname{cis}(-\pi/4), 8 - 8i$
16. $32 \operatorname{cis} 0, 32$ 17. $2 \operatorname{cis} 0, 2$ 18. $16 \operatorname{cis}(-\pi/3), 8 - 8\sqrt{3} i$
19. $\frac{1}{4} \operatorname{cis}(-\pi/3), \frac{1}{8}(1 - \sqrt{3} i)$ 20. $9 \operatorname{cis}(\pi/2), 9i$

Exercise 4E

1. (a) $\pm 2\sqrt{2}(1 - i)$ (b) $\pm(\sqrt{3} + i)$ (c) $2 \operatorname{cis}(-5\pi/12), 2 \operatorname{cis}(7\pi/12)$
   (d) $\sqrt{5} \operatorname{cis}(\theta/2), \sqrt{5} \operatorname{cis}(\pi + \theta/2)$, where $\tan\theta = \frac{3}{4}$, Cartesian form $\pm \frac{(3 + i)}{\sqrt{2}}$

2. (a) $-i, \pm \frac{\sqrt{3}}{2} + \frac{i}{2}$ (b) $-2, 1 \pm \sqrt{3} i$
   (c) $3 \operatorname{cis}\left(\frac{2k\pi}{3} + \frac{\pi}{9}\right), k = 0,1,2 \rightarrow 3 \operatorname{cis}(20°, 140°, 260°)$ (d) $2i, \pm\sqrt{3} - i$

3. (a) $\frac{1}{\sqrt{2}}(\pm 1 \pm i)$ (b) $\sqrt{2}(\pm 1 \pm i)$ (c) $\sqrt{3} - i, 1 + \sqrt{3} i, -\sqrt{3} + i, -1 - \sqrt{3} i$
   (d) $\operatorname{cis}\left(\frac{k\pi}{2} - \frac{\pi}{12}\right), k = 0,1,2,3 \rightarrow \operatorname{cis}(-15°, 75°, 165°, -105°)$

4. (a) $z = 2 \operatorname{cis}\frac{2k\pi}{5}, k = 0,1,2,3,4 \rightarrow z = 2 \operatorname{cis}(0°, 72°, 144°, 216°, 288°)$
   (b) $z = 2 \operatorname{cis}\left(\frac{\pi + 2k\pi}{5}\right), k = 0,1,2,3,4$
   (c) $z = \operatorname{cis}\left(\frac{2k\pi}{5} + \frac{\pi}{6}\right), k = 0,1,2,3,4$
   (d) $z = 2 \operatorname{cis}\left(\frac{2k\pi}{5} + \frac{\pi}{10}\right), k = 0,1,2,3,4$

5. (a) $r^{1/3} \operatorname{cis}\frac{2k\pi + \theta}{3}$ where $r = \sqrt{5}, \tan\theta = \frac{1}{2}$, the roots are $1.29 + 0.201i, -0.820 + 1.02i, 0.472 - 1.22i$
   (b) $-3, i$ (c) $\operatorname{cis}\frac{\pi + 2k\pi}{4}, k = 0,1,2,3 \rightarrow \frac{1}{\sqrt{2}}(\pm 1 \pm i)$
   (d) $2 \operatorname{cis}\left(\frac{k\pi}{2} - \frac{\pi}{8}\right), k = 0,1,2,3$ (e) $2^{1/4} \operatorname{cis}\left(-\frac{\pi}{8}, \frac{7\pi}{8}\right), k = 0,1,2,3$
   (f) $\pm 2, (\pm 1 \pm \sqrt{3} i)$ (six roots)
   (g) $\operatorname{cis}\left(\frac{k\pi}{2} - \frac{\pi}{12}\right), k = 0,1,2,3 \rightarrow \operatorname{cis}(-15°, 75°, 165°, -105°)$
   (h) $\operatorname{cis}\left(-\frac{\pi}{4}, \frac{3\pi}{4}\right) \rightarrow \pm \frac{1}{\sqrt{2}}(1 - i)$

Exercise 4F

($c = \cos\theta$, $s = \sin\theta$, $t = \tan\theta$)

1. (a) $4c^3 - 3c$ (b) $3s - 4s^3$ (c) $\dfrac{3t - t^3}{1 - 3t^2}$

2. (a) $16c^5 - 20c^3 + 5c$ (b) $16s^5 - 20s^3 + 5s$ (c) $\dfrac{5t - 10t^3 + t^5}{1 - 10t^2 + 5t^4}$

3. (a) $c^6 - 15c^4s^2 + 15c^2s^4 - s^6$ (b) $6c^5s - 20c^3s^3 + 6cs^5$

   (c) $\dfrac{6t - 20t^3 + 6t^5}{1 - 15t^2 + 15t^4 - t^6}$

4. (a) $\frac{1}{4}\cos 3\theta + \frac{3}{4}\cos\theta$ (b) $-\frac{1}{4}\sin 3\theta + \frac{3}{4}\sin\theta$

5. (a) $\frac{1}{16}(\cos 5\theta + 5\cos 3\theta + 10\cos\theta)$ (b) $\frac{1}{16}(\sin 5\theta - 5\sin 3\theta + 10\sin\theta)$

   (c) $\frac{1}{16}(\frac{1}{5}\sin 5\theta + \frac{5}{3}\sin 3\theta + 10\sin\theta)$ (d) $-\frac{1}{16}(\frac{1}{5}\cos 5\theta - \frac{5}{3}\cos 3\theta + 10\cos\theta)$

6. (a) $\frac{1}{32}(\cos 6\theta + 6\cos 4\theta + 15\cos 2\theta + 10)$

   (b) $-\frac{1}{32}(\cos 6\theta - 6\cos 4\theta + 15\cos 2\theta - 10)$ (c) $\dfrac{5\pi}{32}$ (d) $\dfrac{5\pi}{32}$

7. (a) $\dfrac{1}{64}, \dfrac{7}{64}, \dfrac{21}{64}, \dfrac{35}{64}$ (b) $\dfrac{16}{35}$

8. (a) $-\dfrac{1}{64}, \dfrac{7}{64}, -\dfrac{21}{64}, \dfrac{35}{64}$ (b) $\dfrac{16}{35}$

Exercise 4G

1. (a) $\pm(2 + i)$ (b) $\pm(2 - i)$ (c) $\pm(\sqrt{6} + i)$ (d) $\pm(3 - \sqrt{2}\,i)$
   (e) $\pm(3 + 2i)$ (f) $\pm(3 + i)$ (g) $\pm\dfrac{1}{\sqrt{2}}(1 + i)$ (h) $\pm(2 - 2i)$

2. (a) $\pm(1 + 4i)$ (b) $\pm\dfrac{1}{\sqrt{2}}(\sqrt{3} + i)$ (c) $\pm(1 + i)$

3. (a) $2 - 3i, -1 - i$ (b) $2 - i, -4 - 3i$ (c) $-1, -3 - 2i$
   (d) $-1 - i, -3 + 3i$

4. (a) $\frac{1}{5}(2 + i)$ (b) $\frac{1}{13}(5 - 12i)$ (c) $12 + 7i$

7. $-\dfrac{3i}{2}$

Exercise 4H

1. (a) (i) $1 - 2i$ (ii) 2 (iii) $4i$ (iv) 5 (v) $\sqrt{5}$ (vi) $\sqrt{5}$ (vii) $\frac{1}{5}(1-2i)$

   (b) (i) $3 + i$ (ii) 6 (iii) $-2i$ (iv) 10 (v) $\sqrt{10}$ (vi) $\sqrt{10}$ (vii) $\frac{1}{10}(3+i)$

7. $\frac{\pi}{3}, \frac{2\pi}{3}, \frac{4\pi}{3}, \frac{5\pi}{3}$

Exercise 4I

2. $z^2 - 3z + 3 = 0$ 6. (b) $z^2 + z - 1 = 0$ (c) Fig. 1 (d) 2.38

7. (b) $\pm 1, \pm \frac{1}{2} \pm \frac{\sqrt{3}}{2}i$, see Fig. 2, area $= \frac{3\sqrt{3}}{2}$

   (c) (i) $z^2 - z + 1 = 0$ (ii) $z^2 + z + 1 = 0$

9. (a) $\pm 1, \pm \frac{1}{2} \pm \frac{\sqrt{3}}{2}i$ (b) $\pm \frac{1}{2} \pm \frac{\sqrt{3}}{2}i$. See Fig. 3.

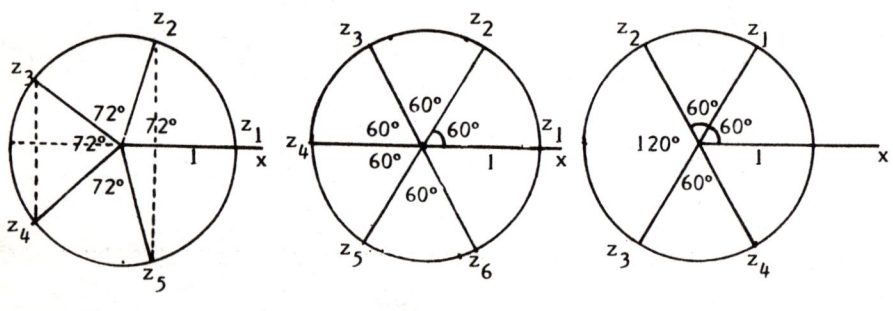

Fig. 1   Fig. 2   Fig. 3

Exercise 4J

3. $\frac{1}{\sqrt{2}}(\pm 1 \pm i)$, see Fig. 1

7. (a) $-1, \pm i$ (b) $-1, \pm \frac{1}{2} \pm \frac{\sqrt{3}}{2}i$

   (c) $\pm \frac{\sqrt{3}}{2} \pm \frac{1}{2}i$ (d) $\pm \frac{1}{2} \pm \frac{\sqrt{3}}{2}i$

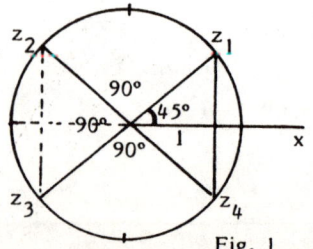

Fig. 1

Exercise 4K

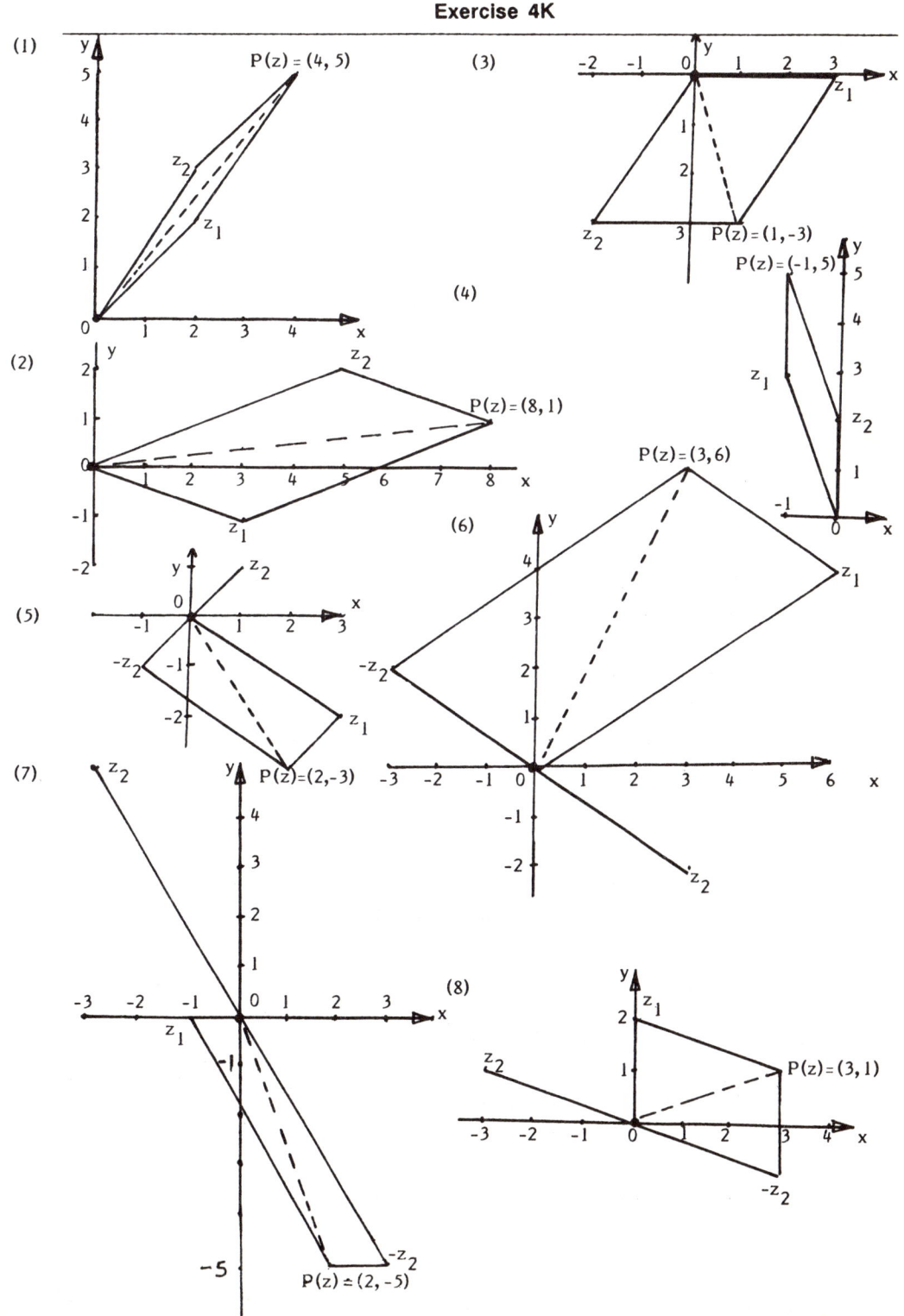

9.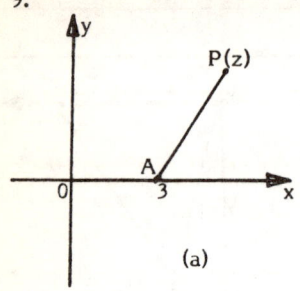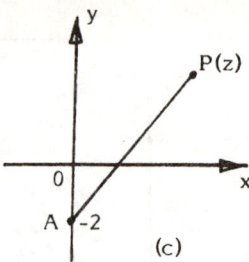

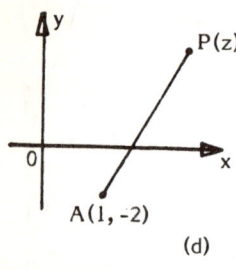 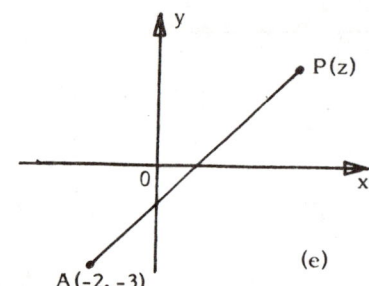

10. $|z| = 1$, $\arg z = \frac{\pi}{2}$, $|\omega| = 1$, $\arg \omega = \frac{\pi}{4}$

11. $R(3, 0)$ or $R(-5, 0)$

12. $z = 3 + 2i$

13. The diagonals of a rhombus intersect at right angles.

14. Equality sign holds when $\arg z_1 = \arg z_2 + \pi$

15. The sum of squares of the diagonals of a parallelogram is equal to the sum of squares of the four sides.

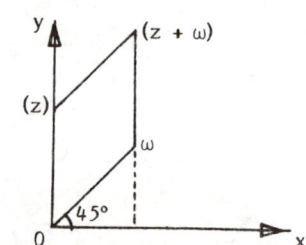

Exercise 4L

1. (a) $z = \frac{\sqrt{3}}{2} - 1 + \left(\frac{1}{2} + \sqrt{3}\right)i$ (b) $z = -\frac{1}{\sqrt{2}} + \frac{3}{\sqrt{2}} i$ (c) $z = -2 + i$

2. $\frac{1 - \sqrt{3}}{2} + \frac{\sqrt{3} + 1}{2} \cdot i$ or $\frac{\sqrt{3} + 1}{2} + \frac{1 - \sqrt{3}}{2} \cdot i$

3. $Q(z_1)$, $z_1 = \sqrt{2} r (\cos 75° + i \sin 75°)$

   $R(z_2)$, $z_2 = -\frac{r}{2} + \frac{\sqrt{3} r}{2} \cdot i$

4. $B(z_1)$, $z_1 = \frac{3}{2} - \sqrt{3} + \left(\frac{\sqrt{3}}{2} + 3\right)i$ $C(z_2)$, $z_2 = \frac{1}{2} - \sqrt{3} + \left(1 + \frac{\sqrt{3}}{2}\right)i$

5. $-1 + 2i$, $-2 + 3i$, $-3 + 2i$, $-2 + i$.

Exercise 4M

1. (a) $|z| = 1$ (b) $|z| = 3$ (c) $|z| = \frac{1}{2}$ (d) $|z| = \frac{\sqrt{2}}{2}$

2. (a) $z\bar{z} = 25$ (b) $z\bar{z} = 64$ (c) $z\bar{z} = \frac{1}{a}$ (d) $z\bar{z} = \frac{5}{3}$

3. (a) $x^2 + y^2 = 16$, $0(0,0)$, $r = 4$ (b) $4x^2 + 4y^2 = 1$, $0(0,0)$, $r = \frac{1}{2}$
   (c) $x^2 + y^2 = 25$, $0(0,0)$, $r = 5$ (d) $4x^2 + 4y^2 = 1$, $0(0,0)$, $r = \frac{1}{2}$

4. (a) $(x - 2)^2 + y^2 = 1$, a circle, $r = 1$, $C(2, 0)$
   (b) $(x + 2)^2 + y^2 = 9$, a circle, $r = 3$, $C(-2, 0)$
   (c) $x^2 + (y - 3)^2 = 4$, a circle, $r = 2$, $C(0, 3)$
   (d) $x^2 + (y + 2)^2 = 25$, a circle, $r = 5$, $C(0, -2)$
   (e) $3x^2 + 3y^2 + 2x - 1 = 0$, a circle, $r = \frac{2}{3}$, $C(-\frac{1}{3}, 0)$
   (f) $(x - 2)^2 + (y - 1)^2 = 4$, a circle, $r = 2$, $C(2, 1)$

5. (a) $|z - 1 - i| = \sqrt{2}$ (b) $|z + 1 + 2i| = 2$ (c) $|z + \frac{1}{2} + \frac{3}{2}i| = \frac{\sqrt{10}}{2}$
   (d) $|z + 1 + \frac{3}{4}i| = \frac{\sqrt{17}}{4}$

6. (a) $C(2, 0)$, $r = 2$ (b) $C(1, 1)$, $r = 1$
   (c) $C(2, -3)$, $r = 2$ (d) $C(1, 1)$, $r = 3$

Exercise 4N

1.

(a) The circle $x^2 + y^2 = 4$, $r = 2$, $C(0, 0)$

(b) The circle $(x - 2)^2 + y^2 = 4$, $C(2, 0)$, $r = 3$

(c) The circle $(x + 2)^2 + y^2 = 9$, $C(-2, 0)$, $r = 3$

(d) The circle $x^2 + (y - 1)^2$, $C(0, 1)$, $r = 2$

(e) The circle $x^2 + (y + 2)^2 = 9$, $C(0, -2)$, $r = 3$

(f) The circle $(x + 2)^2 + (y - 3)^2 = 4$, $C(-2, 3)$, $r = 2$

(g) Locus of z is the perpendicular bisector of OA, $A(1, 0)$, $2x = 1$

(h) Locus of z is the perpendicular bisector of AB, $A(2, 0)$, $B(0, -1)$, $4x + 2y = 3$

(i) Locus of z is the perpendicular bisector of AB, $A(-2, 3)$, $B(-2, -1)$. $y = 1$

(j) The locus is a circle $(x + 4/3)^2 + (y + 2/3)^2 = 20/9$. $C(-4/3, -2/3)$, $r = \sqrt{20}/3$

(k) Locus, a circle $(x + 2)^2 + (y + 7/3)^2 = 64/9$, $C(-2, -7/3)$, $r = 8/3$

(l) $\frac{x^2}{4} + \frac{y^2}{3} = 1$
Locus is the ellipse
Centre $(0, 0)$, Foci $(\pm 1, 0)$

(m) Ellipse Centre $(0, 0)$ Foci $(0, \pm 1)$
$\frac{x^2}{3} + \frac{y^2}{4} = 1$

(n) $\frac{(x - 1/2)^2}{4} + \frac{y^2}{15/4} = 1$
Ellipse Centre $(\frac{1}{2}, 0)$ Foci $(0, 0)$, $(1, 0)$

2.

(a)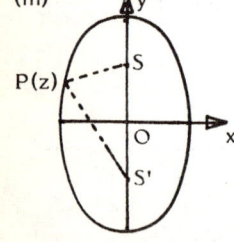
Locus is half ray along the line $y = \sqrt{3}x$ excluding the point $O(0, 0)$, $y > 0$

(b)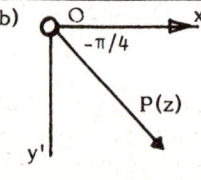
Locus is the half ray along the line $y = -x$ excluding $O(0,0)$ and $y < 0$. $\angle POX = -\pi/4$

(c)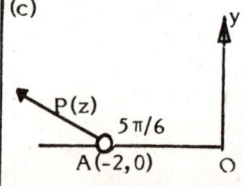
Locus is half ray AP where $A(-2, 0)$ and $y > 0$ excluding A
$\angle PAx = 5\pi/6$
$x + y\sqrt{3} + 2 = 0$

(d)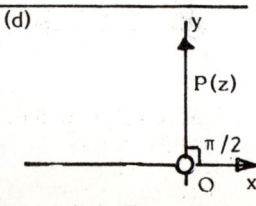
Locus is half-ray from $O(0,0)$, $y > 0$, $x = 0$ excluding O.

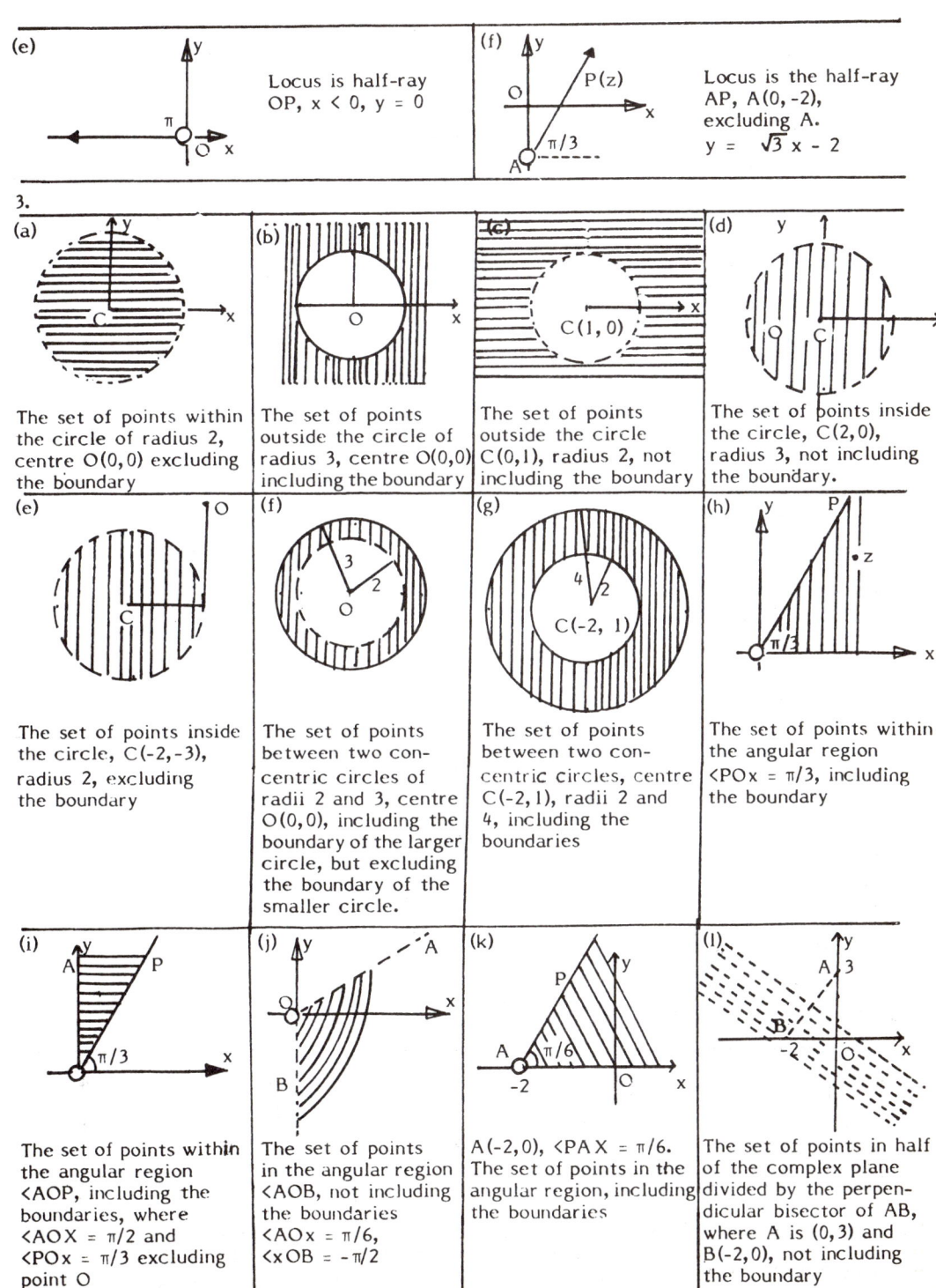

4.

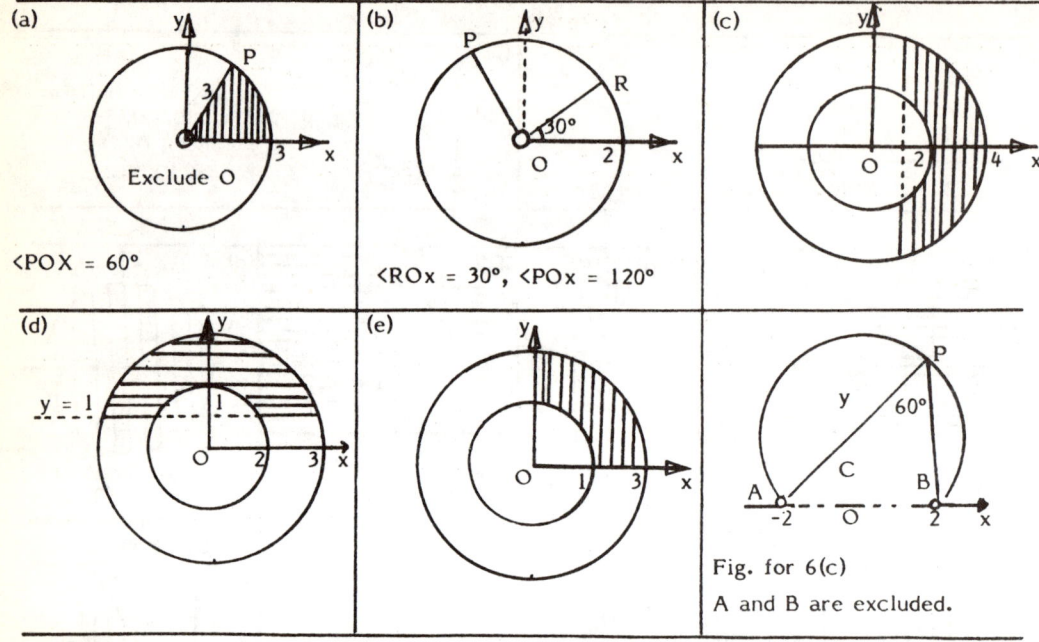

Fig. for 6(c)
A and B are excluded.

5. (a) Locus of w is a circle of radius 3, centre (-2, 0), equation $(x + 2)^2 + y^2 = 9$.
    (b) Locus of w is a circle, radius 2, C(1, 0), equation $(x - 1)^2 + y^2 = 4$
    (c) Locus of w is a circle, radius $\frac{\sqrt{20}}{3}$, $C\left(-\frac{4}{3}, \frac{2}{3}\right)$
    (d) Locus of w is a circle, $r = \frac{\sqrt{5}}{2}$, $C\left(-\frac{3}{2}, 0\right)$

6. (a) The x-axis, y = 0, excluding 0
    (b) Locus is a circle, $r = \frac{\sqrt{5}}{2}$, $C\left(1, \frac{1}{2}\right)$, excluding A(2, 0), AB is the diameter B(0, 1)
    (c) Locus of z is the major arc of the circle on chord AB containing the angle angle of 60°, A(2, 0), B(-2, 0), excluding A and B.
        Equation of the circle is $x^2 + y^2 + \frac{4y}{\sqrt{3}} - 4 = 0$, centre $\left(0, \frac{2}{\sqrt{3}}\right)$, $r = \frac{4}{\sqrt{3}}$
        (see the last fig. above)

Exercise 40

1. (a) 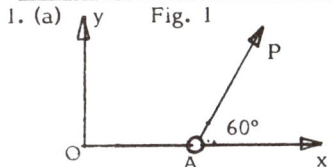 Fig. 1
Locus is a half-ray AP, A(2, 0), excluding A
$\angle PAx = 60°$

1. (b) 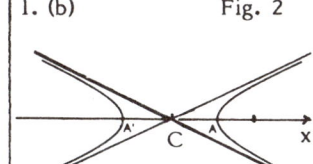 Fig. 2
A hyperbola
$3x^2 - y^2 + 8x + 4 = 0$
centre $\left(-\frac{4}{3}, 0\right)$

1.(c) 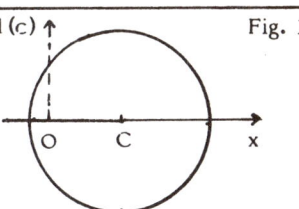 Fig. 3
Locus of z is a circle
$x^2 + y^2 - 8x - 10 = 0$,
C(4, 0), $r = \sqrt{26}$

1.(d) 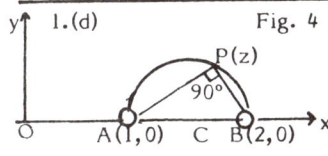 Fig. 4
A semi circle on AB as diameter, excluding A and B

1.(e) 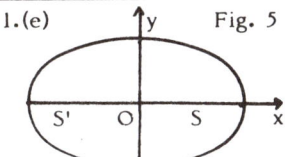 Fig. 5
Locus is an ellipse.
Foci $(\pm 1, 0)$, centre (0, 0)
Centre (0, 0)
Equation
$20x^2 + 36y^2 = 45$

1. 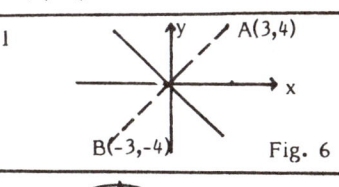 Fig. 6

3. (a) $3 - 2i$ (b) Locus is either a point $(3, -2)$ or the circle $(x - 3)^2 + (y + 2)^2 = 1$

4. (a) $x = 3/2, y = 2$ or $x = -3/2, y = -2$
   (b) (i) $x + 2y + 2 = 0$
   (ii) Circle $x^2 + y^2 + 2x + y = 0$, $C(-1, -1/2)$, $r = \frac{\sqrt{5}}{2}$

5. (a) Locus of z is the perpendicular bisector of AB, A(3, 4), B(-3, -4), its equation $3x + 4y = 0$ (see fig. 6)
   (b) Circle $x^2 + y^2 + \frac{15}{2}x + 10y + 25 = 0$
   $C\left(-\frac{15}{4}, -5\right)$, $r = \frac{15}{4}$

6. A straight line $2x + y = 5$

7. (a) $p = \frac{5}{4}$, $q = -\frac{7}{12}$ (b) $p = 4 - \frac{11}{4}i$, $q = 4 + \frac{11}{4}i$

8. Centres (2, 0), (0, 2), radii 2, 2, the points of intersection are $z = 0$ or $z = 2 + 2i$ (see Fig. 7)

9. $B(z) = \frac{3 - 4\sqrt{3}}{2} + \frac{4 + 3\sqrt{3}}{2}i$
   $D(z) = \frac{-3 - 4\sqrt{3}}{2} + \frac{3\sqrt{3} - 4}{2}i$

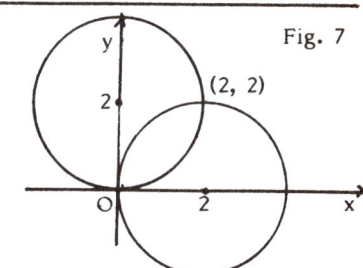
Fig. 7

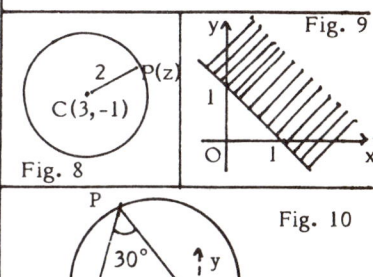
Fig. 8   Fig. 9

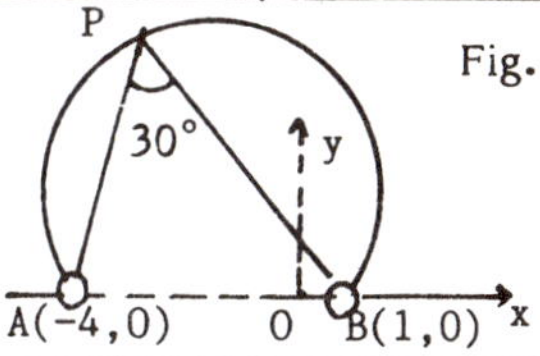

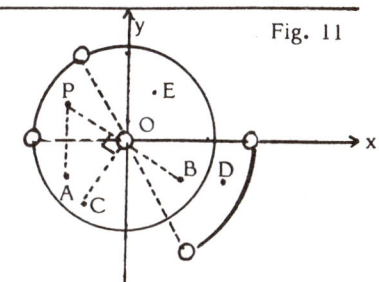
Fig. 10

Fig. 11

10. (a) (i) 1   (ii) 1   (iii) $\sqrt{2}$ (iv) $\pi/4$
    (b) (i) A circle of radius 2, C(3, -1) (see Fig. 8)
        (ii) The half-plane $x + y \geq 1$ (see Fig. 9)
    (c) Locus is the major arc of a circle on AB as a chord,
        A(-4, 0), B(1, 0), with P(z) on the circle, $\angle APB = 60°$,
        excluding A and B (see Fig. 10)
    (d) See Fig. 11

11. (a) $Q(z) = \sqrt{2}\,\text{cis}(\theta + 45°)$, $R(z) = r\,\text{cis}(\theta + \pi/2)$
    (b) $P'(z) = \text{cis}\,90° = i$, $Q'(z) = \sqrt{2}\,\text{cis}\,135° = -1 + i$
        $R'(z) = \text{cis}\,180° = -1$

12. (a) (i) $\frac{\sqrt{13}}{5}$, $\theta = 3.18°$ (ii) $\frac{\sqrt{29}}{5}$, $\theta = 58.67°$
    (c) The circle $x^2 + y^2 = 1$, $r = 1$, $C(0, 0)$

13. See Fig. 12.   14. (a) $p = -20$, $r = -8$

14. (b) (i) Locus of z is a ray AP, A(-2, 0), $\angle PAX = 45°$
        (ii) $\sqrt{2}$, $3\pi/4$ (see Fig. 13)   (iii) $-1 + i$

15. (a) $\sqrt{5}/5$, $\theta = -10.3°$ (b) $\pm(2 + i)$.   (see Fig. 14)

16. (a) $\pm\frac{\sqrt{3}}{2} \pm \frac{i}{2}$, $\pm i$ (see Fig. 15)   (b) $\pm(3 - 5i)$

17. $y^2 = 4a^2(a^2 - x)$, focus (0, 0). The locus of Q is the x-axis,
    if P moves on the y-axis.

19. (3, 0), (-1, -4), $y^2 = 4(3 - x)$

20. (a) (i) 25, $\frac{2\pi}{3}$ (ii) 5, $-\frac{\pi}{3}$ (iii) $\frac{1}{5}$, $-\frac{\pi}{3}$ (iv) 5, $\frac{5\pi}{6}$
    (b) (i) 15   (ii) 5   (c) $8 + 6i$ (d) $-8 - 6i$

21. (a) $\sqrt{2}$, $-15°$, $n = 12$, -64 (b) (i) $4\cos\theta$ (ii) $\frac{1}{4\cos\theta}$, $-\theta$
    (c) $4x = 1$

22. (a) The ellipse $100x^2 + 36y^2 = 225$ (b) The y-axis, excluding the origin.

23. $r = 1.97$, $\theta = -73.5°$ 24. (a) $\pm\frac{\sqrt{3}}{2} - \frac{i}{2}$, i (b) $z = 0$, $-i$, $\frac{3}{2} + \frac{i}{2}$, $\frac{-3}{2} + \frac{i}{2}$

25. a square   27. (a) $(z + 1)(z^2 - z + 1)$ 30. $(-1)^k \sec\left(\frac{4k + 1}{4m}\pi\right)^m \cdot \frac{(1 + i)}{\sqrt{2}}$

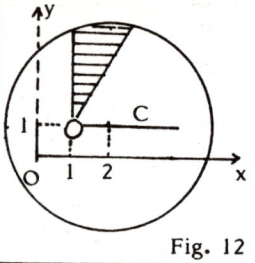
Fig. 12

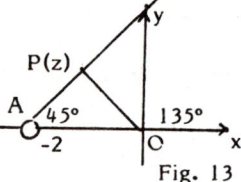
Fig. 13

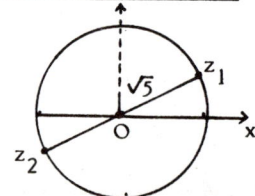
Fig. 14

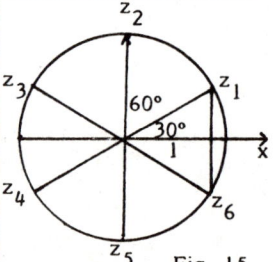
Fig. 15

CHAPTER 5 POLYNOMIALS

Exercise 5A

(Q = quotient,   R = remainder)

1. $Q = x^2 + 3$, $R = 5$ 2. $Q = x^3 - 2x^2 + 2x - 1$, $R = 0$ 3. $Q = x^2 + 2x + 3$, $R = 0$
4. $Q = 2x^2 + x + 2$, $R = 0$ 5. Yes   6. No   7. Yes   8. No
9. -35 10. 464 11. $33/8$ 12. $10 - 4a + 2b$ 13. 1 14. 3
15. -1 16. 3 17. $k = 20$, $x = 5$, $-\dfrac{3 \pm \sqrt{39}i}{6}$
18. $k = 2$, $x = 2$, $\dfrac{1 \pm \sqrt{5}}{2}$ 19. $k = 1$, $x = 1$, $-1 \pm \sqrt{7}$ 20. $k = -2$, $x = 2$, -3, $\pm 2i$

Exercise 5B

1. $1, 1, 5$ 2. $2, 2, -2$ 3. $3, 3, -4$ 4. $-1, -1$
5. (a) $1, 1, 1, -5$ (b) $1, 1, 1, 3$ 6. (a) $(-2, -13)$ (b) $(0, 1)$
7. (a) $k = 4$, $x = -1, -1, -4$; $k = 0$, $x = 0, -3, -3$
   (b) $k = 28$, $x = 2, 2, -7$; $k = -80$, $x = -4, -4, 5$
8. (a) $1, 2, -2$ (b) $-1, 2, -3$ (c) $\dfrac{-1}{2}, 2, 3$ (d) $-1, -1, -2, 3$
   (e) $-1, 2, 3$ (f) $-2, 4, 2 \pm \sqrt{5}$ (g) $\dfrac{-1}{4}, \dfrac{3 \pm \sqrt{5}}{2}$ (h) $\dfrac{-1}{2}, \dfrac{1 \pm \sqrt{17}}{4}$
   (i) $\tan\theta = -1, 2, -3, 4$

Exercise 5C

1. $(x + 2i)(x - 2i)$ 2. $(x + ci)(x - ci)$
3. $(x + \sqrt{5}i)(x - \sqrt{5}i)$ 4. $(x + \dfrac{1}{2} + \dfrac{\sqrt{3}}{2}i)(x + \dfrac{1}{2} - \dfrac{\sqrt{3}}{2}i)$
5. $(x + \dfrac{3}{2} + \dfrac{\sqrt{11}}{2}i)(x + \dfrac{3}{2} - \dfrac{\sqrt{11}}{2}i)$ 6. $3(x + \dfrac{1}{3} + \dfrac{\sqrt{2}}{3}i)(x + \dfrac{1}{3} - \dfrac{\sqrt{2}}{3}i)$
7. $4(x - \dfrac{1}{8} + \dfrac{\sqrt{15}}{8}i)(x - \dfrac{1}{8} - \dfrac{\sqrt{15}}{8}i)$ 8. $2(x + \dfrac{i}{\sqrt{2}})(x - \dfrac{i}{\sqrt{2}})$
9. $\dfrac{1}{2}(1 \pm \sqrt{7}i)$ 10. $\dfrac{1}{2}(-1 \pm \sqrt{5}i)$ 11. $-5, 2 + 3i$ 12. $\dfrac{1}{2}, 1 + i$
13. $2 - i$, $-1 \pm \sqrt{5}$ 14. $-1, 2, -2 + i$ 15. $\dfrac{1}{2}, -2, -2 - i$
16. $(x - x_1)(x - x_2)(x - x_3)(x - x_4)$ where $(x_1, x_2, x_3, x_4) = \pm \dfrac{1}{2} \pm \dfrac{\sqrt{7}}{2}i$
17. With form used in ex. 16 above, $(x_1, x_2, x_3, x_4) = \pm \sqrt{2} \pm \sqrt{2}i$
18. With form used in ex. 16 above, $(x_1, x_2, x_3, x_4) = \pm \dfrac{1}{2} \pm \dfrac{\sqrt{3}}{2}i$
19. $(x + 1)(x - 1)(x - x_1)(x - x_2)(x - x_3)(x - x_4)$ where (x_1, x_2, x_3, x_4) as in ex. 18
20. (a) $-5i$ (b) $-1 - 5i$

Exercise 5D

1. (a) 10 (b) 23 (c) 74 2. (a) -5 (b) 25 (c) -8
3. (a) -1 (b) 2 (c) -3 4. $4, -2, 1$ 5. $-5, -2, 1, 4$
6. ($b = 2$, $c = 3$, $m = 10$, $n = 12$) or ($b = 2$, $c = -3$, $m = -2$, $n = -12$)
7. $2p^3 + 27r = 9pq$ 8. $-\dfrac{2}{3}, \dfrac{1}{2}, 3$ 9. $1, 1, -2, -2$
10. $b = 9$, $x = -1, -4 \pm 2\sqrt{3}$

11. (a) $3x^3 - 4x^2 + 8x + 8 = 0$ (b) $x^3 + 4x^2 - 8x + 24 = 0$ (c) $x^3 - x^2 - 3x + 6 = 0$
    (d) $x^3 + 8x^2 + 18x + 15 = 0$ (e) $x^3 - 8x^2 - 8x - 9 = 0$ (f) $8x^3 + 8x^2 - 4x + 3 = 0$
12. (a) $2x^3 - 9x^2 + 11x - 3 = 0$ (b) $3x^3 - 11x^2 + 9x - 2 = 0$ (c) $4x^3 - 13x^2 + 7x - 1 = 0$
13. (a) $x^3 + 4bx + 8c = 0$ (b) $x^3 + 4bx - 8c = 0$ (c) $cx^3 - bx^2 - 1 = 0$
14. $dx^3 + cx^2 + bx + 1 = 0$ (a) $\frac{-c}{d}$ (b) $\frac{b}{d}$ (c) $\frac{c^2 - 2bd}{d^2}$
15. (a) $x^4 - 4x^2 + 16x + 48 = 0$ (b) $3x^4 + 2x^3 - x^2 + 1 = 0$
    (c) $x^4 - 2x^3 + 7x^2 - 10x + 9 = 0$
16. (a) $x^3 - 4x^2 + 4x - 9 = 0$ (b) $x^3 - 7x^2 + 15x - 18 = 0$ (c) 18

Exercise 5E

1. (a) $(x - 2)(x^2 + 2x + 4)$; $(x - 2)(x + 1 + \sqrt{3}i)(x + 1 - \sqrt{3}i)$
   (b) $(x - 2)(x + 2)(x^2 + 4)$; $(x - 2)(x + 2)(x + 2i)(x - 2i)$
   (c) $(x + 1)(x^2 - x + 1)$; $(x + 1)(x - \frac{1}{2} + \frac{\sqrt{3}}{2}i)(x - \frac{1}{2} - \frac{\sqrt{3}}{2}i)$
2. (a) $(x + 2i)(x - 2i)$ (b) $(x + 4 + \sqrt{8})(x + 4 - \sqrt{8})$
   (c) $(x - 2 + \sqrt{2}i)(x - 2 - \sqrt{2}i)$ (d) $(x + 3)(x + 2i)(x - 2i)$
   (e) $(x + \sqrt{3}i)(x - \sqrt{3}i)(x + i)(x - i)$ (f) $(x - 3)(x + 2 + 2i)(x + 2 - 2i)$
3. (a) $P(x) = K(x^2 - 4x + 5)$ (b) $P(x) = K(x^2 - 6x + 25)$
   (c) $P(x) = K(x^3 - 2x^2 - 3x + 10)$ (d) $P(x) = K[x^2 - (4 + i)x + 3 + 3i]$
   (e) $P(x) = K[x^3 - (3 + i)x^2 + (1 + 2i)x + 1 + i]$ (f) $P(x) = K(x^2 - 7x + 13 + i)$
4. (a) $2 \pm i$ (b) $3, 2 + i$ (c) $-2, 3, 1 + 3i$ (d) $\frac{1}{2}, 3 + 2i$
5. (a) $(x + 1)(x + i)(x - i)$ (b) $(x - 3)(x + 1 + i)(x + 1 - i)$
   (c) $(x - 1)(x - 1 + 2i)(x - 1 - 2i)$ (d) $2(x - 2)(x + \frac{1}{2} + \frac{\sqrt{5}}{2}i)(x + \frac{1}{2} - \frac{\sqrt{5}}{2}i)$
6. (a) $-1, \frac{1 \pm \sqrt{3}i}{2}$ (b) $\pm 2, \pm 2i$ (c) $\pm \sqrt{2}, \pm \sqrt{2}i$
   (d) $\pm i, \pm \sqrt{2}i$ (e) $2, 3, 1 \pm i$
7. $3, 3, \frac{-1 \pm \sqrt{3}i}{2}$ 8. $b = -5, c = 5$ 9. $\frac{-1 \pm \sqrt{3}i}{2}, \frac{-1 \pm \sqrt{15}i}{4}$
11. (b) $\frac{\sqrt{3}}{2} + \frac{i}{2}, i, -\frac{\sqrt{3}}{2} + \frac{i}{2}, -\frac{\sqrt{3}}{2} - \frac{i}{2}, -i, \frac{\sqrt{3}}{2} - \frac{i}{2}$ (c) $\pm \frac{\sqrt{3}}{2} \pm \frac{i}{2}$ (4 roots)
12. (a) (i) $(x - 3)(x^2 - 6x + 13)$ (ii) $(x - 3)(x - 3 + 2i)(x - 3 - 2i)$ (b) $2, 2, 2, 2, -3/2$
14. $x^5 = 1$ has 5 roots cis $\frac{2K}{5}$, $K = 0, 1, 2, 3, 4, 5$. Area is 2.38.
    Roots of $x^4 + x^3 + x^2 + x + 1 = 0$ are: cis $\frac{2K}{5}$, $K = 1, 2, 3, 4$
15. $2 \pm i, -\frac{2}{3}$ 16. cis $(\pm \frac{\pi}{3})$, cis $(\pm \frac{2\pi}{3})$ 17. $K = 0, -4$ 18. $-3 - 2i, K = -13i$

19. (a) $\frac{\pi}{16}, \frac{5\pi}{16}, \frac{9\pi}{16}, \frac{13\pi}{16}$ (c) $\tan(\frac{\pi}{16})$, $\tan(\frac{5\pi}{16})$, $\tan(\frac{9\pi}{16})$, $\tan(\frac{13\pi}{16})$

(d) (i) -4 (ii) 28 20. (a) $\frac{(-3 \pm \sqrt{17})i}{2}$

(b) $z_1 = \frac{1}{2}[-2 + x + i(-3 + y)]$

$z_2 = \frac{1}{2}[-2 - x + i(-3 - y)]$ where $x = \sqrt{\frac{\sqrt{409} - 3}{2}}$, $y = \sqrt{\frac{\sqrt{409} + 3}{2}}$

(c) $z_1 = 3 - i$, $z_2 = 1 + 3i$ (d) $\pm(2 - i)$ (e) $-1, -3 - 2i$ (f) $2 - i, 1 + 2i$

22. $1 + i$, $2 \pm i$

23. (a) $\pm\sqrt{\frac{3}{2}} \pm \sqrt{\frac{1}{2}}i$ (b) $\pm i$, $\pm(\sqrt{7 + \sqrt{48}})i$, $\pm(\sqrt{7 - \sqrt{48}})i$

(c) $\pm(x + iy)$, where $x = \frac{1}{2}\sqrt{\sqrt{2} + 1}$, $y = \frac{1}{2}\sqrt{\sqrt{2} - 1}$, (d) $\pm(4 \pm i)$

24. cis $\frac{2k\pi + \pi}{8}$, $k = 0, 1, 2, 3, 4, 5, 6, 7$

These can be expressed in the form $A + iB$ by evaluating ratios of $\pm 22.5°$, $\pm 112.5°$, $\pm 157.5°$. A great deal of time can be saved by noting that the roots are symmetrically placed with respect to both axes.

$z_1 = 0.924 + 0.382i$, $z_2 = 0.382 + 0.924i$, $z_3 = -0.382 + 0.924i$,
$z_4 = -0.924 + 0.382i$, $z_5 = \bar{z}_4$, $z_6 = \bar{z}_3$, $z_7 = \bar{z}_2$, $z_8 = \bar{z}_1$

25. $a = 1, b = -4; 1 \pm i, -3$ 26. $-\frac{1}{2} + \frac{\sqrt{3}}{2}i$, $\frac{-1 \pm \sqrt{5}}{2}$ 27. $m = -\frac{22}{3}$, $n = 12$

30. $1, 1, 1, 3$ 31. $1 - i(\sqrt{3} + \sqrt{2})$, $-1 + i(\sqrt{3} - \sqrt{2})$

33. $2, 2 \pm \frac{\sqrt{3}}{2}$ 34. $y^3 + 7y^2 - y + 1 = 0$ 35. $4x - 7$

CHAPTER 6 CONIC SECTIONS

Exercise 6A

1. (a) O $(0, 0)$ (b) $\frac{\sqrt{7}}{4}$ (c) $(\pm\sqrt{7}, 0)$ (d) $8, 6$ (e) $x = \frac{\pm 16}{\sqrt{7}}$

2. (a) O $(0, 0)$ (b) $\frac{\sqrt{7}}{4}$ (c) $(0, \pm\sqrt{7})$ (d) $8, 6$ (e) $y = \frac{\pm 16}{\sqrt{7}}$

3. (a) O $(0, 0)$ (b) $\frac{\sqrt{11}}{6}$ (c) $(\pm\sqrt{11}, 0)$ (d) $12, 10$ (e) $x = \frac{\pm 36}{\sqrt{11}}$

4. (a) O $(0, 0)$ (b) $\frac{\sqrt{20}}{6}$ (c) $(0, \pm\sqrt{20})$ (d) $12, 8$ (e) $y = \frac{\pm 18}{\sqrt{5}}$

5. (a) O $(0, 0)$ (b) $\frac{\sqrt{15}}{5}$ (c) $(\pm\sqrt{15}, 0)$ (d) $10, 2\sqrt{10}$ (e) $x = \frac{\pm 25}{\sqrt{15}}$

6. (a) O $(0, 0)$ (b) $\frac{\sqrt{3}}{2}$ (c) $(0, \pm 6)$ (d) $8\sqrt{3}, 4\sqrt{3}$ (e) $y = \pm 8$

7. (a) O $(0, 0)$ (b) $\frac{\sqrt{3}}{2}$ (c) $(0, \pm\sqrt{3})$ (d) $4, 2$ (e) $y = \frac{\pm 4}{\sqrt{3}}$

8. (a) O $(0, 0)$ (b) $\frac{\sqrt{5}}{3}$ (c) $(\pm\frac{\sqrt{5}}{6}, 0)$ (d) $1, \frac{2}{3}$ (e) $x = \frac{\pm 3}{2\sqrt{5}}$

9. (a) O $(0, 0)$ (b) $\frac{\sqrt{5}}{3}$ (c) $(0, \pm\sqrt{5})$ (d) $6, 4$ (e) $y = \frac{\pm 9}{\sqrt{5}}$

10. (a) O $(0, 0)$ (b) $\frac{1}{\sqrt{2}}$ (c) $(\pm\frac{\sqrt{2}}{2}, 0)$ (d) $2, \sqrt{2}$ (e) $x = \pm\sqrt{2}$

11. $\dfrac{x^2}{16} + \dfrac{y^2}{4} = 1$ 12. $\dfrac{x^2}{4} + \dfrac{y^2}{25} = 1$ 13. $\dfrac{x^2}{25} + \dfrac{y^2}{9} = 1$

14. $\dfrac{x^2}{9} + \dfrac{y^2}{14} = 1$ 15. $\dfrac{x^2}{25} + \dfrac{y^2}{16} = 1$ or $\dfrac{x^2}{9} + \dfrac{y^2}{25} = 1$

16. $\dfrac{x^2}{36} + \dfrac{y^2}{52} = 1$ 17. $\dfrac{x^2}{36} + \dfrac{y^2}{20} = 1$ or $\dfrac{x^2}{20} + \dfrac{y^2}{36} = 1$

Exercise 6B

1.

	Foci	Directrices	Vertices
a	$(\pm\sqrt{41}, 0)$	$x = \pm\dfrac{25}{\sqrt{41}}$	$(\pm 5, 0)$ (See Fig. 1)
b	$(0, \pm\sqrt{41})$	$y = \pm\dfrac{16}{\sqrt{41}}$	$(0, \pm 4)$ (See Fig. 2)
c	$(\pm\dfrac{\sqrt{5}}{2}, 0)$	$x = \pm\dfrac{2}{\sqrt{5}}$	$(\pm 1, 0)$ (See Fig. 1)
d	$(\pm\sqrt{5}, 0)$	$x = \pm\dfrac{1}{\sqrt{5}}$	$(\pm 1, 0)$ (See Fig. 1)

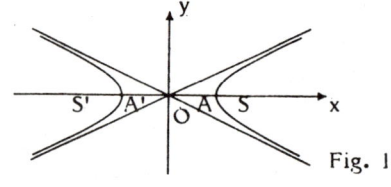
Fig. 1

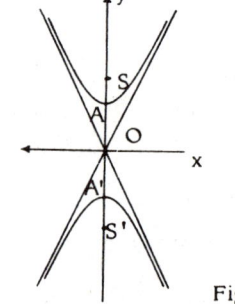
Fig. 2

2. $\tan^{-1}\left(\dfrac{2ab}{a^2 - b^2}\right)$ 3. $90°$

Exercise 6C

(Note: T = tangent, N = normal)

1. T: $x + y = 3$
   N: $x - y = -1$
2. T: $3x - 2y + 5 = 0$
   N: $2x + 3y = 1$
3. T: $2\sqrt{3}x + 3y = 12$
   N: $6x - 4\sqrt{3}y = 5\sqrt{3}$
4. T: $3x + 4y = 12\sqrt{2}$
   N: $\sqrt{2}(4x - 3y) = 7$
5. T: $3x + \sqrt{6}y = 6$
   N: $\sqrt{6}x - 3y = 7\sqrt{6}$
6. T: $x + y + 1 = 0$
   N: $x - y + 3 = 0$
7. T: $3x + 2y = 1$
   N: $2x - 3y = 5$
8. T: $3\sqrt{2}x - 2y = 6$
   N: $2x + 3\sqrt{2}y = 13\sqrt{2}$
9. T: $2x - \sqrt{3}y = 1$
   N: $\sqrt{3}x + 2y = 4\sqrt{3}$
10. T: $x + t^2y = 2ct$
    N: $t^3x - ty = c(t^4 - 1)$
11. $x - 2y = \pm 5$
12. $100x - 45y = 192$
    $P(25/4, 15/16)$
13. T: $x + y = 6$, N: $x - y = 12$, $\left(\dfrac{9}{2}, \dfrac{3}{2}\right)$
14. $P\left(\dfrac{3}{2}, \dfrac{1}{2}\right)$, $63.43°$
15. $\left(\dfrac{16}{5}, \dfrac{9}{5}\right)$
16. $(2,1)$
17. $x + y = \pm 1$, $(3, -2)$, $(-3, 2)$
20. $y = \pm x \pm \sqrt{2}$ (four tangents) ; $\left(\pm\dfrac{1}{\sqrt{2}}, \pm\dfrac{1}{\sqrt{2}}\right)$ (four points)

Exercise 6D

1. (a) $4x + 5\sqrt{3}y = 40$ 1. (b) $10\sqrt{3}x - 8y = 9\sqrt{3}$ 2. (a) $x \pm 2\sqrt{3}y = 2$
2. (b) $8\sqrt{3}x \pm 4y = 3\sqrt{3}$ 3. (a) $y = \pm(x - 1)$ 3. (b) $y = \pm(x - 3)$
4. (a) $3x + 4y = 12\sqrt{2}$ 4. (b) $4\sqrt{2}x - 3\sqrt{2}y = 7$ 5. (a) $4\sqrt{2}x - 5y = 20$
5. (b) $5x + 4\sqrt{2}y = 41\sqrt{2}$
11. (a) Tangents are: $x \pm 3\sqrt{2}y = 9$ (b) Tangents are: $3x \pm \sqrt{5}y = 4$
    Normals are: $3y \pm 9\sqrt{2}x = \mp 5\sqrt{2}$ Normals are: $3y \pm \sqrt{5}x = 6\sqrt{5}$
12. $y = x \pm \sqrt{41}$ 13. $AB = \sqrt{136} = 2\sqrt{34}$ 14. $3x + 2\sqrt{3}y = 12$, $AB = \sqrt{28}$
17. (e) $\sqrt{\frac{(\sqrt{5} - 1)}{2}}$ 22. $\left[\frac{a}{2}(\sec\theta + \csc\theta), \frac{b}{2}(\tan\theta + \cot\theta)\right]$
    or $\left[\frac{a}{2}\left(\frac{1}{\cos\theta} + \frac{1}{\sin\theta}\right), \frac{b}{2\cos\theta\sin\theta}\right]$
23. $\frac{25}{x_1}$ 25. Normal is $(5\sin\theta)x - (3\cos\theta)y = 16\cos\theta\sin\theta$
    Locus is $25x^2 + 9y^2 = 64$, $e = \frac{4}{5}$ (see the sketch below)
27. $(x_1^2 - a^2)m^2 - 2x_1y_1m + y_1^2 - b^2 = 0$, $x^2 + y^2 = a^2 + b^2$
28. $a^2y_1x + b^2x_1y = x_1y_1(a^2 + b^2)$ 30. $R\left(\frac{x_1 + x_2}{2}, \frac{m(x_1 - x_2)}{2}\right)$
    Locus of R is $m^4x^2 + y^2 = K^2m^2$
31. (a) $3x\cos\theta + 4y\sin\theta = 12$ and $3x\sin\theta - 4y\cos\theta = -12$.
    (b) $T\left(-4(\sin\theta - \cos\theta), 3(\sin\theta + \cos\theta)\right)$
33. Area $= c^2$ 37. Area $= \frac{1}{2}ab$
38. 30   39. $x^2 - y^2 = 2$ (a) $x\tan\phi + y\sec\phi = 2\sqrt{2}\sec\phi\tan\phi$
40. $P\left(\frac{a}{\sqrt{2}}, \frac{b}{\sqrt{2}}\right)$, Minimum area is ab.
41. $x + pqy = c(p + q)$ 43. $lx - my = 0$.   44. $2c^2$

(Fig. for ex. 25)

CHAPTER 7 ELEMENTARY PARTICLE DYNAMICS

Exercise 7A

1. $T_1 = 80$ N, $T_2 = 60$ N   2. 656 N   3. $\frac{M(v - u)}{F - R - 10M\sin\theta}$
4. (a) -8 m.s^{-2} (b) 2.08 s   (c) 17.4 m
5. $F = m(f + \sin\theta)$ 6. $a = 4.33$ m.s^{-2}, Reaction 75 N.
7. $a = -6$ m.s^{-2}, Reaction 16 N.   8. -2 m.s^{-2}
9. (a) 8330 N   (b) 8030 N

CHAPTER 8 MOTION PROBLEMS IN TWO DIMENSIONS

Exercise 8A

1. 12.46 p.m
2. (b) $x = \pm \frac{1}{3}$ (c) $2 \pm 2\sqrt{2}$, motion is not S.H.M.
4. Centre at $x = 1$, Amplitude $= \frac{5}{3}$, Max. velocity 5 m/s
5. (a) 2 (b) 1 (c) π
6. (a) $\sqrt{\frac{5}{2}}$ (b) 3.4 (c) 8.32

Exercise 8B

1. (a) $\tan^{-1}(\frac{2}{\sqrt{3}})$ (b) $\tan^{-1}(\frac{5}{\sqrt{3}})$ 2. (b) 82.9° or 16.6°
6. $v^2 = u^2 - 2ug\sin\theta + g^2 t^2$ 8. 45°, 71.57°

Exercise 8C

1. $v = \frac{g}{k}(1 - e^{-kt})$ (2) $\frac{1}{2k}\log_e(4/3)$ 4. $\frac{U}{k}(1 - \log_e 2)$
6. 180 km/h. 8. (a) 3.43 s (b) 76.3 m
10. (a) 2.40 s (b) 32.1 m 12. $v^2 = \dfrac{1}{(1 + c^{-2})e^{2t} - 1}$, 0
13. (b) $\frac{1}{K}\left[-2 + \frac{P}{mk}\log\left(\frac{P - 2mk}{P - 4mk}\right)\right]$ (c) 2.1 m N 16. (i) 10 m/s (ii) 1.44 m
17. (ii) $t = -\frac{1}{k}\log_e\left(1 - \frac{kv}{g}\right)$ (iii) 50 m/s 18. (b) $-kv_x$ and $-g - kv_y$
20. (a) $m\frac{dv}{dt} = -mg - \frac{mv}{k}$ (b) $t = k\log_e(c/g)$, $h = k^2(c - g) + gk^2 \log_e(g/c)$
   (c) The time of descent < the time of ascent, since the gravity opposes the upward motion of the object.

CHAPTER 9 CIRCULAR MOTION

Exercise 9A

1. 5.03 m/s, 10.1 rad 2. 0.262 rad/s, 94 km/h 3. 25.1 rad/s
4. 7.27×10^{-5} rad/s, 1.99×10^{-7} rad/s 5. 468 m/s (1690 km/h)
6. 29.9 km/s (107000 km/h) 7. 5.56 rad/h 8. 5.03 m/s
9. (a) 251 rad/s (b) 1005 rad (c) 377 m/s
10. π rad/h, 31400 km/h 11. 9.59×10^{-3} rad/h, 3690 km/h

Exercise 9B

1. 50 m.s^{-2} 2. 6.25 N   3. 3130 N   4. 6320 m.s^{-2}
5. (a) 465 m/s (b) 0.0338 m.s^{-2} 6. 3000 N
7. (a) 0.262 rad/h (b) 11100 km/h (c) 224 N   8. 8.38 m.s^{-2}

Exercise 9C

1. (a) 1.39 m/s (b) 32.4 N   2. (a) 1.68 m/s (b) 1.87 s (c) 5.66 N
3. (a) 3.01 m/s (b) 33.9 N   4. (a) 19.6 m/s (b) 71.7 N   5. 3.60°

Exercise 9D

1. 6.46°   2. 5.8°   3. 73 km/h   4. 5.62°, 0.0979 m   5. 7.18°   6. 79 km/h

Exercise 9E

4. (a) $\dfrac{-a\omega}{r-a}$ (b) $\dfrac{\omega a^2}{r^2 + a^2}$ 5. 2.5 rad/s, 0.735 rad/s
6. 160 km/h   7. 60 km/h, 60°

Exercise 9F

1. (a) 25110 km/h (b) F = 3050 N
2. (a) 52.4 rad/s (b) 52.4 m/s (c) 2740 m.s^{-2}
3. Angular velocity = 0.524 rad/h   Speed = 18800 km/h
4. 395 N   5. 6.32 m/s
6. (a) 1890 N (b) 22600 km/h (c) 2.89 h
7. 151 revolutions per minute   8. 15 N, 1 kg
10. Tension 71.1 N, θ = 45.3°   11. 3.48 m   12. 4.45 rad/s, 80.4°
13. 5.63°   14. 20.6 m   15. 15.1 m/s
16. 4.47 m/s   17. r = $\sqrt{39}$ m, v = $\sqrt{78}$ m/s
18. (a) 1.99 × 10^{-7} rad/s (b) 5.94 × 10^{-3} m.s^{-2}
19. (a) 2.73 × 10^{-3} m.s^{-2} (b) 1024 m/s   20. (b) 2900 N, 1540 N
22. $\sqrt{\left(\dfrac{M+m}{m}\right)\cdot g}$ 23. 11100 km/h   25. (d) 7.55 m/s

Exercise 10A

8. (a) $\frac{\pi}{4}, \frac{3\pi}{4}, \frac{5\pi}{4}, \frac{7\pi}{4}, \frac{\pi}{12}, \frac{5\pi}{12}, \frac{13\pi}{12}, \frac{17\pi}{12}$

   (b) $0, \pi, 2\pi, \frac{\pi}{5}, \frac{3\pi}{5}, \frac{7\pi}{5}, \frac{9\pi}{5}$

9. (a) $24.2°, 102.7°, 204.2°, 282.7°$

   (b) (in degrees) $0, 30, 60, 120, 150, 180, 210, 240, 300, 330, 360$

10. (a) $\frac{\pi}{12}, \frac{9\pi}{12}, \frac{17\pi}{12}$

Exercise 10B

1. (a) $x^2 + y^2 - x + y = 0$ (b) $x^2 + y^2 - x - 5y + 4 = 0$
2. (a) $(-1, 2), 2$ (b) $(\frac{3}{4}, \frac{-5}{4}), \frac{3}{2}$
3. $x^2 + y^2 - 2x - 9 = 0$ 4. $x^2 + y^2 + 6x + 8y - 56 = 0$
5. $x^2 + y^2 + 2x - 2y + 1 = 0$, $x^2 + y^2 + 10x - 10y + 25 = 0$
6. $x^2 + y^2 - 4x - 8y + 4 = 0$, $x^2 + y^2 - 20x - 40y + 100 = 0$
8. $(-5, -7)$ 9. $x^2 + y^2 - ax - by = 0$ 10. 4
11. (a) $2x + 3y = 22$ (b) $y = 2x - 9$ (c) $3x + 4y = 27$
13. $x + 1 = 0$, $3x + 4y = 5$
14. (a) $x^2 + y^2 - 7x + 3y = 28 = 0$ (b) $x^2 + y^2 - (a + b)x - (a + b)y + 2ab = 0$
    (c) $x^2 + y^2 = 2a^2$

Exercise 10C

8. 12 cm.

Exercise 10F

1. 18 2. 1 3. 4 4. $\frac{\pi^2}{2}$

15. (a) $h(x) = x - \frac{x^2}{2}, \frac{x^2}{2} - 3x + 4$

    (b) $A(1, \frac{1}{2}), B(3, \frac{-1}{2})$

    (c) $\frac{2}{3}$,

    (d) 2

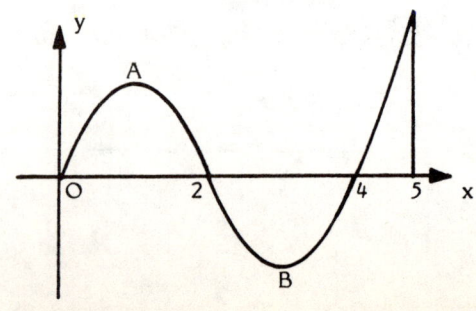